FORBIDDEN
RITES

MAGIC IN HISTORY

FORBIDDEN RITES

A NECROMANCER'S MANUAL OF THE FIFTEENTH CENTURY

RICHARD KIECKHEFER

THE PENNSYLVANIA STATE UNIVERSITY PRESS
UNIVERSITY PARK, PENNSYLVANIA

Copyright © 1997 Richard Kieckhefer

Published in 1998 in the United States of America and Canada by
The Pennsylvania State University Press, University Park, PA 16802

First published in 1997 in the United Kingdom by Sutton Publishing Limited

Library of Congress Cataloging-in-Publication Data

Kieckhefer, Richard.
   Forbidden rites : a necromancer's manual of the fifteenth century
/ Richard Kieckhefer.
      p.   cm.
   Includes bibliographical references and index.
   ISBN 0-271-01750-3 (cloth : alk. paper)
   ISBN 0-271-01751-1 (pbk. : alk. paper)
   1. Bayerische Staatsbibliothek. Manuscript. Clm 849. 2 Magic—History.
3. Demonology—History.   I. Title.
BF1593.K525   1997
133.4'3—dc21   97-26745

Printed in the United States of America

Sixth printing, 2014

It is the policy of The Pennsylvania State University Press to use acid-free paper
for the first printing of all clothbound books. Publications on uncoated stock
satisfy minimum requirements of American National Standard for Information
Sciences—Permanence of Paper for Printed Library Materials, ANSI Z39.48—
1992.

CONTENTS

TABLES

ACKNOWLEDGEMENTS

I am indebted to the Bayerische Staatsbibliothek for providing a microfilm and photographs of Clm 849; to the British Library and Cambridge University Library for providing relevant materials; to Martina Stratmann for supplying a codicological analysis of Clm 849; to Barbara Newman, H.C. Erik Midelfort, Steve Muhlberger, John Leland and Frank Klaassen for reading my analysis, sharing with me their insights, giving me the benefit of their suggestions, and helping to protect me from errors; to Charles Burnett in particular, who read both the analysis and the edition of the manuscript with meticulous care and expertise and helped resolve many problems; to Vincent Cornell and Sani Umar for information about Arabic texts; and to Persephone, a familiar companion who reminds me constantly about the significance of my work.

Cave! terrentia hac in scientia latent, si cupis scire occulta, pericula multa pro te et upupis!

INTRODUCTION: MAGICAL BOOKS AND MAGICAL RITES

We are what we read – and the power of books to transform the minds and personalities of their readers can give cause for anxiety as well as for celebration. A cluster of related developments in late medieval Europe brought heightened concern about what people were reading. The spread of literacy and the rise of a far wider reading public, lay as well as clerical, brought greater demand for written material. The availability of paper, a medium far less costly than parchment, made books more readily accessible than they had previously been, and allowed for more abundant supply of reading matter to feed this demand, even before the invention of printing with movable type. And the emergence of silent reading habits made reading a more private activity.[1] Historians have attended to the impact of these developments on medieval heresy, on churchmen's fear that literacy contributed to the diffusion of heretical views, and on the efforts at censorship that ensued. But less work has been done on the dissemination of *magical* texts, which in some ways represented an even more sinister threat to orthodox culture, and on attempts to control these texts.[2] A book of magic which deliberately and expressly invited contact with demons presented all the hazards of reading in their deepest and most pressing form.

Beginning around the early fourteenth century, possession and use of magical writings becomes a recurrent theme in the records of prosecution. When Bernard Délicieux was accused in 1319 of having used necromancy against the pope, he was cleared of that charge but nevertheless condemned to prison for merely possessing a book of necromancy.[3] Fear of necromancy and of necromantic writings was becoming an obsession at the time, especially at the court of Pope John XXII, who in the previous year had commissioned the bishop of Fréjus and others to investigate a group of clerics and laymen charged with using books of necromancy, geomancy and other magical arts.[4] In 1320 Matteo and Galeazzo Visconti were tried for using necromancy against Pope John; the offence here was actual use of the art, yet when one witness said he had been shown a book filled with experiments for love, hatred, finding of stolen objects and so forth, the very sight of such a book was evidently cause for horror.[5] In 1406–7, informants claimed that a group of clerics had used formulas from magical books against Benedict XIII and the king of France, and the ensuing inquiry uncovered a box filled with booklets containing prayers, hymns and conjurations.[6] But in 1409, at the Council of Pisa, Benedict in turn was charged with using necromancy and hiring necromancers. The pope, it was said, had sought out a book of necromancy available only from the Saracens and had purchased it for some 1,000 francs. A book of necromancy was allegedly found under the pontiff's bed.[7] In such cases the uncovering of necromantic writings made more plausible the charge that necromancy had actually been used, but more fundamentally the books themselves would have impressed contemporaries as unsavoury and incriminating, somewhat as the discovery of Satanic paraphernalia might seem incriminating today. Not surprisingly, inquisitors and other judges used such discoveries as propaganda in their zealous campaigns against magic. In 1382 an inquisitor wrote to the government of Siena about a band of magicians at Rugomagno; one Agnolo di Corso had been found in possession of a book of seventy chapters, which others had copied, and which spoke of invoking evil spirits to murder people or constrain their affections.[8] Two years later Niccolò Consigli was executed at Florence for practicing necromancy and unlicensed exorcisms; his judges confiscated and burned the books of necromancy from which he had taken conjurations.[9] One might even say it was common for books of magic to be set forth as codefendants alongside their owners and users – and indeed, as we shall see, those who condemned books of magic in some ways ascribed to them a kind of personality.[10] When the books were burned, there were those (as we shall see) who heard the voices of demons in the crackling of the flames.

The book-burning might at times be voluntary: according to a fifteenth-century biographer, Gerard Groot studied magic in his youth, and was accused of practising it as well, but when he converted to a life of piety and foreswore the art of necromancy, he consigned his books of magic to the flames.[11] The movement he went on to found, the Devotio Moderna, was one of the most influential forces in the devotional culture of pre-Reformation Europe, a movement of inner piety nurtured by devout reading, manifested in the copying out of pious phrases in personal florilegia, and financially supported by the copying of manuscripts – a movement, in short, firmly grounded in the book-culture of late medieval Europe, and initiated with an act of penitential book-burning.

From the early years of Christianity, conversion to Christ had meant, among other things, doing away with books of magic. The scene at Ephesus, as described in the Acts of the Apostles (18:19–19:20), perhaps epitomized what happened on a smaller scale elsewhere. When Paul arrived in the town and made converts to the new faith, 'a number of those who practised magic arts brought their books together and burned them in the sight of all, and they counted the value of them and found it came to fifty thousand pieces of silver'.[12] (This comes to roughly 1,666 times as many silver pieces as Judas received for betraying Christ.) By the later Middle Ages, treatment of those found with offending literature was often more judicial than pastoral. To be sure, a monk of Sulby monastery was treated leniently when he was found possessing books of magic in 1500. A superior in the Premonstratensian order had heard of a brother named Thomas Wryght who had been using books of experiments and gone about paying people generously to teach him the occult arts.

Faced with the evidence – one of his books of experiments – he insisted that he owned such books only out of curiosity, not for actual use. The matter was treated as a disciplinary one within the monastic setting, and the brother received a light penance.[13] But in an age when books of this sort were held in deep suspicion one could never count on such clemency, as Bernard Délicieux well knew.

Anything that arouses such deep anxiety is a subject of historical interest, and books of magic hold considerable fascination indeed. To know why books of magic aroused fear we must gain a fuller understanding of what the books themselves were likely to contain. Most of them no doubt have perished in the inquisitors' flames, but some eluded detection and have survived. The focus of following chapters in this study is arguably among the most interesting sources we have for the study of medieval magic: a fifteenth-century handbook of explicitly demonic magic, or what contemporaries called 'necromancy'. This compilation is contained in a manuscript in the Bavarian State Library in Munich. To be sure, the text is neither edifying nor profound, nor is it particularly original; in late medieval Europe there were no doubt many compilations equally illustrative of common magical practice, most of them now lost. But among the manuscripts that survive, few are quite as diverse in content, or as full, explicit and candid in their instructions as this work.

Detailed examination of such a compilation may most obviously help us understand the mentality of the necromancers themselves who copied such books, whether for curiosity or for use. But study of this handbook may clarify several other factors in the history of magic, and three in particular. First, examination of a necromancer's manual sheds light on the function and cultural significance of a magical book itself. We will know more about the cultural significance of books generally – and we will know more fully the range of meanings a book could have – when we have grasped the role of this exceptional category of books. Second, the mentality of the necromancers' opponents becomes clearer from examination of such a compilation: the views of the Renaissance mages (such as Marsilio Ficino and Johannes Reuchlin) who insisted that they practised a higher and purer form of magic than did these base necromancers, and those of the demonologists (Heinrich Kramer and his successors) for whom necromancy was a dark filter shading their perception of witchcraft. The reactions of the opponents may be historically more important than the attitudes of the necromancers themselves, because they tell us more about the culture as a whole, but we cannot begin to comprehend these reactions without knowing the realities on which they were based. Third, the rites contained in this compendium illustrate strikingly the links between magical practice and orthodox liturgy. The analogy I will use is that of a tapestry, whose display side implies a reverse side: so too, a society that ascribes a high degree of power to ritual and its users will invite the development of unofficial and transgressive ritual, related in form to its official counterpart, however sharply it may differ in its uses.

A BOOK OF MAGIC AS A CULTURAL ARTIFACT

A book of magic is also a magical book. It not only tells how to perform magical works, but shares in the numinous qualities and powers of the rites it contains. To be sure, not all magic is book magic: much magical practice arises from oral culture, is transmitted orally, and is used without needing inscription on paper or parchment, even if it is the largely accidental circumstance of its having been transcribed at some point that accounts for its survival and its accessibility to us. But in the later Middle Ages certain forms of magic were increasingly assimilated to liturgy and increasingly written, so that a magical act was the performance from a script, or the observance of a rite whose details were enshrined in a text. This development surely owed much to the spread of literacy among the laity, but even more to the practice of magic among the clergy, particularly those on the fringes of the clerical elite. Judicial and anecdotal evidence suggests that explicitly demonic magic, called 'nigromancy' or 'necromancy',[14] was largely the domain of priests, perhaps especially those without full-time parish employment, as well as ordained monks with some education and esoteric interests, university students and others who had been received into minor orders.[15] It was within this context that a book of magic would most naturally be perceived as a magical book, sharing in the numinous quality of the rites it prescribes.

Christian ritual had from early centuries been the enactment not of oral tradition but of texts embodied in books. With the unprecedented late medieval diffusion of literacy, availability of reading matter and expansion of the clergy, books might still be accessible only to an elite, but it was a much expanded elite, and the numbers and varieties of books available were far greater than in previous centuries, so that maintaining control over this diffusion and this variety was scarcely possible, however much hierarchs may have attempted to censor the available reading matter. Little surprise, then, if books of magic found their way onto some readers' shelves, whether for use or for mere curiosity.

Apart from its function as a repository of information and insight, a book can be of interest as a physical object, as a mirror of its writer's life and mind, and as a mirror of the society and culture from which it emanates and to which it returns. The surviving books of medieval demonic magic repay study from each of these perspectives, although their claims to significance differ from those of ordinary texts: a book of magic is a physical object like any other book, but even as object it is perceived as having sinister power, as a kind of negative relic; it reveals something of the writer's life and mind, but more often than in most other cases, and for more obviously compelling reasons, the authorship remains anonymous or pseudonymous; and it serves as a mirror of the surrounding culture, but often the mirror is a distorting one, a deliberately transgressive adaptation of what the society takes to be holy.

Any book of rituals serves as point of contact between sacred texts (permanent, authoritative repositories of power) and their performance (which utilizes this power for specific occasions). The book itself, like a liturgical vessel or a sacred building, is consecrated; when a formula is read from it, the power of the text is enhanced by the sacrality of the book from which it is read. A book of magic may also be consecrated, to confirm the numinous power resident in the physical object. A book of magic is thus significant not only as a source for information about magical practice – generally more reliable than court records, denunciatory treatises and literary accounts – but also as itself a magical object, treasured and closely guarded by its possessors, and condemned to burning by judges in mimickry of the punishment that might await the magicians themselves.

This perception of a book of magic as itself a magical object, and therefore as suspect, is seldom so dramatically manifested as in the canonization proceedings for Archbishop Antoninus of Florence (the man from whom, incidentally, the *Malleus maleficarum* derived most of its misogynist tropes).[16] One witness to the sanctity of the archbishop told how the saint had gone one day to a barber-surgeon of Florence named Master Peter to have his hair cut. During the process the prelate began to wonder how a man who read no Latin was able not only to cut hair but also to cure the sick people who came to him. He learned that the barber had obtained a 'book of surgery' from a Cistercian and had learned from it the art of healing. Antoninus asked Peter to bring forth this book and show it to him; the man readily complied.

> The archbishop recognized that the book was full of incantations, and formulas and signs belonging to the wicked magical arts. So one day he went to San Marco for lunch, and when certain members of the city's nobility were with him in the cloister after the meal, he had fire brought in an earthen vessel, and he set fire to the book. Immediately the air was so darkened that the citizens were afraid, and clung to the archbishop. He comforted them, saying that when the book was fully burned this darkening and clouding of the air would cease, as indeed happened. Then, calling these citizens and Master Peter about him, he explained that the book contained incantations, and that at some point a mass had been celebrated over it for conjuring and summoning demons, so that wherever the book was, a multitude of demons resided there.

The burning thus served as an exorcism; the very pages seemed quite literally infected by demons, who needed to be banished. Once this was accomplished, Antoninus admonished Peter to find some other means for healing the sick; the man obeyed this admonition, and the canonization proceedings assure us that God did not allow his family to go lacking.

The notion that demons could infest a book appears elsewhere: Michael Scot told of a magical book inhabited by spirits who call out when the book is opened, 'What do you want? What do you seek? What do you order? Say what you want and it shall be done forthwith.'[17] The theme admits at least two interpretations. One might see it as a way of symbolizing the ubiquity of malign spirits, their eagerness to seize any opportunity for mischief, and their dense concentration in those places and objects seen as special 'occasions of sin'. Beyond this, it can express obsessive anxiety about the book itself as an object invested with a kind of negative sacrality, something taboo, a source of spiritual and psychological contagion. The difference is not that the first interpretation is cultural and the second psychological; both interpretations function on both levels, relating the concerns of individual observers to the shared perceptions of the society. But the first interpretation places greater weight on the theological assumption that malevolent forces are secretly present in the world, an 'objective' assumption in the sense that it is widely diffused within the culture, eliciting and appealing to a diversity of personal concerns and anxieties, while the second stresses the aversion of the individual observer, a reaction inevitably both experienced and expressed in culturally conditioned terms.

Archbishop Antoninus's authority was perhaps too great for a mere barber-surgeon to challenge his interpretation of the book he had been using, but not all practitioners were so amenable to instruction. In the 1340s, the inquisitor Pietro da l'Aquila charged the Florentine physician Francesco di Simone with having purchased a book on the virtues of herbs, in which (according to the inquisitor) there was necromantic content. The physician testified that he had indeed bought such a book, but that there was no taint of necromancy in it, and if he had known that the volume contained anything prohibited he would never have bought it.[18] It makes little difference for our present purposes whether the inquisitor's or the archbishop's reading of a particular book was correct, or grounded in a careful reading of the volume's contents. Either of them might have been scandalized by simple charms of a sort that a theologian would in principle have deemed innocent but a careless or overly zealous critic might perceive as tainted and implicitly demonic.[19] In other cases it seems more likely that magical books condemned as demonic were in fact collections of expressly demonic magic; Piero di ser Lippo claimed that the book he confiscated from Agnolo di Corso contained formulas for adoration and invocation of spirits such as Satan and Beelzebub, and there is no reason to doubt that the inquisitor encountered a work of genuine demonic magic, of the sort that have on occasion survived.

Less dramatic than the action of Archbishop Antoninus, but similar to it in certain respects, was the judicial treatment of a magical book by the secular authorities at Dijon:

Concerning the execution [*exécution*] of a book of devilry [*deablerie*]. On the sixth day of August, in the year 1463, at the command of my lords of the Chambre des comptes at Dijon, after consultation in this Chambre, a book made of paper and covered with leather that was colored green was brought from the house and residence of the widow and heirs of Thomas of Dampmartin, during his life resident of Dijon. In this book were written many evil and false invocations of devils [*deables*], divinations, charms [*charoyes*], and other things of the magical art, which give very bad example and are against God and the holy Christian faith. In it were contained many depictions of devils and other detestable figures and characters. At the end of this book were several chapters and articles on necromancy [*nigromance*] and chiromancy. This book had been seen by my lords of the Council and the Chambres des comptes. And after they inspected it with great and serious deliberation – in the presence of lord Jehan Bon Varlet, priest of the chapel of my lord the duke of Dijon, dean of Saint-Seigne, vicar and scelleur of the reverend father in God my lord the bishop of Lengres in Dijon; master Jehan de Molesmes, secretary of my lord the duke; Ayme d'Eschenon, mayor of the town and commune of Dijon; Jehan Rabustel, procurator of that town; Aimé Barjod, procurator of my lord in the district of Dijon; and many others – this book was cast into the fire and totally burned to cinders, to the despite and confusion of the evil enemies [of the faith], and so that it could never again be used in any manner.[20]

Here there is no allegation of supernatural phenomena, and the book is not seen as infected or possessed by demons needing to be exorcized. None the less, the book itself is treated as if it were a human subject, to be examined and, once found guilty, executed by burning. Nothing in the account need be taken as implying that the book itself possesses numinous powers, yet the book elicits the loathing and the judicial reaction normally reserved for a personal agent and embodiment of evil. From one perspective there is nothing unusual about investing a book with personality: the reading of any book can be perceived as a kind of dialogue between the reader and the text. Rarely, however, is the perception carried to this extreme.

The numinous quality of a book of magic could resemble that of a liturgical or devotional book, and in some cases the distinction between a devotional and a magical work could be obscure. The chronicle of Saint Denis tells how in 1323 a monk of Morigny was found to possess a book of devotions inspired by curiosity and pride, although he claimed to have been inspired rather by visions of the Virgin Mary. In her honour, he had had many images of the Virgin painted on his pages. He thus sought to renew the 'heresy and sorcery' known as the *ars notoria*, which involves the use of special figures, contemplation of these figures amid prayer and fasting, and invocation of mysterious and presumably demonic names, all for the sake of knowledge, wealth, honour or pleasure. His own book promised such rewards, but required invocations, the special copying of the book (at great expense), and the inscription of one's name in the book itself two times;

the physical object, in other words, needed to be customized for its user. This book was so evil, the chronicle declares, that judges at Paris consigned it to the flames.[21] In other cases the boundary between devotion and magic was complicated by various factors: the combination of devotional and liturgical material with natural magic;[22] the tendency in books of conjuration to juxtapose formulas for invoking angels, demons and spirits of neutral or indeterminate standing, and the use of prayers to God for power over demonic and other spirits. Thus, when the necromantic plot against Benedict XIII was divulged in 1406, and investigation produced a coffin filled with books of prayers as well as conjurations, it is impossible to know whether even the 'prayers' were orthodox or deviant.

Tales of sorcerers' apprentices emphasize that the wondrous powers of a magical book are not easily controlled: one exemplum tells of a pupil who reads a chapter from his master's magical tome and thereby arouses a tempest which can be quelled only when the master comes back and reads a chapter equal in length.[23] One might say that in such a tale it is not the book itself but the magic it contains that is powerful and uncontrollable, but the emphasis on use of a chapter of equal length suggests that the process of reading may have magical, quantifiable efficacy distinguishable from that of the specific contents.

THE *BOOK OF CONSECRATIONS*

The perception of a book of magic as possessing numinous power is not merely an obsession of the inquisitors; it is grounded in the writings of the magicians as well, who guarded the secrecy of their writings perhaps mainly for fear of detection, but also out of a sense that the books themselves were sacred objects.

A late medieval book of demonic magic is in at least one respect decidedly not like a cookbook. If one discovers that the recipes in a cookbook tend to come out badly, one may reasonably wonder whether there are errors in detail – whether, for example, the author meant a teaspoon rather than a tablespoon of salt, or a pinch and not a pound of nutmeg – but to take the faulty book to a priest and have it blessed would normally be thought eccentric at best. Yet that, or the rough equivalent, is indeed what a late medieval necromancer might have done with a defective book of magic. He might suppose that verbal flaws in the conjurations were partly to blame,[24] but, as we will see, the variants in late medieval necromantic texts seem to have been so common that a practitioner might have despaired of ever finding a flawless text to recite. In any case, the problem of verbal flaws was perhaps not the necromancer's greatest concern. A short, anonymous work called the *Liber consecrationum* (*Book of Consecrations*), which circulated in late medieval manuscripts in varying forms, makes clear that the book itself was a sacred object requiring elaborate consecration, and that its contents might lose their magical efficacy.[25] According to this *Book of Consecrations*, the magician must seek to recover the lost efficacy of his formulas by subjecting the book itself to an elaborate process of recharging, or reconsecration.

The prologue to this work insists that its proceedings are especially valuable, being dedicated to the names of God, and should not be used in vain. By invoking God's names, the 'exorcist or operator' can renew the power of a magical experiment which has lost its efficacy. Many people seek to achieve great works, and possess writings by which they will attain their desire, but they accomplish nothing, because their experiments are corrupt. The operator must refrain from every pollution of mind and body, and for nine days must be abstinent in food and drink, must keep from idle or immoderate words, and must be clothed in clean garments. On each of these days he must hear mass, carrying this book with him and placing it on the altar during the mass, which seems to assume the celebrant's complicity, if the owner of the book is not in fact himself a cleric. He must execute this procedure devoutly, with prayer and fasting, so as to attain knowledge of sacred mysteries, and then he must carry the book back home. He should have a secret place, sprinkled with holy water, in which he can place the book, after binding it with a priestly cincture and a stole placed in the form of a cross. Kneeling toward the east he must say seven psalms (presumably the seven penitential psalms), 'the litany' (meaning the litany of the saints), and a further prayer before opening the book. Then he may open the book with humble devotion and with heartfelt desire 'that God may sanctify and bless and consecrate this book, devoted to his most sacred names, so that it may fully obtain the power it should have, that it may have power for consecrating the bond of spirits and for all invocations and conjurations of [spirits], and likewise all other experiments'.

These instructions are followed by a prayer, to be said after the litany of the saints – actually three prayers of varying length. The first is a plea that God may hear the operator's prayers despite his unworthiness. The second, addressed to Christ, repeats this central entreaty, and asks that he may consecrate this book:

> by the power of these your most sacred names, On, Jesus Christ, Alpha and O, El, Eloy, Eloyye, Sithothith, Eon, Sepmelamaton, Ezelphates, Tetragramaton, Elyoram, Ryon, Deseryon, Erystion, Ysyornus, Onela, Baysyn, Moyn, Messias, Sother, Emanuel, Sabaoth, Adonay, and by all your secret names which are contained in this book, so that by the virtue, sanctity, and power of these names this book may be consecrated ✠ and blessed ✠ and confirmed ✠ by the virtue of the sacrament of your body and blood, so that it may effectively, without any deception, [and] truly obtain the power that this book should obtain, for consecrating the bond of spirits, and for consecrating all corrupt experiments, and that they may have the fulness of virtue and power for which they are ordained, through the grace of the Lord Jesus Christ, who is seated on high, to whom be honour and glory throughout unending ages. Amen, amen, amen, amen, amen.

This second prayer then invokes all the heavenly powers to bless the book. The third and briefest simply calls upon Christ to bless the book. The procedure is then complete. If the operator later wishes to consecrate a particular experiment, or add a new one, he should use a series of further prayers, along with which he must say the Confiteor, take holy water, and make the sign of the cross on his forehead. At all times he must take care that this book, which the wise adepts (*sapientissimi phisichi*) dedicated to God's holy names, not fall into the hands of the foolish. Why this caution might be necessary becomes especially clear toward the end of the supplementary prayers, in which the 'exorcist or operator' specifically requests power to summon 'malign spirits' from wherever they may happen to be lurking.

THE MENTALITY OF THE NECROMANCERS AND THEIR OPPONENTS

It would be a mistake to think of necromancy as a peripheral phenomenon in late medieval society and culture. Secular as well as ecclesiastical courts took it seriously and at times executed those charged with its practice; monarchs and popes as well as commoners lived in fear of becoming its victims. This fear may have been in some cases or to some degree feigned or pathological, but it was also grounded in realistic awareness that necromancy was in fact being practised, and in an almost universally shared conviction that it could work.

The history of magic sometimes claims a place in academic study as a field within intellectual history. This claim is plausible when the subject is a writer such as al-Kindi or Marsilio Ficino, deeply concerned with the practical operation of magic but also with the philosophical principles by which magic worked. This is not the type of material I will chiefly be examining in this study. The focus here will be formulas of frankly demonic magic, with only the most meagre of intellectual pretensions; I wish to suggest, perhaps perversely, that such a text none the less repays close examination. The rites contained in a manual of necromancy are flamboyantly transgressive, even carrying transgression toward its furthest imaginable limits, and in today's academic environment one might justify studying them on these grounds. I am impelled more by a simple urge to grapple with late medieval culture in its entirety, including its most problematic and conflicted manifestations – warts and all, to use a fitting cliché – and to explore how the underside of the culture related to the side more often displayed. This too is part of the historian's challenge of discerning how things made sense in an alien culture.

First, then, the surviving necromantic texts provide a useful starting point for the *sources* of late medieval magic. Certain aspects of the necromancy laid out in these writings are clearly derived from the Arabic tradition of astral magic that became widely diffused in Europe from at least the thirteenth century onward. At times, as we shall see, the experiments are indebted to Jewish magical traditions, whether explicitly or implicitly, although the impact of Jewish magic on the forbidden rites of Christendom has been less studied and is harder to trace in detail than the influence of Arabic tradition. There are even materials in late medieval necromantic manuscripts closely resembling the magic of antiquity. It is often tempting to suppose that the forms of magical practice are essentially similar across cultures and throughout time, or at least over a very extended *longue durée*. Indeed, one might easily be persuaded that there is a history of the uses of magic and reactions to magic, but not a history of magic itself: virtually every magical technique one encounters appears so deeply rooted in tradition that magical practice seems essentially timeless and perennial. Indeed, it is possible to cite analogues and possible sources for late medieval magic from widely diverse cultures; in search of such parallels one could wander endlessly through thickets of the history of magic, from the Greek magical papyri of antiquity, through Arabic and Byzantine sources, and on to the grimoires of the early modern era. Yet when certain more or less well defined classes of practitioner take an interest in magic, they will adapt to their own use forms of magic taken from various sources. If the history of magic is to be anything other than a night in which all cats are black, it must attend to the characteristics of specific mélanges of magical tradition. The chief purpose of this study is therefore not to trace the history of individual elements but to reconstruct the configurations into which these elements enter: the patterns of magical practice worked in a particular historical setting, the relationship between these forms of magic and other aspects of the culture, and the perceptions of magic within that culture.

Furthermore, we cannot understand the *opposition* to magic in late medieval Europe without knowing fully what sorts of magic were being practised in that culture. Apart from the exempla by Caesarius of Heisterbach and others telling of the dangers of necromancy, there is considerable literature by late medieval theologians directed against these practices. For instance, the Paris theologians who in 1398 issued a general prohibition of magic were clearly aware of necromantic practices and concerned to eradicate them.[26] The theological literature against necromancy is incomprehensible without knowledge of the necromancers' formulas, and has at times been seriously misunderstood.[27] Nor can we understand the virulence of the critics' assault on magic without knowing the purposes magic was believed to serve. The glorification of the transgressive and the vilification of persecutors has perhaps too often blinded us to the recognition that much magic was intended for sexual coercion and exploitation, or for unscrupulous careerism, or for vigilante action against thieves that could easily lead to false accusations. I do not propose to moralize about these activities, but as a corrective to naive romanticizing I do want to make clear the kinds of magic one can expect to find in a late medieval source. It would be too much to claim that fear of clerical necromancy was a major source of pre-

Reformation anti-clericalism – in Boccaccio, for example, when clerics make pretence of magical power this is exercised in the service of their lechery, and lust rather than magic is the focus of the satire – but the realization that certain clerics were dabbling in conjuration could hardly have made a positive contribution to the image of the clergy at a time when for other reasons there was increasing distrust of priests and priestcraft.[28]

If we neglect the literature of necromancy we cannot grasp what it is that the Humanist mages (Marsilio Ficino, Giovanni Pico, Johannes Reuchlin, Johannes Trithemius and others) so vigorously claimed *not* to be doing, or what they were often suspected of doing despite their protestations. Even the rise of the witch trials in the fifteenth century is related to increasing consciousness of this explicitly demonic magic. It was surely in large part because they were aware of the demonic magic described in these manuals and evidently practised in their midst that orthodox authorities often became sceptical about the notion of non-demonic, natural magic. They seem to have misconstrued ordinary magical procedures, interpreting them as working, like necromancy, through demonic agency.[29] Cesare Lanza hinted at the connection when he remarked in 1579, 'Today a lowly little woman does more than all the necromancers accomplished in the ancient world.'[30] In so far as necromancers contributed to the plausibility of claims about witches, they bear indirect responsibility for the rise of the European witch trials in the fifteenth and following centuries. To the extent that these early witch trials focused on female victims, they thus provide a particularly tragic case of women being blamed and punished for the misconduct of men: women who were not invoking demons could more easily be thought to do so at a time when certain men were in fact so doing.

Natural magic was always, in some quarters, a suspect category, and understandably so: its mechanisms remained unclear, and its claims to empirical confirmation were perhaps even by medieval standards not impressive. Demonic magic, in contrast, was a straightforward notion, and its efficacy was easy for virtually all medieval people to believe. Small wonder if for some authorities in late medieval Europe this became *the* paradigmatic form of magic, and if other forms came to be interpreted as implicitly grounded in demonic aid, so that a theologian, an inquisitor, or an educated lay judge might be sceptical about claims that some magic was natural rather than demonic.

More generally, knowledge of this material adds significantly to our understanding of later medieval *clerical culture*. A society that had a surplus of clergy inevitably spawned an underemployed and largely unsupervised 'clerical underworld' capable of various forms of mischief, including necromancy, and indeed this underworld seems to have been the primary locus for this explicitly demonic magic. Not all those accused of conjuring demons were clerics; the charge was attached at times to laymen and occasionally women.[31] But the examples cited already suggest that clerics were disproportionally represented, and when we examine the Munich handbook of necromancy in following chapters what we will find there is a characteristically clerical form of magic, using Latin texts and presupposing knowledge of mainstream ritual.[32] The beliefs and ritual operations found in necromancy mimic those of established rites, somewhat as the threads are the same on both sides of a tapestry, and the patterns they form on the underside are recognizably related to those on the front. One might even suggest that a culture in which ritual occupies so central a place will naturally if not inevitably engender forbidden rituals, somewhat as the production of a tapestry necessarily produces on the underside a distorted version of the intended image. The study of late medieval necromancy gives an exceptionally clear and forceful picture of the abuses likely to arise in a culture so keenly attentive to ritual display of sacerdotal power. Our own society, more fascinated with sexuality and its abuse, has its own concerns about miscreant priests and their abuse of young boys; the clerical misconduct most feared in the late Middle Ages was of a different order.

DEMONIC MAGIC AND THE THEORY OF RITUAL

I have spoken of demonic magic as the underside of the tapestry of late medieval ritual culture; more must be said about the character of magic as ritual. If the book of magic is on the one hand a magical book, an object possessing preternatural power, a habitation in which demons may even be supposed to reside, it is on the other hand a script whose formulas are meant for enactment, a guide for ritual action. The book of magic thus functions both as a repository of magical power and as a guide to magical process, a liturgical compendium with rites to be observed, scripts to be enacted. The rites of magic suggest questions analogous to those raised by any rites, even if they differ in the sources of power they mean to exploit. Three issues in the study of ritual are of particular relevance to our understanding of a necromantic text: the relationship between official (or public) and unofficial (or private) ritual; the efficacy ascribed to ritual, and the role of language in ritual.

Émile Durkheim and Marcel Mauss took the chief difference between religion and magic to lie in their social context. To paraphrase their perception, religion is the official observance of a collectivity (such as a Church), while magic is the unofficial practice of an individual (often on behalf of a client). But if one takes religion to be the spiritual practice of a community specifically *acting* as a community, one excludes private prayer – while if one takes it to be the spiritual practice *sanctioned* by a community, even when carried out individually, one relegates any and all disapproved practice, regardless of the grounds for disapproval, to the category of magic.[35] Eamon Duffy has emphasized that magical or superstitious formulas in charms share a common vocabulary with liturgical prayers, which already suggests the need for a nuanced sense of the relationship between religion and magic. The complexity of this relationship may be seen with particular clarity in the comparison of exorcism and conjuration. As we shall see in a later chapter, in medieval parlance these terms were used interchangeably, and the practices are in fact in all ways but one identical. What we now call exorcism was practised by an individual, usually a cleric (although some laypeople claimed the role), who addressed demons with formal commands, whose power was derived chiefly from the sacred realities invoked in the formulas of command. What we now call conjuring was also practised by an individual, usually a cleric, who addressed demons with formal commands essentially identical to those of the exorcists, again powerful by virtue of appeal to sacred realities. In neither case was the command automatically efficacious: both exorcists and conjurers reckoned on the possibility that the demons might resist their invocations and refuse compliance, in which case the rituals of command would be redoubled. Both the exorcist and the conjurer were engaged in spiritual wrestling matches with the demons, and in both cases they were keenly aware of the dangers. Exorcism was in principle carried out on behalf of a demoniac; conjurations could be done as ways of afflicting enemies, and could be carried out on behalf of clients. In both cases, then, the ritual performer was acting as an individual but within a social context. If exorcisms were allowed, at least to authorized clergy, while conjuring was prohibited to all, it was because of the one key difference: the exorcist's intent was to dispel the demons, while the conjurer's was to summon them, and mainstream opinion held that it was better to be rid of malign spirits than to invite them into one's life. Study of conjurations in subsequent chapters will suggest that there is no other essential difference between this form of magic and religious practices, and that it is better to perceive demonic magic as an illicit form of religion than as a cultural phenomenon distinct from religion.

The efficacy of magical rites, like that of any rituals, can be seen as real, objective, and (within the historical culture) rational, or as emotional, subjective, and symbolic: the magicians' operations may be viewed as actually accomplishing certain ends, or as symbolic expressions of their emotions and their desires. In Ludwig Wittgenstein's classic formulation, 'Magic . . . gives manifestation to a wish; it expresses a wish.'[36] Echoing such earlier formulations, Joseph Gusfield suggests that 'in symbolic behavior the action is ritualistic and ceremonial in that the goal is reached in the behaviour itself rather than in any state it brings about'.[37] This pragmatist perception of ritual may be useful as a way for an observer to excuse someone else's otherwise irrational practice, but there is little evidence that most practitioners themselves view the effect of their rites as merely expressive and not objectively effective.[38] Magic rituals in medieval Europe were clearly intended to produce results: to arouse passion, to drive people mad, to find stolen goods, and so forth. Judicial evidence makes it clear that the practitioners, the clients and the victims all expected magic to have objective effect, and when it did not this was because the specific practitioners were inept or did not perform rituals with sufficient strength to command the demons they summoned.[39]

In one sense, however, Gusfield's formulation does apply to magic. Magical rites, like prayers of petition, may be used for practical ends, but any goals extrinsic to the ritual presuppose an effect intrinsic to it. The prayers and actions that constitute orthodox ritual first of all transform the relationship between the praying person and God, as also the relationship with the persons prayed for, with others in whose company one is praying, and with others throughout history who have said the prayer in question. If such ritual is transformative, the transformation is in the first instance one that occurs *within* the ritual itself. The participants in the ritual become different, and the network of relations in which they stand is reconfigured. Even if no further results ensue, for the duration of the ritual the world of the participant is transformed. Normally one undertakes a ritual with the expectation of further, extrinsic changes, moral or physical, but these are secondary, at least in a logical sense, however important they are to the participant: they are secondary because they presuppose a prior change within the ritual itself, an empowerment of the participant that then makes extrinsic change possible. Ritual can be effective for other purposes only if it first is effective *as ritual*. It can have secondary efficacy only by virtue of its primary efficacy. The principle holds in the case of magical rites, and perhaps most especially those involving demonic magic: even if they are undertaken for the sake of some practical end, that purpose can be accomplished only because within the ritual there is a transformed relationship between the magician and God, between the magician and the demons, and perhaps also between the magician and other humans. Calling upon the aid of God, the magician seeks power over the demons; the primary purpose of the ritual is to build sufficient power that the magician may compel the spirits to do his will. Only if within the ritual itself this transformation of power is attained can the magician accomplish any other goal.

The efficacy of ritual *ex opere operato* must be perceived in this light. Thomas Aquinas was stating the common perception of theologians in the later Middle Ages when he recognized the mass and sacraments as having objective effect independent of the disposition and moral status of the celebrant and minister. That ritual was inherently efficacious (*ex opere operato*), apart from any further effect to be gained by virtue of the minister's or participants' disposition (*ex opere operantis*), by no means meant that the rite was magical. Whether an operation qualified as magic or not depended chiefly on which powers it invoked: if it called upon celestial or manifest natural powers it was not magic, but if it appealed to demonic or occult natural powers it was magic.[40] Rituals that called upon angelic aid formed an ambiguous category, possibly but not necessarily magical, but mainly because the identity of the angel summoned might be in doubt.[41]

A ritual, magical or otherwise, could have efficacy *ex opere operato* precisely because it transformed the status of the performer and his or her relationship with God, with other spirits, and with humans. It was clearly this fear of the efficacy of magic *ex opere operato* that led an actor playing in the *Jeu de Sainte Barbe* in 1470 to make a notarized counterpact declaring that 'by the invocations and anathemas of the demons which he makes in the play . . . he does not intend to speak from the heart but only in the manner of the play, and that on that account the enemy of human kind, the devil, should not have any claim on his soul'.[42] But the force of magical ritual was not in all respects analogous to that of other rites. Ordinary prayer and official ritual assume that the spirits invoked are in general well disposed toward humankind, and enter readily into a helping relationship. The praying person's invocation of God or a saint is an appeal to a benevolent being. In this respect the rituals of demonic magic differ from other rites: they invoke fallen spirits taken (by the necromancers as well as by their critics) to be unwilling, uncooperative, inimical and treacherous. The operations of demonic magic, more than other rituals, are thus explicit contests of wills. The necromancer recognizes a need to heap conjuration upon conjuration, and to buttress these formulas with supporting means of power, precisely because the demons are reluctant to come, and if they come will do everything in their power to escape the magician's control, threaten him, and deceive him. To gain the upper hand in the contest, the magician must hold the strongest possible means for power over the demons, and must adjure them in the name of all that is holy to come in non-threatening form, to cause no harm, and to tell only the truth. Yet all of these factors, far from undercutting Gusfield's analysis, actually strengthen it: they show how vitally important it was for the magician to focus his attention and his energies on the *immediate* consequences of his ritual action. His rites could be efficacious for extrinsic purposes only if they were first effective *as* rites, as ritual contests with cunning and powerful spiritual adversaries who could nevertheless be induced to fulfill his command.

The function of language within magical ritual is a subject to be explored in detail when we examine formulas of conjuration in a later chapter. The general topic is one S.J. Tambiah has discussed, with focus on the use of special languages, or the use of elements from various languages, in magical practice.[43] Necromantic conjurations of the late Middle Ages are almost entirely in Latin, which marks them not as specifically magical but as similar to ordinary liturgical formulas. Some experiments give formulas in what is said to be Chaldean, thus making an appeal to the authority of ancient Jewish magic analogous to that of later Christian Kabbalists. But when a child medium is used, he is sometimes licensed to conjure the spirits in the vernacular. On one level one might say that the choice of language is a matter of indifference: the demons or other spirits being conjured know all human tongues and can be addressed effectively in any of them. Yet in a different way the selection of language was important, because it was only formulas in Latin that were clearly related to the prayers of mainstream liturgy. Necromancers who had command of Latin and could use it to demonstrate the groundedness of their rites in the liturgical tradition of the Church could no doubt gain readier acceptance as authentic masters of their art. And even if demons could understand other languages, they seemed (like God) to pay special attention when addressed in Latin.

In any case, within medieval culture, magical words were seen as effective not *per se* but rather as means for evoking the effective presence of the archetypal powers to which they refer. Magical language is thus not in a simple sense the *cause* of efficacy but rather its *occasion*; the cause is a network of forces released and coordinated by the magician's verbal cue. The situation is analogous to that of the eucharist: the priest's utterance of the words of consecration is not the cause of transubstantiation but rather the divinely ordained occasion for divine intervention. One might suppose that this distinction is too subtle to have been clear to the common necromancer, but in fact the point is clearly articulated in the conjurations themselves, which not only acknowledge but insist that the sources of their own power are the archetypal forces they bring to bear upon the situation at hand.

The magic we are dealing with, then, borrows the conventions of liturgical prayer and has efficacy resembling that of the sacraments. In other respects, however, the fitting comparison is not so much with liturgy and sacraments as with the private devotions that were proliferating in the late Middle Ages, and the analogue to the book of magic is less the missal than the private prayer book. Ritual magic and devotions alike showed how liturgical formulas could be adapted for private and domestic use; indeed, one central point of devotionalism was to provide a network of connections between church and home, bonding them in an increasingly complex relationship, and imparting to the home some of the fervour and sacrality of the church. Magic resembles the devotionalism of the books of hours and other prayerbooks in its translation of official rites into an unofficial and largely private setting.[44] Books of magic, like books of devotion, proliferated in the expanding marketplace of privately owned and privately read texts.

PLAN OF THIS BOOK

The following chapter will introduce the manuscript to which this study is chiefly devoted. Subsequent chapters fall into two blocks. Chapters 3–5 examine the experiments according to the chief purposes for which they are performed: entertainment (illusionist experiments), power over other individuals (psychological ones), and knowledge (divinatory ones). The chief point of these chapters is to show that within this body of material there are in fact fairly clearly distinguishable subtraditions, and to sketch the common characteristics of each. Chapters 6–8, then, analyse the sources and techniques used to gain magical power, in particular the conjurations (and the demonology assumed by these conjurations), the magic circles, and the formulas of astral magic – techniques that cut across the categories discussed in the earlier chapters, and thus represent elements of continuity within the diversity of necromantic practice.

Throughout the book I will give translations (my own, unless otherwise noted) of source material for the study of late medieval necromancy. Most of these passages are from the Munich handbook; to give a sense of the cultural context, I have included some material from other writings of the magicians and from writings about and against demonic magic. I have opted not to give a complete translation of the Munich handbook; both specialists and general readers, I assume, will be better served by selective translation of representative and particularly interesting passages (selected perhaps disproportionately but not exclusively from the earlier sections of the handbook), integrated into my analysis. This option seems especially appropriate given the largely repetitive nature of the material, and the need to situate it in its cultural context. The Latin text is, in any case, available at the end of the volume for those who wish to probe more deeply.

Notes

1 On the general topic of literacy in the late Middle Ages see Eamon Duffy, *The Stripping of the Altars: Traditional Religion in England, 1400–1580* (New Haven: Yale University Press, 1992), 53–88; Malcolm B. Parkes, 'The literacy of the laity', in David Daiches and Anthony Thorlby, eds, *Literature and Western Civilization*, 2 (London: Aldus, 1973), 555–77; Paul Saenger, 'Silent reading: its impact on late medieval script and society', *Viator*, 13 (1982), 367–414; and, for a somewhat earlier period, Brian Stock, *The Implications of Literacy: Written Language and Models of Interpretation in the Eleventh and Twelfth Centuries* (Princeton, NJ: Princeton University Press, 1983).

2 See especially Peter Biller and Anne Hudson, eds, *Heresy and Literacy, 1000–1530* (Cambridge: Cambridge University Press, 1994), and Nicholas Watson, 'Censorship and cultural change in late-medieval England: vernacular theology, the Oxford translation debate, and Arundel's Constitutions of 1409', *Speculum*, 70 (1995), 822–64. On certain aspects of books as magical objects see Peter Ganz, ed., *Das Buch als magisches und als Repräsentationsobjekt* (Wiesbaden: Harrassowitz, 1992), esp. Brian P. Copenhaver, 'The power of magic and the poverty of erudition: magic in the Universal Library', 159–80.

3 Barthélemy Hauréau, *Bernard Délicieux et l'Inquisition albigeoise, 1300–1320* (Paris, 1877), 143–65; Lea, *History*, vol. 3, 451f.; Conrad Eubel, 'Vom Zaubereiunwesen anfangs des 14. Jahrhunderts (mit urkundlichen Beilagen)', *Historisches Jahrbuch der Görres-Gesellschaft*, 18 (1897), 628f.; Joseph Hansen, *Zauberwahn, Inquisition und Hexenprozeß im Mittelalter, und die Entstehung der großen Hexenverfolgung* (Munich: Oldenbourg, 1900; repr. Aalen: Scientia, 1964), 253f. The relevant documents are now available in Alan Friedlander, ed., *Processus Bernardi Delitiosi: The Trial of Fr. Bernard Délicieux, 3 September–8 December 1319* (Transactions of the American Philosophical Society, 86/1) (Philadelphia: American Philosophical Society, 1996).

4 Joseph Hansen, ed., *Quellen und Untersuchungen zur Geschichte des Hexenwahns und der Hexenverfolgung im Mittelalter* (Bonn: Georgi, 1901; repr. Hildesheim: Olms, 1963), 2–4; Norman Cohn, *Europe's Inner Demons: An Enquiry Inspired by the Great Witch-Hunt* (London: Chatto, 1975), 193.

5 Eubel, 'Vom Zaubereiunwesen', 609–25; Robert Michel, 'Le procès de Matteo et de Galeazzo Visconti: l'accusation de sorcellerie et d'hérésie, Dante et l'affaire de l'envoûtement (1320)', *Mélanges d'archéologie et d'histoire*, 29 (1909); Hansen, *Zauberwahn*, 333f.; Cohn, *Europe's Inner Demons*, 192.

6 Pierre Luc, 'Un complot contre le Papa Benoit XIII (1406–7)', *Mélanges d'archéologie et d'histoire de l'École de Rome*, 55 (1938), 374–402.

7 Margaret Harvey, 'Papal witchcraft: the charges against Benedict XIII', in Derek Baker, ed., *Sanctity and Secularity: The Church and the World* (Oxford: Blackwell, 1973), 109–16; J. Vincke, 'Acta Concilii Pisani', *Römische Quartalschrift*, 46 (1938), esp. 183–208.

8 Gene A. Brucker, 'Sorcery in early Renaissance Florence', *Studies in the Renaissance*, 10 (1963), 19f., 23., citing G. Sanesi, 'Un episodio d'eresia nel 1383', *Bullettino senese di storia patria*, 3 (1896), 384f.

9 Brucker, 'Sorcery', 13–16, 22f.

10 Nicolaus Eymericus: *Directorium inquisitorum*, ii.43.1, (Rome: Georgius Ferrarius, 1587), also tells of having captured necromancers' books and had them burned in public.

11 Lynn Thorndike, *A History of Magic and Experimental Science*, 3 (New York: Columbia University Press, 1934), 511, citing Rudolf Dier de Muiden, *Scriptum de magistro Gerardo*, ed. G. Dumbar in *Analecta seu vetera aliquot scripta inedita* (Deventer, 1719), 1–12.

12 Quotation from the New Revised Standard Version. For a discussion of the distinctive setting at Ephesus see Clinton E. Arnold, *Ephesians: Power and Magic: The Concept of Power in Ephesians in Light of its Historical Setting* (Cambridge: Cambridge University Press, 1989).

13 Francis A. Gasquet, ed., *Collectanea Anglo-Premonstratensia*, 3 (London: Royal Historical Society, 1906), 117f. The text appears corrupt in more than one place, but the sense is sufficiently clear.

14 One might suggest that the term *nigromantia* not be re-Graecicized as 'necromancy' but left as 'nigromancy'. While in some respects preferable, this usage would mistakenly suggest that medieval usage distinguished between two terms. Both DuCange's *Glossarium* (s.v. *nigromantia*) and the *Oxford English Dictionary* (s.v. 'necromancy') make it clear that *nigromantia* was not a term distinct from *necromantia*, but an alternative version of the same word, influenced by the Latin *niger*. *Dives and Pauper*, for example, is quoted as reading (in the 1496 printing), 'nygromancye, that is wytchecrafte done by deed bodyes'. The equivalence thus conflated 'black divination' (construed broadly with reference to the magical arts in general, but at least by implication these arts conceived as demonic) with 'divination by consulting the dead'. The first part of the word was also at times spelled *nygro-*, *negre-*, *egra-*, etc.

15 On this 'clerical underworld' see Richard Kieckhefer, *Magic in the Middle Ages* (Cambridge: Cambridge Univeristy Press, 1989), esp. 153–6.

16 Hjalmar Crohns, 'Die Summa theologica des Antonin von Florenz und die Schätzung des Weibes im Hexenhammer', *Acta Societatis Scientiarum Fennicae*, 32/4 (Helsingfors, 1903).

17 See Lynn Thorndike, *Michael Scot* (London: Nelson, 1965), 120.

18 Mariano da Alatri, 'L'inquisizione a Firenze negli anni 1344/46 da un'istruttoria contro Pietro da l'Aquila', in Isidorus a Villapadierna, ed., *Miscellanea Melchor de Pobladura*, 1 (Rome: Institutum Historicum O.F.M. Cap., 1964), 225–49.

19 On the relationship between licit and illicit charms, see, e.g., Thomas Aquinas, *Summa theologiae*, II/II, q. 96, a. 4, and the comments of Heinrich Kramer (traditionally ascribed to him and

Jakob Sprenger) in *The Malleus maleficarum*, ii.2.6, trans. Montague Summers (London: Pushkin, 1948), 179–88. Johannes Nider, in his *Praeceptorium divinae legis*, summarized in Henry Charles Lea, *Materials Toward a History of Witchcraft*, ed. George Lincoln Burr, 1 (Philadelphia: University of Pennsylvania Press, 1939), 269f., explains that it is licit to adjure demons in an imperative mode but not in the deprecatory mode that he associates (incorrectly) with necromancers.

20   Jacques Paviot, 'Note sur un cas de sorcellerie à Dijon en 1463', *Annales de Bourgogne*, 65 (1993), 43–5.

21   G.G. Coulton, trans., *Life in the Middle Ages*, 1 (Cambridge: Cambridge University Press, 1928), 162–63, from the *Grandes Chroniques de St Denis*, vol. 5, 269.

22   Duffy, *The Stripping of the Altars*, 266–87.

23   Frederic C. Tubach, *Index exemplorum: A Handbook of Medieval Religious Tales* (FF Communications, 204) (Helsinki: Suomalainen Tiedeakatemia, Akademia Scientiarum Fennica, 1969) , 61, no. 737.

24   For a list of possible explanations for the failure of magic, at least in one cultural setting, see E.E. Evans-Pritchard, *Witchcraft, Oracles and Magic among the Azande* (Oxford: Clarendon, 1937), 475–8.

25   There are two copies in Clm 849, on 52r–59v and 135r–139r, and both are edited below. In addition, there is fragmentary version in Bodleian Library Rawlinson MS D252, 85r–87v, and a French *Livre de consecracion* in Trinity College Cambridge MS 0.8.29, fols 183r–186v.

26   Jean Gerson, *Œvres complètes*, ed. Palemon Glorieux (Paris: Desclée, 1961–73), 10, pp. 86–90.

27   For example, Paul Diepgen, in 'Arnaldus de Villanova De improbatione maleficiorum', *Archiv für Kulturgeschichte*, 9 (1912), 385–403, clearly had no notion what necromancy entailed and was thus seriously mistaken regarding the intent of Arnald's work.

28   Giovanni Boccaccio, *The Decameron*, trans. Mark Musa and Peter Bondanella (New York: Mentor, 1982), 7.3, 7.5 (involving an alleged priest), 8.7 (involving a scholar) and 9.10.

29   See Kieckhefer, *Magic in the Middle Ages*, ch. 7.

30   Guido Ruggiero, *Binding Passions: Tales of Magic, Marriage, and Power at the End of the Renaissance* (New York: Oxford University Press, 1993), 211, 227.

31   E.g., Hansen, *Quellen*, 524–26, and Carl Buxtorf-Falkeisen, *Baslerische Stadt- und Landesgeschichten aus dem sechszehnten Jahrhundert* (Basle: Schweighausen, 1863–8), vol. 4, 1–25.

32   Duffy, *The Stripping of the Altars*, Ch. 6, is surely correct in arguing that knowledge of Latin was shared in varying degree by diverse sections of the population, and was not exclusive to the clergy. It is not the language of necromancy alone, but the command of ritual vocabulary and the assumption of entitlement to use that vocabulary that suggests the necromancers were primarily clerical, and this assumption is confirmed by images of the clerical necromancer found in literature as well as in the judicial records.

33   For discussion of a range of issues in the theory of ritual see Roy A. Rappaport, 'The obvious aspects of ritual', in Roy A. Rappaport, *Ecology, Meaning and Religion* (Richmond, CA: North Atlantic Books, 1979), 173–221.

34   Émile Durkheim, *The Elementary Forms of Religious Life*, trans. Karen E. Fields (New York: Free Press, 1995), esp. 39–44; M. Mauss, *A General Theory of Magic*, trans. R. Brain (London: Routledge & Kegan Paul, 1950).

35   Duffy, *The Stripping of the Altars*, ch. 8.

36 Ludwig Wittgenstein, *Remarks on Frazer's 'Golden Bough'/Bemerkungen über Frazer's 'Golden Bough'*, ed. Rush Rhees, trans. A.C. Miles (Retsford: Brynmill, 1979) ('Die Magie aber bringt einen Wunsch zur Darstellung; sie äußert einen Wunsch'), discussed in Stanley Jeyaraja Tambiah, *Magic, Science, Religion, and the Scope of Rationality* (New York: Cambridge University Press, 1990), 54–63, and in Rodney Needham, *Exemplars* (Berkeley: University of California Press, 1985), 149–77.

37 Joseph Gusfield, *Symbolic Crusade: Status Politics and the American Temperance Movement*, 2nd edn (Urbana: University of Illinois Press, 1986), 21.

38 On this point see Richard Kieckhefer, 'The specific rationality of medieval magic', *American Historical Review*, 99 (1994), 813–36.

39 See, for example, the case of Niccolò Consigli, in Gene A. Brucker, ed., *The Society of Renaissance Florence: A Documentary Study* (New York: Harper & Row, 1971), 361–6.

40 Kieckhefer, 'The specific rationality', 813–36.

41 Invoking an angel established as unfallen, such as the archangels Michael or Gabriel, could be *superstitious* if the means of invocation were inappropriate (e.g., if one used circles and conjurations in calling upon them) but would not thereby have qualified as *magical* by medieval definitions.

42 Jacques Chiffoleau, *La comptabilité de l'au-delà: les hommes, la mort et la réligion dans la région d'Avignon à la fin du Moyen Age (vers 1320–vers 1480)* (Rome: Ecole française de Rome, 1980), 389, n. 92; translation from R.N. Swanson, *Religion and Devotion in Europe, c. 1215–c. 1515* (Cambridge: Cambridge University Press, 1995), 188.

43 Stanley J. Tambiah, 'The magical power of words', *Man*, n.s. 3 (1968), 175–208; also in Stanley J. Tambiah, *Culture, Thought and Social Action* (Cambridge, MA: Harvard University Press, 1985), 17–59.

44 For an overview of the subject see Richard Kieckhefer, 'Major currents in late medieval devotion', in Jill Raitt, ed., *Christian Spirituality*, 2 (New York: Crossroad, 1987), 75–108.

2

THE MUNICH HANDBOOK OF NECROMANCY: Clm 849

In other areas of medieval studies, the 'new philology' is urging renewed attention to particular manuscripts, with respect for their variant readings of texts as well as attention to their physical make-up, evidence of the ways they were used, the disposition of text on the page, and the relationship between text and images. The individual manuscript actually put together by medieval hands and used by medieval readers, rather than the artificial standardized edition, is increasingly seen as a means for understanding how texts functioned within their historical culture.[1] In the same vein, I wish to propose that for the history of magic – especially in the late Middle Ages – what we need most is a series of detailed studies of particular representative manuscripts. This more than any other type of study will contribute toward a concrete and realistic sense of how magicians conceived and represented their art, especially if it is possible to divine the process by which a manuscript was compiled, and to say something about the mentality of the compiler as it changed through different stages of compilation.

Clearly there were those in late medieval Europe whose interest in magic was more theoretical than practical. The monk of Sulby mentioned in Chapter 1 claimed that his fascination with the occult was purely theoretical or speculative. We know that William of Auvergne and Nicholas Eymericus studied works of magic in the interest of analysing them, refuting their assumptions, and condemning them more effectively, while Albert the Great and Roger Bacon had theoretical interests in the occult that grew in large part out of their scientific research. There may well have been many less known figures who took a keen interest in knowing about magic through widely disseminated books such as *Picatrix*, even if they did not intend to practise this learning.[2]

The magical texts probably of greatest interest from a theoretical or scientific viewpoint were integrally conceived and titled works, even if these were pseudonymous or anonymous, as opposed to miscellanies. Works integrally composed by single authors, such as al-Kindi or Marsilio Ficino, or pseudonymous works ascribed to Aristotle, were likely not only to prescribe recipes for specific purposes but to develop more or less explicit theories of occult process. Miscellanies might contain material that *implies* an understanding of how magic worked, but they were less likely to develop a theoretical viewpoint explicitly or coherently. To be sure, this distinction between an integrally conceived work and a miscellany is by no means rigid. While *Picatrix* is one of the great works of Arabic astral magic, infused with a more or less coherent theory of how magic operates,[3] it is also in large measure a compilation. The Pseudo-Albertan *Book of Secrets* is systematic in its organizing principles – it surveys the magical properties first of herbs (nettle, wild teasel, periwinkle, and so forth, one by one), then of stones, then of beasts, and finally of the planets – but the contents gathered under these headings might be found in a miscellany as well, without benefit of organizing structure. Yet while the distinction between an integrally conceived work and a miscellany is thus not absolute, it is none the less real.

It is a distinction worth noting, because the works of magic that survive from medieval Europe include large numbers of miscellanies, and in light of their importance they have been too little studied. When we read in a judicial record or a literary work of a magician who owned and used a book of magic, this is at least as likely to have been a miscellany as an integrally composed treatise. For while miscellanies may be of less interest from a theoretical viewpoint, they had compensating features that may often have made them more useful to the practising magician. The materials assembled in them were selected not to round off some theoretical notion of magic and its component parts, but because *individually* they were taken to be effective. They are documents of use, analogous to the Greek magical papyri.[4] A treatise on conjuration, such as the *Thesaurus necromantiae* ascribed to Roger Bacon,[5] may explain systematically how conjuring spirits works, and how different spirits are related to different astronomical bodies; a necromantic miscellany is more likely to lay out a single 'experiment' (*experimentum*, or, less often, *experientia*, a concrete and experienced application of ritual for magical effect), with all of the required preparations and conjurations, step by step. Historians of magic who are mainly interested in the field from the perspective of intellectual history or the history of science are likely to be drawn mostly to single-author treatises, but those interested in the actual practice of magic and its relevance to cultural, social, judicial, religious and political history must take a keen interest in miscellanies as well. Furthermore, whereas an integrated treatise claims to represent a point of view distilled and isolated from the course of its own development, a miscellany can more fully serve as a biographical document illustrating moments in the life of its compiler, presenting its reader with the challenge of discerning the trajectory of its compiler's shifting interests.

Willy Braekman has edited the magical portions of a Middle Dutch miscellany of the fifteenth century, now at the Wellcome Historical Medical Library in London.[6] This manuscript illustrates the variety of magical materials we might expect to find in a miscellany. Included along with non-magical material are experiments to identify the thief who has stolen milk, beer or wax; to become invisible; to see 'extraordinary things'; to learn about past or future events; to ease childbirth; to transport oneself rapidly by use of an ointment (made of seven herbs, goat's fat and bat's blood). Various love charms or summoning experiments are given, as well as a procedure for preventing a wife from having intercourse with another man by tracing a circle around her genitals with the tail of a lizard.

In the category of magical trickery or parlour games are experiments to cause people to grow dirty while bathing; to cause white birds to hatch from the eggs of black birds; to make a newly hatched peacock white; to cause a woman to leap naked from her bath; to cause a dog to dance; to compel a horse to stand still; to hold a serpent in one's hand without harm, and to cause a horse to collapse as if dead. More useful are procedures to expel mice and flies by use of magical images. The manuscript gives the first half of a moon book, explaining the moon's influence under each zodiacal sign. And it includes a set of experiments ascribed to Solomon, and twelve experiments involving snake-skin, widely attributed to Johannes Paulinus but in fact translated from the Arabic. Most of the experiments in this manuscript are of natural magic, but not all: Braekman's no. 20, especially, calls upon 'the power and might of these spirits, Beheydraz, Anleyuz, [and] Manitaynus', to aid in the magical seduction of a woman.

Bodleian MS Rawlinson D 252, a fifteenth-century English manuscript, contains formulas for explicitly demonic magic, to which Frank Klaassen has called my attention, and which he will describe in his own research now in progress. It is devoted chiefly to lengthy conjurations intended for divination, most often to detect thieves, although there are multi-purpose experiments as well. The bulk of the material is in Latin, but the manuscript also gives lengthy passages in Middle English. The manuscript differs from Braekman's Middle Dutch text in various ways, of which three are immediately apparent: it is more consistently devoted to magical experiments, most of its operations are for a particular kind of magic, and it more regularly calls upon the aid of demons. I will refer to this miscellany on occasion in following chapters.

CODEX LATINUS MONACENSIS 849

We turn now to the specific focus of this study, a fifteenth-century manuscript in the Bavarian State Library, Clm 849, and in particular the texts on folios 3 through 108 of this manuscript. (The material on the following folios is related in kind and approximately contemporary but in different hands and different languages, and evidently not intended as part of the same compilation.) The compiler of this main block of material was evidently German; the appended materials seem to have come from various sources, and one passage contains a formula in Italian.[7] The manuscript is a small one, approximately 8¼ inches high and 5¾ inches wide. The description of this manuscript in the published catalogue is nondescript: it appears there as a book of incantations, exorcisms and sundry bewitchments.[8] Lynn Thorndike made no reference to it in his monumental *History of Magic*,[9] and while he did cite it briefly in a later article published in a festschrift,[10] it has generally been neglected in the literature on witchcraft and magic. In my survey of *Magic in the Middle Ages* I highlighted this text, but without examining it fully and systematically.[11] Yet it deserves careful attention, not because it was influential but because of what it represents. It is a rare example, essentially intact, of what must once have been a flourishing genre: the manual of explicitly demonic magic, or necromancy. It is clearly a miscellany, with little linkage, clustering or other organization of its materials, and no effort to develop a coherent theory to support or explain the 'experiments' it contains. Yet its limitations are also its strengths: the lack of a systematic framework means that each section, essentially self-contained, has a coherence and clarity often lacking in more fully developed writings.

The first two folios of the manuscript are missing, a circumstance which may help to explain how the manuscript evaded detection and thus survived. (Indeed, it is not uncommon for the first folio of a magical manuscript to be missing.)[12] The 107 folios that remain in the main block (rectifying an error in foliation gives us one extra folio) are devoted primarily to a series of forty-two magic experiments. Interspersed with these are a version of the *Liber consecracionum* (no. 31); a list of spirits, with descriptions of the forms in which they appear and the functions they perform (no. 34); a manual of astral magic (no. 37); a list of favourable and unfavourable days for writing magical inscriptions (no. 46); and a fragment of a chemical prescription, with a gloss in the German language (no. 47).

All but a few of the experiments fall into the three main categories. There are twelve illusionist experiments, designed to make things appear other than as they are – to conjure forth an illusory banquet or castle, to obtain a wondrous means of transportation (usually a demon in the form of a horse) that will carry the magician across land or water, or to make a dead person seem alive or vice versa. Seven psychological experiments are intended to have influence on people's intellects or wills – to arouse love or hatred, to gain favour at court, to constrain the will of others, or to drive a person mad. Fully seventeen experiments are divinatory techniques for gaining knowledge of future, past, distant or hidden things. Most of these experiments entail catoptromancy, or scrying: the magician's assistant, usually a young boy, stares at a reflecting surface until he sees figures, taken here to be apparitions of spirits, who can reveal the desired information. As should become clear in following chapters, these three types of experiment are significantly different from one another: we find an element of playful fantasy in the illusionist experiments, an often violent effort at coercion in the psychological ones, and an insistence on detecting truth and righting wrongs in most of the divinatory ones. Differences in tone and in purpose are accompanied by variations in technique: conjuring spirits is of central importance in most of the experiments, but the magic circle plays its most prominent role in the illusionist rituals, sympathetic magic is more prevalent in the psychological experiments, and scrying is itself the key to most of the divination. Rather than a single technique, the necromancy of this handbook represents a congeries of distinct procedures, most of which can be sorted fairly neatly into these three categories.

Roughly speaking, we can say that the moving forces behind the magic of the handbook are the exercise of imagination, the hunger for power and the thirst for knowledge. To be sure, all three elements are at work in all the necromantic experiments. One might say that the main issues raised by the practice of necromancy are those of the relationship between sacrality and power: the necromancers perceived their art and office as sacred and saw themselves as invoking the sacred powers of heaven by which they could constrain the equally numinous but malign and treacherous powers of hell. At the same time, one must recognize that all these experiments required exercise of imagination and were inspired in large part by curiosity. Yet the characteristic emphases differ, and we may safely generalize that it is the imaginative element which dominates in the illusionist experiments, the quest for power in psychological experiments, and the yearning for knowledge in the divinatory ones.

All forms of necromancy presupposed and played upon tensions. Basic to illusionist experiments was the tension between fantasy and reality, all within the border realm in which readers and practitioners were asked to suspend their disbelief, or perhaps rather to entertain possibilities that would normally defy belief but within this ritual context might gain credibility. In psychological experiments the tension was chiefly between the will of the necromancer and that of the victim over whom the master sought to exercise his power. In divinatory experiments it was perhaps most importantly a tension between truth and deception; these rituals were intended to ascertain truth but left themselves open to the constant hazard of error.

The materials in the manuscript that do not fit into these three categories are a procedure for gaining knowledge with the aid of a demon tutor (no. 1), a brief experiment called the 'Key of Pluto' for opening all locks (no. 26), a fragmentary operation for averting harm (no. 44), a chemical recipe (no. 47), and generic materials that can serve diverse ends (nos 31, 32, 34, 36, 37, 42 and 46).

Strikingly absent from this compilation are magical rituals for healing and protection and necromantic procedures for inflicting bodily harm or death. The judicial records provide ample evidence of necromancers charged with undermining the health of their victims, and other necromantic literature evidently provided guidelines for such magic. The compiler of this manuscript seems not to have been a man of conventional morality or scrupulous disposition, yet he seems also not to have taken an interest in these kinds of magic. Not all necromantic manuals were squeamish in this regard. The *Key of Solomon* insists that magic must be used only to glorify God and extend kindness to neighbours, but in fact the work prescribes methods for causing enmity, war, death, destruction, and so forth; as E.M. Butler says, the intentions 'seem to have been of the best; but they were literally of the kind which pave the way to hell'.[13]

The following table shows the order of the forty-two experiments and other materials, most of which are assigned to three broad categories: psychological ('Psych.'), illusionist ('Illus.'), and divinatory ('Divin.'). The numbers for each item are editorial additions.

Table A. Experiments in Clm 849, fols 3–108

No.	Purpose	Fols	Type
1.	For gaining knowledge of the liberal arts	3r–5v	
2.	For causing a person to lose his senses	6r–7v	Psych.
3.	For arousing a woman's love	8r–11v	Psych.
4.	For gaining dignity and honour	11v–13v	Psych.
5.	For arousing hatred between friends	13v–15r	Psych.
6.	For obtaining a banquet	15r–18v	Illus.
7.	For obtaining a castle	18v–21r	Illus.
8.	For obtaining a boat	21r–23r	Illus.
9.	For obtaining a horse	23v–25v	Illus.
10.	For resuscitating a dead person	25v–28r	Illus.
11.	For invisibility	28r–29v	Illus.
12.	For obtaining a woman's love	29v–31v	Psych.
13.	For constraining a man, woman, spirit or beast	32r–33r	Psych.
14.	For obtaining a horse	33v–34r	Illus.
15.	For obtaining a flying throne	34r–35v	Illus.
16.	For finding something in sleep	35v–36r	Divin.
17.	For obtaining a horse	36r–36v	Illus.
18.	The mirror of Floron, for revelation of past, present and future	37r–38r	Divin.
19.	The mirror of Floron, second version	38r–39v	Divin.
20.	Another way of using a mirror	39v–40v	Divin.
21.	For invisibility	40v	Illus.
22.	For discovering a thief or murderer by gazing into a vessel	41r–42r	Divin.
23.	First mirror of Lilith	42r–43r	Divin.
24.	For learning about any uncertain thing by gazing into a crystal	43r–43v	Divin.
25.	For information about a theft by gazing into a crystal	43v–44r	Divin.
26.	Key of Pluto, for opening all locks	44v	
27.	For obtaining information about a theft by gazing into a fingernail	44v–45v, 51r, 46v–47v	Divin.
28.	For obtaining information by gazing at a bone	47v–49r	Divin.
29.	The true art of the basin	49r–49v	Divin.
30.	Twelve names for making spirits appear in a boy's hand	49v–50v	Divin.
31.	The Book of Consecrations	52r–59v	
32.	Conjuration of Satan/Mirage	59v–62v	

No.	Purpose	Fols	Type
33.	For obtaining information from a mirror	62v–65r	Divin.
34.	List of spirits	65v–65r bis	
35.	For obtaining a woman's love	65r bis–67v	Psych.
36.	Generic preparation for conjuring spirits	67v–68v	Divin.
37.	Manual of astral magic	68v–96v	
38.	For obtaining information about a theft by gazing into a fingernail	96v–99v	Divin.
39.	For obtaining information by gazing into a fingernail	99v–103r	Divin.
40.	For obtaining information about a theft by gazing into a fingernail	103r–105v	Divin.
41.	For discovering hidden treasure in sleep	106r–106v	Divin.
42.	The name Semiforas	106v–107r	
43.	For obtaining a horse	107r–107v	Illus.
44.	Fragment of an experiment for averting harm	107v	
45.	For invisibility	107v–108r	Illus.
46.	Favourable and unfavourable days of the month for inscriptions	108r–108v	
47.	Fragment of a chemical prescription (with a note in German)	108v	

After the first (truncated) experiment in the manual, an entire series of fourteen experiments can be gathered into four clusters, two psychological and two illusionist:

Cluster I: Nos 2–5 (for inflicting dementia, gaining the love of any woman, obtaining dignity and honour, arousing hatred between friends)

Cluster II: Nos 6–11 (for obtaining a banquet, obtaining a castle, obtaining a boat, obtaining a horse, resuscitating a dead person, obtaining invisibility)

Cluster III: Nos 12–13 (for obtaining a woman's love, constraining a man or woman or spirit or beast)

Cluster IV: Nos 14–15 (for obtaining a horse, obtaining a flying throne)

Much less of the subsequent material falls into clusters, and the groupings that do occur are devoted exclusively to divination (unless we count the astral magic of no. 37 as itself constituting a cluster):

Cluster V: Nos 18–20 (the mirror of Floron, alternative version of same, another way of using a mirror)

Cluster VI: Nos 22–25 (for discover a thief or murderer by gazing into a vessel, first mirror of Lilit[h], for knowing about any uncertain thing by gazing into a crystal, for information about a theft by gazing into a crystal)

Cluster VII: Nos 27–30 (for obtain information about a theft by gazing into a fingernail, for obtaining information by gazing at a bone, the true art of the basin, twelve names to make spirits appear in boy's hand)

Cluster VIII: Nos 38–41 (for obtaining information about a theft by gazing into a fingernail, for obtaining information by gazing into a fingernail, for obtaining information about a theft by gazing into a fingernail, for discovering hidden treasure in sleep)

Before no. 35 the manuscript gives the heading, 'Here begin good and tried experiments', which suggests that the compiler either reordered materials he was taking from elsewhere or copied this particular experiment from the beginning of some other compilation. The arrangement of folios within the gatherings is highly erratic (with many folios excised, and others elsewhere inserted), but apart from the two folios missing from the front of the manuscript, there is in general a high degree of continuity both within and between the gatherings, the main exception being in the apparently careless fragmentation of experiment no. 27.[14] This discontinuity existed already, and the folios in question had already been excised, at the time of the original (fifteenth-century) foliation. In other words, it is likely that we have the necromancer's manual nearly intact, and possible that, despite the codicological complexity, the discontinuities that exist are the result of the compiler's carelessness rather than later loss of text or errors in binding.

Following all this material from fols 3 through 108 are 48 originally separate folios, 109–156, which again contain miscellaneous material: a conjuration of a demon named Mirage (given fols 109r–118r and again fols 139r–146r); German magico-medical prescriptions (fols 119r–132v); a series of divinatory experiments (fols 133r–134v), with a short 'prayer' in Italian (asking God to ensure the truth of the ensuing revelation) to be recited into the ear of a child who serves as medium;[15] the *Liber consecracionum* (fols 135r–139r); a lunar calendar (fol. 146r); instructions for magical circles (fol. 146v); a treatise on astral magic, the *Opus Zoal et angelorum et spirituum eius* (fols 147r–154v), and a German book of lunar astrology (fols 155r–156v). This material will be discussed here mainly in so far as it resembles or otherwise relates to the main block of material. The only materials from folios 109–156 that are edited here are the second version of the *Liber consecracionum* (given along with no. 31, in parallel columns) and the conjuration of Mirage (given alongside no. 32, in parallel columns).

It may seem – and may indeed be – hazardous to devote such attention to a manuscript that survives in this condition. It is possible that the missing first folio contained a title, named an author, or gave other information that would be important for locating this text within its historical context. If we had such information we might be able to tell more confidently whether this compilation is in fact unique or whether there are other copies.[16] While recognizing the hazards of proceeding with this project, I am moved to do so chiefly by the conviction that this is an exceptionally rich and interesting compilation, that one of the most urgent needs in the history of magic is detailed analysis of specific manuscripts representative of the materials magicians are likely to have used, and that such texts thus hold significance going well beyond their meagre intellectual pretensions. I will make some effort to situate the component parts of the text within their literary context – to cite sources and parallels. For the most part, however, I will focus on the contents of this specific compilation, this microcosm of clerical magic as it was known in the late Middle Ages.

NECROMANCY AND NECROMANCERS IN FIFTEENTH-CENTURY MUNICH

The fact that our necromantic manuscript is now in the Bavarian State Library is not, of course, any indication that it came originally from Munich or even from Bavaria, but its inclusion among the earlier codices of the collection suggests that, wherever its materials were first assembled, they may have been brought to Munich and acquired by the ducal library at an early date. Even if this connection is conjectural, it may thus be interesting to inquire what we know of the practice and perception of necromancy in late medieval Munich. The short answer to this question is that not a great deal is known about necromancers and necromancy specifically in and around Munich in the fifteenth century, yet there are some clues that may help place Clm 849 within a general historical context.

The witch trials conducted in the Dauphiné during the years 1428–47 provide an interesting side light of possible relevance. One of the many subjects brought before the judges in this campaign was a sixty-year-old man, Jubertus of Bavaria, from Regensburg, tried in 1437 at Briançon.[17] Apart from accusations more or less typical of the incipient prosecution for conspiratorial witchcraft (flight to nocturnal assemblies, killing of infants, etc.), Jubertus was charged with activities more often found in connection with clerical necromancy:

> First, the aforesaid Jubertus said and confessed, under freely taken oath . . . that he is sixty years of age, and that for ten years and more he served a certain powerful man in Bavaria who was called Johannes Cunalis, who is a priest and *plebanus*, in a city called Munich in Bavaria, near Bohemia.
>
> Likewise, he said and confessed that this Johannes Cunalis had a book of necromancy [*librum de nigromancia*], and that when he who spoke opened this book at once there appeared to him three demons, one named Luxuriosus, another Superbus, and the third Avarus, [all of them] devils. And the first appeared to him in the form of a charming maiden of twelve years, and she slept with him at night and took their pleasure together.

Likewise, during the night he adored that devil as a god, on bended knee, then turned his posterior toward the east and made a cross on the ground, and spat on it three times, and trampled on it three times with his left foot, and urinated and defecated on it, and wherever he saw a cross he spat upon it and thrice denied God.

Likewise, at dawn he adored Superbus in the same way . . .

Likewise, he gave Superbus what was left over when he ate and drank, and to Luxuriosus he gave three or five pence on Holy Friday before Easter, and he committed both his bodily members and his soul after death. And these devils wanted him to deny that God whom they called an accursed prophet [*maledictum prophetam*], and when he adored those three demons as gods he turned his face toward the west and his posterior toward the east, saying what he said, and when he had his dealings with Luxuriosus the others laughed. . . .

Likewise, he said that when he passed along the roads and was with the demons and found a cross, the devils fled from it and made a great detour around it, and they forbade him to do good deeds and to adore the sacred host, and when it was elevated he was to close his eyes, and they forbade him to take holy water and to kiss the cross or the pax [=osculatory], asserting that they alone were almighty gods.

Likewise, he said and confessed that on Sunday, the seventeenth of this month, all three demons were standing with him in prison, and their eyes glowed like sulphurous fire, and they said to the prisoner that they would guard him well if he did not reveal these things. Then he had dealings and mingled carnally with Luxuriosus, and he said furthermore that these demons would have freed him from prison if he had not revealed these things.

Likewise, he said and confessed that these devils then told him that he would be examined more subtly the next day, and that he would have to tell the full truth, and that he would thus be given over to death . . .

Likewise, he said and confessed that once he was passing with his master through a forest in which there were thieves, but they put them to flight with a multitude of devils who appeared in the form of soldiers. He said further that the world is filled with invokers of demons, and that these devils profit greatly from these things, especially because the world is full of sins, wars and dissensions.

Likewise, he said and confessed that one night with the aid of demons his master had a bridge constructed over a river in Bavaria at a place called Sancta Maria Heremitta.[18]

Likewise, he said and confessed that he had proposed to blind Johanneta, the widow of Johannes Paganus of the present place, because she displeased him. With two keys he had traced her image, in a manner and form which he explained in the examination; he did this on a Sunday, depicting her image beneath the name[s] of devils, using implements, materials and techniques described in the examination, just as he had done in the duchy of Austria in the case of a man called Johannes Fabri of Vienna. And he had disclosed this deed and boasted of it before his capture. . . .

Likewise, he said and confessed that about two years ago he was in the city of Vienna in Austria, and one Thursday there were three drunken cooks in a tavern who refused to let him drink, and when they withdrew at a late hour one of them said to the other two, 'Get up, in the devil's name, and let me pass by!' And at once, at the behest of the accused, all three demons of his master seized those three, snatched them out the door, and cast one of them into a well, another into the sewer or privy of the Dominicans, and the third into the privy of the Franciscans, and none of them but the one cast into a well was killed, the others being freed by the friars at the time of matins.

Likewise, he said and confessed that poisons were made by the aid of devils, by which men could be killed, through their working or by the aid of demons, either at once or in a lingering death, according to the will of the one administering, and according as more or less of the poison is administered, in the name of the devil, in a manner and form contained in the examination, and taken from a basilisk, toad, serpent, spider or scorpion. . . .

Likewise, he said and confessed that when he was passing through the roads and saw images of the Virgin Mary or a cross, he spat at them three times in despite of the Father and the Son and the Holy Spirit, and that on the feast of Saint John the Baptist he gathered certain herbs for medicine, as specified in the proceedings, and on bended knees he first adored them, then extracting them in the name of his devils, and in despite of almighty God, the creator of all. . . .

The link between necromancy and witchcraft emerges also from the work of Johannes Hartlieb (c. 1400–68). Hartlieb served the duke of Bavaria in Munich during the last three decades of his life, and between 1456 and 1464 he wrote *Das půch aller verpoten kunst (The Book of All Forbidden Arts)* at the behest of Margrave Johann ('the Alchemist') of Brandenburg-Kulmbach.[19] Some have seen the work as marking a departure from earlier work of Hartlieb's that dealt with the occult arts in a more sympathetic manner, but the attribution of most of these works is at best doubtful: writings that he had in his library and consulted to inform himself about the occult arts were in some instances falsely ascribed to him. Some have read *Das půch aller verpoten kunst* as a clever excuse for relating otherwise forbidden information to a curious reader, but Hartlieb does not give enough particulars for his work to be of much use in magical practice. Frank Fürbeth is surely correct in placing the work in a tradition of catechetical writings for lay instruction, influenced in particular by Nicholas Magni of Jawor and by the work of certain contemporary Viennese writers.[20] Hartlieb lists necromancy (*nigramancia*) as the first of the seven forbidden arts, along with geomancy, hydromancy, aeromancy, pyromancy, chiromancy and spatulamancy. His chapter 22 defines the term:

> *Nygramancia* is the first forbidden art, and is called the black art. This art is the worst of all, because it proceeds with sacrifices and services that must be rendered to the devils. One who wishes to exercise this art must give all sorts of sacrifices to the devils, and must make an oath and pact [*verpintnuß*] with the devils. Then the devils are obedient to him and carry out the will of the master, as far as God permits them. Take note of two great evils in this art. The first is that the master must make sacrifice and tribute to the devils, by which he denies God and renders divine honors to the devils, for we should make sacrifices only to God, who created us and redeemed us by his passion. The other is that he binds [*verpint*] himself with the devil, who is the greatest enemy of all humankind.[21]

Hartlieb's categorization adapts that of Nicholas Magni and harks to much earlier discussions of the branches of the magic arts. Isidore of Seville, who deals with magic and especially magical divination in his *Etymologies*,[22] speaks of four species of divination which employ the four elements (geomancy, hydromancy, aeromancy and pyromancy), but among other forms of divination mentions the *necromantici* who resuscitate and interrogate the dead. Hugh of St Victor's *Didascalicon* borrows from Isidore, but organizes the divisions of magic into five categories, of which the first, *mantice*, includes divination by necromancy and by the four elements.[23] Hartlieb cites Isidore of Seville's more restricted use of the term 'necromancy', for conjuring the shades of the dead, but he himself uses it in the broader sense, essentially interchangeable with 'demonic magic'.[24]

As indicated, Hartlieb's portrayal of necromancy displays close links between this art and the conspiratorial witchcraft that was emerging in both trials and treatises at the time he wrote. The necromancer conjures the Devil with characters and secret words, with fumigations and sacrifices, in addition to making a pact with the Devil.[25] The Devil acts as if the conjurer caused him pain by his exorcizing and conjuring (*beswern und pannen*), although they actually give him great satisfaction. In all these respects he might be taken as describing the conspiratorial witch, although his explicit subject is the necromancer. Hartlieb even discusses early witch trials at Rome and at Heidelberg within the context of necromancy.[26] Hartlieb's reading and experience were wide: he claims to have consulted with Greeks, Tartars, Turks and Jewish women about the practice of these forbidden arts.[27] His book is thus by no means specifically about the magic practised in and around Munich. But it was while serving as counsellor to the Duke of Bavaria that he gathered information from diverse sources, making his study at Munich in effect a clearing house for knowledge about magical activities.

The early history of Clm 849 is not established,[28] and its ownership obviously cannot be demonstrated. It is tempting to speculate that Hartlieb had it at his disposal, along with numerous other books of necromancy and the allied arts. Many of the practices Hartlieb describes are laid out in Clm 849 (e.g., the anointing of a boy's fingernail for scrying, or the conjuring of a demon in the form of a horse for magical transportation), although, to be sure, there is little if anything in his work that he could not have derived from other sources. Those eager to fill in all the blanks might suggest that Jubertus actually consorted with Johannes Cunalis, the priest of Munich, and that the Munich handbook of necromancy was in fact the *liber de nigromancia* owned and used by this cleric. The spontaneous appearance of Luxuriosus, Superbus and Avarus would on this interpretation would have to be a way of talking about the spirits which inform such a book – and it is perhaps no distortion to suggest that the spirit of lust (*luxuria*) is one main incentive for the psychological experiments, the spirit of pride (*superbia*) is a prime factor in the illusionist ones, and the spirit of avarice (*avaritia*) is a key motive of the necromancer, and sometimes of his client, for staging the divinatory ones.

Even if it were possible to establish a clear connection between Clm 849, Jubertus and Hartlieb, one would hesitate to speak of Munich as in any special way a centre for the practice of necromancy, or to postulate a distinctive character to the magic used there. In all likelihood necromancy was studied and practised within a kind of clerical underworld through much if not most of Western Europe in the later Middle Ages. We have no reason to suppose that Munich was in this respect different from any other city.

THE COMPOSITION OF THE MUNICH HANDBOOK

For reasons I have already touched upon, any discussion of how Clm 849 came to be compiled must remain conjectural: the first two folios are missing, the provenance of the manuscript remains obscure, there are no indications of either authorship or ownership, and the disposition of the manuscript is complex. Nonetheless, we can make some reasonable assumptions about the process by which this handbook came into existence, and thus about the workings of the 'clerical necromancy' that would have produced and employed such a book.

We cannot speak of the writer of this manual as its 'author', because we do not know to what extent he devised the formulations that he gives, or how far he merely reproduced other people's work. In some cases he deliberately gave alternative forms of demons' names,[29] which suggests that he was working from a previous manuscript and was unsure of the reading. The writer's own orthography was highly erratic; within the same experiment he sometimes slipped from one version to another in his names for demons, and while the variations were sometimes slight they were not always so.[30] (At the end of the fifteenth century, Humanist mages such as Johannes Reuchlin protested that the debased magic of contemporary necromancers could have no effect because the very names they used for the spirits were corrupt; the present manuscript might have served as a case in point.)[31] Whether the writer composed badly or copied badly, one constant factor in the manuscript is that its Latin usage is unconventional by medieval (let alone classical or Humanist) standards. In one experiment the writer speaks of a 'whole white dove' (*columbam totam albam*) when he means a 'totally white dove' (*columbam totaliter albam*); he writes that a woman 'will love all things above you' (*super te omnia diliget*) when he clearly means the reverse; he confuses 'without' (*sine*) with 'or' (*siue*), and he evidently substitutes 'prepare' (*parare*) for 'obey' (*parere*).[32] More often than one would expect, he leaves other words out altogether. At times his sentences give way to grammatical nonsense. The formula 'May your arts fail . . . as Jamnes and Mambres failed' (*Deficiant ergo artes tuae . . . sicut defecerunt Iamnes et Mambres*), referring to the names of Pharaoh's magicians according to a tradition reflected in II Timothy 3:8, is given once in the main block of Clm 849, and twice in later sections of the manuscript, by two different hands (no. 32). But in the main block the point of the allusion is lost and the comparison comes out in utterly garbled form as 'May your arts fail . . . so you and members have now ceased' (*sic cessauerunt jam vos et membros*), while in the other versions the passage begins 'Your ears will fail' (*Deficient ergo aures tuae . . .*).

What seems quite clear is that the writer was a cleric – probably a priest, and at least a person in minor orders. His use of Latin makes this a *prima facie* likelihood, even if his Latin is bad. The more compelling evidence is his assumption that the user of the manual will, like him, be acquainted with ritual forms used in the Church's services: he gives the opening line of Psalm 50 (from the Vulgate) and assumes the user will know the text (no. 33); he prescribes the seven (penitential) psalms and the litany (of the saints) and presumes that these too will be familiar and accessible (no. 36). In short, the work appears clearly a product of that clerical underworld in which late medieval necromancy seems to have found something of a natural home. It may have been exercised and feared as a means for gaining otherwise elusive power within a competitive clerical establishment. It may have been a pastime for underemployed clerics with time on their hands and a fondness for this quintessentially clerical form of dark and daring entertainment. It may have been a service rendered to credulous clients by unscrupulous providers of ritual. Like the Ouija board in latter day culture, it may well have been all of the above, an amusement constantly in danger of becoming serious, dark and threatening.

In certain important respects there are shifts in the content and tone of the manuscript, suggesting changes in the compiler's interests and his attitudes toward the material. Along with a shift from illusionist and psychological experiments to rites of divination comes a general flattening of the prose. It is in the front of the manual that the writer is inclined to tell entertaining anecdotes and to provide testimonials to the authenticity and efficacy of the rituals. The earlier materials suggest more authorial self-consciousness, a clearer sense of authorial voice. Later sections are less developed with narrative and other embellishments. Even the magic circles required for the experiments and illustrated in the manuscript tend to become less complex and less interesting in the later sections of the compilation. The manual shifts also in its engagement of the reader. In the earlier experiments the writer regularly addresses the reader in a direct and personal manner, urging him to 'attend carefully' (no. 2), taking him into his confidence by entrusting him with secret information (nos 4 and 9), reminding him of a situation in which he has seen the master perform an experiment (no. 6), and referring to his own needs and desires – 'If you want to have the love of any woman . . .' (no. 3), 'If you wish to infuse a spirit into a dead person so that he appears alive . . .' (no. 10), 'If you wish to be taken for invisible and imperceptible . . .' (no. 11), 'If you wish to know about any matter on which you are doubtful . . .' (no. 24). Subsequent experiments are couched in far more impersonal rhetoric; the reader is instructed with blunt imperatives and subjunctives, with no expression of interest in entertaining him or engaging his interest. The later materials are less ambitious in their imaginative depth, but more ambitious in laying out procedures likely to be put to actual use.

The most basic question about the actual composition of the book is whether it is taken from a single source (as a set of excerpts from a cohesive treatise or as a copy of some previous miscellany) or from multiple sources. The latter scenario seems far more plausible, largely because there are occasional discontinuities that suggest the compiler was working with a collection of unbound materials that were not in perfect order, and he was perhaps not certain about where to fit them into his series of experiments. The effect was similar to that of assembling diverse materials in a scrapbook and finding that some of the odds and ends assembled are not complete or entirely coherent. This type of discontinuity would have been possible if the writer had been drawing excerpts from a cohesive work or copying an earlier miscellany, but in the former case one might have expected the individual units to remain cohesive, and in the latter one might have thought the copyist would have rationalized or deleted the incoherent fragments. At any rate, it appears not at all unlikely that the materials bound together with the main handbook are examples of the sort of material from which the compiler worked. My hypothesis is that the compiler and scribe took a lively interest in various kinds of magical materials, put together a personal collection of them from various sources, and had readily at hand perhaps both bound and unbound writings of diverse character and provenance (at least one bit of appended material contains a fragment of Italian); that the materials that he copied into his own anthology represent his own selection (and perhaps, as in the abridgement and reformulation of the conjuration of Mirage,[33] his own adaptation) from this body of material, and that when his own compilation was originally bound, or perhaps when at some later date it was rebound, some of his sources may have been appended to it, perhaps simply those of compatible format, forming fols. 109–56. This hypothesis rests solely on the partial overlapping of contents between the main block and the appended material, not on paleographic or codicological evidence; indeed, it could be argued that at least some of the appended material seems to be by later hands, although the chronological ordering would be difficult to establish with confidence.

Alternative hypotheses cannot be altogether dismissed. It is possible, for example, that the compiler worked simultaneously on two distinct collections of material, perhaps fols 1–51 and fols 52–108, and that what appears to be a shift from one mode of presentation to another results simply from the binding together of what were intended as separate compilations. Had this been the intent, however, one would have expected a clearer and more decisive shift than in fact occurs: it is not the case that all the divinatory experiments, or all the materials of any sort, are grouped together.

We can only speculate about the identity of the compiler. In two passages he represents himself as connected with a court. He could have been a learned courtier with an interest in the occult arts, such as Johannes Hartlieb, although Hartlieb is more likely to have owned and consulted such a manuscript than to have assembled it or used it.[34] A closer model might be Michael Scot, who served at the court of Frederick II and had an interest in astrology, as apparently did the counsellors of several other German emperors, but there is no real evidence that these astrologers dabbled in necromancy.[35] The compiler might have been a cleric, perhaps a member of the lower clergy, possibly a figure such as the priest-necromancer who befriended Jubertus of Bavaria; or, to compromise between these possibilities, he could have been a cleric of higher or middling status who aspired to some position at court. If we could take seriously the unlikely notion that Hartlieb began by taking an active interest in magic and later became its critic and opponent, we might guess that this collection is his and represents an early phase in his own development. To judge by the book's Latinity, I incline toward the hypothesis that what we have here is the work of a man with some but not a great deal of learning, who would have tended more toward the fringes of society than toward court, even if he had aspirations for higher status that found expression in the early sections of his book but waned over the time he worked on it.

While recognizing that this reconstruction is and must be conjectural, I suggest, then, that the compiler of this miscellany was a moderately educated member of the lower or middling clergy who began by writing colourful and imaginative experiments in hopes of establishing a reputation for expertise in the occult, and perhaps a foothold at some court, possibly that of the Duke of Bavaria in Munich, but whose aspirations were thwarted, and who eventually turned his attention to forms of magic that were less fanciful, playful and

Table B. Types of necromancy found in Clm 849

	Illusionist	Psychological	Divinatory
Purposes	causing things to appear other than as they are: illusory banquet, castle, horse or other means of transportation; make a dead person seem alive or vice versa	influence on people's intellects or wills: love or hatred, favour at court, constraint of others' wills, madness	knowledge of future, past, distant, or hidden things: detection if a crime or criminal (usually a thief, less often a murderer), recovery of stolen goods, discovery of hidden treasure
Motivating impulses	imagination	power	knowledge
Tensions	between fantasy and reality	between the will of the necromancer and that of the victim	between the demand for truth and the fear of deception
Affinities*	• with literary fantasies • with the mythology of witchcraft	• with works of astral magic (in translations from Arabic)	• with divinatory practices developed esp. in Judaism
Central features*	• either highly complex (with complicated magic circles, rituals, and repeated conjurations) or very simple (with no circles, relatively simple rituals, and single conjurations) • emphasis on secrecy, although purpose is display • often accompanied by stories or testimonials • themes central to conception of witchcraft	• elaborate preparation and ceremonies (often over more than one day) • purposes and forms resembling those of astral magic • techniques of 'sympathetic' or 'imitative' magic, with meaning explicated by incantations (and less emphasis on circles and conjurations) • violent procedures and results • secrecy, to evade detection and punishment	• scrying (sometimes psychologically interpreted) combined with conjurations emphasized (but with little emphasis on circles) • participation of a medium, usually a young boy, who alone sees the spirits
Correlation with Jubertus's spirits	Superbus – grandeur of display being a matter of primary concern	Luxuriosus – seduction or rape being one of the most common purposes	Avarus – recovery or discovery of goods being a main purpose, and this being a potentially lucrative form of divination

* See Chapters 3–5 for elaboration of these points.

fantastic, but more in demand for practical application and thus more lucrative, and in any case still revealing of the diversities of magic in late medieval culture.

Table B summarizes the characterization already given of the three types of necromantic experiment found in Clm 849 and anticipates further discussion (in the next three chapters) of these categories. As should be obvious, it consists of broad generalizations, which require some qualification and nuance when applied to particular concrete experiments. While I have decided to use this chart in the interest of clarifying the patterns, the distinctions, and the correlations I mean to emphasize, I am aware of the hazards of fixing these categories too sharply and making them rigid when they should remain fluid. In highlighting the affinity of the psychological experiments with those of Arabic astral magic, for example, and the divinatory ones with practices well known in Judaism, I by no means wish to suggest that the techniques in question were exclusively or even specifically Arabic on the one hand, Jewish on the other. The world of magic is clearly more complex than that, and the boundaries between Jewish and Muslim magic too difficult to define. Still, in some ways the heart of this study – at least its attempt to distinguish different elements in the necromancers' own perception of their art – is sketched on this chart in schematic form. I do not adhere strictly in subsequent discussion to the organizing principles that might be suggested by the table, but everything laid out here is covered at some point either above or in following chapters.

Notes

1 Bernard Cerquiglini, *Éloge de la variante: histoire critique de la philologie* (Paris: Seuil, 1989). See also Stephen G. Nichols, 'Introduction: philology in a manuscript culture', *Speculum*, 65, no. 1 (Jan. 1990), 1–10; Siegfried Wenzel, 'Reflections on (new) philology', *ibid.*, 11–18; and the other articles in that issue of the journal.

2 *Picatrix: The Latin Version of the* Ghāyat Al-Hakīm, ed. David Pingree (London: Warburg Institute, 1986).

3 See, among recent works, Jean Clam, 'Philosophisches zu *Picatrix*: Gelehrte Magie und Anthropologie bei einem arabischen Hermetiker des Mittelalters', in Albert Zimmermann and Andreas Speer, eds, *Mensch und Natur im Mittelalter*, 1 (Berlin and New York: de Gruyter, 1991), 481–509, and Toufic Fahd, 'Sciences naturelles et magie dans *Gayat al-Hakim* du Pseudo-Mayriti', in E. García Sánchez, ed., *Ciencias de la naturaleza en al-Andalus*, 1 (Granada: Conseja Superior de Investigaciones Científicas, 1990), 11–21.

4 Hans Dieter Betz, ed., *The Greek Magical Papyri in Translation, Including the Demotic Spells*, 1 (Chicago: University of Chicago Press, 1986). On the cultural significance of miscellanies see Stephen G. Nichols and Siegfried Wenzel, eds., *The Whole Book: Cultural Perspectives on the Medieval Miscellany* (Ann Arbor: University of Michigan Press, 1996).

5 Roger Bacon, *De Nigromancia*, ed. and trans. Michael-Albion Macdonald (Gillette, NJ: Heptangle, 1988).

6 W. Braekman, 'Magische experimenten en toverpraktijken uit een middelnederlands

handschrift', *Verslagen en mededelingen van de Koninklijke Vlaamse Academie voor Taal-en Letterkunde*, 1966, pp. 53–118; also published separately (Ghent: Seminarie voor Volkskunde, 1966).

7 Fol. 134r: '*et postea dicatur in auriola pueri ista oracio: "O dio fare dispiriti spiritale cum lamina bocha te voio pre* [deleted?] *pregare che spiriti a questo puto vergeno in questa angestara diby mandare che diga emonstre lauerita de quelo chio voio domandare".*'

8 *Catalogus codicum Latinorum Bibliothecae Regiae Monacensis*, 2nd edn, vol. 1, pt 1 (Munich: Bibliotheca Regia, 1892), 202 (*Liber incantationum, exorcismorum et fascinationum variarum*).

9 Lynn Thorndike, *The History of Magic and Experimental Science* (New York: Macmillan and Columbia University Press, 1923–58).

10 Lynn Thorndike, 'Imagination and magic: force of imagination on the human body and of magic on the human mind', in *Mélanges Eugène Tisserant*, 7 (Vatican City: Biblioteca Vaticana, 1964), 353–58.

11 Kieckhefer, *Magic in the Middle Ages*, esp. 6–8.

12 I have this information from Frank Klaassen, who is studying manuscripts of ritual magic in English collections.

13 E.M. Butler, *Ritual Magic* (Cambridge: Cambridge University Press, 1949), 62.

14 See the codicological analysis of the manuscript given in the final chapter.

15 See n. 7 above.

16 It is worth noting that Thorndike, 'Imagination and magic', evidently did not recognize the handbook as an example of anything else he had seen.

17 Hansen, *Quellen*, 539–44. On the witch trials in this region and their context see now Pierette Paravy, *De la chrétienté romaine à la Réforme en Dauphiné: evêques, fidèles et déviants (vers 1340–vers 1530)* (Rome: Ecole française de Rome, 1993), and for this case in particular pp. 814–16.

18 Paravy, p. 815 n. 4, suggests that this is a reference to the pilgrimage shrine at Einsiedeln. She also cites literature on the theme of the diabolical bridge, in particular B.M. Galanti, 'Le leggenda del "Ponte del Diavolo" in Italia', *Lares*, 18 (1952), 61–73.

19 Johann Hartlieb, *Das Buch aller verbotenen Künste, des Aberglaubens und der Zauberei*, ed. and trans. Falk Eisermann and Eckhard Graf (Ahlerstedt: Param, 1989).

20 Frank Fürbeth, *Johannes Hartlieb: Untersuchungen zu Leben und Werk* (Tübingen: Niemeyer, 1992), 88–132.

21 Hartlieb, ch. 22, pp. 34f.

22 *Etymologiae*, viii.9, in the *Patrologia latina*, 82:310–14.

23 Hugh of St Victor, *Didascalicon: De studio legendi*, vi.15, ed. Charles Henry Buttimer (Washington, DC: Catholic University of America Press, 1939).

24 Chs 22, 28.

25 Chs 22–24.

26 Chs 33–34.

27 E.g., ch. 85.

28 Otto Hartig, *Die Gründung der Münchener Hofbibliothek durch Albrecht V. und Johann Jakob Fugger* (Abhandlungen der Königlichen Bayerischen Akademie der Wissenschaften, philosoph.-philolog. und hist. Klasse, vol. 28, sect. 3, 1914), gives the history of the library that provided the earliest foundation for the Bavarian State Library, but does not give the provenance of this manuscript.

29 There are two instances in experiment no. 7, and one in no. 27.

30 See the variation in names in nos 4, 7, 9, 10 and 11.

31 The relationship between demonic and other forms of magic in the Renaissance is a primary theme of D.P. Walker, *Spiritual and Demonic Magic, from Ficino to Campanella* (London: Warburg Institute, 1958). See also Charles Zika, 'Reuchlin's *De verbo mirifico* and the magic debate of the late fifteenth century', *Journal of the Warburg and Courtauld Institutes*, 39 (1976), 104–38, esp. 112–14 (see p. 114, n. 30, *Tota Magia, quae in usu est apud modernos, et quam merito exterminat ecclesia, nullam habet firmitatem, nullum fundamentum, nullam veritatem, quia pendet ex manu hostium veritatis, potestatum harum tenebrarum, quae tenebras falsitatis, male dispositis intellectibus obfundunt*).

32 Fols 8r–11v.

33 See no. 32 in the edition, where a conjuration edited from two versions in the later folios is addressed to a spirit named Mirage, while an alternative form in the main block addresses Satan.

34 The *Schriftproben* in Fürbeth, *Johannes Hartlieb*, p. 280, show that Hartlieb's handwriting is not at all like that in fols 3–108 of Clm 849; it more closely resembles that of some later folios, but not enough that any of this material could be assigned to him.

35 Thorndike, *Michael Scot*, esp. 32–39 and 116–21. See also the interesting article of Helmuth Grössing and Franz Stuhlhofer, 'Versuch einer Deutung der Rolle der Astrologie in den persönlichen und politischen Entscheidungen einiger Habsburger des Spätmittelalters', *Anzeiger der Österreichischen Akademie der Wissenschaften*, Philosophisch-historische Klasse, 117 (1980), 267–83. On court astrology in England see Hilary M. Carey, *Courting Disaster: Astrology at the English Court and University in the Later Middle Ages* (New York: St Martin's Press, 1992).

3

BANQUETS, HORSES AND CASTLES: ILLUSIONIST EXPERIMENTS

The fifteenth-century writer of the Rawlinson necromantic manuscript tells how to summon a demon in the form of a horse by using conjurations, a ring with the Tetragrammaton inscribed on it, and a diagram made with the blood of a hoopoe or a bat. The magician must stand in a circle that extends to the east window of his chamber. When the conjuration is complete, a multitude of spirits will appear in the sky, with many horses; the magician must choose the horse with the red bridle, which will descend outside his chamber. He may then ride off, with sceptre and sword in hand. But he must beware of committing any sins while engaged in this experiment, because if he is unclean he can no longer command the demon. The writer then tells a cautionary tale – from his own experience, he says – to impress upon the reader the importance of not sinning in the course of this adventure:

> For I myself once travelled from Alexandria to India in the space of an hour, and there I saw women whom I found very pleasing indeed, and at once I had my will with one of them. But there was no chance of finding a confessor unless I waited quite some time. I returned to my horse, which was standing where it had been conjured [to stand], but when I seized the end of the bridle the horse began to bolt, not allowing me to put my foot in the stirrup because of my uncleanness. I held on to the bridle firmly, and the horse hurled me forty feet into the air. Finally, seeing that I was going to perish miserably, I let go and fell, breaking my leg quite badly. So I lay there in India for four months, and until I had recuperated I could not go and see my horse.
>
> But when I had recovered I went to confession and did penance. Then I prepared a chamber for myself, and had a sceptre, sword and ring newly made, since the ring which I had defiled had lost its power. When these instruments had been fashioned and newly consecrated, I summoned those same spirits as before, and had them bring the same spirit or horse. With conjurations I commanded that horse and mounted him peacefully, and I kept on riding him continually for an entire month, except when I dismounted to sleep and eat or drink, and thus I circled the globe eight times. And I had him carry me through the sky until I was practically suffocated because of the pressure of the air. In circling the globe I discovered many and wondrous treasures, whose virtues I learned later on under the instruction of one of the spirits, whom I then locked up. And thus [by this long riding] I caused my horse much grief.

When I finally dismounted from him and asked him why he had harmed me, he replied that from that point on he was unable to do so, but he said he would rather have been in hell than keep riding for so long a time. So he asked me not to cause him such grief any more, and he would minister to me faithfully when I summoned him, so long as I was clean. And thus I repaid him evil for evil.[1]

The ceremony given here for conjuring the horse is borrowed, perhaps directly, from the *De nigromancia* or *Thesaurus spirituum* ascribed to Roger Bacon.[2] In the cautionary tale the reader will recognize a variation on a story known from *The Thousand and One Nights*, from the French romances (especially *Li Roumans de Cléomadès* of Adenès li Rois), and from Chaucer's abbreviated and mock-naturalistic retelling in *The Squire's Tale*.[3] In the Arabic and French versions, a magical flying horse cannot be made to descend where the rider wishes to land, and the change of plan that results becomes a factor in development of the plot. In the Rawlinson manuscript as in the literary versions of the tale, the Orient is portrayed as exotic and romantically alluring, although the seduction scene has become a peremptory telling of a male fantasy, with little trace of the *écriture féminine* that has been seen in the literary narratives.[4] What concerns the narrator here is less the seduction than its consequences. Very much like Lancelot in the *Quest of the Holy Grail*, the magician is unable to continue his mission until repentance and confession wipe away his disability.[5]

The moral implications of this story need not detain us now, although the moral ambiguity recurs in this manuscript, in a lengthy Confiteor which admits to every manner of sin but terminates in a prayer for power over certain spirits.[6] As for the world of flying horses, it seems not unlike that of Jubertus of Regensburg, who flew to diabolical assemblies with wondrous speed not on the back of a horse but on the excrement of a mule or horse, *ministerio dyabolorum*.[7] For present purposes what is most relevant is that the form of magic related in this story is intended chiefly for the sake of the magician's own entertainment, and the story about its use is, despite the tone of moral seriousness, a means of entertainment presumably both for writer and reader. The compiler of the Munich handbook, too, is most inclined toward the anecdotal when he is telling his reader how to conjure illusions in which demons appear as horses, castles appear out of nowhere, banquets are brought forth with many apparent but illusory courses, and the magician dons a cloak of invisibility so as no longer to appear at all.

Depictions of magic in medieval literature often tease the reader with uncertainties about the boundary between illusion and reality.[8] When the water level off the coast of Brittany is raised so as to cover the rocks, in Chaucer's *Franklin's Tale*, is the transformation real or merely an illusion?[9] When wondrous pageants and spectacles are brought forth by inexplicable means at court, are they genuine or delusory, and are they worked 'by craft or necromancy'? The literature of magic is replete with stories of magicians who produce magical banquets, horses or boats that can transport people over land and sea, castles with armed warriors, all of which have a tendency to vanish abruptly, suggesting that they rest on dubious ontological foundations. From antiquity and through the Middle Ages, critics of magic insisted it was all illusion, by which they could mean many things: that it was a means by which demons deluded and ensnared the gullible, that its accomplishments were unreal and not lasting, that healings as well as spectacles worked by magic were unreliable.[10] The pagan Celsus, taunting his Christian contemporaries in late antiquity, compared the miracles of Jesus with 'the works of sorcerers who profess to do wonderful miracles, and the accomplishments of those who are taught by the Egyptians, who for a few obols make known their sacred lore in the middle of the market-place and drive daemons out of men and blow away diseases and invoke the souls of heroes, displaying expensive banquets and dining-tables and cakes and dishes which are non-existent, and who make things move as though they were alive although they are not really so, but only appear as such in the imagination'.[11] But it was not only the critics who saw at least some types of magic as entailing illusion: the magicians themselves seemed to revel in their role as illusionists. Not surprisingly, then, many of the formulas in our necromantic handbook – and several of the most interesting – involve some form of illusion.

ILLUSIONIST EXPERIMENTS IN THE MUNICH HANDBOOK

Twelve of the experiments in Clm 849 are 'illusionist' ones, intended to make things appear other than as they are: to make people perceive some object or scene that is not in fact present, to obtain a means of transport such as a horse or a boat, to make the dead seem alive or vice versa, or to become invisible. This category might be seen as a subset of the 'psychological' experiments, but the emphasis here is less on deception of the senses than on production of an objective display that seems different from what it is.

The distinguishing features of these experiments are chiefly four. First, either they are highly complex, with complicated magic circles, intricately worked-out rituals, and at least two conjurations, or else (less often) they are very simple, with no circles, relatively simple rituals, and single conjurations. Second, they often emphasize the need for secrecy, yet the basic point of the experiment is the fascinating and awe-inspiring *display* of magical powers. Third, these experiments are often accompanied by stories (such as the one from the Rawlinson manuscript) or by testimonials assuring the reader of their efficacy. Fourth, these illusionist experiments, for all their exuberant fantasy, come closer than any others in the handbook to touching on themes that would become central to the late medieval and early modern conception of witchcraft.

Seven complex experiments (nos 6–11 and 15) involve relatively elaborate magic circles and intricate rituals, with two distinct conjurations (first the master summons the spirits, who appear to him, then he commands them to execute some illusion, and they do so). Among further complications are offerings made to induce the spirits to carry out the commands, oaths required of the spirits, and provisions for repeating on some future occasion, with less effort, an experiment already produced once. The simpler experiments (nos 14, 17, 21, 43 and 45), by way of contrast, require no magic circles at all, and have illusionist effect following directly from a single conjuration, without an intervening apparition of spirits. The difference may be the result of nothing more than the handbook's general tendency toward simpler, less colourful and imaginative formulations in its later sections, a tendency seen even in this most fanciful category of magic.

At certain points in the illusionist experiments of the Munich handbook the writer comments explicitly on the need for secrecy. At the end of one experiment (no. 8) the writer comments that this book, containing generally unknown names and figures of spirits 'according to their characteristics' (*proprietates*), should be kept in a hidden place because its contents have ineffable efficacy. Experiment no. 10, which can make the living appear dead and the dead alive, must be kept secret because of its great power. In this and in no. 11 the master goes to a remote and secret place outside town to carry out his experiment. Experiment no. 15 must be carried out in a high and secret place. This concern with the esoteric nature of necromancy is not exclusively found in the illusionist experiments – no. 5 also emphasizes the importance of performing the ritual in a secret place, and the text insists that this experiment must be kept secret because it has 'ineffable virtue' – but it is a theme found perhaps most often in this category, and the breathless tone thus imparted adds to the entertainment value of these illusionist experiments.[12] Elsewhere, rather than emphasizing the need for secrecy, the writer comments on the rarity of knowledge about certain formulas. He declares that the art of conjuring an illusory banquet in no. 6 is practically unknown in his day, and that 'Matthew the Spaniard' was utterly ignorant of this magic; he notes that the art of obtaining a cloak of invisibility, in no. 11, is also virtually unknown in his day. But the themes of secrecy and obscurity are not unrelated: they are both ways of emphasizing the esoteric nature of these experiments, and stressing that the reader is being initiated into arcane lore that should arouse not only curiosity but also excitement and a sense of privilege. Yet it is in the nature of these experiments that in one way or other most of them are *shared*: in some cases the result of the magical is a spectacle that may be put on for the wonderment of others, and even when the point is for the magician to become invisible, his very state of non-visibility is a way of relating to others.

The testimonials asserting the efficacy of the experiments take various forms. The writer declares that he has seen one experiment (no. 8) worked in various ways, but the way he gives is the best, entailing least effort and no danger. In recounting the effects of another experiment (no. 10) he claims that he has personally experienced them all, and that he leaves unmentioned those effects he has not experienced. Nor is he shy about claiming the testimony of authorities: Socrates himself, he claims, speaks of the power of one circle (no. 9) in his book of magic. More simply, he asserts that experiment (*experiencia*) no. 10 is 'most worthy'. At one point (no. 6) the writer addresses a courtly reader, whether real or imagined, claiming to remind him of occasions when the magic has worked: 'You have often seen me exercise this art in your court, namely that of bringing forth stewards'. In a similar vein he tells how he once carried out experiment no. 7 while the emperor and his nobles were out hunting in a dark wood, causing an illusory castle to appear, with demons in the form of knights who attacked the emperor and his men.

What are we to make of all this? Are we to assume that the illusionist experiments in this manuscript – and the tales that the writer spins, testifying to the efficacy of his own illusions – were intended merely as entertainment? Is it unthinkable that the clerical necromancers actually hoped to visit exotic lands on flying horses, to explore phantom castles, to feast at magical banquets? The question is difficult to answer in any simple way, because what one writer will write tongue in cheek another may intend as fact, and because in many ways the border between imaginative fantasy and perceived fact is readily permeable: fantasies about harm that other people might inflict shade into paranoid fears of harm that they are inflicting; erotic fantasies, encouraged by techniques of erotic magic, can serve as prelude to actual seduction; purely recreational play with a Ouija board or tarot deck gives occasion for traumatic expression of deep-seated fantasies and anxieties; words spoken as playful boasts may be heard as confirmation of sinister powers.

The tales told in this necromantic manuscript are perhaps best described as literary boasts, analogous to those in medieval literature.[13] And yet they are no less fantastic than those recorded in the witch trials of the later fifteenth and following centuries, and in some ways these tales are not unrelated to aspects of witchcraft. Indeed, this category of experiments more than others has points of contact with the 'cumulative concept' of witchcraft that became established in the fifteenth century, even if the parallels are not exact.[14] When the master has the demons take an oath (no. 6), this is conceived as unilateral; it is therefore not a pact. The spirits swear on an unspecified but consecrated book, and they bind themselves first by the God who created them and all things, second by the (presumably demonic) lords whom they fear and adore, and third by 'the law that we observe'. The second and third elements in this oath presuppose what scholastic demonology did in fact generally assume, that demons are bound by a perverse hierarchy of their own – an inversion of the angelic hierarchy – and that there are infernal laws by which the demons are bound.[15] The banquet that demons bring forth is in one particular like the feasts ascribed in later years to witches at their sabbaths: the food does not really exist, so that the more one eats the hungrier one becomes, and a starving man who eats such fare will die just as if he ate nothing at all.[16] And in both no. 17 and no. 43, the magician is told that when he is flying on an illusory horse he must not make the sign of the cross, or the horse (in fact a spirit in the form of a beast) will flee from him, just as the witches were said to be warned.[17] (By way of contrast, the instructions for no. 8 specify that while riding in a magically produced ship the master may invoke holy things, as in true Christian religion, because the spirits involved are between good and evil, neither in hell nor in paradise.) The parallel with notions from the witch trials is extended by a passage from the manuscript edited by Willy Braekman, which suggests that to travel quickly wherever one wishes, one should make an ointment from seven herbs, the fat of a goat and the blood of a bat, and smear it on one's face, hands and chest, while reciting a short formula.[18] While this specific recipe may not be explicitly necromantic, it appears alongside instructions for demonic magic, and is strikingly parallel to the means witches were thought to use for their flight.[19]

AN ILLUSORY BANQUET

The first two illusionist experiments in the Munich handbook have in mind a courtly setting: one is a procedure to conjure forth a lavish banquet, with entertainment of various kinds; the other creates the illusion of a castle in which an unnamed emperor may hold out against demonic troops. While the first illusion is simply for entertainment, the second is an elaborate trick on unwitting victims, though they may be supposed to have taken the hoax in good spirits.

The experiment for obtaining an illusory banquet, with service and entertainment (no. 6), is one of the longest in the manuscript, and illustrates well the complexity so often found in these experiments:

> You have often seen me exercise at your court the art of summoning banquet-bearers.[20] First one must invoke fifteen spirits, in this manner: At the outset one must go outside town, under a waxing moon, on a Thursday or Sunday, at noon, carrying a shining sword and a hoopoe, and with the sword one must trace circles in a remote place. When this is done, inscribe sixteen names with the point of the sword, as will appear below in the figure.
>
> When you have done this, you should draw the sword toward the east within the inner circle, as the diagram shows. When this is done, you should bind the hoopoe to yourself in such a way that it cannot escape from the inner circle, in which you should stand.
>
> Then you should kneel, turn to the east, take the sword in both hands, and say, 'Oymelor, Demefin, Lamair, Masair, Symofor, Rodobayl, Tentetos,

Lotobor, Memoyr, Tamafin, Leutaber, Tatomofon, Faubair, Selutabel, Rimasor, Syrama, most cheerful, glad and joyous spirits, I, so-and-so, adjure you . . . to come to me here in a gentle, pleasing, and cheerful form and make manifest whatever I say.'

When you have said this twelve [*sic*] times – four times facing east, then four times facing south, then four times facing east, then four times facing north – holding the sword in your hand the whole time, and while you are saying the conjuration constantly drawing it in each location, finally position it where it was at first, when the conjuration was first spoken, as has been said.[21]

When you have said this, constantly kneeling, again turn to the east, holding the sword in your right hand, and the hoopoe in your left hand, and say, 'Come, O aforesaid spirits, come to me, come, for I command you by the eternal glory of God. Amen.'

When you have said this once, turn with the sword and the hoopoe toward the west, and you will see sixteen splendid and stalwart knights. They will say to you, 'You summoned us and we have come, obedient to your will. Ask what you will, confident that we are ready to obey.' Say in reply, 'Make me see your power, that I may behold tables with many people reclining at them, with an infinite array of dishes.' They will tell you that they are pleased to do so.

At once many pages [*domicelli*] will come, carrying three-legged tables, towels and other necessary equipment. Then the most noble of folk will come and recline, and butlers to serve, carrying an infinite array of dishes. And you will hear singing and music-making, and you will see dancing and innumerable games. And you may be sure that these twelve [*sic*] will not withdraw from you, but will stand just outside the circle, speaking with you and watching. You should also know that three kings will come to you beside the circle from among those who are reclining, and will ask you to come and eat with them. You should reply that you are quite unable to leave. When you have said this, they will return at once to those who are reclining, and you will hear them telling the others that they were unable to persuade you to move out of the circle. Then they will send a butler with some food or other, which you may safely eat, and you should offer some of it to the sixteen standing beside the circle, and they too will eat of it. Then you will see everyone rise from the tables and mount their horses in order.

At last, all will vanish from your eyes except those twelve, who, standing by you, will say, 'Our spectacle [*ludus*] has pleased you, has it not?' You will reply cheerfully that it has. When you have responded, they will ask you for the hoopoe, which, strange to say, will at once become alarmed.[22] You will say to them, 'I am willing to give you the hoopoe if you swear to come to me and enact this spectacle whenever I please.' They will say that they are ready to swear. You should have some book brought to them at once, and on it you should have them swear in this manner: 'All twelve of us swear on this sacred book . . . to come to you without delay whenever you invoke us, and to have tables laid, such as you have seen and even better.' And they will swear at once.

And when they have sworn, you will give them the hoopoe, and when they have it they will ask your leave to withdraw. You will give it to them, saying, 'Go forth wherever you wish to go, and be attentive to me.' They will say that they remain obliged to you from then on. Having said this, they will go. You too may leave the circles and erase them so that nothing remains, and, taking your sword, you may withdraw.

You should note that the hoopoe is possessed of great virtue for necromancers and invokers of demons [*nigromanticis et demones invocantibus*], on which account we use it much for our safekeeping.

When you want them [the spirits] to come to you, in secret or openly, or in whatever place, gaze at the above-written circles and figures in the book, and in a quiet voice read the names found in them. When you have read them once while thus gazing, read this conjuration once: 'Oymelor, Demefin, Lamair, Masair, Simofor, Rodobail, Tentetos, Lotobor, Memoir, Tamafin, Zeugaber, Tatomofon, Faubair, Belutabel, Rimasor and Sirama, I ask, conjure and adjure you by the true majesty of God to make your subordinates come here and bring dishes, first of all so-and-so and so-and-so, and make a grand banquet, with games, singing, music-making and dancing, and in general all those things that can gladden the hearts of those standing about [cf. Ps. 103:15 Vulg.].' When you have read this [conjuration] once, splendid pages will come and prepare beautiful tables. When these are set up, you will hear trumpets, harps and an untold multitude of songs. When you call out loudly, 'Bring water', it will be brought forth at once. Likewise, 'Bring forth the meal', and at once it will be brought. And there will be butlers and stewards serving excellently, and handsome pages, and players providing countless entertainments. And you can have a thousand types of dish brought, if it pleases you, and those who eat them will find them uncommonly delicious.

You must know that no matter how much they eat, they will be all the more hungry, because they will seem like dishes but they will not exist, so that if a famished person were to gorge himself, believing them to be real, he would no doubt die just as if he ate nothing.

And when you wish to do away with the spectacle, say that they should take away the tables. At once the tables will be removed, but all those standing around will remain. If you wish for them to sing or play or make the entire spectacle, say, 'Do thus and such', and you will see what you wish, for these are spirits of spectacle and all entertainment, and they will do all that they are told. And when you want them to depart, say, 'Withdraw, all of you, and whenever I call you to me, come forth without any excuse.' They will reply, 'We will do so most gladly!' And when they have withdrawn, all will depart, wondering at this art.

And here this art is concluded, which is virtually unknown among people today, and of which Matthew the Spaniard was utterly ignorant, etc.

The circle to be used for this experiment is depicted: a quadruple band with a pentangle inscribed in the centre, a sword depicted at the top (extending downward across all four bands, with its point on the top of the pentangle) and other figures (likewise extending across all four bands) on the upper left, upper right, lower right, and lower left. The cardinal directions are given outside the outermost band, with east on top. Within the bands the names of sixteen spirits are inscribed.[23]

Two points may suffice here by way of commentary. First, the idea of conjuring an illusory banquet is widespread. Celsus compared Christ with a magician who conjures forth an illusory banquet, and the same trick is found in an adjuration in the Greek magical papyri for obtaining a *daimon* as one's assistant. Among the spirit's myriad functions is that of procuring every manner of food except fish or pork. The magician need only imagine a banqueting hall and order the *daimon* to prepare a banquet, and immediately he will create a hall with marble walls and golden ceiling, all of which will seem partly real, partly illusion. He will bring fine wine, and further *daimones* made out as suitably attired servants.[24] Second, this experiment is exceptional for the Munich handbook in the degree of emphasis on the sacrifice of a hoopoe to the demons. This bird is famous for its magical virtues.[25] The present experiment notes explicitly that the hoopoe has great power for necromancers and invokers of demons, and for that reason is much used by such practitioners. Oddly, the text says that necromancers use the hoopoe a great deal for their safekeeping or protection (*ad nostri tutelam*), which perhaps means that they are safer in the company of demons if they have an offering to make them. The safety of the hoopoes seems not to be an issue.

The fading of this insubstantial pageant might well recall that of a more famous illusion:

> Our revels now are ended. These our actors,
> As I foretold you, were all spirits, and
> Are melted into air, into thin air . . .[26]

But of course the books from which *that* experiment derived have not survived for comparison with the Munich handbook.

AN ILLUSORY CASTLE

The following experiment (no. 7) is designed to obtain an illusory castle, with defenders. It is introduced in grandiose manner, as a 'splendid experiment' by which the magician can convoke spirits to produce an elegant castle with armed men. As in the preceding case, there are two phases, first the summoning of spirits and then having them work the illusion, although for reasons that we will see shortly, the second phase does not precisely involve a conjuration.

Here follows another experiment[27] for invoking spirits so that a man can make a fine and well fortified castle appear, or for summoning countless legions of armed men, which can easily be done, and among other things is deemed most beautiful.

First, go out on the tenth [day of] the moon, under a clear sky, outside of town to some remote and secret place, taking milk and honey with you, some of which you must sprinkle in the air. And with bare feet and head, kneeling, read this while facing west: 'O Usyr, Salaul, Silitor, Demor, Zanno, Syrtroy, Risbel, Cutroy, Lytay, Onor, Moloy, Pumotor, Tami, Oor and Ym, squire spirits, whose function it is to bear arms and deceive human senses wherever you wish, I, so-and-so, conjure and exorcize and invoke you . . . that, indissolubly bound to my power, you should come to me without delay, in a form that will not frighten me, subject and prepared to do and reveal for me all that I wish, and to do this willingly, by all things that are in heaven and on earth.' Having read this once facing west, do so again facing south, east, and north.

And from far off you will see a band of armed men coming toward you, who will send ahead a squire to say that those you summoned are coming to you. You should tell him, 'Go to them and tell them to come to me in such a state that they frighten no one, but I may abide safely with them.' When you have said this, he will return at once to them.

After a short interval they will come to you. When you see them, show them at once this circle, which has great power to terrify those fifteen demons;[28] they will see it and say, 'Ask whatever you wish in safety, and it will all come to pass for you through us.' You should then tell them to consecrate their circle so that whenever you gaze on it and invoke them they must come to you quickly and do that which is natural to them, namely make fortifications and castles and moats and a multitude of armed men appear. They will say they are willing to do so. You should extend a book to them, and you will see one of them place his hand on the book and speak certain words, which you will not understand. When this is done, they will restore it to you.

Then they will ask you to permit them to leave, because they cannot depart from you except with permission. You should say to them, 'Make a castle here, so that I may see your power.' Immediately they will make a castle around you, with many other things, and you will see yourself in the middle of the castle, and a great multitude of knights will be present. But these fifteen will not be able to depart from you. After the space of an hour they will ask you that they may depart, and you should say, 'Be ready whenever I gaze on this circle and invoke you to return at once.'[29] They will swear to come immediately. Then tell them to depart wherever they wish. And the entire spectacle [*ludus*] will be destroyed, and no one will remain there.

When all this is done, return home, guarding well the book in which all power is found. And when you wish to work this fine art, gaze at the circle, reading the names, beginning from the east, saying, 'O Usyr, Salaul, Silitol, Denior, Zaimo, Syrtroy, Ristel, Cutroy, Lytoy, Onor, Moloy, Pumiotor, Tamy, Dor, [and] Ym, I summon you to come here, by the consecration of this circle, in which your signs are inscribed, and to make a well fortified castle appear for me, with a deep moat, and a plenteous company of knights and footsoldiers.' And suddenly a splendid castle, with all that is necessary, will appear there. If you wish to enter it, you can, for a knight will at once stand by you, to whom you may command that all you wish should appear, and he will have it done.

Once when I [wished to test] this art I exercised it with the emperor, when many nobles were accompanying him on a hunting expedition through some dark forest. This is how I proceeded. First I gazed at the circle, calling the aforesaid demons with a clear voice. And at once a handsome knight came to me, whom no one but I could see, and who said to me, 'I am one of the spirits you have invoked; I am named Salaul, and the others have sent me. Command what you will, and it will be done.' I said to him, 'I want you to have a legion of armed men appear, whom the emperor and his companions will take to be rebels.' He said, 'It is done.' And then all the counts and the emperor himself turned and looked to the north, and from far off they saw coming to them an innumerable multitude of knights and soldiers. One of them dismounted, and before an hour's time [*ante magne hore spacium*] came to the emperor and said, trembling, 'Lord emperor, behold, an innumerable horde is coming toward us, swearing to put us and all your counts to death and to kill you pitilessly.' On hearing this, the emperor and the counts did not know what to do. Meanwhile, the spirits approached. Seeing and hearing them, and their terrifying weapons, they began to flee, but the others followed them, shooting arrows, and cried with one voice, 'You cannot escape your death today!' Then I said, 'O Salaul, make a wondrous castle before the emperor and his men, so that the emperor and the others can enter it.' And it was done. A perfectly safe castle was made for the counts, with towers and moat, and the drawbridge down. It seemed excellently constructed and filled with mercenaries, who were crying out, 'O lord emperor, enter quickly with your companions!' They entered, and it seemed that servants and many friends of the emperor were in it; he supposed he had come upon people who would defend him manfully. When they had entered, they raised the drawbridge and began to defend themselves. Then the spirits with their war machines attacked the castle with wondrous power, so that the emperor and the others feared all the more. Then Salaul said to me, 'We do not have the power to remain here longer than a quarter of the day, so we must now withdraw.' Then the castle disappeared, and the attackers, and everything else.[30] The emperor and the others then looked around and found themselves in some marsh, which left them greatly astonished. I said to them, 'This episode has been quite an adventure!' And after this experiment I made a dinner for them.

Remember that this art cannot last longer than a quarter of a day, unless it lasts one quarter one time [and is then renewed for another quarter day], etc.

One might have supposed that the trick played on the emperor constituted an act of rebellion deserving of execution; the tale, which must be read as such, asks us to suspend our disbelief and assume the emperor had unlimited capacity for being amused. The milk and honey that the magician sprinkles evidently serve as a kind of offering, which comes this time at the beginning rather than at the end of the ritual, as in no. 6; it is perhaps worthy of note that this theme of sacrifice occurs specifically in illusionist experiments set at court, and one might perhaps speculate that the offering is somehow analogous here to a courtly gift, but two examples provide too little evidence for such generalization. A further aspect of this experiment that calls for attention is the formula for recalling the spirits. Having summoned them, the master proceeds at once to an arrangement which will ensure multiple recurrence of the desired illusion. The formula to be used on further occasions is simple, and does not use the language of conjuration; presumably the demons are already bound by their own consecration of the circle, and need not be bound by the force of a formal conjuration.

While extensive pursuit of parallels would lead to endless digression, two especially interesting ones deserve comment. The first is from *The Quest of the Holy Grail*, in which a lady who seeks in vain the love of Sir Bors threatens that she and her maidens will kill themselves by leaping from a tower unless he satisfies her. As they plunge from the battlements, Sir Bors crosses himself, and immediately is 'enveloped in such a tumult and shrieking that it seemed to him that all the fiends of hell were round about him: and no doubt there were a number present. He looked round, but saw neither the tower nor the lady who had been soliciting his love . . .'. Thus he knew 'it was the enemy who had laid this ambush for him'.[31] In this case the phantom tower is a demonic snare, but not a work of magic created by demons at the behest of a magician. The second parallel, from much further afield, from the eleventh-century life of the Tibetan Buddhist saint Milarepa, is in this way more closely analogous to the tale in our necromantic handbook. When the lama Marpa had Milarepa construct a tall tower, the lama's enemies attacked it, but 'the lama conjured up some phantom soldiers, clad in armor, and put them everywhere, inside and outside the tower. His enemies said, "Where did Marpa get all these soldiers?"' Terror-struck, they prostrated themselves and became disciples of the lama.[32] In this context sainthood and magic may be more closely related than in medieval Christianity; indeed, even in modern Tibet lamas are said to have risked moral defilement by using magical weapons against Chinese invaders.[33] Yet even within Tibet, not all magic is judged morally equivalent: Marpa may work a harmless trick of magical illusion without jeopardizing his standing, but the tower Milarepa is constructing is part of his arduous penance required for works of destructive magic in his life before attaining sainthood.

EXPERIMENTS TO OBTAIN A HORSE

As we have already seen, magical flying horses are part of the stock in trade of magic lore; they migrate not only across the face of the earth but also between the magicians' own writings and courtly literature.[34] Johannes Hartlieb speaks of horses that come into an old house and transport a rider over many miles, and he hints rather vaguely at how it is done: one takes bat's blood and binds oneself to the Devil with secret words such as 'Debra ebra'; after riding one dismounts and takes the bridle; to return to one's place of origin one need only shake the bridle and the horse will appear – but the horse is, of course, only a devil. Magic of this sort, he says, is widely known among princes. He also tells how *unhulden* and others use a salve called the *unguentum pharelis*, made of seven herbs mixed with the blood of a bird and the fat of an animal, smeared on benches, chairs or other objects, on which they then ride; this too counts for him as necromancy.[35]

One might challenge the inclusion of these experiments in the category of magical illusion, since the journeys undertaken are at least represented as real. In one key sense, however, even from the magicians' perspective there is an element of illusion: the creature that appears is not in reality a horse but a demon in the form of a horse. The illusion is perhaps not so complete as in the case of a banquet with food that does not nourish or satisfy hunger, but this is only to say that from a perspective shared by magicians and theologians alike the demons had real but limited power over the natural order, and while they could effect genuine locomotion through assumed bodies they could not confect food with the substantiality of real food. One might ask further why they could not *transport* real food, perhaps even bringing grapes from distant lands in midwinter, and the answer to that would presumably be that they *could* do so but were content in all these cases to create just enough of an illusion to last through the duration of the experiment, and once they began troubling to transport food from abroad they would be extending themselves beyond the contracted arrangement.

However one wishes to resolve these subtleties, the Munich handbook in any event gives four experiments for obtaining a spirit in the form of a horse on which to ride. Let us begin with the most extended of these (no. 9):

> I also wish to explain to you how to obtain a horse – that is, a spirit in the form of a horse – who can bear you across water and land, through hills and across plains, wherever you wish.

First, on the sixth [day] of the moon, a Tuesday, having fasted, you should go out with a bridle that has never been used, and in a secret place, and make a circle with a nail or an iron stylus, as appears here, inscribing in it the names and figures that appear. When this is done, remain in the middle and kneel on the bridle facing east, and in a somewhat loud voice say, 'O Lautrayth, Feremin, [and] Oliroomim, spirits who attend upon sinners, I, so-and-so, trusting in your power, conjure you by Him who spoke and [all things] were made, and who knows all things even before they come to pass, and by heaven and earth, fire and air and water, Sun and Moon and stars . . . to send me three [spirits], who should come to me gently, without causing me fear, but in such a way that I may remain safe, and you should fulfil entirely whatever I command you, and bring it effectively to pass. Likewise, I conjure you aforesaid spirits by Him who is to come to judge the living and the dead and the world by fire, and by the fearful Day of Judgement, and by the sentence that you must hear on that day, and [by] this circle with which you are effectively invoked, that you should be compelled to come here without delay and humbly fulfil my commands.'

When you have said this three times, you will see three knights come from afar. On seeing them, before they arrive in your presence, say, 'I have lifted to you my eyes unto the mountains, from which my help shall come. My help is from the Lord, who made heaven and earth' [Ps. 120:1f. Vulg.; cf. Ps. 122:1]. And when they come to the circle they will at once dismount from their horses and greet you cheerfully. You will say to them, 'May the Lord in his mercy bring you back to your pristine status.' Then the spirits will say, 'O master, we have come to you, all of us prepared to obey your commands. So command us to do that for which you have made us come here, and it will be fully brought about.' You should reply, 'I wish for you to consecrate this bridle' – which you should hold with both hands – 'so that whenever I shake it a horse will come before me, in whose mouth I may place it, and I may be able to mount it and ride safely on it, and proceed wherever I desire.' Then they will say they wish to take the bridle with them and return it on the third day. You will give it to them. And when you have done so, they will mount their horses and withdraw without delay. When they have gone, leave the circle, without erasing it, and withdraw from that place.

Return there on the evening of the third day and you will find the same spirits offering the bridle to you, assuring you that your request has been carried out. When you have taken the bridle, say, 'I conjure you by the God of gods that you will be unable to depart from here without my leave.' Then they will reply that they will remain there as long as you wish. Then shake the bridle, and at once a black horse will come. Place the bridle on him, and ride. Then dismount and remove the bridle, and at once the horse will depart.

When the horse has left, say, 'I conjure you [spirits] by all the aforesaid

things, and by all those things that have power against you, that you should
swear always to compel that horse to come to me.' They will swear and
promise to do so at once. When they have sworn, tell them to withdraw in
safety.[36] When they have gone, leave the circle and erase it totally, and take the
bridle with you.

And when you wish the horse to come, say, shaking the bridle, 'Lutrayth,
Feremim, Oliroomim', and the horse will come at once. Then place the bridle
in its mouth and ride. You should ride a bit back toward its haunches,[37] which
will be gentler, and you should do this each time. And when you want it to
gallop, spur it on or lash it, and it will fly like an arrow, but you will not be
able to fall off, so do not fear. And when you wish to dismount, it will never
depart until you have removed the bridle from its mouth, whereupon it will
disappear at once.

We have made such bridles very thin, so we can carry them in a small place,
and they can never break or wear out because of the consecration.

One should note that if the circle given above is inscribed on horsehide with
the blood of a horse and with the tooth of a white horse, and then is shown to
horses, they will die at once. And if you carry it with you, written in this
manner, no horse can come near you. And Socrates speaks of the power of this
circle in his book of magic.

The figure shown is a single circular band, with a square inscribed, and a circle
inside the square. Short bars extend outward from the middle of each side of the
square and touch the inner side of the circular band. Names of the cardinal
directions flank each of these bars. 'The place of the master' is marked in the
center of the circle. The band contains the names Lantrayth, Feremni and
Oliromim,[38] plus astronomical and other signs.

Four points about this experiment call especially for comment. First, as in
other illusionist experiments, but not typically in other ones, the spirits conjured
come in the form of courtly figures, in this case knights, which reinforces the aura
of courtly romance intended to characterize these texts. Second, the means for
control over the horse is a bridle, which should not be surprising, since that is the
usual purpose of a bridle, except that in this case the instrument of control is used
in unconventional ways and becomes more an effective symbol of the magician's
power than a practical implement. Third, the circle which serves to gain control
over a demon in the form of a horse can also, differently employed, be used to
threaten an actual horse; while these illusionist experiments may not be overtly
concerned with establishment of power relations (as are the psychological
experiments to be examined in the next chapter), they do entail the exercise of
power, sometimes over a human agent such as the emperor, and in this case (as in
the tale from the Rawlinson manuscript) over an animal. Fourth, the term used
for 'shake' or 'shake violently', *squassare*, may possibly suggest that this material

derives from an Italian source. That verb passed over into modern Italian, and may be more expected in Latin texts from Italy than in those from elsewhere.

The three other experiments for obtaining a horse are much simpler. In one (no. 14) the master looks toward the eastern sky, kneeling and with folded hands as if he were in prison, and with firm hope of obtaining his will he says a 'prayer' seven times to the 'most high and benign king of the east', adjuring him to send an 'airy spirit' on which he can ride to a specified place. A horse comes, and the master conjures it to carry him to that place without danger or disturbance. When he arrives at his destination he thanks the king of the east for bestowing this favour, and offers to serve him forever and obey his commands, 'and may his name be praised forever'. Another experiment (no. 17) is exceptional in that it does not begin with a conjuration, but with merely the inscription of magic names. The master writes six of these on the door of a vacant house, at twilight, 'in the Hebrew manner', then he withdraws for a while. When he returns he finds a horse ready. He conjures it to carry him without harm or trouble to a specified place. He may then mount it confidently, for it cannot harm him. When he arrives at his destination he dismounts and takes the horse's bridle. Having finished his business, he shakes the bridle vigorously and repeats the conjuration to summon the horse. In the third of these simple experiments (no. 43) the master again writes a series of names on the door of a vacant house, at dusk, with bat's blood, then withdraws for a brief time. When he returns he finds a horse awaiting him. After he has ridden the animal, he dismounts, removes the bridle, and hides it underground. When he wishes to return, he retrieves the bridle and shakes it, whereupon the horse returns at once. He then repeats the conjuration, plus the words 'kostolya, elogo, yetas', and off he rides.

OTHER EXPERIMENTS FOR ILLUSORY MEANS OF TRANSPORTATION

In addition to these four experiments, the handbook provides two similar ones, both complex, for conjuring a magical ship (no. 8) and a flying throne (no. 15). The ship will sail quickly over the seas, wherever one wants, with whomever one wishes. The master first fasts on a Monday, then goes out under a waxing moon to a remote place with the rib of a dead man or woman. Having sharpened a point on the rib, he uses it to trace a circle with a horizontal band across the centre and a vertical band across the top semicircle (forming an inverted version of the T–O pattern commonly found in medieval world maps). Superimposed on this design is a crescent shape, possibly representing a ship, with two small circles below it. The place of the master and his companions is marked at the bottom of the crescent, and 'East' is marked toward the bottom. This circle is the 'insignia' of the spirits to be invoked. The master enters the circle at the designated spot and fumigates it with the marrow of a dead man. He will hear voices in the air. Holding the rib in his right hand, he conjures eight spirits to come without delay.

He then sees eight sailors, who will announce in reverential tone that they have been sent to fulfil his command. Before the ship may be employed, the spirits must take an oath to fulfil the master's wishes. Then he commands them to transport the circle and those within it to a specified place. They do so, and it will seem as if the company is sailing on the high seas. In a brief time, they arrive at their destination. When he has arrived at his destination he can command the spirits to return him quickly to the point of departure, and they will do so. Then he gives them permission to leave. When they have done so, he destroys the circle and buries the rib. He can make the spirits swear that they will repeat their service upon demand: whenever he wishes to sail again, the master makes a circle with iron, wood, his finger, or anything else, and tells his companions to enter at the specified place without fear, then he invokes the eight spirits by virtue of the oath they have already taken, ordering them once again to transport him where he wishes to go, and eight sailors will appear and transport him, within an hour, in a ship; when he wants to return, they will take him back. In one key respect this experiment differs from others for means of transportation: the transport comes with the spirits' appearance, not at a later stage after they have sent a spirit specifically delegated for the purpose. But as in other experiments involving transportation, the third stage is a return to the master's original location, and then there are measures for repeating the experiment.

The greater part of the elaborate and fanciful experiment to obtain a flying throne (no. 15) is a ritual for summoning the throne itself; spirits themselves do not appear overtly. The text plunges directly into the instructions, with no introduction. The master must go to a high and secret place when the weather is serene, with no wind. He says various prayers (the Ave Maria, part of Psalm 50, the Lesser Doxology, etc.), then makes a circle, into which he places three jars with him, and he casts into one jar ashes and flour, into another fire and salt, into the third water and chalk. He sits in the middle of the circle and calls the king of the clouds to send three guides (or spirits with the rank of duke, *duces*) to carry him without harm or danger to the place he wants to go. A small cloud appears, and from the three jars he hears voices calling, 'Rise up! Rise up! Rise up!' After thrice saying a conjuration, the master sees a throne in the midst of the cloud. He ascends it and conjures the three guides to carry him without delay, without harm or danger to body or soul. The later part of the text is much concerned with defence against adversaries during the flight. If the rider perceives in flight that someone is trying to harm him by causing the throne to descend toward the south, he conjures the spirit Baltim, who comes and brings a storm upon the adversary. If the harm comes from other directions, other spirits are conjured in defence. If storms, serpents, birds or other terrifying things appear above the master on his way, he conjures a certain king to remove these terrors. Perhaps the most extraordinary feature of this experiment is the sense of peril, which comes not from the potential treachery of the spirits conjured, nor from the danger of breaking the charm (perhaps by making the sign of the cross) and plunging from a great height, but rather from unspecified adversaries, presumably spirits inimical to those invoked. Whether the aiding or the opposing spirits qualify as 'spiritual hosts of wickedness in the heavenly places' (Eph. 6:12) remains unclear; the writer might claim that the spirits on both sides are neutral, or capable of both good and evil, help and harm.

EXPERIMENTS FOR INVISIBILITY

The theme of magical invisibility by means of a ring, a cape or some other object is, of course, ancient. The ring of Gyges is one of the best known manifestations because it provides the basis for a classic thought experiment regarding the virtue of a person whose invisibility allows him to act with impunity.[39] Probably the most commonly recommended means for becoming invisible in medieval works on magic was to carry an opal on oneself, so that its brilliance would blind all potential viewers – a method that is supposed to have worked for Constantius Africanus.[40]

The Munich handbook contains one complex experiment and two simple ones to make the magician invisible. The complex one (no. 11) provides a cloak of invisibility:

> I shall treat also of the art of invisibility, unknown in these days to nearly all.
>
> When you wish to become invisible and insensible to all beings, both rational and otherwise, first, under a waxing moon on a Wednesday, in the first hour of the day, having remained chaste for three days beforehand, and with cut hair and beard, and dressed in white, in a secret place outside of town, under a clear sky, on level ground, trace a circle such as appears here, with a magnificent sword, writing these names and everything shown along with them.
>
> When this is done, place the sword toward the west, on [the name] Firiel. And while you have it placed there, have a vessel in which there is fire with frankincense (*thus*), myrrh and other incense (*olibano*), and with the smoke from these go about the circle, suffumigating it, begining and ending with [the name] Firiel. When you have done this, take blessed water and sprinkle yourself and the circle, saying, *Asperges me, Domine, ysopo* . . . [Ps. 50:9 Vulg.]. When you have done this, kneel facing the east, and in a strong voice say, 'I, so-and-so, conjure you, O Fyriel, Mememil, Berith, [and] Taraor, powerful, magnificent, illustrious spirits, in whom I place all my trust, by the one, inseparable and undivided Trinity . . . that all four of you should come here with utmost humility, bound, constrained, and sworn to carry out my command, whatever I ask of you. Come without delay . . .'
>
> When you have said this invocation four times – once toward Firiel, once

toward Melemil and toward Berith and Tarator – four spirits will at once be present in the circle, saying to you, 'Tell us what you wish, and we will obey you completely.' You will say to them, 'I wish a cloak of invisibility, which should be thin and incorruptible, so that when I wear it no one can see me or sense my presence.' When you have said this, one will withdraw, and within an hour will bring forth a cloak, which you asked them to bring you. They will reply that they cannot give it to you until you first give them your white garment; you will give it to them, and when you have do so they will give you the cloak. One of them will at once put on the garment given to them; you likewise should at once put on the cloak. When you put it on, you will say to the spirits, 'Go in peace', and at once they will withdraw. And when they depart, you should leave the circle, carrying the sword.

On the third day, return there with the cloak, and you will find your garment, which you will take. Be sure to remember; if on the third day you do not return, or you do not take the garment left there, on the fourth day you will find nothing, but in seven days you will die. Having taken it on the third day, you will burn it in the same place. And know that when you burn it you will hear great lamenting and complaining. And when you burn it, sprinkle the ashes in the air, saying, 'I conjure you, Firiel, Melemil, Berith, [and] Taraor, by your virtue and power, and by all things having power against you, to have no virtue or power to harm me by this cloak, but may Jesus Christ protect and defend me . . .' When you have said this, take blessed water and sprinkle the cloak, saying, 'I conjure you, cloak, by the Father and the Son and the Holy Spirit, and by this water, that whenever I put you on, no one may sense my presence or see me. . . .'

The figure required here is a plain circle, with the positions east, south, and west labelled, a sword lying toward the east (with its point near the centre), the position of the master inscribed near the center, and the names Firiel toward the west, Melemil to the south, Berith to the east, and Taraor to the north, along with two characters. One of the most striking features of the experiment is the suggestion that when the master burns the returned garment he will hear lamentation and complaint, as if the garment, like the book Antoninus of Florence is said to have burned, was infested with malign spirits, contained within it in such a way that they were subject to the will of the person who disposed of the physical object.

The two simple experiments in this category are in different ways exceptional: the first (no. 21) because the techniques are without parallel in this manual, and the second (no. 45) because it not only entails a sacrificial offering to the demons but explicitly states that these spirits are worthy of sacrifice. The first of these experiments (which again has no introduction) requires the practitioner to eviscerate a black cat born in March, cut out its heart and eyes, and insert a heliotrope seed in place of each eye and two such seeds in the mouth, while saying a conjuration for invisibility. Then he buries the body in a closed garden, and waters it for fifteen days with human blood mixed with water, whereupon a plant will grow. He determines which of the plant's seeds bears the power to make him invisible by testing each seed: repeating a series of names, he takes a mirror and puts the newly grown seeds into his mouth, one by one, beneath his tongue, and when he finds the seed that causes invisibility he vanishes from the mirror.[41] In the second experiment (no. 45) the master takes a white dove and a sheet of virgin parchment and on a Saturday night goes to a stream by a crossroads. He sacrifices the dove and says, 'O you to whom sacrifice is due, aid in fulfilling my will'; he repeats this formula while facing in each of the cardinal directions. Then he inscribes a figure (a complex sign, with mainly horizontal elements and elaborations) with the dove's blood. Before sunrise he returns, and he finds another sheet with a coin enclosed; when he binds this to his hair he becomes invisible. He must be sure to leave the dove and the parchment behind, presumably as sacrifices to the spirit. The text does not say how to undo the invisibility, but presumably it suffices to remove the seed from one's mouth (taking care meanwhile not to swallow) or the sheet from one's hair.

POWER OVER LIFE AND DEATH

As we have seen, the term 'necromancy' was used interchangeably in medieval parlance with various forms of 'nigromancy', which could be taken to mean 'black magic', or more literally 'black divination'. One possible reason for the conflation of these terms and concepts was the widespread assumption that when one engaged in necromancy in the original sense, conjuring the spirits of the deceased, the spirits which in fact appeared were demons in the forms of the dead. Most famously, the shade of Samuel conjured by the witch of Endor (I Samuel 28) was taken to have been a demon in the guise of Samuel.[42] While 'necromancy' was most often used in later medieval parlance for the conjuring of demons, necromancy in its original sense was not unknown in the magic of the era. The Rawlinson necromantic manuscript, for example, gives procedures for raising the shades of the dead.[43] The Munich handbook comes closest in an experiment (no. 10) by which the necromancer can make a living person appear dead or a dead person appear alive:

> When you wish to infuse a spirit into a dead person, so that he appears alive as he was previously, this is the procedure to follow. First have a ring made of gold. Around the outside these names should be carved: Brimer, Suburith, Tranauit; on the inside, these names: Lyroth, Beryen, Damayn. When the names have been carved, on a Sunday before sunrise, go to running water and place the ring in it, and let it remain there for five days.

On the sixth day, take it out and take it to a tomb, and place it inside, so that it remains there on Friday and Saturday. On Sunday, before sunrise, go outside of town under a clear sky, in a remote and secret place, and make a circle with a sword, and on it write with the sword the names and figures that appear here.

When this has been inscribed, enter into it [the circle] as is designated, and place the sword beneath your knees, and, facing south, recite this conjuration: 'I conjure you, all the demons inscribed on this ring' – which you should have in your hand – 'by the Father and the Son and the Holy Spirit, and by almighty God, maker of heaven and earth . . . that all of you, constrained and bound to my will and my power, should proceed hither in benign form, so that I will not fear, and should consecrate this ring in such a way that it may possess this power, namely that whenever I place it on the finger of a dead person, one of you will enter him, and he will appear alive as before, in the same likeness and form . . .'

When you have said this once, six spirits will at once appear at the circle, requesting the ring, which you will give them. When you have given it, they will depart, and you likewise should leave the circle, taking the sword with you, and not destroying the circle.

On the sixth day, return with the sword, and say, facing south, 'I conjure you, O Brimer, Suburith, [etc.] . . . that you should come to me now without delay, bearing the consecrated ring, so that when I place it on the finger or in the hand of a living person he will fall to the ground as if dead, and when I take it away he will return to his former state, and when I place it on a dead person, as aforesaid, a spirit will enter him and he will appear alive as before . . .'

When you have said all this four times, first toward the south, and likewise toward the west, then toward the north and toward the east, you will see toward the east someone coming on horseback, who, when he arrives at the circle, will say, 'So-and-so' – naming the names written above – 'send you this consecrated ring, but they say they cannot come to you because it is not fitting; you will experience [or test] the power of the ring, and if it does not have the power that you requested, they say they are prepared to come to you whenever you wish.' You will take the ring, saying to him, 'Thanks to you and to them.' When you have said this, he will at once withdraw,[44] and you too shall depart from the circle, destroying it completely.

Keep this ring with you, wrapped in a sheet of white cloth. When you wish to cause someone to appear dead, so that he will seem to everyone devoid of life, place this ring on his finger, and he will appear to be a corpse; and when you remove it, he will return to his former state. And when you wish a corpse to appear animated, place the ring as aforesaid, or bind it to a hand or foot, and within an hour it will arise in the form to which it is previously accustomed, and will speak before all with a living voice, and will be able to display this quality for six days, for each of these [spirits] will remain in it for a day. And if you wish it to be as previously before the assigned terminus, remove the ring. And in this manner you can revive a dead person.

This most worthy experiment is to be kept hidden, because it holds great power.

The circle given above has many powers, of which I shall mention three known to me. If you draw it on a Friday with the feather of a hoopoe and with its blood on a freshly prepared sheet of parchment, and touch a person with it, you will be loved by that person above all others forever. And if you place that circle, written as aforesaid, on the head of a sick person without his knowledge, if he is to die he will say that he can by no means recover, and if he is to recover he will see that he is altogether freed. And if you carry this circle, written in like manner, on your person, no dog will be able to bark at you. And I have experienced these effects; I do not mention those I have not experienced.

The figure shown for this experiment is a double circular band with a pentagram inscribed. The names carved on the ring are repeated, along with astrological signs, within the two bands. The position of the master is indicated in the centre of the pentagram, and the cardinal directions are marked outside the bands.

The reference to the *monumentum*, the white shroud, and Sunday morning before dawn all make it clear that this resuscitation is intended as a replication or perhaps a parody of Christ's Resurrection. Yet pretending to resurrect the dead was one specialty associated traditionally with Antichrist. Indeed, the question whether Antichrist could genuinely revive the dead was much discussed in medieval theology. Honorius of Regensburg in his *Elucidarium* had his disciple ask whether Antichrist will truly raise the dead, to which the master replies:

> By no means; rather, the Devil by his bewitchments [*maleficiis*] will enter someone's body and carry it about and speak in it, so that it will appear as if living, as it is said, 'In all signs and lying wonders' [II Thess. 2:9].[45]

Hildegard of Bingen agreed that Antichrist's miracle is an illusion, and insisted that 'he is allowed to do this only occasionally, for a very short time and no longer, lest his presumption bring God's glory into scorn'.[46] The directions in *The Play of Antichrist* say that the person resuscitated is to be a man lying in a coffin and feigning death in battle;[47] here we have pretence of death rather than of resurrection, but the miracle remains an illusion, just as Christian theology from Patristic sources onward saw magic as inherently a delusion.

These experiments in the Munich handbook make no effort at all to dispel or counteract this viewpoint, but rather presuppose it, and indeed revel in it. But there is no sense here that the magician is trying to use his deception to seduce followers. His tricks are meant fundamentally as entertainment, chiefly for himself, perhaps, but potentially for others as well – and certainly for the reader who, in the privacy of his chamber, fantasizes about these wonders much as one might share in the fantasies of romance and related literature.

In commenting on the allegations pressed at the Council of Pisa against Benedict XIII, Margaret Harvey remarks: 'The charges . . . were almost certainly a tissue of nonsense. . . . The folklore [in them] is itself interesting however, and so are the circumstances in which it could be delivered solemnly as fact to auditors at a general council by a powerful group including doctors of law and even a cardinal.'[48] One might add to this that it is not altogether anachronistic to see the notion of necromancy as nonsense. At its most playful, it was a deliberate violation of sense, a fantasy of illusion, perhaps intended more for imaginative entertainment than for actual use. Yet the boundaries between sense and nonsense are rarely quite stable, and themes that seem to an outsider absolutely nonsensical could be taken in deadly earnest by some observers within the culture. What is perhaps most fascinating about these illusionist experiments is precisely their teasing ambiguity, which perhaps made it possible for writers on witchcraft to believe about witches what they had been conditioned to believe just might be true of the necromancers before them. The playful fantasies of the necromancers, then, became sources for the Boschian nightmares of the witch trials.

Notes

1 Rawlinson MS D 252, fols 75v–76v: *Quia seme[l] eram egomet in India ab Alexandria infra horam et ibi mulieres videbam michi placentissimas, et statim compleui cum vna desiderium meum, nec ibi erat oportunitas confessorum pro tunc nisi diucius expectassem, et cum ad equum meum reuenissem stetit vbi coniuratus est, et cum apprendissem* [76] *finem freni equus incepit se mouere non permittendo me ponere pedem in scropam, racione mee inmundicie, et ego tenui fortiter frenum et equus leuauit me in aerem per 40 pedes in altum ac tandem videns me misere periturum remisi manum et cecidi et fregi crus meum mirabiliter, et in India iacui per 4 menses, nec amplius vsque fueram sanus equum videbam. Cum autem sanus fueram, confessus eram et egi penitenciam, et parando michi cameram, feceram nouiter fieri sceptrum et gladium et anulum, quia anulus quem polueram virtutem perdidit. Et factis istis instrumentis, et nouiter consecratis, vocaui istos eosdem spiritus, et eundem spiritum ve[l] equum michi feci apportari* [MS *apportaris*]. *Et factis coniuracionibus eundem coniuraui et ascendebam pacifice, et per vnum mensem continue nisi quando descendebam ad dormiendum et comedendum vel biben-* [76v] *dum semper equitaui 8cies circulando totum orbem. Et in aerem feceram eum me deuehere quousquo ego fere propter inpressiones aeris fueram suffocatus. Sed in circulando orbem plures* [MS *plrures*] *repperi thesauros et mirificos, quos postea noui in virtute docente me vno spirituum, quem postea includebam. Et sic vexaui equ[u]m meum, qui cum vltimate ab eo descendebam et petente me quare me lesit, respondit quod inde* [sic] *facere non potuit, dixit tamen se tam diu cicius in inferno fore quam per tantum tempus amplius equitare. Et isto modo me rogauit vt amplius eum tam diu non vexarem et ipse michi cum fuero mundus fideliter cum vocauero ministraret. Et sic malo pro malo retribuebam ei.*

2 *De Nigromancia of Roger Bacon*, iv.5, ed. and trans. Michael-Albion Macdonald (Gillette, NJ: Heptangle, 1988), 65–70.

3 H.S.V. Jones, 'The Squire's Tale', in W.F. Bryan and Germaine Dempster, eds, *Sources and Analogues of Chaucer's Canterbury Tales* (New York: Humanities, 1958), 357–76. On the general theme of magical horses see Stith Thompson, *Motif-Index of Folk-Literature: A Classification of Narrative Elements in Folktales, Ballads, Myths, Fables, Mediaeval Romances, Exempla, Fabliaux, Jest-Books, and Local Legends*, rev. edn (Bloomington: Indiana University Press, 1955–8), B184.1 (magic horse), D1442.1 (magic bridle restrains all horses), D1626.1 (artificial flying horse), F401.3.1 (spirit in form of horse).

4 Kathryn L. Lynch, 'East meets West in Chaucer's Squire's and Franklin's Tales', *Speculum*, 70 (1995), 530–51, esp. 539f.

5 *The Quest of the Holy Grail*, trans. P.M. Matarasso (Harmondsworth: Penguin, 1969), 134–61.

6 Fols 49r–50r.

7 Hansen, *Quellen*, 539–44.

8 On illusionist magic in medieval literature see W. Eamon, 'Technology as magic in the late Middle Ages and Renaissance', *Janus*, 70 (1983), 171–212; Sydney H. Ball, 'Luminous gems, mythical and real', *Scientific Monthly*, 47 (1938), 496–505; Joan Evans, *Magic Jewels of the Middle Ages and Renaissance* (Oxford: Clarendon, 1922); Laura H. Loomis, 'Secular dramatics in the royal palace, Paris 1378, 1389, and Chaucer's "tragetoures"', *Speculum*, 33 (1958), 242–55; Marvin Alpheus Owings, *The Arts in the Middle English Romances* (New York: Bookman Associates, 1952), 138–64 ('The supernatural'); Helen Cooper, 'Magic that does not work', *Medievalia et Humanistica*, n.s., 7 (1976), 131–46; M. Sherwood, 'Magic and mechanics in medieval fiction', *Studies in Philology*, 44 (1947), 567–92; Haldeen Braddy, 'Cambyuskan's flying horse and Charles VI's "cerf volant"', *Modern Language Review*, 33 (1938), 41–4; W.A. Clouston, *Notes on the Magical Elements in the 'Squire's Tale', and Analogues* (Chaucer Society, ser. 2, vol. 26) (London: Trubner, 1890).

9 Anthony E. Luengo, 'Magic and illusion in the *Franklin's Tale*', *Journal of English and Germanic Philology*, 77 (1978), 1–16; W. Bryant Bachman, Jr., '"To maken illusion": the philosophy of magic and the magic of philosophy in the *Franklin's Tale*', *Chaucer Review*, 12 (1977), 55–67.

10 Several early Christian writers spoke of magic as deception (*fraus*), delusion (*elusio*) or phantasm – which could mean purely natural sleight of hand within the capacity of any skilled human, but it could also apply to tricks only demons could perform, which would still be illusory in the sense that what appeared to be present would not in fact be. On this theme see Francis C.R. Thee, *Julius Africanus and the Early Christian View of Magic* (Tübingen: Mohr, 1984), esp. 349–52 (Irenaeus), 374–6 (Origen) and 394f. (Hippolytus). For a particularly well done fictional exploration of the motif see Anita Mason, *The Illusionist* (New York: Holt, Rinehart & Winston, 1984).

11 Origen, *Contra Celsum*, i.68, trans. Henry Chadwick (Cambridge: Cambridge University Press, 1953), 62–3.

12 It would be pointless to attempt a survey of the theme in other writings, but to take merely one example, see *Picatrix: The Latin Version of the* Ghayat Al-Hakim, ed. David Pingree (London: Warburg Institute, 1986), 17–18.

13 On this wide-ranging subject see, e.g., Lorne Dwight Conquergood, 'The Anglo-Saxon Boast: Structure and Function' (Northwestern University dissertation, 1977), and Daniel Cliness Boughner,

The Braggart in Renaissance Literature: A Study in Comparative Drama from Aristophanes to Shakespeare (Minneapolis: University of Minnesota Press, 1954).

14 See Joseph Hansen, *Zauberwahn, Inquisition und Hexenprozeß im Mittelalter, und die Entstehung der großen Hexenverfolgung* (Munich: Oldenbourg, 1900; repr. Aalen: Scientia, 1964), 1–36, on the formation of a *Sammelbegriff* or *Kollektivbegriff* of witchcraft.

15 *Summa theologiae*, i.109.1; *Malleus maleficarum*, i.4, trans. Montague Summers (London: Rodker, 1928; repr. London: Pushkin, 1948), 28–31.

16 Rossell Hope Robbins, *The Encyclopedia of Witchcraft and Demonology* (New York: Crown, 1959), 420–21 (with a relevant quotation from Lancashire); Francesco Maria Guazzo, *Compendium maleficarum*, i.12, trans. E.A. Ashwin (Secaucus, NJ: University Books, 1974), p. 37.

17 *Malleus maleficarum*, ii.1.3, p. 105; cf. ii.1.1 and ii.1.4, pp. 97 and 113, in which the sign of the cross is said to have similar effect but outside the context of flight. A warning against the sign of the cross outside the context of flight occurs also in Clm 849, no. 1.

18 W. Braekman, 'Magische experimenten en toverpraktijken uit een middelnederlands handschrift', *Verslagen en mededelingen van de Koninklijke Vlaamse Academie voor Taal- en Letterkunde*, 1966, 28–32.

19 See Robbins, *Encyclopedia of Witchcraft and Demonology*, 364–7, and Richard Kieckhefer, *European Witch Trials: Their Foundations in Popular and Learned Culture, 1300–1500* (London: Routledge & Kegan Paul; Berkeley: University of California Press, 1976), 41–2 (and sources in the notes).

20 I translate *dapiferos* thus, rather than as 'stewards', to convey somewhat more clearly that these figures actually produce the illusory banquet rather than serving at a conventional feast.

21 This passage seems to mean that one is to draw the sword itself not only to the east but to the other directions while reciting the conjuration, and then again hold the sword toward the east.

22 As I can attest from personal experience, even in the absence of demons and magicians an excited or agitated hoopoe flutters its crest, which otherwise lies back on its head.

23 Oymelor, Symofos, Manoir and Faubair in the outermost band; Demefin, Rodobayl, Tamafin and Abelutabel in the next; Lamair, Tentetos, Leutaber and Rimasor in the next; and Masair, Lotobor, Tatomofon and Sirama in the innermost. (The forms of the names are exceptionally variable: Symofos appears elsewhere in the experiment as Symofor or Simofor, Manoir as Memoyr or Memoir, Rodobayl as Rodobail, Abelutabel as Selutabel or Belutabel, Leutaber as Zeugaber, Sirama as Syrama.)

24 The spell of Pnouthis, PGM I.42–195, in Hans Dieter Betz, ed., *The Greek Magical Papyri in Translation, Including the Demotic Spells*, 1 (Chicago: University of Chicago Press, 1986), p. 6, lines 107–14.

25 On the lore of this bird see John Gotthold Kunstmann, 'The Hoopoe: A Study in European Folklore' (University of Chicago dissertation, 1938); W.R. Dawson, 'The lore of the hoopoe', *Ibis*, ser. 12, 1 (1925), 31–9; Samia Al Azharia Jahn, 'Zur Volkskunde eines Zugvogels: Der Wiedehopf (*Upupa Epops* L.) in Nordeuropa und in den islamischen Ländern Afrikas', *Anthropos*, 76 (1981), 371–92; and R. Lops, 'La huppe: histoire littéraire et légendaire d'un oiseau', in Q. Mok, et al., eds, *Mélanges de linguistique, de littérature et de philologie offerts à J.R. Smeets* (Leiden, 1982), 171–85. For some of these references I am indebted to Baudouin van den Abeele. Albert the Great, *Man and the Beasts: De animalibus (Books 22–26)*, xxiii.112, trans. James J. Scanlan (Binghamton, NY: CEMERS, 1987), 321,

reports that smearing hoopoe blood on the temples before sleeping causes nightmares, and that enchanters seek the bird's organs (especially its brain, tongue and heart) for 'their own purposes'. See also Betz, *The Greek Magical Papyri*, 1, pp. 13 (PGM II.1–64), 29 (III.424–66), 129 (VII.411–16), and 210 (PDM xiv.116).

26 Prospero, in Shakespeare's *Tempest*, IV.i.

27 For *experiencia*, although the heading gives *experimenta*.

28 A largely conjectural reading of *qui habet multum ipsos 15 demones pauentare uel spanentare*; the writer seems to have been copying from a source and unable to determine what the verb should be.

29 The MS reads *recedetis*, but the context calls for *redeatis* or the equivalent.

30 This translation simplifies and clarifies a somewhat confused passage.

31 P.M. Matarasso, trans. *The Quest of the Holy Grail* (Harmondsworth: Penguin, 1969), 192–94.

32 Lobsang P. Lhalungpa, trans. *The Life of Milarepa* (Boston and London: Shambhala, 1985), 52.

33 On the relationship in medieval Europe, see my article, 'The holy and the unholy: sainthood, witchcraft, and magic in late medieval Europe', *Journal of Medieval and Renaissance Studies*, 24 (1994), 355–85, reprinted in Scott L. Waugh and Peter D. Diehl, eds, *Christendom and its Discontents: Exclusion, Persecution, and Rebellion, 1000–1500* (Cambridge: Cambridge University Press, 1996), 310–37. The information about modern lamas was related to me by Janet Gyatso.

34 See also Frederic C. Tubach, *Index exemplorum: A Handbook of Medieval Religious Tales* (FF Communications, 204) (Helsinki: Suomalainen Tiedeakatemia, Akademia Scientiarum Fennica, 1969), 245, nos 3,130 and 3,134, and the *Malleus maleficarum*, ii.1.3.

35 Chs 31–2.

36 Or perhaps 'with a farewell' (*cum salute*).

37 For *de cuius cluni[bu]s aliquantulum incidere debes*.

38 The nomenclature is again variable: Lantrayth appears also as Lautrayth and Lutrayth, Feremni as Feremin and Feremim, Oliromim as Oliroomim.

39 The classic source is Plato's *Republic*, book 2, 359d–360c. For medieval versions of the tale see Tubach, *Index exemplorum*, 189, no. 2,391. For other examples of using rings for invisibility see Betz, *Greek Magical Papyri*, 1, pp. 136 (VII.628–42) and 109 (V.447–58).

40 Albertus Magnus, *The Book of Secrets of Albertus Magnus, of the Virtues of Herbs, Stones and Certain Beasts, also A Book of the Marvels of the World*, ed. Michael R. Best and Frank H. Brightman (Oxford: Clarendon, 1973), 26f. The assumption was that the brilliant luminosity of the stone would blind people to one's presence; on the general subject of luminous stones, see Sydney H. Ball, 'Luminous gems, mythical and real', *Scientific Monthly*, 47 (1938), 496–505; and Joan Evans, *Magic Jewels of the Middle Ages and Renaissance* (Oxford: Clarendon, 1922).

41 Perhaps the closest classical analogue to this procedure is from the Greek magical papyri, which recommend holding a snapdragon under the tongue while sleeping, and reciting specified names on rising early, to become invisible; see Betz, *Greek Magical Papyri*, 1, p. 135 (PGM VII.619–27, from a collection called the *Diadem of Moses*). See also an Italian experiment for invisibility mentioned by Charles Burnett in *Magic and Divination in the Middle Ages: Texts and Techniques in the Islamic and Christian Worlds* (Aldershot: Variorum, 1996), IX, pp. 6–7, where five beans are placed in a woman's skull and buried.

42 For a survey of relevant sources see Robbins, *Encyclopedia of Witchcraft and Demonology*, 159–60.

43 Fols 66v–67v.

44 The MS uses the second person, but the reference is clearly to the horseman.

45 *Elucidarium*, iii.10, in *Patrologia latina*, 172, col. 1163. See Linus Urban Lucken, *Antichrist and the Prophets of Antichrist in the Chester Cycle* (Washington: Catholic University of America Press, 1940), 63–5. On Antichrist generally see Bernard McGinn, *Antichrist: Two Thousand Years of the Human Fascination with Evil* (San Francisco: Harper, 1994). See also Nancy Caciola, 'Wraiths, revenants and ritual in medieval culture', Past & Present, 152 (August 1996), 3–45.

46 Hildegard of Bingen, *Scivias*, xi.27, trans. Mother Columba Hart and Jane Bishop (New York: Paulist, 1990), 503.

47 *The Play of Antichrist*, trans. John Wright (Toronto: Pontifical Institute of Mediaeval Studies, 1967), 89f.

48 Margaret Harvey, 'Papal witchcraft: the charges against Benedict XIII', in Derek Baker, ed., *Sanctity and Secularity: The Church and the World* (Oxford: Blackwell, 1973), 109.

4

LOVE, FAVOUR AND MADNESS: PSYCHOLOGICAL EXPERIMENTS

When we speak of one individual as 'charming' or 'fascinating' another, we still use the traditional language of magic to suggest the power that personalities can exert over each other. We know that the human mind is subject to subtle and often threatening or frightening influence; it comes as no surprise that practitioners of magic have claimed to make such influence into a kind of science available for their employment. Nor is it surprising if at times magic intended to bend the minds and wills of other persons has its desired effect, since this form of magic more than any other lends itself to the power of suggestion.[1] Outside the context of clerical necromancy, magic of this sort occurs in trials such as that of Matteuccia di Francesco at Todi in 1428. Among the many charges against Matteuccia was this:

> . . . in the month of December of 1427 a certain woman of that territory went to Matteuccia and, after confessing that she loved a certain man, said that she would like to spread her hatred so that her man would abandon his wife and, loving only herself, do everything she wanted. Matteuccia told the woman to wash her hands and feet facing backwards and with her knees bent and when she had done so to take the water and throw it where the man and woman were going to pass, with the spirit, intent and belief that this would generate hatred between them. The woman did this and reported to Matteuccia that the water had generated hatred between the man and the woman as she had intended, so that they could not meet, but instead hated each other.[2]

The alienation of affection in this case is more than usually complicated: the same ritual simultaneously disrupted the married couple's relationship and bound the husband's affections, causing him to love the client so intensely that he complied with her every wish. In other cases Matteuccia prescribed such water rituals as a means for regaining affection and for transferring disease, presumably on the assumption that the fluidity of water made it a fitting symbol and medium for emotional instability, but also perhaps implying that the sort of water one might expect to find in a medieval city could plausibly be viewed as a means for contamination and contagion.

PSYCHOLOGICAL MAGIC IN THE MUNICH HANDBOOK

The Munich manuscript contains seven experiments that might be termed psychological, because they are intended to influence people's minds or wills: to cause madness or hatred, to gain favour with a potentate, to constrain the will of others, or to arouse the love of a woman. Five general features characterize these experiments. First, they typically involve elaborate preparation and ceremonies which may require more than one day. Second, the purposes and forms (other than the conjurations) have much in common with those of astral magic. Third, the basic techniques are those of 'sympathetic' or 'imitative' magic, whose meaning is explicated by accompanying incantations; magic circles either are not used or are simple and relatively unimportant, and conjurations are less significant and elaborate here than in other forms of necromancy. Fourth, the procedures and the expected results are typically more violent than in other experiments, amounting in the erotic experiments to a kind of rape. Fifth, with rare exceptions, the magician works strictly by himself, in secret, without companions (unless one includes the women he sets out to seduce, in erotic forms of this magic); whereas the secrecy in illusionist experiments adds to the sense of excitement and adventure, the point here is more simply to evade detection in circumstances that would be extremely damaging.

The preparation and ritual is sometimes protracted over several days (nos 2, 4, 5), or at least involves multiple operations performed on a single occasion (nos 3, 12, 13, 35). One is tempted to speculate that such magic can best take effect if its victims are aware that it is being used and if they are liable to the power of suggestion, and that the more elaborate the procedures, the greater the chance that the intended victims will learn the fate that is to befall them. Indeed, in one of these experiments (no. 2) the master is instructed to go to the victim and warn him in advance of his fate. John Gager suggests in a similar context that magicians may have been 'less than totally discreet about their business, perhaps intentionally so, and let it be known that a "fix" had been put on so-and-so'.[3] Such deliberate indiscretion would be especially appropriate for magic that depended entirely on psychological effect.

The purposes served by these psychological experiments are among the most common purposes found in the astral magic translated into Latin from Arabic sources such as *Picatrix* and Thabit ibn Qurra's *De imaginibus*.[4] Thabit's treatise is devoted to experiments for such goals as destroying a city or region, becoming ruler of a place, securing the favour of a king, and arousing friendship or enmity between two persons. The magician is in every case expected to use images, not so much as aids to sympathetic magic, but as channels of astrological power; the astrological conditions for use of these images are thus of paramount importance. The psychological experiments in the Munich handbook are generally much longer and more fully developed than the materials in these Arabic sources. What they add are chiefly conjurations and operations of sympathetic magic.

These rituals consistently entail sympathetic procedures: they rely on the basic principle of sympathetic magic, *sicut hic, ita illic*. More often than not the master is supposed to inflict some kind of violence upon the victim's image, so that a corresponding violence will occur to the actual victim. In other words, ritual rape is a means for accomplishing physical rape. A representative object may be consumed or destroyed: a candle melted (no. 2); stones beaten together, buried, heated and crushed (no. 5); an image pierced with needles (no. 12); a bone placed in fire (nos 13 and 35). Elsewhere the representative object is used for an imitative operation symbolizing submission: one metal image is placed in a position of subordination to another (no. 4). The specifically demonic or necromantic element in these experiments is typically an appendage to this sympathetic magic, and the demons generally play a less prominent role than in illusionist or divinatory experiments. Other features of necromancy, while present, are also relegated to a position of secondary significance. The conjurations used in these experiments tend to be relatively simple. Instead of conjurations, incantations explicating the significance of the sympathetic ritual ('Just as . . . so too . . .') occupy a central position. Even the magic circles called for in these experiments are comparatively simple: indeed, in three cases there are no circles at all (nos 4, 5, 35), and in four others there is either a simple circle (nos 2, 3, 12) or a simple shield-figure substituting for a circle (no. 13).

EXPERIMENTS TO INFLICT HARM

Later medieval books of magic are seldom shy about giving straightforwardly harmful formulas. A fifteenth-century *Liber de angelis, annulis, karecteribus et ymaginibus planetarum (Book of angels, rings, characters, and images of the planets)* in the Cambridge University Library contains an experiment called the *Vindicta Troie (Vengeance of Troy)*, which can be used to arouse hatred or to cause bodily harm or even death. The procedure calls for making an image on the day and in the hour of Saturn, in the name of the person to be harmed. The image must be made of wax, preferably from candles used at a funeral. It should be made as ugly as possible; the face should be contorted, and there should be hands in place of feet and vice versa. The victim's name should be inscribed on the forehead of the image, the name of the planet Saturn on its breast, and the seals or characters of Saturn between its shoulders. The operator should call upon the spirits of Saturn to descend from on high and afflict the named victim. The image should be fumigated with various substances, including human bones and hair, then wrapped in a funeral cloth and buried in some unclean place, face downward. If the magician wishes to harm any particular member of the victim's body, there are instructions for binding the corresponding member on the image with a funeral cloth and piercing the image with a needle; to kill the victim, the magician should insert the needle into the spine, from the head down to the heart. To cure the victim afterward (unless, presumably, the experiment has succeeded in killing him), one must unbury the image, remove the needle and anoint the wounds that are left, rub out the inscriptions, and wash the image in a fountain. The *Liber de angelis* also prescribes a technique for arousing discord: the operator makes one image of Saturn and another of Mars (which counted as 'unfortunate' planets), one holding a lance and the other a sword, and buries them positioned over against each other.[5]

If one were to judge from the trial records, one might suppose that necromancy was used chiefly to bring personal harm and death to enemies. Thus, Guichard of Troyes was charged in the early fourteenth century with hiring a witch and a friar to kill the queen of France by image magic and invocation of demons,[6] and in 1441 Eleanor Cobham was accused of employing a witch and two scholars learned in astrology and necromancy, in part to kill the king of England,[7] to cite only two examples. Yet of all the experiments in the Munich manual, only two (nos 2 and 5), are designed specifically and exclusively to cause harm, and the damage is specifically psychological; the manuscript contains no experiments for killing enemies or inflicting physical harm on them. Even these two experiments designed to bring harm provide countermagic for the master to use if he wishes to undo his own mischief (as does the *Liber de angelis*).

Let us look first at an experiment designed to bring enmity between two friends (no. 5):

When you wish to sow hatred and mortal enmity between two men or women, or a man and a woman, you must take two shiny round rocks from a river.[8] On one you must carve the name of one person, with the names Cartutay, Momabel, Sobil and Geteritacon. On the other [you must carve] the name of the other person and the names Puzanil, Pimaton, Folfitoy, and Mansator. These names are highly antipathetic to each other. When they are carved, you must bury one under the threshold of the one in whose name it was made, if you can, and if you cannot, bury them beneath the threshold of any inhabited house, and the other likewise under the threshold of the other, as has been said, or under some house, as is written above.[9] And let them remain there seven days and seven nights.

Then remove them before sunrise, take them to a secret place, and cast them into a fire, saying, 'I conjure you most inimical spirits, by the glory of the everlasting God, to sow and arouse as much hatred between so-and-so and so-and-so, whose names are carved here on these stones, as there is between you.' When you have said this three times, take the stones from the fire, saying, 'When their fury is enkindled against us, perhaps the waters had swallowed them up' [Ps. 123:3f. Vulg.]. Then cast [*proiciamus*] them into very cold water and let them stay there under a clear sky for three days and nights. On the fourth day take them and fumigate them with sulphur, saying, 'I conjure all you hateful and malignant, invidious and discordant demons . . . to arouse at once between so-and-so and so-and-so as much hatred as there was between Cain and Abel. Arouse them and inflame them so much that one cannot stand to see the other, and one will afflict the other with immeasurable hatred, as a rebel.[10] May all love, affection, fraternity and concord be removed from them; let them be turned to enmity and utter hatred.' When you have said this three times, with constant fumigation, store them [the stones] away.

The next night, beat the rocks together and strike one against the other, saying, 'I do not smash these stones, rather I smash so-and-so and so-and-so, whose names are written here, so that one will at once afflict the other and they will torment each other from now on with unconditional hatred.'

And do this three times, each night and day, for several days. And immediately you will see or hear that they have become enemies and hate each other bitterly, so that neither can abide to see the other.

If you wish to separate them altogether, causing one to flee the other, proceed as follows. Arise before sunrise on a Sunday, under a waning moon, especially when it is in combustion, and proceed in the direction of the sunrise.[11] When you have done this, take two stones that you have brought with you there, and rub them together vigorously, pounding one against the other, saying, 'I do not smash these rocks, etc.' When you have said this three times, bury whichever of them you wish. Then withdraw and go toward the west, and make a ditch there and bury the other in that place, saying, 'As I have separated these stones, thus may so-and-so separate himself from so-and-so, and may they be as distant as these stones.' When it has been buried, withdraw. And you will see them estranged, each separated from the other.

This experiment must be kept secret, for it possesses ineffable power, and no remedy is to be found before they have been estranged and hate each other bitterly.

But if you wish to restore them to their initial friendship, unbury the stones and place them in a furnace, and when they are well cooked smash them to little bits, and paste them together with water, and let [the newly formed mass] dry. When it is dried, cast it into the water of a river, saying, 'Let all enmity be taken away that was between so-and-so and so-and-so, and let them return to their former affection, by the mercy of the gracious God, who does not regard the misdeeds of sinners. Amen.' And you may be sure that on account of this they will be joined together at once, and all anger will be taken away, and they will enjoy their initial concord.

Not only is the imitative action with stones at the heart of this experiment, even the conjuration involves an extension of the principle of imitative magic: the enmity produced by the magic is already manifested in the 'hateful and malignant, invidious and discordant demons' whose services are invoked, and the archetypal enmity between Cain and Abel serves as a paradigm for that intended by the magician. Apart from the verbal formulas, the magic is simple to the point of seeming primitive: the symbolic objects are not carved in the forms of the individuals represented, but are mere rocks, and the abuse to which they are subject is fairly simple exposure to the inimical elements of earth, fire and water. One might wonder why the sympathetic reversal provided in this experiment does not have the effect of utterly destroying the victims. The stones have all along symbolized the victims, and the crushing should have dire effects on them if the logic of sympathetic magic is consistently maintained. Obviously, however, this is not how the writer of the manual viewed matters. From his perspective the operations evidently took effect not simply *ex opere operato* but in accordance with the intentions of the operator as expressed in the accompanying words.

Elsewhere the procedures for separation magic were more imaginative but still essentially imitative. Riccola di Puccio of Pisa was executed at Perugia in 1347, in part for using magic to bring disaffection between a husband and wife; she recited charms and conjurations over an egg from a black hen, calling upon 'Mosectus, Barbectus and Belsabuct, the prince of demons', as well as other demons of various ranks, then he cut the egg in half and gave one part to a female cat and the other to a male dog, saying, 'In the name of the aforesaid demons may the love between [the two] be sundered as this egg is divided between the dog and the cat, and let there be such affection between them as between this dog and this cat.'[12]

The other experiment in this category in the Munich handbook (no. 2) is intended to inflict dementia. The practitioner goes to his victim and openly recites a conjuration commanding the malign spirit Mirael to enter and afflict his brain. Then he makes a pen with wood from the victim's door, and he inscribes a brief conjuration and a magic circle – a single band with the names of Mirael and the victim in the centre, and the names of ten demons within the band – on a piece of linen, and conjures the demons thrice. A set of sympathetic operations follows. The master goes to the victim's house, urinates 'in the manner of a camel',[13] and buries the cloth; while doing so he says, 'I bury you, so-and-so, in the name of the demons written round about you, so that these demons may always be around him, and all your power may be buried.' He goes home and makes a candle, inscribed as was the circle. He lights the candle, saying, 'Just as this candle, made for the destruction of N., burns and is consumed, so may all the power and knowledge he possesses be turned to madness . . .' He then extinguishes the candle, saying, 'Just as this candle is extinguished, so may all the power in N. be utterly consumed.' When he has repeated the procedure over seven days, the victim will become demented, and all who see him will marvel, though he himself will not recognize his condition and will assume that others are mad. If he wishes to restore the victim's sanity, the master goes to his house and enjoins the demons to depart, thus counteracting the effects of his triple conjuration. Then he further nullifies the magic by removing the inscribed cloth and casts it into a fire, saying, 'Just as this fire consumes this cloth, so may all this craft (*ars*) done by me against N. be wholly undone,' then he casts the ashes into a flowing stream.[14] While the countermagic is itself sympathetic, it is not (in the same way as with no. 5) strictly a reversal of the original sympathetic magic involving the burning and extinguishing of a candle.

There are recipes for madness in *Picatrix*, which involve not imitative magic but potions (made from the body parts of a cat, a hoopoe, a bat, a toad and other creatures) to be taken in food or drink, or a fume to be inhaled, whereupon the victim will be bedevilled (*demoniabitur*), losing his senses and memory, and not even knowing where he is.[15] The Munich handbook is perhaps remarkable for its thoroughgoing avoidance of such potions. It rarely combines the techniques of demonic with those of natural magic, and avoids giving recipes for potions whose magical virtue would normally be seen as inherent and natural, but does use imitative rituals, more readily seen as signs and signals to demons.

The burial of some symbolic object is a recurrent theme in these psychological experiments, far more than in other types. Parallels can easily be cited in astral magic, for example in one section of *Picatrix*, which prescribes burying astrological images to attain friendship or love, to secure the fondness and obedience of a ruler's subjects or a lord's servant, to separate two friends, to cause a person to fall under the wrath of a king, to bring love between men and women – but also to destroy an enemy or a city or house, to prevent the construction of a building, to release a captive, to put a person to flight, to get rid of scorpions, to increase the fertility of the fields.[16] The psychological experiments of the Munich handbook which prescribe burial of some object may perhaps be borrowed from astral magic and elaborated with conjurations and other embellishments. Burial ensures secrecy, fixes the object's location, and perhaps implies an appeal to demons or other chthonic powers. It makes the most obvious sense when a particular location is to be affected: like dragons hidden beneath the foundations of a building and causing its disruption, a buried image can work insidiously on the place where it lies. When the magic is psychological, the point is presumably to affect the victim's mind by establishing a kind of magical force field within his or her environment. One might even speak of this is as environmental magic, designed to afflict individuals indirectly by planting sinister forces in or near the places they frequent.

AN EXPERIMENT FOR GAINING FAVOUR

Magical techniques for ensuring favour in the eyes of a dignitary, or for prevailing over one's adversaries in a court of law, are common in the literature of medieval magic, although they rarely if ever become subject matter for prosecution. They presuppose a magician connected to court circles or perhaps to the ecclesiastical hierarchy, or else a magician serving a client with political ambitions. In short, the context for use of such magic is precisely the sort that Edward Peters envisages: a courtly world rife with ambitions and ensuing tensions because of the possibilities for upward mobility and the threat of precipitous downward mobility.[17] The magic recommended for such purposes is often fairly simple. One fifteenth-century compilation prescribes writing out the SATOR-AREPO square on virgin parchment with the blood of a white dove, then carrying it on one's person or in one's hand, to ensure favour in the sight of all. The same collection says that various herbs, collected before sunrise in the sign of Virgo, will prevent people from speaking evil against the bearer.[18] Another compilation recommends writing out certain characters and carrying them in one's left hand as a way of obtaining favours from any person.[19]

From one point of view any attempt to manipulate another person's mind or will is a hostile act. There are none the less significant differences from one experiment to another in the apparent attitude of the master and in the expected attitude of the victim: in the experiments we have examined above, the master is overtly hostile to the victims and expects them to undergo experiences that will be unpleasant for them; in the next experiments the master displays no overt hostility and anticipates that the people affected will become favourably disposed toward him, without feeling harmed or afflicted, and if anyone feels aggrieved it will presumably be either a rival claimant to favour or the victim at a later stage, when he realizes his will has been manipulated.

The Munich handbook provides one rather elaborate experiment designed to gain favour with any manner of dignitary (no. 4):

> . . . I wish for you to read a well tested art for obtaining dignity and honour, status, and the supreme and undying love of a king, prelate, lord or, in general, any man you wish.
>
> First, you should have two soft rocks, which you should rub together so that their surfaces are entirely flush. When you have done this, you should carve in one the image of him [whose favour] you wish, beginning from the head and proceeding to the feet, making first the front and then the back side, and carving a crown on the head if it is a king, and so forth according to his dignity. When this is carved, you will carve on the [other] stone your own form, as best you can, beginning with the head, as before, first the front and then the back. When you have done this, inscribe his name on the forehead of the first [image], in the manner of a seal, and your name on yours. When you have done this, in the first hour of Sunday under a waxing moon take silver or tin and melt it over a fire. When it is melted, cast it in his form, saying, 'I, so-and-so, wishing to obtain favour and be revered by him, and honoured and feared forever, form [this] image, made and carved in his name, by virtue of which he should love me without measure forever.'

When you have done this, you should have an iron stylus, and on his forehead carve the name 'Dyacom'; on his chest, the three names 'Pumeon', 'Terminas', and 'Peripaos'; and on [his] shoulders the six names 'Midam', 'Fabni', 'Gebel', 'Darail', 'Vmeloth' and 'Thereoth'; and on his stomach the name 'Byreoth'. When you have inscribed these things, you should have a clean linen cloth, and wrap the image in it, then store it away carefully.

On Thursday, at the first hour of the day, kindle a fire and similarly melt the tin and cast it in your form, saying, 'I, so-and-so, form my own image according to my likeness, by which I may rule forever over so-and-so and be loved and feared by him for all eternity.' When you have made this, wrap it likewise in another linen cloth.

Note that the image of him whose grace you wish to obtain should be the length of one *semis*[20] when it is carved in the stone, and the proportions of the stone should be such that your image may be larger than his by a third. And you should place a sceptre on your image as well.

When you have done these things carefully, as instructed, on the following Friday at the first hour you should fumigate his image with these aromatics – cinnamon, long pepper and the herb agrimony – saying, 'I, so-and-so, exorcize you, image formed in the name of so-and-so, by the inseparable, unique, and undivided Trinity, and by all the thrones, dominations, and powers, and principalities, and [by the virtue] of all creatures, that by your power I may obtain the favour and love of so-and-so, in whose name it is made.'

Having said this three times, continue as follows: 'O Dyacon, Pumeon, Termines, Peripaos, Midain, Fabin, Gebel, Dorayl, Vmeloth, Tereoth and Bireoth, most benevolent spirits who sow concord, with the greatest vehemence I, so-and-so, pray you, I supplicate you, [and] I beg you, by the only Son of God, who by the shedding of his blood raised the dead human race, that by this image made in the name of so-and-so you may bind him to me in such a manner that he will revere me above all mortals, never wavering from agreement with me, but always obeying my commands. May he take pains to please me, by our same Lord Jesus Christ, who lives and reigns unto ages of ages. Amen.'

When you have said this prayer, take your hold your image in your right hand, and the other in your left, and join his image to yours, saying three times, 'He has subjected the nations to us, and the peoples under our feet' [Ps. 46:4 Vulg.]. Then take a small iron chain and bind it to the neck of his image, placing the other end in the right hand of your image. Then, when it is firmly bound, say, 'Just as you, O image formed in the name of so-and-so, are subjected and bound to my image, thus may so-and-so be bound to me utterly for all eternity.' Then take both hands of his image in your hands and bend them behind his back, saying, 'By this image I bind the

hands of so-and-so, that his hands may never have any power against me.'
Bend the head of his image to the ground, saying, 'As this image, made in
the name of so-and-so, stands before me with bended neck, thus may so-
and-so never waver from my will, but follow me at all times and always
serve me and love me and revere me for ever above all others, and strive to
praise me.'

When you have done this, with constant fumigation, take your image and
place the other at its back, so that its face touches the shoulders of your image,
and while holding them thus, say, 'As this image, made and fashioned in the
name of so-and-so, stands in the greatest subjection to this image made in my
name, thus may so-and-so be subjected to me, as long as these images are
preserved.' Then wrap them up, as has been said, in a clean linen cloth. When
they have been wrapped, place them in some kind of vessel and carry them
secretly through the city and before his presence in his dwelling, if you can.
And you should do this for an entire day. In the evening you should bury the
images in such a place and far enough down that they will [not] be discovered,
and you will see wonders. But if you cannot go before him or into his dwelling,
bury [them], as has been said, wherever you will, and you will be loved by him
above all things.

For Parmen[i]des used this experiment to obtain favour from the king of the
Persians.

This experiment requires two conjurations: one addressed to the image of
the dignitary in question, which is thrice 'exorcized' that it may secure honour
from the person represented; the other a 'prayer' addressed to eleven spirits
distinguished for their benevolence and their skill at inspiring concord. But the
heart of the experiment is a series of five imitative rituals involving both
images: first binding the two figures together, second binding the dignitary's
image to the magician's own with a small iron chain, third binding the hands
of the dignitary's image behind its back, fourth bowing the head of the
dignitary's image to the ground, and fifth placing the two figures together,
with the dignitary's face touching the shoulders of his own image as a sign of
subjection.

The sympathetic operations here are complex but suggest a sort of play,
almost like a child's playful use of a toy. Like many experiments in the
manual, this one comes with a historical testimonial: 'Parmenides', we are
told, used this procedure to gain favour with the king of the Persians.
Testimonials of this kind are of course window-dressing, comparable to a
herbal master's fanciful claim that one remedy was used by Plato himself.[21]
The concluding promise that the magician 'will see wonders' is again a
common formula,[22] which blurs any distinction between the magical and the
wondrous or marvellous.

EROTIC MAGIC: BACKGROUND

If certain of these experiments can be seen as 'friendly' and others as hostile, the experiments for love represent a curious mixture. The imitative procedures involve violence: the image or other object that magically represents the desired woman is burned or pierced. The immediate effect on the victim is likewise violent: she is afflicted with obsessive passion, and has no rest until she yields to the master's desires. Ultimately, however, the woman does submit and is made to feel more than mere friendship. The conception of love that is here assumed may owe something at least indirectly to the tradition of courtly literature, and in particular to its Ovidian sense that love is a disease or an affliction. One Netherlandish compilation gives detailed instructions for 'the best and surest experiment in the world to secure friendship or love between a man and a woman', and says that in Latin such love is called '*amor hereos*', and is burning and indissoluble.[23]

The subject of erotic magic is too extensive to cover fully here,[24] but at least eight key points should be made by way of overview. First, magic may be used to persuade or coerce another person to consent to sex (sex-inducing magic), to intensify the sexual experience of already willing partners (sex-enhancing magic), or to induce a lasting amorous relationship (love-magic). Second, the most common technique for love-magic was administration of potions, as can be seen from penitential prohibitions and secular legislation as well as literary sources.[25] Certain objects or substances borne on one's person were also thought to have aphrodisiac qualities, such as the stone allectory and the herb henbane.[26] Third, while various herbs were used as aphrodisiacs (St John's wort, valerian, vervain),[27] there seems to have been a preference for animal parts or human substances (such as semen) either literally or symbolically associated with sex and procreation.[28] Fourth, in trials for erotic magic it was usually women who were charged with alienating men's affections through magical means, but the surviving formulas for sex-inducing magic typically envisage the use of this magic by men to entice unwilling women.[29] Fifth, in both the trials and the manuscript prescriptions, love-magic is most commonly intended to restore the lost affections of a partner.[30] Indeed, certain women accused of witchcraft seem to have been specialists in such restoration of affection.[31] Sixth, in astral magic with erotic intent, the magical virtues whose potency seemed most relevant were, obviously enough, those of Venus. Thus, a stone, metal plate or image might be made on the day of Venus (Friday), at the hour of Venus, and bearing the sign of Venus for use in such magic; one might even be advised to say a 'prayer' to the spirit associated with that planet.[32] Seventh, the power of the sacred might be employed in erotic magic, in ways that would presumably seem blasphemous to authorities: a slip of parchment with a psalm on it might be left where a prospective lover would walk, or a woman who kissed her husband while holding a consecrated host in her mouth might gain his affection.[33] A prayer addressed to God might lead into a conjuration to compel a husband, or a litany adapted to form a coercive spell.[34] Eighth, erotic magic figures prominently in medieval literature – in the romances especially, herbal love potions frequently play a prominent role – but the significance of this magic is often ambiguous. For example, in Thomas of Britain's version of *Tristan* the love potion seems to function as a symbol of the love that Tristan and Iseult have already begun to feel, rather than as in any simple sense the cause of that love.[35]

The techniques for erotic magic mentioned so far were natural rather than demonic, but sexual submission could also be won by necromancy. Oldradus da Ponte explained in the early fourteenth century that invoking demons to tempt women is mortally sinful but is not heresy, because temptation is proper to the nature of demons and their use for this service thus implies no false belief.[36] Formulas for such magic do survive. An experiment for love in the *Liber de angelis* requires going to a crossroads or a gallows, entering a circle traced on the ground, sacrificing a dove, tearing its flesh apart, dispersing the remains in the air, and invoking a spirit of dubious character named Zagam ('O Zagam, accept this dove which I sacrifice to you!'). One must repeat this operation a second and a third time; after the last of these sacrifices one adds, 'I ask you, O Zagam, and all your companions, to bring forth [the desired woman]', who should be burning with love for the magician and should comply with his will. The next morning he must return to the circle and pick up whatever 'figure' he finds there; he need only show this to the desired woman and she will love him without bounds – as has been proven, the text adds.[37] In a trial from the later fifteenth century at Tournai, where a priest was charged with attempting to seduce a girl by drawing her image in charcoal on a tile, baptizing the figure, sprinkling it with holy water, making a second figure out of wax and baptizing it as well, then conjuring demons according to a book of magic.[38]

The case from Tournai is highly reminiscent of the Netherlandish experiment mentioned earlier as a technique for effecting *amor hereos*,[39] combining prayer and conjuration with image magic:

> You must do it on a Friday in the first hour after midnight, under a waxing moon. Take a tile fresh out of the oven and draw a picture, while saying, 'I, N., draw this picture in the form and likeness of the person N., daughter or son of so-and-so.' Make the picture with a steel pin [*punte*]. Begin with the head and proceed downward, saying, 'May Venus help.' . . . When [the image] is done, make fire with any wood you will. Stand up, take the image in your hand, turn south, and read this [Latin] prayer: 'Almighty, eternal God, who in the beginning created heaven and earth, the sea and all that is in them; who created Adam and Eve according to your likeness and placed them in the earthly paradise . . . I invoke you in supplication, most gracious Father; in your

great power hear me as I ask and knock [cf. Mt 7:7], that I may be able to constrain those malign spirits, the angels who have power to bind a man to a woman, and vice versa, a woman to a man, and especially those four spirits who hold dominion and power over those spirits in the four parts of the globe, to wit, Astaroth, Aroch, Godras, [and] Vynicon.' Say this prayer three [more] times [to north, east, and west]. Then say the following [Latin] conjuration, turning first to the south: "O Astaroth, prince of the south, I conjure you with all the [spirits] under your command, who have power to compel the love of a woman or a man, by Alpha and Omega, the first and last, Abios, Abics, Rubeus, Rubet, Caste, Hely, Messias, Sabaoth, Adonay, Sother, Emanuel; I conjure you, N.; by the Annunciation of our Lord Jesus Christ; by his Passion; by his Resurrection . . . by the head of your prince and King Lucifer . . . and by all the infernal powers by whom you can be conjured and entreated, that you should withdraw from your proper place in the south and [carry out my command].'[40]

The case at Tournai is in at least one respect typical necromantic practice : the alleged perpetrator was a cleric. Similarly, the use of Latin formulas in the Dutch experiment suggests that the intended user was clerical, even if he was not in major orders. Analogous cases are easily adduced. When the Carmelite friar Peter Recordi was tried by an inquisitorial tribunal at Carcassonne in 1329, he confessed that over five years he had performed terrible conjurations over wax images, smeared and sprinkled with blood from a toad and from his own nostrils, all as sacrifice to the Devil. He then placed the images beneath thresholds of women he wanted to seduce, and thus he had his way with three women and had been on the verge of success with others. He had believed that these images held power to coerce women, or, if the victims were refractory, to bring down upon them affliction at the hands of demons. On one occasion he pierced one of the images in its stomach, and blood oozed out.[41] Again, an English chaplain named William Netherstreet was charged in 1377 with using 'conjurations and incantations' to bring a married woman to his chamber at night so he could 'take her violently in adultery'. He protested his own innocence.[42]

In other cases it was non-clerical males who were charged with using specifically demonic magic for love. At Carcassonne in 1410, Geraud Cassendi, a notary, was tried by an inquisitor for invoking demons as a means for debauching women and girls. He was said to have placed on his shirt gold scrapings from an image of the Virgin. Then he invoked demons with conjurations read from a book, but when a swarm of evil spirits actually appeared, a witness to the rite was so terror-struck that he hurled a shoe at them and bade them withdraw, which they did. On another occasion as well Cassendi is supposed to have gone into the woods and invoked demons.[43] And when the inquisitor Piero di ser Lippo wrote to the government of Siena in 1382 about magicians in the village of

Rugomagno, he reported that one Agnolo di Corso had worshipped and invoked
Satan and Beelzebub, and had invoked demons to kill people and to compel men
to go to women.[44]

To be sure, there are cases in which women, too, were said to use specifically
demonic magic for erotic effect. In 1324 Alice Kyteler was charged with using
'the intestines and innards of cocks sacrificed . . . to demons', with other
materials, partly for erotic magic,[45] and a woman tried by Heinrich Kramer at
Innsbruck in 1485 was said to have instructed others in the art of invoking the
devil to arouse love or illness.[46] In these cases it seems less clear that the demonic
element was explicit, that the women were in fact making use of necromantic
techniques, and that their magic was marked with the same degree of ritual
complexity as can be seen in the clerical practice of erotic necromancy. What is
perhaps more likely is that women's natural magic was being interpreted as if it
were similar to the demonic magic more often practiced by clerics and at times
by other men.

AN EROTIC EXPERIMENT IN THE MUNICH HANDBOOK

Our necromantic manual in Clm 849 includes four experiments said to induce
love – one may assume sexual compliance is the main intent – and at least three
of them are complex rituals analogous to the erotic necromancy seen in the
judicial records. The first of these experiments (no. 3) is in one sense the least
violent: rather than inflicting physical harm on the woman's image, the master
afflicts it with a kind of spiritual harm by inscribing on it the names of demons
which are to afflict her. In any case, the writer has no scruples at all about
bringing severe psychological pressure to bear in his magical seduction:

> When you wish to have the love of whatever woman you wish, whether she is
> near or far, whether noble or common, on whatever day or night you wish,
> whether for the furtherance of friendship or to its hindrance, first you must
> have a totally white dove and a parchment made from a female dog that is in
> heat, from whom it is most easily to be had [*de qua est habere leuissimum*]. And
> you should know that this kind of parchment is most powerful for gaining the
> love of a woman. You should also have a quill from an eagle. In a secret place,
> take the dove and with your teeth bite into it near the heart,[47] so that the heart
> comes out, and with the eagle's quill write on the parchment with the [dove's]
> blood the name of her whom you wish, and draw the image of a naked woman
> as best you can, saying, 'I draw so-and-so, N., daughter of so-and-so, whom I
> wish to have, in the name of these six hot spirits, namely Tubal, Satan, Reuces,
> Cupido, Afalion, Duliatus, that she may love me above all others living in this
> world.'
> When you have done this, write on the forehead her name and the name

'Tubal', saying, 'You are so-and-so, daughter of so-and-so, from now on disposed to my will, and you are Tubal [inscribed] on her forehead. I command you to remain, binding the senses of her head and causing her to love me alone.'

Then write on her right arm 'Satan', and on her left arm 'Reuces'. When these [names] have been written, say, 'As you, Satan, and you, Reuces, are inscribed on this image made in the name of so-and-so, may you so afflict her arms without delay, so that she can do nothing but desire to embrace me.'

When you have this, write your own name near the heart of the image, saying, 'As I am on the heart of this image, may so-and-so, N., thus have me in her heart day and night.'

When you have done this, write on the genitals of the image the name 'Cupid', saying, 'As you, Cupid, are on the genitals of this image, may you thus remain always on the genitals of so-and-so, arousing her so that she despises all men of this world and desires me alone, and may the fire of love for me torment and inflame her.'

When you have done this, write on the right leg 'Afalion', and on the left leg 'Duliatus'. When these have been written, say, 'As you Afalion, and you Duliatus, are inscribed on this image, may you sit on the legs of so-and-so, afflicting her legs with such vehement love for me that she has no wish or desire to go anywhere but here.'

When you have said this, take the image with both hands, kneel, and say, 'I have drawn the heart and mind of so-and-so with this image, and with powerful invocation I arouse her to love, desire, and yearn for me, and to have me in mind all night in her sleep, through Our Lord Jesus Christ, who lives and reigns and commands forever.'

When you have said this, take myrrh and saffron, kindle a fire, and fumigate the image, saying this conjuration: 'I conjure all you demons inscribed on this image, by your lords to whom you are bound in obedience – Sobedon, Badalam and Berith – that you should inflame so-and-so, whose image is designed in this name, to love of me, so that day and night she may think of me, [and] may hope for me, until she fulfils my will with ardor [*cum affectu*]. And as you are inscribed and fixed on this image, may you thus dwell in her until I do with her whatever I wish.'

When you have said this conjuration three times, and made the fumigation, take a hair from the tail of a horse and suspend the parchment with this hair, so that it moves in the air, and let it hang. On that day, or the next, or some other, or whenever you can, go to that woman, and without doubt she will be very glad to see you, and will say she cannot live without you. And this will occur immediately, and she will do your heart's desire, and will love you above all things for all eternity.

If you keep this image formed in her name, in which there is such power, you will obtain from it, more wondrous yet, this sign: before you have seen her, as soon as this image is made, when you proceed toward her she will be so enamoured [*filocapta*] of you that when she sees you, you will not withdraw from her company deprived, but rather you will attain satisfaction in whatever you desire. If you cannot approach her, whether from fear or because of distance or any other obstacle, you can still have her brought by the aforesaid demons, who are so effective that if you were in the east, within an hour they could carry her without danger from the west, and likewise they could return her, without exposure.

The image having been made as has been said, and suspended on a particular day, at any hour of the day, you may blow on it so that it moves with your breath, and likewise on the second and third day. On the night of the third day, or on the day itself, either alone or with three faithful companions, take the image and hang it around your neck with the [horse's] hair, and have it lie on your chest. And take a sword and make with it a circle on the ground. When you have made the circle, stand inside it and summon your companions (if you have any), who should do nothing but stand in the circle and watch the spectacle [*ludum*] – but it is better if you do not have them. Take an iron stylus and trace [a band with names in it] round the circle, as is shown here, preserving constant silence.

The circle is shown as a single band containing the names Rator, Lampoy, Despan, Brunlo, Dronoth, Maloqui, Satola, Gelbid, Mascifin, Nartim and Lodoni. The centre of the circle is labelled 'Place of the Master'.

When you have done so, say this conjuration: 'I conjure you demons inscribed in this circle, to whom is given the power and capacity to seduce and bind in the love of men, by the virtue and power of the divine majesty; and by the thrones and dominations and powers and principalities of Him who spoke and they were made; and by those who ceaselessly cry with one voice, "Holy, holy, holy . . ."; and by these names which cause you terror, namely Rator, Lampoy, [etc.]; and by this ring that is here; and by the innumerable powers belonging to you and your superiors, that wherever you are, you should rise up from your places without delay and go to so-and-so, and immediately, without deception lead her here, and take her back when I wish. And let no one be aware of this or take account of it.'

When you have said this three times, gazing at a ring, you will hear a voice, saying, 'Behold, we are here!' Immediately you will see six handsome and gentle young men, saying to you with one voice, 'We are here, ready and willing to obey your command. Tell us what you wish, and at once we will do it.' You should say, 'Go to so-and-so and bring her to me without delay.' When you have said this, they will at once depart, and within an hour they will bring her without harm.

You should know that none of these [six] can enter the circle, but they will bring her to it and she will stretch out her hand to you, and you will draw her in. She will be a bit astonished, but quite willing to remain with you. I should inform you that it is better to make the circle as large as possible, because in it you can make a circle [*sic*], and in it you can stretch out more effectively. For if anything of yours [any part of your body?] should go outside the circle, it would be bad for you. When the woman has come, all the spirits will vanish.

You can keep the woman in the circle as long as you please. For when the woman has entered the circle, you should say to the spirits, 'Let one of you go to the place from which you brought so-and-so and remain there in [her] form while I have her here.' When you have said this, they will all depart in silence. On the day or night and month and year when it pleases you to have her return home, say, 'O you spirits, who brought so-and-so here, take her and carry her to her home. And whenever I wish her back, be compliant in carrying her here. Go, therefore, by the wondrous powers which you ineffably exercise.' When you have said this three times, five spirits will come and carry her off in your sight.

When she enters the circle and you greet her, remember to touch her with the image that you have around your neck, and on this account she will love you for all eternity and will not care to see anyone but you. While you are with the woman, the image which you should keep around your neck will always be invisible to the woman herself, and when she leaves you should take it from your neck and lay it aside carefully in some sort of vessel. When it is thus laid aside, erase the entire circle, and you may depart safely. And when you wish to have [her] again come to you, do as is said above.

And note that this experiment is most effective and is not at all dangerous. By this experiment alone, Solomon had whatever women he wished. And let this suffice on the subject of obtaining women. And it should be carried out with the greatest solemnity.

This experiment contains conjurations, but they play a less prominent role than the auxiliary magical techniques, especially the use of an image for sympathetic magic. The sympathetic identification of the image with the woman portrayed is accomplished solely through assignation of her name: the writer does not emphasize that the image should be in any way realistic (e.g., that it should have some specific feature in common with the prototype), nor does he advise that the image be baptized in the woman's name. The suspension of the image to be blown about freely in the air is reminiscent of a type of aeromancy catalogued by Johannes Hartlieb, involving the suspension of a wax image or *atzman*, left to blow in the wind so that the person in whose name it is prepared will thereby be afflicted.[48] The blood of a dove must be used here – and a dove must be offered as sacrifice in the amatory experiment from the *Liber de angelis* given above – presumably because the dove is traditionally associated with Venus.[49]

The experiment contains an elaborate contingency procedure, used to fetch the woman, which differs markedly from the original sympathetic magic. The woman's image is still used: the experimenter wears it around his neck, although it is invisible to her; as she leaves the circle he touches her with it, and from then on she will love only him; when she departs, he should take it off and keep it safe in a vessel. For immediate purposes at hand, however, the image becomes less significant and the role of the demons becomes proportionally greater. It is the demons who fetch the woman in response to a conjuration, and it is a demon who takes the woman's place and prevents others from noting her absence. When the magician orders one of the spirits to go and take the woman's place and assume her form while she is absent, we have an element of illusionist magic embedded in an experiment designed mainly for psychological effect. Both the problem and the solution are obvious enough that it is not surprising to find parallels in other cultures. Thus, Krishna is said to have used his powers of illusion (*māyā*) to fashion replicas of his female devotees (the *gopīs*), so that when they went for trysts with him their doubles could lie beside their husbands.[50] The contingency procedure in the Munich experiment differs from the original formula also in its use of a circle, which is simple in form but important in its effects, serving both as a location for the conjuration and as a place for rendezvous with the woman.

The experiment is referred to as a kind of game or spectacle, a *ludus*, and any companions present are to serve merely as spectators, suggesting that the necromancer's initial ritual may have the character of a performance, contrasting sharply with the privacy of the tryst itself, the sexual games that follow, which not even the spirits may witness. That something more serious than a game is involved is suggested by the reference to the woman as *filocapta*, bound by love, a condition which the *Malleus maleficarum* speaks of as 'the best known and most general form of witchcraft'.[51]

AN EROTIC EXPERIMENT INVOLVING IMAGE MAGIC

For the next experiment in this category (no. 12) the manuscript once again proceeds directly to the instructions, without any introductory heading. The master must first obtain hairs from the woman he wishes to seduce,[52] plus other objects. Again he goes out with companions in the initial stage of the ritual itself. In contrast to the elaborate preparations, the heart of the ceremony is relatively simple, involving two sympathetic stages and a single conjuration.

Take virgin wax, rendered virginal by art [*ceram virgineam, arte virginizatam*], and do this on a Thursday or Sunday, at the hour of Venus or the hour of Jove; and from this wax make an image over burning coals placed in a pot, without smoke. And the master should have some of the hairs of the woman for whom he wishes to act, and three bristles of red hair, and you should have with you a knife with a white handle made for this purpose.[53] And go to the place where a craftsman makes needles, and have the same craftsman make them, from the hour of the Sun until the hour of Saturn. Then the master should take two faithful companions and go to a fruit-bearing tree, and the master should make a circle. And the master should begin this operation, making an image of the woman for whom you perform it, murmuring constantly in your heart, 'Thou, Belial, and thou Astaroth, and thou, Paymon, be my helpers in this undertaking.' Likewise, you should murmur the words, 'I, N., form this image for the love of so-and-so, that it may accomplish that for which it is made. And may thou, Belial, principal prince, be my helper in this undertaking.' Then the master should make the image of this wax, beginning at the hour of Jove, and proceeding until the hour of Saturn. And when the image has thus been made, the master should have nine needles made by an experienced craftsman, who should be bathed and dressed in sparkling clean [*nitidis*] garments when he makes them; he should make the needles from the hour of the Sun until the hour of Saturn. Then the master should fix the needles in the image, placing one in the head, another in the right shoulder, the third in the left, the fourth where people are accustomed to locate the heart, saying, 'Just as this needle is fixed in the heart of this image, so may the love of N. be fixed to the love of N., so that she cannot sleep, wake, lie down, sleep, [or] walk until she burns with love of me.' He should fix the fifth in the navel, the sixth in the thigh, the seventh in the right side, the eighth in the left, the ninth in the anus. When the image has thus been made, you should baptize [*christianizes*] it, giving it the name [of the woman] for whom you perform the operation, immersing it three times and saying, 'How shall it be called?', with the response, 'N.' And you should say, 'I baptize thee, N., in the name of the Father, and of the Son, and of the Holy Spirit. Amen.' And then place the image in a new and clean cloth, leaving it aside from the hour of the Sun until the hour of Mars. Then make this conjuration under the fruit-bearing tree, with the burning coals; turning toward the east, say, 'O so-and-so, N., I conjure your head, your hair, your eyes, your ears [etc.]. O N., I conjure your entire substance, that you may not sleep or sit or lie down or perform any work of craft until you have satisfied my libidinous desire. I conjure you by the Father and the Son and the Holy Spirit . . . I conjure you and exorcize you and command you, that as the deer yearns for a fountain of water [Ps. 41:2 Vulg.], so you, N., should desire my love. And as the raven desires the cadavers of dead men, so should you desire me. And as this wax melts before the face of the fire, so should N. [melt in] desire for my love, so that she cannot, etc.'

The signs [to be sought in] the woman are these: solitude, dizziness [*inuolucio*] of the head, lamenting, sighing, beating [of the breast], wakefulness, [and] wailing. Then the master or the one who is taking action [viz., for whom it is performed?] should go to her, and if he sees her standing or sitting alone, then the master should continue the conjuration unto the fifth day. And if she is anywhere in the countryside, she will be consumed;[54] but if she is in a town or passing through another city, the master should perform the conjuration until she can come.

And in this all the Spanish, Arabic, Hebrew, Chaldaean, Greek and Latin astrological necromancers [*nigromantici omnes astroloyci*] are in accord. And this experiment was taken [from the book] *On the Secret Arts of the Imaginary Art*, [from the book] *On the Flowers of All Experiments*, etc.

In its general form this experiment bears a resemblance to a procedure well known in antiquity and described in a Greek magical papyrus: to obtain a woman, one makes wax or clay figures, one an armed and threatening man with sword in hand, the other a kneeling woman with hands behind her back. One then writes inscriptions on each member of her body, then pierces each with copper needles, thirteen in all, while saying, 'I am piercing your brain, N.', and so forth. Then one inscribes a lead sheet, affixes it with thread knotted 365 times, and places the ensemble beside the tomb of a person who has died a violent or untimely death. One version adds a further spell, which reads in part, 'Let her be in love with me, N. . . . Let her not . . . do anything with another man for pleasure, just with me alone, N., so that she, N., be unable to drink or eat, that she not be contented, not be strong, not have pleace of mind, that she, N., not find sleep without me . . . and do not allow her, N., to accept for pleasure the attempt of another man, not even that of her own husband, just that of mine, N. Instead, drag her, N., by the hair, by the heart, by her soul, to me, N., at every hour of life, day and night, until she comes to me, N., and may she, N., remain inseparable from me.' There is also archeological evidence for such procedures; for example, one Egyptian statue of a naked woman, pierced with thirteen needles, was discovered in a clay pot and is now in the Musée du Louvre.[55] This does not mean there are specific connections between texts of late antiquity and the prescriptions of the Munich handbook; rather the Munich compilation supports its conjurations with a variety of techniques, some of which are widely diffused and of considerable antiquity.

Among the many further parallels to this experiment is a fifteenth-century version given in a mixture of Hebrew and Yiddish. The magician is told to make a female image of virgin wax, showing the sexual organs clearly delineated, and resembling the woman to be enchanted. On both the breast and the back he should write 'N., daughter of N. [father] and N., daughter of N. [mother].' He must recite the words, 'May it be Thy will, O Lord, that N. daughter of N. burn with a mighty passion for me.' Then buries the figure for a time, then washes it in the name of Michael, in that of Gabriel, and in that of Raphael, places it in urine, then dries it off. The image being thus prepared, the magician may use it when he wishes to cause the woman pain, by piercing a needle into whatever part of her body he wishes to afflict, presumably as a way of bending her to his will, very much in keeping with the violent and coercive tendencies generally found in such magic.[56]

It is entirely possible that the piercing with needles was itself meant or taken to have direct sexual significance,[57] but more fundamentally it was a kind of magical acupuncture intended to cause suffering that could only be alleviated through sexual compliance. The piercing with needles is thus no different in principle from that in image magic intended to work bodily harm or death, although here the affliction could be relieved through submission. It is not that the magician brings about bodily pain that is extrinsically related to the erotic goal and can be cured by compliance, nor is it the case that the magic arouses pleasurable feelings of passion. Rather, the sexual passion aroused by the ritual is itself a kind of suffering for which the woman must obtain relief. The victim of magic cannot sleep, sit down, lie down, or pursue any activity until she relents, because she is compelled to share in the obsessive passion of her pursuer.[58] Her state is almost a parody of the mystic's absorption in the Beloved, of Mechthild of Magdeburg's mystical love-sickness: 'I cannot rest, I burn without respite in Thy flaming love.'[59] But, as Richard of Saint-Victor insisted, such obsession was as debasing in human relations as it was elevating in relations with God; that it should be magically induced by experiments such as those in the Munich handbook is a possibility Richard may never have entertained.[60]

EROTIC EXPERIMENTS INVOLVING RITUALS WITH BONES

Two experiments (nos 13 and 35) involve inscribing letters and names on bones and then subjecting the bones to fire. The first is designed primarily to constrain a woman's or man's will, presumably again with erotic intent (the relevant sections are indicated below with [A]), although the experiment may be adapted for constraining a beast [B] or a spirit [C] as well.

By this experiment a person, woman, man, spirit, [or] beast of any condition is constrained.

These names must be written in this manner on a shoulderblade.

When all this is finished, choose which [variant] you want. If you wish to constrain any spirit, write his name on the shoulderblade between B and E, and in the name which is Bel. If you wish to constrain any man, write his name between L and A. And if you wish to constrain any beast, write its name between A and N, and its colour. For spirits and for men and for women, this is to be done at the same hour in which the shoulderblade has been prepared, and it is necessary at the outset to seek out wood from a white thorn or wood floating on water, and make fire with it, and collect coals and place them in a new pot, and gradually place the shoulderblade on them, and gradually increase the fire, until the shoulderblade becomes hot.

And then invoke the aforesaid spirits, and say this conjuration: 'Asyel, Castiel, Lamisniel, Rabam, Erlain, [and] Belam, I command you' – [A1] If [the operation is] for a man or a woman whom you wish to arouse to love for you, say, 'that you should at once, etc.', as given below. [B] If [it is] for a spirit, name that spirit whom you wish, that he may come to you openly, humbly, with comely visage, and gentle speech, saying, 'I conjure you, Asyel, etc., that you should make spirit N., who has power over all that I wish to ask of him, come to me openly, humbly, with gentle speech, in the form that I have specified – that is, of a comely soldier – to carry out all that I wish to command him.' [A2] And if you wish to do this for a man or a woman, first make known to him where you can be found, for he [or she] will go mad with fury on not being able to find you. [C] If [it is] for a beast, [say,] 'I conjure the aforesaid spirits that they should constrain this beast' which you wish, that it may be unable to depart from the place in which it is until you wish.

The experiment concludes with the conjuration used to constrain a man or woman:

'Asyel, Castiel, Lamsiyel, Rabam, Erlain, Elam, Belam, I conjure you by the true God . . .; likewise, I conjure you by the Father and the Son and the Holy Spirit . . ., and by this conjuration I command you to seduce the heart and mind of N. to love me, immediately and swiftly and at once and without delay. And just as this shoulderblade grows hot and burns, so may you cause him or her, N., to burn and grow hot with the fire of love for me, and in such a way that he [or she] may not be able to rest until completing my will. In the name which is Bel, etc.'

The figure depicted is in the shape of a shield, representing the shoulderblade, divided into sixteen horizontal bands, with one vertical band down the centre. Horizontal bands bear the names Asyel, Castyel, Lamsiyel, Rabam, Erlain, Olam and Belam. In the vertical band are the letters A-B-E-L-A-N. Across the intersection of the vertical band and the twelfth horizontal band *Leo* is written. To the side is a note: 'Likewise note that this shoulderblade should be from an ass, a hare, a goose or a capon, according to its diverse [uses].'

The second of these experiments is somewhat simpler, and more unambiguously erotic. The magician compels a woman to passionate love by writing the names of the 'infernal spirits' Bel and Ebal on a rib, and in between his own name and that of the woman he wishes to seduce. Then he burns the rib, and when it is hot he should conjure Bel and Ebal not to rest until they cause the woman's heart to burn, so that she cannot sleep, wake or do anything else until she fulfils his desire. Again, therefore, we find the emphasis on compelling the woman's compliance through erotic affliction, aroused through means that are straightforwardly violent both on the symbolic plane and in their bodily and psychic effect.

In general, then, these psychological experiments are the most manipulative and abusive materials in the necromancer's handbook, and they are quite unabashedly so. The formulas give no hint of a guilty conscience, and they show no awareness of the incongruity involved in appealing to the power of the sacred for the ends here sought. With no evident sense of irony, the writer can recommend formulas such as, 'I conjure you demons inscribed in this circle, to whom is given the power and capacity to seduce and bind in the love of men, by the virtue and power of the divine majesty . . .' Even merely to read the illusionist experiments might be entertaining, and the divinatory ones might be perceived as useful means for gaining true knowledge, but the rituals for psychological magic could claim little by way of redeeming social importance, and thus they help to clarify the aversion to magic found in most of late medieval society. Yet these rites are interesting, in large part because of the way they fuse relatively simple and largely perennial conceptions of image magic with the formulas of Latin conjuration or exorcism derived more specifically from clerical culture. Guichard of Troyes and Eleanor Cobham were accused of employing both learned male magicians and popular female ones, but the psychological rites of the Munich handbook represent with particular clarity the mingling of magical traditions and ritual forms.

Notes

1 See Robert Mathiesen, 'Magic in Slavia Orthodoxa: the written tradition', in Henry Maguire, ed., *Byzantine Magic* (Washington: Dumbarton Oaks, 1995), 174–6.

2 Domenico Mammoli, *The Record of the Trial and Condemnation of a Witch, Matteuccia di Francesco, at Todi, 20 March 1428* (Rome: Res Tudertinæ, 1972), trans. (with slight adaptation), pp. 28–40.

3 John G. Gager, *Curse Tablets and Binding Spells from the Ancient World* (New York: Oxford University Press, 1992), 21.

4 *Picatrix: The Latin Version of the* Ghayat Al-Hakim, ed. David Pingree (London: Warburg Institute, 1986), and 'Thabit ibn Qurra's *De imaginibus*', in Francis J. Carmody, *The Astronomical Works of Thabit b. Qurra* (Berkeley: University of California Press, 1960), 180–97.

5 Cambridge University Library, MS Dd.xi.45, fols 134v–139; Juris G. Lidaka spoke about this manuscript and gave a transcription of the text at the International Congress on Medieval Studies at

Kalamazoo, Michigan, 4 May 1995. The manuscript is associated with 'Bokenham', but its connection with Osbern Bokenham or any other individual is unclear.

6 Abel Rigault, *Le procès de Guichard évêque de Troyes, 1308–1313* (Paris, 1896). Cf. Guillaume Mollat, 'Guichard de Troyes et les révélations de la sorcière de Bourdenay', *Moyen Age*, 21 (ser. 2, 12) (1908), 310–14; Conrad Eubel, 'Vom Zaubereiunwesen anfangs des 14. Jahrhunderts (mit urkundlichen Beilagen)', *Historisches Jahrbuch der Görres-Gesellschaft*, 18 (1897).

7 George Lyman Kittredge, *Witchcraft in Old and New England* (Cambridge, MA: Harvard University Press, 1929; repr. New York: Russell & Russell, 1956), 81–84.

8 A partly conjectural reading of *duos lapides viuos et recondes [rotundos?] vnius ponderis, qui debent esse fluminei.*

9 I am reading *limen* for *limes* throughout.

10 For *ymo vno reliquum in innumerabili odio rebellis affligat.*

11 For *et maxime quando est in combustione, et ire versus solis ortum facias.*

12 Ugolino Nicolini, 'La stregoneria a Perugia e in Umbria nel Medioevo: con i testi di sette processi a Perugia e uno a Bologna', *Bollettino della Deputazione di storia patria per l'Umbria*, 84 for 1987 (1988), 30–38.

13 T.H. White, trans. and ed., *The Book of Beasts, being a translation from a Latin Bestiary of the Twelfth Century* (London: Jonathan Cape, 1954), 79–80, says nothing whatever about the camel's urination, but one is presumably to imagine the man crouching with knees bent outward.

14 Lynn Thorndike described this portion of the MS in his article, 'Imagination and magic: force of imagination on the human body and of magic on the human mind', in *Mélanges Eugène Tisserant*, 7 (Vatican City: Biblioteca Vaticana, 1964), 353–8.

15 *Picatrix*, 161.

16 *Picatrix*, pp. 16 (friendship, love), 17 (obedience), 18 (destruction), 18–19 (construction), 19 (separation, wrath of king, release, flight), 20 (scorpions), 21 (love, destruction), 22 (fertility).

17 Edward Peters, *The Magician, the Witch, and the Law* (Philadelphia: University of Pennsylvania Press, 1978), 110–37.

18 Bodleian Library, MS Wood empt. 18, fol. 32r. On the famous SATOR-AREPO square see especially Heinz Hofmann, *Das Satorquadrat: Zur Geschichte und Deutung eines antiken Wortquadrats* (Bielefelder Papiere zur Linguistik und Literaturwissenschaft, 6) (Bielefeld: Universität Bielefeld, Fakultät für Linguistik und Literaturwissenschaft, 1977) and Richard Kieckhefer, *Magic in the Middle Ages* (Cambridge: Cambridge University Press, 1989), 77–8.

19 Bodleian Library, MS e Mus. 219, fol. 186v.

20 Taking *semissi* for *semissis*, genitive of *semis*, a coin.

21 Jerry Stannard, 'Greco-Roman material medica in medieval Germany', *Bulletin of the History of Medicine*, 46 (1972), 467.

22 E.g., British Library, Sloane MS 38, fols 24v (*multa mirabilia que videbis*) and 25v (*in ista operacione videbis mirabilia*); *De Nigromancia of Roger Bacon*, ed. and trans. Michael-Albion Macdonald (Gillette, N.J.: Heptangle, 1988), 81; *Picatrix: The Latin Version of the Ghayat Al-Hakim*, ed. David Pingree (London: Warburg Institute, 1986), 18–19. See also Shakespeare's *Merry Wives of Windsor*, V. 1, lines 11–12. For an off-colour adaptation of the theme see the text given in Charles Burnett, *Magic and Divination in the Middle Ages: Texts and Techniques in the Islamic and Christian Worlds* (Aldershot: Variorum, 1996), IX, p. 7.

23 W. Braekman, *Magische experimenten en toverpraktijken uit een middelnederlands handschrift* (Ghent: Seminarie voor Volkskunde, 1966), 38–40 (also published separately in *Verslagen en mededelingen van de Koninklijke Vlaamse Academie voor Taal- en Letterkunde*, 1966, 53–118). On the concept of lovesickness, see Mary Frances Wack, *Lovesickness in the Middle Ages: The* Viaticum *and its Commentaries* (Philadelphia: University of Pennsylvania Press, 1990).

24 I have discussed the topic in my article, 'Erotic magic in medieval Europe', in Joyce Salisbury, ed., *Sex in the Middle Ages: A Book of Essays* (New York: Garland, 1991), 30–55, giving fuller discussion and documentation. Ioan P. Couliano, *Eros and Magic in the Renaissance*, trans. Margaret Cook (Chicago: University of Chicago Press, 1987), interprets certain dimensions of the subject. See also Frederic C. Tubach, *Index exemplorum: A Handbook of Medieval Religious Tales* (FF Communications, 204) (Helsinki: Suomalainen Tiedeakatemia, Akademia Scientiarum Fennica, 1969), 242, nos 3,093 and 3,126. For early examples see, e.g., Marvin Meyer and Richard Smith, eds, *Ancient Christian Magic: Coptic Texts of Ritual Power* (1994), 147–69.

25 John T. McNeill and Helena M. Gamer, *Medieval Handbooks of Penance: A Translation of the Principal Libri poenitentiales and Selections from Related Documents* (New York: Columbia University Press, 1938), 90; cf. 252, 305; *Monumenta Germaniae historica, Leges*, sect. 2, 2, ed. Alfred Boretius and Victor Krause (Hannover: Hahn, 1897), 44. The most famous literary example is in *The Romance Tristan & Iseult, as Retold by Joseph Bedier*, trans. Hilaire Belloc and Paul Rosenfeld (New York: Thistle Press, 1960) (and many other translations); see Dorothy James Roberts, *The Enchanted Cup* (New York: Appleton-Century-Crofts, 1953). De La Warr Benjamin Easter, 'A Study of the Magic Elements in the *Romans d'aventure* and the *Romans Bretons*' (Johns Hopkins University diss., 1905), 70–73, cites the love potions in *Cligés*, the *Tristan* romances of Thomas and Béroul, *Partonopeus*, and *La Violette*, and an ambiguous potion in *Dolopathos*.

26 Albertus Magnus, *Book of Minerals*, trans. Dorothy Wyckoff (Oxford: Clarendon, 1967), 73; Michael R. Best and Frank H. Brightman, eds, *The Book of Secrets of Albertus Magnus of the Virtues of Herbs, Stones and Certain Beasts, also A Book of the Marvels of the World* (Oxford: Clarendon, 1973), 21; Evans, *Magical Jewels*, 197; Joan Evans and Mary S. Serjeantson, eds, *English Mediaeval Lapidaries* (Early English Text Society, orig. ser., 190) (London: Oxford University Press, 1933), 59, 68.

27 P.V. Taberner, *Aphrodisiacs: The Science and the Myth* (Philadelphia: University of Pennsylvania Press, 1985), 58; Lynn Thorndike, *The History of Magic and Experimental Science* (New York: Macmillan and Columbia University Press, 1923–58), vol. 2, 555.

28 *Book of Secrets*, ed. Best and Brightman, 81; British Library, Sloane MS 3132, fols 56r–56v; Wardale, 'A Low German-Latin miscellany', 17; Alan Hull Walton, *Aphrodisiacs: From Legend to Prescription: A Study of Aphrodisiacs Throughout the Ages, with sections on Suitable Food, Glandular Extracts, Hormone Stimulation and Rejuvenation* (Westport, CI: Associated Booksellers, 1958), 99; McNeill and Gamer, *Medieval Handbooks of Penance*, 196, no. 15 and n. 94; Aldo Cerlini, 'Una strega reggiana e il suo processo', *Studi storici*, 15 (1906), 67.

29 See, for example, John M. Riddle, *Marbode of Rennes' (1035–1123) De lapidibus, Considered as a Medical Treatise*, with C.W. King's translation (*Sudhoffs Archiv: Zeitschrift für Wissenschaftsgeschichte*, Beiheft 20) (Wiesbaden: Steiner, 1977), 69, lines 445–46. Regarding vervain, see Henry Ellis, 'Extracts in prose and verse from and old English medical manuscript, preserved in the Royal Library at Stockholm', *Archaeologia*, 30 (1844), 395f.; W.L. Wardale, 'A Low German-Latin miscellany of the

early fourteenth century', *Niederdeutsche Mitteilungen*, 8 (1952), 11; British Library, Sloane MS 3,132, 56r–56v; Bodleian Library, Oxford, MS e Mus. 219, fol. 187v, and Wood empt. MS 18, fol. 33v.

30 *Book of Secrets*, ed. Best and Brightman, 8, 45, 91; Evans, *Magical Jewels*, 226; Bodleian Library, Oxford, MS e Mus. 219, fol. 186v (a series of characters to be placed beneath the threshold of a couple who have quarrelled).

31 Candida Peruzzi, 'Un processo di stregoneria a Todi nel "400"', *Lares: Organo della Società di Etnografia Italiana-Roma*, 21 (1955), fasc. I–II, 9–11; Cerlini, 'Una strega reggiana', 64f.

32 *Picatrix: The Latin Version of the* Ghāyat Al-Hakīm, ed. David Pingree (London: Warburg Institute, 1986), 16, 21, 70–72, 113, 115f., 130–32, 156f., 229, 233.

33 Gene A. Brucker, 'Sorcery in early Renaissance Florence', *Studies in the Renaissance*, 10 (1963), 10f.; C. Kayser, 'Gebrauch von Psalmen zur Zauberei', *Zeitschrift der Deutschen Morgenländischen Gesellschaft*, 42 (1888), 460; Peter Browe, 'Die Eucharistie als Zaubermittel im Mittelalter', *Archiv für Kulturgeschichte*, 20 (1930), 134–54. For similar use of holy chrism see Cerlini, 'Una strega reggiana', 67.

34 Jerzy Zathey, 'Modlitwa z XIV wieku o charakterze zaklęcia, majaca zapewnić zonie miłość męza', *Biuletyn Biblioteki Jagiellońskiej*, 34/35 (1984/85), 63–4; Peter Dronke, 'Towards the interpretation of the Leiden love-spell', *Cambridge Medieval Celtic Studies*, 16 (1988), 61–75.

35 Thomas of Britain, *The Romance of Tristram and Ysolt*, ch. 46, trans. Roger Sherman Loomis (New York: Dutton, 1923), 129–35. On the theme see especially Helen Cooper, 'Magic that does not work', *Medievalia et Humanistica*, n.s., 7 (1976), 131–46.

36 Nicolaus Eymericus, *Directorium inquisitorum*, ii.43.8 (Rome: Georgius Ferrarius, 1587); translated in Alan C. Kors and Edward Peters, eds, *Witchcraft in Europe, 1100–1700: A Documentary History* (Philadelphia: University of Pennsylvania Press, 1972), 84–92.

37 Cambridge University Library, MS Dd.xi.45, fols 137v–138.

38 Paul Fredericq, ed., *Corpus documentorum inquisitionis haereticae pravitatis Neerlandicae*, 1 (Ghent and The Hague, 1889–1906), 428f.

39 Braekman, *Magische experimenten*, 38–40.

40 The conjuration breaks off at this point.

41 Lea, *History*, vol. 3, 657–59. Cf. Hansen, *Quellen*, 449; Lea, *History*, vol. 3, 455f.

42 Margaret Aston, *Thomas Arundel: A Study of Church Life in the Reign of Richard II* (Oxford: Clarendon, 1967), 63, 404f.

43 A. Germain, 'Inventaire inédit concernant les Archives de l'Inquisition de Carcassonne', *Mémoires de la Société Archéologique de Montpellier*, 4 (1885), 305; reprinted in Hansen, *Quellen*, 454f.

44 Brucker, 'Sorcery', 19f., 23, from G. Sanesi, 'Un episodio d'eresia nel 1383', *Bullettino senese di storia patria*, 3 (1896), 384f.

45 Thomas Wright, ed., *A Contemporary Narrative of the Proceedings against Dame Alice Kyteler* (Camden Society, 24) (London: Nichols, 1843), 2.

46 Hartmann Ammann, 'Der Innsbrucker Hexenprocess von 1485', *Zeitschrift des Ferdinandeums für Tirol und Vorarlberg*, ser. 3, 34 (1890), 29.

47 See the experiment with a hoopoe heart mentioned in Kieckhefer, *Magic in the Middle Ages*, 142, from British Library, Sloane MS 3,132, fol. 56v.

48 Johann Hartlieb, *Das Buch aller verbotenen Künste, des Aberglaubens und der Zauberei*, ch. 79, ed. and trans. Falk Eisermann and Eckhard Graf (Ahlerstedt: Param, 1989), 90f. On the term *atzmann* in this

context see Leander Petzoldt, *Kleines Lexikon der Dämonen und Elementargeister* (Munich: Beck, 1990), 25–7.

49 For this suggestion I am indebted to John Leland.

50 See Edward C. Dimock, Jr., *The Place of the Hidden Moon: Erotic Mysticism in the Vaisnava – Sahajiya Cult of Bengal*, new edn (Chicago: University of Chicago Press, 1989), 202. I am grateful to Amy Ong for this reference.

51 *Malleus maleficarum*, ii.2.3, trans. Montague Summers (London: Rodker, 1928; repr. London: Pushkin, 1948), 170.

52 The manuscript does not say whether the hair is to be from the woman's head or from her pudenda. A famous instance of the magic requiring a woman's pubic hair occurred in the late sixteenth-century Scottish trial of Doctor Fian, who thought he had the hair of a young woman but in fact worked his magic over the hair from a cow, which became passionately attached to him; see James VI/I, *Dæmonologie, 1597 [and] Newes from Scotland, Declaring the Damnable Life and Death of Doctor Fian* (Bodley Head Quartos, 9) (London: John Lane; New York: Dutton, 1924).

53 One might have expected a black-handled knife; see Richard P.H. Greenfield, *Traditions of Belief in Late Byzantine Demonology* (Amsterdam: Hakkert, 1988), 256, and Richard P.H. Greenfield, 'A contribution to the study of Palaeologan magic', in Henry Maguire, ed., *Byzantine Magic* (Washington, DC: Dumbarton Oaks, 1995), 142, n. 83.

54 Or perhaps, rather, 'if she is anywhere on Earth [*in terra omnino*]'; in either case, I am reading *consumetur* for *consumatur*.

55 PGM IV.296–329, in Hans Dieter Betz, ed., *The Greek Magical Papyri in Translation, Including the Demotic Spells*, 1 (Chicago: University of Chicago Press, 1986), 44–7; also D.G. Martinez, *P. Michigan XVI.: A Greek Love Charm from Egypt (P. Mich. 757)* (Atlanta: Scholars, 1991), and John G. Gager, ed., *Curse Tablets and Binding Spells from the Ancient World* (New York: Oxford University Press, 1992), no. 27, pp. 94–97. For the Egyptian statue see Gager, *Curse Tablets*, p. 98, fig. 13.

56 Joshua Trachtenberg, *Jewish Magic and Superstition: A Study in Folk Religion* (New York: Behrman, 1939; New York: Atheneum, 1970), 125–26. Cf. the love spell of Klaudianos, in Betz, pp. 141–2 (PGM VII.862–918), and the parallels in Greenfield, *Traditions of Belief*, 266–7.

57 Gager, *Curse Tablets*, 81.

58 For one precedent see Meyer and Smith, *Ancient Christian Magic*, 159.

59 *The Revelations of Mechthild of Magdeburg (1210–1297), or The Flowing Light of the Godhead*, ii.25, trans. Lucy Menzies (London: Longmans, 1953), 54–8.

60 Richard of Saint-Victor, 'Of the Four Degrees of Passionate Charity', in *Selected Writings on Contemplation*, trans. Clare Kirchberger, (New York: Harper, 1957), 213–33.

LEARNING HIDDEN AND FUTURE THINGS: DIVINATORY EXPERIMENTS

A fifteenth-century manuscript from Yorkshire tells of a lord from whom food had been stolen.[1] As it happened, a labourer employed in digging, referred to as 'a great worker and eater', was staying in a room in the lord's house, and when he was hungry he would slip downstairs to where meat was hanging, and would cook and eat it, even during Lent.

> The lord of the house, seeing that his meat was thus cut into, asked his servants about the matter. They all denied guilt and purged themselves with oaths, so he threatened to go to a certain necromantic wizard [*maleficum quendam nigromanticum*] and find out through him about this strange affair. On hearing this, the digger was terribly afraid, and went to the friars and confessed his offence in secret and received sacramental absolution. The lord of the house went as threatened to the necromancer, who anointed the fingernail of a young boy, then with his incantations inquired of him what he saw. [The boy] replied, 'I see a menial worker with clipped hair.' [The necromancer] told him, 'Conjure him, then, to appear to you in the most comely form that he can assume.' And the boy did so, and then declared, 'Look at that! I see a really beautiful horse!' And then he saw a man with the appearance of the aforesaid digger going down stairs and cutting off pieces of meat, with the horse following him. And the cleric [i.e., the necromancer] inquired, 'What are the man and the horse doing now?' And the boy replied, 'Look at that! He is cooking and eating those pieces of meat!' [The necromancer] asked further, 'And what is he doing now?' And the boy said, 'They are going to the church of the friars, and the horse is waiting outside, and the man is going in and kneeling and speaking with one of the friars, who is putting his hand on his head.' Again the cleric asked the little boy, 'What are they doing now?' [The boy] answered, 'Both of them have just vanished from my eyes. I cannot see them any more, and I have no idea where they have gone.'[2]

The manuscript clearly suggests not only that such divination can in principle work, but that it works through the cooperation of demons: it gives the tale the caption, 'How a penitent thief after confession vanished from the eyes of a demon', which is to say that the demon who was providing information through the boy could no longer do so once the thief had been absolved. As in other tales of the later Middle Ages, it is assumed that the demon has a certain power over a soul in a state of sin, and the capacity to know the sins in some detail, but the wiping away of sins through sacramental confession removes them from the sphere of demons' knowledge.[3] The narrator also assumes the reader will expect a necromantic wizard to be a cleric: the fact is mentioned quite incidentally, after the story is well under way, as a fact the reader might be trusted already to have known.

The form of magic here related figures prominently in John of Salisbury's catalogue of divinatory techniques in his *Policraticus*. When John himself was studying Latin grammar as a boy, the priest who taught him made John and a fellow pupil participate in such activities. The priest anointed the boys' fingernails, or used a polished basin, to provide a reflecting surface in which figures might be seen. He then recited incantations, which led the fellow pupil to see 'misty figures', although John himself saw nothing.[4] One entry in Robert Reynys's commonplace book reveals that unfallen angels as well as demons could be invoked by such means. In Reynys's version of the ceremony, the conjurer takes a child between seven and thirteen years of age, places the lad between his legs, winds a red silk thread around his thumb, scrapes his thumbnail clean, and writes on it the letters 'AGLA'. He then says devoutly, 'Lord Jesus Christ, king of glory, send us three angels to tell us the truth and not falsehood in all matters about which we shall inquire.' Three angels will appear in the boy's nail. The boy then repeats a formula addressed to these angels: 'Angels of the Lord, I command you by God the Father almighty, who created you and us out of nothing, and by the virginity of Blessed Mary and Blessed John the Evangelist and of all virgins, and by the virtues of all the holy names of God, to show us the truth and not falsehood in all matters about which we shall inquire.'[5]

The general term for such divination is 'scrying', which is sometimes subdivided into specific forms such as catoptromancy (divination by means of a mirror), crystallomancy (by a crystal), cyclicomancy or lecanomancy (by a cup or basin filled with liquid), hydromancy (by water in a natural body), onychomancy (by an anointed nail); 'catoptromancy' is sometimes also used as the generic term.[6] Synodal legislation as early as the fifth century condemned *specularii* who engaged in these practices, and the condemnation was often repeated. The *Fasciculus morum* condemns those *phitonici* and *specularii* who gaze into mirrors, bowls, polished fingernails, and so forth, and claim that marvellous things are thus revealed to them.[7] In 1311 the bishop of Lincoln instructed one of his officials to investigate people who were practising divination by conjuring spirits in their fingernails and in mirrors, as well as in stones and rings.[8] Surely the most famous of these reflecting surfaces is John Dee's 'show-stone', through which Edward Kelly and other mediums communicated with angels.[9] One particularly dramatic notion about the magical properties of mirrors is the legend, most famously associated with Virgil, of a far-seeing mirror by which a ruler could guard his realm.[10] But the notion of perceiving hidden and future realities in a mirror receives its ultimate extension in the Neoplatonic notion of the divine mind itself as a mirror in which particularities can be foreseen, so that it can be said of a saint with the gift of prophecy that 'in the mirror of divinity everything to be was present to him'.[11]

Johannes Hartlieb tells how a *zaubermaister* stands behind a child and recites secret words into his ear in the practice of hydromancy. In pyromancy as well, he says, the master may set an innocent child in his lap and lift his hand so he can see the fingernails; then he conjures the child and his nail with a long conjuration and recites three secret words into his ear. The master may take oil and soot from a pan and anoint the hand of an innocent girl or boy so that it shines brightly, then he speaks secret words into the child's ear, thus making a vow and forming a pact. Another form of pyromancy involves engraving many characters and figures around a steel mirror, then whispering secret words into the ear of boy as a prelude to interrogation. Alternatively, the child may be made to gaze at a polished sword – Hartlieb knew one great prince who used an old executioner's sword for this purpose – or a crystal. When the master is interrogating the boy, he asks if he sees an angel; if so, he asks what colour. If the angel is red that means he is angry, or if black he is very angry, and they must pray more, light more candles, and offer more incense and other gifts to assuage his anger, until the angel who appears is white. Hartlieb, echoing the much earlier judgement of John of Salisbury, confirms the conventional wisdom when he speaks of such dealings with young children as a form of abuse: 'I was often witness to such proceedings and established that the children by exposure to such words suffered not insignificant harm'.[12]

Writers might differ in their interpretation of these phenomena. Ibn Khaldûn explained the scryers' visions as products of their imaginations: the scryer does not actually see a vision on the reflecting surface, but rather imaginative phantoms are projected outward from the eyes onto a sort of misty veil that forms between the eyes and the object.[13] The related interpretation summarized by Pedro García in the late fifteenth century was perhaps more influential and deserves to be quoted at some length:

> From what has been said and from the conclusions reached [in the preceding discussion] it is clear that divination of occult things and the wonders of magical art are brought about by the aid of demons. But because the proponents of natural magic attempt to reduce [the works of magic] to purely natural causes, we must inquire whether the divination of hidden affairs and the accomplishment of wondrous works can be done thru the power of nature. Let us first ask about the divination of hidden matters, concerning which some people say and write that a person can know and divine hidden things naturally, through the power of the soul. The first manner [of doing so] is by

gazing at luminous bodies and instruments. The principle here is that the *acies* of the human mind in one who gazes on such instruments reflects back upon itself, for the luminosity of the instrument prevents direction or concentration of the mind on exterior things, and repels it, and turns it back upon itself, so that it is forced to gaze upon itself. Thus, according to the philosophy of Plato, if it is purged and cleansed of defilements, which come from the body and cling to the soul, they see as in a clear and clean mirror, and when they inquire about all hidden things, or some portion of them, or some particular hidden thing, it is no surprise that the soul, turned back into itself, should see such hidden things, for according to Plato the human soul is created fully inscribed with the forms of all knowable things, in respect of its intellectual power . . .

Thus it is, according to the opinion of these magicians, that these luminous bodies function, and particularly mirrors. When the soul of the gazer is turned back on itself, it absorbs the attention and fixes the *acies* of the intellect in its inward turning, and the more inwardly it is fixed, the more fully and clearly it turns upon itself and knows and divines hidden things – and the more it is filled within by God, so that the beholding is turned into the soul, which can be so turned in to itself and as it were recollected within itself,[14] that the recollection becomes rapture or a state near to rapture, or ecstasy or a condition near to ecstasy. Thus, those who operate in works of this kind close the eyes of children, and hold their eyes tightly closed after they have seen such revelations, until the soul has returned from this recollection to its original state and is extended in the usual manner throughout the body and its organs – which is to say, until it recovers its powers and the organs from which it appears to have withdrawn, at least somewhat. Otherwise, it is said, there is threat of danger to the body of the child, or perhaps madness. According to the philosophy of the Platonists, this is one manner of saving the divinations of hidden matters through [demonstration] of purely natural causes without any aid of demons, explicit or secret.[15]

Garcia goes on to refute these claims, chiefly by mounting an explicitly Aristotelian refutation of what he takes as standard Platonist psychology; most fundamentally, he denies that the mind is capable of grasping truth by being directed to innate knowledge found within itself. Both Ibn Khaldûn and Garcia's opponents believe divination can be explained in natural terms, but the mechanisms they posit are different. For Ibn Khaldûn (a rationalist intending to deflate the claims of magicians to preternatural knowledge) attention is focused on an outward substance that reflects projections of the mind, while for the adversaries of Garcia (Platonist mages intending to defend their practice against the charge of demonic inspiration) it is directed instead within the mind itself. Neither view sufficed to convince most contemporaries that the mind could so readily be converted into an instrument of divination without demonic aid – but the very attempt to formulate an explanation in natural terms is historically interesting, whether the point is to debunk the supernatural pretensions of the diviners or to defend the validity of the art.

Perhaps most often, those who wrote about these matters did so to condemn them and warn of their danger. This was the point of John of Salisbury's tale of his own early experience. Nicolas Oresme, too, warned that if young boys stared for long intervals into polished surfaces they might become blind; worse, they might suffer disfigurement of their faces and disturbing changes in their personalities.[16]

Judging from the cases reported in the judicial records and chronicles – and judging also from the experiments contained in the Rawlinson necromantic manuscript – divination of this sort seems to have been used mostly to recover lost or stolen goods. At London in 1311, unspecified offenders were investigated for invoking spirits to appear in fingernails, mirrors, stones, rings, and so forth, to reveal the future or the location of lost objects.[17] When a band of monks and canons wished to recover stolen money near Paris in 1323, their plans involved standing in a circle made from the skin of a cat; within that circle they were to invoke the demon Berith, who would answer their inquiries.[18] In 1419 a chaplain named Richard Walker was arrested by the prior of Winchester and tried for using magical arts, the evidence against him included two books containing conjurations and figures, and he acknowledged that he had attempted to use the experiments in one of his books, but to no avail, so he did not believe in their power.[19] In 1440 the Augustinian canons at Leicester accused their own abbot, William Sadyngstone, of using such arts: when no one confessed to stealing certain funds, he had allegedly recited incantations, applied ointment to the thumbnail of a boy called Maurice, asked this medium what he saw there revealed, and learned that the culprit was one of the canons, Brother Thomas Asty. The other monks reported the incident to the bishop, who condemned the abbot for sorcery.[20] Again at Westminster during the 1450s, and at London repeatedly in the later fifteenth century, victims of theft were said to have solicited the services of alleged necromancers ('negremaunsers' or 'nigromansiers').[21]

The Devil being notoriously a liar and the father of lies, it is hardly surprising to find much concern with the question whether he could be constrained to tell the truth, even if their keen and subtle minds and long experience gave them command of exceptionally wide knowledge.[22] Peter Brown has spoken of exorcisms as forms of judicial torture, in which the demons, like criminals, were compelled even against their will to confess what they knew.[23] When the divination was intended to identify a thief, the obvious danger – and probably the chief reason for judicial action against the diviners – was that of false accusation. One is not surprised to read in the Rawlinson necromantic manuscript, which is devoted mainly to this kind of magic, that the spirits must be strictly enjoined not to defame any innocent parties.[24] The point is made forcefully in a story from Stephen of Bourbon, who does not hesitate to ascribe a diviner's revelation to demons, but argues how little the spirits can be trusted:

While I was a student at Paris, one Christmas Eve when our companions were at Vespers, a certain most noted thief entered our hostel, and, opening the chamber of one of our fellows, carried off many volumes of law-books. The scholar would have studied in his books after the feast; and, finding them not, he hastened to the wizards, of whom many failed him, but one wrought as follows. Adjuring his demons and holding a sword, he made the boy gaze upon the blade; and he, after many things there seen, beheld at last by a succession of many visions how his books were stolen by one of our fellows, his own cousin, whom he thought the most upright of our fellowship; whom the possessor of the books slandered not only among the scholars but also among his friends, accusing him that he had stolen them. Meanwhile the aforesaid thief stole other things and was detected, whereupon he fled to a certain church where he lay in the belfry, and, having been duly examined, confessed all that he had stolen, and where, and what he had done with his thefts. When therefore certain scholars who lodged hard by our hostel had found by his means a mantle which they had lost and he had stolen, then he who had lost his books could scarce rest until he had gone to enquire of this thief; who answered and told him when and where he had taken his books, and the Jew's house where he had pledged them, where also my friend found them. This I have told that ye may clearly mark the falsehood of those demons who showed the vision in the sword-blade in order that they might slander that good man and break the bonds of charity between those kinsfolk, and bring the man who believed in them to eternal perdition, both him and his.[25]

Not surprisingly, the diviners themselves could be subject to prosecution on the ground of false accusation, as when the sum of £40 was stolen from John Haddon of Coventry in the mid-1480s, and he consulted necromancers to find the thieves; they charged one William Lee, a poor man, who had been seen wearing the same garments that the necromancers had determined were worn by the guilty parties. Lee petitioned on his own behalf, pleading that the accusation rested on false and illicit proceedings:

Humbly showeth and pitiously complaineth unto your good lordship your daily orator William Lee of the city of Coventry, that where forty pounds of money was taken and withdrawn from one John Haddon of the said city, draper, as the said John hath reported and said, whereupon the said John, to get knowledge of the takers of the said money, caused certain persons using the crafts of sorcery, witchcrafts and necromancy [*Nygromancy*] to inquire by their crafts of the takers of the said money, and thereupon the said persons using the said unlawful crafts advised and counseled the said John Haddon to take and examine your said orator for withdrawing of the said money, for as much as they perceived that your said orator used and wore such garments and clothing as they determined by their unlawful witchcrafts that the takers of the said money had and used at the time of the taking of the said money. And thereupon the said John Haddon, having no other cause against your said orator nor matter of suspicion, arrested and put in prison your said orator and kept him there by the space of a month and more. And after this the said John, having no other cause nor nothing of untruth could prove against your said orator, suffered him to depart and go at his large. And after this the said John Haddon, intending the further vexation and trouble of your said orator, made a plaint of trespass before the mayor and sheriffs of the said city against your said orator concerning the taking of the said money, supposing that your said orator the Wednesday next before the feast of the Annunciation of Our Lady last past took and bore away the said money. In the which plaint of trespass your said orator is like to be condemned, for as much as your said orator is in poverty and the said John Haddon is of great might and power and great alliance in the said city. Wherefore and for as much as the said cause of trespass and the said wrongful arresting and keeping of your said orator in prison was by means and judgment of the said persons using the said unlawful crafts of necromancy and witchcraft, to whom credence ought not to be given, for that is contrary to the faith of Holy Church. In consideration whereof that it would please your good lordship to grant a certiorare to be directed to the said mayor and sheriffs, etc.[26]

Divinatory conjuration could, of course, be used for other purposes as well, such as finding buried treasure. A group of men were tried in Norfolk in 1465 for using necromancy to discover such a trove. Allegedly they invoked and made sacrifice to accursed spirits. When a *spiritus aerialis* appeared, at Bunwell, they promised it the body of a Christian man in exchange for its leading them to treasure; the spirit revealed in a crystal the location of a hill filled with treasure, whereupon the adventurers baptized a rooster with a Christian name and sacrificed it to the spirit.[27] Thomas Forde was sentenced to the pillory at London in 1418 for having defrauded women by claims of magical power: he had extorted money from one woman, and attempted to gain her hand in marriage, by suggesting he could determine where her late husband had buried a chest containing over £200; he had told another of his victims that he could recover for her the gold cloth that had been stolen from her.[28] Other cases too may have involved a substantial measure of straightforwardly cynical charlatanry, but in these instances it seems all the more apparent. It is magic of this sort that gives rise to jest in the tale of Mary of Nijmeghen, where the Devil boasts:

I am beginning to teach people how to find hidden treasure; and only yesterday it cost one of them his life. I told him where there was a treasure hidden and growing mouldy, in a stable, underneath a beam on which the whole weight of the stable was resting. I told him that he would have to dig deep into the ground, and he would find pound upon pound of the hidden treasure. At once he started to dig there, but as soon as he had dug so far that he undermined the beam and the posts supporting it, the beam fell to the ground and crushed this poor idiot under it![29]

At least in cases for detection of thieves, however, otherwise responsible individuals seem rather often to have placed credence in the claims of the diviners, perhaps because they were desperate, and perhaps because what they really sought was a way of persuading others to support a suspicion they themselves already harboured.

DIVINATORY EXPERIMENTS IN THE MUNICH HANDBOOK

The largest number of experiments in Clm 849, nineteen in all, is divinatory. While it is sometimes said that these experiments may be used for any of various purposes, the usual end is detection of a crime or criminal (usually a thief, less often a murderer) and recovery of stolen goods, more rarely to determine the location of hidden treasure. The text of one experiment (no. 25) insists that the procedure must not be used for any base or frivolous purpose, but only for a serious one, because one must not take the name of God in vain.

As for the techniques used in these experiments, the characteristic features in most of them are two. First, the primary magical technique is scrying, combined with conjurations; magic circles either are not used or have little significance.[30] Second, cooperation of a medium, usually a young boy, is vital; it is he alone who actually sees the spirits that are conjured.

Approximately half of these experiments entail the use of a circle or some other figure among the means for conjuring the spirits. The medium typically sees the spirits in a mirror, crystal, vessel, bone, polished thumbnail or fingernail. In most cases the medium must be a virginal boy, who actually sees and communicates with the spirits.[31] Sometimes we are told that he must be younger than twelve, and born of legitimate marriage.[32] Occasionally a girl may be used as well as a boy,[33] but this provision is relatively rare. The use of young and putatively innocent boys in divination must be seen as part of a broader clerical fascination with the ideal of innocent boyhood. In liturgical drama young boys dressed and acted 'in the manner of virgin women', at least in part 'to project the theme of virginity', as Nicholas Orme has phrased it.[34]

The use of a medium could well be a means for expression of socially shared convictions about the likeliest suspects, but it is not entirely obvious that this mechanism came importantly into play. Because the ritual was private, it could more easily become a tool for the expression of individual prejudice and animosity. Yet the one who saw the visions was neither the client nor the master but instead a young boy, in all likelihood not one with a personal interest in the outcome of the experiment. Apart from the obvious matter of the youth's sacred non-sexuality, his youth may have been important mainly because it put him at some remove from the preformed judgements of the adult principals and made possible a relatively neutral accusation. It is, of course, also possible that the mere pretence of childish innocence, neutrality and distance from adult biases was more important than any real immunity of this sort.

EXPERIMENTS INVOLVING MIRRORS

In his account of scrying with a steel mirror, Johannes Hartlieb says, 'I have seen masters who maintain they can prepare mirrors such that any man or woman can see in them what they will.' He also says that other reflecting surfaces can be used; there are even priests who will use the very paten that serves at mass to hold the host; they believe (falsely, adds Hartlieb) that only angels and not demons can appear on such a consecrated object.[35] One might suppose that a mirror would make an ideal tool for divination that requires concentration on a reflective surface, because mirrors are designed specifically for reflection. A *modern* mirror, however, might be distinctly inappropriate for this purpose precisely because it reflects too well and too realistically, giving too little scope to imaginative play and the power of suggestion. Perhaps the mirrors used in divinatory experiments were less polished, but at least in some cases the magician is instructed to use a polished mirror. We must assume that the point was not for the child medium who gazed into the mirror to focus closely on his own face but to use the mirror as a means for perceiving more numinous revelations. To be sure, there are cultures in which the spectator's own face reflected in a mirror becomes a point of reference for visionary encounter; after staring for hours at one's own reflection one may identify one's face with that of an ancestor, or one may perceive it as a manifestation of one's own true, inner or archetypal self.[36] In the Munich manuscript, however, there is no suggestion that the medium's own realistic image plays any role whatever.

The handbook contains five such experiments: two versions of the Mirror of Floron (nos 18 and 19), the First Mirror of Lilith (no. 23), and two others (nos 20 and 33). The Mirror of Floron in its first version may serve as a useful introduction to these experiments:

Have a mirror made of pure steel, measuring one palm around, with a handle for holding it, and have it bright and shiny like a sword. And have it made in the name of Floron, and around the rim of the mirror, on the part that is not polished, have these ten names [Latranoy, Iszarin, Bicol, Danmals, Gromon, Zara, Ralkal, Sigtonia, Samah and Meneglasar] inscribed with ten characters, with the name of the aforesaid spirit [Floron] written in the middle. After it has been made, it should be anointed with pure and bright balsam, and fumigated with aloes, ambergris, myrrh and white frankincense.

When this has been done, the master of this work should sit and have this mirror held with both hands by a virgin boy before his chest. The master himself should be bathed and dressed in clean garments. Before he begins to exercise this work he should sprinkle in the air honey, milk and wine, mixed together in equal proportions, while saying, 'O Floron, respond quickly in the mirror, as you are accustomed to appear.'

When he has said this, he should read this conjuration before the mirror: 'Bismille araathe mem lismissa gassim gisim galisim darrgosim samaiaosim ralim ausini taxarim zaloimi hyacabanoy illete laytimi hehelmini betoymi thoma leminao vnuthomin zonim narabanorum azarethia thathitat hinanadon illemay sard lucacef illemegiptimi sitaginatim viaice hamtamice tatiala taltarini alaoht haleytum gaptametuntij morto orfail geibel huabaton albital hualepin halmagrilie hualeon huastanie hualtamemeth huatorzor illenie giptimi tatgnie gathegine lesuma lesanim aptasale albweroahit vlleath alfard vsemeth aptisile abfluwarth vllelath ant clulamoralie hahysitimi waleles lithimi caegine catliegineles mirabolamini abtasile albiwahith alleath halamaton vnitia gaytatalon huaia gay soze cemeselis phalmorath bethathure huaba lagis illemeammitimi gelgine gathegine lesmiraptalibe albiwath vleuth.'

When he has recited this conjuration, the master should look in the mirror, and he will see an armed knight seated on a horse, and his squire accompanying him. The knight will dismount from the horse and his squire will hold the horse. He will greet the knight [with the words], *se desperata, decentissime visibiliter greciomo*. And then the master may ask him about past, present and future things, and he will at once give full response in writing.

This should not seem unbelievable to you, whoever may execute this work, for when you have carried out these things nine times this same spirit will clearly reveal face to face, orally, all things which previously he has indicated in writing.

And so, when you have completed everything according to your will, command this spirit to withdraw in peace, and to return according to the command of his master when he is summoned.

The second version of this Mirror of Floron adds certain details: the mirror should be made on the first hour on Friday, under a waxing moon; the sculptor or workman must be chaste for nine days beforehand, must be bathed, and must wear clean clothes; the words in which the master conjures the spirit are identified, implausibly, as 'Chaldean'; the master's greeting to the knight is *Parate insilitio gytromon*, which approximates an obviously meaningful statement even less than the greeting in the first version; and the knight who has at first answered questions in writing will answer *per exercicium* at night and orally throughout the day, revealing all things beneath the moon.

The First Mirror of Lilith (spelled *Lilit* or *Lylet*) is dedicated to this ancient Hebrew demon and to her followers and her 'knights' – although the text seems to slip into calling the spirit Bylet before the experiment is over.[37] The master commands these 'demons' to appear in non-threatening form and answer questions. The mirror itself can be made in the form of a shield, but need not be. The master prays to Lilith to come in her own appearance, not in that of ravens, conjuring her to sit with him whenever the master wants. She will appear in a mirror with two or more servants, and will tell the truth or give appropriate signs regarding a theft, murder, or other circumstance.

In one of the remaining experiments (no. 20) the master goes to a secret place at a conjunction of Venus and Jupiter, with burning candles and a polished steel mirror, made under a particular phase of the moon. He makes a circle, and puts the mirror on a piece of wood in the form of a knife. He implores God to make the mirror grow and become bright. Then he recites a brief conjuration three times, and the mirror will seem to grow and become bright. Many people will appear, as in a field. The master may ask them anything he wants, and will obtain an answer. After the first time, he may work this procedure whenever and wherever he wishes, though he must always do so in a secret place; once consecrated for that purpose, the mirror can be used repeatedly. In the other experiment (no. 33), the master smears olive oil on a mirror, says a doxology, enters a magic circle that is sprinkled with verbena, turns to the east, and conjures a spirit. When it comes, he conjures it to tell him the truth, without causing any harm. If the spirit refuses, the master reads the unbreakable 'bond of Solomon', an extended conjuration.

As in some of the illusionist experiments, spirits who appear to divulge information are here designated as knights. But three of these experiments are more distinctive in being given titles, taken from the chief spirits to whom they appeal, Lillith and Floron. The former is familiar from Hebrew tradition, while the latter is known from the writings of Cecco d'Ascoli.[38] The conjuration (and presumably also the greeting) in 'Chaldean' (actually garbled Arabic, as we shall see in Chapter 6) adds a touch of exoticism to some of these experiments. But perhaps the most curious feature, found in the Mirror of Floron, is the reference to the spirit's giving written responses, through a mechanism that is not clearly specified; perhaps the master is to see the spirit holding a written message for his inspection, or possibly patterns discerned on the surface of the mirror are to be interpreted as some form of writing.

EXPERIMENTS INVOLVING CRYSTALS

For the use of crystals and related objects in scrying, Johannes Hartlieb is again a helpful source of information:

> Some take a clear, fine, polished crystal or beryl and have it consecrated, then keep it clean, and lay incense, myrrh, and so forth on it. Then when they wish to exercise their art they wait for a clear day, or use a clean room with many consecrated candles. The masters go to a bathing room, taking an innocent child, and dressing themselves in pure white clothes. They sit down and speak magic prayers (*zauber bätt*), and burn magic offerings (*zauber opffer*), then order the boy to look into the stone and whisper secret words into his ear, which are allegedly most holy – but are indeed devilish words.[39]

The Munich handbook gives two divinatory experiments entailing the use of crystals, both of them extremely brief and simple. The implement used may be something like the legendary crystal ball; when the Rawlinson necromantic manuscript refers to crystals it speaks of them as 'stones', which surely were polished, whatever their shape. In one experiment (no. 24) the master first takes a crystal and washes it with wine, then he writes certain names of Christ on it with olive oil, and asks for two or three angels to appear in that crystal and reveal the truth to a virgin boy. The boy conjures these angels to come in the crystal so he may see them. When they come, the boy conjures them thrice to sit on golden seats and not withdraw from the crystal without the master's permission. For the other experiment (no. 25) the master takes a crystal in the form of a seal or mirror and places it in wax. Then he writes the name 'Honely' on it with oil. He prays Christ to bestow wondrous and useful powers upon this stone, as he has done to other stones, to herbs, and to certain words; the text refers to this prayer as a conjuration, but the writer does not have quite the temerity to conjure Christ himself. He does then conjure certain angels to come at once and appear in the crystal, and not withdraw from it until they have answered the questions he has to ask.

It is probably not an accident that in both of these experiments, unlike most, the spirits conjured are expressly referred to as angels, and in one of them names of Christ are invoked (which is not uncommon in these experiments), while in the other the conjuration is preceded by a prayer to Christ (which is altogether uncommon). The other reflecting surfaces have a kind of artificial reflectivity: some of them need to have oil applied to them, and a mirror is a manufactured object. The crystal, however, was thought to have natural luminosity as one of the properties bestowed on it in its creation. Perhaps for this reason it seemed more natural for a crystal to serve as a medium for the conjuring of unfallen spirits, although this explanation would have greater force if it were supported by substantial evidence from other sources.

A COMPLEX EXPERIMENT INVOLVING APPARITIONS IN A THUMBNAIL

Five divinatory experiments in the Munich handbook – as many as those using mirrors – require the medium to gaze into his own polished fingernail or thumbnail. These tend to be elaborate rituals, with preliminary measures followed by multiple conjurations, then interrogation of the spirits who appear, and in some cases procedures for terminating the experiment. Most of these rituals are intended specifically to learn about the circumstances of a theft, although the text indicates that no. 27 (and presumably others as well) can serve to provide information about whether a friend is well or sick, whether someone is on the road, or other matters. A fingernail may seem an odd instrument for divination, and the image of a boy carrying on a conversation with an elaborately described demon moving about on such a small screen may seem somewhat comic, but fixing the boy's attention on so narrow a space may in fact have been an aid to concentration: the smaller the surface, and the closer it is held to the eye, the more it will be in focus and potential distractions will be out of focus.

No. 27 is broken into two 'chapters', the first of which reads as follows:

To find out about a theft, take a virgin boy of legitimate birth, at whatever hour you wish before noon, and scrape well the thumb nail of his left hand with a knife. Then bind to the same thumb, beneath the nail, a slip with the following names written on it. And these are the names: Egippia, Benoham, Beanke vel Beanre, Reranressym, Alredessym, Ebemidyrr, Fetolinie [?], Dysi, Medirini, Alhea, Heresim, Egippia, Benoham [repeated], Haham, Ezirohias, Bohodi, Hohada, Anna, Hohanna, Ohereo, Metaliteps, Aregereo, Agertho, Aliberri, [and] Halba.

When this is done, if the boy does not see something, etc. [sic!]. But if he does see something, bind a strap of sheepskin, which you have had with you while hearing three complete masses, on the slip, around the thumb, while saying this conjuration: 'O you demons, who have appeared before me in the nail of this boy, by Him who is Alpha and Omega, I order and command and conjure you, by the most sacred names Ely, Eloy, Messias, Sother, Emmanuel, Sabaoth, [and] Adonay, and by On, which is the first name of the Lord, Pantoncraton [sic], Anetheten, and by the other names known and unknown to me, that you should have no power to withdraw with your companions until you have fulfilled my will completely, without any falsehood or harm to anyone. And if you disdain to do this, I command you to be bound beneath the deep waters of the sea, by these two names, Joth [and] Nabnoth, by which Solomon bound demons in a glass vessel. I conjure you by the seven signs of Solomon, and by his seal and wisdom, that you should have no licence to withdraw from here until you have told and shown me the truth about all that I ask.'

When you have said this, if the boy does not speak straightaway, recite this conjuration in his ear: 'I conjure you, virginal youth, by the true God Basyon, and by the name[s] On, Berion, Sabaoth, [and] Adonay, [etc.], to have no power of concealing from me, but to manifest all that you see.'

When you have recited these conjurations three times, if the spirits do not hasten to your service, add this conjuration: 'You demons from the east, you demons from the west, you demons from the south, you demons from the north, open up to us, Discobermath, Archidemath, Fritath, Altramat, Pestiferat, Helyberp, Hegergibet, Sathan.'

When you have spoken or repeated this conjuration three times, the boy will see all things clearly.

This experiment is good also if someone wishes to know the condition of his friends, whether they are well or ill, and it will determine whether or not they are under way.

The conjuration over the strap is as follows. When mass has been finished on any particular day, say this conjuration over the strap: 'I conjure you, Sona, by the name of the Lord Tetragrammaton, and by the name of God Joth, and by the name of God Nabnoth, [etc.], to receive such power that wherever you are bound, these spirits will have no power to withdraw until they fulfil the will of the one who binds.'

The second chapter begins with a lengthy conjuration summoning the spirits to appear in the boy's nail, and is followed by another conjuration commanding the boy to gaze into his nail and tell the truth about what is there revealed. The text continues:

Then ask the boy if the nail is brighter than before. If he says not, read the conjuration again from the beginning, and a third time if necessary. If he says it has become brighter, ask if he sees anything. If he says he sees a man, the master should have the boy conjure the one he sees, in the mother tongue, as follows: 'You who are before me, I conjure you by the Father and the Son and the Holy Spirit, and by Saint Mary and her virginity, and by Saint John and his virginity, [etc.], to go quickly for your king and have him come before me, so that I may see and understand him clearly.'

Then ask the boy if the king has come. If not, have the boy conjure again, as before. If he has come, have the boy tell the king to dismount from his horse and have a throne brought forth on which he can sit. Then have the boy ask the king if he wishes to eat. If he says no, then ask about whatever you will. If he says yes, have the boy tell the king to send wherever he will for a ram to be skinned and cooked, and then he should have a table set, and should rise and wash his hands, and sit at the table and have the ram set before him, and he should go ahead and eat it. After he has eaten, he should get up, take water, and wash his hands.

Then have the boy tell the king to remove the crown from his head and place his right hand on top of his head and swear by his crown and by his sceptre and by that which he holds beneath his right hand, to respond truly to all the master's questions. Then the master should ask whatever he wishes, through the boy. After the master's questions have been answered properly, the spirits may be given licence to leave, and the boy should say, 'Go. Peace be between us and you. And when the master calls you, be prepared to obey him in all things and by all things.'

The conception of a demon as a king or prince is not uncommon (see Chapter 7), and it is in keeping with the dignity of the spirit that he is allowed the privilege of a throne and a meal, although he supplies them himself, within the scene played out on the fingernail of the medium. Elsewhere as well the spirits may be instructed or invited to seat themselves on thrones; in the Rawlinson manuscript the medium is told to have three white-robed spirits fetch three gold thrones for themselves.[40] It is perhaps not surprising that apparitions as elaborate as these might require repeated conjuration. No doubt they also assumed child mediums of exceptional virtuosity, and a master who had found such a child must have been proud indeed to have discovered such a resource.

SIMPLER EXPERIMENTS INVOLVING FINGERNAILS OR THUMBNAILS

While the preceding experiment is more complex than most, others resemble it in their essentials. In experiment no. 30, the master obtains a powder by burning resin and collecting the ash from the bottom of a basin that is inscribed with certain characters. He anoints four joints of the boy's left hand with olive oil and with this powder, in alternation, until the boy's fingers shine like a mirror. (Johannes Hartlieb gives a similar account of how child mediums are instructed to gaze not only into their fingernails but into their hands anointed with oil and soot from a pan.[41]) Then he summons twelve spirits. Three times the master makes the sign of the cross with his right thumb on the boy's forehead, each time praying that Christ himself may sign the boy, as he gave his blessing at Cana. Then he repeats the twelve names, and may make the sign of the cross on his own forehead as well as the boy's. The names are recited until six spirits appear on the boy's hand. Then the boy commands them to sit, except for one, who is to rise and answer the master's questions. When the spirits have answered the master's questions, the boy commands them to depart, in the name of the Trinity; if he wishes, the master may at this point sign the boy's forehead again.

The next three experiments all take place within a simple circle, consisting of three concentric bands, within which the boy sits on a three-legged stool, around which are inscriptions (the boy's name, other names, the Tetragrammaton).[42] In no. 38 the master blesses the boy while waving a sword around his head. He gives the sword to the boy, then signs him with the sign of the cross (saying, 'May the cross sanctify you, and may the prayers of all priests bless you'), scrapes his nails with a knife, anoints them with olive oil, then blesses himself and his companions, who sit silently by the circle, with swords in hand. The boy shuts his eyes; the master blesses all those present by reading the opening verses of John's gospel. The boy looks at his anointed nail and conjures specified demons to make the nail grow large and bright so that various information can appear in it: the thief, the circumstances of the theft, and the place where the stolen object is concealed. The master conjures certain demon princes to come in the form of black men and appear in the boy's nail. If the boy cannot yet see any figures in his nail, the master repeats the conjuration. He asks the boy if he sees a demon leaping and rejoicing. The master and his companions speak to the boy to keep him from fear. Again the master conjures the demons to divulge the desired information. At the end of the experiment, the master rubs his fingernail clean with his tunic, and makes the sign of the cross over four parts of his body with the sword. Then the boy takes the sword and holds it before himself while leaving the circle. The companions and the master himself exit in the same manner.

In no. 39 the master scrapes the boy's right thumbnail, using a knife with a handle of black or white horn, and recites psalm verses. He then signs the boy's forehead with the sign of the cross, says a prayer asking God to have the boy tell the truth, and whispers the names of demons three times into the boy's right ear. Then he enters the circle and stands in front of the boy, anoints his nail with olive oil, gives him the knife, and recites a longer series of demons' names. He conjures the demons (repeatedly, if necessary) to make the boy's nail grow large and bright, so that the details of the theft will appear in it. When this happens, the master conjures the demons (again as often as needed) to come and appear to the boy in the forms of the thieves. When the demons appear, the master conjures them to give the boy power, so that he can make the necessary inquiry and behold the desired information. Afterward the master has the boy close his eyes, then he cleans his nail, signs him with the sign of the cross (*super eum, ante eum,* and *retro eum*), takes the knife from his hand, blesses both himself and the boy, erases the circle, and departs along with the boy. The 'kings' will return to their own kingdoms, but the master conjures them to return whenever he wishes.

In no. 40, the master turns to the east, scrapes both of the boy's thumbnails, places one of the boy's thumbs over the other, writes the name of the boy and the name Astaroth on the knife handle, gives the knife to the boy and has him hold it beneath his thumbs, anoints with olive oil the uppermost of the boy's thumbnails, making the form of a cross on it with all devotion, then himself takes a seat, holding the boy between his knees, and instructing him to look carefully at his thumbnail. (The position of the boy suggests an intimacy that is surely erotic, even if subtly so.) The master conjures the demons to appear in the thumbnail in the form of the thief or thieves, 'as they have promised'. He also prays to Christ, to manifest the truth make the boy report it. Again he conjures the demons to appear, and to make the boy's nail grow large and bright. At the end of the experiment, the master says the prayer, 'Protect, save, bless, [and] sanctify all the people by the sign of the Lord's cross. Fend off afflictions of body and soul. Let no peril prevail against this sign. Amen. May Jesus Christ defend us by this sign of the cross. Amen.'

EXPERIMENTS INVOLVING VESSELS

Perhaps among the most ancient and widespread means for divination is gazing at the surface of a fluid in a bowl or other vessel. The materials for such operations would have been available virtually anywhere, even if suitable mirrors were not on hand. A letter to King Psammetichos, included in the Greek magical papyri, gives instructions for bowl divination: one should take a bronze bowl or saucer and fill it with water, then add green olive oil, recite an incantation over it, and ask questions of whatever god one wishes; the deity will reply, after which he can be dismissed with a powerful name of a hundred letters, a name which commands gods and *daimones*, causing the universe to tremble.[43] Elsewhere there are bowls or other vessels on which magical formulas have been inscribed, but these are usually intended for types of magic other than divination.[44]

In two brief experiments from the Munich handbook, the reflecting surfaces that furnish information are vessels or basins. No. 22 involves tracing a circle on the ground with the point of a special knife, entering the circle with a virgin boy or girl, carving various sacred names on a vessel, well cleaned inside and out, and writing on the vessel with a feather from the left wing of a black hen, with accompanying prayers. The master conjures the child to divulge the information revealed regarding a thief or murderer, then he invokes God to grant this knowledge to the child. The child gazes intently into the vessel, and continues doing so until figures appear. In 'The True Art of the Basin' (no. 29), the master recites ten names into a boy's ear, conjures spirits to appear in a basin and divulge information, writes three names on a slip of parchment or paper, and places it in the basin. Then he asks God with humble devotion to give the boy knowledge so that he can respond truly, and he asks Christ to illumine the boy's mind. He conjures the demons to appear to the boy in a mirror or on the blade of a sword. When the demons appear, the boy tells their king to sit down, and has him send for a ram, a feature reminiscent of no. 27. Then follow various conjurations. The experiment terminates with an exchange between the young boy and the demon king, again in the manner of no. 27.

These divinatory experiments are unusual in their emphasis on sitting: the master, the medium, any companions, and the spirits themselves are instructed or invited repeatedly to sit, whether on thrones, at table, on stools, or simply on the ground. It would perhaps be misleading to seek a single meaning in this posture;

the spirits' being enthroned in their capacity as kings can hardly have the same significance as the medium's being seated on a stool. Yet this feature of the experiments is consonant with another peculiarity of this category which distinguishes it from the psychological and illusionist rituals: in these experiments the conjurations are intended specifically to bring about consultation between the magicians and the spirits, rather than their dialogue being a prelude to some further result, and thus the parties on both sides are in effect sitting down to do business. This is not to say that their being seated is necessary, but that it makes a kind of sense here that it would not make elsewhere.

AN EXPERIMENT INVOLVING A BONE

For no. 28 the master anoints the right shoulder blade of a ram with olive oil and puts it beneath the handle of a knife. He holds a lighted candle and conjures six demons to appear in the reflective surface before a virginal boy (under twelve years of age) and answer questions. If the boy sees the shoulder blade grow larger and brighter, the master conjures the demons again to appear. When a spirit appears in the form of a black man, the master asks him questions through the mediation of the boy. The master can conjure the boy so that he has the power to see a spirit, but not the power to lie. The experiment closes with miscellaneous instructions: While making a circle, the master should say 'Sator Arepo Tenet Opera Rotas', then two prayers, one for aid in undertakings, the other for sending the Holy Spirit upon the boy to illumine his mind so that he can see and reveal truths. Names of God are given, to be inscribed on the shoulder blade. And to send the demons away, the master makes the sign of the cross over the shoulder blade and says, 'Behold the cross of the Lord. Take flight, O hostile powers (*Fugite partes aduerse*). The lion of the tribe of Juda, the stem of David, has conquered. Go in peace to the places from which you came.'

Johannes Hartlieb tells how the shoulder blades of various large animals are examined in the form of divination known as spatulamancy,[45] but does not speak of operations performed over these bones in the manner prescribed by the Munich handbook.

EXPERIMENTS INVOLVING VISIONS IN SLEEP

The last two divinatory experiments in the handbook, both short and simple in form, differ from the preceding divinatory rites because they do not involve gazing into reflective surfaces, but rather the inducement of revelatory dream visions. The Egyptians had been famous for their dream interpretation, whether the dreams were induced or spontaneous, and the Greek magical papyri from Egypt contain instructions for obtaining a revelation in sleep:

according to one passage, the person seeking the vision goes to bed in the presence of a lamp fuelled with sesame oil mixed with cinnabar, and recites a prescribed formula; to ensure that the revelation is not lost to oblivion, he must have a small tablet nearby to write it down. No. 16 has the master write a series of sacred names within a double band on virgin parchment, plus specified names. Three times he conjures the names themselves, that they may send the angels Michael, Gabriel and Raphael to reveal whatever information he is seeking. The master then places this parchment beneath his right ear when he goes to sleep.

No. 41, designed to discover hidden treasure, is exceptional for the extent to which it blends magic with pious devotion:

> To know where a treasure is hidden, first a person must make a general confession of all his sins, under a waxing moon, on a Sunday, when the Sun is in Leo, early in the morning. And when you first arise, sprinkle yourself with holy water, saying the antiphon, *Asperges me, domine, ysopo*, etc., in its entirety. Then go to a crucifix and say before it, *Miserere mei, deus* [Ps. 50 Vulg.], in its entirety, gazing constantly at the crucifix, with utter devotion. And when you say these things, then say most devoutly and with contrite heart, 'O rabbi, rabbi, my king and my God, and Lord of lords, you who are creator of all things, hear the prayer which I, a wretched and unworthy creature, make, and [be mindful?] of your redemption in this hour and always, and may my unworthy cry come unto Thee.'
>
> When you have said this, go to your house and into your chamber, which should be thoroughly cleaned, and, facing east, say this prayer as devoutly as you can: 'O gracious Orient . . . strengthen my understanding in this work by the dominion of your kingdom, which is never lost. Guide and fear [?] me in this my supplication. And I pray you by your kings . . . that on the following night Haram, a benign spirit, may come to me in my sleep and enkindle my heart and my mind, that I may know how to find a treasure, if there is any in these parts or elsewhere, and may he lead me and make a sign there, so that I may know it as true, and [I may know] the truth itself. . . . I call out and implore that you may deign to send me a spirit of truth this night in my sleep, that he may reveal to me a hidden treasure.' Say this facing east, and on bended knees. Say this prayer three times.
>
> When you go to bed, say nine times, 'Orient, Orient, Orient, I pray, beg, and ask, O most benign Orient, that you may fulfil my petition and desire to respect my entreaties.' Then a spirit will come to you, who will not displease you, but will make you dream of a treasure, and will lead you directly to the place.
>
> The next morning, when you arise, give three portions of alms in honour of the great knowing King, and go out, accompanied or alone, to the place where

there is treasure in your home [?], and take it. When you have the treasure, have three masses sung: the first in honour of the Holy Trinity, the second for the sins of the deceased, the third for the safeguarding of your life, etc.

It is by no means surprising to find orthodox, traditional prayers used in the practice of magic, or for non-standard petitions to be referred to as prayers, or even for the magician to prepare himself by a regimen of confession and purification. The offering of alms and the subsequent celebration of three masses is perhaps less expected; in any case, what we have here is a mixture of magic and devotion that assumes no incompatibility between the two, and in the mind of the practitioner there presumably was no incongruity.[47]

POSSIBLE JEWISH SOURCES

Magical practices are often so widespread that it is impossible to trace specific patterns of transmission, and the divinatory rituals found in the Munich handbook are at least as widely diffused as any other magical techniques. Nevertheless, there is some reason to suppose that these divinatory practices show the influence of Jewish divination in particular. This should not be surprising, in the light of frequent suggestions that Christians learned or obtained their magic from Jews.[48] One might suspect that this theme merely reflects stereotypes of the reprobate Jew,[49] but there is nothing implausible about Christians seeking to amplify their own repertoire of magical practices by borrowing from those of a people antecedently categorized as having a reprobate subculture. The formulas of the Munich handbook, like those of the Greek magical papyri from antiquity, often imitate those of Judaism, as if in homage to a culture perceived as having superior magic. The centrality of the Tetragrammaton,[50] the occasional use of Hebrew letters, and the use of the pentacle of Solomon in Clm 849 and other necromantic texts are evident signs of Jewish influence, however indirect and distorted the transmission may have been. No. 42 gives 'the great name Semiforas' (meaning the *Shem ham-M'forash*) as a series of Hebrew and pseudo-Hebrew words beginning 'Saday, Hay, Resel'; the scribe seems uncomfortable with the material, and at one point leaves a blank space in his transcription of the name, but does recognize it as a Hebrew name for God, which he says was written on the forehead of Aaron the priest.[51]

Samuel Daiches has edited and analysed a series of Jewish magical texts that resemble the divinatory practices of the Munich manuscript closely.[52] Of special interest are the procedures in three manuscripts from the collection of Theodore Gaster. Codex Gaster 315 tells how to conjure the 'princes of the thumb' by tracing a circle in the earth with a black-handled knife and then placing a young boy in the circle, anointing the boy's thumbnail and forehead with pure olive oil, and whispering a conjuration into his ear while he gazes at his nail. The conjuration reads, in part, 'I adjure you, princes of the nail . . . that you should bring the king Minon in this nail, and the queen shall also come with him, and that his two servants shall come and that they shall bring there two lambs, one black and one white, and they shall slaughter them . . . and that they shall bring there three glass cups . . .' When the king and queen appear in the boy's nail, they should be invited to eat and drink, after which they will give all the information the operator desires.[53] Another ritual from the same manuscript, for conjuring 'the princes of the hand', requires invoking a series of names; if the boy sees nothing in his hand the master must repeat the invocation, then if necessary say, 'I adjure you, Ator, Sator, Somani, Ator' (a garbled version of the SATOR-AREPO formula). If the boy sees a man dressed in black he must have him don white garments, and then he invites him to eat and drink.[54] Similar rituals are prescribed in Codices Gaster 443 and 1,000. They all require as a medium a young boy (seven years old in one ritual) or girl, or in some cases a pregnant woman, in which case Daiches assumes it is the innocence of the unborn child that facilitates the divination.

The manuscripts Daiches uses are all late – from the sixteenth or seventeenth century, or, in the case of Codex Gaster 443, as late as 1775 – but Daiches argues for close parallels with much earlier Jewish and even Babylonian practice. One Babylonian ritual tablet of around 2000 BCE speaks of 'the master of the nail of this finger'; the slaughter of the lambs, the use of three cups, the invitation of the spirits to eat and drink, and the assurance that they will answer questions truly all find parallels in Babylonian divinatory texts. Rashi in the eleventh century referred to 'work of the demons' called 'princes of the thumb' that involved use of a black-handled knife, a glass cup, and so forth. Further evidence for the continuity of such practices in medieval Judaism comes from the *Sefer Hasidim* and related texts, which report visions in which demons or the spirits of the dead were summoned to appear in dreams or on reflecting surfaces, often to identify thieves or to locate lost objects. Around the turn of the thirteenth century, Jacob of Marvège recorded a series of dreams in which he received answers to questions he had posed (*she'elat halom*).[55] None of this evidence proves that the rituals found in the modern manuscripts preserve in detail the formulas used in medieval magic. Yet it seems likely that the divinatory rituals of the Munich handbook can be traced to medieval Jewish precedent, and thus indirectly to Babylonian prototypes; this is in any event more likely than the reverse, that the Gaster manuscripts contain Jewish borrowing from Christian sources.

AN EXPERIMENT FOR INSTRUCTION

The very first experiment in the Munich manuscript fits only loosely into the category of divination: it is intended for acquiring knowledge of all the liberal arts through the instruction of a demon. Because the first two folios of Clm 849 are missing, this experiment begins *in medias res*, yet even in truncated form the experiment is reasonably intelligible; in all likelihood there was either prefatory material or another experiment on folios 1 and 2, and only a small part of the present experiment has been lost. In the missing lines the magician is evidently instructed to take a piece of cloth and draw on it a 'circle', meaning a simple band made of two concentric circles, within which the names of various demons are to be inscribed. The markings on this cloth are to be made with the blood of a bird, perhaps a hoopoe, and evidently the magician is to use the heart of this bird as a writing instrument: at later points in the experiment reference is made to writing with 'the aforementioned blood' by means of a heart.

This experiment is built around four conjurations: the first, addressed to three "kings" among the demons, results in the initial presentation of a teacher to the magician; the second, again addressed to these kings, is for the return of the teacher and inception of lessons; the third, addressed to the same demons plus four others, is for the same effect; the fourth, addressed to the teacher himself, leads directly to his return and to the instruction. The magician commands the demons Apolin, Maraloth and Berith to send yet another demon as a teacher, or *magister*, a term used elsewhere in the manual for the magician himself.

> . . . toward the east. Then you must say: 'Apolin, Maraloth, Berith, I, so-and-so, exorcise and conjure you . . . to send me a certain spirit who is expert in teaching of all the sciences, and may he be kindly, faithful, and pleasing to me, and teach every knowledge that I desire, coming in the form of a master, so that I may feel no sense of fear. . . . Likewise, I conjure you . . . that you three great kings and companions of mine may endeavour to send to me, your petitioner, one of your subordinates, to serve as master of all the sciences and arts, coming to me in a pleasant and splendid human form, and instruct me lovingly, so that within thirty days I may acquire this knowledge, and after I have received this knowledge I may give them licence to withdraw.' And this must be said so many [=three?] times.
>
> When you have said this, put down the sword and wrap it in the aforesaid cloth, and, having made a bundle, lie down on it and sleep for a little while. After sleeping, rise and clothe yourself (for when the bundle has been made a man must undress and enter a chamber, placing this bundle beneath his head). You must know that when these conjurations have been said, sleep comes by divine power. In the sleep, three great kings [will] appear to you with countless servants, knights, and footsoldiers, among whom there will appear a certain master, whom the three kings will command. [You will see] him ready to come to you. For you will see the three kings, shining with wondrous beauty, who will speak to you in this sleep with one voice, saying, 'Behold, we give you what you have many times requested.' And they will say to the master, 'Let him be your student, and we command you to teach him every science or art

that he wishes to hear. Instruct and educate him so that within thirty days he will be regarded among others as supreme in whatever science he wishes.' And you will see him reply, 'My lords, I shall most gladly do whatever you wish.' When this has been said, the kings will depart and the master alone will remain, and will say to you, 'Arise, behold your master.' When this has been said, you will be aroused; at once you will open your eyes, and you will see a master, excellently attired, who will say to you, 'Give me the sword which you have beneath your head.' You will say, 'Behold your student, ready to do whatever you wish.' But you must have a tablet, and must write down all that he tells you.

First you must ask, 'O master, what is your name?' He [will] tell, and you must write it down. Second, from what order, and likewise write it down. When this has all been said, you must ask for the sword, and when you have it he will withdraw, saying, 'Wait until I return.' You will say nothing, but the master will leave and take the sword.[56] After his withdrawal, you must unwrap the cloth, as appears below. And you should write in this circle his name, as you have written it down, and you must write it with the aforementioned blood. When it is written, wrap up the cloth and hide it well.

When all this has been done, you must dine on bread and pure water alone, and that day you must not exit your chamber. And when you have eaten, take the cloth and enter the circle facing Apolin. Say: 'O King Apolin, great, powerful, and venerable, I, your servant, believing and wholly trusting that you are strong and mighty, ask by your incomprehensible majesty that your servant and subject, so-and-so, my master, should come to me as quickly as he can, by your virtue and power, which is great and supremely great unto ages of ages. Amen.' And you must speak likewise facing Maraloth, changing the name. And likewise facing Berich. When all this has been said, take some of the aforesaid blood and write your name in the middle of the circle with the aforesaid heart, as is shown below. Then write these names, as shown here, with this heart on the corners of the cloth. But if the blood of one bird is not enough, you may kill as many as you wish.

When all this has been done, sit in the circle for the entire day, gazing at it, and saying nothing. When evening comes, wrap up the cloth, undress, and enter the chamber, placing it beneath your head. And as you lie down, say in a clear voice, 'O Apolin, Maraloch, Berith, Sathan, Beliath, Belzebuc, [and] Lucifer, I implore you to command the master – here naming his name – to come to me tomorrow before sunrise and teach me thus-and-such science, without any error . . .'

Beware and take caution not to make the sign ✠ of the cross, on account of the great danger in sleeping. You should know that you will see the master speak with you throughout the night, asking you which science you wish to learn. You should reply, 'Thus-and-such', so that, as said, you may speak with him throughout the night. If you awake during that night, rise and light a candle, and take the cloth and unwrap it, and sit on it – that is to say, in the circle, where your name is written on the spot ordained for you – and call on the name of your master, saying, 'O so-and-so, of thus-and-such an order, given to me by your greater kings as a master, I beseech you to come in a kindly form and teach me thus-and-such a science, in which I may become more expert than all mortals, learning it with great joy, without any effort, and with no tedium. . . .'

When you have said this, looking toward the east you will see the master come with many students, and you will ask him to command that they all depart, and at once they will withdraw. Then the master will say, 'Which science do you wish to hear?' You will say, 'This-and-such', and then you will begin.

Bear in mind that you will learn all that he tells you and commit it to memory, and within thirty days you will acquire every science that you wish to have.

And when you wish him to leave the chamber, fold and hide the cloth, and at once he will withdraw. And when you wish him to come, open the cloth, and at once he will appear there, continuing the lessons. After thirty days, having become well learned in science, have him give your sword to you, and then tell him to go, and he will withdraw in peace. You must repeat what you have said when you invoke him to gain knowledge of another science, and he will proclaim himself ready to oblige your will.

This is the end of the chapter on [gaining] knowledge.

The circle required for this first experiment is a single band inscribed within a square. Inscribed in and around the band are the names of seven spirits and the four cardinal directions. 'The name of the master, of such-and-such an order' and 'The name of the student' are marked in the centre.

This experiment contains one incidental feature of some interest: the sword, which the demonic teacher claims at the beginning of the lessons but relinquishes to the magician at the end of the month when instruction is over, may be intended as a kind of sacrifice, albeit a temporary one. It serves, at any rate, to symbolize the relationship between the magician and the demon that exists throughout the thirty days of instruction: although the magician (as the source and ultimate owner of the sword) has conjured the demon and has authority to command his presence, the demon (as temporary keeper of the sword) exercises the authority over his pupil that comes from his possession of superior knowledge. It is only when the demon has imparted knowledge of all the liberal arts that the magician has become, to that extent, his equal and thus regains the sword.

One might suppose that the magician conceives the sword further as a symbol for the power brought by his newly gained knowledge, but the manuscript gives little indication of a coherent and consistent quest for power, least of all in the political sphere. It is true that the writer claims to have connections at court: in one experiment he reminds the reader, 'You have often seen me carry out this work at your court.' Elsewhere he tells of a trick that he played on an emperor and his courtiers. Even if we assume that this is not all pretence, however, the manual gives only meagre hints of specifically courtly interests. Only one experiment is designed to gain the favour of a potentate. Experiments to cause madness or to turn friends into enemies could be used at court, but could just as well be employed elsewhere. On the whole the manual is remarkably devoid of specifically political concern: there is little sense that the writer is intent on building or destroying kingdoms, nor does he display the combination of magical lore and practical engineering found in the real-life courtier Conrad Kyeser.[57] His procedures for divination seem to focus on personal rather than political matters. Some of the illusionist experiments bespeak the fanciful attitude toward magic often found in courtly romance: an illusory banquet is intended as an entertaining spectacle. The writer is perhaps here manifesting a distant fascination with courtly culture rather than a direct involvement in the life of any court. Any common necromancer, after all, might well fantasize about being called into the emperor's service and serving as Michael Scot was supposed to have served Frederick II.[58]

One might seek precedent here too in Jewish magic designed to foster learning. Formulas occur in various early Jewish mystical texts for mastery of the Torah. The assumption is that angels have opposed God's bestowal of the Torah upon humankind, and that this opposition accounts for students' failure to memorize the sacred text. The solution is to adjure the appropriate spirits, particularly the 'Prince of the Torah' (sar ha-torah), by the power of the sacred names; the specific purpose of such adjuration is to master and memorize the Torah.[59] More immediate precedent, however, may be found in the later medieval magic of the so-called ars notoria, which uses prayers and invocation of angels to gain mastery of the liberal and mechanical arts.[60] Although the ars notoria did not call upon demonic aid, and ostensibly revolved around the recitation of devotions to the Virgin and to unfallen angels, its techniques were untraditional and superstitious, and an unsympathetic observer might pardonably have categorized it with this first experiment in the Munich handbook.

It may also be instructive to compare the magic of this experiment with that narrated in a story told by Caesarius of Heisterbach, in the early thirteenth century, 'concerning a schoolboy who made homage to the devil to have verses composed':

> In the church of Saint Simeon in the diocese of Trier there was a little schoolboy. One day his master gave him a subject on which he was to compose

verses, but he was unable to do so, and sat about disconsolate. The Devil appeared to him in human form as he sat by himself, and said to him, 'Why are you so unhappy, little boy, and why are you sitting there looking so sad?' The boy replied, 'I'm afraid of my master, because I cannot compose any verses on the subject he has given me.' The Devil said, 'If you pay homage to me, I will compose the verses for you.' The boy was unaware that he was dealing with the Devil, the enemy of all, who was bent on mischief, so he replied, 'O yes, sir! I am ready to do anything you command, as long as I can have the verses and not get beaten!' For he did not know who it was. He stretched out his hand to the Devil, paying homage to him. At once he received the verses, written on tablets, and then he no longer beheld their writer. When he gave them to his master at the appropriate time, the latter was amazed at the excellence of the verses, and feared that the knowledge he found in them was supernatural [*divinam*] and not that of a human. He said, 'Tell me, who wrote these verses for you?' The boy said, 'I did, master.' But the master, not believing, repeated his interrogation of the lad many times over, until the boy confessed everything he had done, from beginning to end. Then the master said, 'My boy, that versifier was an evil one, the Devil himself.' Then he added, 'My dear child, are you sorry that you paid homage to that seducer?' The boy replied, 'O yes, master.' The master said, 'Now renounce the Devil and his homage, and all his pomps and all his works.' And he did so. Then the master cut off the sleeves of his surplice and offered them to the Devil, saying, 'These sleeves are yours, O seducer of men, but you will possess nothing more of this creature of God!' At once the sleeves were snatched away with a thunderbolt in the sight of all, while the boy's body remained unharmed. All this was told me by a prior from the church of Trier.[61]

The schoolboy's deed is both more innocent and more guilty than the necromancer of the Munich handbook: it is more innocent because he is unaware that the source of his verses is an evil spirit, and also because he does not conjure the spirit but merely accepts his offer, yet in itself his action is more profoundly guilty because he makes homage to the demon. Joseph Hansen sees the concept of homage to a demon as a high medieval innovation inspired by the obvious feudal analogue, the vassal's homage to his lord.[62] It seems to be only in orthodox literature condemning magic, however, that those who profit from the demons are seen as making such homage, or that sacrifices to the spirits are perceived as involving the same worship that would be implied by sacrifice offered to God. The magicians themselves, as in the Munich handbook, typically perceive any sacrifice as merely a *quid pro quo*. Oddly, the lad's schoolmaster recognizes that the demon has some legitimate claim on the boy as a result of the transaction, and offers the spirit the sleeves of the pupil's surplice (*superpellicii*) as his due, even after the boy repeats his baptismal renunciation of Satan's works and pomps. The most basic difference between the two cases, in any event, is that Caesarius's schoolboy, unlike the Munich magician, receives no new knowledge: he has polished verses handed to him but does not himself become an accomplished versifier. The quest of knowledge through magical means seems to be a theme more deeply embedded in Jewish sources, and in the Solomonic literature related to those sources.

Notes

1 M.R. James, 'Twelve medieval ghost-stories', *English Historical Review*, 37 (1922), 420f.

2 *Ambo simul euanuerunt ab oculis meis et amplius non video eos, et nescio sine dubio vbi sunt.*

3 See the analogues in Caesarius of Heisterbach, *The Dialogue on Miracles*, trans. H. von E. Scott and C.C. Swinton Bland, 1 (London: Routledge, 1929), 112–14. Barbara Newman has found parallels in several thirteenth- and fourteenth-century collections of exempla.

4 John of Salisbury, *Frivolities of Courtiers and Footprints of Philosophers*, ii.28, trans. Joseph B. Pike (London: Oxford University Press, 1938), 146–7.

5 *The Commonplace Book of Robert Reynes of Acle: An Edition of Tanner MS 407*, ed. Cameron Louis (New York: Garland, 1980), 169f.; C.L.S. Linnell, ed., 'The commonplace book of Robert Reynys of Acle', *Norfolk Archaeology*, 32 (1958–61), 114 (Linnell's edition of the text is badly flawed).

6 For the following see generally Benjamin Goldberg, *The Mirror and Man* (Charlottesville: University Press of Virginia, 1985), 3–25 (esp. 8–19), and Henry C. Bolton, 'A modern oracle and its prototypes', *Journal of American Folklore*, 6 (1893), 25–37. For early instances see W.R. Halliday, *Greek Divination: A Study of Its Methods and Principles* (London: Macmillan, 1919), 145–62 (which gives numerous parallels from various cultures) and A. Bouch–Leclercq, *Histoire de la divination dans l'Antiquité*, 1 (Paris: Leroux, 1879), 176–88.

7 Siegfried Wenzel, ed. and trans., *Fasciculus morum: A Fourteenth-Century Preacher's Handbook*, v. 30 (University Park: Pennsylvania State University Press, 1989), 578–9.

8 George L. Kittredge, *Witchcraft in Old and New England* (Cambridge, MA: Harvard University Press, 1929), 185.

9 See Peter J. French, *John Dee: The World of an Elizabethan Magus* (London: Routledge & Kegan Paul, 1972).

10 Domenico Comparetti, *Vergil in the Middle Ages*, trans. E.F.M. Benecke (London: Swan Sonnenschein, 1895), 303–5, citing the *Romans des Sept Sages*, *Cleomadès*, and the *Renart contrefait*. For parallels, see *ibid.*, p. 304, n. 9.

11 Charles Plummer, ed., *Vitae sanctorum Hiberniae*, 1 (Oxford: Clarendon, 1910), 150: *in speculo enim diuinitatis omnia futura sibi presentia erant.*

12 Johann Hartlieb, *Das Buch aller verbotenen Künste, des Aberglaubens und der Zauberei*, ed. and trans. Falk Eisermann and Eckhard Graf (Ahlerstedt: Param, 1989), chs 56, 83–84, 86, 88–90.

13 Ibn Khaldûn, *The Muqaddimah: An Introduction to History*, i.194, trans. Franz Rosenthal, 2nd edn, vol. 1 (Princeton, NJ: Princeton University Press, 1967), 216–17; Bolton, 'A modern oracle', 37.

14 Reading *intra* for *infra*.

15 Petrus Garsia, *In determinationes magistrales contra conclusiones apologales Ioannis Pici Mirandulani*

Concordie Comitis proemium (Rome: Eucharius Silber, 1489), sig. k iv verso through k v recto (the discussion continues through l ij recto); see Lynn Thorndike, *History of Magic and Experimental Science*, 4 (New York: Columbia University Press, 1934), 497–507.

16 Thorndike, *History of Magic and Experimental Science*, 3 (New York: Columbia University Press, 1934), 430.

17 *Registrum Radulphi Baldock*, ed. Fowler (Canterbury and York Series, 7), vol. 1, 144f.; Kittredge, *Witchcraft*, 187.

18 Paris, *Les grandes chroniques*, vol. 5, 269–72; *Recueil des historiens*, vol. 20, 633f., 710–12; G.G. Coulton, trans., *Life in the Middle Ages*, 1 (Cambridge: Cambridge University Press, 1928), 160–62. *Willelmi capellani in Brederode postea monachi et procuratoris Egmondensis chronicon*, ed. C. Pijnacker Hordijk (Amsterdam: Müller, 1904), 127–30.

19 Kittredge, *Witchcraft*, 80, 187, from David Wilkins, ed., *Concilia Magnae Britanniae et Hiberniae*, 3 (London, 1737), 393f.

20 Kittredge, *Witchcraft*, 187, from A. Hamilton Thompson, ed., *Visitations of Religious Houses in the Diocese of Lincoln* (London: Canterbury and York Society, 1915–), 208–13.

21 *Reports of the Royal Commission on Historical Manuscripts*, 8 (London: Eyre & Spottiswoode, 1881), 265; William Hale Hale, *A Series of Precedents and Proceedings in Criminal Causes from 1475 to 1640, Extracted from Act Books of Ecclesiastical Courts in the Diocese of London, Illustrative of the Discipline of the Church of England* (London: Rivington, 1847); 10f.; C. Trice Martin, 'Clerical life in the fifteenth century, as illustrated by proceedings of the Court of Chancery', *Archaeologia*, 60 (=ser. 2, vol. 10) (1907), 371f., 377; Kittredge, *Witchcraft*, 188, 195f

22 The demons' capacity for knowledge and foreknowledge is discussed in the influential work of Saint Augustine, 'The divination of demons', in Roy J. Deferrari, ed., *Saint Augustine: Treatises on Marriage and Other Subjects* (New York: Fathers of the Church, 1955), 415–40.

23 Peter Brown, *The Cult of the Saints: Its Rise and Function in Latin Christianity* (Chicago: University of Chicago Press, 1981), 106–13, esp. 109. Brown quotes Victricius of Rouen on the effects of exorcism: 'A torturer bends over the unclean spirit, but is not seen. There are no chains here now, yet the being who suffers is bound. God's anger has other hooks to tear the flesh and other racks to stretch invisible limbs.' The theme is one which Barbara Newman will address in forthcoming research on thirteenth-century accounts of exorcism.

24 Fol. 156r.

25 Translation from G.G. Coulton, ed. and trans., *Life in the Middle Ages*, new edn, 1 (Cambridge: Cambridge University Press, 1967), no. 46, pp. 85f.

26 Translation from C. Trice Martin, 'Clerical life in the fifteenth century, as illustrated by proceedings of the Court of Chancery', *Archaeologia*, 60 (=ser. 2, vol. 10) (1907), 377f.; see Kittredge, *Witchcraft*, 188.

27 Augustus Jessopp, *Random Roaming and Other Papers*, 2nd edn (London, Unwin, 1894), 109–12. Cf. Kittredge, *Witchcraft*, 94, 206.

28 Kittredge, *Witchcraft*, 195.

29 *Mary of Nijmeghen*, attributed to Anna Bijns, in Eric Colledge, trans., *Medieval Netherlands Religious Literature* (New York: London House & Maxwell, 1965), 208; repr. in Elizabeth Alvilda Petroff, ed., *Medieval Women's Visionary Literature* (New York: Oxford University Press, 1986), 364.

30 Nos 19, 24, 25, 27, 29, 30, 41 (not used); nos 18, 20, 23, 33, 38, 39, 40, 22, 28, 16 (not highly significant).

31 For examples of the use of a boy medium in antiquity, see Hans Dieter Betz, ed., *The Greek Magical Papyri in Translation, Including the Demotic Spells*, 1 (Chicago: University of Chicago Press, 1986), PGM IV.88, I.42, VII.540, V.370, IV.850, V.1 and VII.348.

32 No. 28 specifies that the boy should be under twelve. See also Rawlinson MS D 252, fols 109r–109v.

33 No. 22 in the Munich handbook; Rawlinson MS D 252, fol. 114v; Johann Hartlieb, *Das Buch aller verbotenen Künste*, ch. 84.

34 Nicholas Orme, 'Children and the Church in medieval England', *Journal of Ecclesiastical History*, 45 (1994), 580f.

35 Chs 86, 88, 94.

36 On these possibilities see James W. Fernandez, 'Reflections on looking into mirrors', *Semiotica*, 30 (1980), 27–39.

37 The writer's B and L might readily be confused, especially in the lower case; see, for example, the references to Belial in no. 12. One might syppose that Bylet is simply an alternative spelling for Lilit, but there is in fact a spirit known as Beleth, Bileth, Bilet or Byleth, on whom see Gustav Davidson, *A Dictionary of Angels, Including the Fallen Angels* (New York: Free Press, 1967), 73.

38 Lynn Thorndike, *Michael Scot* (London: Nelson, 1965), 120.

39 Ch. 89.

40 Rawl. 8v, 151v.

41 Chs 83–84.

42 In no. 41 he writes 'Tetragrammaton' (probably that word, though possibly the four letters for which it stands) beneath the boy's feet, then he puts two stones on top of this inscribed word, lest the boy touch the sacred name with his feet.

43 Betz, *The Greek Magical Papyri*, 1, pp. 40–43 (PGM IV.154–285).

44 Joseph Naveh and Shaul Shaked, *Amulets and Magic Bowls: Aramaic Incantations of Late Antiquity* (Jerusalem: Magnes Press, Hebrew University; Leiden: Brill, 1985); see Michael Ofori Mankata, *Hohore – the Magic Bowl: A Ghanaian Folk Tale* (Accra: Afram, 1995).

45 Chs 115–31. See also Charles Burnett, *Magic and Divination in the Middle Ages: Texts and Techniques in the Islamic and Christian Worlds* (Aldershot: Variorum, 1996), XII–XV.

46 The dream oracle of Besas, in Betz, *Greek Magical Papyri*, 1, pp. 122–23 (PGM VII.222–49). On Egyptian dream interpretation see Joseph Kaster, trans. and ed., *The Wings of the Falcon* (New York, 1968), 153–8.

47 Bodleian Library, MS e Mus. 219, contains a miscellany of magical experiments, among which are similarly pious recommendations on fol. 187v: to recover a lost object, recall the cross of Christ (which was found) and give bread to four paupers; to avert affliction, recall the blows of Christ; for release from captivity, recall that of Christ; to survive a duel, fast, give as much as possible in alms, have three masses sung (those for the finding of the Holy Cross, the exaltation of the Holy Cross, and the Ascension), and wash the hands and feet of three paupers (or five, seven or thirteen).

48 E.g., Edmond Albe, *Autour de Jean XXII: Hugues Géraud, éveque de Cahors: L'affaire des poisons et des envoûtements en 1317* (Cahors, 1904); Margaret Harvey, 'Papal witchcraft: the charges against Benedict XIII', in Derek Baker, ed., *Sanctity and Secularity: The Church and the World* (Oxford: Blackwell, 1973), 109–16.

49 On this subject see especially Joshua Trachtenberg, *The Devil and the Jews: The Medieval Conception of the Jew and its Relation to Modern Anti-semitism* (New Haven: Yale University Press, 1943), and more recently R. Po–chia Hsia, *The Myth of Ritual Murder: Jews and Magic in Reformation Germany* (New Haven: Yale University Press, 1988) and Jeremy Cohen, ed., *From Witness to Witchcraft: Jews and Judaism in Medieval Christian Thought* (Wiesbaden: Harrassowitz, 1996); on the reputation of Jewish magic in late antiquity see John M. Hull, *Hellenistic Magic and the Synoptic Tradition* (Naperville, IL: Allenson, 1974), 30–35.

50 Jacob Z. Lauterbach, 'Substitutes for the Tetragrammaton', *Proceedings of the American Academy for Jewish Research* (1931), 39–67; Kaufmann Kohler, 'The Tetragrammaton (Shem ham-M'forash) and its uses', *Journal of Jewish Lore and Philosophy*, 1 (1909), 19–32.

51 Robert Eisler, 'Le Mystère du Schem Hammephorasch', *Revue des études Juives*, 82 (1926), 157–9.

52 Samuel Daiches, *Babylonian Oil Magic in the Talmud and in the Later Jewish Literature* (London: Jews' College, 1913).

53 No. B1, text 1, pp. 14–16, with notes on pp. 28–38.

54 No. B1 text 2, p. 16, with notes on p. 38.

55 *Ibid.*, pp. 28–38; *Encyclopaedia Judaica* (Jerusalem: Keter; New York: Macmillan, 1971–2), articles on *Visions* and *Jacob of Marvège*.

56 If one reads *presentare* for *postulare*, the context becomes clearer: rather than asking for the sword, the magician must give it to the spirit; *quo habito* then becomes 'when he has it' rather than 'when you have it'.

57 Conrad Kyeser, *Bellifortis*, ed. and trans. Götz Quarg (Dösseldorf: VDI, 1967).

58 Charles Homer Haskins, *Studies in the History of Mediaeval Science* (Cambridge: Harvard University Press, 1924), 272–98; J. Wood Brown, *An Enquiry into the Life and Legend of Michael Scot* (Edinburgh: Douglas, 1897); Lynn Thorndike, *Michael Scot* (London: Nelson, 1965).

59 Peter Schäfer, *The Hidden and Manifest God: Some Major Themes in Early Jewish Mysticism*, trans. Aubrey Pomerance (Albany: SUNY Press, 1992), esp. 49–53, 73–5, 89–95, 109–17, 150–57; Michael D. Swartz, 'Patterns of mystical prayer in ancient Judaism', in Paul V.M. Flesher, ed., *New Perspectives on Ancient Judaism*, 6 (Lanham, MD: University Press of America, 1989), 173–86; and esp. Michael D. Swartz,, *Scholastic Magic: Ritual and Revelation in Early Jewish Mysticism* (Princeton, NJ: Princeton University Press, 1996).

60 Thorndike, *A History of Magic and Experimental Science*, 2 (New York: Macmillan, 1929), 281–3. Papers from a session on an *ars notoria* manuscript – Nicholas Watson, 'A fifteenth-century ritual magic manuscript in the McMaster University Library', Richard Kieckhefer, 'The historical background of the McMaster manuscript', and Michael Camille, 'Aspects of art in *ars notoria* manuscripts' – delivered at the 30th International Congress on Medieval Studies, Western Michigan University, Kalamazoo, Michigan, 5 May 1995, are to be published in a volume edited by Claire Fanger.

61 Caesarius von Heisterbach, *Die Fragmente der Libri VIII Miraculorum des Caesarius von Heisterbach*, ed. Aloys Meister (*Römische Quartalschrift für christliche Alterthumskunde und für Kirchengeschichte*, supplementary vol. 14) (Rome: Herder, 1901), 85f.

62 Joseph Hansen, *Zauberwahn, Inquisition und Hexenprozeß im Mittelalter, und die Entstehung der großen Hexenverfolgung* (Munich: Oldenbourg, 1900; repr. Aalen: Scientia, 1964), 275–7.

6

FORMULAS FOR COMMANDING SPIRITS: CONJURATIONS AND EXORCISMS

A collection of sermon *exempla* from the 1270s relates a story of considerable interest for later medieval notions of what it meant to conjure demons. The compiler has been discussing the feast of the Assumption, the primary Marian feast of the era, and adds this sidelight for its unexpected relevance to that occasion:

Something further concerning the feast of the Assumption of the glorious Virgin, which was once told to me and to Brother Roger called Bacon at Paris, must not be passed over in silence. A certain surgeon from my home country, and in fact even a native of my very parish, named Master Peter of Ardene, well known to all clerics from Ireland at that time, had taken a wife at Paris and in my day was a Parisian citizen. He told me and Brother Roger Bacon that a certain Spanish magician [*magus*] was on close terms with him. Every now and then he would summon the man, and they would come to his home for company and amusement. So this magician, wishing to return the favour for Master Peter, took him outside the city one night, with companions whom he wished to take with himself, and made a circle according to his art, and called upon his demon [*vocavit demonem suum*], who, on coming, responded to all the questions they asked. The man took them there for five nights, and each night dealt similarly with the demon he summoned. But the fifth night was the vigil of the Blessed Virgin's Assumption, so when the demon was called by the rite of the art as it was passed down he delayed his coming. And so he was summoned repeatedly, to the point that the devilish master became much agitated in regard to the devil. Finally the devil arrived, mourning and sighing, and with deep and plaintive sighs like a boy that has been beaten he said to them, 'You people are really strange [*Mirum est de vobis*], for the angels in heaven are celebrating the feast of the Virgin Mary, and you cannot take your rest here on earth!' Hearing this, they were astonished, and, not surprisingly, quite fearful. And Master Peter himself spoke to the demon, as he swore, taking pity on him, and said, 'What is your problem?' [The demon] said to him, 'Things are very bad for me.' Then they dismissed him and returned to their dwellings. So much for the story [*Explicit exemplum*].

Behold, O Christian, with what joy you should celebrate the Assumption of the Blessed Virgin, when even the devil, the enemy of the glorious Virgin, is compelled to preach that it should be celebrated, and when the angels celebrate it with so much festivity. When the devil said that he was very bad off amid this festive solemnity, the reason for this, as a great man whom I consulted about the matter suggested, is that on the solemnities of the Blessed Virgin and the saints their punishment is augmented. How this happens I leave to the judgement of those wiser than myself.[1]

Among the interesting features of this story, three are of particular relevance here: first, the suggestion that the demon can be made to appear, but that the magician's summons is one element among many in a cosmic network of potentially competing forces; second, the notion that the demons are subject to punishment with varying degrees of severity (so that, as we shall see, the magicians themselves can threaten to bring greater torment upon these fallen spirits); and third, the representation of the magician and his friends as adventurous inquirers daring to conjure the forces of hell to satisfy their curiosity and their quest of forbidden entertainment. The *exemplum* speaks of the magician as summoning the demon by a traditional rite, but, being uninterested in advertising techniques for necromancy, does not give the actual words of conjuration. From other sources, however, we know what such a rite would involve.

Central to most of the experiments in the Munich manual are formulas of varying length that hinge on the terms *coniuro*, *adiuro* and *exorcizo*, which are essentially interchangeable with each other and with other words meaning 'I command'. Indeed, the conjurations are so centrally important to necromantic experiments that the art of necromancy (as that term is commonly used in later medieval parlance) can even be referred to simply as the conjuring of spirits. Reduced to its generic essentials, the typical conjuration is in the form, 'I conjure you, thus-and-such spirits, by the holy names, by all the saints of God, etc., to carry out my will.' We may speak of the declaration ('I conjure you'), the address ('thus-and-such spirits'), the series of invocations ('by the holy names, etc.'), and the instruction ('to carry out my will') as the four primary elements virtually always found in conjurations. While each is of fundamental significance, they are important in different ways: the instruction indicates the nature of the command, the address makes it clear whom or what the necromancer is commanding, the declaration is the expression of intent to command, and the invocations are the sources of power by virtue of which he is able to command. In all these essential elements conjurations are analogous to exorcisms; indeed, the terms 'conjuration' and 'exorcism' are essentially interchangeable in medieval usage, regardless of whether the intent is to summon or to dispel the evil spirits.

Not all the verbal formulas used in the handbook are conjurations: there are also incantations that serve as glosses interpreting sympathetic magic (especially in the psychological experiments), and at times prayers addressed to God (especially in the *Book of Consecrations*, but note also that no. 22 speaks of a *coniuracio* with reference to the prayer *Deus, creator omnium rerum*, while no. 36 uses the term *oraciones* for a series of verses beginning 'I adjure you, King of kings and Lord of lords . . .').[2] But because the most common formulas are conjurations, it is entirely appropriate for necromancy to be known also as the art of conjuring demons.

The conjurations of the necromancer are in certain respects perhaps similar to the liturgical curses that Lester Little has analysed: they adapt ritual language to purposes that seem morally doubtful, although cursing a violator of monastic property rights might have appeared less problematic to a medieval monk than it does to a modern reader.[3] But while the necromancer's formulas do at times curse the spirits and threaten prospective victims,[4] in formal and structural terms the language of the conjurations does not closely resemble that of the curses Little discusses. Further, liturgical curses are inherently the communal acts of a community such as a religious house or cathedral chapter, whereas the conjurations express the will of a single necromancer. The curses assume direct divine agency, while the conjurations presuppose the compliance of created spirits.

The following (from no. 3) may be taken as a representative conjuration:

[Declaration:] I conjure **[Address:]** you demons inscribed in this circle, to whom is given the power of seducing and binding women in the love of men, **[Invocations:]**

- by the virtue and power of the divine majesty,
- and by the thrones and dominations and powers and principalities of Him who spoke and they were made,
- and by those [angels] who do not cease to cry out with one voice, saying, 'Holy, holy, holy, Lord God of Sabaoth, heaven and earth are full of your glory. Hosanna in the highest. Blessed is he who comes in the name of the Lord. Hosanna in the highest,'
- and by these names, which cause you fear and terror: Rator, Lampoy, Despan, Brulo, Dronoth, Maloqui, Satola, Gelbid, Mascifin, Nartim and Lodoni,
- and by this ring which is here,
- and by the innumerable powers that you and your superiors possess,

[Instruction:] that wherever you are, you should rise up from your places without delay and go to so-and-so, and immediately without deception lead her here, and take her back when I wish. And let no one be aware of this or take account of it.

More complex in its structure is this conjuration (from no. 7):

[Address:] O Vsyr, Salaul, Silitor, Demor, Zanno, Syrtroy, Risbel, Cutroy, Lytay, Onor, Moloy, Pumotor, Tami, Oor and Ym, arms-bearing spirits, whose role it is to bear arms and to deceive human senses wherever you wish, **[Declaration:]** I, so-and-so, conjure and exorcize and invoke you, **[Invocations:]**

  * by the Father and the Son and the Holy Spirit, who are called the holy Trinity,
  * and by the creator of heaven and earth and of all things, visible and invisible,
  * and by him who formed man from the mud of the earth,
  * and by the annunciation of our Lord Jesus Christ,
  * and by his nativity,
  * and by his death and passion,
  * and by his resurrection
  * and by his ascension.

Likewise, **[Declaration:]** I conjure **[Address:]** all you aforesaid demons **[Invocations:]**

  * by the gracious and most merciful and undefiled and incorrupt virgin Mary, the mother of our Lord Jesus Christ, who underwent death for us miserable sinners and recalled us to the heavenly fatherland.

Likewise, **[Declaration:]** I conjure **[Address:]** you aforesaid spirits **[Invocations:]**

  * by all the holy men and holy women of God,
  * and by all the apostles, martyrs, confessors, virgins and widows,
  * and by these most precious and ineffable names of the Creator of all, by which you all are bound, and which arouse fear in all things in heaven, on earth, and in hell, to wit Aa, Ely, Sother, Adonay, Cel, Sabaoth, Messyas, Alazabra and Osian.

Likewise, **[Declaration:]** I conjure and exorcize you **[Invocations:]**

  * by the virtue and power of all your princes, kings, lords, and superiors,
  * and by your virtue and capacity and power,
  * and by your dwelling place, of which this [circle] is the form,
  * and by all the figures present within it,

[Instruction:] that, inseparably bound to my power, you should come to me without delay, appearing in such a form that you will in no way frighten me, submissive and prepared to do and manifest to me all that I wish, and that you should do this by [the power of] all things on heaven and on earth.

To 'conjure' or 'adjure' someone meant basically to command him or her, and the terms had broad application. At one point in the Song of Songs the

Bridegroom says, 'I adjure you, daughters of Jerusalem, by the roes and the hinds of the fields, not to arouse or awake the beloved.'[5] In the Merovingian era, a Bishop Nicetius wrote in a letter to one Clotsinda, 'I conjure you, Lady Clotsinda, by the tremendous Day of Judgement, that you both read this letter carefully and often try to expound it to your husband.'[6] Even in this context, where the message is clearly political and has nothing to do directly with incorporeal spirits, the command is supported by appeal to an eschatological event. In the *vita* of Saint Brendan, one sea monster says to another, 'I adjure you in the name of Saint Bridget . . . to leave me alone,' and the efficacy of the adjuration becomes a sore point in Bridget's holy rivalry with Brendan, whose power the monster does not bother to invoke even though he, unlike Bridget, is physically present.[7] In a context closer to that of demonic magic, ghosts too might be conjured, as becomes manifest from a series of fifteenth-century ghost stories emanating from a Cistercian house in Yorkshire. The ghosts typically cause disruption to arouse the attention of the living, but it is only when they have been conjured or commanded by someone with spiritual power, and in the name of that which is holy, that they can speak and accomplish the business for which they have come back to earth. In one case, for example, a spirit who wished poshumously to confess his sins (allegedly including murder) had to be conjured by a parish priest 'in the name of the Holy Trinity and by the power of Jesus Christ' to answer all the priest's questions, whereupon he 'spoke from his inmost bowels, not with his tongue, but as if inside an empty barrel', and received absolution.[8]

The conjurations used in late medieval Europe are no different in principle from those used in other cultures, but the precise forms are in part culturally specific. In medieval Jewish conjurations, many of which survive from the Cairo Geniza, God's authority may be brought to bear on angels or demons to induce them to do the magician's bidding. These formulas are similar in their overall force but different in structure from the conjurations used within Christendom. Typically they are marked by six elements: first, the spirits are invoked in the name of God; second, they are adjured to perform specific tasks; third, the client is identified; fourth, the expected favours are listed; fifth, the requests are repeated and reinforced with quotations from the Bible and elsewhere, and sixth, the formulas conclude with a solemn liturgical 'Amen' or 'Selah'.[9] The resemblance to the conjurations of the Christian world is close enough that one might posit influence of Jewish magic on its Christian equivalent, but not so close as to prove simple and straightforward borrowing from one tradition to the other.

The conjurations of the Munich handbook are not always in the same form. One notable exception is a conjuration given in pseudo-Chaldean (no. 18): *Bismille araathe.* . . . This formula actually derives from an Arabic prototype: *Bismillahi ar-Rahmān ar-Rahīm*, the opening line of the Quran ('in the name of God, the merciful, the beneficent'), is a standard beginning to a Muslim invocation, and other words in the formula appear also to be garbled versions of Arabic. Shorter or longer texts of such pseudo-Chaldean appear elsewhere as well (nos 19, 20 and 21), but in these cases the very esotericism is more important than any vestigial structure.

Normally the language for conjurations in late medieval Western sources was Latin, but at times – perhaps most often when a young child was being used as a medium – the conjuration is translated into the vernacular. The Munich handbook instructs the master at one point to have the child conjure the spirit in the mother tongue (no. 27). In the Rawlinson manuscript, the text shifts to the vernacular particularly for formulas addressed to the spirits when they have come, in one case for a threat addressed to them if they do not come, and once for a 'binding' conjuration (*coniuracio ligacionis*); the intent in at least some of these cases may be that the master's young companion, who might be a mere beginner in Latin, should use the vernacular.

THE DECLARATION

One of the most widespread ways of distinguishing between magic and religion is the notion that magic is coercive whereas religion is petitionary. Martin Buber seems to assume such a contrast when he says that 'Magic desires to obtain its effects without entering into relation.'[11] Yet this distinction is questionable, partly because it is not a mode of distinction that would have been familiar to medieval Europeans, also because it provides little aid in disentangling magical and religious elements that tend to be inextricably intertwined or even fused. It seems more useful to view demonic magic as inherently a kind of religious activity, and natural magic as lending itself readily to the intermingling of devotional elements.[12] It is the case, however, that the necromancers typically saw themselves as commanding, constraining and binding the spirits they invoked, and one of the arguments most insistently made in the theological condemnations of magic in the late Middle Ages is that such constraint is in fact not possible.[13] The magicians' conception of what they were doing is signalled already in the very opening of a formula of conjuration: the declaration is a statement of intent, indicating how the conjurer perceived his relationship with the spirits. They saw themselves as having a power analogous to that by which Christ astonished those about him (Mk 1:27, Lk 4:36), that of commanding unclean spirits and compelling their obedience.

At times the declaration is simple and unrepeated: 'I conjure you' (*coniuro vos* or *coniuro te*) is by far the most common declaration, occurring fully 147 times in the Munich handbook; equivalent formulas, such as 'I order you', 'I adjure you', 'I exorcize you' and 'I invoke you', are also common.[14] Elsewhere the declaration is compound: 'I invoke and adjure you' or 'I conjure you and command you'.[15] In longer conjurations, the declaration may be repeated intermittently as a way of breaking the litany of invocations: 'I conjure you' is in six conjurations repeated once or twice, but may occur as often as five or even eleven times.[16] Elsewhere the recurring declarations vary in their form:

> I conjure . . . I conjure you . . . I conjure you and exorcize you [and] command you . . .

> I conjure you . . . I conjure you and call you to witness . . . I adjure you [followed by eight more occurrences of 'I conjure you'].

At times the recurrence and compounding of declarations becomes forceful and dramatic:

> I conjure you and exorcize you and call you forth . . . I conjure you . . . I conjure you and order and command you . . . I call you forth . . .

> I invoke you powerfully . . . I invoke and conjure you powerfully and exorcize you . . . I invoke and conjure and exorcize and constrain you . . .

> we exorcize and command you . . . we exorcize and manfully command you.

> I invoke you on behalf of [ex parte] the Father, I provoke you on behalf of the Son, I invoke you on behalf of the Holy Spirit[17]

Approximately 43 per cent of the time the second and following declarations are preceded by 'likewise' (item), which reinforces the sense and the force of the serial construction.

But while the declarations are most often statements of command, not infrequently they express supplication: 'I supplicate you'; 'I beseech you'; 'I beseech you, I supplicate you, I request of you'; 'I pray you'; 'I pray, ask, and entreat'.[18] Alternatively, the declaration may be one not of command alone but also of constraint ('I invoke, conjure, and constrain you'), a claim to yet higher power over the spirits.[19] A command may in principle be refused; coercion may not. As with humans, however, so too with demons, the distinction becomes blurred: a command supported by sufficient authority, or coupled with compelling threats, may be as compelling psychologically as brute force is physically.

THE ADDRESS

If the declaration is the conjurer's statement of intent, indicating how he perceives his action vis-à-vis the spirits, the address is the element in the conjuration that shows which spirits were being called upon – not an insignificant matter, either from the magicians' perspective or from the viewpoint of authorities investigating the practice of magic. The address is our chief source of information for the demonology and angelology of the magicians. This topic will be explored more fully in the next chapter, but may be touched upon here. The address is sometimes an apostrophe, in the vocative case ('I conjure you, O Brimer, Suburith, Tranayrt, Lyroth, Berien, Damay'), and sometimes an appositive phrase, in the accusative case ('I conjure all you demons inscribed on this ring').[20] While the spirits are commonly both named and characterized, the name and the description do not always occur in the same part of the conjuration. And the conjuration mentioned above refers first to 'all you demons inscribed on this ring' and then addresses them twice by name. When the declaration is repeated, the address is sometimes replicated exactly as it was first given, but frequently the later declarations addresses merely the 'aforesaid demons' (*prenominatos demones*), as often as ten or eleven times in a single conjuration.[21] When multiple demons are being conjured they are usually all named, but one conjuration addresses the demon Lylet along with her companions (*socii*), who remain unnamed.[22]

In divinatory experiments, not only the informing spirits but also the boy serving as the necromancer's medium are often conjured to tell the truth. In such cases the conjuration is addressed to the boy simply as *puer* (no. 22) or, more often, as 'young virgin' or 'virginal youth' (*virgo iuuenis*).[23] Less often, objects used in the experiments are at times conjured and thus addressed: an image or a cloak. Power-bearing names are also addressed ('O ye most holy names').[24] Two experiments have conjurations addressed to the spirit who has taken the form of a horse.[25] In most contexts, the beings whose support is most needed and whose resistance is most feared are the spirits, and they are thus the ones chiefly subject to the magician's conjuration.

THE INVOCATIONS

As the fundamental source of efficacy by which a conjuration works, the invocations call upon the sacred power of numinous beings, names and events, power that can be wielded against the addressees and can make them to carry out the master's will. For example, a conjuration in one experiment (no. 7) invokes the power of God; events in the life of Christ; various sacred personages (Mary, the saints, then specifically the apostles, martyrs, confessors, virgins, and widows); the sacred names of God (which bring great fear to 'all things in heaven, on earth, and in hell'); the power of the demons' own princes, kings, lords, and superiors; the spirits' own powers; their habitation, of which the circle is a representation, and 'all the figures present within it', although in fact there are no figures thus depicted. The invocations are strung together in a manner reminiscent of a litany, in most cases between two and eight in a single conjuration, but not uncommonly as many as twenty-four. Only four experiments, all divinatory and involving the cooperation of a child medium, have conjurations with more than twenty-four invocations, and one of these runs to fully fifty-eight.[26]

Invocations can be found in mainstream Christian prayers from the late Middle Ages as well as in conjurations. The *Obsecro te* found in the Little Office of the Blessed Virgin, invoked Mary by the joy she experienced at the Annunciation, by the tender care with which the Son of God entered her womb, by the joys she had in her Son, by the compassion she felt before the cross, and so forth.[27] The difference is that here the events are conceived as having psychological force: they are persuasive because they are remembered, and the point of the prayer is to call them to the Virgin's mind so that, moved by the recollection of what she herself experienced, she will have compassion on those for whom the events of Christ's life were performed – just as Christ himself is reminded of his Passion in the *Dies irae* and urged to mercy so that his suffering may not be in vain. In magical conjurations, the sacred persons, events, and objects cited serve more as powerful but impersonal weapons in a contest of wills, by which the magician may gain the upper hand over an unwilling spirit – as *arma nigromantica*, so to speak. A closer orthodox equivalent would be the petitions in the Litany of the Saints in which Christ is asked to 'free' humanity (*libera nos, domine*) by the successive acts of his life and death (*per natiuitatem tuam*, and so forth), but here the wording posits a natural and objective relationship between the sacred events and the desired effect: the normally expected effect of Christ's passion and death is to redeem humankind, not to give necromancers power over demons. Although the invocations are often by far the lengthiest in the elements of a conjuration, their meaning thus depends on the far shorter wording of the declaration and the instruction. If the purpose of the invocations is to call upon the sacred power of persons, objects and events, this power is like electricity, capable of running the most various machines and working diverse effects, both beneficent and brutally maleficent.

The subjects whose power is invoked fall into nine general categories. The examples given here are more than merely illustrative – they include the most common and significant cases within each category – but not exhaustive:

1. God:
'by God' (no. 20)
'by the Father and the Son and the Holy Spirit' (no. 11)
'by the undivided and inseparable Trinity in which are three persons, namely the Father, and the Son, and the Holy Spirit, who proceeds from both' (no. 8)
'by the Father and the Son and the Holy Spirit, to which every name is bowed [*sic* – cf. Phil. 2:10] and every tongue proclaims Hosanna' (no. 11)

'by the living and true God' (no. 25)

'by Him who is everlasting and eternal, and by Him who gave us the grace not to stand in Hell' (no. 8)

'by God almighty, by Jesus Christ his Son, and by his Trinity, and by that providence which God had in [His] mind before the world was made, by the wisdom of God's eternity by which he made heaven stand above and established and perfected the world below . . . and by the prudence by which God separated light from darkness and created both, by the Word of God by which he made heaven and earth . . .' (no. 39)

'by the creator of heaven and earth, and by Him who created all things for the praise and glory of his name, and by the living God, and by the holy God, and by the true God' (no. 43)

'by the virtue and power of the divine majesty' (no. 3)

'by the ineffable virtue and omnipotence of the creator' (no. 33)

2. Sacred names for God or Christ:

'by the names which strike fear and terror in you' (no. 3)

'by the holy names by whose power you are bound' (no. 1)

Tetragrammaton (*passim*)

Adonay (nos 1, 7, 10, 13, 23, 25, 27, 28, 33, 35, 39)

El (nos 14, 28, 33, 39)

Ely (nos 7, 14, 23, 25, 27, 28, 35)

Eloy (nos 25, 27, 28, 33, 35, 39)

Alpha et O (nos 10, 25, 27, 28, 33, 39)

Emanuel (nos 20, 23, 23, 25, 27, 28, 33, 39)

Messyas (nos 7, 10, 23, 27, 28, 39)

Soter (nos 7, 10, 25, 27, 28, 39)

Sabaoth (nos 1, 5, 7, 10, 13, 23, 25, 27, 33, 35, 39)

62 unspecified names of Christ (no. 39)

99 names spoken by the daughters of Israel (no. 33)

3. Events from the life of Christ (usually emphasizing the Passion):

'by the Incarnation of Our Lord Jesus Christ; by the baptism of Christ; by the fast of Christ; by the death of Christ; by the Passion of Christ; by the resurrection of Christ; by the ascension; by the coming of the Holy Spirit, the Paraclete' (no. 40)

'by the annunciation of Our Lord Jesus Christ; by the sacred fast of Our Lord Jesus Christ; by the baptism of Our Lord Jesus Christ; by the temptation of Our Lord Jesus Christ; by the passion of Our Lord Jesus Christ; by the 1,006 wounds of Our Lord Jesus Christ; by the 106 wounds of Our Lord Jesus Christ; by the 56 wounds of Our Lord Jesus Christ, not including the others from his head to his feet; by the crown of thorns which they placed on the head of Our Lord Jesus Christ, and they knelt down [and] mocked him, saying "Hail, king of the Jews"; by the reed and the blows with which they struck Christ; and by the three nails; by the lance with which the sacred body of Our Lord Jesus Christ was pierced, and at once blood and water flowed out; by the outburst of the holiness of Our Lord Jesus Christ, "Into thy hands I commend my spirit"' (no. 38; cf. no. 39)

4. The saints:

'by all the holy men and holy women [*sanctos et sanctas*] of God'

'by the four evangelists, Luke, Mark, Matthew, [and] John; by the four sermons; by the twelve apostles; by the three magi, Caspar, Balthasar, [and] Melchior; by the patriarchs [and] prophets; by the martyrs and confessors; and by all the popes of Rome, and all the virgins and widows; and by all the bishops; and by all the abbots; by all the priors; by all the provosts; by all the archdeacons; and by all deacons; by all monks; by all nuns; by all priests; by all deacons and subdeacons; by all the saints of God; by the merits of all the saints; by all the Christian people; and by all the saints who are in heaven and on earth; and by the 144 thousand innocents . . .' (no. 38)

'by the faith of the prophets, by the proclamations of the patriarchs, by the dignity of the twenty-four elders, by the creed of the apostles, by the passion of the martyrs, by the confessing of the confessors, by the chastity of the virgins, by the gospels of the evangelists . . .' (no. 39)

by the virginity of Mary, John the Evangelist, Catherine, Agatha, Cecilia, and Barbara (nos 27, 28).[28]

'by all the bodies of the saints that lie in Rome' (no. 12)

5. The Virgin Mary:

'by Saint Mary the virgin' (no. 29)

'by the gracious and most merciful and undefiled and uncorrupt virgin Mary, the mother of Our Lord Jesus Christ, who, dying for us wretched sinners, called us to the heavenly fatherland' (no. 7)

by her virginity (no. 28)

by her tears (no. 40)

by her milk (no. 12)

by her names – Queen, Flower, Rose, Lily, Ladder, Wisdom, Life, Sweetness, Mercy, and Hope (no. 10)

6. The angels:

'by the angels and archangels, thrones and dominations, principalities, powers, virtues of the heavens, cherubim and seraphim' (no. 40) 'by the thrones, dominations, powers, and principalities of Our Lord Jesus Christ; and by all the angels and archangels who dwell before the throne of God, crying out with one voice, "Holy, holy, holy, Lord God of Sabaoth, heaven and earth are full of your glory. Hosanna in the highest. Blessed is he who comes in the name of the Lord. Hosanna in the highest."' (no. 9)

'by the nine orders of angels' (no. 29)

by the archangels Michael, Gabriel and Raphael (no. 38)

7. Material creatures:

'by all things that were and are and will be' (no. 2)

'by all things that exist beneath the heavens' (no. 35)

'by all the powers of heaven and earth' (no. 35)

'by heaven and earth, by the sea, by all things that are in them, by all emperors, by all kings, by all princes, by all counts, by all knights, by all citizens' (no. 38)

'by all things that the four parts of the world contain, and by the ages of the world, and by all animals that exist beneath the heavens, and by serpents and flying things, bipeds, tripeds, quadrupeds' (no. 40)

'by heaven and earth, the sea and hell, and all things existing in them' (no. 11)

by the heavenly and earthly Paradise (no. 10)

'by the eternity of all creatures' (no. 5)

by the five *secula* and seven *etates* of the world (no. 39)

'by the Sun and Moon and all the heavenly stars, and by all those things which have [power] to frighten and constrain you, and by the power of which it behoves you to come to us who summon you' (no. 6)

'by all things which have [power] to terrify, constrain, and bind you, and whose command it behoves you to fulfill completely' (no. 11)

'by your virtue and power, and by all things that have power against you' (no. 11)

by the sacraments of baptism (no. 33)

by the eucharist (nos 12, 38, 39)

by the four rivers of Paradise (no. 8)

8. The Last Judgement:

'by the fearful day of judgement' (no. 35)

'by the fearful day of judgement of God most high, and by the fiery consumption, and by the glassy sea which is before the gaze of the divine majesty, and by the four animals . . . before the throne of the divine majesty, with eyes before and behind' (no. 33)

'by the fearful day of judgement, on which you are all to be damned' (no. 40)

9. The rulers of the demons:

'by Toth, your prince; by Zambrim et Mambrim; by Vsuel [and] by Saduel, to whom you are held to obey and tell the truth' (no. 33)

'by the power and dignity of Lucifer, Aphaleon and Neutrion' (no. 8)

'by your master Astaroth' (no. 40)

'by all your princes, kings, lords and superiors, and by your hell, and by all those things that exist in it'. (no. 10)

'by the virtue and power of all your princes, kings, lords and superiors, and by your [own] virtue and potentiality and potency [*possibilitatem ac potenciam*], and by your dwelling place, of which this [circle] is a form, and by all the figures abiding in it' (no. 7)

The invocations used by far most often and consistently are those in the first two categories – those appealing to the power of the divine persons, powers and names. Of these, the most common is the Tetragrammaton, the *nomen altissimum* in no. 14, spelled *Tetragramaton* (nos 1, 10, 13, 14, 25, 27, 28, 35), and also produced as Y-V-E and HX-V-V-HV, while Y-V-E-X is given as a name used by Abraham (no. 33).[29] The most extended and perhaps the most interesting series of invocations referring to the divine names is one (no. 33) with thirty-one specific names associated with events from salvation history, particularly the Exodus:

> We exorcise and command you by the most mighty and potent name of God, El, strong and wondrous; by Him who spoke and it was made; by all his names; and by the Name YVE, which Moses heard and spoke . . . and by the name YVEX, and with the name [Y]V[E]X, which Abraham heard, and he knew the almighty God; and by the name Joth, and with the name Joth, which Jacob heard from the angel accompanying him, and he was freed from the hand of his brother Esau; and by the name Eyzaserie, and with the name Eyzaserie, which Moses heard on the mountain, and he merited to be now with God, and to hear him speaking in the flame; and by the name Anathematon, and with the name Anathematon, which Aaron heard, and he became eloquent and wise . . .

This conjuration proceeds to invoke the names the names Sabaoth, Oristion, Eloy, Yephaton, Arbitrios, Elyon, Adonay, Pantheon and Arimon, by which Moses caused the plagues in Egypt; Geremon, by which he freed the Israelites; Yegeron, by which he divided the Red Sea; Anabona, by which he merited to receive the tablets of the law; Egyryon, by which Joshua overcame his foes; Patheon, by which David was saved from Goliath, and so on.[30]

Names for Christ are sometimes derived from biblical images, especially in one extended series (no. 39):

Messyas, Sother, Emanuel, Sabaoth, Adonay, Panthon, Panthocrathon, Eloy, Theos, Hon, Vision, Saviour, Alpha and Omega, First and Last, First Born, Beginning and End, way, truth, and wisdom, virtue, Paraclete, I am who am, who are, mediator, lamb, sheep, ram, calf, serpent, kid, Word, image, glory, grace, salvation, light, salt, peace, splendour, bread, font, vine, shepherd, prophet, undying hope, king, father, almighty, merciful, eternal, highest good, Trinity, unity, Father, El, Eloy, Eloe, Eleon, Saday, Symator, Tu, Ye, Ye, Prince of Peace, Enstriel, spirit, fear, goodness, thou, unity of unities, threefold godhead.

Occasionally names for God are derived from Hebrew or Greek liturgical formulas: AGLA (no. 33), the common magical abbreviation for the Hebrew *Ata gibor leolam Adonai* ('Thou art mighty for ever, O Lord'); *Theos* (no. 39), *Yschiros* (no. 28), and *Athanatos* (nos 28, 33), names derived from the liturgical *trisagion*, taken over into the Latin liturgy of Good Friday in the original Greek); *Eleyson* (no. 28), from the *Kyrie eleison*. Other names derived from Greek titles are *ho ōn* (nos 14, 23, 27, 28, 33) or simply *Hon* (no. 25) ('The Existing One'), and Pancraton (nos 28, 33) or Panthocrathon (no. 39), presumably variants on *Pantocrator*, 'the Almighty' or 'Ruler of All'.[31]

In short, what Joseph Kaster says about mastery of the divine names in ancient Egyptian ritual applies in Jewish and Christian contexts as well: 'whoever knows the god's real name, secret and ineffable and taboo, has control over him in the sense that he can evoke his power. In all ceremonial magic, the essential portion of the spell is the calling forth of the spirit or deity by *name*; when he is evoked by his real name, he must work the desire of the magician who "controls" him. This is "a name to conjure with".'[32]

On occasion the names of the demons, like those of God and Christ, are represented as possessing power: one invokes the demonic names Apolyn, Gebel, Astaroth, Tereol, Falmar and Tyroces (no. 5); another has an invocation 'by the name of your highest prince' (no. 27).

Certain conjurations invoking events from the life of Christ make explicit what is presumably implied elsewhere, that they are calling not so much upon the events themselves as upon the power manifested in the events: 'by the power by which Our Lord Jesus Christ entered in to his disciples when the doors were closed' (no. 35); 'by the power of Our Lord Jesus Christ, to wit that for us humans he descended from heaven and was born of the virgin Mary, suffered under Pontius Pilate . . .' (no. 38).

On rare occasions the invocations appeal to the very practice of magic, whether historical or present: spirits are conjured by 'all the experiments of Virgil [the necromancer]' (no. 38),[33] by the ring brought for the experiment (no. 3), or by the magical circle used for the experiment, 'by which you are effectively called forth' (no. 9). In view of the magical powers often ascribed to Solomon, it is not surprising to find his rings invoked, along with the signs and names inscribed on them (nos 28, 33); his seven signs, his seal, and his characters (nos 27, 38); or his wisdom (nos 12, 30, 38).[34] Often the invocations show a preference for saints grouped in threes: most especially the three magi, Caspar, Balthasar and Melchior; also the three young men Sydrac, Mysaach and Abdenago and the three patriarchs Abraham, Isaac and Jacob.[35] The virgin child medium conjures spirits by his own virginity, and the master conjures him by the virginity he has maintained and the baptism he has received (nos 27, 28).

When Oriens is conjured, the invocations refer to his own dignities and subordinate spirits: 'by your kings, and by all your royal powers; by Sotuem [and] Sortfen; by your Sun, a most holy and sacred radiant treasure, bright and shining, which your excellence sends forth and which your manifest and benign power sends back; and by all your dignities and commands' (no. 41).

A conjuration from the supplementary material in Clm 849 commands the demons by virtue of two biblical analogies:

> O you demons, and all princes and every kind of demons, whom your guilt cast out from heaven on high, I adjure you and order you to obey my command and my precepts. Just as God commanded the Jordan and it stood still that the children of Israel might walk across without hindrance, so to I command you to obey my precepts day and night, at all hours and moments, [and be subject] to my precepts. Just as the Red Sea obeyed Moses and Aaron when it divided and presented a dry path for the children of Israel, so by invocation of Our Lord Jesus Christ I command you to obey me without delay, without harm or deception to me or any living thing . . .[36]

The Rawlinson necromantic manuscript, too, uses analogies in some of its conjurations: as Christ was 'fixed' to the cross by the Jews, so may the aerial spirits be 'fixed' by the power of the holy names; as the almighty Father (*sic!*) lay in the tomb for two days and arose on the third day, so may the aerial spirits rise up and come forth; may the master proceed securely along his way, as Jesus proceeded through the midst of his enemies and none of them laid a hand on him because his hour had not come.[37] These formulas are similar in form to invocations, and presumably the intended force is the same: the purpose of the analogy is presumably not only to clarify what the conjurer intends (in which case it would be ancillary to the instruction) but to call upon the power of the sacred event that is recalled.

THE INSTRUCTION

The part of the conjuration directing the addressee what to do is typically introduced with the conjunction meaning 'that' (*ut*, or sometimes *quatenus*, more rarely *quod*). The formula of instruction may be repeated once, twice, or more often (in one conjuration for experiment no. 39 as many as ten times), in which case the manuscript may give the full version only the first time and only the incipit for subsequent occurrences.[38] Necromantic texts sometimes speak of 'obediencial conjurations', intended to compel the spirits' submission; 'bonds' or binding conjurations such as the 'bond of Solomon' (*vinculum Solomonis*), used in the Munich handbook's divinatory experiments to keep the spirits from departing until they have answered all questions;[39] and 'licencial conjurations', dismissing the spirits and requiring them to return at the magician's will.[40] The conjurations found in the Munich handbook, however, can most usefully be divided into 'summoning conjurations' and 'executing conjurations'.

Summoning conjurations are used to instruct a spirit or spirits to come before the necromancer ('that you come in a benign form', 'that you should come to me', 'that you should have no rest until you come to me', 'that you should at once proceed here', or 'that you should be compelled to come here').[41] They may be commanded to appear in a reflecting surface as part of a divinatory experiment ('that you should all appear') or to send another spirit or spirits for that purpose ('that you should command your master that he himself should come', 'that you should take pains to send one of your subordinates', 'that you should send me a certain spirit', 'that you should have your subordinates come here', 'that you, N., should make spirit N. come to me').[42]

Executing conjurations, which require the spirit or spirits to carry out the will of the master, are more varied in proportion to the various purposes of the experiments. In psychological experiments the spirits are enjoined to affect the minds and hearts of the individuals singled out as victims ('that you should sow and stir up hatred between them', 'that you should seduce the heart and mind of N. to my love', 'that you should never have rest until you make her heart burn with my love').[43] In divinatory experiments involving a young boy as medium, either the master or the boy may conjure the father of lies or his minions to tell the truth, or the master may conjure the boy himself to do so ('that you should relate to us whatever you see', 'that you should tell me the truth', 'that you should show me the truth', 'that you should have no rest unless you reveal to this boy the thief and the theft').[44] The spirits may be instructed to make possible the conditions for the bestowal of information – to enlighten the boy's mind, or to cause his fingernail to grow bright and appear large.[45] These conjurations may even involve the explicit insistence that the spirit or the child not lie, nor even have the power to conceal or deceive ('that you should have no power of concealing, but should manifest all that you see').[46] The spirits may be conjured to entrust a treasure to the master ('that you should leave me a treasure'), to fetch and replace a woman ('that you should go to so-and-so and immediately fetch her here, and return her when I wish'), to guard some object, not to harm the master in the course of the experiment ('that you should have no power to harm me'), to protect the master ('that you should forthwith have these terrors removed', 'that you should avenge me against him who is trying to harm me'), or to obey the master's command generally ('that you should obey my command').[47] The child medium may be conjured not only to tell the truth but, at an earlier stage, to gaze into his fingernail ('that you should gaze into [your] nail and see whether it becomes bright or not').[48]

In some conjurations, to be sure, the distinction between summons and execution breaks down. In divinatory experiments the spirits may be simultaneously commanded to come, to make themselves seen, and to provide information ('that you should appear to me and give true responses', 'that you should come and appear and tell me the truth', 'that you should come and appear and reveal this to us', 'that you should appear and respond and reveal all the truth', 'that you should appear and reveal to us the truth', 'that you should come and answer me and tell the truth').[49] Elsewhere they may told to come and bring an object ('that you should come to me, bringing a consecrated ring'), to come and transport the necromancer ('that you should come to me without delay, and carry me to such-and-such a place'), to come and consecrate an object ('that you should come here and consecrate this ring'), or simply to come and fulfill the master's will ('that you should come to me and carry out my entire will').[50]

Executing conjurations need not be addressed to the spirits by whose power the operation is done. Experiment no. 12 contains two instructions to the woman whose passionate love is required, although the second of these vacillates between the second and the third person: 'that you should be unable to sleep until you complete my libidinous desire' and 'that, as the hart longs for the fountain of water [Ps. 41:2 Vult.], so you, N., should long for my love; and as the raven longs for the carcasses of dead people, so you should long for me [*sic!*]; and as this wax melts before the fire, so you, N., should long for my love, so that you are unable . . .' In experiment no. 11, for a cloak of invisibility, the master conjures the cloak itself 'that no one may be able to see me'. In the simple experiments to obtain a horse, as in the complex experiment to procure a flying throne, the master conjures the horse or the throne to transport him, usually to a specified location ('that you should carry me', 'that you should lead me to such-and-such a place').[51]

A BOND OF SATAN OR MIRAGE

One lengthy conjuration appears both in the Munich necromancer's handbook (no. 32) and again twice in the appended material; versions of it by three different hands are thus included in Clm 849.[52] The two isolated versions, which agree quite closely in their wording, are addressed to the demon (or 'ancient serpent') named Mirage; the version incorporated into the manual, which differs markedly from these at many points, addresses the Devil, or Satan, 'most wicked enemy of the faith, death of the human race, tempter of righteousness, lover of evils, root and kindling of vices, seducer of humans, and master', 'most wicked dragon', 'accursed and most mendacious spirit' and 'author of diabolical power, inventor of evils'. The conjuration begins anomalously with a statement regarding the powers being brought to bear against the Devil ('may the angels and archangels accuse you . . . may the elect of God accuse you'), followed by a prayer for divine aid ('God . . . I invoke your holy name . . . I humbly implore that you may deign to give me aid against this spirit Satan'). These elements are followed by simply commands addressed to the spirit himself ('Hear, therefore, Devil . . . come forth . . . I adjure you . . . to be subject to my commands and carry them out'). The instructions are for the most part purely generic: 'I adjure you . . . to do quickly whatever I command you', or 'to do quickly whatever I order and command of you', or 'I adjure and constrain and command you . . . to obey me without any impediment or harm or wound or affliction to my body or soul'. At the end, however, the instruction is specific but allows for such variation that the effect is still to make this a generic conjuration, for virtually any purpose:

> [Come] to me in this hour, without any harm or injury or affliction to my soul or my body, or send another [spirit] or have him come, who will know perfectly how to fulfil my every desire, and will not withdraw from me until I have given him leave and he has fully satisfied my will. I conjure you by all that is written above to make a spirit come to me carrying gold and silver [coins] and [hidden] treasures, before I withdraw from this place. And as often as I invoke him, let him appear at once, benign and humble, harming no one, and ministering to me in all things, and fulfilling my will. So be it, so be it, amen. And bring or send me a spirit willing and competent in all knowledge. May he have the power to make me invisible whenever I wish. And let him please me, and be always under my power. And provide him also with the power to consecrate books and experiments, and everything that I wish. Amen, amen, amen.

Repeatedly the will of the conjuror is identified with that of God: the spirit is told that God himself commands him, or that the conjuror does so not by his own power but by that of God, or 'by the power which I have over you, Mirage, given me by God almighty in baptism and the other sacraments'. At one point the conjuration reads, 'The Word made flesh commands you, He who was born of the virgin commands you, Jesus of Nazareth commands you, He who created you commands you to carry out quickly what I ask or wish to have from you or desire to know; the more you delay in doing what I command you, the greater will be your punishment from day to day.' The reminder of the punishment awaiting the spirit on the Day of Judgement, and the threat of heightened torment as a penalty for disobedience, is also repeated – somewhat as elsewhere (no. 2) a spirit is threatened with being cast forever into the depths of the sea.[53]

The conjuration of Mirage, from the supplementary material in the codex, is followed by material that the main block does not take over: a set of instructions for constructing a circle in a secret location, with various prayers, and supplementary conjurations in which Mirage is threatened with intensified pains if he does not present himself: 'If not, I exorcize you that the chains of your punishment may be rife with sulpur and pitch.'[54] The spirit is to be conjured a second and third time, if necessary, but no more.[55]

EXORCISMS AND CONJURATIONS

Adolf Franz published a lengthy formula of exorcism taken from a West Frankish manuscript of the ninth century, which reads in part:

> . . . I conjure you, Devil, Satan, Enemy,
> - by God the Father almighty;
> - and by those virtues which the Lord himself made and makes;
> - by those angels he has before himself in [his] mind; . . .
> - by those four animals which uphold the world itself;
> - by every good creation that God has made in heaven and on earth;
> - and by the light and the earth and all its creeping things;
>
> by all these things I conjure you that you should not have power to remain, for he commands you who ordered you to be cast down from the kingdom of heaven on high. Hear, therefore, and be afraid [*Audi ergo et time ergo*], Devil, Satan, Enemy; you are banned, and again I speak to you and conjure you
> - by that king who rules and commands all things . . .
>
> Again I have said to you, O infernal enemies, by all things that I have had in mind for you [in] so great a conjuration as this, that you should not have power to remain or to do harm or to rebel. . . . I exorcize you, O accursed one, most unclean spirit, basilisk dragon, noxious serpent . . . that you should go out from this temple of God . . . I exorcize you, O unclean spirit, author of sins, deceiver of souls, envious one, insatiable homicide who endeavoured to kill the immortal man whom God created by his power. . . . In the name of Our Lord Jesus Christ I adjure you, O enemy . . . I conjure you and entreat [*obtestor*] you, O enemy, [that] you should not have power to remain here in this person's soul or body . . . I adjure you
> - by the gates of Paradise;
> - by the six golden candlesticks [Apoc 1:12]. . .
>
> I speak to you in truth, O unclean spirit, dragon, I adjure you,
> - by the Holy Spirit;
> - I adjure you by the six fiery furnaces;
> - I adjure you by the cherubim and seraphim;
> - I adjure you by the wings of the winds;

- I adjure you by the mystery of Christ's [passion];
- I adjure you by the resurrection of Christ the Lord;
- I adjure you by the precious pearls;
- I adjure you by the years [and] by the days;
- I adjure you by the passion of the saints;
- I adjure you by him who who freed the people Israel from the Red Sea, who freed Daniel from the lion's den, who illumined the blind, healed the paralytics, [and] cleansed the lepers.

I adjure you now by him, O enemy, unclean one, inveterate dragon, [that] you should depart from the soul and withdraw from the body or from all the inward parts of [this] servant of God. . . .

It is not I who command you, nor my sins, O most unclean spirit, but the immaculate lamb, Jesus Christ Our Lord, the Son of God, commands you.

The angels press upon [*urguent*] you, the archangels press upon you, the prophets press upon you, the apostles press upon you, the martyrs press upon you, the confessors press upon you. Therefore may the arts of the Devil fail [*defici[a]nt ergo artes diaboli*] by day [and] by night . . .

I exorcize you, O author of diabolical power, inventor of malice . . .[56]

The essential elements of this formula are exactly those seen in necromantic conjurations of a much later era. There are, to be sure, distinctive embellishments. First, the devil being expelled is not only named (Devil, Satan, Enemy) but characterized: he is the 'accursed one, most unclean spirit, basilisk dragon, noxious serpent', or the 'unclean spirit, author of sins, deceiver of souls, envious one, insatiable homicide who endeavoured to kill the immortal man whom God created by his power', and as the 'author of diabolical power, the inventor of malice', and so forth. Second, he is expelled from the energumen's body as well as his soul. Third, it is expressly said not merely that the exorcist commands in the name of Christ (as in Acts 16:18) but that Christ himself is the one who commands, even if through the exorcist. Fourth, various sacred figures are represented as participating in the exorcist's struggle with the malign spirit: the angels, archangels, prophets, apostles, martyrs and confessors all place pressure upon the possessing devil (*urguent*, for *urgent*), or denounce him (reading *arguunt*). And fifth, the second-person address is interrupted with a third-person subjunctive urging that the Devil's arts or snares may come to naught. The essential structure of the formula remains unaffected by these elements, but the network of relations is rendered more complex. The exorcist insults the spirit with whom he is engaged in struggle, identifies his own action as that of Christ, and calls upon the angels and saints not simply as possessors of power that can be tapped through invocation but as active participants in the contest. The representation of the exorcism as a cosmic combat, perhaps a local instance of that apocalyptic conflict that Christ initiated in his own exorcisms and carried forward in his passion and resurrection, here becomes exceptionally dramatic and explicit.

As already indicated, the conjurations of the necromancer are identical in form to the exorcisms designed to dispel demons. The resemblance may be seen in a manual for exorcizing the possessed that was printed several times in the late fifteenth century went by the title *The Conjuration of Malign Spirits Dwelling in the Bodies of People, as it is Done in Saint Peter*.[57] The simplest form of exorcism used here is simply, 'I exorcize you, unclean spirit, in the name of God the Father almighty ✠ and in the name of Jesus Christ his Son ✠ and by the power of the Holy Spirit ✠ that you should recede from this servant of God, N.' Like the conjurations of exorcists, however, the formulas used here become extended through repetition of the instruction and through numerous invocations:

I conjure you, O Devil, by the Father and the Son and the Holy Spirit, and by the patriarchs and prophets, apostles, evangelists, martyrs, confessors, virgins, and all the holy men and holy women of God . . . and by our Lord Jesus Christ I conjure you, that you should recede from this servant of God, N. I conjure you, O Devil, by the passion of our Lord Jesus Christ, which he endured for the human race, that you should recede from this servant of God, N. I conjure you, O Devil, by the holy cross on which our Lord [died for] the servant of God, N., that you should not be able to conceal yourself in his body, nor in his members, nor in his head. I conjure you, Devil, by the nails of our Lord Jesus Christ, by which his hands and feet were affixed to the cross, that you should withdraw from this servant of God, N., that you not be able to conceal yourself in his mouth or head. I conjure you, Devil, by the lance that Longinus held, by which he pierced the side of our Lord Jesus Christ, and blood and water flowed out, that you not be able to conceal yourself in his throat or on his tongue or under his tongue, or in his other members. I conjure you, Devil, by the death and burial of Christ, from which he rose from the dead on the third day, that you not be able to conceal yourself in his bowels or inward parts. I conjure you, Devil, by the resurrection of our Lord Jesus Christ, in which he appeared to his disciples, saying, 'It is I, do not be afraid,' and he commanded them, saying, 'Go into all the world and preach the gospel to every creatures; he who believes and is baptized will be saved, but he who does not believe will be condemned'; by the aforesaid words I conjure and admonish you that you should recede from this servant of God, N. I conjure you, O Devil, by the ascension of our Lord Jesus Christ, that you should recede from this servant of God, N. I conjure you, Devil, by the Holy Spirit, the Paraclete most high, whom our Lord Jesus entrusted to his disciples in fiery tongues, that you should recede from this servant of God, N., and not return any more, nor make any [spirit] return to him, and as God separated heaven from earth, truth from falsehood, good from evil, sweet from bitter, so may you be separated from this servant of God and not be able to approach him any more . . .

The exorcist claims directly the authority of Christ, proclaiming that Christ himself commands the spirit to withdraw:

He commands you, accursed devil, who walked on the sea with dry feet. . . . He commands you, accursed devil, who commanded the winds and the sea and the storms. He commands you, accursed devil, who ordered that you be cast from the heights of heaven to the depths of Earth. . . .

He further threatens the spirit by reminding him of the punishments prepared for him: 'Nor should you be unaware, Satan and Belzebuch, that pains and torments will come upon you in the day of judgement and in that eternal day when God will come like a fiery furnace to judge the living and the dead. . . .' Not only the general structure of the formulas but even the precise wording echoes the conjurations of the Munich handbook and other necromantic texts. At one point, for example, the manual for dispelling a demon parallels the conjuration of Mirage:

You, therefore, most evil spirit, enemy of humankind, death's plunderer [*raptor*], evader of justice [*iustitie declinator*], root of evils, font of vices, seducer of humans [*deductor hominum*] . . . master of demons . . .

You, therefore, most evil Mirage, enemy of the faith of humankind, inventor [*repertor*] of death, herald of injustice [*iniusticie declarator*], root of evils, inciter of vices, seducer of humans [*seductor hominis*], master of demons . . .[58]

Unlike the rite in this oft-published work, the exorcism of elves and other 'demons' from a fifteenth-century medico-magical manuscript makes no pretence of official status, yet it is identical in its basic form to other exorcisms and conjurations:

In the name of the Father, and of the Son, and of the Holy Spirit, amen. I conjure you, elves and all kinds of demons, of the night or of the day, by the Father, and the Son, and the Holy Spirit, and the undivided Trinity, and by the intercession of the most blessed and glorious ever virgin Mary, by the prayers of the prophets, by the merits of the patriarchs, by the intercessions [*suffragia*] of the angels and archangels, by the intervention of the apostles, by the passion of the martyrs, by the faith of the confessors, by the chastity of the virgins, and by the intercession of all the saints, and by the Seven Sleepers, whose names are Malchus, Maximian, Dionysius, John, Constantine,

Serapion, [and] Mortian [*MS* Martimanus], and by the name of the Lord God which is blessed forever ✠A✠G✠L✠A✠, that you should cause or inflict no harm or any evil on this servant of God, N., whether in sleep or while awake. ✠ Christ has conquered [*sic*] ✠ Christ reigns ✠ Christ rules ✠ may Christ bless us ✠ [and] defend us from every evil. ✠ Amen.

In the name of the Father, and of the Son, and of the Holy Spirit, amen. ✠ In my name they will cast out demons, they will speak with new tongues, they will take up serpents, and if they drink any poison it will not harm them, [and] they will put their hands on the sick and will cure them. ✠ Wondrous cross, dispeller of sorrow, recovery of health. ✠ Behold the cross of the Lord; flee, adverse ones [*partes adverse*]. ✠ The lion of the tribe of Judah has conquered, the root of David has sprouted [*allam.?*]. ✠ Christ conquers ✠ Christ reigns ✠ Christ rules ✠ may Christ defend this servant of God from every fantasy and every vexation of the Devil, and from every evil, at every hour and everywhere, by the power of the holy cross ✠ Amen ✠ agios ✠ hyskyros ✠ athanathos ✠ eleyson ✠.[59]

The same may be said of an exorcism of 'malignant spirits' found in the same manuscript:

Hear, O accursed Satan, I adjure you by the name of the eternal God and of Our saviour, His Son Jesus Christ. Depart, trembling and sighing, overcome with your envy. Let there be nothing in common between you and your angels and the servant of God, N. Do not harm him or appear visibly before him, in his sleep or while he is awake. Again I conjure you demons or malignant spirits, whoever you are, by the sprinkling of the blood of Jesus Christ on the cross, and by his bloody wounds. Again I conjure you by the death of Jesus Christ on the cross and the giving up of his spirit, which descended into hell and despoiled it, that now and henceforth you should always flee from this servant of God, N., and never enter into him, but go out and withdraw from him. Again I conjure you by the power of the words written here, if thou are or ye are within him, that thou shouldst or ye should (if you are many) go out from him, so that he may have no terror or disturbance from henceforth. This compels you: may the Word made flesh ✠ the holy cross of Christ, the nails, [and] the crown of thorns drenched in the blood of the Lamb of God on the cross save him, defend the bearer here and everywhere from every adversity and perversity of the Devil. In the name of the Father, etc.[60]

In exorcisms the boundary between mainstream tradition and deviant usage is difficult to define with precision, but the extreme cases are easy enough to determine. One late medieval manuscript requires that the energumen be laid before an altar after mass, inside a chalk diagram, with three stoles binding his body; another requires that the possessed person be dressed in a chasuble and stole and made to lie on his back, with feet turned toward the altar, while the exorcist recites a ritual bond (*vinculum*) to control the evil spirits by the power of various divine names.[61] When Niccolò Consigli was tried at Florence in 1384, for example, he was accused not only of summoning demons to work harm but also of exorcizing the possessed and thus usurping clerical prerogatives. When a ten-year-old girl was brought to him he cured her of possession by laying her on a rug, and intoning a diabolical incantation that began 'Tant muructa? tiri?'[62] In comparison, the exorcisms cited above share their basic form (from declaration through instruction) with the necromantic conjurations we have examined, and they all rest on the mainstream theological assumption that the will of the demons can be constrained, with God's permission and aid, and through the power of the sacred. The necromancers shared with fully official exorcists a belief in the power of the holy to command and ultimately constrain the unclean spirits.

Following a suggestion of Lynn White, André Goddu has sought to explain what he sees as the 'failure of exorcism' in the fifteenth century largely in terms of a heightened consciousness of the possibility that exorcism may be ineffective. Faced with these diminished expectations, theologians began to argue that exorcism was indeed effective on the spiritual plane even if residual bodily effects remained. Alternatively, one could fall back on the time-honoured notion that if exorcism did not succeed then *prima facie* the condition was not truly one of demonic possession.[63] Interesting as his argument is, it rests upon the questionable assumption that the use of exorcism in fact declined. What Goddu shows is that in the October volumes of the *Acta sanctorum* there is diminished occurrence of exorcism in materials from the fifteenth century. But he seems to be referring mainly not to actual exorcisms performed by saints while they were alive, but rather expulsion of demons worked at the tombs of deceased saints, which have indirect relevance at most to the study of exorcism. More compelling is the suggestion of Nancy Caciola, that precisely in the fifteenth century there was *increasing* interest in exorcism as a quasi-liturgical ritual, and that extensive manuals on exorcism, with formulas and instructions for its use, are chiefly the produce of this century. To be sure, there were lengthy formulas in earlier eras, mainly derived from baptismal exorcisms, but before the fifteenth century exorcisms tended to be more concise, and the techniques in large measure improvised.[64] The Munich handbook was thus riding on the crest of a new development: what it represents is a particular version (or, from an orthodox perspective, perversion) of a more general interest in the elaboration and assembly of materials for the commanding of malign spirits. Once again we can see conjuration as the reverse side of a tapestry whose obverse consists of orthodox exorcism – both taking on new significance, as it happens, at the same time that literal tapestries were becoming more significant and more elaborate in European artistic practice.

Notes

1 A.G. Little, ed., *Liber exemplorum ad usum praedicantium, saeculo XIII compositus a quodam Fratre Minore Anglico de provincia Hiberniae, secundum codicem Dunelmensem editus* (Aberdeen: Typis Academicis, 1908), 22. Barbara Newman, who is working on the theme of demon-preachers in and around the thirteenth century, called this text to my attention.

2 See Richard P.H. Greenfield, *Traditions of Belief in Late Byzantine Demonology* (Amsterdam: Hakkert, 1988): 277, on texts in which it appears that God is being commanded or conjured.

3 Lester K. Little, *Benedictine Maledictions: Liturgical Cursing in Romanesque France* (Ithaca, NY: Cornell University Press, 1993).

4 See the curse directed against thieves in the Rawlinson necromantic manuscript, fols 121r–121v: *Obscurentur oculi eorum ne videant et dorsum eorum semper incurua. Irruat super eos formido et pauor in magnitudine brachij tui. Fiant inmobiles quasi lapis, donec pertranseat populus tuus, domine, donec pertranceat [sic] populus tuus [sic] iste quem possedisti, etc* . . . . (Cf. 124r–124v.)

5 In the Vulgate, Song of Songs 2:7, *Adiuro vos, filiae Hierusalem, per capreas cervosque camporum, ne suscitetis neque evigilare faciatis dilectam.*

6 C. Stephen Jaeger, *The Origins of Courtliness: Civilizing Trends and the Formation of Courtly Ideals, 939–1210* (Philadelphia, 1985), 238, citing Nicetius, *Epistulae Austrasicae*, in MGH Epp. Merow. et Karol. aev., 1/3/9, 119–22.

7 Charles Plummer, ed., *Vitae sanctorum Hiberniae*, 1 (Oxford: Clarendon, 1910), 143: *illa bestia fugata ad persequentem se uoce humana dixit: 'Adiuro te in nomine Brigide, uirginis Hibernensis, ut me dimittas.'*

8 M.R. James, 'Twelve medieval ghost-stories', *English Historical Review*, 37 (1922), 413–22 (no. 3). On these cases see Jean-Claude Schmitt, *Les revenants: les vivants et les morts dans la société médiévale* (Paris: Gallimard, 1994), 168–73.

9 Michael D. Swartz, 'Scribal magic and its rhetoric: formal patterns in medieval Hebrew and Aramaic incantation texts from the Cairo Genizah', *Harvard Theological Review*, 83 (1990), 163–80.

10 Rawl. 19r–20r, 124v, 139r–142r, 151v, 155r–156r; 148r–149r; 153r.

11 Martin Buber, *I and Thou*, 2nd edn, trans. Ronald Gregor Smith (New York: Scribner, 1958), 83.

12 See Richard Kieckhefer, *Magic in the Middle Ages* (Cambridge: Cambridge University Press, 1989), 78–80.

13 See Iohannes de Francofordia, *Quaestio, utrum potestas cohercendi demonis fieri possit per caracteres, figuras atque verborum prolationes* (1412), in Joseph Hansen, ed., *Quellen und Untersuchungen zur Geschichte des Hexenwahns und der Hexenverfolgung im Mittelalter* (Bonn: Georgi, 1901; repr. Hildesheim: Olms, 1963), 71–82. See also the conclusions of the Paris theologians, from 1398, in Jean Gerson, *Œuvres complètes*, ed. Palemon Glorieux (Paris: Descle, 1961–73), vol. 10, p. 89: article 17 condemns the belief 'That by such arts demons are truly coerced and compelled and do not feign such compulsion to seduce people'.

14 *Precipio vobis* occurs six times (e.g., no. 38 and no. 39); *adiuro vos/te* twice; *exorzizo te, voco vos, invoco vos*, and *absoluo vos* also occur.

15 *Te invoco et adiuro* (no. 14); *coniuro vos et precipio vobis* (no. 39).

16 No. 27 (five times in a single conjuration), no. 39 (eleven times).

17 No. 12 (*coniuro . . . coniuro te . . . coniuro vos et exorcizo vos [et] impero vobis*); no. 39 (*coniuro vos . . .*

coniuro et contestor vos . . . adiuro vos followed by eight more occurrences of *coniuro vos*); no. 8 (*vos coniuro et exorcizo, et prouoco vos . . . coniuro vos . . . coniuro vos et impero atque precipio vobis . . . vos advoco*); no. 15 (*vos potenter invoco . . . vos invoco et coniuro potenter et exorziso . . . vos invoco et coniuro et exorcizo et constringo*); no. 33 (*vos exorcisamus atque imperamus . . . exorcizamus atque viriliter imperamus*); no. 11 (*invoco vos ex parte Patris, prouoco vos ex parte Filij, invoco vos ex parte Spiritus Sancti*). Further examples: *coniuro vos et advoco,* followed by *coniuro vos* twice; *coniuro vos* six times, followed by *precipio vobis; vos exorciso et coniuro . . . coniuro vos; vos coniuro et exorcizo et invoco . . . coniuro vos . . . coniuro vos et exorcizo; vos coniuro . . . coniuro vos . . . precipio vobis; vobis precipio . . . precipio vobis; coniuro vos . . . precipio vobis; vobis impero et precipio coniuro . . . coniuro vos.*

18 No. 1 (*supplico vobis* and *te deprecor*); no. 4 (*vos deprecor, vobis supplico, vos rogito*); no. 22 (*te deprecor*); no. 23 (*te exoramus*); no. 24 (*rogo . . . rogo vos*); no. 29 (*te deprecor*); no. 41 (*precor te . . . vocor et contestor* and *precor, rogo, et peto*).

19 E.g., no. 6 (*rogo vos, coniuro et adiuro*). no. 15 uses the forms *coniuro et constringo te; te invoco, coniuro, et constringo,* and *te invoco et coniuro et constringo.*

20 Both from no. 10; the latter reads *Coniuro vos, omnes demones scriptos in hoc anulo.*

21 No. 39 and no. 40.

22 No. 23.

23 In no. 27 he is addressed several times by that designation and also as simply *virgo* or *infans.*

24 Nos 4 (*ymago*), 11 (*cappa*), 24 (*O vos sanctissima nomina*). no. 40 addresses *Jaspar, Balthasar, Melchior, Smoagel, Emanuel, et deus fortis,* but this appears to be a mistake; these names should appear in invocations rather than in an address.

25 Addressed as *eque bone* in nos 17 and 43.

26 A conjuration in experiment no. 38 has thirty-four, one in no. 40 has forty-six, one in no. 33 has forty-nine, and one in no. 39 has fifty-eight.

27 Eamon Duffy, *The Stripping of the Altars: Traditional Religion in England,* c. *1400–*c. *1580* (New Haven: Yale University Press, 1992), 262f.

28 Cf. *The Commonplace Book of Robert Reynes of Acle: An Edition of Tanner MS 407,* ed. Cameron Louis (New York: Garland, 1980), 169–70.

29 Nos 1, 10, 13, 14 (where it is called the *nomen altissimum*), 25, 27, 28, 33 (where it is said to have been used by Abraham) and 35. On the Jewish background for magical use of the divine name see K. Kohler, 'The Tetragrammaton (Shem ham-M'forash) and its uses', *Journal of Jewish Lore and Philosophy,* 1 (1919), 19–32.

30 Compare the wording of the conjuration in Bodleian Library MS Rawlinson D 252, fols 87v–89v.

31 Nos 33 (AGLA); 39 (Theos); 28 (Yschiros); 28 and 33 (Athanatos); 28 (Eleyson); 14, 23, 27, 28, 33 (On); 25 (Hon); 28, 33 (Pancraton); 39 (Panthocrathon). One of the more extraordinary invocations is *per legem legalem et per spem sperantem et per karitatem karitatiuam* (no. 14), presumably an adaptation or garbling of the three theological virtues.

32 Joseph Kaster, trans. and ed., *The Wings of the Falcon* (New York, 1968), 60.

33 On the lore of Virgil see Domenico Comparetti, *Vergil in the Middle Ages,* trans. E.F.M. Benecke (London: Swan Sonnenschein, 1895), and J.W. Spargo, *Virgil the Necromancer* (Cambridge, MA, 1934).

34 See esp. F.C. Conybeare, 'The Testament of Solomon', *Jewish Quarterly Review,* 11 (1899), 1–45, but also John M. Hull, *Hellenistic Magic and the Synoptic Tradition* (Naperville, IL: Allenson, 1974), 30–35.

35 E.g., no. 20.

36 Fols 141r–141v.

37 Rawl. MS D 252, fols 16v–17v., 72r–72v.

38 E.g., nos 27, 35, 40.

39 No. 25, *vt non recedatis . . . quousque certificati fuerimus de omni re dubitabili*; no. 27, *vt non habeatis licenciam recedendi . . . donec . . . michi dicatis . . . veritatem*, and *vt non habeatis potestatem recedendi . . . donec . . . meam voluntatem adimpleueritis*, and *vt virtutem talem recipias quod quocumque fueris ligata, ipsi spiritus non habeant potestatem recedendi quousque velle ligatoris perficiant*). They may also be used to ensure that the spirits will repeat the desired effect on later occasions, at the master's will (no. 9, *vt iurare vos debeatis vt predictum equum semper ad me venire cogetis*). The term 'bond' (*hoc vinculum est legendum*) occurs in no. 33.

40 E.g., Rawlinson D 252, 4v, 43v (*coniuracio obediencialis*) and 12r, 14v, and 36v (*coniuracio licencialis*).

41 Nos 1, 6, 8, and 9. Also nos 7 and 9, *quatenus . . . ad me venire debeatis*, and *vt hic venire debeatis*; and no. 11, *quatenus . . . huc venire debeatis*.

42 Nos 1, 6, and 13. Also no. 24, *vt mittatis . . . angelos . . . qui dicant michi veritatem*; no. 27, *vt . . . vadas pro rege tuo et facias eum venire*; no. 38, *vt vestrum vnus . . . veniat vt iste puer possit eum . . . videre*; no. 41, *vt michi spiritum veritatis . . . mittere digneris*.

43 Nos 5, 13, and 35. Also no. 2, *vt eatis . . . et relinquatis talem in statu priori*, and *vt . . . [talem] personam . . . circuatis, et sensus eius . . . affligatis*; no. 4, *vt . . . ipsum [?] iuxta me taliter aligetis, vt me . . . veneretur*; and no. 5, *quatenus . . . odium . . . inseratis*.

44 Nos 22, 24, 27, and 38. Also no. 38, *vt michi sitis obedientes et isto puero . . . quod verum est . . . dicatis*, and no. 39, *quod . . . ostendatis et dicetis huic puero . . . vbi acceptum uel reconditum sit hoc furtum*.

45 No. 22, *quatenus isti puero tribuas scienciam et intellectum, vt michi veritatem annunciet*; no. 29, *illumina istius pueri cor [et] mentem, et fac vt michi veritatem . . . dicat . . . vt [?] indicet omnia*, and *vt isti puero tribuas scienciam et intellectum, vt michi veritatem . . . dicat*; no. 38, *vt . . . iste puer . . . possit videre furem cum furto*; no. 39, *quod vobis detis auctoritatem huic puero . . . audiendi, interrogandi, et videndi*, and *vt . . . vngwem huius pueri . . . crescere et clarescere faciatis . . . vt apparere possit . . . et videre in eo furem et furtum*; no. 40, *vt . . . faciatis vngwem istius pueri . . . crescere et clarescere . . . quod iste puer . . . in eo videre possit furem uel fures et furtum*.

46 No. 27.

47 Nos 33, 3, 43, 15, 39, 40.

48 No. 27; cf. no. 22.

49 Nos 23, 27, 28, 29, 33.

50. Nos 10, 15, 10, 39.

51 Nos 14, 15, 17, and 43.

52 The conjuration on fols 59v–69v is abbreviated; the full text is given on fols 109r–118r and 139r–146r. Compare the conjuration in Bodleian Library MS Rawlinson D 252, fols 24r–29r.

53 For parallels see Marvin Meyer and Richard Smith, eds, *Ancient Christian Magic: Coptic Texts of Ritual Power* (1994), 157, and Kaster, *Wings of the Falcon*, 151–2. See also *Malleus maleficarum*, ii.1.13, p. 141.

54 Fols 115v and 144r, *Alioquin exorcizo te ut cathene penales tue fecundantur* [or, on 144r, perhaps *secundantur*] *sulphure et pice*.

55 Fols 111v–118r and 141r–146r.

56 Adolf Franz, *Die kirchlichen Benediktionen im Mittelalter*, 2 (Freiburg im Breisgau, 1909), 587–96.

57 *Coniuratio malignorum spirituum in corporibus hominum existentium prout in Sancto Petro* (Rome: Stephan Plannck, ca. 1492; also Rome: Eucharius Silber, ca. 1495, and other editions).

58 Clm 849, fols 109r–109v, 139v.

59 British Library, MS Sloane 962, fols 9v–10r: *In nomine patris, et filii, et spiritus sancti, amen. Coniuro uos elues et omnia genera demonum nocturna siue diuturna per patrem, et filium, et spiritum sanctum, atque indiuiduam trinitatem, et per intercessionem beatissime et gloriose semperque virginis Marie, per oraciones prophetarum, per merita patriarcharum, per suffragia angelorum et archangelorum, per int[er.?]uentum apostolorum, per passionem martyrum, per fidem confessorum, per castitatem virginum, et per intercessionem omnium sanctorum, et per septem dormientes, hos quorum nomina sunt hec: Malchus, Maximianus, Dionisius, Iohennes, Constantinus, Seraphion, Martimanus, et per nomen domini dei quod est benedictum in secula ✠ A ✠ G ✠ L ✠ A ✠ vt non noceatis neque aliquid mali faciatis vel inferatis huic famulo dei N. neque dormiendo neque vigilando. ✠ Christus uicit [sic] ✠ Christus regnat ✠ Christus imperat ✠ Christus nos benedicat ✠ [et] ab omni malo deffendat ✠ Amen. In nomine patris, et filii, et spiritus sancti, amen. ✠ In nomine meo demonia eicient, linguis loquentur nouis, serpentes tollent, et si mortiferum quid biberint non eis nocebit, super egros manos imponent et bene habebunt. ✠ Crux admirabilis, euacuacio doloris, restitucio sanitatis. ✠ Ecce crucem domini, fugite partes [sic.?] adverse. ✠ Vicit leo de tribu iuda, radix Dauid [Apoc 5:5] allam [sic.?]. ✠ Christus vincit ✠ Christus regnat ✠ Christus imperat ✠ Christus hunc famulum dei N. ab omni fantasia et ab omni vexacione diaboli et ab omni malo omni hora et vbique per virtutem sancte crucis deffendat ✠ Amen ✠ agios ✠ hyskyros ✠ athanathos ✠ eleyson ✠.*

60 Fol. 10r: *Contra malignos spiritus. Audi maledicte Sathana, adiuro te per nomen eterni dei et saluatoris nostri filij eius Ihesu Christi, cum tua victus inuidia, tremens gemensque, discede. Nichil tibi neque angelis tuis sit commune cum famulo dei N., neque noceas ei, neque appareas coram illo visibiliter, sompniendo neque vigilando, et iterum coniuro vos demones siue spiritus malignos, quicumque sitis, per aspercionem sanguinis Ihesu Christi in cruce, et eius vulnera cruentata. Et iterum coniuro vos per mortem Ihesu Christi in cruce et spiritus emissionem, qui ad infernum descendit et ilum spoliauit, vt nunc et a modo semper fugiatis ab hoc famulo dei N. et nunquam in eum introeatis sed exeatis et recedatis ab eo. Et iterum coniuro vos per virtutem verborum istorum infrascriptorum hic [MS hoc?], si infra eum sis vel sitis, vt exeas vel exeatis, si plures sitis, ab illo vt nullum a modo habeat terrorem neque vexacionem. Hoc vos cogat, verbum caro factum ✠ crux Christi sancta [MS sancea or santea], claui, corona spinea in sanguine agni dei in cruce perfusa, saluent ei, deffendant hic et vbique ferentem [sic] ista ab omni aduersitate diaboli et peruersa. In nomine patris, etc.*

61 Franz, *Die kirchlichen Benediktionen*, 2, p. 573.

62 Gene A. Brucker, ed., *The Society of Renaissance Florence: A Documentary Study* (New York: Harper & Row, 1971), 261–6; Gene A. Brucker, 'Sorcery in early Renaissance Florence', *Studies in the Renaissance*, 10 (1963), 13–16, 22f.

63 André Goddu, 'The failure of exorcism in the Middle Ages', in A. Zimmermann, ed., *Soziale Ordnungen im Selbstverständnis des Mittelalters* (Berlin, 1980), 540–57.

64 Nancy Caciola, 'Discerning Spirits: Sanctity and Possession in the Later Middle Ages' (University of Michigan dissertation, 1994), Ch. V: 'Exorcism from spectacle to ritual'.

7

DEMONS AND DAIMONS:
THE SPIRITS CONJURED

In his recent study of late Byzantine demonology, Richard Greenfield distinguishes between a 'standard orthodox' tradition of demonology and 'alternative' traditions. The former sees demons as immaterial, as ranked under a single chief (Satan, the Devil), and as acting only with God's permission or through illusion (which they use because, weakened by Christ, they must dupe humans into believing they still wield power). The latter ascribe some degree of materiality to them, classify them in various hierarchies with multiple leaders, and ascribe some power to the demons themselves.[1] Greenfield says that in the alternative traditions, 'it is always assumed that the demons are free to obey the practitioner or are capable of doing what he wants as long as sufficient or coercion is provided. There is no suggestion that they can only do so if allowed to by God for the ends of divine providence or economy, the state of affairs required by standard belief – indeed, many of the purposes for which they are employed would seem to be most inappropriate, if not actually contradictory to normal Christian concepts of God's purposes.'[2] Greenfield does not mean to suggest a clear or sharp dichotomy, but rather a strong difference in tendency between the theological purists and those with alternative and at least implicitly non-orthodox views.

With perhaps some differences in nuance, one can make the same rough distinction for the later medieval West as well, and some if not all of the specific contrasts that Greenfield isolates would apply in the West. Most fundamentally, one can discern – in the Munich manuscript, as in Western magic generally – a tension between the early Christian notion of demons as fallen angels, whose status is determined by their free moral act of rebellion against God, and the Graeco-Roman conception of *daimones* (or *daemones* in Latin) as spirits linked with the world of nature, whose status is fixed by their natural position within the hierarchy of beings. Apuleius's *De deo Socratis* remained long influential in Christian tradition, despite its incongruence with the notion of demons as fallen angels; for Apuleius, *daemones* were rational beings whose natural sphere was the sublunary air, just as gods and humans are rational beings residing in the ether and on earth respectively. They are not naturally evil, but may be either good or evil.[3] The conjurations of late medieval necromancers, resembling as they do the exorcisms intended for the possessed, presuppose that the spirits in question are the same sort of fallen ones that Christ expelled from the energumens of first-century Palestine. But intermingled with references to such manifestly maleficent beings are notions of benign or neutral spirits, neither angels nor demons in classical Christian terms, a category not recognized in the orthodox theology of the late Middle Ages.[4] One might thus say that the conjurations betray a tension between 'demonology' and what we might call 'daimonology'.

Theologians as well as necromancers believed that the demons held various ranks, in a kind of hierarchy that parodied that of God's heavenly court, or rather a 'Lowerarchy', as C.S. Lewis called it.[5] The notion of a demonic hierarchy, with a multiplicity of named and ranked spirits, stems chiefly from the Neoplatonists, and above all Iamblichus. Proclus, drawing on Iamblichus's elaborate categorization, spoke of *daimones* as ruling the fire, the air, the water, the earth and the underground region; to this system Psellus added lucifugues (or light-fleeing) demons, and Johannes Trithemius lent the weight of his authority to this system.[6] The basic notion became part of mainstream theological tradition: that demons are organized into an infernal parody of the celestial hierarchy is an assumption that the *Malleus maleficarum* shared with Thomas Aquinas.[7] For the later medieval West, at least, one thus cannot speak of such conceptions as part of an alternative tradition, although it is true that a fascination with the details of the infernal hierarchy was left to the fringes of the theological community.

Altogether 189 spirits are addressed by name in the Munich handbook's conjurations, of whom 88 are referred to expressly as *demones*. Further specification is common: 'malign demons'; 'most inimical spirits'; 'all hateful and malign, invidious and discordant demons'; 'arms-bearing [or squire] spirits, whose role it is to bear arms and . . . deceive human senses'; 'spirits who dwell in the water [and] endanger ships'; 'spirits who attend to sinners'; 'infernal spirits'; 'fornicator, tempter, seducer, possessor of humans'.[8] In short, the compiler of this manual was far from squeamish about invoking clearly and explicitly fallen angels.

The conjurations of the Munich handbook sometimes refer to demons by their rank in the infernal hierarchy: five are 'princes of the demons'; three are powerful, magnificent, and illustrious spirits; Bartha is a king; Baltim, Galtim, and Saltim are dukes; Belial is 'foremost prince'; seven demons are 'subjects' of Lytim.[9] On rare occasion the spirits referred to in the Munich handbook are clearly conceived as unfallen – a claim that would elicit skepticism from orthodox authorities. Experiments no. 24 and no. 25 both refer to 'angels', and in other cases as well the characterizations could be taken as implying unfallen angels: 'most benign spirits, who sow concord'; 'most pleasant, happy, joyful spirits'; 'powerful, magnificent, and illustrious spirits, in whom I place full trust'.[10] In two experiments the spirit addressed is named Orient, and in both cases he is explicitly conceived as a benevolent figure: he is addressed, 'O most high and benign king Orient', 'O benign Orient, maker of the greater part of the world, heaven, and earth, at whose command all things on heaven and on earth were wisely made'.[11] It would be hazardous to posit a direct connection here with the goddess-figure Oriente said to have been venerated in the territory of Milan in the late fourteenth century,[12] but in both cases the traditional medieval primacy of the direction east obviously lies behind the construction of a chief deity. In several experiments God himself is addressed: 'God, creator of all things'; 'Almighty, everlasting God, Lord Jesus Christ'; 'God of heaven, God of earth, God of the angels, God of the archangels, you who are king of all the saints, the patriarchs, and the prophets'; 'Lord Jesus Christ, Son of the living God, who, according to the will of the Father, with the cooperation of the Holy Spirit, by your death gave life to the world'; and 'King of Kings and Lord of Lords, eternal and unchanging Lord God'.[13]

Sometimes the nature of the spirit addressed cannot be determined. In one case the subject of the address is the indeterminate 'N.' (no. 12), and elsewhere the spirit who appears to a boy is addressed simply as 'you who are before me' (no. 27). Another experiment provides a conjuration with the indeterminate address, 'O so-and-so, of thus-and-such an order' (no. 1).

A few of the experiments list demons whose names are familiar from other sources: Astaroth, Baruch, Belial, Belzebub, Berith, Castiel, Lucifer, Mirael, Paymon and Satan or Sathan.[14] The experiments that list such familiar spirits do not restrict themselves to these, however, but also address less familiar or entirely unfamiliar names: one conjures not only Belzebub, Berith, Lucifer and Sathan, but also Apolin, Beliath and Maraloch; another addresses not only Mirael and Astaroth but also Belferith, Camoy, Noryoth, Ocel, Oreoth, Pinen, Sismael, Sobronoy and Tryboy; a third gives the altogether well established name Satan (spelled 'Sathan') but also the exceptional ones Altramat, Archidemath, Discobermath, Fritath, Hegergibet, Helyberp, Pestiferat and Sona; a fourth lists not only Berith, Belzebub and Astaroth, but also Althes, Cormes, Dies, Diles, Dilia, Fabar, Felsmes, Mithiomo, Molbet, Natheus, Onaris, Pist, Progemon, Thobar, Vmon and Vralchim.[15] In some cases the names listed could be corrupt or variant forms of more familiar ones: Apolin could be Apollion, Arath could be Arathiel, Astra could be Astrael, Damay could be Dahnay, Erlain could be Erel(l)im, Gana could be Ganael, Gebel could be Gebiel, Lamair could be Lama, Oor could be Or, Safrit could be Safriel, Tami could be Tamiel, Taraor could be Tara, Tatomofon could be Tatonon, Thomo could be Thomax, Ym could be Im, and Zanno or Zaimo could be Zainon.[16] Even so, of the 189 names addressed in the conjurations, only 17 per cent at most seem to be well established ones. Of the eleven spirits named in experiment no. 34, only Curson has broad currency (unless Hanni is equated with Haniel). When the list of spirits in this manual is compared with that in *Picatrix*, what is striking is the singular lack of correspondence.

The crucial question for the necromancers of Western Europe is whether the demons can be compelled to appear, and their own assumption – that the demons can be so compelled, but only with God's permission and aid – is not fundamentally different from the assumption that underlies orthodox exorcism and mainstream theology. John of Frankfurt devoted a treatise in 1412 to the question, 'whether it is possible to have the power of coercing a demon through characters, figures, and recitation of words' (*utrum potestas cohercendi demonis fieri possit per caracteres, figuras atque verborum prolationes*), and he insisted that it was not – that the demons may pretend to be compelled only to lure the conjurers deeper into their own perfidy, but that they come, if at all, of their own free will.[17] He seems not to have taken fully into account that the necromancers, exactly like orthodox exorcists, claimed the power of coercing demons specifically with divine aid. To be sure, their goals were at variance with orthodox morality, yet they saw their appeal to sacred powers as itself a sacred activity, and if it led to the killing and coercion of other individuals, that did not sway them from this conviction.[18] In any event, while their critics and judges saw the necromancers as in league with the demons, they perceived themselves as calling upon God to help them control and exploit the spirits.

One reason it appeared to critics that the necromancers were bound to the spirits they conjured, rather than vice versa, is that they seemed to make sacrifice to these spirits: fumigations and other acts could readily be seen as sacrifices. Nicholas Eymericus explains that some conjurers exhibit the honour of latria to the demons they invoke by sacrificing to them, adoring them, reciting execrable prayers to them, dedicating themselves and promising obedience to the demons, swearing by them and adjuring one demon by the name of a higher one, singing songs in their honour, genuflecting and making prostrations, observing chastity out of respect for them, fasting and otherwise macerating the flesh in their honour, wearing black or white out of reverence to them, using characters and unknown names, lighting lamps and offering fumigations, sacrificing birds and beasts and even their own blood, and so forth.[19]

Some of the experiments in the Munich handbook and elsewhere do indeed involve offering something, such as a hoopoe, to the demons. Whether such offerings count as sacrificial depends on one's definition of sacrifice. If any exchange with spirits implying *do ut des* is a sacrifice, then the term applies. From the necromancers' perspective, however, a fumigation would surely be more a means for alluring and gaining power over the spirits, and the offering of a hoopoe would be payment for services rendered. There is no explicit acknowledgement in the handbook that the magician is *serving* the spirits; to the contrary, he sees himself as commanding and exploiting them.

The spirits invoked may on occasion be represented as unfallen ones. Some are referred to as 'most benign', which could suggest but does not prove that they are unfallen; even an evil spirit may relate in a kindly manner toward his own. In one experiment (no. 9) the master greets the spirits when they appear with a wish that God may restore them to their original status, which makes it clear that they are fallen yet suggests that they are none the less redeemable.[20] Most interesting is the suggestion that the spirits who provide a magic ship (no. 8) are of intermediate status: 'And you should note carefully that in this ship you are able to mention holy things, as in true Christianity, because these spirits are between good and evil, dwelling neither in Hell nor in Paradise.' The Paris theologians in 1398 condemned the belief that there are good and benign demons, omniscient demons, and demons who are neither saved nor damned but somewhere in between.[21] At times the spirits summoned are threatened with damnation if they refuse to obey the master, which assumes either that they are unfallen spirits or that they occupy some middle ground, perhaps being fallen but capable of redemption.[22]

The problem of distinguishing between fallen and unfallen spirits had long been a vexed one, and it was not made easier by the necromancers' habit of calling more or less indiscriminately on spirits of both kinds, as well as allegedly neutral spirits. The Rawlinson necromantic manuscript, for example, sometimes prays for power over all malign spirits, or for power over Satan, or for protection from malign spirits. It explicitly invokes Satan and other 'infernal demons'.[23] At other times it implicitly identifies the invoked spirits as demons, conjuring them 'by the power by which [Christ] destroyed hell and despoiled and tormented your companions [socios]' or 'by him who cast you from heaven'. While magicians were not at all shy about conjuring angels directly, the tendency in the Rawlinson manuscript perhaps more often than in other manuscripts is to pray that good angels be sent. It even includes a lengthy prayer to the master's guardian angel for protection. At one juncture it conjures 'benevolent spirits and demons', without making altogether clear whether these are distinct categories.[24]

One rule of thumb was that spirits explicitly known from traditional sources as unfallen angels could be prayed to, but others were at best suspect. The archangels mentioned in the Bible and the Old Testament apocrypha (Gabriel, Michael, Raphael) were mentioned from the seventh century onward in the Litany of the Saints, although it was not until the twentieth century that Benedict XV made the feast of the last two obligatory. The names of other angels were deemed apocryphal: the Book of Enoch adds Uriel, Raguel, Seraqael and Haniel to the list of archangels. In the mid-eighth century a Frankish priest named Adalbert was condemned, inter alia, for praying to Uriel, Raguel, Tubuel, Adin, Tubuas, Sabaok and Samiel, all of whom a Roman synod declared to be in fact demons. In 789, Charlemagne's Admonitio generalis condemned the invocation of 'unknown angels', presumably for the same reason.[25] Even if a petitioner intended to call upon unfallen angels, the spirits he summoned might not be the spirits he got.

Johann von Frankfurt noted in the early fifteenth century that Plato distinguished between good daimons (calodemones) and evil (cacodemones), but for scriptural and dogmatic reasons he rejects this distinction and insists on a rigid dichotomy between unfallen angels and demons, the latter being always evil.[26] Invoking demons, he says, is prohibited both by scripture (Deut 2:18, also IV

Kgs 1 and I Kgs 28) and by canon law (the canon *Episcopi*). He insists that demons cannot be coerced: they are free agents, with intellect and will, and cannot be bound by human actions; Job attests that no power on earth is comparable to the Devil;[27] and many later medieval authorities are cited to confirm this stance. He argues that 'although demons often do come when they are summoned by invocations, they do so not coerced, but fraudulently, so as to deceive them [the conjurers] and others" (p. 78). (Not long before Johann wrote, the theologians at the University of Paris had in 1398 condemned the belief that God is induced to compel demons to obey invocations, and that by magical arts the demons are compelled to speak truthfully.[28]) To be sure, Solomon is said to have exorcized or commanded demons, but if he did so at the time that he himself had the spirit of God, then he expelled the demons by divine power and with the cooperation of God, whereas if he do so after he had fallen into idolatry (III Kgs 11 Vulg.), then *fuit factum arte magica*, and the demons pretended to be expelled so as to lead people into error. When Tobias placed a fish's liver on coals, demons were expelled (Tob 6) – but the book of Tobias is not canonical, so it may have edifying value but no probative force. Experience itself may suggest that demons come or depart when certain words are uttered, but it is prayer and not fumigation that has the effect of expelling demons.

Notions of demonic corporeality are more rarely expressed but not unknown. The Rawlinson manuscript says at one juncture that if the spirit refuses to withdraw, the master should trace a circle with the point of his sword and then 'strike' the spirit who is left standing outside the circle. The text goes on to explain that the reader should not be astonished at this reference to striking, because the spirits can indeed be struck when they assume bodies for the sake of apparition.[29] More extraordinary is the tale – involving a ghost rather than a demon, to be sure – of 'a woman who captured a spirit, carried it into a house on her back in the presence of certain men, one of whom later told that he saw the hands of the woman sunk deep into the spirit's flesh, as if its flesh were putrid and not solid, but fantastic'.[30] More often the spirits' corporeality is presupposed but not the subject of comment: they presumably cannot carry the magicians about in the form of horses or usher forth elaborate banquets without some sort of bodies, but the precise nature of their flesh seems not to have concerned the writer of the Munich handbook.

When the demons appear, they presumably do so either through phantasms impressed directly on the viewers' senses or in assumed bodies.[31] They may be able to take on any appearance they wish, conceivably even that of a famed beauty such as Helen of Troy, since their bodies are in any event assumed, but it seems to have been agreed that their most natural shape is terrifying. The Munich handbook thus routinely conjures the spirits to appear in pleasing and non-threatening form, the implication being that it is natural for them to appear otherwise. Indeed, the treatise on necromancy ascribed to Roger Bacon warns that demons will try to frighten the magician with illusions, with hissing like that of a serpent, and with terrifying shapes, but bold use of the Tetragrammaton and the sign of the cross will compel them to adopt pleasing forms.[32] The spirits are conjured to appear in human form, because they are assumed closer to beasts, and thus it is more natural for them to assume grotesque versions of bestial appearance,[33] as they did in hagiography since the life of Saint Anthony.[34] In one case they are told to take on the pleasing form of a ten-year-old boy, evidently by cross-fertilization of the instruction with the requirements for a medium.[35]

The most sustained discussion of demons in the Munich manual is an extended list which names and describes eleven spirits (no. 34). Each has a rank: marquis, 'president' (*preses*), count, duke, prince or king. They appear in diverse forms: as a seneschal; as a man with large teeth and three horns, carrying a sharp sword in his hand; as a crowned man with leonine face, bearing a viper in hand, riding horseback, and preceded by trumpets; as a splendid knight, with lance, banner, and sceptre; as a boy with the wings of an angel, riding on a dragon with two heads;[36] as a beautiful and crowned woman, riding on a camel; as a knight, riding on a black horse; as a benevolent man with a woman's face. Hanni comes in a fiery flame, but also takes human form. Curson is said readily to assume a human and aerial body; presumably the others as well take on aerial bodies when they come visibly.[37] Their functions are likewise diverse. Six of the spirits are said to disclose the location of hidden treasure, or to reveal and open treasures, and although in one case it is specified that the treasure must not be protected by magic or charms, in another case the spirit in question can reveal treasures guarded by other spirits. Four of them respond to questions about present, past, future, and hidden matters; Curson can reveal divine and hidden matters, even regarding divinity and the creation of the world. Another gives knowledge about occult matters and duels. Three specialize in imparting particular knowledge: the trivium, astronomy and other liberal arts, and languages. Two can procure the love of women, especially beautiful women in one case, widows in the other; a third makes women burn with love for men, on demand will transform them into another form until they come to their beloved, and makes them sterile. Others can enable a person to cross seas and rivers quickly, or to pass quickly from one region to another. Four can secure the favour of all, enemies as well as friends, or that of magnates and princes, or of all kings, marquises and knights. One gives dignities; another gives an exorcist power over serpents; yet others provide excellent familiars or knights. Each has command of legions of subordinate spirits (perhaps an allusion to Mark 5:9), as few as twenty-two, and as many as fifty.

Identical in form but independent in content is the list contained in *Le livre des esperitz* found in a fifteenth-century French manuscript (Trinity College, Cambridge, MS 0.8.29). This compilation lists forty-seven spirits: the triad Lucifer, Bezlebuth and Satan; four associated with the cardinal directions; then others for whom title, appearance, function, and number of subordinate legions are given, as in the Munich handbook. Most commonly the spirits here listed are said to give accurate response to the master's questions (Vaal, Bucal, Oze, Bulfas, Artis, Gazon, Diusion, Orient, Poymon, Am[m]oymon, Barthas, Samson, Vipos, Berteth, Distolas, Asmoday, Flauos, Carmola, Abugor, Caap, Bune, Amon). They also furnish instruction (Bezlebuth, Barthas, Artis), sometimes in all sciences (Cerbere, Parcas, Tudiras hoho, Am[m]oymon), often regarding more specific matters: the virtues of herbs and precious stones (Machin, Parcas, Forcas, Gemer); transformation of metals into gold or silver (Berteth); all language (Ducay, Agarat); astronomy and other sciences (Barthas, Furfur); the sounds of birds and dogs (Barbas). They disclose or provide buried treasure (Diusion, Parcas, Abugor, Bezlebuth, Barbas, Samson, Forcas). They make a person invisible (Parcas, Beal, Forcas). They obtain the love of women (Ducay, Furfur [?], Bitur), or of queens and women generally, whether maidens or not (Samson). They secure provision of dignities, seigneuries and favour (Agarat, Bitur, Vaal, Am[m]oymon, Poymon, Berteth, Gazon, Artis, Beal), as well as wealth (Bune, Cerbere, Distolas), or specifically of gold and silver (Caap, Dam, Bezlebuth). They can furnish means by which the 'master' or someone else at the master's will may be transported from place to place (Ducay, Machin, Malpharas, Bune, Parcas), and the spirit Distolas can provide a horse to transport the master in an hour 100, 200 or 300 leagues but no further. Unlike the list of spirits in the Munich handbook, however, the *Livre des esperitz* also indicates that certain spirits specialize in maleficent magic: they can bring death or illness, deformity, destruction of adversaries, discord and battles. The service Bezlebuth performs, which would have endeared him to Faustus, is to reveal all the secrets of hell.

Such lists of demons derived their basic conception from early Jewish sources such as the *Testament of Solomon*, which listed various demons and told how Solomon employed them.[38] These catalogues were especially common in the treatises and grimoires of the early modern era (Johannes Weyer's *Pseudomonarchia daemonum* lists sixty-nine demons with their offices and functions), but the basic idea can be traced to medieval sources. Trithemius speaks of a *Liber officiorum* that catalogues four emperors and various kings, dukes, marquises, and counts. The *Lemegeton* lists seventy-two demons with their functions, including Asmoday (a great king with three heads, who furnishes a ring of virtues, teaches mathematics, answers questions truly, makes a person invisible, reveals hidden treasure, and so forth), Berith, and others.[39]

Among other specializations, there were demons who ruled over one or another of the cardinal directions. Thus, the Paris theologians repudiated the notion that one demon is king of the east and holds special prominence, known in the Munich handbook and elsewhere simply as Oriens, while others ruled the west, the north and the south.[40] No doubt the identification of these demons with special competence had much practical value for those wishing to make use of their services, but the formation of the lists was in itself a display of theoretical knowledge that might appeal greatly to those curious about the secrets of hell. One can perhaps understand why stern medieval moralists, never favourable to *curiositas* in the first place, would condemn this particular sort of curiosity in particular as vain and perilous.

Presupposed throughout the Munich handbook is that the experiments described are worked through the power of spirits, often overtly referred to as demons. The writer makes no pretence that his magic is in any way 'natural', as opposed to demonic. Classical notions of magic as either implicitly or explicitly grounded in the instruction and aid of demons come here to their fullest development: far from shrinking from this suggestion or defending himself against it, the writer candidly acknowledges and perhaps even boasts, no doubt like other necromancers of the era, that the commanding of malign spirits is the essence of his art.

Table C. Spirits named in the conjurations

Abgo (*demon*, no. 39)

Abgoth (*demon*, no. 40)

Achalas (*spiritus*, no. 26)

Althes (*demon*, no. 38)

Altramat (*demon* [from cardinal direction], no. 27)

Andyron (*demon*, *subditus* of Lytim, no. 39)

Apolin (or Apolyn) (no. 1) (no. 5 inv.)

Arath (*demon*, no. 40)

Arbas (or Arbes?) (no. 28)

Archidemath (*demon* [from cardinal direction], no. 27)

Astaroth (or Astoroth or Astarotht) (*demon malignus*, no. 2; no. 12; no. 33; *princeps demoniorum*, no. 38) (no. 5 inv.)

Astra (no. 33)

Asyel (no. 13)

Azathi (*demon*, no. 39)

Baltim (or Balthym? or Balthim or Baltym) (*dux*, no. 15)

Bartha (or Bartham?) (*rex*, no. 15)

Baruth (*demon*, *subditus* of Lytim, no. 39)

Basal (no. 29)

Bel (*spiritus infernalis*, no. 35)

Belam (no. 13)

Belferith (*demon malignus*, no. 2)

Belial (*inicialis princeps*, no. 12)

Beliath (no. 1)

Belzebub (or Belzebuc?) (no. 1; *princeps demoniorum*, no. 38)

Berien (or Beryen, no. 10)

Berith (or Berit) (no. 1; *spiritus potens, magnificus, et illustris*, no. 11; *princeps demoniorum, fornicator, temptator, et seductor, possessor hominum*, no. 38)

Bireoth (*spiritus benignissimus*, no. 4)

Bos (*demon*, no. 39)

Brimer (no. 10)

Spirits named in the conjugations

Camoy (or Canay) (*demon malignus*, no. 2)

Carab (or Careb?) (no. 29)

Cargie (no. 28)

Castiel (no. 13)

Cebal (no. 33)

Cormes (*demon*, no. 38)

Cutroy (or Cotroy?) (*spiritus armigerus, sensus* [*decipiens*], no. 7; *spiritus habitator aque*, no. 8)

Damay (or Damayn, no. 10)

Demefin (*spiritus iocundissimus*, no. 6)

Demor (or Denior) (*spiritus armigerus, sensus* [*decipiens*], no. 7)

Dies (*demon*, no. 38)

Diles (*demon*, no. 38)

Dilia (*demon*, no. 38)

Discobermath (*demon* [from cardinal direction], no. 27)

Dorayl (*spiritus benignissimus*, no. 4)

Dyacon (*spiritus benignissimus*, no. 4)

Dydones (*demon*, no. 40)

Dyrus (*demon*, no. 39 and no. 40)

Dyspil (or Dyspyl) (*spiritus habitator aque*, no. 8)

Ebal (*spiritus infernalis*, no. 35)

Elam (no. 13)

Emogeni (*demon*, no. 40)

Ergarrandras (no. 28)

Erlain (no. 13)

Fabanin (no. 29)

Fabar (*demon*, no. 38)

Fabath (*demon*, no. 40)

Fabin (*spiritus benignissimus*, no. 4)

Falmar (no. 5 inv.)

Faubair (*spiritus iocundissimus*, no. 6)

Febat (*demon*, no. 39)

Felsmes (*demon*, no. 38)

Feremin (*spiritus peccatoribus insistens*, no. 9)

Finibet (*demon*, no. 40)

Foliath (*demon*, no. 39)

Fritath (*demon* [from cardinal direction], no. 27)

Fyriel (or Firiel) (*spiritus potens, magnificus, et illustris*, no. 11)

Fyrin (or Syrim) (*spiritus habitator aque*, no. 8)

Fyrus (*demon*, no. 40)

Gallath (*demon*, no. 40)

Galtim (or Galtym? or Galtyra?) (*dux*, no. 15)

Gana (*demon*, no. 39)

Gebat (or Gebath?) (*demon*, no. 39)

Gebel (*spiritus benignissimus*, no. 4) (no. 5 inv.)

Gemitias (*demon*, no. 39)

Geremittarum (*demon*, no. 40)

Gyton (*demon*, no. 40)

Haram (*spiritus benignus*, no. 39)

Hegergibet (*demon* [from cardinal direction], no. 27)

Helyberp (*demon* [from cardinal direction], no. 27)

Jubutzis (*demon*, no. 40)

Lamair (*spiritus iocundissimus*, no. 6)

Lamisniel (or Lamsiyel, no. 13)

Lautrayth (*spiritus peccatoribus insistens*, no. 9)

Leutaber (or Zeugaber) (*spiritus iocundissimus*, no. 6)

Lotobor (*spiritus iocundissimus*, no. 6)

Lucifer (no. 1)

Lylet (or Bylet or Bylent) (no. 24; *demon, subditus* of Lytim, no. 39)

Lyroth (no. 10)

Lytay (or Lytoy or Litor) (*spiritus armigerus, sensus* [*decipiens*], no. 7)

Lytim (*demon*, no. 39)

Maraloch (no. 1)

Masair (*spiritus iocundissimus*, no. 6)

Mememil (or Melemil) (*spiritus potens,*

Spirits named in the conjugations

magnificus, et illustris, no. 11)

Memoyr (or Memoir) (*spiritus iocundissimus,* no. 6)

Midain (*spiritus benignissimus,* no. 4)

Mirael (no. 2)

Mistal (no. 29)

Mithiomo (*demon,* no. 38)

Molbet (*princeps demoniorum,* no. 38)

Moloy (*spiritus armigerus, sensus [decipiens],* no. 7)

Motmyo (*demon,* no. 39)

Natheus (*princeps demoniorum,* no. 38)

Neyilon (*spiritus,* no. 26)

Non (no. 29)

Noryoth (or Moryoth) (*demon malignus,* no. 2)

Nubar (*demon,* no. 39)

Ocel (*demon malignus,* no. 2)

Oliroomim (*spiritus peccatoribus insistens,* no. 9)

Onaris (*demon,* no. 38)

Onor (*spiritus armigerus, sensus [decipiens],* no. 7)

Onoroy (*spiritus habitator aque,* no. 8)

Oor (or Dor) (*spiritus armigerus, sensus [decipiens],* no. 7)

Oreoth (*demon malignus,* no. 2)

Oriens (or rex Orientis) (*altissimus et benignissimus rex,* no. 4; *benign[issim]e,* no. 41)

Ornis (no. 28)

Oronothel (no. 29)

Orooth (*spiritus habitator aque,* no. 8)

Oymelor (*spiritus iocundissimus,* no. 6)

Panite (or Panyte) (*demon,* no. 38 and no. 40)

Paymon (no. 12)

Peamde (*demon,* no. 39)

Peripaos (*spiritus benignissimus,* no. 4)

Pestiferat (*demon* [from cardinal direction], no. 27)

Pharachte (*demon,* no. 39)

Pinen (*demon malignus,* no. 2)

Pist (*demon,* no. 38)

Progemon (*demon,* no. 38)

Pumeon (*spiritus benignissimus,* no. 4)

Pumotor (or Pumiotor) (*spiritus armigerus, sensus [decipiens],* no. 7)

Rabam (no. 13)

Rayma (*demon,* no. 40)

Riasteli (no. 29)

Rimasor (*spiritus iocundissimus,* no. 6)

Rimel (*spiritus habitator aque,* no. 8)

Risbel (or Ristel) (*spiritus armigerus, sensus [decipiens],* no. 7)

Rodobayl (or Rodobail) (*spiritus iocundissimus,* no. 6)

Rofanes (*demon,* no. 40)

Safrit (*demon,* no. 39)

Salaul (*spiritus armigerus, sensus [decipiens],* no. 7)

Saltim (*dux,* no. 15)

Sanfrielis (*demon,* no. 40)

Sathan (no. 1; *demon* [from cardinal direction], no. 27)

Selentis (*demon,* no. 40)

Selutabel (or Belutabel) (*spiritus iocundissimus,* no. 6)

Sertugidis (*demon,* no. 40)

Silitor (or Silitol) (*spiritus armigerus, sensus [decipiens],* no. 7)

Sismael (*demon malignus,* no. 2)

Sobronoy (*demon malignus,* no. 2)

Sona (no. 27)

Suburith (no. 10)

Symofor (or Simofor) (*spiritus iocundissimus,* no. 6)

Syrama (or Sirama) (*spiritus iocundissimus,* no. 6)

Syrtroy (*spiritus armigerus, sensus*

Spirits named in the conjugations

[*decipiens*], no. 7)

Sysabel (or Sisabel) (*spiritus habitator aque*, no. 8)

Tamafin (*spiritus iocundissimus*, no. 6)

Tami (or Tamy – Tamer?) (*spiritus armigerus, sensus* [*decipiens*], no. 7)

Taraor (*spiritus potens, magnificus, et illustris*, no. 11)

Tatomofon (*spiritus iocundissimus*, no. 6)

Tentetos (*spiritus iocundissimus*, no. 6)

Tereol (no. 5 inv.)

Tereoth (*spiritus benignissimus*, no. 4)

Termines (*spiritus benignissimus*, no. 4)

Thitodens [?] (*demon*, no. 39)

Thobar (*demon*, no. 38)

Thomo (*demon*, no. 40)

Tranayrt (or Tramayrt, no. 10)

Tryboy (or Triay) (*demon malignus*, no. 2)

Tyroces (no. 5 inv.)

Tyros (*demon*, no. 39)

Tyroy (*spiritus habitator aque*, no. 8)

Va (no. 29)

Vatuel (no. 29)

Vijas (*demon*, no. 39)

Virus (*demon*, no. 39)

Virytus (*demon*, no. 40)

Vm (*demon*, no. 39)

Vmeloth (*spiritus benignissimus*, no. 4)

Vmon (*demon*, no. 38)

Vniueny (*demon*, no. 40)

Vnyrus (*demon*, no. 39)

Vom (*demon*, no. 39)

Vralchim (*demon*, no. 38)

Vresius (*demon*, no. 39)

Vsyr (*spiritus armigerus, sensus* [*decipiens*], no. 7)

Vtimo (*demon*, no. 40)

Vzmyas (*demon, subditus* of Lytim, no. 39)

Ygrim (*demon, subditus* of Lytim, no. 39)

Ym (*spiritus armigerus, sensus* [*decipiens*], no. 7)

Ytelteos (*demon, subditus* of Lytim, no. 39)

Zanno (or Zaimo) (*spiritus armigerus, sensus* [*decipiens*], no. 7)

Zelentes (*demon*, no. 39)

Zymens (*demon, subditus* of Lytim, no. 39)

Table D. Spirits listed in no. 34

Name	*Rank*	*Appearance*	*Function*	*Number of legions*
Barbarus	count and duke		discloses treasures not protected by magic	36
Cason	duke	seneschal	responds about present, past, future, and hidden things; gives favour of friends and enemies; gives dignities	45
Otius	*preses* and count	human, with large teeth and	responds about present, future, and hidden matters; gives	36

Name	Rank	Appearance	Function	Number of legions
		3 horns, sharp sword in hand	favour of friends and enemies	
Curson	king	man, with crowned leonine face, viper in hand; rides horseback, trumpets proceeding	reveals present, past, future, and hidden matters; reveals and opens treasures; assumes human and aerial body and responds about divine and hidden matters (including deity and creation of world); gives excellent familiars	22
Alugor	duke	splendid knight, with lance, banner, and sceptre	responds about occult matters and duels; provides knights; gives favour of all kings, marquises, and knights	50
Taob	prince	human	excellent physician for women, making them burn with love for men, on request transforming them into another form until they come to their beloved; makes sterile	25
Volach	president	boy, with wings of angel; rides on dragon; has two heads	responds about hidden treasures; serpents appear, gives over serpents into the hands of exorcist	27
Gaeneron	duke	beautiful woman, crowned, riding on camel	responds about present, past, and future matters, and hidden treasures; gives love of women, especially beautiful ones	27
{ Tvueries Tuveries?	marquis	knight, riding on black horse	teaches trivium, reveals hidden treasures and other hidden things; causes person to cross sea and rivers quickly	30
Hanni	president	fiery flame, but takes human form	teaches astronomy and other liberal arts; gives excellent familiars; gives favour of magnates and princes;	30

Name	Rank	Appearance	Function	Number of legions
Sucax	marquis	man, with woman's face; appears benevolent	reveals treasures guarded by spirits gives love of women, especially widows; gives command of languages; makes person pass quickly from region to region	23

Notes

1 Richard P.H. Greenfield, *Traditions of Belief in Late Byzantine Demonology* (Amsterdam: Hakkert, 1988), *passim*, esp. 307–26.

2 *Ibid.*, 275–6.

3 C.S. Lewis, *The Discarded Image: An Introduction to Medieval and Renaissance Literature* (Cambridge: Cambridge University Press, 1967), esp. 40–44 and 117.

4 See the Paris conclusions of 1398, in Jean Gerson, *Œuvres complètes*, 10, ed. Palemon Glorieux (Paris: Desclée, 1961–73), p. 89: the 23rd condemned article is 'That some demons are good, some benign, some omniscient, others neither saved nor damned'.

5 Thomas Aquinas, *Summa theologiae*, i.109.1; *Malleus maleficarum*, i.4, trans. Montague Summers (London: Rodker, 1928; repr. London: Pushkin, 1948), 28–31; C.S. Lewis, *The Screwtape Letters*, xx (New York: Macmillan, 1962), 102.

6 E.M. Butler, *Ritual Magic* (Cambridge: Cambridge University Press, 1949), 29–36, esp. 35.

7 *Summa theologiae*, i.109.1; *Malleus maleficarum*, i.4, 28–31.

8 No. 2 (ten named *demones maligni*); no. 5 (*spiritus inimicissimos*); no. 5 (*omnes demones odiosos et malignos, inuidios et discordes*); no. 7 (fifteen named *spiritus armigeri, quibus proprium est arma deferre et . . . sensus humanos decipere*); no. 8 (*spiritus habitatores aque, qui naues . . . periclitare conamini*); no. 9 (three named *spiritus peccatoribus insistentes*); no. 35 (*spiritus infernales*); no. 38 (Berith, described as *fornicator, temptator, et seductor, possessor hominum*). See also no. 3 (*omnes demones in hac ymagine scriptos* and *demones in hoc circulo sculptos*) and no. 5 (*spiritus inimicissimos* and *omnes demones odiosos et malignos, inuidios et discordes*).

9 No. 38 (*principes demoniorum*); no. 11 (*spiritus potentes, magnifici, et illustres*); no. 15 (Bartha as *rex*, and Baltim, Galtim, and Saltim as *duces*); no. 12 (Belial as *inicialis princeps*); no. 39 (seven demons as *subditi* of Lytim).

10 No. 4 (eleven *spiritus benignissimi et concordiam seminantes*); no. 6 (sixteen *spiritus iocundissimi, ylares, et gaudentes*); no. 11 (*spiritus potentes, magnifici, et illustres, in quibus omnino confido*).

11 No. 14 (*O altissime et benignissime rex Orientis*); no. 41 (*O Oriens benigne, maior pars mundi, celi, terreque sator, cuius nuta [sic] omnia, tam celestia quam terrestria, prouide facta sunt; benignissime Oriens*).

12 Ettore Vergo, 'Intorno a due inediti documenti di stregheria Milanese del secolo XIV.', *Rendiconti del Reale Instituto Lombardo si Scienze e Lettere*, ser. 2, vol. 32 (1899), 166–8; on Madonna Oriente see Carlo Ginzburg, *Ecstasies: Deciphering the Witches' Sabbath*, trans. Raymond Rosenthal (New York: Pantheon, 1991), esp. 92–6, 100–102, 131–6, 247–8.

13 No. 22 (*Deus, creator omnium rerum*); no. 25 (*Omnipotens, sempiterne deus, Domine Ihesu Christe*); no. 29

(*Deus celi, deus terre, deus angelorum, deus archangelorum, qui es rex sanctorum omnium, patriarcharum ac prophetarum* and *Domine Ihesu Christe, fili dei viui, qui ex voluntate Patris, cooperante Spiritu Sancto, per mortem tuam mundum viuificasti*); no. 36 (*rex regum et dominus dominancium, eterne et incommutabilis deus dominus*).

14 Nos 2, 5, 12, 33, and 38 (Astaroth); no. 20 (Baruch); no. 12 (Belial); nos 1 and 38 (Belzebub); nos 1, 3, 11, and 39 (Berith); no. 13 (Castiel); no. 1 (Lucifer); no. 2 (Mirael); no. 12 (Paymon); nos 1 and 27 (Sathan). See the listings for each of these in Gustav Davidson, *A Dictionary of Angels, Including the Fallen Angels* (New York: Free Press, 1967), and for general information on demons see also Leander Petzoldt, *Kleines Lexikon der Dämonen und Elementargeister* (Munich: Beck, 1990). On the naming of demons see Jeffrey Burton Russell, *Lucifer: The Devil in the Middle Ages* (Ithaca, NY: Cornell University Press, 1984), 248–50.

15 Nos. 1, 2, 27, and 38.

16 Nos 1 and 5 (Apolin or Apolyn); no. 40 (Arath); no. 33 (Astra); no. 10 (Damay); no. 13 (Erlain); no. 39 (Gana); nos 4 and 5 (Gebel); no. 6 (Lamair); no. 7 (Oor); no. 39 (Safrit); no. 7 (Tami); no. 11 (Taraor); no. 6 (Tatomofon); no. 40 (Thomo); no. 7 (Ym); no. 7 (Zanno or Zaimo). For these too see Davidson's *Dictionary*.

17 Hansen, *Quellen und Untersuchungen*, 71–82.

18 Richard Kieckhefer, 'The holy and the unholy: sainthood, witchcraft, and magic in late medieval Europe', *Journal of Medieval and Renaissance Studies*, 24 (1994), 355–85; and in Scott L. Waugh and Peter D. Diehl, eds, *Christendom and its Discontents: Exclusion, Persecution, and Rebellion, 1000–1500* (Cambridge: Cambridge University Press, 1996), 310–37.

19 Nicolaus Eymericus, *Directorium inquisitorum*, ii. 42–3 (Rome: Georgius Ferrarius, 1587), translated in Alan C. Kors and Edward Peters, eds., *Witchcraft in Europe, 1100–1700: A Documentary History* (Philadelphia: University of Pennsylvania Press, 1972), 84–92. See also Greenfield, *Traditions of Belief*, 252–5.

20 The classic source of the notion that Satan and the demons are redeemable is Origen; see on this theme Joseph Wilson Trigg, *Origen: The Bible and Philosophy in the Third-century Church* (Atlanta: John Knox, 1983), 89, 106, 138f., 206, 208. Whatever indirect influence Origen may have had on the necromantic tradition, it is difficult to believe that writers such as the compiler of the Munich handbook had any direct acquaintance with his works.

21 Ch. 23.

22 Rawlinson MS, 148r–149r, 150v, 154r.

23 *Coniuros vos demones infernales* (fol. 121v).

24 Bodleian Library, Oxford, Rawlinson MS D 252, fols 24r (prayer for power over all malign spirits); 40v (prayer for power over Satan); 37r, 50r–50v, and 72r (prayers for protection from malign spirits); 152r (invocation of Satan); 121v (*Coniuro vos demones infernales*); 4v and 5v (implicit identification of spirits as demons); 78r–78v (prayer for vision of good angels); 123v (prayer that good angels be sent); 159v (prayer for three good angels to appear in a crystal); 135v–139r (prayer to guardian angel); 73r (*Coniuro vos spiritus beneuolos et demones*).

25 Aron Gurevich, *Medieval Popular Culture: Problems of Belief and Perception*, trans. János M. Bak and Paul A. Hollingsworth (Cambridge: Cambridge University Press; Paris: Editions de la Maison des Sciences de l'Homme, 1988), 65–8 and Jeffrey B. Russell, 'Saint Bonaventure and the eccentrics', *Church History*, 33, (1964), 235–47, esp. 237–8. For general information on the cult of angels see A.A.

Bialas, 'Devotion to angels', *The New Catholic Encyclopedia*, 1 (New York: McGraw-Hill, 1967), 514–15, and the sources cited there.

26 Iohannes de Francofordia, *Quaestio, utrum potestas cohercendi demonis fieri possit per caracteres, figuras atque verborum prolationes*, in Joseph Hansen, ed., *Quellen und Untersuchungen zur Geschichte des Hexenwahns und der Hexenverfolgung im Mittelalter* (Bonn: Georgi, 1901; repr. Hildesheim: Olms, 1963), 71–82.

27 Page 72, citing the depiction of Leviathan: *Et eciam Iob 4*. [i.e. 41:24 Vulg.] *dicitur: non est potestas super terram, qui ei comparetur, et textus ibidem loquitur de dyabolo.*

28 Gerson, *Œuvres complètes*, 10, pp. 88f., art. 9, 17.

29 Fols 77v–78r.

30 M.R. James, 'Twelve medieval ghost-stories', *English Historical Review*, 37 (1922), 418f.

31 The *Malleus maleficarum*, ii.1.4, pp. 109–14, discusses the nature of these assumed bodies in connection with the nature of incubi, and concludes that the demons confect ad hoc flesh from the elements in the surrounding air.

32 *De Nigromancia of Roger Bacon*, iv.3, ed. and trans. Michael-Albion Macdonald (Gillette, NJ: Heptangle, 1988), 33, 56f.

33 On demons in the form of beasts, see Russell, *Lucifer*, 209: 'Until the eleventh century the Devil was generally portrayed either as a human or as an imp, and this tendency persisted in Byzantine art. In the West, beginning in England about 1000 and spreading to Germany about 1020 and then beyond, the Devil tends to be a monstrous composite of human and animal.'

34 St. Athanasius, 'Life of St. Anthony', ch. 9, in Roy J. Deferrari, et al., trans., *Early Christian Biographies* (Washington: Catholic University of America Press, 1952), 144.

35 Fol. 27v.

36 It is evidently the dragon that is two-headed, although the context does not make the point clear.

37 On this point see the *Malleus maleficarum*, ii.1.4 (p. 109), and Thomas Aquinas's *Summa theologiae*, I.51.2 ad 4.

38 F.C. Conybeare, 'The Testament of Solomon', *Jewish Quarterly Review*, 11 (1899), 1–45.

39 On this material see generally Butler, *Ritual Magic*, 47–89, and Arthur Edward Waite, *The Book of Ceremonial Magic* (repr. Secaucus, NJ: Citadel, 1961), 58–66.

40 Gerson, *Œvres complètes*, 10, p. 90, art. 25.

8

THE MAGIC OF CIRCLES
AND SPHERES

If necromancy was in one sense chiefly the art of conjuring, it was also widely associated in the popular mind with the drawing of magic circles. The *Fasciculus morum* says of necromancers (*nigromantici*) first of all that they 'raise devils in their circles that are expected to answer their questions', and only secondly that they also 'make figures of people in wax or some other soft material in order to kill them'.[1] In *The Pilgrimage of the Life of Man*, the messenger of Necromancy traces a circle on the ground, with characters and figures, and informs the Pilgrim that his invocation causes the spirits to answer and obey, and they cannot withstand his prayers, characters, and conjurations because he holds a commission from 'the King', meaning God, to whom they are subject.[2] The Yorkshire manuscript mentioned earlier tells how one man used a magic circle in conjuring not a demon but a ghost:

> . . . he came to the assigned place and made a large circle with a cross, and it had on it [the opening words of?] the four gospels and other sacred words, and he stood in the middle of the circle, placing four small reliquaries in the form of a cross on the rim of the circle, and saving words such as 'Jesus of Nazareth' and so forth were inscribed on the reliquaries. Then he waited for the spirit to arrive. Finally he came, in the form of a goat, and three times he went around the circle, going 'a-a-a, a-a-a, a-a-a'. But when he was conjured he fell to the ground and rose up again in the form of a man of great height, horrid and gaunt, like one of the dead kings shown in paintings.[3]

Like conjuration, the use of magic circles appears to have spread beyond the sphere of clerical necromancy. For example, a woman charged with witchcraft at Provins in 1452 was said to have belonged to a 'sect' of witches that conjured the Devil by tracing three evidently concentric circles on the ground.[4] What this incident probably represents is not a popular tradition parallel to that of the necromancers, but influence from their tradition.

FORM AND PREPARATION OF THE MAGIC CIRCLE

These magic circles could at times be very simple, but sometimes they were elaborate diagrams made on specially constructed platforms.[5] The *Sworn Book* ascribed to one 'Honourius, son of Euclid', gives elaborate instructions for constructing a magic circle. The magician must construct a square platform fourteen feet across of good and well dressed stone, or of tile, or (if necessary because of poverty) of pure earth. On top of it he must fashion a circular platform, seven feet across and three feet high. The site must be ritually purified and consecrated, with blessings, incense, and invocation of angels. Then, presumably on top of the circular platform, he must make two concentric circles, carved with a new knife or inscribed in chalk, with the names written in the band between the circles. In a later chapter the magician is told that in an elaborate ceremony of consecration he should carve or inscribe four concentric circles, the smallest nine feet and the largest twelve feet across, with names of God and of angels in the bands and the seal of Solomon in the centre. Then there must be two concentric squares around these circles, with the corners pointing in the cardinal directions, names of God between the squares, and lighted censers placed within two smaller concentric circles at each of the four corners.[6]

The *De nigromancia* associated with Roger Bacon provides even fuller and more elaborate instructions for preparing and consecrating a magic circle. The magician must have a square 'secret vault' constructed in some remote place, twenty feet to each side at most, and twenty feet high at least, with windows facing the cardinal directions. Inside this building he must inscribe two concentric circles in chalk, fifteen feet at the most across, with characters and names of spirits inscribed. There are distinct kinds of circles for spirits of the air, fire, water, and earth, but the treatise is not altogether clear regarding the distinguishing features. The consecration entails, among other things, having a priest say a mass in honour of Saint Cyprian, famous for having been a magician.[7] A later chapter gives further details: the pentacle of Solomon should circumscribe the circle; the Tetragrammaton must be inscribed on all circles, because without it 'all conjurations of the spirits will fail, and no spirit will answer truth, but falsehood'; and an appropriate time must be observed for making the circle.[8] Elsewhere the treatise recommends a circle for discovery of hidden treasure that is inscribed on a circular sheet of vellum eight feet in compass, which should have ten loops with which it can be pinned to the ground.[9]

The Rawlinson necromantic manuscript is more interested in conjurations than in circles, but does prescribe and depict circles in connection with some of its conjurations, sometimes very simple, sometimes with pentangles and words and characters inscribed, and says at one point that the master should trace a circle with the point of his sword. There as elsewhere, however, circles may be inscribed not on the ground, as a location for conjuring, but on a moveable object, as a means for gaining power over the spirits: at one point the reader is told to draw a circle on a tablet, with the name 'Satan' inscribed in it.[10]

MAGIC CIRCLES IN THE MUNICH HANDBOOK

The circles in Clm 849 consist most fundamentally of single circular bands or varying numbers of concentric bands, between two and four.[11] Beyond this simple composition are various complicating factors: a single band inscribed within a square (no. 1); an inverted triangle inscribed within the outer boundary of a single band (no. 15); a double band divided into ten segments, and a rectangle inside the circle divided into six sections (no. 18); a double band with its interior divided into six wedges (no. 22); a triple band with a cross dividing the interior into four wedges (no. 40); a square inscribed in a single band, with a circle inside the square, and short bars extending outward from the middle of each side of the square and touching the inner side of the circular band (no. 9); a single band bisected by a horizontal band, while a vertical band bisects the upper portion of the circle, and a closed crescent shape (presumably representing a ship) appears in the upper two-thirds of the circle, with two dots beneath it at the prow and the stern (no. 8). Another experiment (no. 13) is unusual in having not a circle but a shield with a single band around its edge.

Inscriptions are of various kinds:

1. Four cardinal directions, with east on top in the fashion of traditional medieval cartogarphy: nos 1, 6, 9, 15, 36; at times not all the directions are explicitly given (nos 8, 10, 11).

2. Positions of the master and child medium: The position of the master is often marked in the centre of the circle, with the term *Locus magistri* (nos 3, 7, 9, 12) or simply *Magister* (nos 10, 11). The circle for no. 8 marks the position with the inscription *Hic magister cum suis sociis.* No. 1 has *Nomen magistri, de tali ordine* and *Nomen discipuli* are marked in the center. The positions for no. 22 are in the literal sense eccentric: inscriptions indicate that the master and boy are to sit on top of pentagrams on opposite sides of the circle: *Hic sederat* [=*sedeat*] *puer super signum* (at the top), and *Hic sedeat magister super signum a latere sinistro* (at the bottom). Toward the middle of the circle for no. 40 are word fragments and *N.p.* (presumably for *Nomen pueri*).

3. Names of spirits, given most frequently within the bands: no. 1 has the names of the spirits Belial, Satan, Osendior, Matalot, Belzebub, Lucifer, Sententino and Apolin inscribed in and around its band; no. 2 has Oreoth, Pinen, Otel, Tryboy, Noryoth, Belferith, Camoy, Astaroth, Sobronoy and Sismael inscribed in its band, and the names Mirael and N. (for the name of the intended victim) inscribed in its centre; no. 3 has the names Rator, Lampoy, Despan, Brunlo, Dronoth, Maloqui, Satola, Gelbid, Mascifin, Nartim and Lodoni; no. 6 has the names Oymelor, Symofos, Manoir, Faubair, Demefin, Rodobayl, Tamafin, Abelutabel, Lamair, Tentetos, Leutaber,

Rimasor, Masair, Lotobor, Tatomofon and Sirama; no. 7 has O Vsyr, Salaul, Silitor, Demor, Zanno, Syrtroy, Risbel, Cutroy, Litor Onor, Moloy, Pumotor, Tami, Oor and Ym, *spiritus armigeri*, in its bands; no. 8 has the names Fyron, Dyspil, Onoroy, Sysabel, Cotroy, Tyroy, Rimel and Orooth; no. 9 has the names Lantrayth, Feremni and Oliromim; no. 10 has O Brimer, Suburith, Tranauit, Lyroth, *vnq* (?) Berien, Damayn; no. 11 has the names Firiel to the west, Melemil to the south, Berith to the east, and Taraor to the north; no. 18 has the names Latranoy, Iszarin, Bicol, Danmals, Gromon, Zara, Ralkal, Sigtonia, Samah and Meneglasar written in the ten segments of its outer band, corresponding figures in its inner band, and the letters F-L-O-R-O-N in the six sections of its inner rectangle; no. 12 has the invocation *Tu Belial, tu Astaroth, tu Paymon, ad hoc sitis opus michi adiutores*; no. 13 has the names Asyel, Castyel, Lamsiyel, Rabam, Erlain, Olam and Belam in horizontal bands; no. 23 has the name Lylet (or Bylet) inscribed in its centre.

4. Sacred names: no. 16 has *Agla / Michael virtus dei / Gabriel fortitudo / Emanuel Paraclitus / Raphael medicina dei / Alpha et O, Oli, Ely / Tetragrmaton, amen / Agla* inscribed inside a double band, with a cross inside a square before and after each line of text; no. 36 has four divine names outside its triple band: Sabaoth at the top, Tetragramaton at the right, and Adonay at the bottom, Agla at the left.

5. Miscellaneous inscriptions: no. 15 has characters in what appears to be pseudo-Hebrew; to the right of the circle for no. 22 is a rectangular *signum* with the inscription *Esto altissimus, vnus, eternus, amen*, on five horizontal bands; no. 40 shows the word *onus* (possibly for *On*) four times.

Various types of sign and other objects also appear:

1. Pentagrams (or pentangles). No. 6 has a pentagram inscribed in its centre; no. 10 has a pentagram inscribed; no. 23 contains two pentagrams with the name *On* just beyond each point inscribed in the upper and lower wedges, and two more to the lower left and right of the circle.

2. Astronomical characters and miscellaneous figures: no. 6 shows radiating figures extending across its bands on the upper left, upper right, lower right, and lower left; nos 9 and 10 show astronomical and other signs alongside the names of spirits; no. 11 has two figures.[12]

3. Objects to be used in the experiments: no. 6 shows a sword at the top, extending downward, with its point on the top of a pentangle); no. 11 shows a sword lying toward the east with its point near the centre; no. 15 has dots evidently denoting positions for jars. These objects are presumably not meant to be drawn, but rather positioned where they are shown. Alongside the circle

for no. 2 runs a vertical band labelled *Hoc* [or *hic*] *est candela* and inscribed with the names Oreoth, Pinen, Ocel, Triboy, Norioth, Belferith, Camoy, Astaroth, Sobronoy.

When prayers are shown inscribed on the bands, these may be meant to be inscribed, but are perhaps more often to be recited as the circles themselves are traced:

The first circle for no. 39 has *In nomine Patris et Filij et Spiritus Sancti; In nomine indiuidue trinitatis, Alpha et O, deus et homo*; and *Ego te facio per illum qui creauit celum et terram, mare et omnia que in eis sunt* in its three bands.

The second circle for no. 39 has *In nomine Patris et Filij et Spiritus Sancti, Celi enarrant* in the middle band, and *Deus tuum* [sic] *regi da* in its three bands.

No. 36 has inscriptions in each of its three bands: ✠ *Hunc circulum facio in nomine dei Patris omnipotentis, qui solo verbo vniuersa creauit* in the outermost; ✠ *Hunc circulum facio in nomine dei viui qui humanum genus humano sangwine redemit* in the middle, and ✠ *Hunc circulum facio in nomine Spiritus Sancti paracliti, quia* [sic] *apostolorum et prophetarum corda sua gracia illustrauit* in the innermost. In the upper left, a further inscription begins in the outer circle and ends in the middle one: *Per hoc signum sancte crucis gracia dei defendat nos ab omni malo.*

No. 40 has ✠ *Hunc circulum facio in nomine Patris omnipotentis dei, qui solo verbo cuncta creauit. Dextera domini fecit virtutem, dextera domini exaltauit me, non moriar sed viuam et narrabo opera domini. Castigans castigauit dominus* in (and extending beyond) its outermost band; ✠ *Hunc circulum facio in nomine filij unigeniti dei viui, qui humanum genus proprio sangwine redemit. Dextera domini fecit virtutem, dextera domini exaltauit me, non moriar sed viuam et narrabo opera* in its middle band; and ✠ *Hunc circulum facio in nomine Spiritus Sancti paracliti, qui corda apostolorum et prophetarum suorum sanctissimam graciam* [sic] *illustrauit. Dextera domini fecit virtutem, etc.* in its outermost band.

No. 23 has *Deus sanctus, deus omnipotens, deus fortis, deus inmortalis, pater futuri seculi.*

No. 12 gives a modified conjuration that is shown on the circle for no. 12: *Tu Belial, tu Astaroth, tu Paymon, ad hoc sitis* [*michi* deleted] *opus michi adiutores.*

One of the experiments in the Munich handbook (no. 7) speaks of the circle as a representation of the spirits' habitation, perhaps implying a conception of Hell related to Dante's, but the point remains implicit and undeveloped. And in one of the handbook's experiments (no. 33) an unusual kind of magic circle is required: the master goes to a cemetery and gathers as many stones as there are verses in Psalm 50, and with them he makes a circle, then sprinkles it with verbena.

THE FUNCTION OF THE MAGIC CIRCLE:
PROTECTION OR HEIGHTENING OF POWER

Magic circles are usually represented in histories of magic as protective devices,[13] and at least sometimes they performed that function. In one of the *exempla* told by Caesarius of Heisterbach, a cleric famed for his skill in necromancy agrees to conjure demons to persuade a knight who does not believe in them. The cleric inscribes a circle on the ground at a crossroads, and warns the knight that he must remain within the circle as protection from the demons, and within this protective confine the knight remains secure (albeit terrified) when demons and the Devil himself arrive. In another *exemplum*, individuals who dare to step outside the circle are immediately attacked by the fiends.[14]

This notion of the magic circle as a protective device occurs at times in the magicians' own writings. In the Rawlinson necromantic manuscript the spirits are commanded to approach the master 'beside the circle here inscribed' (*iuxta circulum hic circumscriptum*). Elsewhere the spirits are commanded to come to the 'place and circle' (*locum et circulum*) ordained for their appearance. The master is to 'sign' or bless the circle with his rod, saying 'I make this circle in honour of the Holy Trinity, that [it] may be for him and his companions a place of protection and a refuge which the demons cannot violate, enter, defile, touch, or even fly over; they must appear in a place designated for them outside the circle.'[15] The notion of the circle as a protective device is found again in an early sixteenth-century text pseudonymously ascribed to Cornelius Agrippa.[16] But it is probably not the magicians' original understanding of how the magic circle functioned. The circle as a locus of power, enhancing the power of the operator, is ancient; it appears, for example, in the early Jewish story of Honi the Circle-Drawer and in the Greek magical papyri.[17] The further notion that the circle protects the magician from demons may well have originated with moralists such as Caesarius, as a symbolic way of talking about how hazardous it is to conjure demons, even if it was eventually taken over by the necromancers themselves.

In the Munich handbook it is clear that the circle is a focus of power meant to gain control over spirits. The circles have power to convoke the demons (no. 9) and to terrify them (no. 7). In one case the circle is identified as the insignia of the spirits being conjured (no. 8). In another experiment the circle seems to be identified as a representation of the spirits' dwelling place (no. 7). Apart from its power over spirits, a circle may be inscribed on horsehide, and then it will exert power over any horses to whom it is displayed, or keep unwanted horses from approaching its bearer (no. 9). At one point it is said that the spirits cannot enter a circle (no. 3), but elsewhere they are said in fact to do so (no. 11). The instructions for conjuring Mirage in the supplementary sections of the codex do suggest that the circle has a protective function, more for the magician's companion than for the master himself: the master makes a circle with a knife and has his companion sit inside it, carefully instructing him not to stretch hand, foot, clothes or hair outside it until all is done, 'lest through some error he should seem to enter into danger'.[18] The role of the circle in one of the manual's erotic experiments (no. 3) is ambiguous: it is clearly a focus of magical power, and it may also play a protective role. The text says that the larger the circle, the better; if anything of the master's should extend beyond the circle, 'it would be bad for you'. Does this imply that the circle is a protective enclosure against the assaults of the demons? Perhaps, but this function is not clearly expressed. At no point does the author expressly state that the demons may cause harm and that the circle is necessary for protection; indeed, the experiment is explicitly said to be without danger. While the master sports with the woman inside his capacious circle the demons have in fact vanished; there is no sense that they remain as invisible yet menacing presences. The master's greatest fear may be not assault but interruption: having gone to such effort to secure the woman's presence and guard the secrecy of his magic, he does not want to be disturbed in his love-making by forces demonic or otherwise, and the circle provides an enclosure within which his privacy is secure. Exceeding the bounds of this enclosure will probably have the worst result he envisions: the spell will be broken and he will be disappointed in his love.

ASTRAL MAGIC

Magic circles are not explicitly linked with the celestial spheres, at least in the Munich handbook, yet the magic of circles and that involving heavenly bodies are perhaps related, at least indirectly. In each case the circular form – the perfect shape, according to ancient Greek thought – was conceived as a centre of power that radiated outward. The elegance of the simple form, made with a single and uniform line, seems to have been suggestive of inward-looking strength combined with maximal power to influence other beings. Even if the magic circle could also serve as a protective boundary, defining a safe space within itself, the Munich handbook makes it clear that the circle exerted force over demons, whether traced on the ground or transferred to a sheet of parchment. More clearly and perhaps more obviously, in medieval thought, the stars and planets emitted powers that affected life on earth and could be put to use by a magician for good or for ill. The possibility of such astral magic was not merely a belief of the magicians themselves; philosophers and theologians, indeed educated people generally, accepted the premise that the heavenly bodies influenced affairs here below.[19]

In 1441 Eleanor Cobham, the Duchess of Bedford, was tried for treasonous magic along with accomplices who included Roger Bolingbroke. His part in the matter is summarized by one contemporary source in these terms:

And a certain clerk, one of the most renowned in all the world in astronomy and the magical art, master Roger Bolingbroke, was arrested, and publicly in the cemetery of St Paul's, with the vestments of his magic and with waxen images, and with many other magical instruments, he sat in a certain high throne, so that people from everywhere might see his works; afterwards he was hanged, drawn and quartered, and his head placed on London Bridge. This master Roger was one of the most notable clerks in the whole world, and he was accused on account of . . . Lady Elianora [Cobham], to whom he was an advisor in the magic art, and after his death many lamented exceedingly greatly.

For our purposes it is not necessary to explore all details and implications of the affair.[20] Suffice it to point out that this Bolingbroke clearly was an 'astronomer' or astrologer, and surely had cast the horoscope of Henry VI, already an activity that smacked of treason, but whether he had actually compassed the monarch's demise is another matter. In any case, we have here a classic case of the intersection between astrology, astral magic and necromancy. Whether or not this particular astrologer was also a necromancer, to lend further force to its conjurations necromancy clearly did borrow techniques, however superficially, from the traditions of astral magic derived from Arabic treatises such as *Picatrix*. This and similar writings had been translated from Arabic into Western European languages in and around the thirteenth century and seem to have had profound influence on necromantic practice. This influence manifests itself in the Munich manual chiefly in instructions to observe certain astrological conditions and in the use of fumigations.

In various ways the magical apparatus contained in the Munich manual draws from the tradition of astral magic. Eleven experiments specify that their operations, or certain of them, should be done under specified astrological conditions, which most often entail phases of the moon: the work should be done under a waxing or waning moon, or in a particular phase of the moon. The day of the week is sometimes specified. The time of the day may be indicated: the first hour, before sunrise, morning or noon. Thus, an erotic experiment (no. 12) must be initiated in the hour of Venus or the hour of Jove, not simply because of the obvious erotic associations of Venus, but because Venus and Jupiter were seen as 'favourable' planets. At times the manual says that operations should be carried out under a clear sky. Astrological specifications of slightly greater sophistication occur only rarely: an experiment is to be carried out under a conjunction of Venus and Jupiter, or when the Sun is in Leo.[21]

Fumigations (or suffumigations) occur in eight of the manual's experiments. In psychological experiments it is the image or the object sympathetically representing the victim that is fumigated: with myrrh and saffron (no. 3); with cinnamon, pepper and agrimonia (no. 4), or with sulphur fumes (no. 5). In illusionist experiments it is the circle that is thus treated: with the marrow of a dead person (no. 8), or with incense and myrrh (no. 11). An all-purpose experiment (no. 36) likewise instructs the master to place incense and myrrh in a thurible (presumably of gold) and walk around the outer edge of the circle, saying, 'I make this fumigation in the name of the Father, and of the Son, and of the Holy Spirit.' Both versions of the Mirror of Floron require that the mirror itself be fumigated.

The portion of the manual most fully reflecting the influence of Arabic astral magic is the compendium devoted specifically to the subject (no. 37). This section of the manuscript, which is deeply indebted to works such as *Picatrix* and other manuals of astral magic,[22] contains two types of material: integrated instructions for magical rites utilizing the powers of the heavenly bodies, and lists of supplementary information regarding each day of the week (the seals to be used, the names of angels and other spirits who rule and serve on each day, suffumigations to be employed) and each hour of the day and night (the name and function of each, names of angels that rule each hour, images to be used for each hour, and so forth).[23] The latter form of material can perhaps best be conveyed in tabular form (see Tables E–G), even if some nuance is lost in this presentation. Those subsections which give integrated instructions for rites are, in particular, no. 37a (conjurations for each day of the week), nos 37m and 37n (uses of images for each day and night hour), and no. 37q (uses of images and conjurations for each day of the week).

Two examples (one from no. 37m, the other from no. 37q) will illustrate how the integrated experiments draw upon the schemata found in the mere lists:

During the fifth day hour one should make an image to tame wild beasts, such as lions, bears, wolves, and any other wild and harmful beasts. At this hour cast an image of the animal of the sort you wish to control or tame, and on the head of the image carve the name of the animal, and on the chest the name of the hour and the name of the lord of the hour, and on the stomach the seven names of the first hour, and fumigate the image with Indian wood and with red sandalwood, and bury the image in a place of your choosing, and with the Lord's help aiding you, you will see that all those animals will be turned to your will.

Somewhat more elaborate is a procedure for bringing concord between humans:

The fifth image is that of Thursday, and the angels constituted over it are Satquiel, Pattar, Constiel, [and] Assassayel, and these are the winds

constituted over the image: Silite, Maraben, Halharit, and their helpers
are Yse, Riron, Naasay, [and] Eladab. And when you wish to perform this
work, make an image of yellow bronze or of yellow wax on a Thursday,
and tint it with green, and make it for a man [or] for a woman, if you
wish thereby to bring friendship between two men or women, or between
a man and a woman. Make two images of green wax in the month of May,
at the height of Pisces, or in the month of January in the height of
Sagittarius, and write the name of the man on the heart of the woman's
image, and the name of the woman on the heart of the male, and say this
conjuration:

'O Lord God, almighty creator of [all] things, visible and invisible,
establish gentle concord between thus-and-such woman, daughter of so-and-
so, and so-and-so, son of so-and-so, such as you established between Adam
and Eve, and between Jacob and Rachel, and between Michael and Gabriel
(one of whom is fiery and the other watery, [yet] the one does not harm the
other, but there is great concord between them), and such concord as you
established between the angel whose medium is fire and the one whose
medium is snow, so that the snow does not extinguish the fire, nor does the
fire consume the snow, and so you likewise turn envy into concord. Thus, O
Lord, by your most holy kindness and mercy, may you cause so-and-so,
daughter of so-and-so, to accord with, to love, and to cherish so-and-so, son
of so-and-so. I conjure you angels by the name Yafaa, Safaa, Alleya, Hayala,
Haya, Halix, Hayul, Ataya, Hytoia, Saffetaba, Coffossol, Remlestar, El, Lord
God, you who know the secrets of [all] hearts and are the end and the
beginning, [and] who never die. Hasten, Sarafem [and] Custyeli, and
command Amaris and his helpers, that they may quickly carry out and
accomplish my request.'

And bury the image in a place by which they pass, and you will see the
marvels of almighty God.

No. 37a consists chiefly of conjurations for the days of the week; the conjurations
differ in two main ways from those found in the main block of material: their
purpose is left unspecified, there being no explicit instruction to the spirits
conjured; and they involve word play and near repetition of a sort often
associated with Kabbalah: 'In the name Adonay, Adonay, Eye, Eye, Eyu . . . Eye,
Aloraye; in the name Sadaye, Saday, Cados, Cados, Cados, the high one, sitting
upon the cherubim . . .'; 'In the name Adonay, Adonay, Adonay, Eye, Eye, Eye,
Cados, Cados, Cados, Hatyn, Hatyn, Hatyn, Va, Va, strong one, Va, who
appeared on Mount Sinai with glorification of his reign, Ya, Adonay, Saday,
Sabaoth, Hanath, Hu, Haxi, Ya, Ya, Ya, Marmalita, Abym, Yea . . .'; and 'by the
name Ya, Ya, Ya, A, A, Va, Hy, Hy, Haa, Haai, Va, Va, Han, Han, Hon, Hy,
Hyen, Haya, Haya, Hol, Hol, Hay, Hael, Hon; by the names of the Lord Adonay,

Haya, Hol, creator of the ages, Cados, Cados, Cados, Ebel, El, Ya, Ya, Ya, Eloy, Arar, Eloym, Eloym . . .'

Elements of simple lunar astrology, too, are found toward the end of the compilation, in a listing of what were called *lunationes*, or days of the lunar cycle that are good or bad for making magical inscriptions (no. 46). In general, lunar astrology lent itself more to popular use than did the more technical science of solar astrology; while it is found in varying degrees of complexity, it could easily be reduced to a simple list of days in the lunar cycle, identified as favourable or unfavourable, whether in general or for a particular operation such as the working of magic.[24]

When all is said and done, however, the use of astrology and astral magic in the Munich handbook – and probably in other, similar necromantic texts – is fairly superficial. One does not find detailed or rationalized efforts to exploit the powers of celestial bodies, and even the concise treatise of astral magic is more a catalogue than a fully developed work, presumably included simply because the compiler was highly eclectic, but not genuinely integrated into the drift of the compilation as a whole.

The *Speculum astronomiae*, probably written by Albert the Great, explains the basic principles of astrology, then touches at the end on necromancy and related arts. The author says he does not mean to speak in favour of astrological images, because of their similarity to necromantic (*necromanticas*) ones. He then goes on to say that necromantic books should be set aside without being destroyed, 'For perhaps the time is already at hand, when, for certain reasons about which I am now silent, it will be useful on occasion to have inspected them, but, nevertheless, their inspectors should be wary of using them.'[25] Coy as it is, this statement makes clear that the boundary between astral magic and necromancy was fluid in practice even if in theory it could be stated with clarity: astral magic invoked the natural powers of the stars and planets, while necromancy called upon demons; but if there were spirits associated with the heavenly bodies, these might be difficult to distinguish from the spirits of the air traditionally conceived as demonic.[26] One can well understand why orthodox authorities and writers would be suspicious of that which even bordered on the forbidden. The works translated from the Arabic might include a great deal of material that was straightforwardly astrological and clearly non-demonic, but a work such as *Picatrix* appealed to both the powers of the planets and those of spirits, and identified its art as that of necromancy. The Munich handbook is important in part because it extends the spectrum to the furthest extreme, giving us nearly in its entirety a work expressly devoted to demonic magic, worked out in considerable detail and for the most part with only token borrowing from the astral magic with which necromancy was so richly intertwined.

Table E. Specifications for each day of the week

	Angels serving (37a, 37b, 37d, cf. 37h)	Spirits ruling (and co-adjutors) (37e)	Suffumi-gations (37f)	Purposes (37g)	Images (37q)
Sun.	Raphael	King Saytam (Taatus, Candas, Vanibal)	yellow or red sandalwood	binding tongues otherwise binding people	gold or yellow wax, for binding tongues
Mon.	Gabriel	King Almodab (Sylol, Millalu, Abuzaba)	aloes, *anacap*	benevolence, concord, friendship	gold or steel or white wax, for concord
Tues.	Samael	'*rex filius dyabuli*' (Carmath, Utanaual, Pascami)	pepper, *abana, cyg*	illness and destruction	red copper or red wax, for depopulating a house, causing bloodshed or illness, or other harm
Wed.	Michael	King Saba (Conas, Pactas, Sanbras)	*altast*	enmity and hatred	lead, for enmity
Thurs.	Satquiel	Madrath, son of Arath (Hyrti, Ignaro Quiron, Saalalebeth)	yellow incense	peace	yellow copper or yellow wax, for concord between man and woman
Fri.	Anael	King Saabotes (Nassath, Ynasa)	*almastic* or *lignum radim*	friendship	white wax, for love of a woman
Sat.	Captiel= Caffriel	Hayton, Assayby (Abimalyb, Haybalydoth, Yfla)	*assandaron,* sulphur	binding locations	*pix clara*, for binding tongues or places, for discord

Table F. Specifications for day hours

	Names (37j)	Functions (37j)	Ruling angels (37l)	Functions of images (37m)
1st	Yayn	binding tongues	Raphael	binding tongues
2nd	Yan, Or	friendship, favour of potentates	Anael	benevolence
3rd	Nassura	hunting, fishing	Michael	congregating birds and fish
4th	Sala	binding wild beasts	Gabriel	dispelling beasts
5th	Sadadat	binding beasts	Gaffriel	taming wild beasts
6th	Tamhut	freeing captives	Satquiel	freeing captives
7th	Caror	peace between kings	Samael	hunting and fishing
8th	Tariel	discord	Raphael	destroying houses and other places
9th	Karon	travel, safe passage among robbers	Anael	travelling without harm
10th	Hyon	work with demons or demoniacs, foul wind, aid to ladies	Michael	obtaining one's will with kings and princes
11th	Nathalon	causing bleeding in women, binding men to women and vice versa	Gabriel	concord
12th	Abat	peace (between men and women)	Cafriel	binding tongues

Table G. Specifications for night hours

	Names (37k)	Functions (37k)	Ruling angels (37l)	Images (37n)
1st	Leron	working with demoniacs, foul winds	Satquiel	illuminating dark places
2nd	Latol	working with fish	Samael	knowing fortunes
3rd	Hami	working with fire	Raphael	dispelling reptiles
4th	Atyn	destroying houses, expelling people	Anael	destroying or depopulating villages, causing enmity
5th	Caron	asking questions of sleepers	Michael	scattering armies

	Names (37k)	Functions (37k)	Ruling angels (37l)	Images (37n)
6th	Zaia	working with fruit trees and other plants	Gabriel	putting enemies to flight
7th	Nectius	expelling people, causing sickness and death	Cafriel	burning vegetation
8th	Tafat	causing enmity	Satquiel	gathering bees or birds
9th	Conassuor	binding tongues, entering before kinds and lords	Samael	attracting and capturing birds
10th	Algo	destroying evil speech or thought	Raphael	scattering besieging armies
11th	Caltrua	binding or catching birds	Anael	Not to be used for making images
12th	Salaij	telling fortunes, disclosing theft or other crime	Michael	

Notes

1 Siegfried Wenzel, ed. and trans., *Fasciculus morum: A Fourteenth-Century Preacher's Handbook* (University Park: Pennsylvania State University Press, 1989), v. 30, pp. 578–79.

2 Guillaume de Deguileville, *The Pilgrimage of the Life of Man, Englisht by John Lydgate, A.D. 1426, from the French of Guillaume de Deguileville, A.D. 1330, 1355*, ed. F.J. Furnivall (London: K. Paul, Trench, Trübner, 1899–1904), vol. 2, pp. 493–505, lines 18,471–924. See Richard Kieckhefer, *Magic in the Middle Ages* (Cambridge: Cambridge University Press, 1989), 172–3, where the drawing of the meeting with the necromancer is reproduced.

3 M.R. James, 'Twelve medieval ghost-stories', *English Historical Review*, 37 (1922), 416f.

4 Hansen, *Quellen*, 556–9; *Bibliothèque de l'Ecole des Chartes*, ser. 2, vol. 3 (1846).

5 A classic Byzantine treatise on magic instructed its reader to make two concentric circles wide enough to accommodate two people; they should be drawn inside a square, with an entrance corridor to the south, and various words and signs are to be inscribed. See Richard P.H. Greenfield, *Traditions of Belief in Late Byzantine Demonology* (Amsterdam: Hakkert, 1988), 286–7.

6 *The Sworn Book of Honourius* [sic] *the Magician, as Composed by Honourius through Counsel with the Angel Hocroell*, ed. and trans. Daniel J. Driscoll (Gillette, NJ: Heptangle, 1983), chs 26 and 38.

7 *De Nigromancia of Roger Bacon*, ii.4–6, ed. and trans. Michael-Albion Macdonald (Gillette, NJ: Heptangle, 1988), 13–26. On the legend of St Cyprian of Antioch see *Butler's Lives of the Saints*, ed. Herbert Thurston and Donald Attwater (New York: Kenedy, 1956), under 26 September.

8 *De Nigromancia.*, iii.1, 28f.

9 *Ibid.*, 51.

10 Rawl. 29r, 73r, 77v–78r, 79r, 103v, 104v.

11 One (nos 1, 2, 3, 8, 9, 12, 15), two (nos 7, 10, 16, 18, 22), three (nos 36, two in 39, 40), or four (no. 6).

12 For parallels and possible sources in Arabic culture see H.A. Winkler, *Siegel und Charaktere in der muhammedanischen Zauberei* (Berlin and Leipzig: de Gruyter, 1930).

13 E.g., Greenfield, *Traditions of Belief*, 286.

14 Caesarius of Heisterbach, *The Dialogue on Miracles*, trans. H. von E. Scott and C.C. Swinton Bland, vol. 1 (London: Routledge, 1929), 315–17. See also Stith Thompson, *Motif-Index of Folk-Literature: A Classification of Narrative Elements in Folktales, Ballads, Myths, Fables, Mediaeval Romances, Exempla, Fabliaux, Jest-Books, and Local Legends*, rev. edn (Bloomington: Indiana University Press, 1955–58), nos. D1272 (magic circle), D1381.11 (magic circle protects from devil) and G303.16.19.15 (devil cannot enter magic circle made to keep him out); and Frederic C. Tubach, *Index exemplorum: A Handbook of Medieval Religious Tales* (FF Communications, 204) (Helsinki: Suomalainen Tiedeakatemia, Akademia Scientiarum Fennica, 1969), p. 86, nos. 1,069–71.

15 Bodleian Library, Oxford, Rawlinson MS 252, fols 25v, 59v–61v.

16 Cornelius Agrippa, *Of Occult Philosophy, Book Four: Magical Ceremonies*, ed. and trans. Robert Turner (Gillette, NJ: Heptangle, 1985), 72.

17 *Taanith*, 3.8, in C.K. Barrett, *New Testament Background: Selected Documents* (London: SPCK, 1956; rev. edn 1987), pp. 191–2; and Hans Dieter Betz, ed., *The Greek Magical Papyri in Translation, Including the Demotic Spells*, 1 (Chicago: University of Chicago Press, 1986), 141 (PGM VII.846–61), 73 (IV.2006–2125).

18 Fols 112v–113v, 142r–142v: *magister facit circulum cum cutello, et faciat socium suum intus sedere, et precipiat sibi magister quod nec pedes neque manus nec vestes nec capillos foras extendat, donec magister exeat expeditus ab omnibus ordinatis. . . . Postea faciat circulum cum cultello suo, et assignat locum in quo socius suus sedere debeat. Postea iubet eum sedere, et ostendit ei sub qua forma sedere debeat in circulo, et qualiter se regere in omnibus debeat, et qualiter spiritum in aduentu suo recipere debeat, et quomodo exire debeat de circulo, et qualiter in recessu suo eum licenciare tenetur, et quomodo exire debeat de circulo, et quo debeat se diuertere. Et hec omnia debet magister socio suo ostendere antequam eum in circulo incurrere permittit, ne ex defectu periculum intrare videatur.*

19 See Richard Kieckhefer, *Magic in the Middle Ages* (Cambridge: Cambridge University Press, 1989), 131–3.

20 See Hilary M. Carey, *Courting Disaster: Astrology at the English Court and University in the Later Middle Ages* (New York: St Martin's Press, 1992), ch. 8, from which the translation is taken.

21 Nos 4, 6, 8, 11, 19, 41 (waxing moon); 2, 5 (waning moon); 7 [?] (first phase of the moon); 9 (sixth phase); 20 (other phases); 4, 41 (Sunday), 9 (Tuesday), 11 (Wednesday), 6 (Thursday or Sunday), 2, 5 (Saturday); 4, 11 (first hour); 5 (before sunrise); 41 (morning [*de mane*]); 6 (noon); 7, 8 (clear sky); 20 (conjunction of Venus and Jupiter); 41 (Sun in Leo); 5 (under a waning moon *et maxime quando est in combustione*).

22 *Picatrix: The Latin Version of the Ghāyat Al-Hakīm*, ed. David Pingree (London: Warburg Institute, 1986), esp. passages such as those on pp. 15–22 (images to effect peace, love, the favour of a lore, etc.); pp. 68–73 (images of planets), and 200–2 (fumigations for various planets); for further examples see 'Thabit ibn Qurra's *De imaginibus*', in Francis J. Carmody, *The Astronomical Works of Thabit b. Qurra* (Berkeley: University of California Press, 1960), 180–97. See Lynn Thorndike, 'Traditional medieval tracts concerning engraved astrological images', in *Mélanges Auguste Pelzer: Etudes d'histoire littéraire et doctrinale de la Scolastique médiévale offertes à Monseigneur Auguste Pelzer* (Louvain: Bibliothèque de l'Université, 1947), 217–73.

23 Nos 37a (conjurations for days of week), 37b (signs of angels), 37c (signs of days), 37d (angels ruling days), 37e (spirits ruling days), 37f (fumigations for days), 37g (purposes served each day), 37h (angels of days), 37i (names of God), 37j (names and functions of day hours), 37k (names and functions of night hours), 37l (names and functions of hourly angels), 37m (images for day hours), 37n (images for night hours), 37o (angels of times), 37p (names of planets and parts of Earth), 37q (images and conjurations for days) and 37r (summary). The association of angels and demons with specific days and hours had been worked out in Byzantine sources; see Armand Delatte, *Anecdota Atheniensia*, 1 (Liège: Bibliothèque de la Faculté de Philosophie et Lettres de l'Université de Liège, 1927), 403–4, 434–8. For material similar to that in no. 37j, see Charles Burnett, *Magic and Divination in the Middle Ages: Texts and Techniques in the Islamic and Christian Worlds* (Aldershot: Variorum, 1996), IX, p. 2.

24 On the tradition from which this text draws see Ute Müller, *Deutsche Mondwahrsagetexte aus dem Spätmittelalter* (diss. Berlin: Freie Universität Berlin, 1971); *The Works of John Metham, including The Romance of Amoryus and Cleopes*, ed. Hardin Craig (EETS, o.s. 132) (London: Kegan Paul, Trench, Trübner, 1916), xxxviii–xlii (a survey of the genre), 148–56; L. Braswell, 'Popular lunar astrology in the late Middle Ages', *University of Ottawa Quarterly*, 48 (1978), 187–94.; Robert Vian, ed., *Ein Mondwahrsagebuch: Zwei altdeutsche Handschriften des XIV. und XV. Jahrhunderts* (Halle, 1910); and Frank Fürbeth, *Johannes Hartlieb: Untersuchungen zu Leben und Werk* (Tübingen: Niemeyer, 1992), 49–57. W. Braekman, 'Magische experimenten en toverpraktijken uit een middelnederlands handschrift', *Verslagen en mededelingen van de Koninklijke Vlaamse Academie voor Taal- en Letterkunde*, 1966, 54–68, gives the first six sections of a moon-book for when the moon is in each zodiacal sign.

25 Paola Zambelli, *The 'Speculum astronomiae' and its Enigmas: Astrology, Theology and Science in Albertus Magnus and His Contemporaries* (Dordrecht, Boston, and London: Kluwer, 1992), chs 16–17, pp. 270–73.

26 On this issue see especially D.P. Walker, *Spiritual and Demonic Magic, from Ficino to Campanella* (London: Warburg Institute, 1958; repr. Notre Dame, ID: University of Notre Dame Press, 1975).

9

CONCLUSION

Some time around the 1530s, Benvenuto Cellini witnessed the conjuring of demons in the Colosseum at Rome – or at least so he reports in his autobiography.[1] He had met a Sicilian priest who knew Latin and Greek, and who agreed to introduce him to the art of necromancy. Along with two companions they went to the Colosseum, traced circles on the ground, and undertook 'the finest ceremonies that can be imagined', amid various suffumigations and an hour and a half of conjurations. When legions of demons filled the Colosseum, the priest urged Cellini to make some inquiry, and he asked them to restore to him his Sicilian girlfriend, Angelica, to which they made no reply. Cellini and the priest went to the Colosseum a second time, with a twelve-year-old boy and two other companions. In Hebrew and Greek as well as Latin, the necromancer conjured multitudinous demons by name, invoking the power of God, and there appeared a hundred times as many spirits as previously. Cellini repeated his request, and the spirits promised that within a month he would be together with Angelica. But the ceremony was soon out of control: the necromancer declared that the demons were a thousand times more than he had conjured, and they were the most dangerous of spirits; the boy shrieked that a million threatening figures were swarming around them, while four 'giants' were endeavouring to break into the circle. Eventually, however, the numbers of spirits dwindled, so that by the time the conjurers left their circle the boy reported there were only two demons left, skipping along the road or on the rooftops. The necromancer insisted that he had never before encountered such a ferocious display of demons. The experience did not dissuade him, however, from urging Cellini to join him in another ritual, the consecration of a book by which they could discover buried treasure. Cellini agreed, but was soon so preoccupied with his work that he abandoned both this new project and his hopes regarding Angelica.

E.M. Butler inclined to accept Cellini's story essentially at face value, although she noted that only the boy seems actually to have seen the conjured spirits – the rest of the party relied chiefly on the lad's reports – and she ascribed the exceptional success of the necromancer's rituals to the boy's impressionable nature.[2] No doubt it could have happened. Conjuring demons is hardly the most implausible undertaking humans have devoted themselves to, and it seems *prima facie* unlikely that books of necromancy would have circulated in late medieval and early modern Europe without occasional use of the experiments they contained. The results may more often have been those experienced by Gilles de Rais, who engaged more than one clerical necromancer in an effort to recoup his finances with demonic aid, but who found the conjurations utterly without effect – except when he was not looking, at which point the necromancer would assure him that ferocious spirits had come and beaten him mercilessly.[3] Gilles de Rais's necromancers were perhaps typical in their skilful deception of a gullible client. One is reminded of the necromancers, including a former Templar, who strung Cardinal Francesco Caetani along, begging for time to complete their experiments, and pleading that they could not do so because they were unable to locate such necessary items as a hoopoe.[4] The necromancer appears often to have been a mountebank, and the most important factor in his success was perhaps the credulity of his client. Yet one hesitates to generalize; if clients could place faith in necromancy, this was in part because the broader culture took the matter seriously enough to prosecute people for exercising the art, and few doubted in principle that conjuring could succeed, so there must have been necromancers and would-be necromancers who copied out experiments into their books in the hope of having close encounters with malign but potentially useful spirits.

In some respects the story of Benvenuto Cellini is consonant with the picture of necromancy given in the Munich handbook, while in other ways it is not. The use of circles, conjurations and suffumigations, the recruitment of a young boy, and the presence of a few companions – all this is typical of what we have seen in the necromancer's manual. The use of a classical language is again expected, although Greek and Hebrew may have been exceptional. The experiments in the Munich handbook sometimes instruct the spirits to come in pleasant and non-threatening form, as if the conjurers were aware that the experience of Cellini and his friends – a veritable temptation of Saint Anthony – might befall them. What is most unusual about Cellini's report is precisely its drama. The demons foreseen in the Munich manuscript are made tame, domesticated, even docile in comparison. The conjurations are intended to coerce the spirits, and the expectation is that these spirits will present themselves in a mood of submission to the necromancer's constraint. Yet the writer surely knew the alternative possibility, and if he insisted on using conjurations as spiritual weapons against the spirits he did so because he knew that precautions were necessary, that docility did not come naturally to demons.

I have argued that material such as the Munich handbook is historically important because it helps us grapple with the mentality of the clerical necromancers, but that this mentality was not a simple or stable entity. Its variations depended largely on the type of ritual in question. The illusionist experiments display a playful and imaginative impulse, but one that could nurture the profoundly serious anxieties seen in the early witch trials. In the psychological rites we find a quest for power over other people's minds, wills, and bodies, often manifesting itself as an expression of violent impulse, and in any case revealing tension in the clash of wills. In the divinatory operations a desire for knowledge often combines with pecuniary motives, and we see an almost obsessive concern with the truth of the knowledge gained, in the face of the danger of falsehood. In the Munich handbook we find all three types of material, but in shifting proportions: if I am right in my hypothesis that we have the experiments substantially in their original order, the compiler seems to have become less interested in the glamorous forms of magic, more absorbed in workaday divination, and more prosaic in his manner of presentation as he pursued his task. To read the work in this way is to find in it an element of implicit autobiography, even when the first person is not used. It is also to see the compiler as reflecting both synchronically and diachronically the diversities of magical tradition: not only does he bring disparate practices into fusion, combining sympathetic magic or scrying with conjuring and other techniques, but as he continues the process his work loses some of its earlier brio and he settles for kinds of magic more likely to draw money-bearing clients.

Furthermore, I have suggested that books such as the Munich manual of necromancy are significant for the light they shed on broader tendencies in late medieval culture. First, attention to such a compilation expands our conception of how a book could function and how it could be perceived in late medieval culture. Cellini's story reminds us of what we have already seen, that a book was a sacred object, particularly when consecrated, and that its sacrality was a factor enabling the necromancer better to attain his goals. Second, awareness of what magicians set out to do is needed for a realistic of their enemies' reactions and refutations. Cellini knew, as everyone at the time knew, that the behaviour of his priest friend was transgressive. One might view it as frivolous transgression; it certainly had no obvious political significance. Be that as it may, it takes on more sober significance in light of the virulent attacks on necromancy by people whose opinion weighed heavily, including popes and theologians, inquisitors and secular judges, those instrumental in forging the cumulative concept of witchcraft as a hammer for crushing women in particular, and the Humanist mages who wished to distance themselves as effectively as possible from common and vulgar necromancers. Third, study of this material helps us see the essential continuity in form between necromancy and exorcism, and the grounding of both in the established liturgy of the medieval Church. As the reverse side of the liturgical tapestry, the necromancer's experiments help us to see how ritual could be perceived and perverted by those making private use of it for transgressive purposes.

From a slightly different perspective, we might say that a text such as the Munich handbook is historically significant because it elucidates the connection between dreams and nightmares. The necromancers and their clients dreamed of discovering wealth, sexual fulfilment, favour and promotion, power over adversaries, entertainment, and knowledge of secret and future matters. In pursuing these dreams they risked entering into nightmares that they shared with those about them. Cellini experienced what any necromancer other than a sheer impostor must have feared, the traumatic disruption of psychic and spiritual security, the terrifying irruption of sinister forces into the private space they occupied. The thrill of flirting with such danger was surely one reason for the art's powerful appeal. Like the Ouija board, the necromancer's circle could begin as a game but turn unexpectedly nasty and threatening. On a purely rationalist reading, the danger of the means might be balanced against the allurement of the ends. More realistically speaking, the hazards were surely among the attractions of such activity, and as Freud would remind us, the nightmare was itself the distorted fulfilment of a wish, at least for those mysterious souls who took delight at venturing into a Boschian landscape, in the hope that when they finished they would not be trapped within its frame.

Notes

1 *The Autobiography of Benvenuto Cellini*, lxiv–lxv, trans. John Addington Symonds (repr. Garden City, NY: Doubleday, 1946), 118–22. For background see Franco Cardini, 'I diavoli al Colosseo: note su alcuni luogli "magici" della città di Roma nel Medioero', in F. Troncarelli, ed., *La città dei segreti: magia, astrologia e cultura esoterica a Roma (XV–XVIII secolo)* (Milan: Angeli, 1985), 43–54.

2 E.M. Butler, *Ritual Magic* (Cambridge: Cambridge University Press, 1949), 118–29.

3 Reginald Hyatte, intro. and trans., *Laughter for the Devil: The Trials of Gilles de Rais, Companion-in-Arms of Joan of Arc (1440)* (Rutherford, NJ: Fairleigh Dickinson University Press; London: Associated University Presses, 1984).

4 Charles Victor Langlois, 'L'affaire du cardinal Francesco Caetani (Avril 1316)', *Revue historique*, 63 (1897), 56–71; Conrad Eubel, 'Vom Zaubereiunwesen anfangs des 14. Jahrhunderts (mit urkundlichen Beilagen)', *Historisches Jahrbuch der Görres-Gesellschaft*, 18 (1897), 628.

The Necromancer's Handbook
in Clm 849: Fols 3r–108v

THE DISPOSITION OF THE MANUSCRIPT

The manuscript is from the first half of the fifteenth century, of unknown provenence. It is not mentioned in Otto Hartig, *Die Gründung der Münchener Hofbibliothek durch Albrecht V. und Johann Jakob Fugger* (Abhandlungen der Königlichen Bayerischen Akademie der Wissenschaften, philosoph.-philolog. und hist. Klasse, vol. 28, sect. 3, 1914). It is on paper, without discernible watermark. The present binding is probably from the end of the nineteenth or beginning of the twentieth century; the inner side of the rear binding bears a sticker referring to Georg Winkler Buchbinderei KB, Hoflieferant, München, Kreuzstr. 9. Fol. 3 is heavily worn. In the middle of the lower margin of fol. 3r (as on fol. 156v) is a stamp with the inscription *Bibliotheca Regia Monacensis*. In the middle of the upper margin of fol. 3r, *Clm 849* is marked in pencil. The manuscript is 14.7 cm wide and 21 cm high. The text is in a single column, with lineation still discernible on almost all pages. Initials are rubricated. Foliation runs from fol. 3 through fol. 152, and was probably executed after the earliest binding; earlier foliation occurs on individual folios, and is largely erroneous. Various hands are represented, but these do not always correspond to the gatherings of the manuscript; gatherings 12 through 14, however, are written by entirely different hands from those that precede, and the condition of the paper is also different from that in gatherings 1 through 11.

There are fifteen gatherings:

Table H. Gatherings of Clm 849

	Folios	*Experiments*	*Codicological particularities*
1	3–11	No. 1 to beginning of no. 4	Sheet with fol. 10 is separately inserted.
2	12–23	End of no. 4 to beginning of no. 9	Sheet with fols 12–13 is separately inserted.
3	24–35	End of no. 9 to beginning of no. 16	Sheet with fols 24–25 is separately inserted.
4	36–45	End of no. 16 to beginning of no. 27	Fol. 45 is also marked as fol. 59 (in earlier hand).

	Folios	Experiments	Codicological particularities
5	46–50	End of no. 27 through no. 30	Postponement of the middle of no. 27 results in textual discontinuity at the beginning of this gathering. After fol. 50 (on which no. 30 is completed), five uncounted folios (i.e., the second half of the gathering) are excised.
6	51–59	Middle of no. 27, then no. 31 and beginning of no. 32	Between fol. 51 (which is inscribed only recto) and 52 (which begins with an incipit) five uncounted folios are excised. Fol. 59r is also marked as 79 (in earlier hand).
7	60–68	End of no. 32 to beginning of no. 37	Between fol. 66 and fol. 67 is fol. 65 bis.
8	69–82	Continuation of no. 37	Fol. 70r is also marked as fol. 89 (in earlier hand). Fol. 71r is also marked as fol. 70 (in later hand). Fol. 82 is also marked as fol. 9 (in earlier hand).
9	83–95	Continuation of no. 37	Three sheets – fols 91, 92, and 94 – are separately inserted. Fol. 94 is also marked as fol. 10 (in earlier hand).
10	96–103	End of no. 37 to beginning of no. 40	Fol. 96r is also marked as fol. 104 (in later hand).
11	104–108	End of no. 40 through no. 47	After fol. 108, three uncounted folios are excised. Fols 106–7 are also marked as fols. 114–5 (in later hand). No. 44 is a fragment on the middle of fol. 107v. No. 47 is a fragment on the middle of fol. 108v.
12	109–118	Related materials, written by various hands	After fol. 118, two uncounted folios are excised. In this gathering there is no lineation.
13	119–32		
14	133–146		Fols 133–139 are also marked as fols 1–7.
15	147–156		Six sheets – fols 147–151 and 156 – are separately inserted.

TEXTUAL DISCONTINUITIES

Apart from the abrupt beginning of the text at the beginning of the main block (on fol. 3r) and the occurrence of textual fragments at the end of this block (on the middle of fol. 107v and on the middle of fol. 108v), discernible breaks in textual continuity occur at three points within the block: (1) Between fols 45 and 46, one text ends abruptly (45v) at the end of the fourth gathering, the fifth gathering begins with a blank page (46r), and a new text begins *in medias res* (46v). (2) Between fols 50 and 51, one text ends with an *explicit* (50v), five folios are excised at the end of the fifth gathering, and the sixth gathering begins *in medias res* (51r). (3) Between 51 and 52, one text ends abruptly (51r) even though the verso is blank, five following folios are excised within the gathering, and the same gathering resumes with an *incipit* (52).

The discontinuities on fols 45–51 are related, in the sense that the central portion of an experiment (no. 28) has been postponed to fol. 51r, which evidently supplies the missing link between the beginning (fols 44v–45v) and the end (fols 46v–47v) of this experiment. Note that experiment no. 28 is divided into two 'chapters': the end of the first is marked by the words *Explicit primum capitulum* near the bottom of fol. 46r; the second begins with a list of names at the very bottom of that folio, which continues at the top of fol. 51r and continues with a conjuration that occupies the remainder of fol. 51r (fol. 51v is blank), only to conclude with the material on fols 46v–47v, which terminated with the notation *Explicit secundum capitulum.* The textual continuity produced by this rearrangement is corroborated by the identification of two chapters as part of a continuing experiment. The discontinuity is not fully explainable in terms of erroneous binding, which would not account for the scribe's not using the verso of fol. 51. Rather, the lack of continuity is more plausibly explained on the assumption that the scribe recognized belatedly that he had material at hand that belonged to an earlier experiment; he may not have taken the trouble to determine exactly where the fragment inserted on fol. 51r belonged.

It is possible that the only material actually deleted from the miscellany is that on the first two folios. Although folios are elsewhere excised (between fols 50 and 51, between fols 51 and 52, and between fols 108 and 109), the evident textual discontinuities can be emended by rearrangement, and there are no further deletions from the original foliation.

At the end of this block, three folios between 108 and 109 are excised at the end of a gathering, after which new material begins, written by different hands. Within this new material there are three further breaks in textual continuity: between 118 and 119, where two folios are excised at the end of a gathering; between 132 and 133, with the beginning of a new gathering; and between 146 and 147, again with the beginning of a new gathering.

EDITORIAL PRINCIPLES

Punctuation and capitalization have been standardized. Non-standard but clearly intentional forms and spellings have been allowed to stand: *abilem* for *habilem* (no. 34), *aparuisti* for *apparuisti* (no. 31), *beniuolus* for *beneuolus* (no. 34), *blica* for *plica* (no. 1), *colido* for *collido* (no. 5), *commitantem* for *comitantem* (no. 19), *commitiuam and commitiua* for *comitiuam and comitiua* (no. 7), *decim* for *decem* (no. 18), *desparsit* for *dispersit* (no. 33), *dissipulos* for *discipulos* (no. 35), *duodecim* for *duodecem* (no. 27), *genubus* for *genibus* (nos 10 & 11), *hillariter* for *hilariter* (no. 6), *hostio* for *ostio* (no. 17), *inungas* for *inunguas* (no. 22), *karacteribus* for *characteribus* (no. 19), *karitatem karitatiuam* for *caritatem caritatiuam* (no. 14), *kathedram* for *cathedram* (no. 15), *legittimo* for *legitimo* (no. 27), *letania* for *litania* (no. 31), *lingnum* for *lignum* (no. 13), *loycam* for *logicam* (no. 34), *magestas* for *majestas* (no. 1), *magestatis* for *majestatis* (no. 33), *navim* for *navem* (no. 8), *optinere* for *obtinere* (no. 31), *pallificando* for *paleficando* (no. 19), *patifacere* for *patefacere* (no. 6), *pulcherimi* for *pulcherrimi* (no. 13), *quadruuio* for *quadriuio* (no. 26), *rethoricam* for *rhetoricam* (no. 34), *ribelles* for *rebelles* (no. 33), *senephali* for *seneschali* (no. 34), *sepellire* for *sepelire* (no. 4), *sepellitur and desepelliendo* for *sepelitur and desepeliendo* (no. 2), *Septemtrione* for *Septentrione* (fols 115r and 144r), *thesaurum* for *thesaurus* (no. 43), *vppupa* for *upupa* (no. 6). The text has been corrected conservatively when it was necessary to do so for the sense of a passage, but not simply to correct errors; e.g., on fol. 56r *quod vij die hominem ad ymaginem plasmasti tuam* is corrected to *qui vij[a] die hominem ad ymaginem plasmasti tuam* but *vij* is not corrected to *vi*, and on fol. 13r *discedat . . . seruiet* [for *seruiat*] *. . . diligat* has been allowed to stand. Necessary additions have been made in square brackets; deletions and substitutions are indicated in the notes. Lower-case *c* and *t* are sometimes distinguished but often not; when the context allows either, *c* is used. In occult names and 'Chaldean' formulas especially it is often impossible to distinguish between *c* and *t*, to determine whether a superscript line over a vowel represents *m* or *n*, or to make other editorial judgements which depend on context; in these cases the transcription is perforce largely arbitrary.

Italics are used for ritual text that is to be recited, but not for dialogue. In the conjurations, chains of invocations given in unbroken sequence in the manuscript are broken into individual units (beginning with *per* or *et per*), each marked with a bullet, to clarify the structure of each invocation.

NO. 1. FOR GAINING KNOWLEDGE OF THE LIBERAL ARTS (FOLS 3r–5v)

[. . .] versus orientem. Deinde dicere [debes]:

Apolin, Maraloth, Berith, ego, talis, vos exorciso[a] et coniuro ex parte dei omnipotentis, qui vos vestra eleccione iussit antra subire profundi, ut debeatis michi mittere quendam spiritum peritum dogmate omnium scienciarum, qui michi sit beniuolus, fidelis, et placidus, ad docendum omnem scienciam quam voluero,[b] veniens in forma magistri, vt nullam formidinem doleam percipere. Fiat. Fiat. Item coniuro vos

---

a   *Corrected from* exorcisor.

b   *MS* volueris, *although the final letter is uncharacteristic for this hand.*

- *per Patrem et Filium et Spiritum Sanctum,*
- *et [per] hec sancta nomina quorum virtute ligamini – scilicet Dobel, Vriel, Sabaoth, Semoni, Adonay, Tetragramaton, Albumay, Siloth, Moreth, Sadabin, Rodobel, Domiel, Perarabiel,[c] Alatuel, nominem, nominam,[d] [et] Vsobel,*

quatenus vos tres reges maximi et michi socii michi petenti vnum de subditis vestris mittere laboretis, qui sit magister omnium scienciarum et arcium, veniens in forma humana placabilis [et] splendens[e] michi, et erudiens me cum amore, ita et taliter quod in termino 30a[rum] dierum talem scienciam valeam adipisci, permittens post sumpcionem sciencie dare sibi [3v] licenciam recedendi.

Et hoc eciam tociens dici debet.

Hec vero dicta,[f] depone ensem et involue in dicto panno, et facto fasciculo cuba super ipso, et aliquantulum dormias. Post sompnum vero surge et induas te, quia facto fasciculo homo se spoliat et intrat cubiculum, ponendo dictum fasciculum sub capite. Est autem sciendum quod dictis hiis coniuracionibus sompnus accidit virtute diuina. In sompno apparent tibi tres maximi reges cum famulis innumeris, militibus et peditibus, inter quos est eciam quidam magister apparens, cui ipsi tres reges iubent. A[d] te ipsum venire paratum videbis. [Videbis] enim tres reges fulgentes mira pulchritudine, qui tibi in dicto sompno viua voce loquentur, dicentes, 'Ecce, tibi damus quod multociens postulasti.' Et dicent illi magistro, 'Sit iste tuus discipulus, quem docere te iubemus omnem scienciam siue artem quam audire voluerit. Doce ipsum taliter et erudi, vt in termino 30a[rum] dierum in quacumque sciencia[g] voluerit summus inter alios habeatur.' Et videbis ipsum respondere, 'Domini mei, libentissime faciam quidquid [4r] wltis.' Hiis dictis, reges abient et magister solus remanebit, qui tibi dicet, 'Surge, ecce magister tuus.' Hiis vero dictis, excitaberis; statim apperies oculos, et videbis quendam magistrum optime indutum, qui tibi dicet, 'Da michi ensem quam[h] sub capite tenes.' Tu vero dices, 'Ecce discipulus vester, paratus facere quidquid wltis.' Tamen debes habere pugillarem, et scribere omnia que tibi dicet.

Primo debes querere, 'O magister, quod[i] est nomen vestrum?' Ipse dicit,[j] et tu

c   *Or* Pararabiel.
d   Sic *in MS.*
e   *MS* splandens.
f   Sic in *MS.*
g   *MS* in quam scienciam.
h   Sic in *MS.*
i   Sic in *MS.*
j   Sic in *MS.*

scribas. Secundo, de quo ordine, et similiter scribe. Hiis scriptis, debes sibi postulare[k] ensem; quo habito ipse recedit, dicens, 'Expecta me donec veniam.' Tu nichil dices. Magister vero recedet et fert ensem. Post cuius recessum, tu dissolues pannum vt ap[p]aret inferius. Etiam scribas in dicto circulo nomen eius scriptum per te, et scribi debet per te cum predicto sangwine. Quo scripto, involue dictum pannum et bene reconde.

Hiis factis, debes prandere solo pane et pura aqua, et illa die non egredi cameram. Et cum pransus fueris, accipe pannum et intres circulum versus Apolin. Dic sic: 'O rex Apolin, magne, potens, et venerabilis, [4v] ego famulus tuus, in te credens et omnino confidens quod tu es fortis et valens, rogo per incomprehensibilem magestatem tuam vt famulus et subiectus tuus, talis, magister meus, debeat ad me venire quam[l] cicius fieri potest, per virtutem et potenciam tuam, que est magna et maxima in secula seculorum. Amen.' Et similiter dicere [debes] versus Maraloth, mutando nomen. Et versus Berich similiter. Hiis dictis, accipe de dicto sangwine et scribe in medio circuli nomen tuum cum supradicto corde, vt hic apparet inferius.[m] Deinde scribe cum dicto corde in angulis panni illa nomina, vt hic apparent. [5r] Si autem sangwis unius auis non sufficeret, potes interficere quantum tibi placet.

Quibus omnibus factis, sedebis per totam diem in circulo, aspiciens ipsum, nichil loquendo. Cum vero sero[n] fuerit, blica dictum pannum, spolia te, et intra in cubiculum, ponendo ipsum sub capite tuo. Et cum posueris,[o] dic sic plana voce:

O Apolin, Maraloch, Berith, Sathan, Beliath, Belzebuc, [et] Lucifer, supplico vobis vt precipiatis magistro – in eo [loco] (nominando eius nomen) – vt ipse debeat venire cras ante solis ortum ad me et docere me talem scienciam sine aliqua fallacia, per illum qui venturus est iudicare viuos et mortuos et seculum per ignem. Amen.

Caue igitur et precaue ne signum ✠ crucis facias, propter magnum periculum in sompno. Scias quod videbis magistrum tota nocte loqui tecum, interrogans a te quam scienciam velis addiscere. Et cum dices, 'Talem', ita quod, vt dictum est,

---

k   *Meaning* presentare*?*

l   *Followed by* ci *(?), deleted.*

m   *Circle at the bottom of fol. 4ᵛ: a single band inscribed within a square. The names of the spirits* Belial, Satan, Mendior Matalot, Belzebub, Lucifer, Sententino *and* Apolin *are inscribed in and around the band, as are the four cardinal directions.* Nomen magistri, de tali ordine *and* Nomen discipuli *are marked in the centre.*

n   *The final* o, *written with a superscript line, has been corrected, with the correct form* sero *also in the margin.*

o   *Meaning* reposueris*?*

tota nocte cum eo hoc loqueris. Cum itaque excitatus fueris, quod e[s]t in ipsa nocte, surge et accende candelam, et accipe dictum pannum et devolue, et in eo sede, videlicet in circulo vbi nomen tuum scriptum est ad tuum commodum, et voca nomen magistri tui, sic dicens:

> *O talis, de tali ordi-* [5v] *ne, et in magistrum michi deditus per maiores reges tuos, te deprecor vt venies*[p] *in forma benigna, doctum me talem scienciam,* [in] *qua*[q] *sim promcior omnibus mortalibus, discens ipsam cum magno gaudio, sine aliquo labore, et omni tedio derelicto. Veni igitur ex tuorum parte maiorum, qui regnant per infinita secula seculorum. Amen. Fiat, fiat, fiat.*

Hiis itaque dictis, tunc aspiciens versus occidentem videbis magistrum venire cum multis discipulis, quem rogabis vt omnes abire iubeat, et statim recedunt.[r] Quo facto, ipse magister dicet, 'Quam scientiam audire desideras?' Tu dices, 'Talem,' et tunc incipies.

Memento enim quod quantum tibi dicet, tantum addisces[s] et memorie commendabis, et omnem scienciam quam habere volueris addisces in termino xxx[a[rum]] dierum.

Et quando ipsum de camera abire volueris, plica pannum et reconde,[t] et statim recedet. Et quando ipsum venire volueris, aperi pannum, et subito ibidem apparebit, continuando lecciones. Post vero terminum 30a[rum] dierum, doctus optime in scientia, fac tibi dare[u] ensem tuum et dic vt vadat, et cum pace recedat. Debes iterum dicere cum pro alia ipsum invocabis habenda sciencia, qui tibi dicit ad tui libitum esse paratum.

Finis est capituli sciencie, etc.

NO. 2. FOR CAUSING A PERSON TO LOSE HIS SENSES (FOLS 6r–7v)

Ad hoc igitur, vt sciencia siue ars possit ab aliquo auferri, vnde diligenter attende.[a] Debes enim primo decrescente luna die sabbati ire ad illum quem ad mentem venire volueris et coram eo sic dicere plana voce:

---

p   Sic *in MS.*

q   *MS* quam.

r   Sic *in MS.*

s   *MS* addiscens.

t   *MS* retunde.

u   Sic *in MS.*

a   Sic *in MS.*

Subintret Mirael cerebrum tuum et omnem sapienciam, sensum,[b] discrecionem, [et]
cogitationem diluat et aboleat. Coniuro te, Mirael,
- *per omnes principes et maiores,*
- *et per omnia que facere voles,*

vt in tali quem aspicio debeas permanere donec michi libuerit, et ipsum obfuscare,[c] et omne quod
agnoscit ammittat,[d] alioquin mittam te in maris profundum, quod non egredieris in secula.

Quibus dictis, recede et prestolare donec sero fuerit. Quo facto, vade ad
hostium eius et incide de ligno ipsius hostij tantum quod de ipso calamum facere
possis, et ad domum redeas, et fac de ipso calamum, et de sangwine murilogi in
panno lini cum ipso calamo scribe:

O Mirael, ablator sapiencie, sciencie, cognicionis, et artis, adsis in sensibus talis, et spiritum
facere debeas animo dementem.[e]

Qua conuocacione scripta, fit in dicto panno circulus cum dicto sangwine vt hic
apparet,[f] vbi scribitur vt sequitur: nomen illius quem priuare volueris in medio
circuli conscribitur, [cum] hoc nomine 'Mirael'. Quibus factis, debes dicere sic:

Coniuro vos decem demones [6v] *malignos, videlicet Oreoth, Pinen, Ocel, Tryboy, Noryoth,*
Belferith, Camoy, Astaroth, Sobronoy, Sismael,
- *per indiuiduam trinitatem, videlicet Patrem et Filium et Spiritum Sanctum ab vtroque*
  procedentem,
- *et per tremendam et timendam diem judicij,[g]*
- *et per omnia que fuerunt et sunt et erunt,*

vt[h] sicut in hoc circulo figurati,[i] circuitis talem,[j] ita vere et efficaciter et existenter personam
eius circuatis, et sensus eius taliter affligatis quod ignorans, demens, stultus, et mente captus[k]

---

b   *Followed by* et.

c   *Corrected in margin from* abfuscare.

d   *MS* amittit.

e   Sic *in MS.*

f   *Figure on fol. 6ᵛ: a single circular band, with* Oreoth, Pinen, Otel, Tryboy, Noryoth, Belferith, Camoy,
Astaroth, Sobronoy *and* Sismael *inscribed in it. In the centre of the circle* Mirael *and* N. *(for the name of the*
intended victim) are inscribed. Along the left side of 6v is a band labelled Hoc [*or* hic] est candela *and the following*
names inscribed along it: Oreoth, Pinen, Ocel, Triboy, Norioth, Camoy, Astaroth, Sobronoy.

g   *The writer began to write* judij-, *then corrected the second* j *to* c.

h   *MS* et.

i   *Followed by* estis.

j   *Followed by* vt.

k   *MS* capitis.

[7r] *efficiatur. Et tu, Mirael, de cerebro eius nunquam egrediaris, manens in eo die noctuque donec ab eo abire iubebo.*

Quibus sic dictis ter, iterum redeas in eadem nocte ad domum ipsius cum dicto panno et cum quodam cultello, et cum ibi fueris, volue humeros versus suum hostium, et flectens te in terram, minge in parte eius more cameli. Faciendo foueam subter[r]ando dictum pannum in eius limite,[1] dic sic:

Subterro te, talem, in nomine demoniorum scriptorum circa te, quod semper ipsi demones [sint] circa te et omnis tua virtus sepulta sit.

Et cooperto dicto circulo cum terra, redeas iterum ad domum, et fac candelam, in qua sint scripta omnia contenta in circulo. Et debes ipsam facere de cera primo empta, [in] nomine et [pro] destrvccione eius, cum vna acu similiter empta. Qua facta, accende ipsam et dic sic:

Sicut hec candela,[m] facta in destruccionem talis, comburitur et consumatur,[n] ita omnis virtus et sciencia existens in ipso in demenciam conuertatur, per virtutem demoniorum in hac candela scriptorum. Et sicut vos demones hic scripti ardetis, ita nullam requiem habere possitis donec hoc duxeritis ad effectum.[o]

Quibus verbis semel prolatis, dictam candelam extingwe, dicendo hec verba:

Sicut hec candela extingwitur, ita omnis virtus in tali permanens penitus consumetur.

Mane vero ipsam accende, dicendo, *Sicut hec* [7v] *candela, etc.* Item alio mane, vsque ad terminum septum dierum, computato primo die; in octavo vero die, videbis istum dementem omnino, de quo omnes mirabuntur. Mirabile est autem quod non credit se aliquem habere defectum, et omnes alios mente putat esse carentes.

Hanc igitur experienciam apud te tene, quia magne virtutis est.

Cum autem ipsum volueris in statum priorem deuenire, optime fieri potest. Die iouis, 1. hora noctis, vade ad suum hostium vbi sepelisti pannum, quod dum sepellitur debet poni pannus in quodam vase vt non putrescat; sic factis omnino ipsum liberandi, et ipsum pannum desepelliendo, sic dicas:

1   *Corrected from* limate.
m   *Followed by* est.
n   *Presumably meaning* consumitur.
o   *MS* affectum.

O Mirael, Oreoth, Pinen, Ocel, Triay, Moryoth, Belferith, Canay, Astaroth, Sobronoy, [et]
Sismael, ego, talis, absoluo vos vt eatis ad vestri libitum, et relinquatis talem in statu priori.

Quibus dictis, fer domi^p istum pannum, et accenso igne ligni oliue et^q prouincula
et herba verbena,^r priocias dictum pannum sub dicto igne, dicendo,

Sicut ignis iste consumit hunc pannum, ita omnis ars facta per^s me contra talem penitus
consumetur.

Combusto igne, proice dictum puluerem in aqua currenti, et omnis ars destructa
erit. Cognoscet eciam se postea vir quod fuerit primo omni prefectura priuatus,
credens se habuisse egritudinem, cuius occasione hec accessisse putabit, etc.

NO. 3. FOR AROUSING A WOMAN'S LOVE (FOLS 8r–11v)

. . . maxima diligencia probaui ipsam, et est periculosa, cum hec scilicet in
persona, et . . .^a

Cum volueris habere amorem a quacumque muliere vis, siue longinqua siue
propinqua, tam nobili quam prolipia,^b in quacumque die vel nocte vis, siue in
augmento siue in amicicie detrimento, primo debes habere quandam columbam
totam albam et cartam factam de cane femina dum est in amore, de qua est habere
leuissimum. Et debes scire quod predicta carta potentissima est ad amorem
mulieris habendum. Debes eciam habere calamum aquile. Et in loco occulto accipe
dictam columbam et cum dentibus morde eam penes cor ita vt cor egrediatur, et
cum calamo aquile in dicta carta cum dicto sangwine scribe nomen illius quam vis.
[Debes] formare ymaginem mulieris nude quam melius scis,^c dicendo,

Formo talem, N., filiam talis, quam habere desidero, nomine^d istorum sex spirituum
calidorum, videlicet Tubal, Sathan, Reuces, Cupido, Afalion, Duliatus, quod ipsa me diligat
super omnes viuentes istius mundi.

---

p   *Sic, for* domum.?
q   *Meaning* cum.?
r   *MS* herbam verbenam.
s   *Inserted above the and in margin.*
a   *Introductory line at top of folio, partly cut off.*
b   *Meaning* plebeia.?
c   Sic *in MS.*
d   *Meaning* in nomine.?

Qua facta, scribe in fronte nomen eius et hoc numen 'Tubal', dicendo,

> *Tu es talis, filia talis, de cetero ad meam voluntatem disposita, et tu es Tubal in fronte eius.*
> *Te iubeo permanere, ligando sensus eius capitis sui[e] ad me tantummodo cupientem.*

Postea adhuc scribe in brachio suo dextro 'Sathan', et in [8v] sinistro 'Reuces'. Quibus scriptis, sic dic:

> *Sicut tu, Sathan, et tu, Reuces, estis scripti in hac ymagine facta nomine talis, ita continuo*
> *affligatis brachia ista sua vt aliquid facere nequeat sed me amplecti desideret.*

Quo facto, iterum scribe penes cor ymaginis nomen tuum, dicendo,

> *Sicut in corde istius ymaginis sum, ita talis, N., die noctuque me in corde suo habeat.*

Quo facto, scribe supra wuluam imaginis hoc nomen 'Cupido', dicendo sic:

> *Sicut tu, Cupido, es super wuluam istius ymaginis, ita semper maneas super wuluam talis,*
> *accendendo ipsam vt omnes viros istius mundi despiciat et me tantummodo cupiat, et ignis*
> *amoris mei ipsam torqueat et inflammet.*

Quo facto, scribe in crure dextro 'Afalion', in sinistro 'Duliatus'. Quibus scriptis, dic:

> *Sicut tu Afalion et tu Duliatus estis scripti in hac ymagine, ita sedeatis in cruribus talis,*
> *affligendo crura eius propter amorem vehementem mei, quod non velit ire nec ire desideret*
> *aliquo nisi huc.*

Quibus dictis, accipe[f] ipsam ymaginem ambabus manibus, et flexis genibus dic sic:

> *Adtraxi cor et mentem talis per hanc ymaginem, et prouoco in ipsam invocacione forti quod*
> *ipsa me diligat, cupiat, et affectet, et eciam tota nocte in sompno aspiciat, per dominum*
> *nostrum Iesum Christum, qui viuit [9r] et regnat et imperat in eternum.*

Quibus dictis, habeas mirram et saffranum, et facto igne, dictam ymaginem suffumiga, dicendo hanc coniuracionem:

---

e   Sic *in MS.*
f   *MS* accipit.

Coniuro vos omnes demones in hac ymagine scriptos, per dominos vestros quibus obedire tenemini: Sobedon, Badalam, et Berith,ᵍ quatenus talem, cuius ymago est hoc nomine figurata, in amore meo accendere debeatis, vt die noctuque in me cogitet, in me speret, donec cum affectu meam compleuerit voluntatem. Et sicut in hac ymagine scripti et fixi estis, ita in ipsa recumbaris donec de ea faciam quidquid velim.

Hac igitur coniuracione ter dicta, et facta suffumigacione, habeasʰ caude pilum cuiusdam equi, et suspende dictam cartam cum dicto pilo, ita vt moueatur ab aere, et dimitte stare; illaⁱ vero die, vel sequenti, vel alia, vel quando potes, ad illam mulierem accedas, et procul dubio libentissime te videbit, dicens [se] sine te stare non posse. Et hoc habeas pro constanti, et tuo animoʲ faciet voluntatem, et super te omnia diligetᵏ in eternum.

Si bene seruaueris ymaginem eius nomine figuratam, in qua virtus talis existit, ymmo et de hoc magis est admirandum: hoc est signum: antequam vidisses ipsam, statim facta hac ymagine [9v] cum ad eam accesseris erit de [te] taliter filocapta quod dum te viderit, quod non recedas ab ipsius coniunccione priuatus, ymmo de omni quod volueris contentus habebis.ˡ

Si vero ad eam non possis accedere, siueᵐ timore aut loci distancia aut aliquo interueniente, tamen potes ipsam apportari facere per supradictos demones, qui ita efficaces sunt quod si esses in Oriente in vna hora ipsam ab Occasu portarent sine aliquo periculo, et similiter reportarent sine aliqua diwlgacione. Et vt sit facta ymago vt dictum est et suspensa illa die, in aliqua hora diei, sufflas in ipsa ita quod flatu tuo moueatur. Et similiter secunda die et tercia die. In nocte vero ipsius diei tercij, vel eciam in ipsa die, solus uel cum tribus sociis fidelibus, accipe dictam ymaginem et cum illo pilo liga ipsam ad collum tuum, et pendet in pectore tibi. Et habeas quandam ensem, et in terra fac circulum cum dicto ense. Facto circulo, stans intus, voca socios si habeas, qui nichil faciant nisi quod in circulo sedeant et ludum videant; quos si non habueris, quod melius est.ⁿ Habeas stilum ferreum, et circa circulum scribe vt hic apparet,ᵒ cum silentio semper.

g   *MS* Lerith.

h   *MS* habeat *or* habeac.

i   *MS* illam.

j   *Perhaps for* tui animi.

k   Sic *in MS.*

l   Sic *in MS.*

m   *MS* sine.

n   Sic *in MS.*

o   *The upper portion of 10ʳ is occupied by a single circular band containing the names* Rator, Lampoy, Despan, Brunlo, Dronoth, Maloqui, Satola, Gelbid, Mascifin, Nartim *and* Lodoni. *The centre is labelled* Locus magistri.

Quo facto,[p] [10r] dic hanc coniuracionem:

Coniuro vos demones in hoc circulo sculptos, quibus data est potestas et potencia ducendi et
alligandi mulieres in amore virorum,
  • *per virtutem et potentiam maiestatis diuine,*
  • *et per thronos et dominaciones et potestates et principatus illius qui dixit et facta sunt,*
  • *et per illos qui non cessant clamare vna voce, dicentes, 'Sanctus, sanctus, sanctus,*
    dominus deus sabaoth, pleni sunt celi et terra gloria tua. Osanna in excelsis. [10v]
    Benedictus qui venit in nomine domini. Osanna in excelsis',
  • *et per hec nomina pauencia et tremencia vos,[q] scilicet Rator, Lampoy, Despan, Brulo,*
    Dronoth, Maloqui, Satola, Gelbid, Mascifin, Nartim, et Lodoni,
  • *et per anulum istum qui hic est,*
  • *et per innumerabiles potencias vestras et maiorum vestrorum,*
quod vbicumque sitis de locis vestris sine mora surgatis et ad talem pergatis, et statim sine
fallacia ipsam huc ducatis, et cum voluero ipsam reportabitis. Et de hoc nemo senciat vel
perpendat.

Qua[r] dicta ter, versus anulum aspiciendo, audies quandam vocem dicentem,
'Ecce nos sumus,' et statim eos videbis sex domicellos pulcriores et mites, tibi eadem
voce dicentes, 'Assumus hic, parati tibi parere[s] benigne. Dic igitur quid vis, et statim
subito faciemus.' Tu autem dices, 'Eatis ad talem et michi ipsam sine mora ducatis.'
Quibus dictis, subito recedent; ante horam ipsam sine lesione portabunt.

Et scias quod nullus ipsorum potest ingredi circulum, sed ipsam apportent
apud ipsum, et ipsa porriget tibi manum, et intus ipsam trahis, que aliquantulum
est attonita tamen wult libentissime [11r] tecum stare. Doceo eciam te quod
quanto maiorem circulum facis, melius est tibi, quia in eo potes facere circulum
et in ipso melius extendere. Si enim aliquid tui esset vltra signum circuli, malum
esset tibi. Venta itaque muliere, omnes spiritus euanent.

Potes enim retinere hanc mulierem in dicto circulo quantum tibi placet, quia
cum mulier ingreditur circulum dicere debes illis spiritibus, 'Vnus vestrum vadat
ad locum a quo[t] talem a[p]portauistis, et in forma [eius] ibidem maneat donec
ipsam hic habuero.' Hiis dictis, omnes abient cum silencio. Cum autem, illa die
ac nocte ac mense ac anno quando tibi placuerit quod ipsam ad domum volueris
reuertere,[u] dic sic:

p   Quo facto *repeated at top of 10^r.*
q   Sic *in MS.*
r   *Sc.* coniuracione.
s   *MS* parare.
t   *Corrected from* qua.
u   Sic *in MS.*

O vos spiritus, qui talem huc duxistis, accipite ipsam et ad domum suam portate. Et quotiens ipsam reuoluero, ipsam sitis in reportando subiecti. Venite igitur per miras valencias quas ineffabiliter exercimini.

Quibus ter dictis, venient quinque spiritus, qui eam te vidente portabunt.

Memento enim, quando ipsa egreditur circulum, in dicendo 'Vale', tangere ipsam cum ymagine quam habes ad collum, quia in eternum pro hac te diliget et neminem preter te videre curabit; ymaginem semper interim quod cum muliere [11v] moraris, ad collum retinere debes, qui semper ipsi mulieri invisibilis apparebit, et cum ipsa abierit, dissolue ipsam a collo tuo et in quoddam vasculum diligenter reconde. Et ipsa recondita, dilue totum circulum et secure egrediaris. Et quando [eam] iterum ad te venire volueris, fac vt desuper dictum est.

Et nota quod experimentum est efficacissimum, et in eo nullum periculum est. Quo solo experimento Salomon habebat quascumque mulieres volebat. Et hec dicta sufficiant pro habendis mulieribus. Et debet fieri cum sollempnitatibus maximis, etc.

NO. 4. FOR GAINING DIGNITY AND HONOUR (FOLS 11v–13v)

Dicto de habendo amore mulieris, volo tibi legare artem probatissimam ad obtinendum dignitatem et honorem, statum et maximam incorruptibilem dileccionem a rege uel a pelato siue domino, et generaliter a quocumque viro volueris.

Primo igitur habeas duos lapides molles quos ad inuicem ita fricabis vt superficies ipso[rum] plane eque concordent. Quo facto, in vno sculpes formam illius quem volueris,[a] incipiendo a capite, deinde vsque ad pedes, faciendo primo a parte anteriori, deinde a posteriori, sculpendo eciam coronam in capite si rex est, et sic [12r] secundum dignitatem. Qua sculpita,[b] formabis in illo eciam lapide apud aliam formam tuam figuram, quam melius scieris, incipiendo a capite, vt dictum est, et a parte anteriori deinde a tergo. Quibus factis, scribe in fronte primo more sigilli nomen illius, et in tua nomen tuum. Quo facto, luna crescente die dominica in prima hora diei, habeas argentum siue stagnum, et ad ignem decola. Quo decolato, proicias in formam illius, dicendo sic:

Ego, talis, volens talem graciam obtinere et ab eo venerari, semper honorari, similiter et timeri, formo[c] ymaginem factam et sculptam nomine eius virtute cuius ipse me perpetue diligat vltra modum.

a   *Followed by* jncip, *deleted.*
b   Sic *in MS, for* sculpta.
c   *MS* formam.

Qua^d facta, habeas stilum ferreum, et in eius fronte sculpes hoc nomen 'Dyacom'; in pectore eius hec tria nomina, scilicet 'Pumeon', 'Terminas', et 'Peripaos'; et in spatulis hec sex nomina, videlicet 'Midam', 'Fabni', 'Gebel', 'Darail', 'Vmeloth', et 'Thereoth'; et in vmblico hoc nomen 'Byreoth'.^e Quibus scriptis, habeas pannum lineum candidissimum, et hanc ymaginem in ipsam involve. Quam involutam bene recondas.

Die vero iouis, in prima hora diei, facto igne, cola similiter stagnum et in tua forma ipsum infunde, dicendo,

Ego, talis, formo ymaginem meam et ad mei similitudi- [12v] *nem, qua ego semper dominer tali et ab ipso diligar et timear in eternum.*

Qua formata, similiter in alio linteolo involuas.

Et est aduertendum quod ymago illius cuius vis graciam obtinere debet esse longitudinis ipsius unius semissi, cum sculpitur in ipso lapide. Qui eciam lapis tantus debet esse quod ymago tua tercia parte ymaginis illius debeat esse maior. Et eciam in ymagine tua^f debes imponere sceptrum.

Quibus factis omnibus diligenter, ut dictum est, in sequenti die veneris, prima hora eius, suffumiga ymaginem illius ad fumum horum aromaticum, scilicet cinamomi, piperis longi, et herba agrimonia, dicendo sic:

Ego, talis, exorzizo^g te, ymaginem,^h nomine talis formatam,
- *per inseparabilem vnicam et indiuiduam trinitatem,*
- *et per omnes thronos, dominaciones, et potestates, et principatus,*
- *et [per potenciam] omnium creaturarum,*

vt per tui virtutem obtineam graciam et amorem talis cuius nomine facta es.

Quibus ter dictis, sic proferas:

O Dyacon, Pumeon, Termines, Peripaos, Midain, Fabin, Gebel, Dorayl, Vmeloth, Tereoth, et Bireoth, spiritus benignissimi et concordiamⁱ seminantes, ego, talis, cum instantia magna vos deprecor, vobis supplico, vos rogito, per vnicum dei filium, qui sui

---

d   *Sc.* ymagine.

e   *The forms of these names vary even within this experiment:* Dyacom *appears on fol. 12^v as* Dyacon; Terminas *as* Termines; Midam *as* Midain; Fabni *as* Fabin; Darail *as* Dorayl; Thereoth *as* Tereoth, *and* Byreoth *as* Bireoth.

f   *Corrected in MS from* tuam.

g   *Sic in MS, corrected from what appears to be* exerzizo.

h   Sic *in MS.*

i   *MS* concordium.

sangwinis effusione humanum genus mortuum suscitauit, vt per hanc ymaginem forma-
[13r] *tam nomine talis ipsum iuxta me taliter aligetis, vt me super omnes mortales*
veneretur, nunquam a meo consensu̇ discendens, sed meis semper parens preceptibus. Michi
studeat complacere, per eundem dominum nostrum Ihesum Christum, qui viuit et regnat in
secula seculorum. Amen.

Qua oractione dicta, accipe tuam ymaginem et ipsam in dextra teneas, aliam autem in sinistra, et iunge illam tue, sic dicendo ter: 'Subiecit populos nobis, et gentes sub pedibus nostris' [Ps. 46:4 Vulg.]. Quo dicto, habeas quandam catenulam ferream, et ad collum ipsius ymaginis liga, ponendo aliud capud in manu dextera tue ymaginis. Quo posito, bene ligato, ita sic dices:

Sicut tu, ymago formata nomine talis, es subpedita et ligata mee ymagini, ita talis in
eternum sit michi penitus alligatus.

Quo dicto, capias cum tuis manibus ambas manus ymaginis, et retro flectens dic,[k]

Ligo per hanc ymaginem manus talis, quod manus eius perpetuo nullam vim habeant contra
me.

Flecte eciam predicte ymaginis caput versus terram, sic dicendo:

Sicut ymago hec, facta nomine talis, manet coram me flexa ceruice, ita talis nunquam a mei
voluntate discedat, sed me continue sequatur et michi semper seruiet[l] et me in eternum diligat
super omnes, me veneretur, et michi studeat applaudere.

Quo dicto, faciendo semper suffumigacionem, accipe [13v] tuam ymaginem et a tergo ipsius pone aliam, ita quod os suum tangat humeros tue ymaginis, et ponendo sic dicas:

Sicut hec ymago, facta et condita nomine talis, stat apud istam ymaginem factam nomine mei
cum maxima subieccione; ita talis sit subtritus et subiectus michi donec iste ymagines fuerint
conseruate.

Quibus dictis, involue ipsas, vt dictum est, in quodam alio linteolo mundissimo.
   Quas involutas in quodam vasculo pone et clam porta per ciuitatem et coram eius presenciam in habitaculo eius, si potes; et hoc facere debes per totam diem.

---

j   *Corrected in both text and margin from* sensu.

k   *MS* dicendo.

l   Sic *in MS for* seruiat.

In sero, autem, debes sepellire has ymagines in tali loco et ita infra, vt [non] reperiantur, et videbis mirabilia. Si autem coram ipso aut eius habitaculum pergere non valeres, subterra, vt dictum est, et ipsas^m vbicumque tibi placet, et ab ipso super omnia diligeris.

Hoc enim experimentum^n vsus fuit Parmen[i]des ad regis Persarum graciam obtinendam.

NO. 5. FOR AROUSING HATRED BETWEEN FRIENDS (FOLS 13v–15r)

Ad faciendum odium inter diligentes.^a

Restat etiam vt de odio et inimicitia inter diligentes ponere pertractemus.

Cum igitur inter duos viros siue mulieres siue masculum et feminam seminare volueris inimiciciam et^b odium capitalem, necesse est vt accipias duos lapides viuos et recondes^c vnius ponderis, qui debent esse fluminei, et in vno debes sculpire nomen vnius cum hiis [14r] nominibus: Cartutay, Momabel, Sobil, et Geteritacon. Et in altero, nomen alt[er]ius et hec nomina, scilicet Puzanil, Pimaton, Folfitoy, et Mansator. Que nomina sunt valde se odencia. Quibus sculptis, vni videlicet illum qui factus est nomine illius, debes sub ianua eius limine^d subterrare si potes, si autem non, sepelias sub limine^e cuiusdam domus inhabitate, et similiter alium sub limine^f alterius, vt dictum est, vel sub cuiusdam domus, vt supra scriptum est, et^g ibi stare permittas septem diebus et septem noctibus.

Quo facto, ante solis ortum remoueas et in locum ocultum ambas facias^h et ipsas in ignem

proicias, sic dicendo:

Coniuro vos spiritus inimicissimos, per eterni dei gloriam, quod inter talem et talem, quorum nomina hic in illis lapidibus sculpta permanent, quantum odium inter vos est, tantum inter ipsos seminetis et inseratis.

m Sic *in MS; meaning not altogether clear, but perhaps* et *should be deleted.*
n Sic *in MS.*
a *Title repeated in margin.*
b ac *added between lines.*
c vn *deleted.*
d *MS* limite.
e *MS* limite.
f *MS* limite.
g *MS* et et.
h Sic *in MS.*

Quibus ter dictis, ipso[s] lapides de igne afferas, sic dicendo: 'Cum irascetur furor eorum in nos, forsitan aqua absorbuisset nos' [Ps. 123:3f. Vulg.]. Quo dicto, proiciamus[i] ipsos in aqua frigidissima, et in ipsa stare permitte sereno celo tribus diebus et noctibus.

Quarto autem die, accipias ipsos et suffumiga eum cum fumo sulphuris, dicendo sic:

Coniuro vos omnes demones odiosos et malignos, inuidios et discordes,
- *per vnitatem Sancti Spiritus Paracliti manentis in Patre et Filio et Spiritu Sancto,[j]*
- *et per eternitatem omnium creatorum,*
- *et per omnes sanctos et sanctas dei,*
- *et per hec sancta nomina, virtute quorum dominator olimpi celum et terram est formare dignatus, scilicet 'Aa', [14v] 'Sabaoth', 'Helyn', et 'Abacel',*
- *et per omnes reges et dominatores inferni,*
- *et per hec nomina demonum, videlicet 'Apolyn', 'Gebel', 'Astaroth', 'Tereol', 'Falmar', et 'Tyroces',*

quatenus quantum odium inter vos existit et quantum inter Caym et Abel fuit, tantum inter talem et talem protinus inseratis. Accendite itaque ipsos, et taliter inflametis quod vnus alterum videre non valeat, ymo vno reliquum in innumerabili odio rebellis affligat.[k] Remoueatur ab ipsis omnis amor, dileccio, fraternitas, et compago; ad inimiciciam ac omne odium maximum conuertantur.

Quibus ter dictis, suffumigando ipsos semper, reconde.

Nocte vero sequenti, colidas dictos lapides simul et vnum super reliquum proicias, sic dicendo:

Non collido hos lapides, ymo col[l]ido talem et talem, quorum nomina hic sculpta sunt, quod vnus alterum continuo affligat et inmitigabili odio se ad inuicem de cetrero crucient.

Et sic facias singula nocte et singula die ter per aliquos dies. Et videbis statim siue audies quod inimici efficientur et se odient animo, et vnus alterum videre non valent.[l]

Si enim omnino ipsos disiungere voles, et voles vnum ab altero disgregare et vnus alterum fugiat, facias hoc modo. Surge die sabbati ante solis ortum, decrescente luna, et maxime quando est in combustione, et ire versus solis ortum

---

i   Sic *in MS, for* proice.?

j   Sic *in MS.*

k   Sic *in MS.*

l   Sic *in MS.*

facias.^m Qua facta, habeas dictos lapides illuc tecum [15r] latos, et fortiter ipsos ad inuicem frica, pulsando vnum super alterum, sic dicendo:

Non colido has^n lapides, etc.

Quo dicto ter, sepelias quem volueris. Deinde recede et versus occidentum vade et ibi fac foueam, et aliam^o ibi sepelias, dicendo sic:

Sicut disiunxi hos lapides, ita talis^p se disiungat a tali, et oppositi sint sicut isti lapides.

Quo sepulto, rec
ede. Et videbis disiungi et vnum ab altero separari.

Hoc enim experimentum occultandum est, quia ineffabilis in eo virtus existit. Nullum enim remedium invenitur ante^q ipsi disiungantur et se mordaciter odiant.

Cum vero volueris ad primam amiciciam remeare, desepeliendi sunt predicti lapides et in fornace ponendi; qui, bene cocti, minutissime terantur, et ipsos cum aqua ad invicem inpasta et siccare permitte. Quo siccato, in fluminis aqua proicias, dicendo,

Tollatur omnis inimicicia et ira que fuit inter talem et talem, et in amorem pristinum reuertantur, per misericordiam pii dei, qui non respicit malicias peccatorum. Amen.

Et scias quod per hec statim coniunguntur, et omnis ira tollitur, et pristina pace fruuntur.

NO. 6. FOR OBTAINING A BANQUET (FOLS 15r–18v)

Artem quam in tua curia vidisti me tociens exercere, videlicet ad prouocandum dapiferos. Primo debet fieri invocacio xv^a spirituum hoc modo: In primo, extra villam debes accedere, luna crescente, die iouis [15v] vel die dominica, in meridie, et debes tecum ferre ensem lucidissimum et auem vppupam, et cum dicto ense in quodam remoto loco facere circulos. Quibus factis, cum acie predicte^b ensis scribere debes xvj nomina vt inferius apparebit in^c illa figura. Quibus factis, debes

---

m Sic *in MS.*

n Sic *in MS for* hos.

o Sic *in MS.*

p *MS* talis et talis.

q Sic *in MS.*

a Sic *in MS.*

b Sic *in MS.*

c *MS* et.

figere versus orientem in interiori circulo dictum ensem, vt hec racio demonstrat.[d]
Quo facto, debes tibi taliter alligare dictam vppupam vt discedere non valeat de
in- [16r] teriori circulo, in quo tu stare debes.

 Quo facto, genibus flexis, respiciendo versus orientem et capiendo dictum
ensem ambabus manibus, sic[e] proferas:

*Oymelor, Demefin, Lamair, Masair, Symofor, Rodobayl, Tentetos, Lotobor, Memoyr,
Tamafin, Leutaber, Tatomofon, Faubair, Selutabel, Rimasor, Syrama, spiritus iocundissimi,
ylares, et gaudentes, ego, talis, vos adiuro*

- *per Patrem et Filium et Spiritum Sanctum,*
- *et [per] filium vnici dei potentissimi, viui et veri, qui propter nos et nostram salutem
  descendit de celis et incarnatus est de Spiritu Sancto, ex pura et intemerata ac
  incorrupta virgine Maria,*
- *et per natiuitatem et passionem ac resurreccionem domini nostri Iesu Christi, filij dei
  veri,*
- *et per sanctum lauacrum baptismatis quo quisque saluatur,*
- *et per solem et lunam et omnia sidera celestia,*
- *et per omnia illa que [potenciam] habent vos terrere et constringere, et virtute quorum
  ad nos vocantibus[f] oportet accedere,*

*quatenus huc sine mora ad me venire debeatis in forma miti, placida, et iocunda, patifacere
quidquid dicam.*

Qua dicta duodecies[g] – videlicet primo quater versus orientem, secundo quater
versus meridiem, tercio quater versus occidentem, quarto et vltimo quater versus
aquilonem – portando semper ensem in manu, et cum [16v] dicis
coniuracionem, figiendo[h] semper ipsum in quolibet loco; deinde pone vbi primo
erat dicta coniuracio, vt dictum est.

---

d   *Diagram on fol. 15ᵛ: a quadruple band with a pentangle inscribed in the centre, a sword depicted at the top
(extending downward across all four bands, with its point on the top of the pentangle) and other figures (likewise
extending across all four bands) on the upper left, upper right, lower right, and lower left. The cardinal directions are
given outside the outermost band, with* Oriens *on top. Within the bands sixteen names are inscribed:* Oymelor,
Symofos [*on 16ʳ:* Symofor; *on 17ᵛ:* Simofor], Manoir [*on 16ʳ:* Memoyr; *on 17ᵛ:* Memoir] *and* Faubair *in
the outermost band;* Demefin, Rodobayl [*on 17ᵛ:* Rodobail], Tamafin *and* Abelutabel [*on 16ʳ:* Selutabel;
on 17ᵛ: Belutabel] *in the next;* Lamair, Tentetos, Leutaber [*on 17ᵛ:* Zeugaber] *and* Rimasor *in the next; and*
Masair, Lotobor, Tatomofon *and* Sirama [*on 16ʳ:* Syrama] *in the innermost.*

e   *Corrected in MS from* sicut.

f   Sic *in MS, for* ad nos vocantes oportet vos accedere*?*

g   *Sic in* MS.

h   Sic *in MS for* figendo *or, rather,* fige.

Qua dicta, semper genibus flexis, iterum volue te versus orientem, tenendo nunc ensem per

manum dexteram, et accipiendo vppupam per sinistram, sic dicas:

Venite, o prenominati[i] spiritus, venite ad me, venite, quoniam ego precipio vobis per eternam dei gloriam. Amen.

Qua dicta semel, volue te cum ense et vppupa versus occidentem, et videbis xvi milites decoros et strenuos, qui tibi dicent, 'Vocasti nos et ad te venimus, parare[j] subiecti. Pete secure quid vis, quoniam tibi sumus in obediendo parati.' Tu autem dices, 'Facite michi videre vestram potenciam, vt aspiciam mensas cum discumbentibus multis cum inprandionibus infinitis.' Qui tibi respondebunt [se] libenter velle facere.

Et statim venient domicelli multi, apportantes mensas tripedes, manutergia, et alia necessaria. Post hec venient nobilissime gentes, qui discumbent, et pincernas ibidem seruientes et apportantes infinita cibaria. Et audies cantus, melodias, et tripudiantes videbis et ludos innumeros. Et scias quod illi duodecim[k] non discedant a te, stantes apud circulos et extra, et tecum loquentes et videntes. [Debes] eciam scire quod ad te de illis discumbentibus apud circulos venient tres reges, [17r] rogantes te vt cum ipsis commestum vadas. Et tum respondebis te aliquo modo non posse discedere. Quibus dictis, ipsi subito ad discumbentes reuertentur, dicentes eis de circulo te mouere non velle, quos audies. Quibus dictis, mittebunt[l] per vnum pincernam de qualibet dape, de qua secure comedas, et de ipsa porrige illis xvi apud circulum stantibus, et ipsi eciam de ea comedent.[m] Post hec, videbis omnes a mensis discedere et ordinate equos ascendere.

Et demum omnes a tuis oculis euanebunt, preter illos xij,[n] qui, stantes coram te, dicent, 'Nonne placuit tibi ludus noster?' Quibus tu hillariter respondebis quod sic. Et facta responsione, ipsi petent a te vppupam, que continuo trepidabit, quod mirum est. Quibus tu sic dices: 'Volo vobis vppupam dare si iurabitis ad me venire, faciendo hunc ludum quotiens michi placuerit.' Qui dicent se esse iurare paratos. [Ad] quos librum quendam facias apportare, quem subito apportabunt, et in ipso hoc modo iurare facias:

i   *Corrected from* prenominate.

j   Sic *in MS for* pareti et *or* parere?

k   Sic *in MS.*

l   *MS* mittentibus.

m   *MS* comedentur.

n   Sic *in MS.*

Iuramus omnes duodecim[o] *in hoc sacrato libro*

- *per illum deum viuum et verum, qui nos et omnia creauit,*
- *et per dominos quos timemus et adoramus,*
- *et per legem quam obseruamus,*

ad te sine mora venire quocienscumque vocaueris nos, et mensas parari facere, [17v] *sicut et adhuc melius vt vidisti.*

Et statim iurabunt.

Et cum iurauerint, dabis eis vppupam, quam cum habuerint a te petent licenciam recedendi. Quibus dabis hoc modo, dicendo, 'Pergite quo affectatis accedere, et estote solliciti[p] michi.' Qui dicent [se] esse tibi de cetero obligatos. Hiis dictis, abeunt, similiter et tu egredere de circulis et ipsos aboleas vt nullus appareat, et tuum ensem ferendo recedas.

Debes igitur attendere quod vppupa magne virtutis est nigromanticis et demones invocantibus,[q] quapropter ipsa multo[r] vtimur ad[s] nostri tutelam.

Cum enim clam aut palam aut vbicumque ipsos ad te venire volueris, respicias in libro suprascriptos circulos et figuras, legendo submissa voce nomina in ipsis existencia. Quibus inspectis et semel lectis, lege hanc coniuracionem semel:

Oymelor, Demefin, Lamair, Masair, Simofor, Rodobail, Tentetos, Lotobor, Memoir, Tamafin, Zeugaber, Tatomofon, Faubair, Belutabel, Rimasor, et Sirama, rogo vos, coniuro et adiuro per dei veram maiestatem, vt hic venire faciatis subditos vestros, qui apportent huc cibaria, et primo talem et talem, et faciant pulcherimum festum cum iocis, canticis, choreis, et tripudiis, et ge- [18r] *neraliter cum omnibus que*[t] *circumstantibus corda letificent* [cf. Ps. 103:15 Vulg.].

Qua semel lecta, splendidissimi venient domicelli parantes mensas pulcherrimas. Quibus paratis, audies tubas, cytaras, et cantus innumeros. Cum enim alta voce dices, 'Apportate aquam', statim apportabitur. Et similiter, 'Ferantur epule', et statim feruntur. Et erunt pincerne et dappiferi optime seruientes, et domicelle pulcherrime, et instrventes, facientes innumerabilia sollacia. Et potes facere apportari, si tibi placet, inprandioni[um] mille maneries, que valde et[u] ultra modum sapient comedentibus.

o *Sic in* MS.

p *MS* sollicite.

q *Followed by* quem.

r *MS* multa.

s *MS* in ad.

t *MS* qui.

u *Followed by* p, *deleted.*

Debes itaque scire quod quanto magis comedunt, multo plus famescunt, quia apparentur sicut dapes, tamen non[v] existent, ita quod si famelicus in illis esset credens illis dapibus saciari, vt si non comederet procul dubio moreretur.

Et quando volueris ludum destruere, dic vt mensas accipiant. Eciam acceptis statim mensis,[w] omnes astantes ibidem permanebunt. Quos si voles cantare aut sonare aut omnem ludum facere, dic, 'Sic fiat,' et videbis affectum,[x] quoniam hij sunt spiritus ludi et omnis solacij, qui facient omnia dicta sibi. Et cum volueris ipsos abire, dic sic: 'O vos omnes, recedite, et quociens vos vocabo ad me, omni causa remota pergetis.' Qui respondebunt, 'Libentissime faciemus.' Et ipsis recessis, omnes [18v] exiuerint, de hac arte stupentes.

Et hic finitur ars illa, que est quasi apud hodiernos ignota, quam Matheus Hispanus totaliter ignorauit, etc.

NO. 7. FOR OBTAINING A CASTLE (FOLS 18v–21r)

Experimenta formosissima ad conuocandum spiritus vt homo faciat[a] apparere castrum pulcherrimum et fulcitum, siue ad prouocandum armatorum innumeras[b] legiones.[c]

Et eciam[d] vna[e] alia experiencia ad prouocandum spiritus vt homo faciat apparere castrum pulcherimum et fulcitum, siue ad prouocandum armatorum innumeras legiones,[f] quod leuiter fieri potest, et intra alia pulcherimum reputatur.

Vade primo, luna 10, sereno celo, extra villam ad aliquem locum segregatum et secretum, portans tecum lac et mel, de quo per aerem aspergere debes. Et discalciatus, nudo capite, genibus flexis, versus occidentem sic lege:

O Vsyr, Salaul, Silitor, Demor, Zanno, Syrtroy, Risbel, Cutroy, Lytay, Onor, Moloy, Pumotor, Tami, Oor, et Ym,[g] spiritus armigeri, quibus proprium est arma deferre et vbicumque wltis sensus humano[s] decipere, ego, talis, vos coniuro et exorcizo et invoco,

---

v   *Followed by* sunt.

w   *MS* mensas.

x   *Meaning* effectum.*?*

a   *MS* faciant.

b   *MS* innumerasl.

c   *Heading underlined in text and repeated in margin.*

d   enim *written above, invading preceding line.*

e   *Written above* alia, *also invading preceding line.*

f   *This repetition may be erroneous, or may be a reference to the repetition of the experiment (fol. 20r) or to the testimonial anecdote (fols 20r–21r).*

g   Silitor *appears on fol. 20r as* Silitol; Demor *appears on fol. 20r as* Denior; Zanno *appears on fol. 19r as* Zanno, *with the note added* uel Zaimo, *and on fol. 20r as* Zaimo; Risbel *appears on fol. 20r as* Ristel; Lytay *appears on fol. 19r as* Litor *and on fol. 20r as* Lytoy; Pumotor *appears on fol. 20r as* Pumiotor; Tami *appears on fol. 20r as* Tamy; Oor *appears on fol. 19r as* Oor, *with the note added* uel Dor, *and on fol. 20r as* Dor.

- *per Patrem et Filium et Spiritum Sanctum, que sancta trinitas nu[n]cupatur,*
- *et per creatorem celi et terre et visibilium omnium et invisibilium,*
- *et per illum qui hominem de limo terre formauit,*
- *et per enunciacionem domini nostri Ihesu Christi,*
- *et per eius natiuitatem,*
- *et per eius mortem et passionem,*
- *et per eius resurrexionem,*
- *et per eius ascensionem.*

Item [19r] *ego coniuro vos omnes prenominatos[h] demones,*

- *per piam et misericordissimam et intemeratam ac incorruptam virginem Mariam, matrem domini nostri Ihesu Christi, qui pro miseris peccatoribus mortem sumens nos ad celestem patriam reuocauit.*

Item ego coniuro vos supradictos spiritus,

- *per omnes sanctos et sanctas dei,*
- *et per omnes apostolos, martires, confessores, virgines, et viduas,*
- *et per hec preciosissima ac ineffabilia nomina omnium creatoris, quibus omnes ligamini, et que[i] terrent omnia celestia, terrestria, et infernalia, scilicet Aa, Ely, Sother, Adonay, Cel,[j] Sabaoth, Messyas, Alazabra, et Osian.*

Item ego coniuro vos et exorcizo

- *per virtutem et potenciam omnium principum, regum, dominorum, et maiorum vestrorum,*
- *et per virtutem et possibilitatem ac potenciam vestram,*
- *et per habitaculum vestrum, cuius hec est forma,[k]*
- *et per omnes figuras in ipso permanentes,*

quatenus vos, insolubiliter ad mei potenciam alligati, ad me sine prestolacione venire debeatis, in tali habitu vt me aliqualiter non terreatis, [19v] *subiecti et parati facere ac demonstrare michi omnia que voluero, et hoc facere debeatis et velit[is] per omnia que in celo et in terra morantur.*

Qua lecta semel versus occidentem, similiter [lege] versus meridiem, orientem, et aquilonem.

Et a longe videbis continuam commitiuam turbam armatorum versus te venientem, qui premittent[l] tibi quendam scutiferum, dicentem quod illi ad te

---

h *Followed by* spiritus, *deleted.*

i *MS* quem.

j *Meaning* El?

k *Figure at bottom of fol. 19r: double band, with* O Vsyr, Salaul, Silitor, Demor, Zanno [*outside outer band:* uel Zaimo], Syrtroy, Risbel, Cutroy, Litor *in the outer band, and* Onor, Moloy, Pumotor, Tami, Oor [*inside inner band:* uel Dor], et Ym, spiritus armigeri, *in the inner band.* Locus magistri *is marked in centre.*

l *MS* permittent.

veniunt quos vocasti. Cui dices sic: 'Vade ad eos, et dic ipsis vt in tali condicione ad me veniant vt nullum timeam,[m] sed secure permaneam cum ipsis.' Quo dicto, statim ad eos redibit.

Qui post modicum interuallum venient ad te. Quibus visis, ostende eis[n] statim hunc circulum, qui habet multum ipsos 15 demones pauentare (uel spanentare),[o] quem ipsi aspicient, dicentes, 'Secure quid vis pete, quoniam per nos tibi omnino fiet.' Quibus tunc dices quod istum suum circulum taliter debeant consecrare vt quandocumque ipsum aspexeris, vocando ipsos, ad te debeant velociter venire,[p] debentes illud facere quod est in ipsis naturale, scilicet facere[q] apparere fortilicias et castra cum foueis et cum multitudine armatorum. Qui dicent [se] hoc facere velle. Quibus porriges librum, et videbis quemlibet ipsorum super ipsum manum inponere et aliqua verba loqui, que non intelliges. Hoc facto, ipsum tibi restituent.

Quo restituto, rogabunt te vt ipsos abire permittas, quia a te non possunt nisi licencia petita. Quibus dices, 'Facite hic castrum, vt vi- [20r] deam vestri efficaciam.' Qui statim circa te castrum facient, cum multis aliis, in medio cuius castri te videbis, et ibidem militum maxima multitudo [erit]. Tamen isti quindecim a te discedere non valebunt. Post enim huius hore spacium, te[r] rogabunt vt a te discedere possint. Quibus dic, 'Estote michi parati quocienscumque hunc circulum aspiciam, vocando vos, et subito recedetis.'[s] Qui iurabunt a[d] te venire continuo. Quo dicto, dic vt recedant quocumque ire desiderant. Et tunc ludus totaliter destruetur, et nullus ibidem apparebit.

Hiis factis, domum remea, custodiendo librum bene in quo virtus totalis existit. Quando vero enim pulcherime artem volueris operari, aspicias circulum, legendo nomina; incipiendo ab oriente, sic dices:

O Vsyr, Salaul, Silitol, Denior, Zaimo, Syrtroy, Ristel, Cutroy, Lytoy, Onor, Moloy, Pumiotor, Tamy, Dor, Ym, voco vos vt hic venire debeatis per consecracionem huius circuli, in quo signa vestra permanent, et michi in omnibus istis apparere faciatis castrum fortissimum, cum profundis foueis, et militum et peditum cum maxima commitiua.

---

m   *First two letters corrected in MS.*

n   *Followed by* hoc circulum, *deleted.*

o   *Parentheses inserted on the assumption that* uel spanentare *is meant as an alternative reading. For* qui habet . . . pauentare uel spanentare *read perhaps* qui facit . . . pavere *or* pavescere.

p   *Followed by* et proficisti, *deleted.*

q   *MS* faciendi.

r   *The* e *is misshapen, and another* e *is written above it.*

s   Sic *in MS.*

Et subito videbitur ibi castrum pulcherrimum[t] cum omnibus necessariis. Quod si vis ingredi, poteris, quia continuo miles tecum stabit,[u] cui omne quod voles apparere precipias et fieri faciat.

Cum semel ego hanc artem [probare volebam], exercui eam cum imperatore, quem multi nobiles comitabant, qui venando per quandam obscuram siluam pergabant. Et hunc modum tenui. Primo inspexi circulum, vocando supradictos demones [20v] plana voce. Et tunc statim venit ad me quidam speciosus miles, quem nullus preter me valebat aspicere, qui ad me dixit, 'Ego sum vnus de vocatis spiritibus, ab aliis ad te missus, qui nominor Salaul, cui precipias quid tibi placet petere, et statim fiet.' Cui dixi, 'Volo vt apparere facias istis vnam legionem armatorum, quam imperator et alij secum stantes ipsos[v] credent esse rebelles.' Qui dixit, 'Factum est.' Et tunc omnes comites et eciam imperator[w] respexerunt versus aquilonem, et a longe viderunt versus ipsos venire et equitum et militum innumerabilem multitudinem, a quibus vnus discessit, et ante magne hore spacium venit ad imperatorem, tremendo dicens, 'Domine imperator, ecce videte gentes sine numero qui contra vos veniunt, iurantes vos et omnes vestros comites mori tradere, et vestros dure[x] interficere.' Quo audito, imperator et comites[y] quid deberent agere nesciebant.[z] Et interim ipsi spiritus apropinquabant. Quos imperator et alij videntes et audientes, ipsorum instrumenta terrencia fugere tunc ceperunt, et isti sequentes ipsos et sagitando vna voce clamabant, 'Fugere non potestis hodie mortem!' Et tunc ego dixi, 'O Salaul, fac ante imperatorem et suos unum castrum mirantissimum,[a] quod imperator et alij ingredientur.' Et factum est. Tunc factum est tutissimum castrum comitum optime,[b] cum turribus et foueis, depresso[c] ponte, quod vide-[21r] batur optime et plenum esse[d] dispendiariis, clamantibus, 'O domine imperator, ingredere cum tuis sociis festinanter!' Qui ipsum intrauerunt, in quo videbantur esse famuli et multi amici imperatoris; existimauit se ibi invenisse se viriliter defendentes. Quibus ingressis, leuauerunt pontem et se defendere

---

t   *Added in margin.*

u   *Note added in bottom margin:* uel quia continuo quidam milites tecum stabunt.

v   Sic *in MS.*

w   *MS* imperator et eciam.

x   e *repeated above line.*

y   *Followed by* territus, *deleted.*

z   *MS* nesciebat.

a   *Followed by* comitum, *deleted.*

b   optime *added in margin.*

c   *MS* depresse.

d   *Followed by* stipendariis, *deleted.*

ceperunt. Tunc illi spiritus cum machinis[e] castrum mirifice totaliter expugnabant. Quapropter imperator et alij sui, valde territi, magis timebant.

Tunc dixit michi Salaul, 'Non habemus potenciam hic[f] morandi nisi vno quadrante, ita quod recedere nos oportet.' Et tunc, recesso castro et expugnantes[g] et ipsis recedentibus castrum et omnia euanerunt.[h] Imperator et alij sui tunc viderunt et invenerunt se in quadam[i] palude, de quo admirati sunt valde. Quibus dixi, 'Negocium ex hoc maximum fuit festum.' Et ad ciuitatem remeatis, de sero cenauimus. Quibus sequentem experienciam post cenam feci.

Memento quod ars predicta nisi vno quadrante durare non potest, nisi durabit vnum quadrantem vna vice, etc.

NO. 8. FOR OBTAINING A BOAT (FOLS 21r–23r)

Vt vbicumque sis possis habere nauem, in qua tu cum quibuscumque voles quocumque ferris[a] vadas: ieiunus[b] die lune; ipsa die, luna crescente, ad celum serenum, id est sereno celo, solus [sis] in loco remoto, et fer tecum vnam [21v] costam hominis siue mulieris mortui, quam primo acuere debes, et facere cum ipsa in terra has figuras cum nominibus et aliis omnibus contentis in ipso circulo, vt hic apparet.[c] Quo facto, debes ingredi signatum locum, et voluendo te circa circulum, suffumiga ipsum cum medulla mortui, vt dictum est.

Quo facto, audies per aerem voces, facta suffumigacione; quibus auditis, hanc coniuracionem dices versus occidentem, vt scriptum est:

Fyrin (quod[d] sic dicas: *O Fyrin*), *Dyspil, Onoroy, Sysabel, Cotroy, Tyroy, Orooth,* [22r]

---

e　*Followed by* et.

f　*Followed by* manendi, *deleted.*

g　*MS* expungnantes.

h　*Perhaps for:* recesso castro, et expugnantibus recedentibus, castrum et omnia euanuerunt.

i　*Followed by* plade *(deleted)* plaude *(deleted)* uel.

a　*Meaning* voles?

b　u *partly covered by blot.*

c　*Figure on fol. 21ᵛ: a single circular band in which are inscribed the names* Fyron, Dyspil, Onoroy, Sysabel, Cotroy, Tyroy, Rimel *and* Orooth. *A horizontal band bisects the circle, and a vertical band bisects the upper portion of the circle. A closed crescent shape (presumably representing a ship) appears in the upper two-thirds of the circle, with two dots beneath it at the prow and the stern. Within this crescent shape, below the horizontal band, is the inscription* Hic magister cum suis sociis. *The position* Occidens *is marked just inside the circular band, at the bottom.*

d　*MS* qui.

Rimel, spiritus^e habitatores aque, qui naues nauigantium periclitare conamini, ego vos coniuro et exorcizo, et prouoco vos, vbicumque sitis, aut in oriente aut in occidente aut in meridie aut in aquilone, aut in aquis aut in terris,

- *per indiuiduam ac inseparabilem trinitatem que in tribus personis existit, scilicet Patrem et Filium et Spiritum Sanctum ab vtroque procedentem,*
- *et per illum qui perpetuus et eternus est,*
- *et per illum qui concessit nobis graciam in inferno non stare.*

Item, ego coniuro vos^f et constringo vos

- *per quatuor flumina paradysi,*
- *et per aduentum domini nostri Ihesu Christi, qui frangens vectes ferreos sanctos patres de tenebris extraxit ad lucem.*

Item ego coniuro vos

- *per wltum, manus et pedes, atque plagas Ihesu Christi,*

vt hic venire debeatis, vos octo^g spiritus prenominati, vt vos videam in forma na[u]tarum, et hoc sine prestolacione^h aliqua faciatis. Item ego coniuro vos et impero atque precipio vobis

- *per potenciam et dignitatem Luciferi, Aphaleon, et Neutrion,*

vt nullam requiem habeatis donec ad me veniatis,ⁱ vt dixi. Venite, quia ego vos advoco ex parte domini dei Sabaoth, quo et gloria cuius celi et vniuersa terra est repleta.

Qua semel dicta, tenendo costam semper in manu dextra, videbis octo nautas^j cum magna reuerencia et timore dicentes, [22v] 'Ecce, mittimur ad te; precipe nobis de omnibus ad nos pertinentibus, et erit sine mora fulcitum.' Quibus dicis, 'Volo vos coniurare ac promittere michi tot debeatis ad me venire teneamini cum a me fueritis coniurati.' Qui maximum^k facient sacramentum ad te venire et redire quandocumque libuerit, tuam parati facere voluntatem. Hoc iurato, sic dices: 'Ego precipio vobis vt hunc circulum cum naui capiatis et ad talem locum sine mora me feratis.' Hiis dictis, videbis ipsos cum ramis^l ingredi nauim et imponere vela, et incipient nauigare. Et scias quod tibi videbitur esse in profundo maris, et in paruo temporis spacio voles quocumque ferris.^m Quibus eciam

---

e   *Followed by* habitares, *deleted.*

f   *MS* te.

g   *Initial* o *corrected from* v.

h   *MS* prestilacione.

i   *MS* veneatis.

j   *MS* naues.

k   *MS has extraneous line over the* x.

l   *MS* romis.

m   *Sic in MS, perhaps for* quocumque vis te feret *or* volabis quocumque vis.

precipias vt ad locum a quo acceperunt te instantissime reportent, qui statim
facient. Et cum illic[n] fueris reportatus, dic eis eciam quod revenient, quod hec
omnia sine fraude facient, eis quocienscumque iubebis, qui statim iurabunt ad te
venire velociter quando eis vocaueris, et te solum vel cum quibus volueris in naui
portare quocumque tibi placuerit accedere.

Quibus iuratis, des licenciam recedenti. Quibus recessis, aboleas circulum, et
costam subterra ibi.

Cum igitur tu solus uel cum aliis voluntatem habueris nauigandi, cum ferro uel
cum ligno uel digito vel cum aliquo signante fac circulum cum aliis, vt superius
demonstraui, et cum aliis ingredere supradictum locum, dicens eis vt timere non
de- [23r] beant, fingens eis aliquid.[o] Et cum omnes ingressi fuerint, sic legas
semel:

O Syrim, Dyspyl, Onoroy, Sisabel, Cotroy, Tyroy, Orooth, [et] Rimel, sculpti in hoc circulo,
ego invoco vos per vestram subieccionem michi factam, vt statim sine mora subito et
incontinenti hinc[p] debeatis accedere, mites, subiecti, parati et obedire michi et tanquam
na[u]te hunc circulum cum hac naui figuram vestram debeatis assumere, et nauigando
debeatis nos portare ad talem locum ad quem intendimus profiscissi.[q]

Et[r] conuocatione lecta, venient statim in naui octo naute placabiles, dicentes tibi,
'O viri,[s] quo ire intenditis?' Quibus tu dices, omnibus audientibus, 'Ad talem
locum.' Tunc nauis et omnes[t] in aqua esse videbuntur,[u] et istos velociter nauigare,
aspiciens qui nauigant,[v] et[w] ad locum optatum [venietis] vnius in[fra] hore
spacium. Et cum ibi fueris, si in ipso loco manere volueris, dic nautis vt abiant,
parati ipsum officium reassumere[x] et execucioni mandare quando eos
invocaueris. Qui[y] subito, hoc audito, recedent. Et cum volueris remeare vel alias
pergere, voca ipsos vt dictum est, et omnia facient.

n   *MS* illis.

o   Sic *in MS.*

p   Sic *in MS, meaning* huc.

q   *Corrected in margin from* perfecisti.

r   *MS* Aut.

s   O viri *added in margin.*

t   et omnes *added in margin.*

u   *MS* videbitur, *assuming* nauis *alone as the subject.*

v   Sic *in MS.*

w   *Followed by* epulent, *deleted.*

x   *MS* reasumere.

y   *MS* Quo.

Et scias diligenter quod in ipsa naui similiter potest fiere nominacio sanctorum, sicut in vera cristianitate, quia hij spiritus sunt inter bonum et malum, non in inferno, non in paradyso morantes, quibus hanc artem facere proprium est. Et circulus ille insignia sua est.

Hoc enim experimentum vidi multos esse peritos, tamen aliter et aliter; hic autem modus est verus, pauci laboris,z et nullius periculi.

Et nota quod in isto libro sunt nomina et figure spirituum secundum suas proprietates, que ignota sunt; igitur occultande sunt et celande, propter ipsorum ineffabilem efficaciam pro certo, etc.

NO. 9. FOR OBTAINING A HORSE (FOLS 23v–25v)

Volo eciam tibi mitterea quomodo equus, hoc est spiritus in equi forma, possit haberi, ferentis te tam per aquas quam per terram, tam per colles quam per planicies, quocumque volueris.

Primo enim, 6a luna, die Martis, ieiunus, forinsecus egrediaris cum quodam freno nunquam operato, et in loco secreto cum quodam clauo siue stilo ferreo fac circulum, vt hic apparet,b sculpiens in eo nomina et figuras ibidem apparentes.c Quibus factis, permanens in medio, genibus flexis, super freno versus orientem aliquantulum alta voce sic dicas:

O Lautrayth, Feremin, [et] Oliroomim, spiritus peccatoribus insistentes, ego, talis, in vestra [24r] *virtute confidens, vos coniuro*
- *per illum qui dixit et facta sunt, et omnia scit et cognoscit antequam fiant,*
- *et per celum et terram, ignem et aerem et aquam, solem et lunam et stellas,*
- *et per thronos, dominaciones, potestates, atque principatus domini nostri Ihesu Christi,*
- *ac per omnes angelos et archangelos qui morantur ante thronum dei simili voce clamantes, 'Sanctus, sanctus, sanctus, dominus deus Sabaoth, pleni sunt celi et terra*

---

z   *MS* laborum.

a   Sic *in MS.*

b   *Figure on fol. 23ᵛ: a single circular band, with a square inscribed, and a circle inside the square. Short bars extend outward from the middle of each side of the square and touch the inner side of the circular band. Names of the cardinal directions flank each of these bars.* Locus magistri *is marked in the centre of the circle. The band contains the names* Lantrayth, Feremni *and* Oliromim, *plus astronomical and other signs.*

Lantrayth *appears as* Lautrayth *in the text on the same folio, and as* Lutrayth *on fol. 25ʳ.* Feremni *is given as* Feremin *on the same folio, and as* Feremim *(with a misshapen final m) on fol. 25ʳ.* Oliromim *appears as* Oliroomim *in both later contexts.*

c   *MS* apparencias.

gloria tua, osanna in excelsis; benedictus qui venit in nomine domini, osanna in excelsis',

quatenus vos tres ad me venire debeatis suauiter, vt non terr[e]ar nec timeam, sed securus existam,[d] et quidquid vobis imperabo debeatis totaliter adimplere et cum maxima efficacia execucioni mandare. Item ego coniuro vos supradictos spiritus

- *per illum qui venturus est judicare viuos et mortuos et seculum per ignem,*
- *et per tremendam diem judicij,*
- *et per sentenciam quam audire debetis in ipsa die,*
- *et [per] hunc circulum, quo efficaciter prouocamini,*

vt sine mora huc meare cogamini, et precepta mea suppliciter obseruetis.

Quibus dictis ter, tres equites videbis a longe venire. Quos cum videris, dic donec ad te fuerint, *Leuaui ad te oculos meos in montes, vnde veniet auxilium michi. Auxilium* [24v] *meum a domino, qui fecit celum et terram* [Ps. 120:1f. Vulg.; cf. Ps. 122:1]. Et quando apud circulum fuerint, statim descendent equos, et tunc hilariter [te] salutabunt. Quibus dices, 'Dominus per sui misericordiam in statum pristinum vos reducat.' Hoc dicto, ipsi dicent, 'O magister, ad te venimus, vnanimes tuis preceptis seruire parati. Precipe igitur nobis illud, propter quod[e] nos huc venire fecisti, et erit penitus expeditum.' Quibus respondere debes, 'Volo vt presens frenum' – tenendo ipsum ambabus manibus – 'taliter consecretis vt quocienscumque ipsum squassauero ante me veniat equus, ori cuius ipsum possim imponere, et ipsum ascendere possim, ipsum equitare tute et accedere quo michi libuerit proficisci.' Hoc dicto, ipsi asserunt[f] dictum frenum velle secum ferre et ibidem tercio die reportare. Quibus ipsum[g] dabis. Et cum dederis, ascendent equos et sine mora recedent. Quibus recessis, egredere circulum, non abolendo [illum], et deinde recedas.

Tercia vero dei, in vesperis, reuertaris illuc, et invenies ibidem predictos spiritus offerentes tibi dictum frenum, asserentes tuam peticionem esse fulcitam. Et accepto freno, sic dicas: 'Ego coniuro vos per deum deorum vt sine mei licencia de hinc[h] discedere non possitis.' Hoc dicto, tibi respondebunt quod quantum voles ibidem [25r] permanebunt. Quo dicto, squassabis frenum, et subito illuc veniet equus niger, cui inpones frenum, et equitabis. Hoc facto, descendes[i] et remouebis frenum, et subito equus abibit.

---

d   *Followed by* t, *deleted.*

e   *MS* illud, quidquid.

f   Sic *in MS.*

g   *MS* ipsius.

h   *Followed by* poss, *deleted.*

i   *MS* descendens.

Quo recesso, sic dices:

Ego iterum coniuro vos,
* *per omnia antedicta,*
* *et per omnia habencia contra vos potestatem,*
vt iurare vos debeatis vt predictum equum semper[j] ad me venire cogetis.

Qui iurabunt et promittent expresse hoc continuo cum efficacia facere. Quod cum iurauerint, dic quod cum salute recedant. Quibus recessis, egredere circulum et ipsum totum aboleas, et frenum tecum portes.

Et cum volueris equum venire, dic, squassando frenum, *Lutrayth, Feremim, Oliroomim,* et statim equuus veniet, cui[us] ori inpones frenum, et equitabis. De cuius cluni[bu]s aliquantulum incidere debes, quia micior erit, et hoc omni vice facere debes. Et cum volueris ipsum currere, punge ipsum uel verberes, quia illic more sagitte [volabit], de quo nunquam cadere poteris, nec timere poteris. Et quando voles descendere, nunquam recedet donec frenum de ore eius auferes.[k] Quo ablato, subito euanescet.

Facimus enim talia frena tenuissima, ita quod in paruo loco portare possimus, que nunquam frangi possi[n]t nec putrefieri, [25v] propter ipsam consecracionem.

Item est aduertendum quod si supradictum circulum, in corio equi cum sangwine equi scriptum, cum dente eciam equi, est[l] ostensum equis, subito moriuntur. Et si ipsum, vt dictum est scriptum, erga te tuleris, nullus equus ad te poterit appropinquare. Et [de] virtute huius circuli eciam ait Socrates in libro magice.

NO. 10. FOR RESUSCITATING A DEAD PERSON (FOLS 25v–28r)

Cum volueris [in] aliquem mortuum infundere spiritum, ita quod viuus, [vt] erat prius,[a] videbitur, talis ordo tenendus est. Primo quidem ex auro anulum fieri facias. Eciam sculpta sint[b] in parte[c] exteriori hec nomina: Brimer, Suburith, Tranauit; in parte vero interiori sculpta sint hec nomina: Lyroth, Beryen,

---

j   *MS* predictum equum semper vt.

k   *MS has* recedent *and* euanescent, *but the line over the last* e *in* euanescent *is faint. Evidently the writer meant to correct the plural to the singular.*

l   *MS* eciam.

a   *MS* primo; *cf. fol. 27ʳ.*

b   *MS gives* sit, *with a line over the* t, *which elsewhere in the MS is used for* sicut.

c   *MS* ex parte.

Damayn.^d Quibus sculptis, die dominico ante ortum solis accedas ad aquam currentem et in ipsa pone dictum anulum, et quinque diebus ipsum in ea stare permittas.

Sexta vero die, ipsum extrahe et fer ad quoddam monumentum, et in ipso pone, ita quod moretur ipsa die Veneris et Sabbati die. Vero dominica die, ante solis ortum, accedas extra villam, sereno celo, in loco occulto et remoto, et fac circulum cum quodam ense, et in ipso scribe cum dicto ense nomina et figura[s] vt hic apparet.^e [26r] Quibus scriptis,^f ingredere in eum vt signatum est, et pone ensem sub genubus tuis, dicendo versus meridiem hanc coniuracionem:

Coniuro vos, omnes demones scriptos in hoc anulo – quem in manibus habeas,
- *per Patrem et Filium et Spiritum Sanctum,*
- *et per omnipotentem deum, factorem celi et terre,*
- *et per dominum nostrum Iesum Christum, eius filium, qui propter humani generis salutem mortem sufferre dignatus est,*
- *et per gloriosam virginem Mariam, matrem eius,*
- *et per lac* [26v] *eius sanctissimum Christi,^g per quod angeli denunciando pastoribus locuti sunt, 'Gloria in excelsis deo, etc.'*

Item ego coniuro vos, O Brimer, Suburith, Tranayrt, Lyroth, Berien, Damay,
- *per omnes sanctos et sanctas dei,*
- *et per hec nomina sancta dei: Tetragramaton, Oel,^h Messyas, Soter, Adonay, Alpha et O, Sabaoth,*
- *et per hec sancta nomina virginis Marie, scilicet regina, flos, rosa, lilium, scala, sapiencia, vita, dulcedo, misericordia, et spes,*
- *et per paradisum celestem et terrestrem,*
- *et per omnes angelos et archangelos, thronos, dominaciones, potestates, atque principatus, et maiestates et glorias regis celi et terre,*
- *et per omnes principes, reges, dominos, et maiores vestros,*

---

d   *The names are given on fols. 25v, 26r, 26v, and 27r. Spelling is consistent, except that* Tranauit *appears on 26v as* Tranayrt *and on and 27r as* Tramayrt, Beryen *is given on 26r and 26v as* Berien, *and* Damayn *lacks the final n on 26v.*

e   *Figure on fol. 26r: a double circular band, with a pentagram inscribed. O Brimer, Suburith, Tranauit is inscribed in the outer band, with astronomical signs;* Lyroth, vnq *(sic)* Berien, Damayn *is inscribed in the inner band, with further signs.* Magister *is written in the centre of the pentagram. The cardinal directions* meridies, occidens *and* oriens *are marked outside the band. For alternative forms of the names, see above, n. e.*

f   *Followed by* ingrediar, *deleted.*

g   *Something missing – perhaps* et per cantum? *?*

h   *Presumably for* O El.

- *et per infernum vestrum,*
- *et per omnia in eodem existencia*

quatenus vos omnes, constricti et ligati in voluntate mea et in potestate mea, debeatis huc accedere in benigna forma, vt nullum timeam, et consecrare ita et taliter presentum anulum, vt in eo hec virtus existat, videlicet quod quandocumque inposuero ipsum in digito alicuius mortui, vnus vestrum ipsum ingrediatur, et vt primo viuus[i] appareat in illa similitudine et forma, per illum qui viuit et regnat in vnitate Spiritus Sancti deus, per omnia secula seculorum. Amen.

Hiis semel dictis, apparebunt subito apud circulum 6 spiritus, [27r] petentes dictum anulum; quibus dabis. Quo dato, ipsi abient, et similiter tu egredere circulos, ferens tecum ensem, non destruens circulum.

Sexta vero die, cum predicto ense, reuerteris et versus meridiem sic dices:

Ego coniuro vos, O Brimer, Suburith, Tramayrt, Lyroth, Beryen, Damayn, per deum vnum, viuum, solum, et verum, vt nunc sine mora ad me venire debeatis, apportando anulum consecratum, ita quod quando inposuero ipsum in digito siue in manu alicuius persone viue cadat in terram sicut mortua, et quando abstulero ab ipsa in statum pristinum reuertatur, et eciam in quocumque[j] mortuo inposuero, vt dictum est, ipsum spiritus ingrediatur et viuus vt prius fuerat videatur, per omnia que possunt vos terrere et omnino constringere.

Hiis dictis quater, videlicet primo versus meridiem semel, et similiter versus occidentem, deinde versus aquilonem et versus orientem,[k] videbis versus orientem venire quendam equitem, qui cum fuerit apud circulum sic dicet: 'Tales mittunt' – nominando[l] nomina suprascripta – 'tibi hunc anulum consecratum, dicentes [se] ad te venire non posse, quia non expediens est; experieris anuli virtutem, et si non habuerit virtutem a te postulatam, dicent quod quandocumque [vis] sunt ad te venire parati.' Quem anulum accipies,[m] dicendo ei, [27v] 'Graciam tibi et ipsis.' Hoc dicto, statim recedet,[n] et tu eciam exies de circulo, ipsum totaliter destruendo.

Et predictum anulum bene teneas involutum in syndone albo. Cum vero volueris vt aliquis viuus mortuus videatur et ab omnibus videtur vita carere, pone in digito eius hunc anulum, et cadauer videbitur; et quando remouebis, veniet in

---

i *MS* vnus.
j *MS* cuicumque.
k *Followed by* et.
l *MS* nominando nominando.
m *MS* accipiens.
n *MS* recedes.

primum statum. Et quando volueris aliquod cadauer animatum apparere, pone vt dictum est anulum, uel ad manum siue ad pedem liga, et ante horam surget in forma primo habita, et viua voce coram omnibus loquetur, et hoc monstrare poterit sex diebus, quia quilibet eorum sua die in ipso permanebit. Et si volueris [illum] ante dictum terminum vt primo erat esse, remoue anulum. Et hoc modo resurgere poteris defunctum.

Hec enim experiencia dignissima est et occultanda, quia in ipsa magna virtus existit.

Circulus eciam suprascriptus multas virtutes habet, cuius tres per me notas[o] exponam. Si enim die Veneris ipsum cum calamo vppupe et cum eius sangwine in carta edina nouata[p] scripseris,[q] et aliquam personam cum eo tetigeris, in eternum super omnes ab ipsa diligeris. Et si predictum circulum, scriptum vt dictum est, posueris super caput egroti, ipso ignoranti, si mori debet dicet se nullatenus euadere posse; et si debet euadere dicet se omnino [28r] liberatum. Et si predictum circulum, scriptum similiter, super te habueris, nullus canis tibi latrare valebit. Et ista sunt per me experta; inexperta[r] vero per me relinquo.

NO. 11. FOR INVISIBILITY (FOLS 28r–29v)

Tracto eciam de arte invisibilitatis, hodie quasi ab omnibus ignorata.[a]

Cum itaque volueris apud omnia, tam racionabilia quam non, invisibilis ac insensibilis haberi, primo, crescente luna die Mercurij, in prima hora diei, castus ante per triduum, et tonsus capillos et barbam, et albo indutus, extra villam in loco occulto, sereno celo, in plano solo, cum ense splendidissimo fac circulum vt hic apparet,[b] scribendo hec nomina [et] cum eis omnia ibidem apparencia. [28v] Hoc facto, fingas versus occidentem super Firiel dictum ensem. Et cum figeris, habeas vas in quo sit ignis cum thure, mirra, et olibano, et cum fumo ipsorum [circum]vade circulum, suffumigando ipsum, incipiendo a Fyriel et ibi finiendo. Hoc facto, habeas aquam benedictam et aspergas te et circulum, dicendo,

o   *MS* notans.

p   Sic *in MS.*

q   *In margin:* Nota.

r   *MS* inexperto.

a   *At top of page, in margin:* de invisibilitate.

b   *Figure on fol. 28r: a plain circle, with the positions* oriens, meridies *and* occidens *labelled, a sword lying toward the east with its point near the centre,* Magister *inscribed near the centre (with* Firiel *to the west,* Melemil *to the south,* Berith *to the east, and* Taraor *to the north), and two figures.*

The names occur on fols 28r, 28v, 29r, and 29v. Spelling is consistent, except that Firiel *occurs twice on 28v as* Fyriel, Melemil *appears on 28v as* Mememil, *and* Taraor *is given on 29r as* Tarator.

Asperges^c me, domine, ysopo et mundabor; lauabis me et super niuem dealbabor [Ps. 50:9 Vulg.]. Quo facto, voluendo te genubus flexis versus occidentem, emissa voce, sic dicas:

Ego, talis, coniuro vos, O Fyriel, Mememil, Berith, [*et*] *Taraor, spiritus potentes, magnifici, et illustres,^d in quibus omnino confido,*

- *per vnicam, inseparabilem, ac indiuiduam trinitatem, scilicet Patrem et Filium et Spiritum Sanctum,*
- *et per deum vnicum, solum, viuum, et verum, qui omnia de nichilo formauit, et cui subdita sunt omnia, celestia, terrestria,^e et infernalia,*
- *per celum et terram, mare et infernum, et omnia in ipsis existencia,*
- *et per omnes principes, reges, et dominos vestros,*
- *et per illum deum quem timetis et adoratis,*
- *et per omnia que habent* [*potenciam*] *vos terrere, constringere, et alligare, et quorum preceptum vos oportet totaliter adimplere,*

quatenus vos omnes 4or cum humilitate maxima huc venire debeatis, ligati, constricti, et iurati ad execucioni mandandum quidquid a uobis petiero. Venite sine mora; venite, quia invoco vos ex parte Patris, prouoco [29r] *vos ex parte Filij, invoco vos ex parte Spiritus Sancti.*

Hac invocacione dicta quater, scilicet semel versus Firiel, semel versus Melemil et versus Berith et Tarator, aderunt subito in circulo 4or spiritus, dicentes tibi, 'Dic nobis quid vis, et plene tibi obediemus.' Quibus dices, 'Ego volo quandam cappam invisibilitatis, que sit tenuis et incorruptibilis, qua cum indutus fuero nullus videre nec me sentire valeat.' Hoc dicto, vnus discedet, et ante horam apportabit ibi quandam cappam, quam ab ipsis petebas^f vt tibi dare deberent. Qui respondebunt tibi dare non posse si primo ipsis non das tuum indutum album; quibus dabis, et cum dederis eis, ipsi tibi dabunt cappam. Quorum vnus statim induet indutum eis datum; similiter tu statim induas cappam. Quam cum indueris, illis spiritibus dices, 'Abite cum pace,' et statim recedent. Et cum abierint, debes dimittere circulum, ferendo ensem.

Tercia vero dei, cum cappa illuc reuertere, et invenies tuum indutum, quem accipies. Memento enim, si ipsa tercia die non reuerteris, siue tuum indutum ibi dimissum non accipias, quarta die nullum invenires, sed in septem diebus moreris. Accepto enim tercia die induto, ipsum in eodem loco combures. Et scias

---

c   *MS* Asperiges.

d   *MS* illustros.

e   *The second* t *appears marked for deletion, erroneously.*

f   *MS* petiebas.

quod quando ipsum combures audies maximos planctus [29v] et querelas. Et cum combureris, aspergas cinerem per aerem, sic dicendo:

Coniuro vos, Firiel, Melemil, Berith, [et] Taraor,
- *per virtutem et potenciam vestram,*
- *et per omnia habencia contra vos potestatem,*

vt non habeatis virtutem nec potenciam ledendi me per hanc cappam, sed Ihesus Christus protegat et defendat me per omnia secula seculorum. Amen.

Quo dicto, habeas aquam benedictam et aspergas dictam cappam, sic dicendo:

Ego coniuro te, cappa,
- *per Patrem et Filium et Spiritum Sanctum,*
- *et per hanc aquam,*

vt quandocumque te indutus fuero, nullus sentire nec videre me valeat, per dominum nostrum Ihesum Christum, filium dei viuum, qui viuit et regnat per omnia secula seculorum. Amen.

NO. 12. FOR OBTAINING A WOMAN'S LOVE (FOLS 29v–31v)[a]

Recipe ceram virgineam, arte virginizatam, et hoc[b] in die Jouis vel in die dominico, hora Veneris vel hora Jouis; ex dicta cera facias ymaginem ad carbones accensas sine fumo in vna olla positos. Et habeat magister de capillis mulieris pro qua wult facere, et tres fillos sete rubee, et habeas tecum cultellum albi manubrij ad hoc facti. Et vade ad locum vbi artifex facit acus, et tu facias facere ab eodem artifice, hora Solis vsque ad horam Saturni. Deinde magister [30r] habeat duos socios fideles, et vadat ad arborem fructiferam, et faciat magister circulum.[c] Et incipiat magister artem facere, siue ymaginem mulieris pro qua facis, semper murmurando in corde tuo,

Tu Belial, tu Astarotht,[d] tu Paymon, ad hoc sitis opus michi adiutores.

Et similiter murmurando dices,

a   *In margin:* de amore.

b   *Inserted above line.*

c   *Figure on fol. 30ʳ: a double circular band, with* Tu Belial, tu Astaroth, tu Paymon, ad hoc sitis [michi *deleted*] opus michi adiutores *inscribed in the band, and* Locus magistri *marked in the centre.*

   The names appear on the same folio in the text. Spelling is consistent for two of them, but Astaroth *is rendered in the text as* Astarotht.

d   Sic *in MS.*

Ego, N., formo istam ymaginem in amorem talis, vt valeat ad quod facta est. Et tu, Belial,
inicialis princeps, ad hoc opus sis michi adiutor.

Et tunc^e magister faciat ymaginem de predicta cera, incipiens hora Jouis,
descendendo vsque ad horam Saturni. Et sic formata ymagine, faciat fieri [30v]
magister ab artifice perito nouem acus, qui eas faciat corpore balneatus et nitidis
vestibus indutus; faciat dictas acus hora Solis vsque ad horam Saturni. Postea
magister fingat dictas acus in ymagine, ita collocando vnam in capite, aliam in
humero dextro, terciam in sinistro, 4am vbi cor consueuit ab hominibus
assignari, ita dicendo:

Sicut ista acus fingitur in cor istius ymaginis, ita fingatur amor N. in amorem N., quod non
possit dormire, vigilare, iacere, sedere, [uel] ambulare,^f quousque in meum exardescat
amorem,

quintam in vmbilico, sextam in femore, septimam in latere^g dextro, octauam in
sinistro, nonam in ano. Sic formata ymagine, christianizes ipsam, inponendo sibi
nomen [mulieris] pro qua facis, submergendo ter et dicendo, 'Quomodo vocatur?';
et respondetur, 'N.' Et tu debes dicere, *Ego baptizo te, N., in nomine Patris, et Filij, et*
Spiritus Sancti. Amen. Et postea pone ymaginem in panno nouo et mundo, dimittendo
ab hora Solis vsque ad horam Martis. Deinde facias istam coniuracionem sub
arbore fructifera ad carbones accensos, et voluas te versus orientem, et dicas,

Coniuro, talis, N., caput tuum, crines tuos, oculos tuos, aures tuas, genas tuas; coniuro, talis,
cerebrum tuum; coniuro, N., tunicas^h [31r] cerebri^i tui, scilicet duram et piam matrem;
coniuro, N., oculos tuos; coniuro, N., tunicas oculorum tuorum; coniuro, N., frontem tuam;
coniuro, N., dentes tuos; coniuro, N., os tuum; coniuro, N., mentum tuum; coniuro, N.,
nasum tuum; coniuro, N., nares tuas; coniuro, N., palatum tuum; coniuro, N., gingiuas tuas;
coniuro, N., guttur tuum; coniuro, N., humeros tuos; coniuro, N., spatulas tuas; coniuro, N.,
pectus tuum; coniuro, N., mammillas tuas; coniuro, N., corpus tuum; coniuro vmbilicum
tuum; coniuro, N., femur tuum; coniuro, N., renes tuos; coniuro, N., latera tua; coniuro, N.,
anum tuum; coniuro, N., costas tuas; coniuro, N., wuluam tuam; coniuro, N., genua tua;
coniuro, N., crura tua; coniuro, N., talos^j pedum tuarum; coniuro, N., brachia tua; coniuro,

e   *Added both between lines and in margin.*

f   *Followed by* sic.

g   *MS* lattere *or* lactere.

h   *Followed by* tuas, *deleted.*

i   *MS* cerebrum.

j   *MS* tales.

N., digitos manuum tuarum; coniuro, N., manus tuas; coniuro, N. vngwes manuum tuarum; coniuro, N., cor tuum; coniuro, N., pulmonem tuum; coniuro, N., bucellas tuas; coniuro, N., stomachum tuum; coniuro, N., totam personam tuam; coniuro, N., totam substanciam tuam, vt non possis dormire nec sedere nec iacere nec aliud artificiale facere donec meam libidinosam compleueris voluntatem. Coniuro te

- *per Patrem et Filium et Spiritum Sanctum,*
- *per magistratum[k] artis,*
- *per virtutem ipsius,[l]*
- *per sapienciam Salomonis,*
- *per verum Sabaoth,*
- *per verum seraphin,*
- *per verum Emanuel,*
- *per omnia corpora sanctorum* [31v] *que iacent in Roma,*
- *per lunam et solem et dominum maiorem,*
- *et per lac virginis,*
- *per sanctam Mariam, matrem domini nostri Ihesu Christi,*
- *per eukarisma sanctum,*
- *per corpus et sangwinem Ihesu Christi.*

Coniuro vos ex exorcizo vos [et] *impero vobis, vt sicut ceruus desiderat fontem aquarum* [Ps. 41:2 Vulg.], *ita desideres,[m] N., ad meum amorem. Et sicut coruus desiderat cadauera mortuorum, ita desideres[n] tu me. Et sicut cera ista liquefacit a facie ignis, ita desideret N. in meum amorem, quod non possit, etc.*

Signa autem mulieris hec sunt et sequentur: solitudo, inuolucio capitis, ploratus, gemitus, percussiones, euigilaciones, [et] eiulaciones. Tunc magister siue ille qui facit vadat ad illam, et si viderit illam solam stantem aut[o] sedentem, tunc corroboret magister coniuracionem vsque ad quintam diem. Et si illa in terra omnino fuerit, consumatur; si autem fuerit in villa aut aliam ciuitatem transierit, tamdiu magister faciat coniuracionem quousque illa possit venire.

Et in hoc fuerunt concordes nigromantici omnes astroloyci Hyspanici, Arabici, Hebrei, Caldei, Greci, et Latini. Et extractum fuit istud experimentum [ex libro] de secretis artibus ymaginarie artis, [ex libro] de floribus omnium experimentorum, etc.

---

k   *MS* mgrm *with line over last three characters.*

l   *Presumably either incomplete or intended with reference to the previous phrase.*

m   *MS* desiderat, *following the Psalm verse.*

n   *MS* desideras.

o   *MS* et.

NO. 13. FOR CONSTRAINING A MAN, WOMAN, SPIRIT, OR BEAST
(FOLS 32r–33r)

Per hoc experimentum constringitur homo, mulier, vir, spiritus, [vel] bestia, cuiuscumque condicionis existat.

Hec nomina in hunc modum sint scripta in spatula.[a] Postquam hoc totum adinpletum fuerit, quod vis eligere tibi. Si aliquem spiritum constringere volueris, scribe nomen eius in spatula inter b et e et in nomine quod est Bel. Si aliquem hominem constringere volueris, scribe nomen illius inter l et a. Si vero aliquam bestiam constringere volueris, scribe nomen eius inter a et n, et colorem eius. Pro spiritibus vero atque hominibus et pro mulieribus, agendum est ita et in eadem hora in qua expleta spatula fuerit ab accione,[b] ibi oportet vt in primis perquirantur lingna ex spina alba vel lingna que vagantur in aquis, et faciat inde ignem, carbonesque collige et in ollam nouam mitte, et desuper paulatim pone spatulam, et paulatim augmentando ignem donec spatula calefiat.

Et tunc invoca predictos spiritus, et dic hanc coniuracionem:

Asyel, Castiel, Lamisniel, Rabam, Erlain, [et] Belam,[c] vobis precipio

[A1] Si pro homine uel muliere quem uel qua[m] in tuo amore accendere volueris, sic dicas:

vt statim, etc.

secundum quod infra continetur.[d] [B] Si vero pro spiritu, [32v] nomina illum spiritum quem vis vt veniat ad te patenter, humiliter, pulcra facie, et blando sermone, dicendo,

---

a *Figure at the bottom of fol. 33[r] (i.e., at the end of the experiment): a shield divided into 16 horizontal bands, with one vertical band down the centre. In the top band is inscribed,* Hec est figura spatule. *Succeeding bands bear the names* Asyel, Castyel, Lamsiyel, Rabam, Erlain, Olam *and* Belam, *each of which straddles the vertical band. In the vertical band are the letters* A *(at the intersection with the second horizontal band),* B *(fifth),* E *(seventh),* L *(ninth),* A *(eleventh) and* N *(thirteenth). Across the intersection of the vertical band and the twelfth horizontal band* Leo *is written.*

To the side is the note: Item nota quod spatula supradicta debet esse asinina vel leporina vel anserina vel caponina, secundum diuersos [usus?].

b Sic *in MS.*

c *Corrected in lower margin from* Bolam.

d *This phrasing occurs toward the end of the conjuration given in the next paragraph.*

Coniuro vos, Asyel, etc., vt N. spiritum N.,ᵉ qui potestatem habet super omne quod ab eo querere volo, ad me venire faciatis patenter, humiliter, blando sermone, eius forma vt dixi, scilicet militis [et] pulcherimi, ad complendum omnia que ei precipere voluero.

[A2] Et cum pro viro aut muliere hoc facere volueris, fac ei prius notum vbi te invenire possit, quia nisi te inveniet pro cuius furore suo insaniet.ᶠ [C] Si pro bestia, [dic:]

Coniuro predictos spiritus vt constringant illam bestiam

quam vis, ne de loco in quo est se remouere valeat donec volueris.

[A3] [Conjuration to constrain a man or woman:]

Asyel, Castiel, Lamsiyel, Rabam, Erlain, Elam, Belam, ego vos coniuro
- *per deum verum,*
- *per deum viuum, qui vos creauit,*
- *et per eum qui Adam et Euam formauit,*
- *et per eum qui mare creauit aridamque fundauit, qui facit angelos suos spiritus et ministros suos ignem vrentem* [Ps. 103:4 Vulg.], *qui nouit ea que non sunt sicut ea que sunt, qui habet claues mortis [et] inferni, ipse enim primus et nouissimus, principium et finis, Alpha et O, et qui viuit et fuit mortuus et revixit,ᵍ qui vocauit deum patrem eius.*
- *Alphagramaton, per hoc nomen*

vos coniuro,
- *et per sanctum et ineffabile nomen dei Tetragramaton,*
- *et per id nomen quod nemo nouit nisi ipse* [33r] *qui est verbum dei,*
- *et per hec nomina dei: Hely, Heloy, Heloe, Sabaoth, Elion, Adonay, Saday,*
- *et per omnia nomina eius,*
- *et per ipsius virtutem,*
- *et per omnes virtutes celorum;*

item coniuro vos
- *per Patrem et Filium et Spiritum Sanctum,*
- *et per sanctam trinitatem et vnitatem dei,*
- *et per illam coronam quam dominus noster Ihesus Christus in suo capite habuit,*
- *et per lac beate Marie virginis,*
- *et per hec predicta nomina et per omnes virtutes eorundem,*

---

e   Sic *in MS.*

f   Sic *in MS.*

g   *Corrected above line from* refixit.

et per istam coniuracionem precipio vobis, vt statim et cito et velociter et sine mora seducatis cor et mentem N. in amorem meum. Et sicut hec spatula calefit et incenditur, ita illum vel illam, N., incendatis et calefaciatis igne mei amoris, et ita vt nu[n]quam quiescere valeat donec meam adimpleuerit voluntatem. In nomine quod est Bel, etc.

NO. 14. FOR OBTAINING A HORSE (FOLS 33v–34r)

Vt equum habeas ad eundum quo vis, [debes] respicere aerem versus orientem, flexis genibus [et] iunctis manibus et si esses[a] in carcere, et dic cum magna fiducia et spe firmissima obtinendi,

O altissime et benignissime rex Orientis, exaudi oracionem meam et clamor meus ad te veniat; fiant aures tue intendentes in vocem deprecacionis mee [Pss. 101:2, 129:2 Vulg.], *per nobilissimam sedem maiestatis tue. Te invoco et adiuro*
- *per illum dominum quem cones[b] diligis, confidis, et speras,*
- *per legem legalem[c] et per spem sperantem et per karitatem karitatiuam,*
- *per On, El, Ely, [et] Tetragramaton, quod est nomen altissimum,*
- *et per locum vbi sedes in solio magne nobilitatis tue.*

Mitte ad me spiritum aereum, quo[d] in eo valeam ad plenum, quod opto, proficere. Potens es,[e] domine, ipsum mittere, vt michi in hac hora tua magna potencia in omnibus et per omnia sit obediens et legalis.[f] Et ideo te, domine, invoco, adoro, et laudo nomen tuum in eternum, qui oriens omnes benedicte et gloriossisimus[g] per infinita secula seculorum. Amen.

Hoc igitur dicto septies, dic audaciter:

Volo ire ad talem partem, et statim veni.

Vt si volueris spiritus uel equus, vel dormiendo uel vigilando.[h] Cum equus venerit, dic,

Coniuro te per dominum, qui creauit celum et terram, mare, et omnia que in eis sunt, tam

---

a   *MS* esset, *perhaps meaning* vt si esses?

b   *Or* tones, *perhaps intending* toto corde?

c   *Meaning* fidem fiducialem, *corresponding to the other theological virtues?*

d   *Meaning* vt?

e   *MS* est.

f   Sic *in MS.*

g   *Perhaps meaning* qui Oriens es, benedictus et gloriosissimus.

h   *Probably meaning* Et si volueris spiritum uel equum, uel dormiendo uel vigilando.

visibilia quam invisibilia, vt^i sine strepitu et timore, dampno aliquo uel periculo seu^j angustia mei cor- [34r] *poris et anime portes me suauiter et depones me sine aliqua lesione presenti uel futuri, vsque ad talem locum suauiter me deponas.*

Cum enim deposuerit te vbi affectabis, dicas humiliter,

Gracias tibi ago, Oriens, qui dignum me fecisti in hac parte mea^k et pro tanta gracia et beneficio meo,^{l} et me tibi offero, seruire et semper tuis obedire mandatis. Benedictum [et] laudatum sit semper nomen tuum, regnaturum super omnia secula seculorum. Et tibi eciam gracias ago, qui per coniuracionem nominum altissimi dei per me fatigare^m dignatus es, etc.

NO. 15. FOR OBTAINING A FLYING THRONE (FOLS 34r–35v)

Vade ad locum secretum et altum, tempore sereno et absque ventu, et dic: *Sancta Maria, ora pro nobis, Secundum magnam misericordiam tuam* [Ps. 50 Vulg.], cum *Gloria Patri* totum,^{a} *In manus tuas, domine, commendo spiritum et totum spiritum et corpus meum,*^{b} *Domine deus, Pater omnipotens,* [et] *Iudica me* [Ps. 42 Vulg.]. Postea fac talem circulum vt inferius designabitur,^{c} cum ollis, et [34v] pone in ollam septentrionis cinerem et farinam, et in orient[al]em ignem cum sale, in occidentalem^d aquam et calcem. Et sede in medio circuli et verte te versus septentrionem, et voca regem nubium, nomine Bartha, vt mittat 3es de ducibus qui habent posse^e [super] nubibus et ventris, scilicet Saltim,^{f} Balthim, Gehim, qui ducent te absque lesione et absque periculo tui corporis et anime ad locum quem volueris. Et tunc apparebit tibi parua nubes, et de tribus ollis exibunt tres alie olle, dicen[te]s, *Ascende, ascende, ascende.* Tunc autem inperterrite ac et cum audacia parate^g sellam

---

i   *MS* et.

j   *Followed by* et.

k   Sic *in MS.*

l   *MS* mea.

m   *Probably meaning* pro me fatigari.

a   Sic *in MS.*

b   Sic *in MS; cf. Lk. 24:46.*

c   *Figure at bottom of fol. 34^v: a single circular band, with an inverted triangle inscribed within its outer boundary. Characters (in pseudo-Hebrew?) are inscribed along two sides of the triangle, within the band. In the intersections of the band and the triangle, circles with dots in them (evidently denoting positions for jars) are marked. Cardinal directions are shown.*

d   *MS* occidentali.

e   *Possibly meaning* potenciam; *followed by* michi, *deleted.*

f   *Followed by redundant* Baltim, *deleted.*

g   Sic *in MS.*

magistro, hec dicas ter. Tunc videbis kathedram in medio nubis, et tu ascende illam, et dic,

Rex Bartha, et duces Saltim, Baltim, [et] Galtim, portate me placabiliter, sine timore et inpedimento et periculo aliquo mei corporis[h] et anime, vsque ad talem locum, et suauiter me leuate et suauiter me deponite. O tu rex Bartha, et o vos principes Saltim, Balthim, Galtyra,[i] vos potenter invoco vt cito et velociter me ducatis vsque ad talem locum sine omni timore et periculo mei corporis et anime, et ad hoc[j] vos invoco et coniuro potenter et exorziso per hec angelorum nomina altissima qui in aere sunt potentes: Mastiesel,[k] Emedel, Emethel, Sangel, Eymeal, Venoel, Gerbon, Seutan, Ty- [35r] *robay, Teneyn, Teregey, Gerebon, Gamelorum, Tubairum, Ficary, Gysay, Austeron, Boreal, Gemeloy, Garoen, Sypro, Ebely, Aurora, Subseloy, Siego, Afonei, et Zephirim, Boreoth, Beolthoray, Aforax,[l] Aquelyo, Eureal, Fauelyon. Per hec nomina vos invoco et coniuro et exorcizo et constringo, vt sine mora veniatis ad me existentem in hoc loco, et multum[m] me suauiter et benigne deferatis et ducatis ad talem locum, sine omni timore, lesione, et periculo mei corporis et anime. Sic fiat, fiat, amen.*

Vade securus et non timeas, quia portabunt te quo volueris. Si forte socios habere volueris in via et in opere, oportet quod sitis impares, tamen plus.[n] Hec nomina dices, scilicet Semegibetelye, Sabolaay,[o] Saroten, Saramey, Cerbelli, Tyaurax.[p] Et sic ire poteris in omnem partem et terram securus quo volueris.

Si quis tibi forte nocere voluerit vel attemptauerit: Si a parte septentrionali senseris kathedram descendere, dic,

O Balthym, te invoco, coniuro, et constringo vt vindices me de isto qui michi nocere temptatur,[q] per hec septem nomina que in omnibus potestatem habent, scilicet Flegely, Stygeloy,[r] Melyon, Babaia, Regale, Setgaboy, Guitipabey.

---

h   *Corrected in MS from* corperis.?.

i   Sic *in MS.*

j   *Or* hec.

k   *Or* Masciesel.

l   *Or* Afforax.

m   Sic *in MS.*

n   Sic *in MS.*

o   *Corrected in MS from* Sabalaay.

p   *Or* Tyanrax.

q   *Meaning* temptat?

r   *Or* Scygeloy.

Et statim veniet tempestas super eum et timeas.[s] Si vero a parte occidentali quis tibi nocere temptauerit, dic audacter,

> *O Saltim, coniuro et constringo te per ista semptem nomina, [35v] scilicet Sebegyol, Sebely, Serbaton, Tymelyy,[t] Gerotal, Tyboel, Galtym. Fiat vt sit pluuia et nubes super illum, in tantum quod non possit videre nubem.*

Si vero ex parte orientali quis temptare voluerit, dic,

> *Veniatis, Galtym [et] Baltym, per ista nomina, scilicet Flegely, Stygeloy, Melyon, Barbaia, Regale, Segaboy, Guitipabey, et cadant tonitrua super[u] illum et nubes et tempestas, ita [quod] me temptare non audeat.*

Si forte in via videris super te tempestates uel serpentes aut aues aut alia terribilia, quibus forte posses terreri, dicas,

> *O tu rex Bartham, ego te invoco et coniuro et constringo, rex sapiens et fortis, per hec nomina, scilicet Alrogen, Segeuratetho, Spitalote, Frigonay, Gebelsey, vt hec terribilia[v] facias protinus remoueri statim.*

Dictis hiis verbis, sine mora recedent, et vltra non habebis contrarium.
  Hic circulus debet fieri ad istud opus, etc.[w]

NO. 16. FOR FINDING SOMETHING IN SLEEP (FOLS 35v–36r)

Ad inveniendum in sompnis que vis, scribe hec nomina in carta virginea cum nominibus illius diei in hunc modum sicut inferius patebit. Postea pone sub dextra aure quando vadis dormitum, et videbis quidquid vis de preteritis, presentibus, et futuris.
  Hec est con- [36r] iuracio que debet fieri super cartam:

> *O vos gloriosa nomina summi dei, cui omnia, presencia, preterita, et futura presencia sunt,*

---

s   *Possibly meaning* et timebit *or* quem times.

t   Sic *in MS.*

u   *Partly covered by blot.*

v   *MS* terrebilia.

w   That is, the circle given already on fol. 34r, but perhaps drawn at the end of the experiment in an earlier manuscript.

rogo vos ego, seruus et subditus vester, quod mittatis michi angelos vestros[a], qui scripti sunt in
circulo isto, vt michi reuelare debeatis

quidquid super talem rem, uel de quocumque vis negocio quod venturum est. Et
hec dicas tribus[b] vicibus, et videbis quidquid vis, per potenciam dei.

Hic est circulus qui debet scribi cum ibis dormitum.[c]

NO. 17. FOR OBTAINING A HORSE (FOL 36r–v)

Ad equum habendum[a] scriba[n]tur in hostio domus vacui, in crepusculo noctis,
more he- [36v] brayco, hec nomina cum sangwine vespertilionis: Tuditha,
Stelpha, Alpha, Draco, Mariodo, Ypation. Quibus scriptis, recede modicum a
loco.

Post horam paruam reuertaris, et inuenies equum paratum, quem[b] cum
uolueris ascendere pone sinistrum pedem ad strepam et dic hanc coniuracionem:

Coniuro te, eque bone,
- *per creatorem celi et terre,*
- *et per illum qui creauit vniuersa et omnia ad laudem et gloriam sui nominis,*
- *et per deum viuum,*
- *et per deum sanctum,*
- *et per deum verum,[c]*

vt non in corpore nec in anima nec in minimo membro meo vere obesse[d] valeas, nec in aliquo
me perturbes, sed me, N., ad locum talem deferas, placide, hilariter, jocunde, et velociter,
absque omni inpedimento.

Deinde ascende audacter et secure, quia omnino tibi nocere non potest. Signo
vere crucis non te signabis, quia ipsum a te fugabis.

Cum autem perveneris ad locum prenominatum, descende de equo et accipe

---

a   *Blot between* o *and* s.

b   *MS* dicat.

c   *Figure on fol. 36*ᵛ*: a double circular band, with eight lines of text inscribed within it:* Agla / Michael virtus
dei / Gabriel fortitudo / Emanuel Paraclitus / Raphael medicina dei / Alpha et O, Oli, Ely /
Tetragramaton, amen / Agla. *Each line of text has a cross inside a square at either end.*

a   *Followed by* hec.

b   *MS* quod.

c   *Followed by a blot.*

d   *Corrected from* abesse.

frenum, et absconde sub terra. Peracto autem tuo negocio, recipias frenum et scucte[e] firmissime, et statim veniet. Cum autem ascendere volueris, dic[f] precedentem coniuracionem et hec tria verba: *Rastelya, Elogo, Yetas,* etc.

NO. 18. THE MIRROR OF FLORON, FOR REVELATION OF PAST, PRESENT, AND FUTURE (FOLS 37r–38r)

Hic incipit speculum Floron.

Fac fieri speculum de puro calibe, ad mensuram palme vnius in rotundo; habeatque manubrium ad tenendum, et sit illuminatum et lucidum vt ensis. Sitque factum in nomine Floron, et in circuitu istius speculi ex alia parte non lucida sint hec decim nomina, cum hiis decem caracteribus descripta, et nomen spiritus predicti sit in medio scriptum.[a] Postquam fuerit factum, in loco secreto vngatur ex puro balsamo ex parte lucida, et subfumiga, scilicet [37v] cum ligno aloes, ambra, et mirra, et olibano albo.

Hoc peracto, magister huius operis sedens faciat ipsum speculum teneri per manubrium cum ambabus manibus pueri virginis ante pectus suum, et ipse magister sit balneatus, eciam mundis vestibus indutus, qui antequam incipiat exercere hoc opus mel, lac, et vinum equaliter insimul mixtum in aerem aspergat, dicendo,

O Floron, in speculo sicut solitus es apparere citissime respondeas.

Hoc dicto, hanc coniuracionem coram speculo legat:

Bismille araathe mem[b] bismissa gassim gisim galisim darrgosim samaiaosim ralim ausini taxarim zaloimi hyacabanoy illete laytimi hehelmini betoymi thoma leminao vnuthomin zonim narabanorum azarethia thathitat hinanadon illemay sard hucacef illemegiptimi sitaginatim viaice hamtamice tatiala taltarini alaoht haleytum gaptametuntij mortoorfail geibel huabaton albital hualepin halmagrilie hualeon huastanie hualtamemeth huatorzor illenie giptimi tatgnie gathegine lesuma lesanim aptasale albweroahit vlleath alfard vsemeth aptisile abfluwarth vllelath ant clulamoralie hahysitimi waleles [38r] lithimi caegine

---

e   Sic *in MS.*

f   *MS* ac.

---

a   *Figure on fol. 37[r]: a double circular band, divided into ten segments. Outer band has the names* Latranoy, Iszarin, Bicol, Danmals, Gromon, Zara, Ralkal, Sigtonia, Samah *and* Meneglasar *written in the ten segments; inner band contains corresponding figures. Inscribed within the bands is a rectangle, subdivided into six sections, which contain the letters* F-L-O-R-O-N.

b   *Second* m *written with superscript line over it.*

catliegineles mirabolamini abtasile albiwahith alleath halamaton vnitia gaytatalon huia gay
soze cemeselis phalmorath bethathure huaba lagis illemeammitimi gelgine gathegine
lesmirapta libe albiwath vleuth.[c]

Dicta vero hac coniuracione, magister in speculo aspiciat, et videbit militem armatum in equo sedentem et armigerum suum comitantem secum, qui miles de equo descendet, et armiger eius equum tenebit. Cui militi sic dicet: 'Se desperata, decentissime visibiliter greciomo.'[d] Et tunc magister ipsum interrogat de preteritis, presentibus, et futuris, et ipse continuo certo scripto interrogata plenius insinuabit.

Non ergo tibi incredibile sit, quicumque fuerit[e] huius operis artifex, quia dum nouies ista perfeceris, idem spiritus manifeste vniuersa que prius per scripta insinuauerat ore ad os viua voce palificando denunciabit.

Dum ergo cuncta pro tuo velle perfeceris, eidem spiritui[f] cum pace precipe vt recedat, et iuxta preceptum sui domini redeat cum fuerit vocatus.

No. 19. The Mirror of Floron, Second Version (fols 38r–39v)

Hic incipit speculum Floron, et alio modo quam supra sit notatum, quamuis cum eisdem regulis.

Fac fieri speculum de puro calibe, ad mensuram palme vnius in rotundo, et habeat manu- [38v] brium ad tenendum, et sit illuminatum et lucidum vt ensis. Sitque factum in honore et in nomine spirituum inferiorum, et in circuitu speculi et ex alia parte non lucida sint 10 nomina cum decem karacteribus suprascriptis, vt pateat in speculo, et hoc nomen Floron in medio sit sculptum. Et postquam factum fuerit, in loco tali secreto sicut scis vngatur puro balsamo in parte lucida. Et sit subfumigatum hiis speciebus, scilicet ligno aloes, ambra, mirra, splendenti,[a] et olibano albo.

Hoc facto, magister huius operis sedens faciat ipsum speculum teneri ambabus manibus alicuius pueri virginis[b] ante pectus suum. Et ipse magister sit primo balneatus et mundis vestibus indutus, et ab omnibus aliis modis, vt bene nosti, ordinatus,[c] antequam incipiat hoc opus exercere. Mel, lac, et vinum mixta aspergantur in aere, et magister predictum spiritum proprio

---

c   *Individual words in almost all cases separated by punctus.*

d   Sic *in MS.*

e   *Meaning* fueris?

f   Sic *in MS.*

a   Sic *in MS.*

b   *MS* alicui puero virgini.

c   Sic *in MS.*

nomine^d advocet vt in speculum sicut solitus est veniat et vera responsa de omnibus interrogatis per certa scripta vel verba respondeat.

Hoc dicto, magister coniuracionem sequentem C[h]aldaycis verbis scripta[m] perlegat hoc modo:

Brismassa cassini gossini gaissini gratagossini samalaosini raxini gratini caraxini maraxini sobohini herura banor allegalte alitisti alaro haletum ha- [39r] *maymon hyalermon bispelimi bristedelimin hybelim bytho yhan bythoimin chosuma lonym lonynti torrimernum vitabanor atheretatat hyathet huyazalon vtaref illemegyptum biragyarius hyarite^e heramenice conolar ganstraximi aloryoli helytum gayta mementum montoro lazyabel hubaton albnetal^f hyxalepini almagarie hualeon hyaltanixe hualenyefet huatosor allemegitum cagine satogyne laminy lesymaybdo abtysilthi alluhuait valehat arfard huzeniecht aptihle abimerahit vllehath enzebula morabe balitum veralesucum teagyne lesmyro valanum aptalile asugnathecht valleaath hyamatharon hyabia gaytatalon hya yagapolozol phalmolmeth bethaure huaba laygip illenietentum taygine oragine deragrineles myraptalile vlleytith setrataha conox.^g*

Magister inspiciat in speculo et videbit militem armatum in equo sedentem et armigerum suum commitantem secum. Qui miles de equo descendet, et armiger eius equum tenebit. Cui militi sic dicet: 'Parate insilitio gytromon.' Tunc magister interroget ipsum de preteritis, presentibus, et futuris, et ipse continuo certo scripto interrogata plenarie inti- [39v] mabit. Non sit igitur incredibile tibi, quicumque fueris huius operis artifex, quod cum con[iuracionem] predicta[m] feceris, idem spiritus qui prius manifeste insinuauerat per scripta postea vna nocte per exercicium et in die omni hora ore ad os pallificando denunciabit, et eciam omnia que sub circulo lune sunt et eciam in terra et super terram, visibiliter et^h aperte demonstrabit.

Cum igitur cuncta perfeceris, precipe vt in pace recedat et iuxta preceptum magistri quacumqueⁱ hora vocatus fuerit quod festinanter veniat et sine mora.

Nota quod 10 nomina cum suis caracteribus debent sculpi in speculo prima die Veneris, luna^j crescente, et eciam speculum eadem die debet fieri. Et si non potest ex toto perfici eodem die Veneris, compleatur [secunda] uel tercia die Veneris, et semper luna crescente. Videat bene sculptor vel faber quod non sint poluti luxuria per 9 dies antequam accedant ad opus. Sint eciam balneati et loti et mundis vestibus induti, vt scis.

---

d   *Partly covered by blot.*

e   *Followed by* heramite, *deleted.*

f   *Or* albuetal.

g   *Or possibly* conrox.

h   *Followed by* apere, *deleted.*

i   *MS* quecumque.

j   *MS* lune.

NO. 20. ANOTHER WAY OF USING A MIRROR (FOLS 39v–40v)

Item, secundum alium modum.

In coniunccione Veneris et Jouis, vade ad locum secretum ac secretissimum, vt infra assignabitur. Et habeas tecum candelas accensas, et tene tecum speculum calibeum limpidum et politum, factum luna 4a uel 7a vel xiija.[a] [40r] Et in sequenti die ieiunabis. Et cum operare volueris, vade ad locum vt supra dictum est, et fac circulum, et finge ibi speculum supradictum supra[b] lignum ad modum cultelli factum, et dicas hec verba:

Siclis piclis ticlis moturas baruch cortex garyn ruent hismuie haruel fuganes furtym fermal faruc cornalis bosuo zelades pasapa phirpa tirph. Tu qui es deus, Alpha et O, fac hoc speculum crescere et clarescere donec ad visum meum sufficiat.

Hic non est defectus.

Sequitur [alia] coniuracio:

Coniuro te
- *per deum,*
- *et per tres pueros Sydrac, Mysaach, et Abdenago,*
- *et per tres magos Caspar, Balthasar, et Melchior,*
- *et per tres patriarchas Abraham, Ysaac, et Iacob,*
- *et per illum cui nomen est Theoden, Lien, Elyon, Vergiton, Christus, Deus fortis, Emanuel, Caspar, Caspan, Caspar, Corpion, Asmal.*

Hec dic tribus vicibus, et videbitur tibi clarescere et crescere, et apparebunt tibi multi in speculo tamquam in campo.[c] Tunc inquire secure de quacumque re quod volueris, et sufficienter tibi respondebunt.

Post primam autem vicem, [40v] quandocumque vis, vbicumque vis, in secreto tamen loco, hoc facere poteris dicens verba supradicta. Hoc enim speculum tibi consecrabitur ad illam quam tu vnquam plus affectasti in circulo nobilissimo de tribus militibus.[d]

Et nota quod omnis circulus et dicti circuli debent fieri quando[e] nubes non appareant, quod si postea apparuerint non est timendum, quia spiritus sunt, etc.

---

a   xiija *duplicated in lower margin.*

b   *MS* supera.

c   *MS* canpo.

d   Sic *in MS.*

e   *MS* quod.

NO. 21. FOR INVISIBILITY (FOL. 40v)

Studeas invenire vnam cattam nigram, natam in mense Martij, et exviscera eam, corde tamen remanente; tunc abscide cor cum cultello qui sit de Venere facto,[a] et oculos erue dicte catte cum eodem cultello, et imple[b] foramina oculorum semine cuiusdam herbe que elyotropia dicitur, vnum in oculo dextro et aliud in sinistro, et tercium in cor[de], semper hec verba dicendo: *Sapreson lampsones sampsanay, invisibilis fiat homo.* Et reple eam cora,[c] et sepeli eam in ortu tuo in quo nemo intrat, et eam riga[d] cum sangwine humano et aqua commistis, hoc continuando per xv dies vsque quo crescit herba alba, cuius semen suo opere[e] semper illa verba repetendo. Scias tamen quod quelibet herba dabit semen, sed granum unum bonum, quod quidem sic eligere debes, et nomina semper repetendo. Habeas igitur speculum coram te, et respiciendo vnum granum post aliud in speculo, et ponas omnia grana in ore tuo sub lingwa tua, et bene semper consideras granum illud quod ponis in os tuum. Et si in[f] quocumque grano posito in ore te videre non poteris in speculo, scias id esse bonum et vtile pro te, etc.

NO. 22. FOR DISCOVERING A THIEF OR MURDERER BY GAZING INTO A VESSEL (FOL. 41r–42r)

Ad furtum inveniendum, recipe cultellum cum manubrio nigro vel albo, et facias circulum in terra,[a] dicendo has oraciones: *Deus, qui corda fidelium Sancti Spiritus, etc., Concede nos famulos tuos, etc.,* et *Homines sancti tui.* Et habeas puerum uel puellam virginem. Et magister intret[b] cum ea vel cum eo in circulum, et accipiet[c] magister

---

a　*Meaning* cum cultello die Veneris facto*? The* e *in* de *is blotted out, but the word is replicated in the margin.*

b　*Followed by* fro, *deleted.*

c　Sic, *an alternative form of* cera.

d　*MS* rega.

e　Sic *in MS.*

f　*Meaning* cum*?*

a　*Figure at the top of fol. 42ʳ: double circular band, the interior of which is divided into six wedges. Pentagrams with* On *just beyond each point are inscribed in the upper and lower wedges, and to the lower left and right of the circle. Within the circle is inscribed* Hic sederat [=sedeat] puer super signum *(in the inner band, at top);* Hic sedeat magister super signum *(in the inner band, at bottom) a latere sinistro (in the outer band, at bottom). To the right of this figure is a column containing five horizontal bands and labelled* Istud est signum; *in the bands is inscribed* Esto altissimus, vnus, eternus; amen, *with one word per band.*

b　*Followed by blot.*

c　*Altered in MS from* accipiat.

serraginem bene mundatam intus et extra, et scribat super eum predicto cultello hoc signum et hec nomina similiter:

Onel,[d] On, Adonay, Emanuel, sanctus deus fortis, sanctus Ely, sanctus Elyon, sanctus dominus deus Sabaoth, mirabilis splendor, Alpha et O. Fiat.

Quo scripto, accipias lumen et invngas desuper serraginem cum penna galline nigre, et de sinistra ala, hoc modo dicendo *Pater Noster* ter, tot cum *Kyrieleison, Christeleison, Kyrieleison* tribus vicibus, *Christus ab antiqua fraude, magnus, magnus et eternus; fiat, amen, Exaudi nos* tribus vicibus, *Pater de celis, miserere nobis; sancta Maria, ora pro nobis; sancte Michahel, orate pro nobis; sancte Raphahel, ora pro nobis; sancte Johannes Baptista, precursor domini, ora pro nobis; omnes sancti et sancte, ora pro nobis; Kyrieleison, Christeleison, Kyrieleison; Christe, audi nos.*

Hoc vero supra scriptum periurato,[e] dicat magister in auriculo pueri coniuracionem istam:

Coniuro te, puer,
- *per Patrem et Filium et Spiritum Sanctum, cui omne nomen flectitur et omnis lingwa proclamat Osanna* [cf. Phil. 2:10];

coniuro te
- *per sanctam Mariam semper virginem,*
- *per angelos et archangelos,*
- *per xxiiijor seniores,*
- *et per cxla milia martirum* [41v] *qui pro nomine Christi iugulati sunt,*
- *et per sanctum Johannem Baptistam,*
- *et per omnes patriarchas et prophetas,*
- *et per xij apostolos,*
- *et per 4or ewangelistas,*
- *et per septuaginta discipulos domini,*
- *et per omnes sanctos et sanctas dei,*
- *et per omnes virtutes omnipotentis dei, celestes, terrestres, et infernales,*

vt quidquid tu videas nobis insinues, et vt tu veraciter videre posses quis vel qui eciam sit vel sint qui furtum istud uel homicidium fecerunt, virtute omnipotentis dei[f] et gracia.

Coniuracione vero facta, dicas super caput pueri hanc coniuracionem:

---

d   *Meaning* On, El.

e   Sic *in MS.*

f   *MS* virtute dei omnipotentis dei.

Deus, creator omnium rerum, te deprecor humili deuocione, per tuam mirabilem potenciam, quatenus isti puero tribuas scienciam et intellectum, vt[g] michi veritatem annunciet de furtis uel homicidiis, vt[h] cogatis, omni fallacia remota, inimicos,[i] vt exaltent nomen tuum, quod est benedictum in secula seculorum. Amen. Domine Ihesu Christe, qui cooperante Spiritu Sancto per mortem tuam mundum viuificasti, illumina cor[j] et corpus istius pueri, vt veritatem michi annunciet de furtis que interrogauero, per hec sanctissima nomina: Nazarenus, Messyas, Adonay, qui cum Patre et Filio et Spiritu Sancto viuit et regnat per omnia secula seculorum.

Precipiat magister puero vt intente inspiciat in vase illo idem ehimurili,[k] hoc vero modo vt alibi non respiciat aut aliquo modo visum suum ab eo auertat. Et si aliquo modo puer in prima vice nichil viderit, iterum coniuret illum puerum secunda vice, quousque videat puer hoc furtum vel homicidium et rem illam de qua dubitas. Etc.

NO. 23. FIRST MIRROR OF LILITH (FOL. 42r–43r)

Hoc est primum speculum Lilit et suorum virorum suorumque militum seniorum. Et hoc speculum debet fieri in magistratu sui speculi, et in memoria omnium nominum suorum seruorum, qui omnes res ante Caym faciunt in mundissimo loco.[a]

Coniuro vos demones vt veniatis et compareatis et dicatis michi de quocumque interrogauero vos omnem veritatem, in nomine Patris et Filij et Spiritus Sancti. Amen. Christus ✠ vincit ipsum ✠ Balbieit ✠ Zelans,[b] Zelles, Dimedero, Cadar, es qui cottidie astra celorum ascendunt vbi sunt tres dogie[c] cruci uel breues actu uel ictu seculorum in quatuor partes seculi, ad faciendam totam voluntatem in eam, per deum vbi probabilit[er][d]et licencia placabiliter et effabiliter, sine terrore, absque tocius ineffabili poten- [42v] *cia deitatis summi viui, in hac veri dei virtute te exoramus, Lylet, per honorem patris tui Arieth, et per illud sacramentum quod tu Nocma matri tue fecisti verbo, vt in similitudine tua et non in*

g   t *malformed, and duplicated above line.*

h   *Meaning* et?

i   *MS* inimici.

j   c *blotted out, and word duplicated in margin.*

k   Sic *in MS.*

a   Sic *in MS.*

b   *Followed by* zo *(?), deleted.*

c   Sic *in MS.*

d   Sic *in MS?*

coruorum similitudine, ad sermocinandum et ad sedendum nobiscum in quacumque hora requisierimus te in speculo isto, pacifice ac humiliter ac sine vlla deformitate, te michi ostendas; et amplius vt duo uel plures de seruis tuis, qui vero tam de furto quam de homicidio aut de quacumque alia re dubitabili de qua scire voluero michi dent vera responsa vel signa, in dei virtute et obediencia.

Istud vero speculum debet formari ad modum Clypei, vel[e] alio modo [si] volueris, in cuius giro hec nomina depingantur: *Deus sanctus, deus omnipotens, deus fortis, deus inmortalis, pater futuri seculi.* Et circa duo lattera superiora sigilla Salomonis depingantur majora, in fine vero clypei minus sigillum Salomonis, et in medio speculi hoc nomen 'Lylet'[f] depingatur, prout in hac patebit figura que infra ponitur.[g] [43r] Postea vero sicut alio vitro, sicut alia specula solent, circumdetur.[h] Quo vero facto, tacite et secrete defer ad quadriuium vel ad sepulc[r]um alicuius hominis interfecti, in crepusculo noctis, diei Martis vel Saturni, dicendo hanc coniuracionem:

Coniuro te, Lylet,[i] ac socios tuos,
  * *per Alpha et O,*
  * *per primum et nouissimum, Abiel, Rotbons, Cafre, O deus, O male Christe, inclitus, On, Ely, Elyon, Messyas, Sabaoth, Adonay, Emanuel;*
coniuro [te] eciam, Lylet,[j] atque socios tuos,
  * *per annunciacionem domini nostri Ihesu Christi,*
  * *et per natiuitatem eius,*
  * *et per aduentum Spiritus Sancti paracliti,*
vt in quacumque hora te vocauero, in hoc speculo michi appareas cum tuis sociis atque de re illa de qua scire voluero michi vera dando responsa vel signa.

Oracione vero ista completa, per aliam viam reuertaris ad hospicium tuum. Postea vero, eadem hora ac die, ad quadriuium vade et accipe speculum, et cum de re aliqua volueris scire dubitabili, ipsos per coniuracionem iam dictam venire compellas. Et quere quidquid volueris, et dicent tibi. Etc.

---

e *Largely blotted out.*

f *MS* Bylet.

g *Figure given at bottom right of fol. 42v: shield with a single band around its edge. In the band is inscribed,* Deus sanctus, deus omnipotens, deus fortis, deus inmortalis, pater futuri seculi. *The name* Bylet [=Lylet] *appears in the centre. In the upper left- and right-hand corners are pentagrams with* On *just beyond each point; smaller version appears at bottom.*

h *Perhaps meaning:* Postea vero vitro, sicut alia specula solent, circumdetur.

i *MS* Bylet.

j *MS* Bylet.

NO. 24. FOR LEARNING ABOUT ANY UNCERTAIN THING
BY GAZING INTO A CRYSTAL (FOL. 43r–v)

Si vis scire de omni re de qua dubitaueris, accipe puerum virginem et cristallum, quem laua cum vino. Deinde scribe in illo cum oleo oliue hec nomina: [43v] Hon, Hely, Sabaoth, Adonay, Hel, Hely, Heloym, Sother, Emanuel, Alpha et O, [et dic,]

> *O vos sanctissima nomina, rogo vt mittatis michi duos angelos uel tres in hunc cristallum, qui dicant michi veritatem de hiis que ego inquiram. Et rogo vos angelos vt dicatis michi veritatem quam[a] ego inquiram a vobis.*

Primo hec[b] dicat puer:

> *Coniuro vos in nomine Dedeon, et dij Egarias et Semisonay, et ex parte magistri mei, quod veniatis in hunc cristallum, ita quod aperte[c] possim videre.*

Et repete nomina superius habita donec venerint.

Et cum venerint, puer dicat nomina supradicta et coniuret eos *in nomine Dedeon et dij, etc.*; quod fiat ter. Et super sedes aureas sedeant, et cum sedeant puer dicat,

> *Coniuro vos in nomine Bessabes, et Hint, et Serem, et Salaboni, et Lethem, vt non recedatis ab hoc cristallo sine licencia mei magistri, qui hic presens est.*

NO. 25. FOR INFORMATION ABOUT A THEFT BY GAZING INTO A CRYSTAL
(FOLS 43v–44r)

Experimentum cristalli ad inveniendum furtum.

Accipias cristallum planum et lucidum, ad modum sigilli factum vel speculi, quem in cera reconde ex una parte virginea. Postea scribas in ipso cum oleo viridi hoc nomen: Honely. Postea dicas hanc coniuracionem:

> *Omnipotens, sempiterne deus, Domine Ihesu Christe, fili[a] dei viui, qui lapidibus, herbis, [et] predicacionibus virtutes michi gentissimas[b] atque [44r] mirabiles contulisti, [et] lapidem istam; item,*
> - *per natiuitatem sanctam tuam,*
> - *ac per passionem ac gloriosam resurreccionem tuam et ascensionem,*

---

a   *MS* que.
b   *Or* hoc.
c   *MS* apperte.
a   *MS* filij.
b   *Meaning* gratissimas?

- *atque per hec sancta nomina tua: Adonay, Sabaoth, Hon, Ely, Eloy, Elyon, Honely, Sother, Tetragramaton, Emanuel, Alpha et O,*

consecrare [et] benedicere digneris, per^c tui honorem et gloria[m], qui viuis et regnas deus, per omnia secula seculorum. Amen. Agla, Otmonta, Panoneogens, Origmaria, non obstet Asya, Africa, nec Europa,^d nec eius partes, quin ad nos veniatis. Fiat, fiat, fiat sine mora.

Postquam vero apparuerint tibi in cristallo, dicas hanc coniuracionem:

Coniuro vos angelos,
- *per deum viuum et verum,*
- *et per natiuitatem^e sanctam eius,*
- *et per eius passionem,^f*
- *et per eius resurreccionem sanctam,*
- *et per eius missionem Sancti Spiriti paracliti,*
- *et per sanctam eius aduentum,*
- *et per hec sancta nomina dei: Honay, Sabaoth, Onel, Ely, Eloym, Sother, Emanuel, vt superius dictum est,*
- *et per omnia nomina sancta dei,*

vt non recedatis ab hoc lapide quousque certificati fuerimus de omni re dubitabili de quo scire voluerimus, virtute dei omnipotentis et obediencia. Amen.

Notandum eciam est quod non debet aliquis vti hoc experimento pro re vili vel modica, sed pro causa^g ardua, et ne eciam secundum quod dictum est alibi, 'Ne sumas nomen dei tui in vanum [Ex 19:7], nec invoces invtiliter, etc.'^h

NO. 26. KEY OF PLUTO, TO OPEN ALL LOCKS (FOL. 44v)

Sume tibi ferrum inventum ex inprouisu, et fac tibi fieri clauem huiusmodi, factam die Veneris.^a Et cum facta fuerit, repone eam per noctem cum sacrificio galli albi in quadruuio, dicens,

O spiritus Neyilon [et] Achalas, accipite sacrificium vt nichil contra me et contra clauem istam valeat sera vbi ista clauis ponetur.

---

c   *Followed by* te.
d   *MS* Eroupa.
e   *MS* natifitatem.
f   *Followed by two (?) deleted words.*
g   *MS* casa.
h   *Ex. 20:7 Vulg.:* Non adsumes nomen domini dei tui in vanum.
a   *Figure on upper right of fol. 44v: a key, with a single tooth extending to the left and a single tooth to the right.*

Et fac super istam clauem antequam posueris subtus terram hanc figuram de sangwine galli albi.[b] Et dimitte ibi tribus diebus. Tercia autem nocte, ante gallicinium, accipe eam inde. Cum transieris vrbem, recipe clauem cum sinistra manu de occidente in orientem, omnesque[c] seras aperiat. Et[d] dicitur hec[e] clauis Plutonis.

NO. 27-A. FOR OBTAINING INFORMATION ABOUT A THEFT BY GAZING INTO A FINGERNAIL (FOLS 44v–45v)

Ad furtum inveniendum, accipe puerum virginem de legittimo thoro, hora qua vis ante meridiem, et illius vngwem de pollice sinistre manus cum cultello bene purgabis. Deinde cedulam subnotatis nominibus scriptam in eodem digito ligabis sub ungwe. Et hec sunt nomina: Egippia, Benoham, Beanke (vel Beanre), Reranressym, Alredessym, Ebemidyri, Fecolinie, Dysi, Medirini, Alhea, Heresim, Egippia, Benoham,[a] Haham, Ezirohias, Bohodi, Hohada, Anna, Hohanna, Ohereo, Metaliteps, Aregereo, Agertho, Aliberri, Halba.

Hoc facto, si puer non vi- [45r] det aliquid, etc.[b] Si autem videt, liga corrigiam ouinam, quam ad tres missas quas perfecte audiuisti tecum habuisti, supra cedulam circa digitum, dicendo hanc coniuracionem:

O vos demones, qui coram me in vngwe istius pueri apparuistis,
> • *per eum qui est Alpha et O,*

vobis impero et precipio et coniuro,
> • *per hec sacratissima nomina: Ely, Eloy, Messyas, Sother, Emanuel, Sabaoth, Adonay,*
> • *et per On, quod est primum nomen domini Pantoncraton,[c] Anetheten,*
> • *et per alia nomina michi cognita et incognita,*

vt non habeatis potestatem recedendi cum vestris sociis donec omnino omnem meam voluntatem adimpleueritis, et sine omni mendacio et lesione alicuius. Et si hoc facere contempseritis, iubeo vos ligari sub profunditate aquarum maris, per hec duo nomina: Ioth [et] Nabnoth, per que Salomon constringebat in vase vitreo demones. Coniuro vos
> • *per vij signa Salomonis,*
> • *et per sigillum et sapienciam eius,*

---

b *Figure part-way down fol. 44v: a large cross, followed by* XL.

c *MS* omnia qui.

d *Deleted, but re-added in margin.*

e *Or* hoc.

a *These two names, already given at the outset of the series, are here repeated.*

b *Partly blotted out.*

c Sic in *MS, for* Pantocrator?

vt non habeatis licenciam recedendi hinc donec de quacumque re interrogauero michi dicatis et ostendatis veritatem.

Hiis dictis, si puer non dicat directe, dic in aure eius hanc coniuracionem:

Coniuro te, virgo iuuenis,
- *per deum verum Basyon,*
- *et per nomen On, Berion, Sabaoth, Adonay;*

coniuro te
- *per baptismum* [45v] *et castitatem tuam sacratam, qua te regenerauit ex aqua et Spiritu Sancto,*

vt non habeas potestatem celandi, sed omnia que videris manifestes.

Hiis coniuracionibus ter dictis, si te expedire[d] non expediant spiritus, adde hanc coniuracionem:

Vos demones ab oriente,[e] vos demones ab occidente, vos demones ab meridie, vos demones a septentrione, aperite nobis, Discobermath, Archidemath, Fritath, Altramat, Pestiferat, Helyberp, Hegergibet, Sathan.

Qua coniuracione ter dicta seu repetita, clare videbit puer omnia.

Hoc eciam experimentum valet adhoc si aliquis vellet scire statum amicorum suorum, vtrum essent sani vel egri, et denunciat si essent in via vel non.

Coniuracio super corrigiam, de qua iam dictum est: Finita missa qualibet die, ter dicas hanc coniuracionem super corrigiam:

Coniuro te, Sona,
- *per hoc nomen domini: Tetragramaton,*
- *et per hoc nomen dei: Ioth,*
- *et per hoc nomen dei: Nabnoth,*
- *et per omnes virtutes et potestates herbarum et lapidum et verborum,*

vt virtutem talem recipias quod quocumque fueris ligata, ipsi spiritus non habeant potestatem recedendi quousque velle ligatoris perficiant.

Explicit primum capitulum.

Cemay edo cuscutas, feferaton, San.[f]

---

d   *Or possibly* expedite.

e   *Followed by* ab occidente, *deleted.*

f   *Fol. 46ʳ, following, is blank.*

NO. 27-C. FOR OBTAINING INFORMATION (FOLS 46v–47v)ᵃ

[. . .] *pueri; et*

- *per nomen principis vestri summi,*
- *per coronam capitis sui,*
- *per obedienciam quam sibi debetis,*

vt veniatis ab omnibus partibus mundi, omni occasione postposita, et in vngwe istius pueri appareatis, et nobis sine dubio et sine fallacia illud quod a vobis scire volumus veraciter manifestetis. Fiat, fiat, fiat.

Coniuro te, virgo iuuenis,

- *perᵇ deum On, Orion, Sabaoth, Adonay,*

vt non habeas potestatem menciendi uel celandi de quocumque interrogauero; itemᶜ coniuro te, virgo juuenis,

- *per deum tuum, Alpha et O, qui est primus et nouissimus,*

vt michi veritatem dicas de hac re de qua te requiro; item coniuro te, virgo,

- *per baptismum quemᵈ recepisti in nomine sancte et indiuidue trinitatis,*
- *per castitatem et potenciam qua te reg[e]nerauit ex aqua et Spiritu Sancto,*

vt non habeas potenciam neque licenciam celandi uel menciendi quodcumque videris; item coniuro te, virgo iuuenis,

- *per Patrem et Filium et Spiritum Sanctum,*
- *per sanctum nomen dei Elthie,*
- *per sanctum Tetragramaton,*
- *per sancta nomina dei On, Ely, Eloy, Eloe,*

vt non habeas licenciam seu potestatem celandiᵉ quodcumque sciueris; coniuro te, virgo iuuenis,

- *per baptismum quem accepisti de sancta credulitate, per castitatem et potenciam sacramenti qua te reg[e]nerauit de anima Spiritus Sancti,*

vt tam cito et sine mora, aperte et breuiter, in vngwe istius pueri veritatem [47r] *nobis ostendas, aliter, etc.ᶠ Infans, coniuro te*

- *per Patrem et Filium et Spiritum Sanctum,*
- *per nomenᵍ deiʰ Elthie,*

---

a   *Text continued from fol. 51r.*

b   per *repeated.*

c   *Followed by blot.*

d   *MS* quod.

e   *MS* scelandi.

f   *This element of conjuration, addressed to the spirit, seems misplaced in the midst of a conjuration addressed to the boy.*

g   *MS* nomina.

h   *Followed by* Elith, *deleted.*

- *per Tetragramaton,*
- *per hec nomina domini nostri Ihesu Christi: Ely, Eloy, Eloem,*
- *et per baptismum quem accepisti in nomine sancte et indiuidue trinitatis,*
- *per caritatem dei, Alpha et O, quod est principium et finis,*

vt aspicias in vngwe ita vt si deveniat clarus uel non.

Tunc interroga puerum si vngwis sit clarior quam ante. Si dicat non, lege iterum coniuracionem ab inicio, et tercia vice si necesse fuerit. Si dicit quod sit clarior, quere si videat aliquid. Si dicit quod videat hominem, faciat magister coniurare puerum illum[i] quem videt, in materna lingwa, sic:

Tu qui es coram me, coniuro te
- *per Patrem et Filium et Spiritum Sanctum,*
- *et per sanctam Mariam et eius virginitatem,*
- *per sanctum Iohannem et eius virginitatem,*
- *per sanctam Katherinam et eius virginitatem,*
- *per omnes sanctos et sanctas virgines,*
- *et per virginitatem meam,*

vt cito vadas pro rege tuo et facias eum venire coram me, ita vt ipsum possim expresse videre et intelligere.

Postea quere a puero si rex venit. Si non, coniuret iterum puer vt prius. Si venit, dicat puer regi quod descendat de equo suo et faciat afferri cathedram super quam sedeat. Tunc querat puer a rege si velit comedere. Si dicit quod non, tunc de quo volueris queras. Si dicit quod sic, dicat puer regi quod mittat pro vno ariete [47v] ad quemcumque locum voluerit et faciat ipsum excorriari et decoqui, et tunc dicat quod faciat poni mensam, et surgat et lauet manus, et sedeat ad mensam et faciat arietem poni coram se, et cito comedat. Postquam comedit, surgat et accipiat aquam et lauet manus.

Postea dicat puer regi quod remoueat coronam de capite et ponat manum dextram super caput suum et iuret per coronam suam et per ceptrum suum et per illod quod tenet sub manu sua dextra quod veraciter respondeat ad omnes questiones magistri. Deinde querat magister per puerum quidquid voluerit. Postquam satis factum questionibus magistri, detur spiritibus licencia, et puer sic dicat: 'Ite. Pax sit inter nos et vos. Et quando magister vos vocauerit, estote parati sibi obedire in omnibus per omnia.'

Explicit secundum capitulum.[j]

---

i   *Followed by* quod, *blotted out.*

j   *Written twice.*

NO. 28. FOR OBTAINING INFORMATION
BY GAZING AT A BONE (FOLS 47v–49r)

De[a] omni re dubitabili, eciam incerta, [pro] veritate habenda, accipe spatulam arietis dextram, oleo oliue invnctam, quam ponendo super manubrium cultelli, inspiciat puer[b] virgo. Tu vero ex alia parte, tenendo candelam accensam, dicas hoc modo:

Ergarrandras, Ornis, Arbes, Cargie, Ornis, Arbas, ego in virtute domini nostri Ihesu Christi, qui est Alpha et O, primus et nouissimus, inicium et finis, coniuro vos demones et advoco,

- *per eum qui dixit omnia et facta sunt,*
- *et per [48r] eum cui obediunt omnes creature,*
- *et per eum [ante] quem tremunt omnes exercitus angelorum, celestium et terrestrium et infernorum,*
- *et per ipsius virtutem et omnipotenciam,*
- *et per tremendum diem iudicij summi dei,*
- *et per ipsius nomina hec sancta: On, El, Ely, Eloy, Adonay, Alpha et O, Messyas, Soter, Emanuel, Pancraton, Occinomos, Tetragramaton, Agyos, Otheos, Athanatos, Yschiros, Kirios, Alleluia, Eleyson, Ymas,[c]*

quatenus sine mora visibiliter in hac spatula compareatis, ante faciem istius pueri virginis, et respondeatis et demonstretis omnem veritatem de hac re,[d] N., nobis dubitabili[e] et incerta. Britonia, Bresis, Diton, Crasis, Sanete, Garbamion, libera nos famulos ab omni malo. Pater noster, etc.

Item coniuro vos demones

- *per caput et coronam principis vestri,*
- *et per vestram potestatem, vobis a summo deo datam,*
- *per anulum Salomonis, et per signa et sancta nomina in ipsis descripta,*
- *et per vij celos et per omnes angelos in ipsis dispositos,*
- *et per omnes potestates aereas[f] et infernales,*

quatenus cito, etc. Gospar, Dasper, Gespar, Lapir, Sparsis, Nota, Calius,[g] Asper. Item coniuro vos demones

---

a   *Repeated in margin.*

b   *Followed by* vr, *deleted.*

c   Sic *in MS.*

d   *Followed by* nob, *deleted.*

e   *Corrected from* dubitabile.

f   r *blotted out, and replaced above line.*

g   *Or* Talius.

- *per caput et coronam principis vestri,*
- *et per*[h] *vestram potestatem, vobis a summo deo datam,*
- *per anulos Salomonis et per signa et sancta nomina in ipsis descripta;*[i]
- *per angelos et archangelos, per thronos et dominaciones, per principatus et potestates* [48v] [*et*] *virtutes, per cherubin et seraphin, et per omnes virtutes celorum,*
- *per celum et terram et mare et omnia que in eis sunt,*
- *per xij apostolos,*
- *per martires et confessores, virgines* [*et*] *viduas,*
- *per patriarchas et prophetas et ewangelistas,*
- *per*[j] *xxiij seniores,*
- *per cxl milia innocentum,*
- *et per omnes sanctos et electos dei qui sunt in celo et in terra,*

quatenus cito et sine mora, etc.

Tunc inquiras a puero si videat spatulam crescere et clarescere, quod si sic, tunc dicat postea hanc coniuracionem:

Coniuro vos spiritus
- *per virtutem domini nostri Ihesu Christi,*
- *et per virginitatem sancte Marie,*
- *et per virginitatem sancte Katerine et sancte Lucie et sancte Agate et sancte Cecilie et sancte Barbare,*
- *et per virginitatem sancti Johannis ewangeliste,*[k]
- *et per caput sancti Johannis ewangeliste,*
- *et per virginitatem meam,*

vt cito in hac spatula a[*p*]*pareatis, vt vos videre possim.*

Quo spiritu viso in forma humana nigra, inquire ab ipso de tuo negocio, prout melius videris expedire, puero mediante[l] et per virginitatem[m] ipsum spiritum constringente.

Sit puer infra xij annos existens. Et post mane et in crepusculo noctis, circulum protrahendo, dicas,

---

h   *Followed by* virtutem, *deleted.*

i   *The lines* Item coniuro vos demones . . . per signa et sancta nomina in ipsis descripta *are repeated verbatim.*

j   *Formation is irregular, as if the scribe began writing the sign for* et *and then changed it to that for* per.

k   Sic *in MS, meaning* Baptiste.

l   *Initial letter blotted out.*

m   *Changed in MS to (or from?)* virginitates.

Sator, arepo, tenet, opera, rotas. In nomine Patris et Filij et Spiritus Sancti. Amen. Acciones nostras, quesumus, domine, aspirando preueni et adiuuando persequere, vt cuncta nostra opera a te semper incipiant et per te cepta finiantur. Per Christum dominum nostrum. Amen. Deus, qui misisti Spiritum Sanctum super [49r] *apostolos tuos, mitte Spiritum Sanctum tuum paraclitum super istum puerum, et illumina et clarifica intellectum ipsius atque animam, vt in spiritu videre possit creaturas tuas, et nobis reuelare omnem veritatem de hac re nobis dubitabili et incerta.*

Scribantur in spatula hec sancta nomina dei: On, El, Eloy, Adonay, Alpha et O, Pancraton, Occinomos, Tetragramaton. Dum volueris eos licenciare, fac signum crucis supra spatulam, dicendo,

In nomine Patris, et Filij, et Spiritus Sancti. Amen. Ecce crux[n] domini; fugite, partes aduerse; vicit leo de triba Juda, stirps Dauid. Ite in pace ad loca vnde venistis.

Poteris eciam coniurare puerum per virginitatem vt habeat potestatem videndi spiritum et non menciendi.

Explicit.

NO. 29. THE TRUE ART OF THE BASIN (FOL. 49r–v)

Incipit ars verissima de bacimine.

Hec nomina dices in aurem pueri virginis:

Carab, Riasteli, Careb, Basal, Mistal, Oronothel, Fabanin, Non, Va, Vatuel. Coniuro vos
- *per Patrem et Filium et Spiritum Sanctum,*
- *per[a] sanctam Mariam virginem,*
- *per ix ordines angelorum,*
- *per patriarchas,*
- *per prophetas [et] apostolos,*
- *per martires,*
- *per confessores,*
- *per virgines,*

vt appareatis in bacimine isto, vt veraciter huius rei veritatem nobis ostendatis, vt non sit michi aliquod impedimentum veritatis in ista questione. Rabuel, Astena, Hytatol, cogitate facere voluntatem meam per predictas potestates.

---

n   *MS* crucem.

a   *Followed by* patriarches et prophetas, *deleted, and by a redundant* per *that is not deleted.*

Hec tria nomina scribentur in cedula [49v] que ponitur in bacimine dum ars fiet. Postea dic,

Deus celi, deus terre, deus angelorum, deus archangelorum, qui es rex sanctorum omnium, patriarcharum ac prophetarum, te deprecor humili deuocione vt isti puero tribuas scienciam et intellectum, vt michi veritatem de quibus[cumque] interrogauero dicat, per hec sancta nomina tua: Ely, Eloe, Sabaoth, Adonay, Elyon, On, qui viuis et regnas per infinita secula seculorum. Amen. Domine Ihesu Christe, fili[b] dei viui, qui ex voluntate Patris, cooperante Spiritu Sancto, per mortem tuam mundum viuificasti, illumina istius pueri cor [et] mentem, et fac vt michi veritatem de hiis que interrogauero dicat, per hec sancta nomina tua: Jesus Nazarenus, Messyas, Sother, Emanuel, Fortis, Fons, Leo, Petra, vt indicet omnia de quibus postulo veritatem.

Explicit.

Coniuracionem facio, tu qui es Alpha et O. Coniuro vos demones,
- *per tres reges, Caspar, Balthasar, Melchior,*
- *et per tres pueros, Sydrac, Misac, Abdenago,*
vt omnes appareatis huic puero in hoc speculo uel ense, Abiniabyndo, Abyncola, Abracalos, Pyel, Thyel, Syel.

Quibus apparentibus,[c] dicet puer regi vt sedeat et mittat pro ariete, sic[ut] alias dictum est ante in secundo capitulo istius tractatus.

Postea sequatur coniuracio pueri sicut eciam ibidem dictum est.

Explicit.

No. 30. Twelve Names to Make Spirits Appear in a Boy's Hand (fols 49v–50v)

Bethala, Pamelon, Anguis, Floris, Ereth,[a] Alya, Cabyona, Ely, Eloy, Sadamay, Melgry, Asmyacre, intretis in nomine domini. Karacteres isti [50r] scribendi sunt vt infra docetur: A, Q,[b] O, P, E, V.

In nomine Patris et Filij et Spiritus Sancti, signum sancte crucis sit in fronte tuo, hoc modo

---

b   *MS* filij.

c   *MS* aparantibus.

a   *Corrected in MS from* Areth.

b   *MS has sign for* quod.

signet te dominus Ihesus Christus, hoc modo signet te dominus sicut signauit in Chana Galilee. In nomine Patris et Filij et Spiritus Sancti.

Hoc ter dicatur, qualibet vice signando frontem pueri cum pollice tuo dextre[c] manus. Hec nomina predicta xij, scilicet Bethela,[d] etc., tociens repetantur, quousque sex spiritus compareant in manu pueri. Postquam[e] comparuerint, precipiat puer eis in nomine Patris et Filij et Spiritus Sancti vt sedeant, et vnus eorum surgat, qui det vera responsa ex parte magistri sui.

Modus operandi idem: Accipe resinam albam quam accendes per candelam super lapidem aliquem planum sub pelui desuper aliquantulum eleuata. Postea cum penna noua colligas in pergamen[t]o aliquo uel corio albo puluerem illum adherentem pelui ex vaporacione resine predicte, et reserua quousque operari volueris. Tunc enim intinges digitum medium[f] dextre manus primo in oleo oliue, et linies inferiores quatuor articulos sinistre manus pueri masculi virginis. Deinde eundem digitum tuum intingas in puluerem prefatum,[g] et similiter lineas articulos pueri, sicut prius, et sic alternando, nunc cum oleo, nunc cum puluere, donec articuli predicti fiant sicut speculum clarum et resplendens.

Post[ea] dic verba illa duodecim supra nominata: Bethala, Pamelon, etc. Deinde cum signaueris frontem pueri et frontem tuam, si vis, dicendo, *In nomine Patris et Filij et Spiritus Sancti*, signum sancte crucis sit in fronte, etc., vt supra.

[50v] Cum autem predictos spiritus vis licenciare, puer dicat,

Precipio vobis quod recedatis, in nomine Patris et Filij et Spiritus Sancti.

Et iterum signare poteris frontem pueri et tuam si vis tercio, modo quo prius et verbis. Nota eciam quod in parte peluis predicte eleuata interius per circuitum cum cultello inscribendi sunt sex illi karacteres, qui supra in isto capitulo sunt nominati – scilicet A, Q,[h] etc. – antequam ipsa resina sub ipsa pelui accenditur.

Explicit. Etc.[i]

---

c *MS* dextro.

d Sic *in MS.*

e *Preceded by* Qui.

f u *misshapen, as if scribe began writing* e.

g *MS* prefato.

h *Formed as before.*

i *Remainder of fol. 50ᵉ is blank.*

No. 27-B. For obtaining information (fol. 51r)[a]

[. . .] *Cedon, Zephata, Eloym, Eloyay, venite et apparete in vngwe istius pueri sub forma humana, et ipsum[b] vngwem faciatis crescere et clarescere in tantum vt sufficiat ei ad videndum de quocumque ipsum interrogauero. Coniuro vos spiritus,*

- *per tres reges, Caspar, Baltasar, Melchior, quibus stella apparuit,*
- *[et] per virtutem domini nostri Ihesu Christi, vt natiuitatem suam manifestaret,[c]*

vt in vngwe istius pueri appareatis, et quod a vobis inquirere volumus nobis absque fallacia et sine dubio manifestetis. Coniuro vos spiritus qui vocati estis,

- *per tres pueros Sydrac, Misac, Abdenago,*

vt in vngwe istius pueri appareatis, nec ipsi puero timorem uel terrorem aut lesionem faciatis, et nos de omnibus que a uobis scire volumus certos faciatis. Coniuro vos spiritus qui vocati estis,

- *per Patrem et Filium et Spiritum Sanctum,*
- *et per omnipotenciam eius et virtutem,*
- *per cherubin et seraphin,*
- *per thronos et dominaciones,*
- *per principatus et potestates et virtutes,*
- *per angelos et archangelos,*
- *per patriarchas,*
- *per prophetas,*
- *per apostolos,*
- *per confessores,*
- *per martyres,*
- *per monachos,*
- *per virgines et viduas,*
- *per omnes sanctos et electos dei,*
- *per ix ordines angelorum,*
- *per sanctam Mariam matrem domini nostri Ihesu Christi,*
- *per virginitatem istius [. . .][d]*

---

a   *Continuation of text from fol. 45v.*

b   *MS* ipsam.

c   *Meaning* qua natiuitatem suam manifestauit?

d   *Fol. 51ᵛ is blank; text continues on fol. 46v.*

No. 31. The Book of Consecrations
(FOLS 52r–59v AND FOLS 135r–139r)

Incipit prologus libri consecracionum,[a] dividens[b] ac demonstrans ad quid inventus fuerit, et quid sit eius effectus. Quicumque aliquod opus inceptum perficere voluerit vt perveniat ad effectum, prevideat sibi prius in omnibus et caueat ne in vanum operetur, et precipue in opere isto, quod pre cunctis locis aliis preciosissimum et magis laudabile atque certissimum, quod dei nominibus est consecratum et confirmatum, ne aliquis operator falli possit, si spem et fidem bonam habeat et certam in domino Ihesu Christo, a quo omnia bona procedunt, vt testatur sacra littera, qui non firmiter fideliterque crediderit, saluari non poterit.[c] Sic ergo fideliter crede[re] vnicuique operatori est necesse, ne fallatur.

Scias ergo pro certo hoc opus esse inventum propter [errorem] quorundam experimentorum remouendum, scilicet florum, vt per virtutem et invocacionem sanctorum dei nominum [et per] ineffabilem ipsius misericordiam, virtutem et potestatem efficaciter obtineant

[135r] Incipit prologus libri consecracionum dicens aut [demonstrans] ad quod inventus sint et quid sint eius[a] effectus. Quicumque enim aliquot opus inceptum et finire voluerit ut preueniat ad effectum, prouideat sibi primo que sibi[b] necessaria sunt, ne in vanum operetur, et precipue in opere isto[c] quod pre cunctis alijs magistris[d] est laudabile atque certissimum, quod sacris nominibus est consecratum ac confirmatum, ne aliquis operare possit falli, si spem et fidem firmam habeat in domino Ihesu Christo, a quo omnia bona procedunt, sicut sacra scriptura dicit, qui firmiter et fideliter non crediderit, saluus esse non poterit. Si[c] ergo credere vnicuique operatori necesse est, ut non fallatur.

Scias ergo pro certo quod opus est inventum propter errorem quorundam experimentorum remouendum, ut per virtutem et invocacionem sanctorum nominum dei et per

---

a   *Heading duplicated in MS.*

b   Sic *in MS.*

c   *Cf. Is 7:9, Lk 1:20, Lk 8:12, Rom 10:9, I Cor 1:21.*

a   Sic *in MS.*

b   *MS* scilicet.

c   *Followed by* que, *deleted.*

d   Sic *in MS.*

quem debeant obtinere, sicut inferius declarabitur. Quando aliquod experimentum virtutem et potestatem suam sana[d] amisit tali modo sicut postea declarabitur potest recuperari.

Nota quod multi sunt qui multa et magna querunt et multa eciam scripta habent et credunt de die in [52v] diem ad effectum pervenire, sed nunquam pervenient. Et sic se ipsos decipiunt, et opera sua amittunt, et melius valet virtus vnius verbi istorum quam pondus auri. Vnde dicitur, 'Melius est sciencia quam secularis potencia.'[e] Sic ista sciencia preualet omnibus aliis, quia omnia alia vera experimenta sunt corrupta, quorum quedam sunt ficta et sic omnia pene falsa.

Hiis igitur diligenter prenotatis, ad nostrum propositum recurras, et videamus quando et qualiter[f] exorcista siue operator habere debeat, et quid ei sit vtile ad operandum, ne fallatur.

In primis, quicumque hoc opus sit facturus

ineffabilem ipsius misericordiam, veritatem[g] atque potestatem efficaciter obtineant quod optinere debea[n]t, sicut inferius declarabitur. Cum igitur hoc experimentum virtutem ac potenciam suam amiserit, tali modo sicud postea docebitur recuperari poterit.

Nota. Multi sunt querentes magna scripta, et credunt de die in diem peruenire ad effectum, et non perueniunt. Sed se ipsos sic decipiunt, quod tempora[f] sua amittunt, et melius est scire virtutem vnius verbi quam pondus[g] auri, vnde dicitur, 'Melius est sciencia quam secularis[h] potencia.' Sic ista sciencia plus valet omnibus scienciis, que omnia experimenta sunt victa et corrupta, et sic pene omnia vniuersa.

Hijs igitur diligenter prenominatis prenotatis ad imum recordamus ipso situm volentes quando operari et qualiter exorcista se habere debeat, et quit[i] sit ei vtile ne fallatur.

In primis, igitur, quicumque hoc opus sit

---

d   Sic *in MS.*

e   *This quotation conveys the spirit of the Pseudo-Aristotelian tradition most fully conveyed in the* Secretum secretorum; *see M.A. Manzalaoui, ed.,* Secretum secretorum: Nine English Versions *(Oxford: Oxford University Press, 1977–).*

f   *MS* equaliter.?

e   *MS* et veritatem.

f   Sic *in MS.*

g   *Corrected in MS to* pondeus.

h   *MS* solis aris.?

i   Sic *in MS.*

ad quod vocatur liber consecracionum, ab omni pollucione mentis et corporis se debet abstinere in cibo [et] potu, in verbis ociosis siue inmoderatis, et sit mundis indutus^g vestibus, nouem diebus ante opus inceptum, et debet audire in qualibet missam vnam, et librum istum secum deferre et pone super^h altari donec missa finiatur quolibet die, quousque transacti fuerint omnia,ⁱ et hec devotissime faciat, cum oracionibus et ieiuniis, quia sicut scriptum est, per ieiunium et oraciones occulta ministeriorum celestium reuelatorque diuini sacramenti archana pendunt.^j Et cottidie post missam librum portabis domi. Et habeas locum secretum [53r] ab omnibus absconditum, ne aliquis sit presens operi suo,^k et prius aspergat locum aqua benedicta vbi librum istum^l ponet, et cum cingulo sacerdotali et stola dedicata liget eum in modum crucis circumquaque, et flexis genibus versus orientem, dicat vij psalmos cum le-

facturus, quod vocatur liber consecracionum, ab omni pollucione mentis et corporis debet se abstinere, in cibo et in potu atque verbis ociosis, sit moderatus et sit mundis vestibus indutus ix diebus antequam^j opus incipiatur, et debet audire qualibet die vnam missam [135v] et istum librum ferre secum et ponere in altari quousque missa finiatur, et hoc deuotissime faciat, cum oracionibus et ieiunijs, sicut scriptum est, 'Per ieiunia et oraciones occulta misteriorum celestium reuelantur, archana diuine sacramenta pandantur.' Et cottidie post missam portatur librum domu et habeat locum secretum,^k ab omnibus inquinamentis mundum, nec aliquis sit presens huic operi, et aspergat locum aqua benedicta, scilicet vbi ponat librum et eum cingulo sacerdotis et stola benedicta liget^l librum in modum crucis circumquaque, et flexis genibus ponat librum versus Orientem, dicens vij psalmos cum oracione longa et letaniam, sanctificet et benedicat et consecret istum librum suis sanctis nominibus insignitum, cum omni deuocione ac toto cordis affectu, et deus omnipotens sua bonitate ac misericordia sanctificet hunc librum, benedicat,

---

g   *MS* indutis.

h   su *(?) duplicated above line.*

i   *MS* omnes.

j   *Meaning, perhaps,* occulta misteriorum celestium reuelantur, et diuini sacramenti archana panduntur?

k   Sic *in MS.*

l   *Partly blotted out.*

j   *MS* antequem.

k   *Followed by* abhominibus, *struck through.*

l   *MS* ligat.

tania et oracionem sequentem
antequam liber aperiatur. Et supra^m
librum predictum debet aperire cum
humili deuocione et toto cordisⁿ
affectu, vt omnipotens deus
misericordia et bonitate sua sanctificet
ac benedicat et consecret istum librum
sanctissimis nominibus suis insignitum,
vt virtutem quam obtinere debeat
potenter obtineat, vt valeat ad
consecrandum vinculum spirituum et
ad omnes invocaciones et
coniuraciones ipsorum, et sic omnia
alia experimenta.

Similiter nota hunc librum non
valere habenti nisi ab ipso denuo
consecretur.

Letania autem finita, aperi et dic
hanc oracionem humiliter et animo
perfecto et mente sincera.

Oracio. *Deus meus, miserere^o mei et parce
malis meis. Sana animam meam, quia peccaui
tibi. Non obneges michi umquam que pluribus
aliis contulisti. Exaudi, deus, oracionem
famuli tui, N., et^p quacumque die* [53v]
*invocauero te exaudi me velociter, sicut exaudisti
sanctam Mariam matrem tuam. Suscipe,*

et^m consecraret suis sanctissimis
nominibusⁿ insignitum ut virtutem
quem obtinere debeat videlicet ad
consecrandum vinculatum spiritum,^o
valens ad omnes invocaciones et
coniuraciones ipsorum et ad omnia^p
alia experimenta.

Item nota. Quicumque polluit hunc
librum sciat eum vltra non valere nisi^q
ab ipso de nouo consecretur,^r tunc
oracione et letania viuificat librum.

Aperiat et dicat hanc oracionem
humili corde et anima deuota, tunc
incipe sicut sequitur:

*Deus meus, miserere mei et parce malis meis,
sana animam meam, quia peccaui tibi. Non
abneges vni quod pluribus contulisti. Exaudi,
deus, oracionem meam, famuli tui N., et^s*

m Followed by an extraneous stroke.
n Followed by et.
o Sic in MS.
p alii deleted.
q Followed by abip and a space.
r MS consecratur.
s MS ut.

m Sic in MS.
n MS corde.
o MS miscerere.
p MS vt.

domine, clamorem[q] confitentis. Audi[r] vocem precantis, per merita beatissime Marie wirginis matris tue atque omnium sanctorum tuorum, vt oraciones et preces perveniant ad aures pietatis tue, quas ego pro hoc libro consecracionum effundo coram te in hac hora, vt per tua sanctissima nomina que in ipso continentur sit consecratus et confirmatus a quocumque voluero, prestante domino nostro Ihesu Christo, qui viuit et regnat per omnia secula seculorum. Amen.

Oracio. *Domine Ihesu Christe, per ineffabilem misericordiam tuam, parce michi seu miserere mei et exaudi nunc per invocacionem nominis tui, scilicet Patris et Filij et Spiritus Sancti, vt accepta habeas et tibi placeant verba et oraciones oris mei, per invocaciones sanctorum tuorum nominum in hoc libro descriptorum. Humiliter et fideliter, deprecantissime, licet ego indignus, cum in te confidens vt sanctifices et benedicas librum istum sanctis nominibus tuis insignitum et consecres istum, vt per hec nomina tua sanctissima – On, Ihesus,*

in quacumque die invocauero te, velociter exaudi me, sicut exaudisti Mariam matrem tuam. Suscipe, domine, clamorem confitentis anime. Exaudi, domine, vocem deprecantis, per merita et oraciones beatissime virginis[t] Maria matris tue, atque omnium sanctorum, et oraciones et preces mee ad aures tue pietatis, quas ego pro[u] hoc libro consecracionum effundo coram te in hac hora, per tua sanctissima nomina, que in hoc libro continentur, sit consecratus et confirmatus, ad quodcumque voluero, prestante domino nostro Ihesu Christo, qui viuit et regnat in secula seculorum.

[136r] Domine Ihesu Christe, per ineffabilem misericordiam tuam, parce michi et miserere mei. Exaudi me nunc per inuocacionem nominis tui trini, scilicet Patrem et Filium et Spiritum Sanctum, ut accepta habeas et placea[n]t tibi verba oracionis mee, per inuocacionem sanctorum nominum tuorum in hoc libro scriptorum. Humiliter et fideliter deprecans, licet ego indignus peccator, tamen in te confidens, ut sanctifices ac benedicas[v] librum istum tuis sanctis nominibus insignitum, et consecres

---

q   *Followed by* confide, *deleted.*

r   *Extraneous letter between* d *and* i *appears blotted out.*

t   *Followed by* matris, *deleted.*

u   *MS* per.

v   *MS* benedices.

Christus, Alpha et O, El, Eloy, Eloyye,
Sithothith,ˢ Eon, Sepmelamaton, Ezelpha-
[54r] tes,ᵗ Tetragramaton, Elyoram, Ryon,
Deseryon, Erystion, Ysyornus, Onela, Baysyn,
Moyn, Messyas, Sother,ᵘ Emanuel, Sabaoth,
Adonay — et per omnia secreta nomina tua que
in hoc libro continentur, quatenus virtute,
sanctitate, ac potestate eorundem nominum sit
liber iste consecratus ✠ *et benedictus* ✠ *et*
confirmatus ✠ *per virtutem sacramenti corporis*
et sangwinis tui, vt virtutem quam liber iste
debet obtinere efficaciter, sine aliqua fallacia,
veraciter obtineat, ad consecrandum vinculum
spirituum et ad consecrandum omnia
experimenta corrupta, et perfectam virtutem et
potestatem habeant ad quam sunt constituta,
prestante domino Ihesu Christo, qui sedet in
altissimis, cuiusᵛ honor et gloria per infinita
secula seculorum. Amen, amen, amen, amen,
amen.

per hec sanctissima nomina tua, scilicet On,
Ihesus Christus, Alpha et O, El, Ely, Eloye,
On, Otheon, Stimlamathon,ʷ Ezelphares,
Tetragramaton, Elyoraz,ˣ Eygiraem,ʸ Vsirion,
Oristion,ᶻ Orona, Anellabiassim, Noyn,
Messias, Cother,ᵃ Emanuel, Sabaoth, Adonay,
et per omnia nomina secreta que in hoc libro
continentur, quatenus sanctitate,ᵇ virtute, ac
potestate eorundem nominum tuorum, [per]
virtutem et potestatem tuam diuinam, sit iste
liber consecratus ✠ *benedictus* ✠ *sanctificatus*
✠ *et confirmatus, per virtutem corporis et*
sangwinis tui, ut virtutem quam debet obtinere
obtineat efficaciter, sine aliqua fallacia, ad
consecrandumᶜ vinculatum spiritum,ᵈ ad
consecranda omnia experimenta corrupta, ut
perfectam virtutem habeant ad ea ad que ipsa
sunt constituta, prestante domino, qui sedet in
altissimis. Tui est honor et gloria per infinita

w Sic *in MS?*

x *Followed by* ey, *struck through.*

y Sic *in MS?*

z Sic *in MS?*

s *Or* Sichochich*?*

t *Malformed, and duplicated below line.*

u *Followed by* ::: v.

v *Meaning* cui sit*?*

a Sic *in MS.*

b *MS* sanctificati.

c *Followed by* vinctum spiritum, *deleted.*

d Sic *in MS.*

Bene✠dicat te Pater. Bene✠dicat te Filius.
Bene✠dicat te Spiritus Sanctus. Amen. Sancta
Maria, mater domini nostri Ihesu Christi, te
bene✠dicat et sanctificet, vt virtutem
sacramenti in te obtineas quam obtinere
debeas. Bene✠dicant te omnes sancte virgines.
Bene✠dicant te hodie et omni tempore sancti et
electi dei. Omnes virtutes celestes te
bene✠dicant et confirment, omnes angeli et
archangeli, virtutes et potestates, principatus,
throni et [54v] *dominaciones, cherubin et*
seraphin, et ex auctoritate et licencia dei te
bene✠dicant, per merita et oraciones et
invocaciones omnium sanctorum tuorum.

Oracio. *Domine Ihesu Christe,*
bene✠dicas et sanctifices librum istum, et
confirmes per omnipotenciam tuam, vt virtutem
et potestatem obtineat ad quam institutus est et
confirmatus, prestante domino Ihesu Christo,
cuius regnum et imperium sine fine permanet
in secula seculorum. Amen.

Et sic in dei virtute confisus ad librum
consecracionum accedas securus, et
invenies quod optas. Hoc facto per ix
dies, erit liber consecratus, et
quocienscumque aliud consecrare
volueris, incipias primam oracionem
legere, scilicet *Deus invisibilis*, cum reliquis

secula seculorum. Amen.

Oracio. *Benedicat te Pater, benedicat te*
Filius, benedicat te Spiritus Sanctus. Sancta
Maria, mater domini nostri Ihesu Christi,
benedicat et sanctificet te, ut virtutem
sacramenti obtinere debeas quam obtinere
debes. Benedicant te omnes sancte virgines.
Benedicant te hodie et in omni tempore omnes
sancti et electi dei, omnes virtutes celestes, te
benedicant et confirmant omnes angeli et
archangeli, principatus, virtutes, potestates,
troni, et dominaciones, cherubin et seraphin, ex
auctoritate et licencia^e dei te benedicant, per
merita et oraciones ac inuocaciones omnium
sanctorum tuorum. Domine Ihesu Christe,
benedic, consecra, [136v] *et sanctifica librum*
istum, et confirma per omnem potenciam tuam,
ut virtutem et potestatem optineat^f ad quam
constitutus et confirmatus est, prestante domino
nostro Ihesu Christo, cuius regnum et
imperium permanet sine fine in secula
seculorum. Amen.

Et sic in dei virtute^g confisus, ac
tute ad librum consecracionum
accedas et inuenies quod hoc facto
per ix dies, erit consecratus, et

---

e   *MS* lancea.

f   *MS* optineant.

g   *MS* in die Iouis.

sequentibus, et^w in vtroque tuum
Confiteor debes dicere, et aqua
benedicta respergi, et signum sancte
crucis fronti tuo inpone, vt deus
infundat graciam^x Spiritus Sancti ad
opus tuum perficiendum.

Et sic vtere hoc exemplar et non
fallaris. Et caue prudenter ne in
manibus insipientium hoc magnum
secretum deueniat, quod a
sapientissimis phisichis est mag[n]is et
sanctis dei nominibus consecratum.

Et si alicui experimento deficit
documentum ante consecracionem,
[55r] habeas istud preparatum, et sic
cum documentis docens debes
experimenta tua consecrare, et ponas
vnum uel plura coram te, et dic primo
et principaliter tuum Confiteor, et
postmodum versus istos: *Ne derelinquas
me, domine deus meus, ne disceseris a me.
Intende in adiutorium meum, domine deus
salutis mee* [Ps 37:22–23 Vulg.]. *Fiat
misericordia tua, domine, super nos,
quemadmodum spera[ui]mus in te* [Ps
32:22 Vulg.]. *In te, domine, speraui; non
confundar in eternum.* [Ps 70:1 Vulg.].
Intret in conspectu tuo oracio mea.

quociescumque aliquid consecrare
volueris, incipe primam oracionem
legere, scilicet 'Deus inuisibilis,' cum
tribus reliquis subsequentibus, et inter
utrumque debes dicere tuum Confiteor,
et aqua benedicta te aspergere, et
signum crucis in fronti tuo pone, ut
deus infundat graciam Sancti Spiritus,
ad opus tuum perficiendum.

Et vtere hoc exemplari, et non
fallaris.^h Et caue diligenter ne hoc
magnum secretum in manus
insipiencium deueniat, quod
sapientissimis et paratissimis
philosophis fuit absconditum, et
nominibus dei sanctis insignitum.

Item si alicui experimento deerit
documentum ante consecracionem,
habeas illud in prompto et hijs^i debes tua
experimenta consecrare et ponas vnum
uel plura circa te et dic primo et
principaliter tuum Confiteor, etc., *Ne
derelinquas me, [domine] deus meus, ne
discesseris a me. Intende in adiutorium meum,
domine deus salutis mee* [Ps 37:22–23 Vulg.].
*Fiat misericordia tua, domine, super me,
quemadmodum speraui [in] te* [cf. Ps 32:22
Vulg.]. *In te, domine, speraui, non confundar in
eternum. In iusticia tua libera me et eripe me* [Ps
70:1–2 Vulg.]. *Intret in conspectu tuo oracio
mea. Inclina aurem tuam ad precem*

---

w   *MS* et et.

x   *MS* qm.

h   *MS* vallaris.

i   Sic *in MS?*

Inclina aurem tuam ad preces nostras [cf. Ps 87:3 Vulg.]. *Domine, exaudi oracionem meam, et clamor meus ad te veniat* [Ps 101:2 Vulg.].

Oracio. *Deus invisibilis, deus inestimabilis, deus incorruptibilis, deus püssime, deus excelse, deus gloriose, deus inmense, deus tocius misericordie, ego, licet indignus et plenus iniquitate, dolo, et malicia, suppliciter ad tuam venio misericordiam, orans et deprecans vt non respicias ad vniuersa et innumerabilia peccata mea, sed sicut consueuisti peccatori miserere*[y] *et preces humilium exaudire, ita quod me famulum tuum, N., licet indignum, exaudire digneris clamantem ad te, quod hoc experimento sanctissimis nominibus insignito vt virtutem quam obtinere debeat potenter obtineat, sed adereas*[z] *potestates et infernales principes, quod hanc [55v] oracionem consecratam mirabiliter constringant vt cum voluerit humano voluntati obediant, et cum exorcista voluerit in unum omnes congregare, et cum voluerit dispergat, et per sanctissimum nomen tuum quod scribitur 4or litteris, loth, hoth, vel hec, vel A G L A, g, e, he, van, quo audito*[a]

meam [Ps 87:3 Vulg.]. *Domine, exaudi oracionem meam, et clamor meus ad te veniat* [Ps 101:2 Vulg.].

Oracio. *Deus inuisibilis, deus inestimabilis, deus ineffabilis, deus incommutabilis, deus incorruptibilis, deus püssime, deus dilectissime, deus potentissime, deus fortissime, deus summe, deus gloriose, deus immense, deus totius misericordie, ego licet indignus et plenus iniquitate, dolo, et malicia, suplex*[j] *ad tuam venio misericordiam,* [137r] *orans et deprecans ne despicias ad uniuersa et innumerabilia peccata mea sed sicut consweuisti peccatorum misereri et preces humilium exaudire, ite me famulum tuum, N., licet indignum, exaudire digneris, clamantem ad te pro hoc experimento tuis sanctissimis nominibus insignito, ut virtutem quam obtinere debeat potenter obtineat, scilicet aereas potestates et insanabiles*[k] *principes, per hanc oracionem consecratam, humiliter et mirabiliter constringat, vt velint vel nolint humani*[l] *voluntati obediant. Et cum exorcista voluerit, eos omnes in vnum*

---

y   *Corrected in MS from* misesere.

z   *Meaning* ad aereas?

a   *MS* auditu.

j   Sic *in MS.*

k   Sic *in MS.*

l   Sic *in MS.*

mare regreditur, aer commutatur,[b] vel N.
concitatur,[c] terra tremit, ignis extingwitur,
omnisque celestis exercitus, terrenus et
infernalis, tremit et turbatur, et per hec
sanctissima nomina tua – On, Alpha et O,
Principium et Finis, E, El, Ely, Elyo, Eloe,
Elyon, Sother, Emanuel, Sabaoth, Adonay,
Egge, Yaya, Eeye – consecratur hoc
experimentum, eo potestate, cuius[d] honor et
gloria [per] infinita seculorum secula. Amen.

Si autem quodcumque
experimentum consecrare volueris
quod pertinet ad invocaciones
spirituum, tunc dicere debes: *Me[e]*
exaudire digneris, clamantem ad te, quod hoc
experimento[f] vt virtutem quam obtinere debeat
potenter obtineat, per sanctissimum nomen
tuum quod scribitur, et sic in qualibet
consecracionem, vt supra dictum est.
Finita oracione, procede vlterius:

congreget,[m] et cum voluerit eos dispergat.[n]

Oracio. *O summe deus, per*
sanctissimum nomen tuum quod scribitur per
quatuor litteras,[o] scilicet ioth, varo, hee, thet,
quo audito mare retrogreditur, aer commutatur
et concitatur, terra[p] timet, ignis extingwitur,
omnisque exercitus terrenus et infernalis tremet
[et] turbatur, et hec sanctissima nomina tua,
On, Alpha et O, Principium et finis, El, Ely,
Eloy, Eloy, Elyon, Sother, Emanuel, Sabaoth,
Adonay, Eggie, Ye, Ye, Ya, Ya, consecretur hoc
experimentum, prestante illo cui est laus,
honor, et gloria per infinita secula seculorum.
Amen.

Rubrica. Si autem aliquis aliud
experimentum consecrare voluerit,
quod non pertinet ad consecracionum
spirituum,[q] tunc debes dicere quater, *Me*
exaudire digneris clamantem ad te, ut hoc
experimentum virtutem obtineat quam obtinere
debet potenter, per sanctissimum nomen tuum
quod scribitur per iiij litteras, scilicet Ioth,
Varo, Hee, Teth, etc.

---

b   Sic *in MS.*
c   Sic *in MS.*
d   *Presumably meaning* eius . . . cui.
e   *MS* Mi[e].
f   Sic *in MS.*

m   *MS* congregat.
n   *MS* dispergit.
o   *MS* litteris.
p   *Followed by* tremet, *struck through.*
q   Sic *in MS.*

Deus, vniuersi conditor orbis, qui celum
super altitudinem nubum extendisti et terram
in sua stabilitate super aquas fundasti, [56r]
et mari terminum suum quem preteriri non
poterit [Ps 109:9 Vulg.] *tribuisti; qui solem*
et lunam et stellas in summo aere collocasti;
qui omnia in sapiencia fecisti [Ps 103:24*
Vulg.]; *qui^g vij[a]^h die hominem ad*
ymaginem plasmasti tuam et de spiritu tuo in
eum inspirasti; quem^i eciam cum Euam
propter preua[r]icacionem eiecisti; qui genus
humanum in aqua diluuij perdidisti; qui Noe
et eos qui cum eo erant in archa saluasti; qui
Abrahe sub triplici persona ad radicem
manibus^j apparuisti; qui Loth de submersione
Sodome et Gomorre liberasti; qui Moysi in
medio rubi in flamma ignis locutus fuisti; qui
populum tuum de captiuitate Egyptorum
deduxisti et ei per medium^k maris viam
aperuisti;^l qui legem Moysi in Monte Synay
dedisti; qui de petra aquas exire fecisti; qui Da-

Oracio. *Deus, vniuersi orbis conditor et*
redemptor, qui celum super altitudinem
nubium extendisti et terram in stabilitate sua
super aquas fundasti, et mari terminum quem
preterire non potest tribuisti [cf. Ps 103:5, 9,
Vulg.], *et solem et lunam ac stellas in celo*
collocasti; qui omnia in sapiencia fecisti [Ps
103:24 Vulg.]; *qui vja die hominem ad*
ymaginem ac similitudinem tuam formasti et
ei spiraculum vite inspirasti, [137v] *quem*
vna cum Eua propter preuaricacionem de
Paradiso eiecisti; qui genus humanum aquis
diluuij saluasti; qui Abraham sub triplici
persona ad Iheem^r Mambre aparuisti; qui
Loth de submersione Sodome et Gomorre
liberasti; qui Moysi in medio rubi in flamma
ignis aparuisti et ei locutus fuisti; qui
populum tuum per manum Moysi et Aaron de
captiuitate Egiptiaca eduxisti et eos per
medium Maris Rubri viam fecisti; qui Moysi
legem in Monte Sinay dedisti; qui aquas de
petra Oreb exire fecisti; qui aquas amaras in
Amarat per inmissionem ligni in dulcorem
conuertisti; qui solem et lunam per
inuocacionem Iosue stare fecisti; qui flumen
Iordanis in ingressu filiorum Israhel diuidisti;
qui Danielem de lacu leonum eripuisti; qui
tres pueros, scilicet Sidrach, Misach, et
Abdenago, de igne [camini] *ardentis abire il-*

g   *MS* quod.

h   Sic *in MS.*

i   *MS* quam.

j   Sic *in MS.*

k   *MS* modum.

l   *MS* apperuisti.

r   Sic *in MS.*

nielem de lacu leonum rapuisti;^m qui tres → *nielem de lacu leonum rapuisti;[m] qui tres*

nielem de lacu leonum rapuisti;[m] qui tres
pueros de camino ardenti, scilicet Sydrach,
Mysaac, Abdenago, illesos abire fecisti; qui
Susannam in te confidentem de falso crimine
liberasti; [*et qui*] *Ŷonam de ventre ceti*
saluasti, per hec et alia multa miracula que
fecisti, exaudi propicius, pie Ihesu, oracionem
famuli tui, N., et da huic experimento virtutem
et potestatem super malignos spiritus, ad
congregandum ipsos et ligandum et sol- [56v]
uendum et maledicendum et in profundum
abyssiⁿ proiciendum si non obseruauerunt
mandata exorciste, qui es sanctus et
benedictus, et regnas per omnia secula
seculorum. Amen.

Oracio. *O gloriose Adonay, per quem*
creantur omnia et hec regenerantur et
constituunt[*ur*]*, adesto propicius*
invocacionibus meis, et clementer presta vt hoc
experimentum perfecte virtutem obtineat ad
cogendum malignos spiritus, velint^o humiliter
obediant et eius mandatum impleant, te
iuuante et iubente, qui sedes in altissimis et
cuncta custodis, etc. Honor sit et potestas per
infinita secula seculorum. Amen.

On pie, On iuste, Adonay sanctissime, qui

lesos fecisti; qui Susannam in te confidentem
de falso crimine liberasti; qui Ionam de uentre
ceti saluasti – per hec et alia multa mirabilia
que fecisti, exaudi, pie Ihesu Christe,
oracionem famuli tui N., et da huic
experimento potestatem et virtutem super
malignos spiritus, ad ipsos^s congregandum,
ligandum, soluendum, et maledicendum, et in
profundum abissi proiciendum si non seruant
precepta et si non obediant mandatis exorciste,
prestante domino, qui est sanctus et benedictus,
regnans in secula seculorum. Amen.

Gloriose Adonay, per quem creantur et
generantur omnia, et que^t subsistunt vniuersa,
adesto propicius invocacionibus meis, et clementer
michi presta ut hoc experimentum perfectam
virtutem obtineat ad subiugandum malignos
spiritus, vtrum velint vel nolint, semper exorciste
obediant humiliter atque mandata eius impleant,
adiuuante et iubente qui sedet in altissimis et
cuncta custodit, et cui est laus et honor per
infinita secula seculorum. Amen.

[138r] *On pie, on iuste, Adonay sanctissi-*

---

m *MS* capuisti.

n *MS* abyssus.

o *MS has* velint *(?), followed by a space, possibly*
meaning vt [humiliter obediant].

s *Followed by* ad.

t Sic *in MS.*

es fons misericordie et pietatis, origo, rex regum, et dominus dominancium, qui sedes in magestate tua, intuens profundum abyssi, omnia cernens, omnia regens, omnia continens, et virtute tua moderaris,[p] *qui hominem ad ymaginem et similitudinem tuam de limo terre formasti, vt in terra sicut in celo lauderis et glorificeris, vnde omnis terra adoret te et psallat tibi, et ego, licet indignus, psalmum dicam nomini tuo. Vnde piissime et misericordissime magestatem tuam imploro et cum humili deuocione expostulo suppliciter vt in virtute tua et gracia dono tuo consecrantur et confirmantur omnes consecraciones, coniuraciones, et invocaciones que in hoc libro continentur, vt virtutem* [57r] *et efficaciam ad quam institute*[q] *sunt potenter obtineant et potestatem exorciste super malignos spiritus perfecte tribuant cum invocati et exorcisati fuerint statim ex omni parte conueniant et responsa certa et vera reddant*[r] *et mandata exorcistarum perficiant, illo prestante cui laus et potestas, qui per omnia regnat et imperat, per omnia secula* [*secul*]*orum. Amen.*

Oracio. *Adonay, Meloth, Adonay, Ioiloth,*

me, qui es fons misericordie et pietatis, origo, rex regum et dominus dominancium, qui sedes in maiestate tua intuens in profundum abissi, omnia regens, omnia cernens, omnia contuens, omnia gubernans, omnia tua virtute moderans, qui hominem de limo terre et ad ymaginem et similitudinem tuam formasti, ut in terra sicut in celo glorificeris et lauderis, quia omnis terra adoret te et psallat tibi, et ego licet indignus peccator psallam tibi ac psalmum[u] *dicam nomini tuo, pijssime et misericordissime deus, maiestatem tuam suppliciter exoro et cum humili deuocione tuam immensam sanctitatem imploro et expostulo, ut in uirtute tua et dona gracie tue consecrantur et confirmantur oraciones et consecraciones, coniuraciones, et inuocaciones que in hoc libro continentur, ut virtutem et efficaciam ad quam instituta sunt potenter obtineant et potestatem super malignos spiritus exorcisare perfecte tribuant, et cum exorcisati et inuocati fuerint, statim ex omni parte conueniant et responsa veritatis reddant et mandata exorciste perficiant, prestante illo cui est laus et potestas, qui regnat* [*et*] *imperat per eterna secula seculorum. Amen.*

Adonay, Meloth, Adonay, Naioloth,[v] *Leo-*

p *Meaning* moderans?

q *Final* e *blotted out.*

r *MS* reddunt.

u *MS* psallmum.

v Sic *in MS?*

Exclaui, Azeth, Adonay, in quo cuncta creata
sunt et sanctificata, [per] misericordiam tuam
et ineffabilem karitatem tuam, per hec
sanctissima nomina invoco te, vt N.,[s] *michi*
postulanti, licet indigno famulo tuo, N.,
auxilium gracie tue prestare digneris super has
consecraciones [et] invocaciones tuis
sanctissimis nominibus insignitas, que in hoc
libro continentur:[t] *On, El, Eloe, Adonay,*
Sadoy, Alpha et O, Ya, He,[u] *Yhe, Aseroye,*
Esyon, Prearraton, Tetragramaton,
Ezelphares, Otaizomos, Onoyteon, Stimulacio,
On, Ely, Araz, Messyas, Sother, Emanuel,
Saboath, Panttra,[v] *Pramelius,*[w] *Principium,*
Primogenitus, Sapiencia, Virtus, Grabaton,[x]
Osanna, Sol, Splendor, Gloria, Lux, Panis,
Fons, Vitis, Mens, Hostium, Ianua, Petra,
Lapis, Os, Verbum, Salus, Angelus, Sponsus,
Sacerdos, Philosophia, Mediator, Agnus, Ouis,
Vitulus, Serpens, Aries, Leo, Vermis,
Athanatos, Kyrios, Ayos, Theos. Per hec
nomina sanctissima, et per alia que

lam, Naoch, Adonay, per quem cuncta creata
et significata sunt, [per] misericordias tuas et
ineffabilem potestatem tuam, per sanctissima
nomina tua te inuoco, ut michi postulanti
licet indigno famulo tuo, N., auxilium gracie
tue prestare digneris super has oraciones et
invocaciones tuis sanctissimis nominibus
insignitas, que in hoc libro continentur, On,
El, Eloe, Adonay, Saday, Alpha et O, Ye, Ye,
Aserie, Vsion, Pantrathon,[w] *Tetragramaton,*
Acomiamos, Occinomos, Onoydeon,[x] *On,*
Elioram, Messias, Sother, Stimulamaton,
Emanuel, [138v] Sabaoth, Pantrather,[y]
Premelus,[z] *Principium et finis, Primogenitus,*
Sapiencia, Virtus, Hrabathon,[a] *Osanna,*
Sol, Splendor, Gloria, Lux, Panis, Fons,
Vitis, Mons, Hostium, Ianua, Petra, lapis,
Os, Verbum, Salus, Angelus, Sacerdos,
Pastor, Propheta, Mediator, Agnus, Ouis,
Vitulus, Serpens, Aries, Leo, Vermis,
Athanathos,[b] *Kirios, Ayos, Otheos – per hec*
sanctissima nomina tua et per omnia que
nominare non licet, suppliciter expostulo

---

s   *Added above line; probably intended to be added*
after michi.

t   *Pointing hand drawn in margin.*

u   *Duplicated in margin.*

v   Sic *in MS?*

w   Sic *in MS?*

x   Sic *in MS?*

w   Sic *in MS.*

x   Sic *in MS?*

y   Sic *in MS.*

z   Sic *in MS?*

a   Sic *in MS?*

b   Sic *in MS.*

[57v] *nominare non licet, te suppliciter*
expostulo vt oracionibus, consecracionibus,
atque invocacionibus istis, que continentur in
hoc libro, virtutem et potestatem tribuas, per
virtutem tuam diuinam, ad consecrandum^y
omnia experimenta et invocaciones demonium,
vt vbicumque maligni spiritus in virtute
tuorum nominum fuerint advocati et
exorcizati, statim [ex] omni parte conveniant
et exorcizatoris voluntatem adimpleant,^z *nichil*
nocentes, neque timorem inferentes, sed pocius
obedientes et ministrantes ad tua districta^a
virtute mandata perficientes. Fiat. Fiat.
Amen.

Notandum: si denuo aliquod^b
experimentum componere volueris, ad
placitum inpone ei documentum et
consecra ipsum sicut prius dictum est,
et cum est consecratum pervenit ad
effectum.

Oracio. *Omnipotens, sempiterne deus, qui*
in principio omnia creasti ex nichilo; cui
obediunt omnes creature; cui omne genus
flectitur, celestium, terrestrium, et infernorum;
quem timent angeli et archangeli, dominaciones,
potestates, adorant et tremunt; qui

vt^c *oracionibus et consecracionibus istis, scilicet*
in hoc libro contentis, virtutem et potestatem
tribuas ut per virtutem diuinam ad
consecrandum^d *omnia experimenta et*
[in]vocaciones^e *demonium vt*^f *vbicumque*
maligni spiritus in uirtute tuorum nominum
invocati fuerint et exorcisati, statim ex omni
parte conueniant et voluntatem^g *exorciste*
diligenter adimpleant, nichil ei nocentes nec
terrorem ei inferentes, sed pocius ei ministrantes
et^h *obedientes, per tremendum iudicium tuum et*
omnia mandata exorciste perficiant. Amen.

---

c   *MS* et.

d   *MS* sacrandam.

e   *Followed by* demonum, *struck through.*

f   *Followed by* vbique, *struck through.*

g   *Followed by* d, *struck through.*

h   *Written above line.*

y   *MS* consecrandam.

z   *Followed by* et, *deleted.*

a   *MS* districti *?*

b   *MS* alique*?*

manu claudis omnia; [qui] Adam et Euam ad
similitudinem [tuam] formasti et angelos tuos
incredulos per superbiam eorum in profundum
Thartari eiecisti, te rogo, te peto, clementissime
pater omnipotens, et sic obsecro, per Ihesum
Christum filium tuum, in cuius potestate sunt
omnia, qui sedes*c* ad dexteram Patris
omnipotentis, iudicaturus viuos et mortuos, tu
qui es Alpha et O, primus [58r] et
novissimus, rex regum, dominus dominancium,
Joth, Agla, Nabuoth, El, Elyel, Enay,
Enacuel, Ananyel, Aniazyel, Sodamel,
Agyten, Colymas, Elyas, Schyros,*d*
Athanathos,*e* Ymas, Ely, Messyas.

- Per hec tua sancta nomina,
- et per alia tua nomina

aduoco te et obsecro te,

- per natiuitatem domini nostri Ihesu
  Christi,
- per puerum baiulantem,*f*
- per baptismum tuum,
- per passionem tuam,
- per resurrexionem*g* tuam,
- per spiritum paraclitum tuum,

c   *Note shift to second person, addressing Christ.*

d   Sic *in MS?*

e   Sic *in MS?*

f   Sic *in MS?*

g   *MS* resurrexicionem.

- *per amaritudinem anime tue quando exiuit de corpore,*
- *et per v wulnera tua,*
- *per mortem tuam,*
- *et per sangwinem et aquam que exiuerunt de corpore tuo,*
- *per misericordiam et omnipotenciam et virtutem ineffabilem tuam,*
- *per sacramentum quod discipulis tuis dedisti pridie quam passus fuisti,*
- *per sanctam trinitatem et indiuiduam,*
- *per beatam Mariam, matrem tuam,*
- *per angelos et archangelos tuos,*
- *per omnes sanctos et sanctas tuas,*
- *per omnia sacra misteria et beneficia que sunt in honore tuo,*
- *per sanctissima nomina, cognita et incognita,*

adoro te et invoco, obsecro te et benedico te et rogo te, vt accepta habeas omnes coniuraciones et verba oris mei quibus vti. Peto, des virtutem et potestatem super angelos tuos qui de celo eiecti sunt, ad decipiendum genus eorum et loquelam eorum contrahendum, ad constringendum, ad soluendum, ad ligandum, ad cogendum[h] eos coram te, ad precipiendum, ad omnia que sunt eis [58v] possibilia, et verba mea et vocem meam vllo modo acceptent et me

h   *MS* cog'endu.

timeant. Per humilitatem et misericordiam et graciam tuam deprecor et peto te, Athon, Onay, Anay, Anathon, Vegeido, Ya, Yayay, El, Blemutum, Vsyon, Vsy, Elyas,

- *per omnia nomina tua,*
- *per sanctos et sanctas,*
- *per archangelos, angelos, potestates, dominaciones, virtutes,*
- *et per nomen[i] per quod Solomon astringebat dyabolos et conclusit eos, Shoeth, Hebatit, Het, Agla, Jocht, Othot, Vanecht, Nabuthi,*
- *et per omnia sacra nomina tua que scripta sunt in hoc libro,*
- *et per virtutem eorundem,*

quatenus michi compareant et michi respondere de omnibus permittas que queram, sine lesione corporis et anime mee, per dominum nostrum Ihesum Christum, filium tuum, qui tecum vivit, etc.

Oracio. *Pater de celis deus, unus in substancia, trinus in personis, qui Adam et Euam et plurimos[j] peccare permisisti, et filium tuum vnigenitum pro eorum peccatis crucifigi et mori voluisti, clementissime igitur pater, te rogo*

Pater de celis, vnus in substancia,[i] trinus in personis, qui Adam et Euam in pomum[j] peccare permisisti, et tuum vnigenitum filium pro eorum peccatis cruci et morti[k] tradidisti, clementissime pater, te igitur rogo et peto ac sup-

---

i   *Followed by* quod, *deleted.*

j   Sic *in MS.*

i   b *added in margin.*

j   Sic *in MS.?*

k   *MS* morte.

et peto supplex metis[k] omnibus quibus possum,[l] per Alpha et O, Christum filium tuum,[m] vt me congregare et me adunare quosdam angelos tuos incredulos permittas, qui michi hanc[n] potestatem alloquendi et faciendi, quod volo et desidero, et hoc[o] sine lesione al[i]qua vel alicuius nocumento. Et per virtutem lapidum, harbarum, et verborum, et nominum tuorum, michi des potestatem soluendi et ligandi demones, verbis meis et auxilio tuo. Quod michi concedas per innumerabilem virtutem et omnipotenciam tuam. Amen.

[59r] **Oracio.** *O summa et eterna deitas, et virtus altissima, qui te disponente hiis vero iudicio vocaris nominibus: Emoytho, On, Strinolamaton, Elzephares, Tetragramaton, Elyeyon, Egyrion, Vsyrion, Oristion, Eryono, Vsy, Ormis, Euella, Brasym, Moym, Ioseph, Messyas, Sother, E, Emanuel, Sabaoth, Adonay, et eciam sicut superius scribuntur, te invoco, te*

pliciter[l] per omnia nomina tua quibus possum, per Alpha et O, per Ihesum Christum[m] filium tuum, ut me, famulum tuum, N., facias congregare, adiurare angelos siue spiritus qui habent potestatem michi loqui et facere que volo ac desidero, sine lesione et nocumento corporis et anime mee et omnium viuencium, precipue qui dedisti potestatem et uirtutem herbis, lapidibus, verbis, per uirtutem omnium herbarum, lapidum, et verborum, et precipue sanctissima nomina tua[n] concede potestatem ligandi [et] soluendi demones verbis meis et auxilio tuo. Hoc michi concedas per mirabilem uirtutem et omnem potenciam tuam. Amen.

[139r] *O summa et eterna diuinitas, O[o] virtus altissima, qui [te] disponente hys nominaris nominibus: Oneytheon, Stimula, Mathon, Elelpharos, Tetragramathon,[p] Osorion, E, Egyrion, Vsyrion, Oristion, Orrona,[q] Vsiorius, Ouel, Byasim, Neym, Ioseph, Messias, Sother, Emanuel, Sabaoth, Adonay, etc., sicut*

---

k   *Meaning* mentis?

l   Sic *in MS.*

m   *MS* Christi filij [*altered from* filium] tui.

n   *MS* hunc.

o   *Or* hec.

l   Sic *in MS.*

m   *Followed by* fli, *struck through.*

n   *MS* sanctissimos nominum tuos.

o   Sic *in MS?*

p   Sic *in MS.*

q   Sic *in MS?*

adoro, tocius mentis viribus imploro, quatenus
per te presentes oraciones, consecraciones, et
invocaciones in hoc libro existentes
consecrentur et preparentur,[p] quemadmodum
conuenit, scilicet vbicumque maligni[q] spiritus
in virtute tuorum nominum fuerint invocati seu
exorcizati, statym ex omni parte conveniant[r] et
voluntatem exorcistarum adimpleant diligenter,
quod nichil nocentes nec timorem inferentes, sed
pocius obedientes et ministrantes districta
virtute mandata exorciste[s] perficientes. Fiat.
Fiat. Amen.

In nomine domini nostri Ihesu Christi,
Patris et Filij et Spiritus Sancti, tam trinitas
et inseparabilis vnitas, te invoco vt sis salus,
defensio, et proteccio corporis[t] et anime mee,
nunc et in perpetuum, per virtutem crucis et
passionis tue. Te deprecor, domine Ihesu
Christe, fili dei viui, per merita et oraciones et
intercessiones beatissime matris tue Marie
atque omnium sanctorum, vt michi concedas
graciam tuam atque potestatem diuinam super
omnes malignos spiritus, vt quemcumque in

modicum superius scribit[ur], te inuoco, te
adoro, te totis mentibus et verbis inploro,
quatenus presentes oraciones, consecraciones, et
invocaciones in hoc libro existentes consecrentur[r] et preparentur, quemadmodum
conuenit, scilicet ut vbicumque maligni spiritus
per virtutem[s] tuorum nominum fuerant
aduocati et exorcisati, statim ex omni parte
conueniant et voluntatem exorciste adimpleant[t]
diligenter, ei nichil nocentes, nec timorem ei
aliquem inferentes, sed pocius ei obedientes et
ministrantes, et tua uirtute ac iudicio tuo
districto mandata exorciste perficientes. Amen.
Finis.

---

p   *MS* preparantur.
q   *MS* malignus.
r   Sic *in MS?*
s   *MS* exorcisti.
t   *MS* corperis.

r   *MS* consecrantur.
s   *MS* iuret?
t   *Followed by* et.

virtute tuorum nominum invocauero, statim ex
omni parte [59v] *conueniant[u] et voluntatem*
meam perfecte adimpleant, quod nichil
nocentes[v] nec timore[m] inferentes, sed pocius
obedientes et ministrantes, et tua districta
virtute mandata mea perficientes.[w] Amen.

NO. 32. CONJURATION OF SATAN/MIRAGE

From fols 59v–62v

Per invocacionem domini nostri Ihesu Christi,
imperatoris et agni inmaculati,[a] quod inde[b]
arguant te angeli et archangeli; argua[n]t te
Michael et Gabriel [et] Raphahel; arguant te
tres patriarche Abraham, Ysaac, et Jacob, et
prophete; arguant te apostoli Christi, sancti et
electi dei. Deficiant ergo artes tue de die in
hora et in mense et in momento, sic[ut]
cessauerunt jam vos et membros,[c] vt cito et sine
aliqua condicione obediatis dictis meis et

From fols 109r–111v [A] & 139r–140r [B]

Per inuocacionem nominis domini Ihesu Cristi,
Mirage, imperat tibi agnus immaculatus;
perinde arguant te angeli et archangeli,
Michael, Gabriel, Raphael; arguant te tres
patriarche, scilicet Abraham, Ysaac, et Iacob;
arguant te prophete et omnes apostoli Christi;
arguant te omnes sancti et electi dei. Deficient
ergo aures[a] tue in die et in nocte in hora et in
mense et in momento,[b] sicut defecerunt Iamnes
et Mambres [II Tim 3:8], *nisi cito sine*
aliqua mora dictis meis obedias et voluntati
mee subiciaris.

---

u   *MS* conueniunt.

v   *Corrected in MS, with second vowel blotted out*
and e *substituted.*

w   *MS* perficiem.

a   *MS* imperatori et angnus inmaculatus.

b   Sic *in MS?*

c   Sic *in MS.*

a   Sic *in MS.*

b   momentu AB.

voluntati mee subiciatis.^d Amen.

Deus angelorum, deus archangelorum, deus prophetarum, deus apostolorum, deus martyrum, deus confessorum, deus virginum et viduarum, deus pater [domini] nostri Ihesu Christi, invoco nomen sanctum tuum preclare magestatis tue potencie.^e Supplex exposco vt michi auxilium prestare digneris adversus istum spiritum Sathanam, vt vbicumque lateat, audito nomine tuo, velociter de loco suo exeat et ad me festinanter accedat. Ipse imperat tibi, dyabole, qui de supremis sedibus te in inferiora mire mergi iussit. Audi ergo, dyabole, et [60r] tu, victus et prostratus, accede in nomine domini nostri Ihesu Christi. Tu ergo, nequissime, inimicus fidei, generis humani mortis temptator iusticie, delectator malorum, radix [et] fomes viciorum,^f seductor hominum, et^g magister, et stas et resistis cum scis te perdere vires tuas. Istum metue qui in Ysaac immolatus est, in Ioseph venundatus est, in agno occisus est, in homine crucifixus est, deum^h surrexus triumphator. Audi ergo, diabole, et timeas verba dei, et esto michi paratus in omni-

Deus angelorum, deus archangelorum, deus prophetarum, deus apostolorum, deus ewangelistarum, deus martirum, deus confessorum, deus domini nostri Ihesu Christi, inuoco nomen sanctum tuum in hac preclara tue maiestatis potencia. Supplex exposco ut michi auxilium tuum preparare digneris aduersus illum spiritum Miragem, ut vbicumque iacet, [B 139v] audito nomine tuo, velociter de loco suo exeat et festinanter^c ad me accedat. Ipse imperat tibi, dyabole, qui te de supernis celorum sedibus in inferiora terre demergi^d precepit. Audi, ergo, Mirage nequissime, et time,^e victus et prostratus, accede in nomine dei^f nostri Ihesu Christi. Tu ergo, Mirage nequissime, inimicus fidei, humani generis mortis repertor,^g iniusticie declarator, malorum radix, fomes viciorum, [A 109v] seductor hominis, demonum magister, qui stas et resistis^h cum scis te perdere vires tuas. Illum metue qui in Ysaac est ymmolatus, in Ioseph venundatus, in agno

---

d   *Meaning* subiciaris?

e   Sic *in MS.*

f   *MS* vincorum.

g   et *added above line.*

h   Sic *in MS, for* deus *or* deinde?

c   vestinanter B.

d   demerge A.

e   tunc A.

f   *Sic* AB, *presumably for* domini.

g   *Corrected from* reperator *in* B.

h   resipis A.

bus negociis meis perficiendis. Amen.

occisus, in homine crucifixus, deum[i] surrexit triumphator. Audi ergo, Mirage, et time verba dei, et esto michi preparatus in omnibus negociis prouidendis.[j]

Adiuro te, serpens antique, per iudicem viuorum et mortuorum, per eum qui habet potestatem te mittere in Iehennam, vt facias cito quidquid precipio tibi, illo iubente qui sedet in altissimis. Amen.

Adiuro te, non mea infirmitate sed virtute Spiritus Sancti, vt subiectus sis meis mandatis perficiendis. Cede michi et ministris Christi illius, dyabole. Arguat te potencia [eius] qui se[i] crucis[j] patibulo subiungauit, te illius brachium contremat,[k] qui te uictus gemitibus inferni[l] animas ad lucem perduxit. Sit timor tibi corpus hominis. Sit tibi formido ymago dei, quam sancta morte sua redemit. Nec resistes, nec moreris ap[p]ropinquare michi et velle meum adimplere, et ne me in infernum putes condempnandum,[m] dum me peccatorem nimis esse cognoscis.

Adiuro te, Mirage, non mea vi set uirtute Spiritus Sancti, ut sis subiectus mandatis meis, ea sine mora perficienda. Cede ministris Ihesu Christi. Illius potestas te vrgeat qui se pro nobis affligendo crucis patibulo subiugauit, illius enim brachium contremisce qui de victis gemitibus inferni animas ad lucem produxit. Sit tibi tremor cor[p]us hominis. Sit tibi formido ymago dei, quam[k] Christus sancta morte redemit. Ne resistas, ne moreris[l] apropinquare michi, et uelle meum implere, et ne me infirmum putes ad condempnandum te.

Imperat tibi dominus. Imperat tibi magestas. Imperat tibi deus Pater. Imperat tibi

Tibi imperat deus Pater. Tibi imperat deus Filius. Tibi imperat Spiritus Sanctus. Tibi

---

i   *Followed by* ab asseris[us] *(?), deleted.*

j   *Followed by* suo, *deleted.*

k   *Corrected in MS from* contremiat?

l   inferni *duplicated in margin.*

m   *MS* condempnendum.

i   *Sic* AB, *for* demum?

j   perfidend' B.

k   quatenus A.

l   moretis B.

Filius. Imperat tibi Spiritus Sanctus. Imperat tibi apostolorum sedes, scilicet Petri et Pauli ceterorumque apostolorum. Imperat tibi indulgencia confessorum. Imperat tibi martyrum sangwis. Imperat tibi sacramentum crucis. Imperat tibiⁿ mysteriorum virtus. Imperat tibi virtus [60v] *in quo nichil invenisti de corporibus tuis.^o* [*Imperat tibi Christus,*] *qui te spoliauit, qui regnum tuum destruxit, qui te vinctum ligauit et vasa tua disrupit, qui te proiecit in tenebras, vt tibi cum ministris tuis erit preparatus interitus, sed quem nunc crudelem te recogitas, quem^p temerarie retractas.*

Reus [*es*] *omnipotentis dei, cuius statuta^q transgressus es; reus^r filij eius Ihesu Christi, quem temptare ausus es et crucifigere presumpsisti; reus humani generis, cui^s mors tuis*

imperat apostolorum fides, scilicet Petri et Pauli et ceterorum apostolorum. Imperat tibi indulgencia confessorum. Imperat tibi sa[*n*]*gwis martirum. Imperat tibi mundicia virginum. Imperat tibi continencia viduarum.* [A 110r] *Imperant tibi pia opera coniugatorum. Imperant tibi oraciones omnium bonorum hominum in ecclesia dei militancium. Imperat tibi sacramentum* [B 140r] *crucis. Imperat tibi virtus corporis et sa*[*n*]*guinis domini nostri Ihesu Christi. Imperat tibi misteriorum virtus. Imperat tibi Ihesus Christus in quo nichil iurauisti^m de operibus tuis, qui te exspoliauit, qui regnum tuum destruxit, qui victum te ligauit et vasa tua disrupit, qui te proiecit in tenebras exteriores vbi tibi et ministris tuis est preparatus eternus interitus. Sed quid nunc, truculente dyabole retractus, qui temperie redardas?ⁿ*

Reus es omnipotenti[*s*]*, cuius statuta transgressus es; reus Ihesu Christi filij^o eius, quem temptare ausus fuisti et crucifigere permisisti; reus humani generis, cui mors persuasionibus tuis euenit. Impero^p tibi, nequissime, per imperium diuinum. Adiuro te per agnum inma-*

---

n   *Followed by* minstriorum virtus, *deleted.*

o   Sic *in MS.*

p   Sic *in MS?*

q   *MS* statera, *with* r *inserted above line, after another interlinear letter which is blotted out.*

r   *Followed by* esse (?), *deleted.*

s   *MS* tibi.

m   *Sic* AB.

n   *Meaning* redardescis?

o   Christo filio AB.

p   imperat AB.

persuasionibus euenit. Impero tibi, draco
nequissime, per imperium dominicum. Adiuro
te in nomine agni inmaculati,[t] qui ambulat
super aspidem et basiliscum, qui conculcauit
leonem et draconem [Ps 90:13 Vulg.], *vt*
facias cito quidquid precipiam. Contremisce et
time, invocato nomine dei, quem inferi timent,
quem celorum virtutes et potestates,
dominaciones et virtutes, [et] alie subiecte sunt
et timent et adorant, quem cherubin et seraphin
indefessis vocibus laudant. Imperat tibi
verbum qui[u] caro factum.[v] Imperat tibi natus
ex virgine.[w] Imperat tibi Iesus Nazarenus, qui
te creauit, vt cito impleas omnia que a te
petam uel habere voluero uel scire desidero.[x]
Quia quanto tardius feceris que tibi precipio
vel precipiam, tibi supplicium magis crescit et
crescat de die in diem.

   Exorcizo te, maledicte et mendacissime
spiritus,
- *per verba veritatis,*
- *per omnipotentem,*

culatum, qui ambulat super aspidem et
basiliscum, qui conculcat leonem et draconem
[Ps 90:13 Vulg.], *ut facias cito quidquid*
impero tibi et precipio. Contremisce et time.
Inuoco nomen domini, illum time cui uirtutes
celorum, potestates, dominaciones, et
principatus subiecti sunt, timent, et honorant,[q]
quem cherubin et[r] seraphin indefessis vocibus
laudant. Imperat tibi verbum caro factum,[s]
imperat tibi natus de uirgine. Imperat tibi
Ihesus Nazarenus. Imperat tibi qui te creauit,
ut impleas cito omnia que peto a te uel habere
voluero uel scire cupio. Quia[t] [A 110v]
quanto tardius feceris ea que tibi precipio,
tanto[u] magis supplicium tibi erit de die in
diem.

   Exorcizo te, maledicte et[v] nequissime ac[w]
mendacissime spiritus,

---

		q	honorent A.
		r	*Followed by* serahp, *struck through* B.
t	*MS* inmaculatij?	s	*Followed by* est, *struck through (?)* B.
u	*Inserted above line.*	t	que AB.
v	*MS* caro factum est.	u	tantum B, *but with the letter* o *written twice in*
w	*Followed by interlinear marking, apparently an* m		the margin.
	(presumably for Maria*), which appears to be struck*	v	ac B.
	through.	w	et B.
x	desidero *added in margin.*		

- *per Ihesum Christim Naza-* [61r]
  renum, agnum immaculatum, de
  altissimo progressu[m], de Spiritu
  Sancto conceptum, ex Maria virgine
  natum, quem Gabriel angelus
  nunciauit venturum, quem cum
  vidisset centurio[y] *exclamauit, dicens,*
  'Vere hic est filius dei' [cf. Matt
  27:54].

Exorciso te, auctor dyabolice potestatis,
inventor malorum, cum omnibus subditis tuis,
in nomine Patris et Filij et Spiritus Sancti; in
nomine gloriose deitatis, cuius ix ordines
angelorum, throni, dominaciones, patriarche[z] *et*
apostoli, et omnes sancti[a] *diebus ac noctibus*
proclamant, dicentes, 'Sanctus, sanctus, sanctus,
qui erat et qui est[b] *et qui venturus est, et qui est*
omnipotens' [Apoc 4:8], *vt non presumas*
transgredi precepta mea, N. Nec tibi[c] *lateat,*[d]
N., inminere tibi penas, inminere tibi tormenta,
diem iudicij, diem supplicij, sempiterni diem,
qui venturus est[e] *velut clibanus ar-*

- *per verbum veritatis,*
- *per deum omnipotentem,*
- *per Ihesum Christum Nazarenum,*
- *per agnum inmaculatum de*
  altissimis progressum, de Spiritu
  Sancto conceptum, ex Maria virgine
  natum, quem Gabriel nunciauit,
  quem cum vidisset Johannes[x]
  exclamauit, dicens 'Hic est filius
  dei.'

Exorcizo te, auctor dyabolice potestatis,
inuentor malicie, cum omnibus subditis tuis, in
nomine Patris et Filij et Spritus Sancti, et in
nomine gloriose deitatis, cui nouem chori
angelorum, patriarche et prophete, apostoli,
martires, confessores,[y] *virgines et* [B 140v]
vidue, et omnes electi dei diebus ac noctibus
indefessa voce collaudant, dicentes, 'Sanctus,
sanctus, sanctus, qui erat, qui est, et qui est
venturus, et qui est omnipotens' [Apoc 4:8],
ut non presumas transgredi precepta mea. Nec
tibi[z] *lateat tibi imminere penas, tibi imminere*
tormenta, tibi imminere diem iudicij, tibi
imminere diem suplicij sempiterni, per deum
qui venturus est velud clibanus[a] *ignis ardentis,*

y   centurio *duplicated in margin.*

z   *Corrected in MS from* patriarchi*?*

a   et omnes sancti *added in margin.*

b   et qui est *added above line.*

c   *MS* te.

d   latet *altered in MS to* lataet.

e   est *added above line.*

x   Sic *in MS.*

y   martires et confessores B.

z   te AB.

a   clibanum AB.

dens, in quo tibi atque vniuersis angelis tuis sempiternus erit preparatus interitus. Et ideo pro tua nequicia dampno te atque dampnabo. Da honorem deo viuo et vero, et michi subditus esto in omnibus operibus meis preparandis ac proficiendis. Da honorem deo viuo et vero; da honorem Ihesu Christo et^f Spiritui Sancto Paraclito, in cuius nomine ac virtute precipio tibi ego,^g N., vt nomini eius^h et verbis meis obedias, cui omnis creatura deseruit, quem cherubyn et seraphym laudant, dicentes, 'Sanctus, sanctus, sanctus, dominus deusⁱ exercituum [Is 6:3], qui regnat et dominatur^j per infinita secula. Amen, amen, amen.'

[61v] *Coniuro et constringo atque precipio tibi, vt sine aliquo nocumento michi nunc et semper obedias, sine lesione et grauamine corporis et anime mee. Coniuro te, diabole,*
- *per^k omnia predicta sacramenta facta,^l*
- *et per omnia scripta, dicta, facta, creata, viua [et] mortua,*

in quo tibi et angelis tuis preparatus est semp[i]ternus introitus. Et ideo pro tua nequicia, dampnate^b atque dampnande, da honorem deo viuo et vero, et esto^c michi subiectus, ut omnia precepta mea adimpleas. Da honorem Ihesu Christo filio eius, da honorem Spiritui^d Sancto Paraclito, in cuius nomine atque virtute precipio tibi, Mirage, ut nomini eius ac preceptis meis obedias, cui omnis creatura deseruit, quem cherubin et seraphin laudant, dicentes, 'Sanctus, sanctus, sanctus, dominus deus exercituum [cf. Is 6:3], qui regnat et dominatur [A 111r] per infinita secula seculorum. Amen.'

Adiuro ac constringo et^e precipio tibi, Mirage, ut michi obedias sine aliquo impedimento uel nocumento uel lesione et grauamine corporis et anime mee, nunc et semper. Iterum coniuro te, Mirage,
- *per omnia predicta sacramenta facta et facienda,*
- *per omnia scripta sancta, creata, viua et mortua,*
- *per illum qui te de celo proiecit.*

f   deo viuo . . . Christo et *added in margin.*

g   ego *added above line.*

h   eius *deleted and* eus *substituted.*

i   deus *added above line.*

j   *Followed by* -turus, *deleted.*

k   *Followed by* omnes, *deleted.*

l   *Followed by duplication of* et per omnia sacramenta facta.

b   dampnante A.

c   est A.

d   Spiritu AB.

e   ac B.

- *et per istum qui te de paradyso eiecit.*

Coniuro te et precipio tibi, N.,

- *per hostiam sacram,*
- *per hostiam inmaculatam,*
- *per hostiam conscriptam et benedictam atque deo placentem.*

Coniuro te atque precipio tibi, Diabole,[m]

- *per omnia quibus constringi et ligari possis.*

Exorciso te

- *per nomen tuum et potestatem omnium spirituum,*
- *et per omnes karacteres,*
- *et per sigillum Salominis,*
- *et per anulum*[n] *eius, ix candarias celestes, in malediccione et confusione et augmentacione penarum*[o] *tuarum*[p] *dupla,*[q] *de die in diem,*

quod tu, Diabole, non requiescas[r] *nec cesses a labore continuo in eodem loco in quo modo es remouearis*[s] *et ab officio tuo et ab omni soci-*

Coniuro te et precipio tibi

- *per hostiam sanctam et per hostiam inmaculatam,*
- *per hostiam scriptam et per hostiam benedictam atque deo placentem.*

Coniuro te ac precipio tibi, Mirage,

- *per omnia per que ligari et constringi possis.*

Exorcizo te

- *per nomen domini,*
- *per potestatem omnium spirituum,*
- *per omnes caractares,*
- *per sigillum Salominis,*
- *per annulos eius,*
- *per septem candelabra aurea ante dominum lucencia,*

ut tibi, Mirage, augmentatur penarum acerbitas de die in diem, ita vt non requiescas nec cessas a labore tuo continuo in eodem loco vbi nunc es remouere,[f] *et ut remouearis ab omni officio tuo et ab omni societate et temptacione et decepcione, ut priuaris statim per verba coniuracionis tibi inflicta. Maledico* [B 141r] *te et nomen tuum confundo in eternum*

---

m *Followed by* quibus, *deleted.*

n *Corrected in MS from* annulum.

o *MS* puerum.

p *Followed by* fide (?), *deleted.*

q *MS* duplo.

r -equi- *erroneously struck through.*

s *Followed by* abo, *deleted.*

f *Sic* AB.

etate et temptacione et decepcione alicuius[t]
priuatus statim, per verba et coniuraciones tibi
predicta. Maledico te, dyabole, et nomen tuum
confundo in eternum,

- *et per omnes dies vite tue,*
- *et per potestatem quam[u] habeo super*
  te hic michi ab omnipotenti deo[v] data
  in baptissmo et in aliis sacramentis,
- *et per eukaristiam que est corpus*
  Christi.

Eciam te excommunico et maledico tibi et
   omne illud quod ad te pertinet [62r]
   et confundo [te]*,*

- *per On,*
- *et per[w] Alph*[a] *et O,*
- *et per Emanuel,*
- *et per nomen dei ineffabile,*
- *et per sanctum Tetragramaton,*
- *et per omnia verba que dicta sunt*
  tibi,[x] N.,

vt facias statim, sine aliqua mora, mandatum
meum et peticionem quam tibi manifestabo,
dum vtinam comparas quod michi alloquaris.

   In nomine Patris veni, et in nomine Filij

- *per omnes dies vite mee,*
- *per potestatem quam habeo super te,*
  Mirage, michi ab omnipotenti deo
  data in baptismo et alijs sacramentis,
- *per corpus domini nostri Ihesu*
  Christi.

Eciam te excom[m]unico, tibi maledico et
   omne id quod a[d] *te pertinet, et*
   confundo te et omnia tua,

- *per On,*
- *per Alpha et O,*
- *per Emanuel,*
- *per nomen dei ineffabile,*
- *per sanctum Tetragramaton,*
- *per omnia nomina et verba que dicta*
  sunt,

ut statim venias, Mirage, sine aliqua [A
111v] *mora, mandatum et potestatem meam*
quam tibi manifestabo, quam michi loqueris.

   In nomine Patris veni. In nomine Filij veni.
In nomine Spiritus Sancti veni. In nomine
sancte Trinitatis veni. Tibi dico, in nomine dei
summi veni. In nomine creatoris et omnium
creaturarum veni ad me in hac hora, sine
aliquo nocumento, lesione, atque grauamine
corporis et anime mee, uel alium mittas,

---

t   Sic *in MS.*

u   *Corrected in MS from* quem.

v   deo *added above line.*

w   *Added above line.*

x   *Followed by* etc.*?*

veni, et in nomine Spiritus Sancti veni, et in nomine sancte trinitatis tibi dico veni, in nomine summi dei creatoris omnium creaturarum veni ad me in hac hora, sine aliquo nocumento, lesione, atque grauamine anime mee et corporis mei, uel alium mittas uel venire facias, qui sciat perfecte omne desiderium meum adimplere, et nullo modo a me recedat,ʸ nisi licenciatus fuerit a me, et voluntatem meam plenarie perfecerit. Coniuro te per hec et per hocᵃ, et ita vt supradicta sunt, vt facias michi venire vnum spiritum, qui auferat secum aurum et argentum denarios, et thesauros, antequam a loco isto recedam; et quocienscumque ipsum invocauero statim compareat,ᵇ benignus ac humilis, nulli nocens, et michi in omnibus ministrans, et voluntatem meam perficiens, fiat, fiat, amen; vt ducas uel mittas michi vnum spiritum prom[þ]tum et ydoneum in omnia sciencia; vt habeat potestatem facere me invisibilem quandocumque voluero;ᶜ [62v] et

velᵍ venire facias, qui sciat perfecte desiderium meum adimplere, et nullo modo a me recedere, nisi a me fuerit licenciatus uel uoluntatem meam plenarie perficiat. Item coniuro te per hec que supradicta sunt, ut facias michi venire vnum spiritum qui portetʰ michi aurum et argentum uel thesauros absconditos, antequam de isto loco recedam; ut sit michi ministrans in omni uoluntate mea, etⁱ quocienscumque ipsum inuocauero statim compareat michi, benignus ac humilis, nulli nocens, sed uoluntatem meam in omnibus adimplens et perficiens, fiat, fiat, fiat, amen; ut adducas michi vnum spiritum promptum et ydoneum in omni sciencia, et ut habeat potestatem me faciendi inuisibilem quandocumque voluero; et michi placuerit, et quod semper sit sub potestate mea; et concedas ei similiter [potestatem] consecrandi libros, experimenta, et omnia quecumque voluero. Amen.

---

y   *Followed by* dare *(?), deleted.*

a   *Or* hec.

b   *MS* comparaeat.

c   *The clauses marked here as [B] and [C] are given at the end of 62r, after* Fiat, fiat, amen, *but are evidently intended as alternatives to the material here given as [A]. The lines on the top of 62v (*Et michi placuerit . . . Amen. Amen. Amen.*) may also be intended for reading here.*

g   fere AB.

h   portat AB.

i   ut B.

michi placuerit, et eciam quod semper sit sub
potestate mea; et concedas ei similiter
potestatem consecrandi libros et experimenta et
omnia quecumque voluero.[d] *Amen, amen,*
amen.

d   *MS* volueris.

NO. 33. FOR OBTAINING INFORMATION FROM A MIRROR (FOLS 62v–65r)

Circue cimiterium et collige tot lapides quot[a] sunt versus in psalmo *Misereri mei deus* [Ps 50 Vulg.].[b] Cum hiis lapidibus, pone circulum quando vis, et inpone herbam que vocatur verbena. Postea accipe speculum, et line ipsum cum oleo oliue cum pollice, dicendo *Gloria in excelsis deo, etc.* Et intres circulum. Stes supra herbam, et verte primo ad orientem, dicens,

Coniuro te, Astra, Astaroth, Cebal,
- *per Patrem et Filium et Spiritum Sanctum,*
- *per xxiiijor seniores,*
- *et per tres pueros Sydrach, Mysaac, et Abdenago,*
- *per Toth,[c] principem vestrum,*
- *per Zambrim et Mambrim,*
- *per Vsuel [et] per Saduel, quibus obedire tenemini de veritate,[d]*
- *et per baptismum quod recipitur in fonte a sacerdote,*

vt obediatis michi.[e]

Cum venerit spiritus, dic si volueris, 'Deum qui te genuit dereliquisti, et oblitus [es] domini creatoris tui.' Cui tunc dicet spiritus, 'Verum est.' Tunc dic, 'Ligo[f] et constringo vos demones, per verba que audistis a creatore vestro pendente[g] in cruce, vt nulli noceatis, sed[h] dei[i] veritate respondeatis michi.' Quod si noluerint, lege vinculum Salomonis; de vinculo spirituum non est soluendum, sed ymo pocius diuidendum et ymitandum.[j]

[63r] Sed tamen, vt predictum est, cauendum est ne in manus quorundam insipiencium hoc secretum deueniat. Eructuamus sapientissimum filium, per quod[k] predicti reges et principes [cum] omnibus subditis suis valeant subpeditari

a   *MS* quod.

b   *Added in upper margin:* Nota: 47 versus sunt in isto psalmo.

c   *Perhaps a reference to Thoth?*

d   Sic *in MS.*

e   *Followed in MS by* et per baptismum quod recepi in fonte a sacerdote meo, vt obediatis michi, *whether by way of pleonasm or as a correction.*

f   *Followed in MS by* uel *(?).*

g   *MS* pendens.

h   *Followed in MS by extraneous* de *(?), deleted.*

i   *Followed in MS by* virtute, *deleted.*

j   Sic *in MS.*

k   Sic *in MS. Perhaps* Eruct[u]amus sapientissimum verbum *(Ps. 18:3 Vulg.) is intended, which would explain the neuter* quod.

et cogi et ligari et in abissum proici. Si vero sunt ribelles et contradicentes et inobedientes exorciste semper, et si in omnibus non obedierint uel precepta exorciste non conseruauerint, hoc vinculum est legendum,[l] quod sic incipit:

- *Per corroboratum et potentissimum nomen dei El, forte et ammirabile,*

vos exorcisamus atque imperamus,

   - *per eum qui dixit et factum est,*
   - *per omnia nomina ipsius,*
   - *et per nomen Y et V et E, quod Moyses audiuit et locutus est,*
   - *per nomen Genery, et in nomine Genery, quod Noe audiuit et locutus est, cum viija familia de linea sua,*
   - *et per nomen Y et V et E et X, et in nomine V et X,[m] quod Abraham audiuit et cognouit omnipotentem deum,*
   - *et per nomen Joth, et in nomine Joth, quod audiuit Jacob ab angelo secum comitante, et liberatus est de manu fratris sui Esav,*
   - *et per nomen Eyzaserie, et in nomine Eyzaserie, quod Moyses in monte audiuit, et meruit quod nunc est cum deo, et audire ipsum cum flamma loquentem,[n]*
   - *et per nomen[o] Anathematon, et in nomine Anathematon, quod Aron audiuit, et eloquens et sapiens [63v] factus est,*
   - *et per nomen Sabaoth, et in nomine Sabaoth, quod Moyses audiuit et inde nominauit, et omnes aque egredi de terra ceperunt palidum,[p] et verse sunt in sangwinem, et putruerunt,[q]*
   - *et per nomen Oristion, et in nomine Oristion, quod Moyses nominauit, et fluuij omnes ebulierunt ranas,[r] et absconderunt in domibus Egyptorum,*
   - *et per nomen Eloy, et in nomine Eloy, quod Moyses audiuit, percuciens puluerem terre, et factus est cinifes in hominibus et iumentis,[s]*
   - *et per nomen Artifontite, et in nomine Artifontite, quod Moyses nominauit, et omne genus muscarum misit in Egyptum, et inter[t] Egyptios,*
   - *et per nomen Yephaton, et in nomine Yephaton, quod Moyses audiuit, et quod Moyses nominauit, percuciens terram, et grauis pestis percussit equos, asynos, et camelos, oues et boues interierunt,*

l   *MS* ledendum.

m   Sic *in MS.*

n   Sic *in MS.*

o   *MS* votum.

p   Sic *in MS – evidently an echo of the biblical* paludes, *which would fit equally little into the present context.*

q   *Cf. Ex. 7:17–21.*

r   *Cf. Ex. 8:3.*

s   *Cf. Ex. 8:17.*

t   *Followed in MS by* in, *deleted.*

- *et per nomen Arbitrios, quod Moyses nominauit, et tulit cinerem de cymiterio, et desparsit in celum, et facta sunt wlnera visicarum vrgentium in hominibus et iumentis, et in omni terra Egyptorum,*

- *et per nomen Elyon, et in nomine Elyon, quod Moyses nominauit, et [facta est] grando talis qualis non fuerat ab inicio mundi, vsque ad presens tempus, ita quod homines et iumenta que erant in agris ceciderunt et interierunt,*

- *et per nomen Adonay, et in nomine Adonay, quod Moyses voluit, et facte sunt locuste et apparuerunt super omnem terram, et quidquid residuum grandis erat [64r] deuorauerunt,*

- *et per nomen Pantheon, et in nomine Pantheon, quod Moyses nominauit, et facte sunt vmbre horribiles tribus diebus et tribus noctibus,*

- *et per nomen Arimon, et in nomine Arimon, quod Moyses media nocte nominauit, et omnia primogenita Egypti perierunt et mortua fuerunt,*

- *et per nomen Geremon, et in nomine Geremon, quod Moyses nominauit et totum Ysraheliticum populum in captiuitate*[u] *liberauit,*

- *et per nomen Yegeron, et in nomine Yegeron, quod mare audiuit, et diuisum est,*

- *et per nomen Ysiston, et in nomine Ysiston, quod mare audiuit et submersit omnes currus pharaonis,*

- *et per nomen On, et in nomine On, quod petre audiuerunt, et innumerabiles emanuerunt,*

- *et per nomen Anabona, et in nomine Anabona, quod Moyses in monte Synay audiuit, et meruit tabulas manu*[v] *saluatoris scriptas accipere,*

- *et per nomen Egyryon, et in nomine Egyryon, cum quo Yosue pugnauit et inimicos destruxit suos et victoriam obtinuit,*

- *et per nomen Patheon, et in nomine Patheon, vt*[w] *sanctus Dauid nominauit et liberatus est de manu Golye,*

- *et per nomen Eya, et in nomine Eya, quod Salomon audiuit et Gabaon et meruit in sompnis postulare et inpetrare sanctam sapienciam,*

- *et [64v] per nomen Pancraton, et in nomine Pancraton, quod Elyas orauit quod non plueret, et non pluit tribus annis et mensibus sex,*

- *et per nomen Symayon, et in nomine Symayon, quod Elyas orauit et celum dedit pluuiam, et terra dedit fructum suum,*

- *et per nomen Eloy, et in nomine Eloy, quod Elyseus nominauit et Esunamitis filium liberauit,*

- *et per nomen Athanatos, et in nomine Athanatos, quod Yeremias nominauit et preteri[i]t captiuitatem Jerusalem ciuitatis,*

u   *MS* captificate.

v   *MS* manus.

w   Sic *in MS.*

- *et per nomen Alpha et O, et in nomine Alpha et O, quod Daniel nominauit, et per illud Bel destruxit et draconem interfecit,*
- *et per nomen Emanuel, et in nomine Emanuel, quod tres pueri in camino ignis ardentis[x] nominauerunt, et per hoc illesi exierunt et liberati,*
- *et per hec nomina et omnia alia nomina omnipotentis dei viui et veri, qui vos de excelso throno primum[y] de vestra culpa eiecit et vsque ad abissum locum vos proiecit.*

Exorcizamus[z] atque viriliter imperamus,
- *per eum qui dixit et factum est, cui obediunt omnes creature,*
- *et per tremendum diem iudicij dei summi,*
- *et per igneam deuoracionem,*
- *et per mare vitreum[a]* [cf. Apoc. 4:6] *quod est ante conspectum diuine magestatis,[b]*
- *et per 4or animalia contra sedem diuine magestatis gaudencia (uel gradiencia), oculos ante et retro ha-* [65r] *bencia* [cf. Apoc. 4:6–8],
- *et per sanctam trinitatem, que[c] est verus deus vnus,*
- *et[d] per nonaginta nouem nomina que dicunt filie Israel,[e]*
- *et per ineffabilem ipsius creatoris virtutem et omnipotenciam,*
- *et per[f] xxiiijor seniores ante[g] thronum circumstantes,*
- *et per angelos celorum, potestates et dominaciones, que sub eo creatore nominantur,*
- *et per summam sapienciam,*
- *et per anulum Salomonis* [et] *sigillum,*
- *et per sacratissimum nomen illius, quod omne seculum timet, quod scribitur 4or literis,[h] HV, V, et V, HV, AGLA,*
- *et per ix celestes candarias,*
- *et per earum virtutes,*

[A] *quatenus hodierno die vsque ad talem terminum rei michi integre custodiatis;[i]* [B] *quatenus thesaurum istum quem huc vsque custoditis penitus michi relinquatis, sine aliqua*

---

x   *MS* ardenter.

y   Sic *in MS.*

z   *MS* Exorcistamus.

a   *MS* viacum.

b   *Followed by* gaudencia uel gradiencia, *deleted.*

c   *MS* qui.

d   *Added above the line.*

e   *MS* Israeli.

f   *Followed by* ignem ar, *deleted.*

g   *Added in margin.*

h   *Followed by a blot, or by* scilicet *(?).*

i   Sic *in MS.*

diminucione, ita quod faciatis quod a nullo^j valeat seperari; [C] et iam in hac hora veniatis^k et debeatis michi respondere, de re et de rebus integre^l de quibus vobis interrogauero veritatem dicere.^m

Item, si invenires spiritum vel spiritus rebelles uel contrariantes, sic dices:

Per nomen Pneumaton, et in nomine Pneumaton, quod Moyses nominauit et absorpti fuerunt a cauernis terre, Dath, An, et Abyron, et virtute illius sacratissimi nominis dei Pneumaton, maledicimus vos in profundum abyssi; vsque ad vltimum diem iudicij ponimus vos atque religamus, nisi precepto meo^n obediatis et desiderium meum duxeritis ad effectum.

NO. 34. LIST OF DEMONS (FOLS 65v–65r bis)

Barbarus [est] magnus comes et dux, et apparet in signo Sagitarij siluestris cum 4or regibus ferentibus tubas. Intellectus autem cum latratus canum inimicus boum et omnium animalium.^a Loca thesauriorum facit aperiri que non custodiunt[ur] a magicis et a cantacionibus. Et est de ordine virtutum, et habet sub se xxxvj legiones.

Cason magnus dux est et fortis, et a[p]paret in similitudine senaphali. Dat ad plenitudinem vera responsiua^b de presentibus, preteritis, et futuris, et occultis.^c Dat graciam amicorum et inimicorum. Dat dignitates et confirmat. Habet sub se xlv legiones.

Otius magnus preses et comes [est], et apparet in signo Vipere, et habet deterrimam hominis speciem, sed cum suscipit formam humanam habet dentes magnos et tria cornua. In manu portat gladium acutum. Dat ad plenitudinem vera responsiua^d de presentibus et futuris et occultis rebus. Dat graciam amicorum et inimicorum. Habet sub se xxxvj legiones.

Cvrson magnus rex est et fortis, et apparet in similitudine hominis. Facies

---

j   *Meaning* a me nunquam?

k   Sic *in MS?*

l   Sic *in MS?*

m   *Alternative C added in margin.*

n   Sic *in MS?*

a   Sic *in MS.*

b   Sic *in MS.*

c   *MS* occulte, *perhaps intended to modify* dat, *but more plausibly construed as parallel to the preceding substantives, as in the following paragraph.*

d   Sic *in MS.*

leonina coronatus est dyademate. In manu fere[n]s^e viperam fortissimam, equitat super [66r] dorsum feruentissimum, et ante ipsum semper precedunt tube.^{f} Bene scit presencia, preterita, et futura [et] occulta pandere. Loca thesaurorum ostendit et aperirir^g facit.^{h} Libenter suscipit corpus humanum et aereum, et dat vera responsa de diuinis et occultis rebus, de deitate et mundi creacione. Dat optimos familiares. Habet sub se xxij legiones, partim de ordine virtutum et partim de ordine thronorum.^{i}

Alugor magnus^j dux est. Apparet in similitudine militis pulcherrimi, ferens lanceam, vexillum, et sceptrum. Ad plenitudinem dat vera responsa de occultis rebus et de duellis, quarum^k fieri debeant et quarum^l aduentura sunt. Dat eciam milites in occursum, et dat graciam omnium regum, marchionum, et omnium militum. Habet sub se l^m legiones.

Taob magnus est et princeps. Apparet in signo medici cum suscipit figuram humanam; [est] doctor opti[m]us mulierum, et facit ardere in amorem virorum. Si sibi iussum fuerit, facit eas transmutari in aliam formam, quousque veneri[n]t coram dilectis; finis^n facit eas steriles. Habet sub se 25° legiones, etc.

[66v] Volach magnus preses est. Apparet [in forma] pueri, et habet alas ad modum angeli. Equitat super draconem. Duo habet capita. Dat ad plenitudinem vera responsa de occultis thesauris, in quibus [locis] videntur et apparent. Serpentes et absque illis custodibus^p posse omnium serpentum tradit in manus exorciste. Habet sub se xxvij legiones.

Gaeneron dux est fortis et potens, et apparet in similitudine pulcherrime mulieris. Ductili coronatur coria.^{q} Equitat super camelum. Dat ad plenitudinem vera responsiua de presentibus, preteritis, et futuris, et de occultis thesauris, in quibus locis videntur et apparent. Dat optime amorem mulierum, et precipue puellarum. Habet sub se xxvij legiones.

---

e   *Or perhaps meaning* fert.

f   Sic *in MS.*

g   *MS* apperui, *but either* aperiri *or* apparere *is presumably intended.*

h   *MS has extraneous vertical line between* c *and* i.

i   *MS* throni.

j   *Followed by a blot.*

k   *Meaning* quando *or* quomodo?

l   *Meaning* quomodo?

m   Sic *in MS?*

n   *Meaning* si vis?

o   *Duplicated in margin.*

p   Sic *in MS.*

q   *Meaning* ducali coronatur corona?

Tvueries marchio magnus et fortis [est], regnans et imperans in Afforanis[r] partibus. Docet ad plenitudinem gramaticam, loycam, rethoricam, ac dictata,[s] et facit loca thesaurorum aperiri,[t] et occulta ostendi[u] facit. Eciam hominem velocissimo cursu mare et flumina transire uel transmeare [facit]. In specie militis apparet. Equitat super equum nigerrimum et superbitatem.[v] Habet sub se xxx legiones.

Hanni preses magnus [est], et apparet in flamma ignea, sed cum suscipit formam humanam [65r bis][w] mirabilem reddit hominem abilem in astronomia et[x] in aliis artibus liberalibus. Dat optimos familiares et graciam magnatum et principum, et loca thesaurorum que a spiritibus custodiunt[ur] mirabiliter ostendit. Habet sub se xxx legiones.

Svcax magnus marchio est, et apparet in similitudine hominis. Wltum habet femineum. Videtur beniuolus. Multum mirabiliter dat amorem mulierum, et maxime omnium viduarum. Dat ad plenitudinem omnia genera li[n]gwarum. Facit hominem transire de regione in regionem velocissimo cursu. Habet sub se 23 legiones.

NO. 35. FOR OBTAINING A WOMAN'S LOVE (FOLS 65r bis–67v)

Incipiunt experimenta bona[a] et probata et verissima, primo de modo scribendi[b] Bel et Ebal.

Nota: in feria quinta, nouis vestibus indutus et balneatus, in crepusculo, scribe in costam nomen tuum et mulieris, Bel et Ebal – Bel in principio, et in medio nomen tuum et nomen mulieris, in fine Ebal – et pone ad ignem et fac cremari costam, et quando est in maximo calore uel furore lege coniuracionem que sequitur, et consequeris desideratum:

[65v bis] *Coniuro vos spiritus infernales Bel et Ebal, quorum nomina in ista costa scripta sunt et in igne ardescunt,*

---

r   *Meaning* Africanis?

s   *MS* dictate.

t   *MS* apperire.

u   *MS* ostendere, *followed by a blot.*

v   *Meaning* superbum?

w   *Fol. 65 bis occurs between fols. 66 and 67.*

x   et *duplicated.*

a   *These three words occur twice, the first time as a heading.*

b   *Followed by a blank space.*

- *per omnes virtutes celorum et terre,*
- *per thronos, principatus et potestates, et dominaciones,*
- *per cherubin et seraphin,*
- *et per omnia que sub celo sunt,*

vt nunquam requiem habeatis, quin[c] cor eius in amore mei ita ardere faciatis vt nunquam dormire, comedere nec bibere, nec ire nec stare, nec flere nec ridere, nec aliquod opus perficiat, quin cordis mei desiderium prius adimpleat. Item coniuro vos, Bel et Ebal, quorum nomina in[d] igne ardescunt,

- *per dominum omnipotentem,*
- *et per Ihesum Christum filium eius,*
- *et per Spiritum Sanctum,*
- *et per virtutem sancti dei,*
- *et per ipsam prouidenciam dei,*
- *et per terram, mare, et profundum abissi,*
- *et per clemenciam [dei],*
- *et per visionem dei,*
- *per noctem et tenebras,*
- *et per tremendum diem iudicij,*

vt nunquam requiem habeatis quin cor[e] eius in amore mei ita ardere faciatis vt nunquam dormire, comedere nec bibere, ire nec stare nec iacere, nec flere nec ridere, nec aliquod opus perficere valeat, quin cordis mei desiderium penitus adimpleat.[f] Item coniuro vos, Bel et Ebal, quorum nomina in igne ardescunt,

- *per deum* [67r] *verum, per deum viuum, per deum sanctum, qui vos et cuncta creauit, qui Adam et Euam de limo creauit, qui fecit angelos suos spiritus* [Ps. 103:4 Vulg.], *qui scit presencia, preterita, et futura, qui habet claues celi, [qui] claudit et aperit, [qui] claudit et nemo aperit* [Apoc. 3:7],
- *per eum qui fuit mortuus et resurrexit, qui est principium et finis, Alpha et O, primus et nouissimus* [cf. Apoc. 21:6, 22:13],

vt nunquam, etc. Coniuro vos, O Bel et Ebal, quorum nomina in igne ardescunt,

- *per hec sancta nomina dei: Ely, Eloy, Eleon, Tetragramaton, Tupanoel, Fabanoel, Sabaoth, Sathay, Adonay.*

Coniuro vos

- *per virtutem qua dominus noster Ihesus Christus ianuis clausis ad dissipulos suos intrauit.*

Coniuro vos, Bel et Ebal, quorum nomina in igne ardescunt,

---

c *MS* quoniam.

d *Followed by* ige.

e *MS* corus.

f *MS* adimpleatis.

- *per spineam coronam quam dominus noster Ihesus Christus in capite sustinuit,*
- *et per fixuram clauorum qui pias manus et pedes transfixerunt,*
- *et per sangwinem et aquam de latere fluentem,*
- *et per lacrimas beate virginis Marie,*
- *et per mortem et sepulturam Christi,*
- *per resurreccionem et ascensionem Christi,*

vt nunquam requiem habeatis, quin cor mulieris in amore ita ardere faciatis quod nunquam dormire, comedere nec bibere, nec stare nec sedere, [nec flere] nec ridere, nec aliquod opus perficere valeat, quin cordis mei desiderium [67v] penitus adimpleat, et quod illud nullatenus obmittat.[g] *Hoc*[h] *precipio vobis, per eum qui viuit et regnat in secula seculorum. Amen. Amen. Amen. Etc.*

NO. 36. GENERIC PREPARATION FOR CONJURING SPIRITS (FOLS 67v–68v)

De responsione spirituum.[a]

Cum magister voluerit vocare spiritus, vadat ad locum[b] secretum cum duobis sociis, et[c] habeat cultellum cum manubrio albo uel nigro, in cuius lamina hec nomina ex utraque parte sunt scripta: Agla [et] Sabaoth. Et faciat[d] cum eodem cultello exteriorem circulum,[e] dicendo, *Hunc circulum facio in nomine dei Patris omnipotentis, qui solo verbo vniuersa creauit.* Et in eodem circulo scribat cum cultello prelibato hec nomina: contra orientem, Agla; contra occidentem, Tetragramaton; contra septentrionem, Adonay; contra meridiem, Sabaoth. Deinde faciat secundum circulum, dicendo, *Hunc circulum facio in nomine dei viui, qui humanum genus humano sangwine redemit.* Tercium vero circulum faciat dicendo, *Hunc*

---

g   *MS* obmittatis.

h   *Or* hec.

a   *Line duplicated in margin of MS.*

b   *MS* locrum.

c   *MS* aut.

d   *MS* faciendo.

e   *Figure at top of fol. 68ᵛ: a triple circular band, with* Sabaoth *and* meridies *marked just outside at the top,* occidens *and* Tetragramaton *at the right,* septentrion [sic] *and* Adonay *at the bottom,* oriens *and* Agla *at the left. The outermost circle bears the inscription,* ✠ Hunc circulum facio in nomine dei Patris omnipotentis, qui solo verbo vniuersa creauit. *The middle circle has the inscription,* ✠ Hunc circulum facio in nomine dei viui qui humanum genus humano sangwine redemit. *The innermost contains the inscription,* ✠ Hunc circulum facio in nomine Spiritus Sancti paracliti, qui [*MS* quia] apostolorum et prophetarum corda sua gracia illustrauit. *In the upper left, a further inscription begins in the outer circle and ends in the middle one:* Per hoc signum sancte crucis gracia dei defendat nos ab omni malo. *The interior is left blank.*

circulum facio in nomine Spiritus Sancti paracliti, qui[f] apostolorum et prophetarum corda sua gracia illustrauit. Post hec faciet crucem per omnes circulos, [dicens], *Per hoc signum sancte crucis gracia dei defendat nos ab omni malo.* Tunc accipe turribulum, inposito thure[g] et mirra, [et] circuas[h] ex- [68r] teriora circuli,[i] dicens, *Hanc fumigacionem facio in nomine Patris et Filij et Spiritus Sancti.* Et post hec,[j] stans contra orientem extra circulum,[k] dicat vij psalmos cum letania,[l] deuote et humiliter, et has oraciones:

Adiuro[m] te, rex regum et dominus dominancium, eterne et incommutabilis deus,[n] intellige clamorem meum nunc et spiritus mei gemitumque cordis mei,[o] vt respirem[p] in te saluatorem meum. Da[q] michi intellectum sanctum et bonum, et aufer a me quod malum est; et commutans me in omnem dileccionem tuam qua formasti me et saluasti, tribuas[r] incrementum michi. Exaudi, domine, precem meam qua clamaui ad te, et exaudi me. Reuela et illumina oculos mentis mee et carnis, vt considerem et intelligam mirabilia tua. Viuifica me in iustificacionibus tuis, vt preualeam in conspectu aduersariorum[s] meorum et dyaboli.[t]

NO. 37. MANUAL OF ASTRAL MAGIC (FOLS 68V–96V)

37a. Conjurations for each day of the week

Incipiunt coniuraciones dierum super composicionem sacrificiorum, quod fiet quando debuerit aliquid operare[a] antequam illud incipiat. Coniura ergo cum alia

f   *MS* quia.

g   *MS* thus.

h   *MS* circuat.

i   *MS* circulum.

j   *Or* hoc.

k   *Followed by* in, *deleted.*

l   *Followed by* et.

m   *Redundant a struck through.*

n   *Followed by* dominus, *deleted.*

o   Sic *in MS.*

p   Sic *in MS.*

q   *MS* dat.

r   *Followed by* in- *(?), deleted.*

s   *Followed by* et.

t   *Followed by a blank space left for the title of the following material, and by this fragment (evidently in the same hand, but less careful than usual):* Aloe epacium quando im aracum *(?)* pliwis wirnies *(?).*

a   *Note that* operari *and* operare *are used interchangeably.*

coniuracione sequentium dierum quibus operabis, et scribenda fuerint. Scribe ea die suo.

Coniuracio diei dominici sequitur, etc.

[1.] [69r] Coniuracio diei solis.[b]

Coniuro et confirmo super vos, angeli fortes et sancti,

- ☩ *In nomine Adonay, Adonay, Eye, Eye, Eyu, qui est ille qui fuit, est, et erit, Eye, Aloraye,*
- *in nomine Sadaye, Saday, Cados, Cados, Cados, altus, super cherubin sedens,*
- *et per nomen ipsius magni, sancti, fortis, potentis, et exaltati, super omnes celos, Eye, Saraye, Plasmatoris seculorum, qui creauit mundum, celum, et terram, mare, et omnia que in eis sunt in primo die celorum, et sigillauit super eos cum nomine sancto suo,[c] Yhon, super terram que sigilla terra est, honorato, precioso nomine suo Yhaa,*
- *et per nomina sanctorum angelorum qui dominantur in primo exercitu et seruiunt coram potentissimo Salamia, angelo magno et honorato,*
- *et per nomen stelle que est Sol,*
- *et per signum inmensissimum dei viui et quod omnia per predicta.[d]*

Coniuro
- *super Raphael angelum[e] qui est prepositus diei dominici,[f]*
- *et per nomen Adonay, dei Israel, qui creauit mundum et quicquid est in eo,*

quod pro me labores et adimpleas omnem voluntatem meam et peticionem iuxta meum velle et votum in negocio et causa mea.

Dicas autem secundum quod tibi videbitur.

[2.] Coniuracio diei lune.[g]

[69v] *Coniuro et confirmo et sigillo super vos, angeli fortes et sancti,*
- *in nomine Adonay, Adonay, Adonay, Eye, Eye, Eye, Cados, Cados, Cados, Hatyn, Hatyn,[h] Hatyn, Va, Va, fortis, Va, qui apparuit[i] in monte Synay cum glorificacione regni sui, Ya, Adonay, Saday, Sabaoth, Hanath, Hu, Haxi, Ya, Ya, Ya, Marmalita, Abym, Yea, qui maria creauit, stagna, et omnes aquas in secunda die, quosdam in*

---

b   *Heading duplicated in margin.*

c   u *corrected from another letter, which is blotted out.*

d   Sic *in MS.*

e   *MS* angele.

f   *Meaning* dominico.

g   *Heading duplicated in margin, and again at top of fol. 69v.*

h   *Corrected both times from* Hatym.

i   *MS* apparauit

celis,[j] quosdam in terra, et sigillauit mare cum virtute sua et alto nomine suo vt terminum quem sibi posuit non preterierent [Ps. 103:9 Vulg.],

- *et per nomina angelorum qui dominantur in secundo exercitu, qui seruiunt Oraphaniely, angelo magno, precioso, et honorato,[k]*
- *et per nomen stelle que est Luna,*
- *et per sigilla et per nomina predicta.[l]*

Coniuro super te Gabriel, qui est prepositus diei secundo, scilicet Lune, quod pro me labores et adimpleas omnem meam peticionem. Amen.

[3.] Coniuracio diei Martis.[m]

Coniuro et confirmo et sigillo super vos, angeli fortes et sancti,
- *per nomen Ya, Ya, Ya, A, A, Va, Hy, Hy, Haa, Haai, Va, Va, Han, Han, Hon, Hy, Hyen, Haya, Haya, Hol, Hol, Hay, Hael, Hon,*
- *per nomina[n] domini Adonay, Haya, Hol, Plasmatori seculorum, Cados, Cados, Cados,* [70r] *Ebel, El, Ya, Ya, Ya, Eloy, Arar, Eloym, Eloym,*
- *et per nomen ipsius alti dei qui fecit aridam apparere et vocauit eam terram et produxit arbores et herbas de ea, et sigillauit super eam precioso et honorato [et] metuendo nomine suo,*
- *et per nomina angelorum dominancium exercitui tertio et ministrando Acynerim, angelo magno, forti, potenti, et honorato,*
- *et per nomen stelle que est[o] Mars,*
- *et per nomen Adonay, dei viui et veri.*

Coniuro super te, Samael, angelo qui est[p] prepositus diei tercio, scilicet Marti, quod pro me laboretis et adimpleatis omnem meam voluntatem et totam meam peticionem, vt sicut in primo capitulo, etc., etc.

[4.] Coniuracio diei Mercurij.[q]

Coniuro et confirmo et sigillo super vos, angeli fortes et sancti et potentes,

---

j   *MS* celos.

k   *MS* honorata.

l   *MS* predictos.

m   *Heading duplicated in margin.*

n   *Followed in MS by* men, *deleted.*

o   *MS* qui.

p   Sic *in MS.*

q   *Heading duplicated in margin.*

- *in nomine fortis, metuendi, et benedicendi, Ya, Adonay, Eleoym, Saday, Saday, Saday, Eye, Eye, Eye, Asaame, Asaomie, Asamye,*
- *in nomine domini Adonay, cum quo super verba hominum sigillauit Saa, quid, Sayguans,^r Capym, Say, Saaqui,*
- *et per nomina^s Cryasy, Adonay, Taguaasas, Adonay, dei Israel, quia ipse est^t [qui creauit] diem et noctem,*
- *et per nomina omnium^u angelorum seruiencium* [70v] *exercitui 4o, quorum Thytagora, angelo maiori, forti atque potenti,^v*
- *et per nomen stelle que est Mercurius,*
- *et per nomen sigilli cum quo sigillatur Adon, fortissimo et honorato,^w*
- *et per omnia predicta.*

Coniuro super te, angele magne Michahel, qui es prepositus diei 4o,
- *et per nomen sanctum quod in fronte Aaron sacerdotis altissimi creatoris^x erat,*
- *et per nomina angelorum qui in gracia confirmati sunt creatoris,*
- *et per nouem sedes animalium habencium seuas^y et alas,*

vt pro me laboretis in [causa] mea, vt cicius ducatur ad effectum optatum, etc.

[5.] Coniuracio diei Veneris.^z

Coniuro et confirmo et sigillo super vos, angeli fortes et sancti atque potentes,
- *in nomine Hay, Hey, Hea, Ya, A, Ya, Ya, Ananey,*
- *in nomine Saday, qui creauit quadrupedia et animalia reptilia et hominem in sexto die, et dedit Ade potestatem super omnia animalia – inde benedictus sit nomen creatoris in loco suo,*
- *et per nomen angelorum qui seruiunt exercitui sexto coram Daghyel, angelo magno principi, forte^a atque potenti,*
- *et per nomen stelle que^b est Venus,*
- *et per sigillum eius, quod quoddam sigillum est sacratum,*

---

r   Sic *in MS?*

s   *Followed in MS by* et.

t   *Followed by* ide, *struck through.*

u   omnium *added below line in MS.*

v   Sic *in MS.*

w   Sic *in MS.*

x   *Corrected in MS from* creatis.

y   Sic *in MS?*

z   *Heading duplicated in margin.*

a   *Corrected in MS from* fortem.

b   *MS* qui.

- *et per omnia predicta.*

Coniuro super te, angele magne Anael, qui es prepositus diei sexto, vt pro me labores, vt supra.

[6.] [71r] Coniuracio diei Jouis.[c]

Coniuro et confirmo et sigillo super vos, angeli fortes et sancti atque potentes,
- *per nomen Cados, Cados, Cados, Eseraye,[d] Esoraye, Eseraye, Hatym, Va, fortis firmatoris seculorum, Catiney, Yaheiz, Yaruc, Yarac, Calloac, Allae, Assaf, Maataf, Barifay, Abnaym,*
- *et per nomen Adonay, qui creauit[e] pisces et reptilia in aquis et aues volantes super faciem terre versus celos die quinto,*
- *et per nomina angelorum seruiencium exercitui quinto, pastore angelo magno sancto et potenti principi,*
- *et per nomen stelle que[f] est Jupiter,*
- *et per nomen sigilli sui,*
- *et per nomen Adonay, supremi diei omnium creatoris,[g]*
- *et per nomina omnium stellarum, et per vim et virtutem eorum,*
- *et per nomina predicta.*

Coniuro super te, Satquiel, angele magne qui est[h] prepositus diei Jouis, quod pro me labores vt meus affectus ad effectum deueniat.[i]

[7.] Coniuracio diei Saturni.[j]

Coniuro et confirmo et presciendo[k] super vos, Captiel, Matatori, Sartaquidi, angeli fortes et potentes,
- *per nomen Adonay, Adonay, Eye, Ey, E, Eye, Hacyn, Hacyn, Hacyn, Cados, Cados, Cados, Yma, Yma, Yma, Saday, Ya, Sar, domini formatoris seculorum, [qui] die septimo quieuit, et illam in beneplacito suo filiis Israel in hereditatem [71v] et obsequium dedit, vt eum firmiter seruarent et custodirent et sanctificarent ad habenda*

---

c   *Heading duplicated in margin at bottom of fol. 70v.*

d   *Corrected in MS from* Esaraye.

e   *Followed by* pissces, *struck through.*

f   *MS* qui.

g   *Presumably meaning* supremi dei, omnium creatoris.

h   Sic *in MS.*

i   *MS* deueniant.

j   *Heading duplicated in margin.*

k   Sic *in MS.*

inde bona et in alio seculo remuneraciones, et nomina angelorum seruiencium exercitui
septimo coram Boel, angelo magno, potenti principi,
- *et per nomen stelle que^l est Saturnus,*
- *et per sanctum^m sigillum eius,*
- *et per omnia predicta.*

Coniuro Captiel, qui prepositus es^n diei septimo, qui est^o dies sabbati, vt pro me labores^p et non desistas^q donec totum affectum ad effectum perducas. Amen.

37b. Seals for seven angels

Sequitur videre et scire septem sigilla que^a signanda sunt in quolibet opere secundum diem septimane.

Hec sunt sigilla vij planetarum discurrencium vij celos, secundum quod dixerunt vij physici sapientes, quotquod opus facies, quod si non scies non complebitur sine signis istis sequentibus, quoniam quelibet dies suum sigillum et suam^b planetam et suos angelos et suum regem spirituum cum adiutoriis suis et sua[s] creatura[s] et suffumigium suum, secundum quod inferius tibi dicetur, et quando feceris hec,^{c} scias quod perfectum ipsum fuisse et magnum qui hunc librum composuit. Et scias quod quidquid quesieris perficietur,^{d} et virtute dei, cuius nomen sit benedictum per infinita secula seculorum, amen.

[1.] [72r] Ecce sigillum Raphahelis, angeli cuius stella est Sol. Fac illud die Solis in signo Leonis.^{e}

[2.] Ecce sigillum Gabrielis, angeli cuius stella est Luna. Fac illud die Lune, hora Lune, in signo Cancri, etc.^{f}

[3.] Ecce sigillum Samaelis, angeli cuius stella est Mars. Fac illa die Martis, hora Martis, in signo Arietis uel Scorpionis.^{g}

l   *MS* qui.
m   *Followed by* g, *struck through.*
n   Sic *in MS.*
o   *MS* es.
p   *MS* laboras.
q   *MS* desistac *or* desistat.
a   *MS* qui.
b   *MS* suum.
c   *Or* hoc.
d   perficietur *duplicated in MS.*
e   *Followed by seal.*
f   *Followed by seal.*
g   *Followed by seal.*

[4.] Ecce sigillum Michahelis, angeli cuius stella est Mercurius. Fac illa die Mercurij et hora Mercurij, in signo Capricorni uel Gemini uel Virginis.[h]

[5.] Ecce sigillum Satquielis, angeli cuius stella est Jupiter. Fac illa die Jouis, et hora Jouis, signo Sagittarij et Pissis, etc.[i]

[6.] [72v] Ecce sigillum Anaelis, angeli cuius stella est Venus. Fac illa die Veneris, hora Veneris, in signo Thauri et Libre, etc.[j]

[7.] Ecce sigillum Caffrielis,[k] angeli cuius stella est Saturnus. Fac illa die Sabbati, hora Saturni, in signo Capricorni et Aquarij.[l]

37c. Seals for days of the week

[1.] Ecce sigillum diei dominici, quod fieri debet Sole ascendente.[a]
[73r] Ecce signum Solis, quod[b] est planeta die[i] dominice.[c]
[2.] Ecce sigillum Lune, quod fieri debet Luna ascendente.[d]
Ecce signum Lune, quod est planeta diei Lune.[e]
[3.] Sigillum diei Martis, quod debet fieri Marte ascendente.[f]
[73v] Signum die[i] Martis, quod est planeta diei Martis.[g]
[4.] Sigillum Mercurij debet fieri Mercurio ascendente.[h]
Signum Mercurij, quod est planeta Mercurij diei.[i]
[5.] Sigillum Jouis, quod fieri debet Joue ascendente.[j]
[74r] Signum Jouis, quod est planeta diei Jouis.[k]
[6.] Sigillum Veneris, quod debet fieri Venere ascendente.[l]

---

h　*Followed by seal.*

i　*Followed by seal on top of 72ᵛ.*

j　*Followed by seal.*

k　*Or* Casfrielis*?*

l　*Followed by seal.*

a　*Followed by four lines of seals.*

b　Sic *in MS, here and in following cases.*

c　*Followed by two lines of seals.*

d　*Followed by two lines of seals.*

e　*Followed by one line of seals.*

f　*Followed by five lines of seals.*

g　*Followed by two lines of seals.*

h　*Followed by five lines of seals.*

i　*Followed by one line of seals.*

j　*Followed by two lines of seals, and three further lines at the top of 74ʳ.*

k　*Followed by one line of signs.*

l　*Followed by four lines of signs.*

Signum Veneris, quod est planeta diei Veneris.[m]

[7.] Sigillum Saturni, quod debet fieri Saturno ascendente.[n]

[74v] Note de signis vij planetarum, id est septem dierum. Conpleta signa vij dierum ebdomade super planetis et signis eorum. Caue igitur in illis tibi, quia[o] maxima virtus est in eis, quare quia in eis complebuntur opera tua.

37d. Names of the angels who rule over the days of the week

Nomina angelorum regnancium a diebus septimane sunt dicenda, et sequitur que opera habet[a] nominare in operibus septimane.

[1.] Angelus diei dominici est Raphahel.

[2.] Angelus diei Lune est Gabriel.[b]

[3.] Angelus diei Martis est Samael.

[4.] Angelus diei Mercurij est Michael.

[5.] Angelus diei Jouis [75r] est Satquiel.

[6.] Angelus diei Veneris est Anael.

[7.] Angelus diei Saturni, id est Sabbati, est Captiel.[c]

In isto igitur opere nominabis angelum diei in quo facies opus tuum, et scribe illa, quare[d] si fuerint scripta multum iuuabunt te cum potencia creatoris.

37e. Spirits who rule over the days of the week

Regum spirituum vij diebus in septimana regnancium nomina subscribentur super eos angelos dominantes diei quando facies opus et sic venient et complebunt voluntatem tuam et respondebunt tibi in omnibus que quesieris.[a]

[1.] Die ergo dominico regnat et seruit rex Saytam. Coadiutores sui sunt[b] Taatus, Candas, Vanibal.

[2.] Et die Lune regnat et seruit rex Almodab. Coadiutores sui sunt Sylol, Millalu, Abuzaba.

[3.] Die Martis regnat et seruit rex filius dyabuli.[c] Coadiutores sunt Carmath, Utanaual, Pascami.

---

m   *Followed by one line of signs.*

n   *Followed by 6 lines of signs at the top of 74ᵛ.*

o   Sic *in MS.*

a   Sic *in MS.*

b   r *in* Gabriel *partly blotted out in MS.*

c   *Or* Capciel*?*

d   Sic *in MS.*

a   Sic *in MS.*

b   *Followed in MS by* Sylol, Candas, *struck through.*

c   Sic *in MS.*

[4.] Die Mercurij regnat et seruit rex Saba. Coadiutores sui sunt[d] Conas, Pactas, Sanbras.

[5.] Die Jouis regnat et seruit rex Madrath, filius Arath. Coadiutores sui sunt Hyrti uel Hyiti, Ignaro,[e] Quiron, Saalalebeth.

[6.] Die Veneris [75v] regnat rex et seruit Saabotes. Coadiutores sui sunt Nassath, Ynasa.

[7.] Die Saturni regnat Hayton, Assayby. Coadiutores sui sunt Abimalyb et Haybalydoth et Yfla.

Conpleta sunt nomina regum spirituum regnancium et seruiencium septem diebus septimane.

37f. Suffumigations for each day of the week

Quilibet enim dies septimane habet suffumigium sibi appropriatum, cum quo suffumigabis[a] opus tuum quod facies in ea, et complebitur opus tuum sine dubio.

[1.] Suffumigium dies dominice assandalum croceum vel rubeum uel simile sibi.

[2.] Die Lune est aloes, anacap, uel simile sibi.

[3.] Die Martis est piper aut abana, cyg[b] uel sibi simile.

[4.] Die Mercurij est altast aut ei simile.

[5.] Die Jouis est olibanum aut croceum uel ei simile.

[6.] Die Veneris est almastic aut lignum radim uel ei simile.

[7.] Die Saturni est assandaron et sulphur aut ei simile.

Et si in die Saturni operare volueris ad ligandas lignas,[c] erit suffumigium thus Odee Capre.[d] Hec[e] sunt suffumigia dierum septimane.

37g. Purposes served in each day of the week

[1.] In die dominico operari poteris ad ligandas li[n]gwas aut ad alias ligaciones hominum.

[2.] Die Lune operandum est ad beniuolenciam et ad concordiam et amiciciam.

[3.] Die Martis [76r] operandum est ad infirmandum homines et destruendum.

---

d   *Followed in MS by* Comas, *deleted.*

e   Sic *in MS?*

a   fumi *blotted out in MS.*

b   Sic *in MS, for* cygminus?

c   *Meaning* linguas?

d   Sic *in MS?*

e   *MS* Hee.

[4.] Die Mercurij operandum est ad ponendum inimiciciam siue odium inter homines.

[5.] Die Jouis operandum est ad faciendum pacem inter homines discordantes.

[6.] Die Veneris operandum est ad coniu[n]gendum homines in amicicia uel prouocandos de loco ad locum ad beniuolenciam.

[7.] Die Saturni operari poteris ad ligandum[a] interiora[b] balnea, molendina, aut similia.[c]

Dictum est de operibus dierum septimane in qua operandum est.

Quacumque die septimane operari volueris ad beniuolenciam aut quo[d]libet bonum uel malum, attende diligenter quod illa sit operi faciendo conueniens,[d] nec dimittas opus tuum de die in diem uel differas, quare si illud opus non confirmaretur uel non duceretur ad effectum forsitan putaret[ur] illud esse falsum.

37h. Angels serving on each day of the week

Sciendum quod qualibet[a] die septimane presunt tres angeli ad seruiendum homini et opera eius perficienda.

[1.] Diei dominico presunt tres angeli, scilicet Raphahel, Dardiel et[b] Vrlacafel.

[2.] Die Lune presunt[c] hij: Gab[ri]el, Michael, Sammyel.

[3.] Diei Martis presunt hij, scilicet Satyel, Sanyel, Barma- [76v] ly.

[4.] Diei Mercurij presunt hij, scilicet Gemi, Sabael, Sarpiel, Muriel.

[5.] Diei Jouis presunt hij, scilicet Pacta, Castiel, Assassael.

[6.] Diei Veneris presunt hij, scilicet Anael, Sarquiel, Sacquiel.

[7.] Diei Saturni presunt hij, scilicet Captiel, Mataton, Sartquiel, id est Satraquel.

In omni opere quod facies, invocabis angelos illius die[i] quo operari volueris, et ipsi tuam complebunt voluntatem et ducent ad effectum opus tuum.

37i. Names of God

Sequuntur consequenter nomina que scribere habent in principio cuiuslibet operis quod facies ei et respondebunt voluntati tue. Et sunt ex nominibus

---

a   um *blotted out in MS.*

b   *Initial* i *blotted out in MS.*

c   *Followed by* Quacumque die septimane.

d   *Meaning* quod illa sint operi faciendo conueniencia?

a   *MS* quilibet.

b   *MS* uel.

c   *MS* prosunt *(here and in the following five cases).*

creatoris. Ista ergo nomina cum nominari volueris invocanda sunt, scilicet Anguas, Yna, Dei Israel, Ybae,[a] Subae, Guabas, Ynissamon, Haa, Dosa, Barian. In omnia alia karta quam scribes opus hoc vt scribat in ea vbi sit alique ex materia carte quod si fuerit de amicicia et si fuerit de inimicicia et si ad medicinam similiter sic obseruet[ur] in omnibus.[b]

37j. Names of the hours of the day, and their functions

Scribere nos oportet nomina horarum[a] diei quibus horis perficientur opera que facies.

[1.] [77r] Prima ergo diei hora dicitur Yayn. In hac hora facienda est carta ad destruendas voces hominum et mala verba eorum et lingwas ligandas.

[2.] Secunda enim hora diei dicitur Yan, Or, et in ea operaberis ad amiciciam et graciam et beneficium obtinendum et ad societatem hominum aduittandum[b] ad reges et ad potentes.

[3.] Tercia vero hora diei dicitur Nassura. In ea facias cartam uel ymagines ad venerandum[c] feras vel aues, siue ad inplicandum pisces, uel aliquod quodlibet nascencia perhibenda.[d]

[4.] Quarta hora diei dicitur Sala. In ea fac cartam uel ymaginem ad ligandum omnes bestias siluestres, leones, vrsos, et similia.

[5.] Quinta hora diei dicitur Sadadat. In ea fac cartas ad ligaciones et ad applicandas quaslibet bestias, et ad quidquid vis aliud.

[6.] Sexta hora diei dicitur Tamhut. In ea operari poteris ad extrahendum captiuos de carcere, ad ligatos soluendos.

[7.] Septima hora diei dicitur Caror. In ea operatur ad ponendum pacem inter reges.

[8.] Octaua hora diei dicitur Tariel. In ea operari poteris ad mandeolenam et discor- [77v] diam[e] ponendam inter homines.

[9.] Nona hora diei dicitur Karon. In ea facienda est carta ad itinerandum[f] uel ad eundum inter latrones sine timore.

[10.] Decima hora diei dicitur Hyon. In ea operari poteris ad demonia uel demoniacos uel ventum malum uel pauorem uel iuuandum ad dominas.

---

a   *Corrected in MS from* Ybas *(?).*

b   *This entire paragraph seems obscurely written.*

a   *MS* horas.

b   *Meaning* admittendam *or* admittendorum?

c   *Presumably meaning* venandum.

d   Sic *in MS.*

e   c *added above line in MS.*

f   *MS* itenerandum.

[11.] Vndecima hora diei dicitur Nathalon. In ea operari poteris ad prouocandum sangwinis fluxum in mulieribus et ad ligandum virum cum muliere uel e contrario.

[12.] Duodecima hora diei dicitur Abat. In ea operari poteris inter maliuolos ad pacem ponendam inter virum et mulierem.

37k. Names of the hours of the night, and their functions

[1.] Iste sunt hore diei, et operibus sibi pertinentibus.[a]
Prima hora noctis dicitur Leron. In ea fac ad demoniacos opera tua, aut ad uentos malos aut ad congregandas et loquitur cum eis.[b]

[2.] Secunda hora noctis dicitur Latol. In ea operari poteris ad piscariam et ad omina nascencia aque.

[3.] Tercia hora noctis dicitur Hami. In ea operari poteris ad accendendum uel ad exti[n]gwendum ignem et ad omnia que in eo volueris operari.

[4.] Quarta hora noctis dicitur Atyn. In ea operari [78r] poteris ad destruendum domum uel huiusmodi ad expellendum homines de loco ad locum.

[5.] Quinta hora noctis dicitur Caron. In ea fac questiones vt in sompnis videat quod futurum est in mundo uel in diebus uel in annis et ad secreta reuelanda.

[6.] Sexta hora noctis dicitur Zaia. In ea operari poteris ad arbores et fructus earum et ad ceteras plantas terre et ad omne quod operandum est in terra.

[7.] Septima hora dicitur Nectius. In ea operari poteris ad expellendum homines de domo sua uel quod infirmetur uel quod moriatur.

[8.] Octaua hora noctis[c] dicitur Tafat. In ea poteris operari ad inimicicaam ponendam inter quos volueris.

[9.] Nona hora noctis dicitur Conassuor. In ea poteris operari ad ligaciones li[n]gwarum aut ad intrandum ad reges et dominos.

[10.] Decima hora noctis dicitur Algo. In ea operari poteris ad destruendas li[n]gwas uel omnem cogitacionem super te aut concilium malum quod super te cogitatum fuerit.

[11.] Vndecima hora noctis dicitur Caltrua. In ea operari poteris que volueris in auibus, ad eas ligandas[d] uel capiendas.

[12.] Duodecima hora noctis dicitur Salaij. In ea poteris [78v] operari ad inveniendum quidquid predictum est uel ad reuelacionem furti uel malorum factorum.

---

a   *Presumably meaning* opera eis pertinencia.
b   Sic *in MS.*
c   *Corrected in margin of MS from* nothis.
d   *First* a *inserted above line, substituting for a letter that is blotted out.*

371. Names of angels that rule each hour of the day and of the night

Cvm aliquod opus uel cartam volueris scribere, nomen hore et nomen angeli et hore et qui ei dominatur uel ministratur oportet te nominare. Hec sunt nomina angelorum dominancium omnibus horis diei noxium[a] septimane. Prime hore diei dominatur Raphael. 2e hore Anael. 3e Michael. 4e Gabriel. 5e Gaffriel. 6e Satquiel. 7e[b] Samael. 8ue Raphael. 9e Anael. 10e Michael. Vndecime Gabriel. 12e Cafriel.

Nocte diei Lune prima hora dominatur Satquiel. 2e hore Samael. 3e Raphael. 4e Anael. 5e Michael. 6e Gabriel. 7e Cafriel. 8e Satquiel. 9e Samael. 10e Raphael. 11e[c] Anael. 12e Michael. Sic autem intelligere debes de omnibus aliis noctium et dierum prenominatis quidem enim angeli dominatur et ministrat horis secundum dominacionem planetarum uel ministracionem in eis. Omni hora Solis ministrat uel dominatur Raphael. Hora Veneris, Anael. Hora Mercurij, Michael. Hora Lune, Gabriel. Hora Saturni, Caffriel. Hora Jouis, Satquiel. Hora Martis, Samuel. Diei eciam cuiuslibet planete cum angelis suis signaque planetarum distributa horum angelorum nomina debent concordare et respondere [79r] nominibus capitulis supra proxime positus et angelo qui continetur infra in coniuracionibus cuiuslibet diei et in capitulis de ymaginibus deorum quibus ministrant adinuicem.[d]

Diei dominici ergo ministrat Sol, et angelus eius Raphael, eiusque signum Leo. Diei lune[e] ministrat Luna, et angelus eius Gabriel, eiusque signum Aries et Scorpio. Diei Martis ministrat Mars, et angelus eius Samael, eiusque signum Cancer. Diei Mercurij ministrat planeta Mercurij, et eius angelus Michael uel Mathael, eiusque signum Gemini uel Virgo. Diei Jouis ministrat Jupiter, et angelus eius Samael, eiusque signum Sagitarius et Pisces. Diei Veneris ministrat Venus, et angelus eius[f] Anael, eiusque signum Thaurus et Libra. Diei Sabbati ministrat Saturnus, et angelus eius Caffriel, eiusque signum Capricornus et Aquarius.

Nomina[g] siue istis v nominibus opus tuum perficere non poteris. Prima hora diei Lune ministrat uel dominatur Gabriel. Secunda hora Caffriel. 3a hora Satquiel. 4a hora Samael. 5a hora Raphael. 6a hora Anael. 7a hora Michael. 8a hora Gabriel. Nona hora Caffriel. Decima hora Satquiel. Vndecima hora Samael. Duodecima hora Raphael.

---

a   Sic *in MS.*
b   *Blotted out in MS.*
c   *MS* 12.
d   Sic *in MS.*
e   *Corrected in MS from* luna.
f   *MS* eiusque.
g   Sic *in MS.*

37m. Images to be used for each hour of the day

[79v] De operibus ymaginum diei.

[1.] Nota primo malas li[n]gwas. Prima hora diei facienda est ymago ad ligandas li[n]gwas, et li[n]gwa que ligata fuit illa hora nunquam erit potens loquendi malum verbum de te. Prima hora diei fac ymaginem canis ex argento uel stanno^a puro, et sculpe in capite ymaginis nomen illius super quem operaris et nomen domini hore et diei in quo hec^b facis, et in ventre ymaginis nomen potentissimi et altissimi domini, et suffumigabis ymaginem suffumigio supra dicto, et cum sangwine rubeo et involues eam in panno albo nouo, et sepelies eam ad partem illius de quo volueris, tunc non loquitur de te malum. Et sic ligabunt omnia ora et oculi hominum, et tibi nunquam nocere poterit quamdiu durabit ymago ista. In ventrem ymaginis scribe nomen Lune et nomen signi et angelorum tempore quo hoc^c facies. Hec autem nomina sunt nomina creatoris multum preciosa et benedicta, quibus creatum fuit^d celum et terra.^e Hic^f autem cum sculpes, sculpe eam totaliter vt bene appareat.^g Et hec sunt nomina: Lyara, Lyalguana, Loaffar, Vialuarab, Lebara, Lebarion, Layasales. Hec sunt vij nomina que scribes in ventre forme, et scribes ea in omnibus operibus omnium rerum pertinencium hominibus, aut auibus et bestiis et omnibus creaturis de concordia et amicicia.

[2.] [80r] Secunda hora diei facienda est ymago benivolencie, et vna ymago viri et altera mulieris de purissimo stanno fusile et [in] capite ymaginis mulieris nomen viri, et in capite viri nomen mulieris, in pectore vero et in ventre ymaginis^h sculpes vijtem subsequencia nomina simul cum vijtem nominibus supradictis, et iunges ymagines, conglutinandoⁱ eas cum cera, ita quod inter se bene firmantur, et sepelias^j in domo illius quem volueris alium sequi, et fiet inter eos amicicia durabilis quamdiu ymagines durabunt. Et hec sunt ista vij nomina, hec scribes: Malthayl, Caramel, Azariel, Zaraimayl,^k Parsail, Porbayl, Seralabelis. Et hec^l quod^m legi possunt.

---

a *MS* stangno.

b *Or* hoc.

c *Or* hec.

d *Presumably meaning* quibus creauit.

e *In margin of MS:* Nota nomina, *and pointing hand.*

f *Meaning* hanc [ymaginem]?

g *MS* appariat *or* apperiat [appiat].

h *MS* ymaginem.

i *MS* conglutinaando.

j *MS* sepelieas.

k Sic *in MS?*

l *Or* hoc.

m *Meaning* quoque?

[3.] Tercia hora diei facienda est ymago ad prouocandas omnes aues et tota omnia piscaminaⁿ ad locum signatum. In hac hora fac ex ere rubeo ymaginem animalis quod applicare volueris, et sculpe in capite ymaginis nomen domini hore et in pectore similiter et in ventre vij nomina prime hore, et suffumiga eam cum feniculo aut ordeo yndo, et sepeli eam in loco ad quem volueris applicare animalia sub quorum similitudine ymaginem formasti, et videbis mirabilia creatoris quando veniant ad locum istum.

[4.] [80v] Quarta hora diei facienda est ymago ad animalia prouocanda uel effuganda, vt scorpiones et omnia reptilia et bestias siluestras. In hac hora fac ymaginem ex ere croceo ad similitudinem animalis cuius genus [ge9] in loco signato volueris applicare, sculpe nomen animalis in capite ymaginis et in pectore nomen domini hore, et vij supradicta nomina, prima hora^o sculpe in ventre ymaginis et sepeli ymaginem in loco quo vis applicari. Hec quidem ymago applicabit omnia animalia que tunc non in loco erant.

[5.] Qvinta hora diei facienda est ymago ad feras mitigandas, vt leones, vrsos, et lupos, aut^p quaslibet alias feras nocentes. In hac hora funde ymaginem animalis cuius genus volueris applicari uel mittigari, et sculpe in capite ymaginis nomen animalis, et in pectore nomen hore et nomen domini hore, et in ventre vij nomina prime hore, et suffumiga ymaginem cum ligno yndo et cum sandalo rubeo, et sepeli ymaginem in loco vbi volueris, et auxilio domini te adiuuante videbis quod omnia illa animalia ad voluntatem tuam reuertentur.

[6.] Ad liberandos incarceratos. Sexta hora diei facienda est ymago pro captiuis aut incarceratis, uel dampnandis ad mortem uel saluandis. In hac [81r] hora funde ymaginem illius uel istorum quos saluari volueris ex argento uel stanno, et sculpe in capite ymaginis nomen viri saluandi, et in pectore nomen hore, et in ventre^q septem nomina prime hore, et^r dona^s ymaginem alicui eorum, quod eam secum teneat carcere et ista nocte euadent a carcere cum potencia dei creatoris.

[7.] Ad uenandum uel ad piscandum.^t Septima hora diei facienda est ymago pro uenacione et piscacione, et est fortis et vtilis multum. Funde ymaginem ex optimo argento in hac hora, et sculpe in capite ymaginis nomen domini hore, et in pectore ymaginis vij nomina 2e hore, et omni hora qua piscatum vel venatum

---

n   Sic *in MS.*

o   *MS* hore.

p   *MS* aut.

q   *MS* virtute.

r   et *slightly malformed, and duplicated above line in MS.*

s   *MS* tona.

t   *Heading added in margin of MS.*

ieris ymaginem tecum porta et[u] applicacionem, venacionem, uel piscacionem quam volueris.

[8.] Ad maliuolenciam et discordiam ponendam inter homines. Octaua hora diei facienda est ymago ad domos uel ad loca destruenda[v] et deponenda. In hac hora funde ymaginem ex ere rubeo cum duobus capitibus, quorum vnum sit asininum, reliquum vero hominis, et sculpe in capite asinino nomen loci quod deletum esse volueris, et in capite humano sculpe nomen domini loci, et ministratores domini loci et in pectore ymaginis nomen domini hore, et suffumiga ymaginem cum sangwine hominis inter- [81v] fecti uel cum auxugia carnis, et sepeli eam in loco quem depopulatum rem[w] volueris et fugient omnes homines et depopulabitur iste locus talis quod nec quoddam[x] brutum animal remanebit.

[9.] Quod poteris transire vbicumque volueris et nullus tibi nocere potest. Nona hora diei facienda est ymago ad ambulandum sine timore inter leones aut feras et transire per eas sine timore [uel] terrore, et ad omnia itineranda secure. In ea hora funde ymaginem sub similitudine de qua quesieris,[y] et scribe in capite ymaginis nomen domini hore, in ventre vij nomina prime hore, et suffumiga ymaginem cum supradicto[z] fuste et croco. Portans eam tecum, transibis per quemcumque locum volueris sine timore, qui[a] oculi cunctorum videre te non poterunt et eorum li[n]gwe obmutescent. Poterisque transire, [et non] fiet tibi dampnum, cum potencia dei.

[10.] Ad optinendum quidquid volueris coram[a] regibus et[b] principibus. Decima hora diei facienda est ymago ad intrandum ad reges et potestates. In hac hora funde ymaginem hominis ex argento, et sculpe in capite ymaginis nomen hominis, et in pectore nomen hore et nomen domini hore, et in ventre vij nomina prime hore, et suffumiga ymaginem cum croco et fuste supra- [82r] dicto, et involue eam in panno nouo lineo et albo, et hora qua ad aliquem volueris intrare vel ire porta eam tecum, et obtinebis quid volueris cum adiutorio dei.

[11.] Ad faciendum concordare discordantes. Vndecima hora diei facienda est ymago ad prouocandam concordiam inter discordantes uel inter virum et mulierem. In hac hora funde duas ymagines, vnius ponderis et vnius quantitatis

---

u *Meaning* ad?

v *Meaning* depopulaturum?

w Sic *in MS?*

x *Followed in MS by* p, *struck through.*

y *Perhaps meaning* sub similitudine bestie de qua quesieris?

z Sic *in MS.*

a *Followed in MS by* te, *struck through.*

b *Followed in MS by* pueri (?), *struck through.*

et qualitatis, et sculpe nomen viri in capite femine, et nomen femine in capite masculi, et in pectoribus ambarum ymaginum sculpes nomen hore et nomen domini hore, et in ventris nomina 2e hore, et pone eas facie ad faciem, et suffumiga eas cum croco et fuste supradicto, et pone eas in secreto ad stellas, et videbis mirabilia, quomodo vnus inqui[e]tet alium et non poterit vnus sine alio stare.

[12.] Ad ligandas li[n]gwas. Dvodecima hora diei facienda est ymago ad ligandas li[n]gwas. In hac hora fac ymaginem hominis ex optimo stanno, et sculpe in capite nomen eius, et in pectore nomen hore, et in ventre nomina prime hore, et suffumiga cum croco et fuste supradicto, et pone ad stellas vij noctes, et cum mochazat et cum sandaras, et coniura eam cum qui sic incipiunt Samahil, et non erit potens loqui super eum malum verbum.

[82v] Finite sunt vij ymagines que faciende sunt in similibus horis diei cum omnibus suffumigacionibus et operibus suis. Caue igitur in illis, quia exanimate sunt et vere et ne per te mentiantur,[c] quia per eas totam perficies tuam voluntatem, in gracia dei, cuius nomen sit benedictum. Amen.

37n. Images to be used for each hour of the night

De operibus ymaginum noctis.

Modo dicam operacionem ymaginum noctis, sicut studuerunt antiqui qui nominati sunt; invocantur qui ipsi eas composuerunt, vt omnes homines operantes eas scirent de lucerna que nunquam exti[n]gwi possit.

[1.] Prima hora noctis facienda est ymago ad illuminanda loca tenebrosa uel quemlibet alium locum obscurum. In hac hora funde candelam eream quasi crucibulum habens vij ora, et sculpa in quo[libet] ore crucibuli hec nomina: Sarastan, Hasas, Dalas, Sassa; et pone in quolibet ore crucibuli lignum[a] de bombace, et scribe super os crucibuli hec xij nomina: Bezat, Berith, Zenit, Caffan, Dalfat, Dana, Aneth, Beas, Manith, Hassas, Dalaph, Sefa. Et fac ex eo super crucibulum ymaginem hominis tenentis secum quasi formam vasis in similitudinem fundentis oleum in candela, et imple candelam oleo quod non fuerit expressum manibus, et sculpe super faciem ymaginis istud [83r] nomen: Leorphahel [uel] Leorpahel, et super formam nomen istud: Rosahal. Et similiter supra candelam crucibuli, et cooperi faciem ymaginis quod non possit discooperiri, et accende ora crucibuli, et nunquam

---

c   Sic *in MS.*

a   *MS* lignium.

exti[n]gwetur. Poteris facere ymaginem in loco quod nulla mulier poterit transire, nec ibi stare, nec ibi stetur.[b]

[2.] Secunda hora noctis faciendum est ymago ad presciendum fortunium. Istud testificatus est homo Almera, qui fuit ex sapientibus antiquis, qui cum ingressus fuisset quamdam ciuitatem quam nominabant Alandar fecit in ea ymaginem istam et vlterius ingressa non fuit mulier in eam. In hac hora funde ymaginem ex ere lympide, et scribe super faciem ymaginis hec nomina: Notooa,[c] Har, Beel, Cead, Vasas, Naaya, Haat. Et hec alia sculpes in quodam folio oris[d] et ponas in manu ymaginis; hec sunt nomina, scilicet, Raagor, Ralaz, Branar, Cundaz,[e] Natho, Jany. Et sepeli ymaginem in medio ciuitatis siue ville, vt nullus te videat dum hoc[f] feceris. Et cum hac ymagine poteris prescindere scorpiones aut cetera nocencia de loco.

[3.] Ad fugandum omnia reptilia. Tercia hora noctis facienda est ymago ad predestinendum reptilia nocencia aut bestias malas aut locustas, vt viperas aut omnem rem malam. In hac hora funde ymaginem [83v] eream ad similitudinem reptilis quod volueris fugari et scribe in facie eius hec nomina: Vabros, Wiez, Bercca,[g] Beror, Berabut, Baramel. Et sepely ymaginem vbi volueris, et omnia de dictis effugabunt.

[4.] Ad destinandum villam aut locum quem volueris depopulari, aut inimiciciam. Qvarta hora noctis facienda est ymago ad villam vel locum destruendum quem volueris depopulari, aut inimiciciam.[h] In hac hora minge tu ipse retro in ore cameli uel catti, et collige in panno hominis, et vade ad domum inimici tui, et [scribe] ista nomina cum ista aqua in porta domus eius: *Raccedi,[i] Palicos, Pytalas, Pila, coniuro vos quod cito destruetis domum illius*, N., et tam cito factum erit.

[5.] Ad dispergendum exercitum. Qvinta hora noctis faciendum est ymago ad dispergendum exercitum congregatum super castrum aut quemlibet alium locum, aut malas nubes aut grandinem. In hac hora funde ymaginem ex plumbo et ere rubeo equaliter mixtum sitque 4or librarum, et sculpe in ea hec nomina: Baraa, Atle, Hate, Carbara, Garglale, Ha, Conadiuro Famal,[j] Alul, Beaali, Aguel,

---

b   Sic *in MS.*

c   Sic *in MS?*

d   Sic *in MS.*

e   Sic *in MS?*

f   *Or* hec.

g   Sic *in MS?*

h   Sic *in MS.*

i   Sic *in MS?*

j   Sic *in MS.*

et Arpa, Nafaca, Paluo. Et suffumiga ymaginem suffumigiis que docuimus, et[k] coniura super eam vij nomina scripta, et sepeli[l] ymaginem in altori loco, et tale infor- [84r] tunium eueniet quod totus exercitus dispergetur, [et] fugiet. Et si operatus fuerit ad dispergendas nubes, sepeli eam in altiori loco et propinquiori monte, ville, morce, uel loco seminato, et dispergetur nubes et complebitur quod quesieris, videbisque mirabilia et potenciam creatoris.

[6.] Ad faciendum fugere inimicos uel inimicum. Sexta hora noctis facienda est ymago ad expellendum inimicum a villa de domo in qua moratur. In hac hora funde ymaginem ex ere rubeo, et sculpe in ea hec nomina: Tartarath, Acuta, Col, Cafra, Cal, Guabrath, Afah, Audena, Cal, Matha, Coltasia, Bal, Mathail, Cafia, Falduc, Atal, Parclena,[m] Cul, Mathiel, Fustaul, Gaulyar, Etal, Patath, Cicubael, Barath, Cabuel, Athael, Pera, Patua. Et in capite ymaginis sculpe nomina illius pro quo ymaginem facis, et suffumiga ymaginem supradictis suffumigiis, et pone eam prope[n] habitacionem eius, et recedet maliuolus fugiendo de villa vel domo, nec quiescet, et pauescet, et distruetur eius sensus totalis.

[7.] Ad comburendum[o] nascencia terre. Septima hora noctis facienda est ymago ad comburenda nascencia terre. In hac [84v] hora funde ymaginem ex ere rubeo, et sculpe in ea hec nomina: Agug, Cantzit, Totman, Catua, Via, Meracuat, Vanath, Gara, Turat,[p] Nuxae, Artha, Nar. Descendat ignis de celis in terram, qui[q] tremat totum terminum istum. Adrat, Mararat, Beguayl, Algayl, Carat.[r] Et sepeli ymaginem in termino ville, et in toto termino folium viride non[s] cremabit.

[8.] Ad congregandum apes aut columbas uel alias quascumque aues. Octaua hora noctis facienda est ymago ad applicandas apes ad aluarium suum, aut columbas ad columbarium suum, aut quascumque alias aues ad locum signatum de longinquis partibus terminis in circuitu. In hac hora funde ymaginem apis de auro ad pondus vnius aurei, et sculpe in ea ista nomina: Cadota, Carosa, Astab, Yatyon,[t] Vetartuna, Taracta. Et sepely ymaginem in altiori loco illius termini et applicabunt illuc omnes[u] apes qui erunt in circuitu loci illius aut columbe ad

---

k   *Followed in MS by sign for* con-, *blotted out.*

l   *Followed in MS by* eam, *deleted.*

m   Sic *in MS?*

n   *MS* proprie.

o   *MS* comburendam.

p   Sic *in MS?*

q   *Followed in MS by* creauit te, *struck through.*

r   Sic *in MS.*

s   Sic *in MS.*

t   *Followed in MS by* Vertart, *struck through.*

u   *Followed in MS by* aues, *deleted.*

columbarium suum vbi fuerit ymago columbe facta secundum quod supra dictum est. Similiter et omnes alie aues.

[9.] Hanc ymaginem facies ad omnia que volueris prouocare ad capiendum aues quas volueris. [85r] Nona hora noctis facienda est ymago ad prouocandas aues quarumlibet ad quemlibet locum volueris. In hac hora fac ymaginem illarum auium quas volueris prouocare, et sculpe in ea ista nomina: Totarati, Tuata, Berhantual, Toluhaya, Ya. Et pone eam quo volueris aues applicari, et applicabunt.

[10.] Ad dispergendum exercitum obsidentem^v villam uel castrum. Decima hora noctis facienda est ymago ad dispergendum exercitum obsidentem villam uel castrum. In hac hora funde duas ymagines ex duobus generibus diuersorum metallorum: vna sit ex ere rubeo, 2a ex plumbo, 3a de stanno, 4a de argento, 5a de ferro. Sint autem hee due ymagines in vno corpore, et ista ymago habeat duo capita, vnum leonis, reliquum vero thauri, habens cornva a parte anteriori,^w et sculpe in testis illis ista nomina: Horata, Taramat, Bata, Velaheia, Laa, Veda, Eaeffaxa, Lylatrala, Calmaatur, Mantut, Caatuas. Et sculpe in ventre formam leonis et formam bouis, et pone inter eas de sepo bouis et de sepo colubri, et suffumiga ymaginem cum eis et sepely eam vbi sedet exercitus, et cadit in eo talis occisio quod ipsimet se occident, et nunquam reuertatur medietas ad terram suam de ordine.

[11.–12.] [85v] Vndecima et duodecima hora noctis nichil per ymagines manuum est operandum, nisi per oracionem et postulacionem, sic enim dixerunt sapientes: Qui de hac sapiencia inquirere uel addiscere voluerit, oportet eum primitus scire horar et nomina dierum, quia in hiis est tota virtus magisterij, et cum hiis perficies opera tua in virtute creatoris, cuius nomen est benedictum in secula [secul]orum. Amen.

37o. Names of angels serving specific times

Qvando volueris operari ex libro isto adnomina nomen Terre in tempore suo quolibet eorum 4or nominum, videlicet in quolibet opere vnum. Et quia hoc^a precipitur, quia si fieret aliqua transgressio per operantem, nullum^b veniret ad effectum, etc.

Cvm autem aliquod opus aut ymaginem operare volueris ad precidendum^c

---

v   *MS* absidentem.

w   Sic *in MS?*

a   *Or* hec.

b   *MS* nullo.

c   Sic *in MS.*

da[m]pnum hominibus siue seminibus aut gregibus, accipiet[d] tempus diei quo hec[e] facies, et si de nocte operatus fueris, accipiet tempus noctis cum nominibus angelorum mendancium[f] tempus in quo operaberis, in nomen non prohibende vt lucuste grandis et malorum nubium aut rei que tibi videbitur, et hec sunt nomina que scribes in primo tempore.[g]

Nomina angelorum primi temporis: Gatrat,[h] Cassa, Tait, Amatyel, Gramsatos, et nomen potentis super istos est Oamquiel, et nomen capitis Singlytiel, et Venatyel, Atatyel, [86r] nomen vero auium est Nerastas.

Nomina angelorum secundi temporis sunt hec: Bartatel, Turiel, Vlmiel, et nomen capitis signi Labael.

Nomina angelorum seruiencium tempori 3o sunt hec: Tarquayl, Acartayl, Acayl, Gaabarayl, et nomen capitis signi Calguarath.

Nomina angelorum seruiencium tempori 4o sunt hec: Amabel, Terayl, Atraa, Atratrayl.

Cvm autem operari volueris, accipe nomen temporis quo hoc[i] facies, et scribe alia nomina aut signa secundum quod fuerit opus, et omnia venient ad effectum in virtute et potencia creatoris, cuius nomen est benedictum in secula [secul]orum. Amen.

37p. Names of the planets and of parts of the earth

Nota de nominibus Solis.

Dicere nos oportet et docere cupiditates scire ista sciencia[j] ymaginum et nomina Solis et Lune et Terre, et 4or parcium mundi, in quolibet tempore.

Nomen igitur Solis in primo tempore est Abrayn. In secundo tempore Acamon. In 3o Abragon. In 4o Rifar.

Primo tempore Solis sunt hec nomina signorum eius: Aries, Thaurus, Gemini. Tempore 2o Cancer, Leo, Virgo. Tempore 3o sunt hec: Libra, Scorpio, Sagitarius. Tempore vero 4o sunt hec: Capricornius, Aquarius, Pisses.[k]

De nominibus Lune. [86v] Primo tempore nomen Lune est Lunatulant. Secundo tempore Albora. Tercio tempore Alladyn. Quarto tempore Saarbaquia.

---

d   Sic *in MS.*

e   *Or* hoc.

f   *Presumably meaning* ministrancium.

g   *This entire paragraph appears to be obscurely written.*

h   Sic *in MS?*

i   *Or* hec.

j   *Possibly meaning* et cupitis scire istam scienciam.

k   Sic *in MS.*

De nominibus celorum. Primo tempore celorum est Asaptaa, Tima. Secundo tempora Armatrassi. Tercio Mafatyn, Gnam.[l] Quarto Safatem.

De nominibus Terre. Primo tempore Terre nomen Inamodon. Secundo tempore Festaen.[m] Tercio Tabian vel Rathbil. Quarto Yemat uel Yaneaa.

De nominibus 4or parcium mundi, scilicet Orientis, Occidentis, Meridiei, et Septentrionis.

Primo nomen 4or parcium mundi, scilicet Orientis in primo 4or temporum est Gnaandon. 2o Pibdaya. 3o Aldebath. 4o Pedioth. Nomen Occidentis tempore primo Amana. 2o Tana. 3o Ytadaon. Quarto Malchaam.[n] Nomen Meridiei tempore primo Mantham. 2o Yasaory. 3o Azut. Quarto Danor. Nomen Septentrionis tempore primo Manbasut. 2o Gasson. 3o Mascyel. Quarto Yamhor.

De aliis 4or nominibus Terre: alia nomina Terre in 4or temporibus: In primo tempore Talyn. 2o Cosmaaram.[o] Tercio Aydarael. Quarto Saybath.

Vt scias que sunt 4or tempora.

Scias quod primum tempus incipit a medio Marcij et finit in medio Junij, et menses[p] Aprilis [87r] et Maij sunt in medio, et sunt de tempore primo. Secundum tempus incipit a medio Junij et finit in medio Septembri, et Julius et Augustus sunt in medio, et sunt de tempore 2o. Tercium tempus incipit a medio Septembri et finit in medio Decembri, et October et Nouember[q] sunt in medio, et sunt de tempore 3o. Quartum tempus incipit a medio Decembris et finit in medio Marcij, et Januarius et Februarius sunt in medio, et sunt de tempore 4o.

37q. Images and conjurations for days of the week

De ymaginibus vij dierum ebdomade.

Sapientes philosophi et experti qui composuerunt istum librum confidentes in deo qui est super omnes deus ordinauerunt ymagines vij dierum ebdomade ad faciendum peticiones, et est sciencia altissima et honorata et multum secreta et non conceditur omnibus hominibus nisi viris magni et profundissimi sensus et intelligencie.

Caue igitur tibi in illis, et proba, et invenies veritatem sanctissimam.

[1.] De ymagine diei dominice. Prima ymago est diei dominici. Forma eam ex

---

l   Sic *in MS?*

m   Sic *in MS?*

n   Sic *in MS?*

o   Sic *in MS?*

p   *MS* mensis.

q   *MS* Octobri et Nouembri.

auro uel auricalco aut cera crocea, et scribe super eam nomina sequencia, et si in altitudine dicitur ascensio Leonis in mense Augusti aut Aprilis. Hec sunt nomina angelorum man- [87v] dancium Leonem: Raphael, Dardyel, Vrlathafel. Nomina ventorum sunt hec uel spirituum qui semper mandant Leonem: Baythan, et eius adiutores Cahatus, Cardas, Yabal. Cum volueris ligare li[n]gwas, fac ymaginem istam in horis nominatis que tibi conuenit[r] et altitudine dicta, et coniura super eam per ista coniuracionem:

> *Coniuro vos, angeli sigillo Solis consignati: Banarga, Lyon, Cylon, Bamayon, Admyon, Assuerop, Tayuf, Rem, Letana, Baupa, Yanoth, Haralyl, Quilil, Casub, Nubtub, Caytuli, Catub,[s] per creatorem celi et terre et 4or parcium mundi et ventorum qui[t] sunt inter celum et terram, qui est super omnes deus, fortissimus et altissimus, et non est alius deus preter eum, et ipse est rerum et conditor omnium naturarum: Yat, Faoli, Ydardyel, Ycalatasyel. Item coniuro vos per hec nomina: Vasamiaa,[u] Licaa, Cassaa, Lamubatub, Olot, Elos, Cymehalod, ipse est qui scit sciencias secretas et apertas, Yfael, Cardiel, Telataph, El, laborate et complete peticionem meam et opus quod cupio compleri.*

[2.] Secunda ymago est [diei] Lune, et est facienda ex auro vel ex stanno aut ex cera alba. Ymago hec est ad maximam beniuolenciam et concordiam, et hi[v] sunt angeli super eam dominantes: Gab[ri]el, [88r] Michael, Samuel. Cum autem volueris facere concordiam et magnam beniuolenciam, fac ymaginem istam 2a hora[w] diei Lune, in altitudine Cancri,[x] in mense Julij aut Martis, uel in mense Piscium. Hec sunt nomina ventorum qui[y] manda[n]t Cancrum: Heletel, Halmital, et huius adiutores sunt Bellomilalum,[z] Abuzaba. Et coniura super eam per istam coniuracionem:

> *Coniuro vos angeli quibus commissum est signum Lune, Comoha, Bamoha, Zihil, Bephaha, Casal, Nata, Vada. Coniuro vos per honorem dei vt compleatis hanc peticionem, nec in aliam rem laboretis donec festinetis[a] compleueritis. Rogo te, G[abriel], M[ichael], et S[amuel],*

---

r   Sic *in MS?*

s   *Followed in MS by* et.

t   *MS* que.

u   Sic *in MS?*

v   *MS* si.

w   *MS* 2[am] horam.

x   *MS* Cancer.

y   *MS* que.

z   Sic *in MS?*

a   -ne- *accompanied by dots normally indicating deletion. Perhaps an adverb is intended?*

quod hec[b] *mea peticione adimplere confirmare non remaneat*[c] *quousque eam perfecte adimplebitis et confirmabitis, diuina nobis concessa gracia et virtute.*[d]

[3.] Tercia ymago est die[i] Martis. Forma eam ex ere rubeo aut cera rubea, die Martis et hora Martis, mense[e] Aprilis aut Decembri.[f] Et scias quod hoc opus est multum honoratum et forte, quando volueris istud opus operari. Nomina angelorum commissorum sigillo Martis sunt hec, scilicet Sariel, Taryel, Harmalil, et nomina ventorum qui seruiunt ei super[g] hec: Harmabia, Blisacana, Ababob, et eius 3es adiutores Coaamal,[h] Vmial,[i] Perasas. Et coniura per istam coniuracionem:

Coniuro vos [88v] *principes angelorum et ventorum eius, Edus, Mafraas, Dadayus, et Hydus, Habat, Alat, Nays, Madasia, Yaral, Fastriath, Ysamtiel, Ytatel, Haramalil, nomine Cabar, Carachar, Ycidanis, Yalens, Harab, et dominum lucis altum Bathaquius, diuinÿ Honris,*[k] *Tortur, Hamahe, Dana, Cadara, dominum celorum et terre, nec est alius deus preter ipsum, deum Salciel, Tariel, Hatamalil, precipe*[l] *Hamar, Benall,*[m] *et adiutoribus eius, quod faciant et compleant quod ab ipsis postulaui.*

Si volueris depopulare domum, ad sa[n]gwinis fluxum prouocare, aut aliquem infirmari, aut quodlibet aliud dampnum facere, forma[n] ymaginem ex ere rubeo et sepely ymaginem iuxta aquam currentem.

[4.] Qvarta ymago est diei Mercurij, et hec sunt nomina angelorum quibus super eam constituunt: Michael, Fanuel,[o] Sarpiel; et nomina ventorum sunt hec mandantium eam, scilicet Tobha et adiutores eius Danhas, Paclas, Sambas. Forma ymaginem mense Julij aut Octobris, et plumbo; sculpe in ea nomina ista

b   *Or* hoc.

c   Sic *in MS.*

d   *MS* virtus.

e   *MS* mensis.

f   *MS* Decembris.

g   *Meaning* sunt?

h   Sic *in MS?*

i   Sic *in MS?*

j   *Meaning* dominum?

k   Sic *in MS?*

l   Sic *in MS.*

m   Sic *in MS?*

n   *MS* formam.

o   Sic *in MS?*

ad seperandos beniuolentes et ponendas inimicicas inter eos,[p] et coniura sic per ista coniuracionem:

Coniuro vos angeli per nomen creatoris, preter quem nullus est vince[n]s, ipse enim est creator et preceptor, et omnis potestas est in manu sua, uel eius sibi eciam est virtus insuperabilis, quia ipse est potens et invincibilis rex, sub cuius [89r] *auctoritate omnia sistunt et viuunt. Coniuro vos, Michael, Sarpiel, Muriel, Peruerl,*[q] *Yeserie, Adonay, Sabaoth, Yo, Yo, domini celorum et terre, venite per bonitatem veri fortis qui solus fuit, est, et erit. Michael, Sarquiel, Muriel, complete peticionem meam,*[r] *vt veniat ad effectum.*

[5.] Qvinta ymago est diei Jouis, et angeli super eam constituti sunt Satquiel, Pattar,[s] Constiel, Assassayel, et hij sunt venti constituti super ymaginem: Silite, Maraben, Halharit, et sui adiutores sunt Yse, Riron, Naasay, Eladab. Et quando igitur volueris hoc opus operari, forma ymaginem ex ere croceo aut ex cera crocea die Jouis, et intinge eam cum viridi, et fac pro viro et pro muliere, [si] hoc modo volueris ponere amiciciam inter duos viros aut mulieres aut inter virum et mulierem. Forma duas ymagines ex cera viridi mense Maij, scilicet in altitudine Piscium, aut mense Januarij in altitudine Sagitarij, et scribe nomen viri super cor ymaginis femine et nomen femine super cor masculi, et dic coniuracionem istam:

Domine deus, omnipotens creator rerum visibilium tam invisibilium, pone beniuolenciam et mansuetam concordiam inter mulierem talem, filia[m] *talis, et talem, filium talis, quam posuisti inter Adam et Euam, et inter Jacob et Rachelem, et inter Michaelem et Gabrielem, quorum vnus est igneus et alter aqueus, vnus* [*autem*] *alteri non* [89v] *nocet, sed est inter eos concordia magna, et quemadmodum posuisti concordiam in angelo cuius medietas est ignea, altera niuea, vt nix ignem non extingwit, nec ignis niuem consumit, et tu pariter inuidiam concordare facis. Ita, domine, tua sanctissima pietate et misericordia*[t] *talem, filiam talis, concordare, diligere, et amare cum tali, filio talis, facias. Coniuro vos angeli nomine Yafaa, Safaa,*[u] *Alleya, Hayala, Haya, Halix, Hayul, Ataya, Hytoia, Saffetaba, Coffossol, Remlestar,*[v] *El, domine deus, qui scis secreta cordium et es finis et principium, qui nunquam morieris. Festina, Sarafem, Custyeli, et precipe Amaris*[w] *et adiutoribus eius, vt cito faciant et compleant peticionem meam.*

p *MS* eas.

q Sic *in MS?*

r *MS* mean.

s Sic *in MS?*

t *MS* misericordiam.

u *Corrected in MS from* Safea *(?).*

v Sic *in MS?*

w Sic *in MS?*

Et sepeli ymaginem in loco per quem transeant, et videbis mirabilia omnipotentis dei.

[6.] Sexta ymago est diei Veneris, et angeli mandantes eam sunt Anael, Naquiel, Sagriel, et venti sunt Sarabores, et 3es adiutores Trathacas, Nasat, Nasaa. Quando de ymaginibus operari volueris, formas illas die Veneris ex cera alba mense Maij, in altitudine Thauri, aut in mense Octobris, et scribe nomen viri super cor ymaginis mulieris, et nomen mulieris in capite ymaginis viri, et suspende eas ad stellas, et percute eos cum virga oliue, et coniura eas cum ista coniuracione:

Venite, Anael, Tarquiel, Samuel, [90r] Hassahaa, Saaca, Giraca, Adtulia,[x] Archalia, Aler, Gnad, Alualia, Saana, Samorie, Mahyra, Cartel, Harat, Maslatym,[y] Caci, Yca, Yca, Dad, Dada, per ipsum qui est Cados, Salba, dominum angelorum et ventorum, Heyt, Asseveye, Adonay, El, Salday, Saraoth, Sabaoth, Lyaste, Ady, Gualbroa,[z] vir fortissimus, virorum fortissimum,[a] deus altus et magnus, creator noster, preter cuius potenciam non est alia, A, Cya, Ya, Barquissaquil, Sabguyel, et per istam coniuracionem quam super vos coniuro, et per virtutem El, Veneris, bene fortunate, coniuro vos vt bene proficiatis in hac mea causa,[b] et compleatis cito meam voluntatem, commemorando filium talis, et talem filiam[c] talis, sicut ferrebat[d] cor Eue per amorem Ade in omnibus, Haycrab, Hayclas, Canael, Taltoth, Scarpe, cor talis, filie tali[s], pro loco condenso vbi cottidie transeat.[e]

[7.] Septima ymago est diei sabbati, cuius planeta est Saturnus, et hec ymago est multum honorata et preciosa, super omnes alias ymagines, eo quod Saturnus est in septimo celo. Hanc autem ymaginem mandant isti angeli: Castuel, Maratron uel Matraton, Satael. Et venti huic seruientes sunt hij: Memmi, Aloybain, Aflas, Analuabith. Quando autem volueris ligare li[n]gwas aut balneum [90v] aut[f] molendinum aut centorium, uel ponere discordiam inter duos diligentes se, forma ymaginem ei et[g] sculpe in ea nomina dicta, et porta eam

---

x   Sic *in MS?*

y   Sic *in MS?*

z   Sic *in MS?*

a   Sic *in MS.*

b   *MS* meam casam.

c   *MS* tali filia.

d   *Perhaps intended for* furebat.

e   *The final words read like fragments of instruction that do not belong to the conjuration, but the passage is evidently confused.*

f   *MS* ad.

g   *Meaning* eorum?

tecum, necessaria cum ea, per portam ciuitatis aut ville uel domus, et sepeli eam
in medio vbi volueris, et ligabunt omnes li[n]gwe hominum loci illius. Et si
volueris ponere discordiam inter duos beniuolos, uel inter virum et mulierem,
forma duas ymagines de pice clara, sitque facies ymaginis viri facies porci, et
facies ymaginis mulieris facies canis, et pone eas tergo ad tergum, et scribe in
cartha virginem[h] sequencia verba, et ponis[i] eam inter costas ymaginis, et hec sunt
verba que faciunt inter eos vt istos discordiam et inimiciciam, maliuolenciam,
pec[t]orum percussio, capillorum depilacio, abhominaciones, et fuga, vt
nunquam vnus ab altero possit diligi, sed ab inuicem sibi tristes obuient. Et sepeli
ymaginem sub porta domus vnius illorum, et videbis mirabilia. Et coniura super
eam[j] cum ista coniuracione:

> Venite, Cya, Mutaron, Sathauel,[k] angeli commissi sigillo Saturni Stigis[l] quod in hac hora in
> adiutorium michi, et precipite spiritibus Amamni[m] et Astaba, Hertanalit,[n] vt venia[n]t cito,
> meum completum[o] mandatum, per nomen domini benedictum Albilfael, Fiel, Ignaborum,
> Yada, Yaffla, Tasagaf, Hyaalym, Anagodyny, [91r] Dymas, Anazana, Salodaya, Athym,
> Adyr, Elsyday, Adaptinor, Sabath, Adoray, Eloym, Eloe, Gna, Cithe, Sereaye, Alssylayessus,
> Agnibora,[p] Osatietas, angelorum Cassie, Mittaron, Satquiel, precipite me Mira et Affla, et
> Alualuaht, Sayp, Aladep, vt idem meam compleant voluntatem per[q] sanctitatem coniuracionis
> huius, quam super vos scripsi.

37r. Summary

Cvm operare volueris, accipe semper tempus, siue de die siue de nocte, cum
nominibus angelorum mandancium tempus in quo operaberis, et nomen rei, et
ibi sunt nomina supradictorum angelorum mandancium tempus, que[a] scribere
debes in primo tempore et in 2o tempore et in 3o et 4o, et eciam nomina
signorum eius, sicut ibi iacet, in quolibet tempore suo, et isti sunt angeli cerciores

---

h   *Meaning* virginea?
i   *Meaning* ponas?
j   *MS* eas.
k   Sic *in MS?*
l   *I.e., Saturn (the spirit) of Styx.*
m   Sic *in MS?*
n   Sic *in MS?*
o   Sic *in MS.*
p   *Followed in MS by* Osan (?), *struck through.*
q   *MS* pre.
a   *MS* qui.

et meliores, secundum librum quendam illi quod dedit, uidetis et quod[b] vocas principes xij mensium, vt sequitur infra, et loco istorum nominabis et pones istos supradictos. Nota quod sicut supradicti angeli sunt nominandi, sicut eciam nomina dierum in quo operaberis,[c] sicut continentur in capitulo quod incipit, 'Conplete sunt vij signa dierum'. Ista sunt dicta Iudei.[d]

Nota quod isti sunt principes angelorum xij [91v] mensium, qui dominantur in suis thronis in quinto celo, qui habe[n]t thronos 4or. Primus thronus est in parte orientali, in quo dominantur tres angeli qui sunt principles. Secundus thronus est in parte occidentali, et ibi dominantur alij 3es angeli et principes. Tercius thronus est in parte septentrionali, et ibi dominantur 3es alij angeli, vt infra statim melius declarabitur.

Nota quod semper vni throno[e] deseruiunt tres menses, et vnum tempus, vt infra patebit. Primus ergo angelus est princeps, qui est in primo throno et in parte orientali, dominatur primo tempore et mense primo, et iste vocatur Aysansasyel, et iste et[f] alij principes supradicti[g] habent plures alios seruientes eis[h] et obedientibus eorum imperiis ornare quilibet princeps dominus est invocandus et nominandus secundum tempus et ordinem suum cum suis seruitoribus, et imo iste primus angelus concordat cum primo tempore et mense, et secundus[i] [sic] cum 2o, et 3us cum 3o, 4us cum 4o, et sic de aliis.

Primum tempus:[j]

2o mense regnat et dominatur princeps Ragiel cum suis seruitoribus.

3o mense regnat et dominatur princeps Dyrnaot cum suis seruitoribus.

[92r] Secundum tempus:[k]

4o mense regnat et seruit princeps Tanenon cum suis seruitoribus.

Quinto mense regnat et dominatur[l] princeps Terogat cum suis seruitoribus.

Sexto mense regnat et dominatur princeps Morel cum suis seruitoribus.

3m tempus:[m]

---

b   *This passage appears confused.*

c   Sic *in MS.*

d   Sic *in MS?*

e   *MS* throni.

f   et *added above line in MS.*

g   *MS* supradicte.

h   *MS* eius.

i   *MS* secundo.

j   *Written on right side of page.*

k   *Written on right side of page.*

l   *Followed in MS by* Terogat, *struck through.*

m   *Written on right side of page.*

Septimo mense regnat et dominatur princeps Patderon cum suis seruitoribus.

Octauo mense regnat et dominatur princeps Illdegage cum suis seruitoribus.

Nono mense regnat et dominatur princeps Andegor cum suis seruitoribus.

4m tempus:[n]

Decimo mense regnat et dominatur princeps Macgmel cum suis seruitoribus.

Vndecimo mense regnat et dominatur princeps Assandaran cum suis seruitoribus.

Duodecimo mense regnat et dominatur princeps[o] Abarthiel cum suis seruitoribus.

Nota eciam quod sicut mensium sunt nominandi sic eciam nomina dierum sunt in quo operaberis, quorum nomina sunt: Prima enim dies dominica[p] vocatur Metraton. Et 2a Yaspel, Tercia Geminiel. 4a Gabriel. 5a Michael. 6a Raphael. 7a Sarphiel uel Captiel, vt scribitur in sacra scriptura. Distingwe tempora et concordabis scripturis,[q] et ideo primo distingwenda sunt tempora et cognoscenda, [92v] et 2o in quolibet opere quod operare volueris si vis opus tuum perficere et vt posses tempora disti[n]gwere et cognoscere, scias quod primum tempus cum fiunt 4or tempora incipit a medio Marcij et finitur in medio Junij, et menses[r] Aprilis et Maij sunt in medio, et sunt de primo tempore, et[s] sic continentur ad tale signum.[t]

Et cum tempus summum[u] continentur 3es menses supradicti, 3es menses et eorum principes, possunt eis adaptari et coniungi et cum eis nominari et invocari quo ad primum tempus, quia sunt primo tempore orientali et in primo throno orientali.

Cvm eciam secundum tempus contineat 3es menses et eorum principes presente 2o tempore adaptari, nominari, et [in]vocari, cum sunt dicitur[v] tempore occidentali et throno occidentali.

Cvm eciam 3m tempus continet 3es menses et eorum principes, possunt 3o tempore adaptari nominari et invocari, cum eciam sunt de 3o tempore et throno meridionali.

Cvm 4m tempus eciam continet 3es menses et suos principes presunt [p͡nt] 4o

n   *Written on right side of page.*

o   *Followed in MS by* Abra, *struck through.*

p   *MS* dominice.

q   *Followed in MS by an extraneous* et, *struck through.*

r   *MS* mensis.

s   *MS* etc.

t   Sic *in MS.*

u   Sic *in MS.*

v   *This passage appears confused.*

tempore[w] adaptari et nominari et invocari cum sunt de 4o tempore et throno septentrionali, ad tale signum invenies angelos cerciores et meliores, qui habent concordare cum 4or temporibus.

Cvm volueris coniurare seu cartham scribere vel nomina invocare, dic nomina angelorum [93r] dominancium tempore et mensi et altitudini qua facies opus. Prima enim altitudo mensis est Nysan, 2a est Yar, et sic de aliis, quod si operatus fueris ad bonas[x] vel ad bonum, narrabis angelos bonos, et si ad malum malos, et sic facies in omnibus que volueris operari, et ita complebitur opus tuum, et probatum libri doctrina est vera et cetera.[y]

Cvm eciam oporteat te nominare nomina Solis et signorum et Lune et terre et parcium 4or mundi, et cum nomina Solis sunt 4or et 4or sunt[z] tempora, concordabit primum cum primo, atque nominabis et invocabis, et secundum cum 2o, et 3m cum 3o, et 4m cum 4o. Et cum sint 3a nomina signorum eius in quolibet tempore, facies idem. Et cum sint eciam 4or nomina Lune concordabis cum predictis et nominabis primum cum primo tempore, et secundum cum 2o, et 3m cum 3o, 4m cum 4o. Et cum eciam sint 4or nomina terre quod eciam oportet te nominare, facies eciam quod primum nominabis cum primis et secundum cum 2is, et 3m cum 3is, et 4m cum 4is, sic[ut] habetur superius in capitulo. Dicere oportet et ita facies de 4or nominibus quod terra signabit [sigibt] aliter ibi in fine dicti capituli.[a] Et eciam oportet te nominare 4or partes[b] mundi, videlicet orientis, occidentis, et meridiei, et septentrionis, et cum quolibet istorum habeat 4or nomina secundum tempus suum, primum nominabis et invocabis cum primis, secundum cum 2o, [93v] 3m cum 3o, 4m cum 4o, et sic de aliis.

Et auertas quod sigillum et signum diei scribatur seu depingatur dies et hora est in qua debes opus tuum facere seu incipere, quia magna virtus est in eis, quare cum eis complebunt opera tua, et nomina angelorum regnancium in diebus septimane dicenda sunt, et sequitur que nomina habet[c] nominare in operibus septimane secundum diem suum.

Angelus diei dominici est Raphael, et si operatus fueris in die dominico istum nominabis et [in]vocabis, et sic de omnibus aliis, vt continetur in supradicto capitulo completa, etc. In omni igitur opere nominabis angelum diei in quo

---

w   *MS* tempori.

x   Sic *in MS.*

y   *Meaning* certa?

z   *Changed in margin to* sint.

a   *MS* capitulum.

b   *MS* parcium.

c   *Meaning* habes?

facies opus, et scribe illud, quia si fuerit inscripto,[d] quia multum iuuabit te cum potencia creatoris.

Regum eciam spirituum vij diebus septimane regnancium nomina subscribentur, seu omnes angelos dominantes diei quo facies opus, et sic veniunt et complebunt voluntatem tuam, [et] respondebunt tibi in omnibus que quesieris.

Diei ergo dominico regnat et seruit Baytan rex, coadiutores sui sunt Caatus, Candas, Vambal, et sic de aliis, vt ibi invenies.

Nota eciam quod quilibet dies septimane habet suffumigium suum sibi a[p]propriatum, cum quo [94r] suffumigari oportet opus quod facies in ea, et complebitur opus tuum sine dubio. Suffumigium diei dominice est assandalis croceum uel rubeum vel sibi simile, et sic de aliis, vt ibidem continetur, et eciam ibi subsequentur[e] invenies qualia opera facere debes in quolibet die.

Nota quod eciam oportet te scribere nomina horarum die[i] quibus quidem horis perfic[i]entur opera que facies. Prima ergo diei hora dicitur Yayn. In hac hora facienda est cartha ad destruendas[f] voces hominum et mala verba eorum, et li[n]gwas ligandas, et sic invenies ibi de aliis horis, tam diurnis quam nocturnis.

Nota eciam quod cum aliquod opus aut cartham scribere volueris, nomen hore et nomen domini hore, id est angeli qui ei dominatur uel ministrat, oportet te nominare. Vnde hec sunt nomina angelorum dominancium omnibus horis diei septimane. Prima enim hora diei dominatur Raphael, et sic de alijs que ibi invenies quo ad idem, et sic eciam est de nocte. Vnde nocte diei Lune prima hora dominatur Sarquiel, et sic eciam de aliis, vt ibi invenies, etc.

Nota eciam quod sic est de omnibus horis supradictis, ita eciam est et intelligere debis, quod quidam angeli dominantur uel ministrant horis secundum dominacionem planetarum uel ministracionem in eis. Omni enim hora Solis dominatur uel ministrat Raphael, et sic de aliis, vt ibi invenies, etc.

[94v] Nota eciam diligenter de concordia, quod eciam habens,[g] debes facere de omnibus supradictis, et coniunccione eorum est regula talis. Diei eciam cuilibet planete cum angelis suis signaque planetarum distributa horum angelorum nomina debent concordare et respondere nominibus et capitulis supra scriptis, et angelo qui[h] continetur in coniuracionibus cuiuslibet diei, vt supra in capitulis de ymaginibus dierum quibus ministrant adinvicem diei, ergo dominico ministrat Sol, et angelus eius est Raphael, eiusque signum est Leo, et sic de aliis, vt ibi invenies.

---

d   Sic *in MS.*

e   *Meaning* subsequenter?

f   *MS* destruandas.

g   *Followed in MS by* de, *struck through.*

h   *MS* que.

Omnia predicta oportet te seruare quandocumque volueris operare secundum istum librum, et in aliquo deficere non posses, quia hec per ordinem invenies quomodo et qualiter habere te debes, et opus tuum secundum istum librum facias et nichil dimittas, si non vis errare, et primo semper respicere mensem lunarem, quia mensis lunaris dierum alij boni sunt, alij sunt mali, vt habetur supra in libro isto, et ideo regula est talis, quod quocumque die septimane operare volueris ad quo[d]libet bonum siue malum facere vis, attende diligenter, quod illa dies sit operi fiendo respiciendo mensem lunarem, vt dictum est. Et si illa dies sit bona et conueniens, non dimittas opus tuum de die in diem, uel differas, quare quia[i] opus tuum non veniret ad effectum, et forsitan putares illud esse falsum.

[95r] Avertas eciam diligenter quod in principio vnius cuiusque tui operis debes scribere nomina que respondebunt voluntati tue, et sunt hec nomina ex nominibus creatoris. Cum igitur illa nomina altissima nominare volueris, flexis genibus humiliter, invocabis sic:

Invoco et humiliter supplico vobis nomina altissima dei, vt nos adiuuetis in opere tali, ad complendum, ad perficiendum:[j] Agnas, Yana, dei Israhel, Ybat, Suliat, Gnalas, Yemssamon, Haa, Dosa, Barian, Barian, etc.[k]

Inuoco et appello te, Captiel, angele qui es[l] prepositus diei[m] septimo, qui es dies sabbati, quod pro me labores[n] et [non] desistas donec totum meum effectum et desiderium ad[o] effectum perducas. Rex Mayron, Assayby, invoco te et appello et tuos adiutores Abymalib et Haybaly, Dot et Yfla, quod pro me laboretis et non desistetis donec totum meum affectum et desiderium compleuerit[is].

Vos[p] angeli qui presidetis diei sabbati, Captiel, Mataton, Sarquiel, id est Satraquiel, invoco et appello vos vt pro me laboretis et non deficiatis donec totum meum affectum compleueritis. O sanctissima nomina dei, Agmas,[q] Yana, dei Israel, Ydar, Subar, Gnabas, Yemssamon, Haa, Dosa, Ba- [95v] *rian,[r] invoco vos et requiro toto corde et ore vt dignemini me exaudire et adiuuare, et totum meum desiderium complere, vt valeam videre mille armatos in meo seruicio.*

Cyayn, prima hora diei invoco te vt adiuues me, vt facias me videre predictos spiritus

---

i   Sic *in MS.*

j   *Followed in MS by* Agnas, Yna, Yana, dei Israel, Ybat, Subat, *struck through.*

k   *Pointing hand drawn in margin, with inscription* Nota nomina.

l   *MS* est.

m   *MS* dei.

n   *MS* laboras.

o   *Followed in MS by blot.*

p   *MS* Quos.

q   *Or* Aginas?

r   *Second pointing hand shown in margin of fol. 95[r].*

armatos, et te eciam, Yan, oportet, que es^s 2a hora, et te eciam, 3a hora Dasura, et te eciam, 4a hora, Sala.

Invoco eciam et appello angelos dominantes predictis horis, Raphael, 2o Anael, 3o Michael, 4o Gabriel. Invoco eciam Saturnum et eius angelum Captielem, et eius signum Capricornum et Aquarium, et suum sigillum quod est hoc quod hic pono,^t vt me adiuuent et faciant michi apparere predictos spiritus armator in meo seruicio.

Terra, que^u in 4o tempore vocaris^v Yemat vel Yaneaa, invoco te et appello, vt tu adiuues me et facias apparere predictos spiritus armatos in meo seruicio. O nomina angelorum qui seruitis 4o tempore, Amabel, Terayl, Atrarayl, invoco vos et appello, vt faciatis michi [96r] venire spiritus in forma militum armatos in meo seruicio. O angeli fortes, Castiel, Matraton, Fatael, invoco vos vt meum desiderium compleatis et predictos spiritos venire faciatis. Et vos ventos, Genuum, Altibayn, Aflas,^w Analuabet,^x venite Eya, Mittaton, Sathane, uel angeli promissi, sigillo Saturni, sitisque in hac hora in adiutorium michi, et precipite spiritibus Amamim^y et Astabam et Hactanaabit, vt veniant cito meum comple^z mandatum, per nomen benedictum Abilfaelfiel, Anogodym, Dymaon, Ana, Ana, Saoday, Athym, Adyr, Essiday, A, Daymior, Sabat, Adonay, Eloym, Eloe, Gna, Cythe, Seredye, Assylla, Yssessus, Agnabora. O societas^a angelorum, Cassie, Matraton, Satquiel, precipite me Mira et Affla et Abralualit, Sayp, Aladep,^b vt iam meam compleatis voluntatem, per sanctitatem coniuracionis huius, et per coniuracionem quam super vos feci. O Tomitat, nomen Solis in 4o tempore, invoco te vt tu adiuues ad faciendum venire supradictos spiritus in forma militum in seruicio meo. O nomina signorum 4ti temporis, invoco vos vt adiuuetis me quod supradicti spiritus venient in meo seruicio, Capricornus, Aquarius, et Pisces. O Saarlaquia, nomen Lune in 4o tempore, rogo te et invoco vt tu adiuues me, quod fa- [96v] cies venire supradictos spiritus in forma militum in meo seruicio. O Safaten, nomen celorum in 4o tempore, rogo te et invoco vt tu adiuues me, quod facias venire supradictos spiritus in forma militum in meo seruicio. O nomina 4or parcium^c mundi, Orientis Pedyoth, Malchaam,^d Mendie, Danoe, Septentrionis Yamhor, vos invoco et rogo vt vos adiuuetis me et faciatis venire supradictos spiritus in forma militum in servicio meo.

---

s   *MS* est.

t   *Followed in MS by three signs, given next to each other across the page.*

u   *MS* quod.

v   s *struck through in MS?*

w   Sic *in MS?*

x   Sic *in MS?*

y   Sic *in MS?*

z   Sic *in MS.*

a   *Followed in MS by* ange, *struck through.*

b   Sic *in MS? Third letter is blotted out.*

c   *MS* temporum.

d   Sic *in MS?*

NO. 38. FOR OBTAINING INFORMATION ABOUT A THEFT
BY GAZING INTO A FINGERNAIL (FOLS 96v–99v)[a]

Accipe puerum virgineum de legittimo thoro, et socios quos tibi placuerint, et vadas ad locum secretum, et facias circulos 3es cum gladio. Ad primum dic, *In nomine Patris et Filij et Spiritus Sancti.* Ad secundum dic, *In nomine indiuidue trinitatis, Alpha et O, deus et homo.* Ad 3m dic, *Ego te facio per illum qui creauit celum et terram, mare et omnia que in eis sunt.*[b]

Hoc finito, fac quod vnusquisque habeat gladium suum, et non minus 4or gladiis extractis, et accipe sedem tripedem, et pone inferiorem circulum, et scribas [97r] nomen pueri ad sedem, et benedic puerum per hanc benediccionem, circu[i]endo per caput eius cum gladio, dicens,

Crux Christi tecum. Crux Christi est quam semper adoro. Crux Christi est vera salus. Crux Christi soluit vinculum mortis. Crux Christi est invincibilis per arma. Crux Christi est mobile signum. Crux Christi superat omne malum.

Et da[c] puero gladium tenere ad manus, et fac illi crucem ad frontem, dicendo,

Crux sancta sanctificet[d] te et omnes oraciones sacerdotum benedicant te.

Et fac puerum sedere ad sedem, et radas sibi vngwem cum cultello, et vnge sibi vngwem cum oleo oliue, et tunc benedicas socios tuos, semper vnum post alium, et te ipsum cum predicta benediccione, sicut tu puerum benedixisti. Et facias eos sedere, vnum post alium, ad inferiorem circulum, et da vnicuique gladium suum tenere ad manum, et facias eos habere silencium, et fac puerum cla[u]dere oculos, et benedic puerum et te ipsum et omnes socios tuos per inicium sancti ewangelij secundum Johannem: *In principio erat verbum, et verbum erat aput deum, etc.* [Jn 1:1].

Hoc finito, fac puerum inspicere vngwem quousque se reuertat et ipse coniurare,

Vmon, Progemon, Mithiomo, Pist, Vralchim, Althes, Panite, Fabar, Thobar, Cormes,

---

a   *This experiment begins a section that is labelled on fol. 96v as follows:* Incipiunt experimenta verissima et probata: Incipiunt experimenta verissima et probata, primum ad omnia indaganda que volueris, siue presencia, siue preterita, siue futura, etc.

b   *Cf. Ps. 145:6 Vulg.*

c   *MS* dat.

d   *MS* sanctificat.

Felsmes, Diles, Dilia, Dies, Onaris, coniuro vos demones prenominatos, per hec nomina sancta, On, Ton, [97v] Gon, Ron, Apt,ᵉ Galapt,ᶠ Ivs,ᵍ Calens, Timel, vt citissime iam nullam requiem habeatis, nec in celo nec sub celo, nec in terra nec sub terra, nec in pluuiis nec in ventis, nec in nubibus nec in aeribus, nec in ignibus nec in aquis, nec in abissis nec in arundinibus, nec in ponisʰ nec in aliis quibus[cumque] locis, nisi furem cum furto isto puero ostendensⁱ vngwem istius pueri virginei oleo linito crescere, clarescere, tanta latitudinis apparere, vt poterit euidenter videre in eo furem et furtum factum nobis ablatum, et locum vbi adhuc latet,ʲ et quicumque cum ipso furto actum.

Tunc sibyla ter. Ad primum dic, *O domineᵏ Ihesu Christe.* Ad secundum dic, *O deus fortis.* Ad 3m dic, *O potestas.*

Hoc finito, dic coniuracionem:

Coniuro vos, principes omnium demoniorum, Astaroth, Belzebub, Berit, Fornicator, Temptator, et Seductor, Possessor hominum, Natheus, Molbet.ˡ Precipio vobis vt vestrum vnus in forma nigra veniat vt iste puer possit eum euidenter videre in sua vngwe.

Hoc finito, queras a puero si videt latitudinem at altitudinem in suo vngwe. Si non, dimittas formam nigram et incipe predictam coniuracionem vsque quod videbit omnia.ᵐ Tunc facias venire sicut prius posui, eciam precipias ipsis per hec nomina:

El, Eloy, Elyon, Aloe, Sappa, Sother, Emanuel, Tetragramaton, Saday, Luamay, Athanatos, Ysos, Kyrie, Primogenitus, Vita, Finis, Via, Flos, Fons, Ve- [98r] *ritas, Sapiencia, Virtus, Paraclitus, Ego sum qui sum, Mediator, Agnus, Ouis, Vitulus, Serpens, Aries, Leo, Os, Verbum, Ianua, Ymago, Gloria, Lux, Sol, Splendor, Lapis angularis, Sponsus, Pastor, Propheta, Sacerdos, Immortalis, Lex, Rex, Christus, Pater, Filius, Spiritus Sanctus, Agla, Petra, Eternitas, Neon, Burnon, Parli, Caon, Aepton, Alpha et O, Omnipotens, Misericors, Caritas, Eternus Creator et Redemptor, Primus et Nouissimus, Dator et Receptor, Ayos, Otheos, Yschyros, Sanctus Deus, Fortis et Paciens, Iustus Iudex in vltimo die. Per ista lxxija*

---

e   Sic *in MS?*

f   Sic *in MS?*

g   Sic *in MS?*

h   *Meaning* pontibus*?*

i   *MS* ostendans.

j   *MS* iatet.

k   *Followed in MS by first stroke of an* x, *struck through.*

l   Sic *in MS?*

m   omnia, *written in margin of MS, probably belongs here.*

nomina Christi precipio vobis vt michi sitis obedientes et isto puero virgineo de qua re et de qua interrogacione quod factum est [nichil] retineatis, quod verum est numeretis et dicatis.

Hoc finito, queras si videt demonem saltantem et gaudentem. Tunc dic ad puerum, et facias ad socios tuos simul loqui quod puer non habeat timorem. Hoc finito, incipe coniurare et fac istum recedere et furem cum furto minare:[n]

Coniuro vos, prenominatos demones,
- *per istum qui creauit celum et terram et omnia que in eis sunt,*
- *et per istum qui nos et vos creauit et nos redemit cum suo precioso sangwine,*
- *et per istum qui venturus est,*
- *per Patrem et Filium et Spiritum Sanctum,*
- *et per sanctam obedienciam,*
- *et per corpus domini nostri Ihesu Christi, qui hodie et cottidie celebratur per vniuersum mundum,*
- *et per sanctam trinitatem,*
- *per deitatem,*
- *[98v] per humanitatem,*
- *per deum verum,*
- *per deum viuum,*
- *per deum sanctum,*
- *per deum omnipotentem,*
- *per sanctam Mariam, matrem domini nostri Ihesu Christi,*
- *per eius vnicum filium,*
- *et per tremendum diem iudicij,*
- *per resurrex[i]onem omnium mortuorum,*

vt recedas et furem cum furto [et] loco, cui adducas, vt iste puer euidenter possit videre furem cum furto N.

Non[o] dicas aliam coniuracionem:

Coniuro vos, prenominatos demones,
- *per annunciacionem domini nostri Ihesu Christi,*
- *per sacrum ieiunium domini nostri Ihesu Christi,*
- *per baptismum domini nostri Ihesu Christi,*
- *per temptacionem domini nostri Ihesu Christi,*
- *per passionem domini nostri Ihesu Christi,*

n   *Presumably for* minari.
o   *Meaning* nunc?

- *per milia sex wlnera domini nostri Ihesu Christi,*
- *per centum sex wlnera domini nostri Ihesu Christi,*
- *per quinquaginta sex wlnera domini nostri Ihesu Christi, sine alijs de capite vsque ad plantas,*
- *per spineam coronam quam in capite domini nostri Ihesu Christi posuerunt et genua flectebant [et] illudebant sibi, dicentes, 'Aue rex Iudeorum',*
- *per arundinem et alapas, quibus Christum cedebant,*
- *et per 3es clauos,*
- *per lanceam qua sacratum corpus domini nostri Ihesu Christi perforatum est dum continuo exiuit sa[n]gwis et aqua,*
- *per emissionem sue sanctitatis domini nostri Ihesu Christi, 'In manus tuas commendo spiritum meum',*
- *per anxietatem quam beata virgo Maria, mater domini nostri Ihesu Christi, habuit dum vidit filium eius pendentem in cruce, dicens, 'Flecte ramos, arbor alta,' et non secundum quod compositum est ex 4or litteris, scilicet Alpha et O, deus et homo factus.*[p]

Coniuro vos prenominatos demones

- *per omnes sanctos angelos, thronos, et dominaciones, principatus, potestates, virtutes celorum, cherubin et seraphin, qui non cessant* [99r] *clamare, dicen[te]s, 'Sanctus, sanctus, sanctus',*
- *et per virtutem domini nostri Ihesu Christi, scilicet propter nos homines descendit de celis et natus ext ex Maria virgine, sub Poncio Pylato passus est,*
- *et per 3es angelos, scilicet Michael, Gabriel, [et] Raphael,*
- *et per dominicam oracionem, scilicet Pater noster,*
- *per vij candelabra que in manibus angelorum odoriferum,*
- *per eorum miracula deo beneplacita, qui sunt sub christiana.*[q]

Hoc finito, queras a puero si videt. Si non, tunc dic hanc coniuracionem:

Coniuro vos, prenominati demones,
- *per 4or ewangelistas, Lucam, Marcum, Matheum, Johannem,*
- *per 4or sermones,*
- *per xij apostolos,*
- *per 3es magos, scilicet Caspar, Balthasar, [et] Melchior,*
- *per patriarchas [et] prophetas,*
- *per martires et confessores,*
- *et per omnes papas Romanorum, et omnes virgines et viduas,*

---

p   Sic *in MS.*

q   Sic *in MS.*

- *et per omnes episcopos,*
- *et per omnes abbates,*
- *per omnes priores,*
- *per omnes preponitos,*
- *per omnes archidiaconos,*
- *et per omnes deconos,*
- *per omnes monachos,*
- *per omnes moniales,*
- *per omnes sacerdotes,*
- *per omnes dyaconos et subdyaconos,*
- *per omnes sanctos dei,*
- *per merita omnium sanctorum,*
- *per omnem populum Christianorum,*
- *et per omnes sanctos qui sunt in celo et in tera,*
- *et per centum et^r xliiij milia innocentum qui non sunt loquentes loqui in puericia, passi sunt supplicia,*
- *per omnes karacteres Salomonis,*
- *per sapienciam suam,*
- *per omnia experimenta Virgilij,*
- *per celum et terram,*
- *per mare,*
- *per omnia que in eis sunt,*
- *per omnes Cesares,*
- *per omnes* [99v] *reges,*
- *per omnes principes,*
- *per comites,*
- *per omnes milites,*
- *per omnes ciues.*

Hoc finito, queras si videt furem cum furto et si venisti ad finem. Tunc terge puero vngwem tunica tua, et accipias vnugla[m] pueri,^s et benedicas puerum tali modo, faciendo crucem cum gladio ad 4or partes corporis sui, dicendo, *Pater, Filius, Spiritus Sanctus, sancti,^t custodiant te.* Et fac puerum gladium recipere ante se, et exire de circulo, et omnibus sociis tuis ita facies et tibi.

r   *Followed in MS by* l, *struck through.*

s   *MS* domini.

t   Sic *in MS.*

NO. 39. FOR OBTAINING INFORMATION
BY GAZING INTO A FINGERNAIL (FOLS 99v–103r)

Incipit secundum [experimentum] bonum et probatum.[a]

[100r] Accipe puerum virginem de legittimo thoro, et fac 3es circulos. Ad primum circulum dic, *In nomine Patris et Filij et Spiritus Sancti.* Ad secundum dic psalmum *Celi enarrant.*[b] Ad 3m dic *Deus tuum regi da.*[c] Post hec,[d] accipe sedem tripedem quercinium, et subtus scribe nomen pueri, et sub pedibus pueri scribatur hoc nomen Tetragramaton, et ponantur desuper duo lapides, ne puer tangat nomen pedibus. Postea scribe in manubrio cultelli et nomen pueri et hec nomina: Istath, Hoaz, Abays, Fastich; et in pollice scribe Alpha et O. Deinde rada vngwem dextri pollicis[e] cultello, cuius manubrium sit factum de cornu nigro uel albo.

Deinde dic, *Domine, secundum peccata, etc.*[f] Postea fac crucem ✠ tali modo in fronte pueri, dicens, *Tu qui es Alpha et O, fac verum dicere puerum virginem istum, N., qui est creatura tua. In nomine Patris et Filij et Spiritus Sancti.* Et dic, *Domine Ihesu, fili dei viui, qui pro nobis peccatoribus de synu Patris descendisti ad terram, ostende nobis veritatem. Amen.* Deinde susurra puero ad aurem dextram, *Sathan, Belzebub, Astaroth, Berith, Azraro, Rotunda;* hec[g] dic ter.

Deinde intra circulos et pone te contra faciem pueri, et tunc lineas vngwem pueri rasum cum oleo oliue, et da puero cultellum ad manum, et dic,

Abgo, Safrit, Bos, Zelentes, Vm, Vom, Motmyo, Thitodens,[h] Gemitias,[i] Gana, Vresius, Pharachte, Foliath, Gebath, Dyrus, [100v] *Virus, Vnyrus, Peamde, Febat, Gebat, Tyros, Vijas,[j] Nubar, Azathi, coniuro vos prenominatos demones*

---

a *This line is given twice; between the two occurrences is the following figure: a triple circlar band, with the inscription* In nomine Patris et Filij et Spiritus Sancti *in the outermost band;* In nomine indiuidue trinitatis, Alpha et O, deus et homo *in the middle band, and* Ego te facio per illum qui creauit celum et terram, mare et omnia que in eis sunt *in the innermost band.*

b *Ps. 18 Vulg.*

c *Cf. Ps. 71:2 Vulg.* (deus, iudicium tuum regi da). *Figure at top of fol. 103^r: a triple circular band, with* In nomine Patris et Filij et Spiritus Sancti *in the outer band,* Celi enarrant *in the middle band, and* Deus tuum *[sic]* regi da *in the innermost.*

d *Or* hoc.

e *Followed in MS by* cuius.

f *Cf. Ps. 102:10 Vulg.* (non secundum peccata nostra fecit nobis) *and Ps. 118:65 Vulg.* (Domine, secundum verbum tuum).

g *Or* hoc.

h *Or* Chitodens.

i Sic *in MS?*

j Sic *in MS?*

- *per Patrem et Filium et Spiritum Sanctum,*
- *per deum omnipotentem,*
- *per Ihesum Christum filium eius,*
- *et per trinitatem illius,*
- *et per ipsam prouidenciam quam deus in mente habuit prius quam mundus fieret,*

[vt] obediatis imperio meo, non per virtutem meam sed per virtutem magestatis omnipotentis dei. Coniuro et contestor vos demones

- *per sapienciam eternitatis dei, qua celum supra stare fecit, terram autem deorsum fundauit et perfecit, elementorum que^k in opus mundi connexit,*
- *et per prudenciam qua deus lucem a tenebris separauit et vtrumque creauit,*

vt arte et magisterio, a magistro vestro Astaroth vobis concessa, vngwem huius pueri, N., oleo linitum, crescere et clarescere faciatis et procreare latitudinem, vt apparere possit euidenter et videre in eo furem et furtum nobis ablatum, et^l locum de quo ablatum est, et in quem locum translatum est, et vbi adhuc positum est, et quidquid ex ipso furto^m actum est. Item adiuro vos prenominatos demones

- *per verbum dei, quo celum et terram creauit et herbam virentem in ea genere suo, solem et lunam et stellas et signum et tempora, fulgura et tonitrua, voces,^{n} et omnia quecumque sint in terra, mare, et inferno,*

vt arte, etc. Item coniuro vos prenominatos demones

- *per annunciacionem,*
- *per natiuitatem,*
- *per circumcisionem,*
- *per baptismum Christi,*
- *et per omnia que fecit Ihesus in Chana Galylee quando conuertit aquam et vinum,*

[101r] ut arte, etc. Item coniuro vos prenominatos demones

- *per ieiunium Christi,*
- *et per istum gressum quando in Monte Oliuete ascendere voluerit adorandum Patrem, dicendo, 'Pater, si fieri potest, transeat a me calix iste';^{o}*
- *et per sudorem sa[n]gwineum Ihesu Christi, qui de suo corpore emanauit pro nobis peccatoribus,*
- *et per omnia archana secretorum,*
- *per sa[n]gwineas guttas sudoris Christi,*
- *per solem obscuratum,*
- *per lunam conuersam in sa[n]gwinem et terribilem clamorem Christi pendentis in ligno crucis,*

k   *MS* quos.

l   *Followed in MS by* in.

m   *MS* furtu.

n   *MS* tunitrua.

o   *Cf. Matt. 26:39.*

- *per sup[p]licium mortis,*
- *et per emissionem sui sanctissimi spiritus,*
- *et per istam virtutem qua velum templi cissum est, et inquinamenta aperta sunt,*
- *et per misterium sacri sepulchri,*
- *et per virtutem dei,*
- *et per dispositionem[p] diuine ordinacionis,*
- *et per[q] dominum nostrum Ihesum Christum, quem adoramus, crucifixum, passum, et sepultum credimus, et scimus resurrexisse et [in] celos ascendisse confitemus,*

vt arte, etc. Coniuro vos prenominatos demones

- *per celum et terram, mare et omnia que in eis sunt;*
- *et per omnia que concludunt 4or partes mundi,*
- *et per serpencia et volatilia celi, bipedia, tripedia, [et] quadrupedia,*
- *et per omnes aereas potestates, vt arte (vt supra).*

Item coniuro vos prenominatos demones

- *per angelos et archangelos, per thronos et dominaciones, principatus et potestates, per virtutes celorum, per cherubin et seraphin,*
- *et per diuinum officium miseracionis,*
- *et per eos qui prosunt,*
- *et per omnia [101v] que subiecta sunt omnipotenti deo,*
- *et[r] per ipsum omnipotentem deum qui ex nichilo creauit cuncta [et] ad laudem et ad gloriam nominis sui fecit,*

vt arte, etc. Coniuro vos prenominatos demones

- *per v secula et vij etates mundi,*
- *et per tremendum diem iudicij*
- *et per lxij nomina Christi,*
- *[et per] etatem et claritatem Christi, quam habuit prius quam mundus fieret,*
- *et per centum et xliiij milia innocentum ante deum astancium,*
- *et omnes ordines ecclesiasticos,*

vt arte, etc. Coniuro vos prenominatos demones

- *per coeternam sapienciam dei, qua deus hominem creauit cum non esset, et Adam[s] ad ymaginem et similitudinem suam formauit,*

vt arte, [etc.]. Coniuro vos prenominatos demones

- *per sanctissima nomina Christi: Messyas, Sother, Emanuel, Sabaoth, Adonay, Panthon, Panthocrathon, Eloy, Theos, Hon,[t] Visio, Saluator, Alpha et O, primus et*

---

p *MS* disponsicionis.

q *Followed in MS by* Ihesum.

r *MS* vt.

s Sic *in MS?* adia – *should be a form of 'adicio', but 'adam' is required.*

t *For Greek* ho on.

nouissimus, primogenitus, principium et finis, via, veritas, et sapiencia, virtus, paraclitus, ego sum qui sum, qui es, mediator, agnus, ouis, aries, vitulus, serpens, edus, verbum, ymago, gloria, gracia, salus, lux, sal, pax, splendor, panis, fons, vitis, pastor, propheta, spes immortalis, rex, pater, omnipotens, misericors, eternus,[u] summum bonum, trinitas, vnitas, pater, El, Eloy, Eloe, Eleon, Saday, Symator, Tu, Ye, Ye, princeps pacis, Enstriel, [102r] spiritus, timor, pietas, tu, vnitas vnitatis, trina deitas,

vt arte, etc. Coniuro vos prenominatos demones

- *per fidem prophetarum,*
- *per preconia patriarcharum,*
- *per dignitatem xxiiijor seniorum,*
- *et per symbolum apostolorum,*
- *et per passionem sanctissimorum martyrum,*
- *per confessionem piorum confessorum,*
- *et per continenciam sanctarum virginum ac viduarum,*
- *et per omnes sanctos et electos dei,*
- *et per 4or ewangeliastas et eorum ewangelia,*

vt arte, etc. Coniuro vos prenominatos demones

- *per salutem omnium sanctorum, viuorum et mortuorum,*
- *et per sancta sacrificia sacerdotum,*
- *et per omnes diuinos oraciones sanctorum,*
- *et per omnia corpora sanctorum dei,*
- *et per eorum animas in statu salutis eterne,*

vt arte, etc.

Si puer non videt ad tunc,[v] dicas,

Jaspar, Balthasar, Melchior, Smoagel, Emanuel, et deus fortis, te deprecor vt ungula N. efficiatur lata et crescat et clarescat.

Ad quamlibet coniuracionem debet operans puerum interrogare si vngwis crescat. Si non, repetatur eadem coniuracio, *Jaspar, etc.*, donec videat crescentem, latam, et magnam, quousque sufficiat. Quere a puero si aliquid videat. Si[w] videt, dic statim sub ungwe hanc coniuracionem:

Lytim, cum tuis subditis Ygrim, Andyron, Vzmyas, Ytelteos, Zymens, Bylent, Baruth, precipio vobis, demones,

---

u   *Line over* u *deleted in MS.*

v   *Meaning* adhuc?

w   *MS* etc.

- *per omnipotentem deum, viuum et verum,*
- *et per tres magos Jaspar, Balthasar, [et] Melchior,*

vt veniatis, vbicumque sitis, ad visionem istius pueri, N., veris^x in specie humana, et in specie istorum qui hoc furtum perpetra- [102v] *uerunt.*

Quere a puero si aliquid videat. Si non, repetatur eadem oratio, Lytmy, donec appareant.

Ipsis autem apparentibus, dic hanc coniuracionem:

Precipio vobis, demones, per trinitatem et inseparabilem vnitatem que facta fuit super ipsum in Iordanis flumine, in^y columbe specie, quod vos ostendatis et dicetis huic puero, N., vbi acceptum uel reconditum sit hoc furtum, et in quo loco adhuc restat.

Si adhuc non prodest, dic hanc coniuracionem:

Coniuro vos demones et precipio vobis per nomen Naamay, Syy, qui Syrum de lepra mundauit, et Danielem de lacu leonum liberauit, et 3es pueros^z de camino ignis illesos abire fecit, quod vobis detis auctoritatem huic puero, N., audiendi, interrogandi, et videndi.

Post coniuracionem factam, fac puerum claudere oculos, et purga sibi vngwem, et fac crucem super eum, ante eum, [et] retro eum, et accipe sibi cultellum de manu. Postea benedic te et ipsum, et dele circulum, et exeas secure cum eo, scilicet puero. Cum autem vis exire circulum, dic, *Pax ipsi^a sit nobis et vobis.* Tunc reges recedunt ad propria regna, et dic,

Cum vos iterum^b vocauero, sitis parati obedire michi. Hoc^c vobis precipio
- *per eternum et viuum deum, qui in cruce passus [est] et ex latere eius exiuit sa[n]gwis et aqua.*

Insuper precipio vobis
- *per hostiam sanctam, per hostiam puram, per hostiam inmaculatam, qui est Ihesus Christus,*

vt cito michi tunc veniatis et omnem voluntatem meam adimpleatis. Amen. Etc.

---

x *Meaning* venientes*?*

y *MS* eciam.

z *MS* puero.

a *Meaning* Christi*?*

b *Followed in MS by* vobi, *deleted.*

c *Or* hec.

NO. 40. FOR OBTAINING INFORMATION ABOUT A THEFT
BY GAZING INTO A FINGERNAIL (FOLS 103r–105v)

Experimentum verum de furto et probatum.

In ortu solis fac 3es circulos, et crucem in medietate circulorum,[a] et fac tibi porrigere sedem tripedem de quercu et cultellum cum manubrio albo et linito cum oleo oliue. Hoc facto, scribe diuisim hec[b] xxiijor nomina; sunt 4or literas uel lapides parum latos et 3es literas pone subtus sedem et vnam subtus pedem[c] pueri, et ipsa omnia nomina subscripta [103v] scribe super vnam literam, quam pones super caput pueri. Hoc facto, tolle puerum ad circulos et loca puerum super sedem. Vertas sibi faciem contra orientem, et scabe puero ambas ungwes pollicis, et pone sibi vnum pollicem super alium, et scribe super manubrium nomen pueri et Astaroth, et des puero cultellum ad manus, ita quod cultellus sit subtus pollices. Hoc facto, vnge puero ungwem superiorem cum oleo oliue ad modum crucis, in omni pietate electa, vt illictis et districtis appareatis in vngwe istius pueri, N. Tu vero sede super sedem qualemcumque volueris, et tu tene puerum inter genua, et dic vt diligenter inspiciat ad vngwem. Hoc facto, caues ne aliquas operaciones habeas sextis aut sabbatis diebus.

Hec sunt nomina que scribi debent: in nomine Progeneri, Mutimo, Possunt, Thomopest, Vtany, Votanes, Filij, Fibos, Fibet, Baruth, Sachith, Propiietas, Voltam, Panyte, Farum, Farum, Farum, Cubarum, Crutines, Tyrygel, Dyrus, Formys, Fembusalk, Berith, Sathanas.

Incipe coniuracionem:

Coniuro vos, demones,
- *per Patrem et Filium et Spiritum Sanctam,*
- *et per incarnacionem domini nostri Ihesu Christi,*

---

a   *Figure at bottom of fol. 105ᵉ: a triple circular band, with a cross dividing the interior into four wedges. The outermost circle has the inscription,* ✠ Hunc circulum facio in nomine Patris omnipotentis dei, qui solo verbo cuncta creauit. Dextera domini fecit virtutem, dextera domini exaltauit me, non moriar sed viuam et narrabo opera domini. Castigans ca- *(finished outside the circle:* stigauit dominus*). The middle circle bears the inscription,* ✠ Hunc circulum facio in nomine filij unigeniti dei viui, qui humanum genus proprio sangwine redemit. Dextera domini fecit virtutem, dextera domini exaltauit me, non moriar sed viuam et narrabo opera. *The innermost band contains the inscription,* ✠ Hunc circulum facio in nomine Spiritus Sancti paracliti, qui corda apostolorum et prophetarum suorum sanctissima gracia *[MS sanctissimam graciam] illustrauit. Dextera domini fecit virtutem, etc. The word onus appears at the edge of each wedge. Toward the middle are the fragments Fren, ---p'on (?), on and N.p (presumably for Nomen pueri).*

b   *Followed in MS by* nomina, *deleted.*

c   m *blotted out in MS.*

- *per baptismum Christi,*
- *per ieiunium Christi,*
- *per mortem Christi,*
- *per passionem Christi,*
- *per resurrexionem Christi,*
- *per ascensionem,*
- *per adventum Spiritus Sancti paracliti,*
- *per* [104r] *tremendum diem iudicij, in^d quo omnes estis dampnandi,*

vt appareatis in vngwe istius pueri, N., in specie furis uel furum qui rem aut res istius hominis, N., accepit; absque omni decepcione appareatis, sicut promisistis. Emogeni, Thomo, Gyton, Sertugidis,^{e} Jubutzis.

Tu qui es Alpha et O, fac verum dicere hunc puerum, N., virgineum, qui est creatura tua. Justus es,^{f} domine, et rectum iudicium tuum.^{g} In circuito tuo, domine, lumen, est et non deficiet. Nichil occultum quod non reueletur, et coopertum quod non sciatur. Domine Ihesu Christe, fili dei viui, qui propter nos peccatores de sinu Patris descendisti ad terram, ostende nobis tuam [veritatem] *et veritatem huius rei.*

Abgoth, Sanfrielis, Selentis, Vniueny, Vtimo, Geremittarum, Dydones, Rayma, Rofanes, Panyte, Fabath, Gallath, Dyrus, Fyrus, Virytus, Finibet, Arath. Coniuro vos prenominatos demones

- *per Patrem et Filium et Spiritum Sanctum, et deum omnipotentem, Ihesum Christum filium eius vnigenitum,*
- *et per deitatem ipsius,*
- *et per ipsam prouidenciam quam deus habuit prius quam mundus fieret,*

vt obediatis imperio meo. Coniuro vos prenominatos demones

- *per sapienciam dei, qua deus celum sursum stare fecit et terram deorsum fundauit, et mare in termino suo collocauit,*
- *et per virtutem qua deus confusionem elementorum in opus mundi convertit,*
- *et per* [104v] *sapienciam dei, qua deus lucem et tenebras creauit, qui diem ac noctem adunauit,*

vt arte et magisterio a magistro vestro Asef Caroth vobis concessa sicut^h sunt vt faciatis vngwem istius pueri, N., oleo linitum, crescere et clarescere et tante latitudinis comparere, quod euidenter iste puer, N., in eo videre possit furem uel fures et furtum furis nobis ablatum,

d   in *blotted out in MS.*

e   Sic *in MS?*

f   *MS* est.

g   *Ps. 118:137 Vulg.*

h   Sic *in MS.*

et rei locus[i] de quo ablatum est, et locum in quem deportatum est, et locum in quo adhuc latet, et quidquid cum ipso furto est, vt huic reueletis. Item coniuro vos prenominatos demones

• per magistrum vestrum Astaroth,

vt compareatis[j] in forma furis et furti, et quidquid cum hoc furto factum est ad nostram faciatis noticiam pervenire. Item coniuro vos prenominatos demones

• per illum qui fecit celum et terram et herbam virentem in genere suo, solem et lunam et stellas celi, signa et tempora, fulgura et tunitrua, voces et omnia quecumque in terra, in mari, [et] in inferno sunt,

vt arte, etc. Item coniuro vos prenominatos demones

• per ieiunium domini nostri Ihesu Christi,

• et per iter quod fecit ad montem Oliueti ad orandum Patrem, 'Pater, si fieri potest, transeat a me calix iste',

vt arte, etc. Coniuro vos prenominatos demones

• per v wlnera domini nostri Ihesu Christi, et fixuras cla- [105r] uorum,

• et per lanceam et clauos quibus crucifixus est dominus.

Coniuro [vos] prenominatos demones

• per omnia que concludunt 4or partes mundi,

• et per etates mundi,

• et per omnia animalia que sub celo sunt,

• et per serpencia et volatilia, bipedia, tripedia, [et] quadrupedia,

• et per omnes aereas potestates,

vt arte, etc. Coniuro vos prenominatos demones

• per tollerancia[m] spinee corone[k] quam sustinuit dominus suo capite,

• et per poculum quo potatus est in cruce felle et aceto.[l]

Item coniuro vos prenominatos demones

• per angelos et archangelos, thronos et dominaciones, principatus, potestates, virtutes celorum, cherubin et seraphin,

• et per dominicum sacrificium et officium miseracionis,

• et per eos qui presunt aliis,

• et per omnia que sunt deo subiecta,

• et per deum omnipotentem,

• et per deum qui ex nichilo omnia creauit ad laudem et ad gloriam sui nominis ac magestatis,[m]

vt arte, etc. Item coniuro vos prenominatos demones

---

i   Sic *in MS.*

j   *MS* comparaeatis.

k   *MS* corane.

l   *MS* acceto.

m   *Followed in MS by* fecit.

- *per coeternam sapienciam qua^n deus hominem creauit cum non esset, condidit ad ymaginem et similitudinem suam,*

vt arte, etc. Item coniuro vos prenominatos demones

- *per fidem prophetarum,*
- *per preconia patriarcharum,*
- *per dignitatem xxiiij seniorum,*
- *per symbolum apostolorum,*
- *per passionem sanctissimorum martyrum,*
- *per confessionem piorum confessorum,*
- *et per continenciam sanctarum virginum ac viduarum,*
- *et per lacrimas beate Marie virginis, quas fudit,* [105v] *et per planctum sancti Johannis ewangeliste, cum viderunt Ihesum Christum in cruce exspiratum,*
- *et per solis obscuracionem et lunam versam in sa[n]gwinem in signa transacta Filij dei,*
- *et per tremendum diem iudicij in quo omnes estis dampnandi,*

vt appareatis in vngwe istius pueri, N., in specie furis uel furum qui^o rem uel res istius hominis, N., ac[c]eperit ad nostram noticiam faciatis peruenire.^{p}

Finito experimento, dic hunc versam:

Protege, salua, benedic, sanctifica populum cunctum per crucis signum domini. Morbos auerte corporis et anime. Hoc contra signum nullum stet periculum. Amen. Per crucis hoc signum defendat nos Ihesus Christus. Amen.

NO. 41. FOR DISCOVERING HIDDEN TREASURE IN SLEEP (FOL. 106r–106v)

A[d] sciendum vbi thesaurum sit absconditum, primum est quod oportet hominem confiteri generaliter peccata sua, luna crescente, videlicet die dominico, sole existente in leone, de mane. Et cum a prima surrexeris, asperge te aqua benedicta, dicens antyfonam, *Asperges me, domine, ysopo, etc.* totam, cum *Gloria Patri*. Postea vade ad crucifixum et dic coram eo *Miserere mei, deus* totum, semper respiciendo crucifixum, cum omni deuocione. Et cum hec dixeris, tunc dic deuotissime corde et contrito, *O rabi, rabi, rex meus et deus meus ac dominus dominancium, qui conditor es vniuersorum, exaudi oracionem mei, misere et indigne^a creature, et redempcionis tue in hac hora et semper,^{b} et indignus clamor meus ad te perueniat.*

---

n   *MS* quo.

o   *MS* uel.

p   *Followed in MS by* vt arte, etc., *extraneously added.*

a   *MS* miserere et indige.

b   Sic *in MS.*

Hoc dicto, vade ad domum tuum et cameram tuam optime mundatam, et versus orientem dic hanc oracionem deuotissime quam potes:

O Oriens benigne, maior pars mundi, celi, terreque sator, cuius nutu^c omnia, tam celestia quam terrestria, prouide facta sunt, confirma intellectum meum in hoc opere per tui regni dominium, quod nunquam dimittitur. Rege et paue me in hac mea supplicacione. Et precor te

- *per tuos reges quod tenet et stringit, sanat et confirmat,^d*
- *et per omnes regias tuas potestas,*
- *per Sotuem, Sortfen,*

vt in nocte sequenti veniat ad me in sompnis Haram, spiritus benignus, et inflammet cor meum et mentem meam, vt sciam thesaurum [106v] *invenire, si aliquis est in partibus istis uel in aliis, et ducat me et signum ibi faciat vt cognoscam verum et ipsam veritatem,^e*

- *per tuum solem sanctissimum et sacratissimum thesaurum nitidissimum, candidum et fulgentissimum, quod mittit tua excellencia et remittit tua manifesta et benigna potestas,*
- *et per omnes dignitates tuas et regimina*

vocor^f et contestor vt mich[i] spiritum veritatis in sompnis mittere digneris hac nocte, vt michi reuelet^g thesaurum absconditum.

Hoc fiat versus orientem et genibus flexis. Hanc oracionem ter dicas.

Q[u]ando autem intras lectum, dicas nouem vicibus,

Oriens, Oriens, Oriens, precor, rogo, et peto, benignissime Oriens, vt votum meum adimpleas, et velis respicere ad offensiones meas.

Et tunc veniet ad te spiritus qui te non offendet, sed sompniare te faciet thesaurum, et ducet te recte ad locum.

Mane autem facto, quando surrexeris, fac 3es elimosinas in honore magni regis scientis, et vade associatus uel solus ad locum vbi est thesaurus in domo tua, et recipe eam. Postquam habebis thesaurum, fac cantare 3es missas: primam ad honorem sancte trinitatis, 2am pro peccatis mortuorum, terciam pro^h [in]columitate vite tue, etc.

---

c *MS* nuta.
d Sic *in MS.*
e Sic *in MS.*
f Sic *in MS.*
g *MS* reuelent.
h *MS* pro pro.

NO. 42. THE NAME SEMIFORAS (FOLS 106v–107r)

Nota: hoc est nomen magnum Semiforas, quod erat [107r] scriptum in fronte
Aaron, sacerdotis creatoris. Crescat in me virtus tua, omnipotens deus, creator
celi et terre, quemadmodum locutus fuisti, dicendo,

*Saday, Hay, Resel,*ᵃ *H, Q.,*ᵇ *Ayn, Yemino, Selatados, Braruth, Huy, Adonay, Eya, Yen, Yhn
uel Tunehy, Vo,*ᶜ *Da, Ey, Aha, Heye, Heye, Heye, Haya, Haya, Haya, Ey, Ey, Ey, Ya, Ya,
Ya, Han, Han, Han, Ga, Ga, Ga.*

Conpletum est nomen Semiforas, benedictum nomen eius cuius regni non erit
finis per infinita seculorum secula. Amen.

NO. 43. FOR OBTAINING A HORSE (FOL. 107r–v)

Ad equum habendum, hoc scribatur in hostio domus vacue in crepusculo
noctis, more Hebrayco, hec nomina cum sa[n]gwine vespertilionis: Tuditha,
Stehiha, Alpha, Draco, Mariodo, Ypanon. Quibus scriptis, recede modicum a
loco.

Post horam paruam, reuertaris et invenies eqqum paratum, quem cum volueris
ascendere, pone sinistrum pedem ad screpam et dic hanc coniuracionem:

Coniuro te, eque bone,
- *per creatorem celi et terre,*
- *et per illum qui creauit vniuersa et omnia ad laudem et gloriam sui nominis,*
- *et per deum viuuum*
- *et per deum sanctum*
- *et per deum verum,*

*vt non in corpore nec in anima nec in minimo membro meo vere obesse valeas, nec in aliquo
me perturbes, sed me, N., ad locum talem deferas, placide, hilariter, jocunde, et velociter,
absque omni inpedimento.*

Deinde ascende audacter et secure, [107v] qu[i]a omnino tibi nocere non
potest. Signo vere crucis non te signabis, quia ipsum a te fugabit.

Cum autem perueneris ad locum prenominatum, descende de equo et accipe
frenum, et absconde sub terra. Peracto autem tuo negocio, recipias frenum et

---

a   *Followed in MS by blank space.*
b   Sic *in MS?*
c   Sic *in MS?*

scucte firmissime, et statim veniet. Cum autem ascendere volueris, dic precedentem coniuracionem et hec tria verba:[d] kostolya, elogo, yetas.

NO. 44. FRAGMENT OF AN EXPERIMENT FOR AVERTING HARM (FOL. 107v)[a]

[. . .] creauit[b] mundum et septem dies, in quibus cuncta creata fuerint in vna torta, et obseruabis cartam, et cum hoc prohibes omnia dampna hominibus, cunctaque nocencia arboribus et nascoiciis,[c] nominabisque hec nomina sursum posita et deorsum. Et hec sunt nomina, scilicet: Layalym, Lyalgnea, Yalgnal, Narath, Lybarye, Lymbaros, Lyaslam. Cum hiis igitur signis prohibes omnia mala et dampna in mundo, et numquam ad locum reuerte[n]tur vnde fuerint expulsa.

NO. 45. FOR INVISIBILITY (FOLS 107v–108r)

Nunc igitur sume albam columbam, die Sabbati de nocte, et cartam agni virgineam, pergasque ad riuum iuxta quadruuium et occide columbam, dicens,

O vos quibus sacrificium debetur, estote michi completium votum meum.[a]

Hoc dicas contra occidentem primo, postea ad meridiem, deinde ad[b] orientem, post[e]a ad [108r] septentrionem. Et scribe de huius[c] collumbe sangwine hanc figuram.[d]

Reuertansque de mane ante solis ortum, invenies ibi aliam literam et as quodam involutum, illudque ligabis in capillis tuis cum volueris esse invisibilis. Et precaue tamen quod ibi dimittas columbam et cartam, ne ipsam accipias modo aliquo.

---

d   *Followed by* kostelia, *deleted.*

a   *This fragment occurs on the middle of fol. 107v, separated by double horizontal lines from the preceding and subsequent material.*

b   *Followed by* mundum, *deleted.*

c   *Meaning* nascenciis?

a   Sic *in MS, for* completio voti mei?

b   *Inserted above line in MS.*

c   *MS* hac.

d   *Figure toward top of fol. 108ʳ: a complex horizontal design.*

NO. 46. FAVOURABLE AND UNFAVOURABLE DAYS OF
THE MONTH FOR INSCRIPTIONS (FOL. 108r–v)

Mensis lunaris dierum alij sunt boni, alij mali ad scribendas[a] cartas. Prima dies mensis, scilicet lunaris, tota est bona. Secunda die mane est bona, et non plus. Tercia nil facere debes. Quarta dies tota bona. Quinta vsque ad horam terciam, et vltra non. Sexta die nichil facies. Septima die, prima hora bona est, et non plus. Octaua, mane bona. Nona nichil facies. Decima die omnino nichil facias,[b] quia mala[c] est ad omnia facienda. Vndecima bona est tota. Duodecima bona est vsque ad terciam uel quartam [horam]. 13a nichil facias. 14a tota bona est. 15a die[d] nichil facies. 16[a] mane tota bona est, postea nichil valet. 17a et 18a vsque ad meridiem mala est, et postea est bona. 19a nichil in ea agas. 20a et 21a et 22a [108v] dies, mane sunt bone, et non plus. 23a [et] 24a,[e] nichil facias. 25a mala, nec bona. 26a et 27a, nichil facias. 28a et 29a et 30a bona est toto. Etc.

NO. 47. FRAGMENT OF A CHEMICAL PRESCRIPTION
(WITH A NOTE IN GERMAN) (FOL. 108v)

Item recipe salis petri, vitrioli, rorani,[a] ana tere, et fac aquam fortem ex eis, et dissolue in ea lune limaturam quantum soluere potes,[b] et quando non plus soluit lunam, tunc recipe illam aquam in qua luna est soluta et inpone mercurij crudi quantum coagulare potest. Istum mixtum sit coagulatum. Accipe et pone eum in crusibulum super stratum istarum rerum. Recipe ceram nouam, thuris albi, gummi arabicum, oxicroceum, asafetidam, serabiuum, boracem, semen orobi, cantarides, puluis buffonum,[c] cerusam, sal nitri, sal commune, vernicium, terebentinam, euforbium, ouum, ana partes equales, et fac similiter fluere. Etc.

---

a   *MS* scribendos.

b   *Followed in MS by* quare.

c   *MS* male.

d   *MS* hora.

e   *Followed in MS by* u, *struck through (?).*

a   Sic *in MS?*

b   *Corrected in MS from* potest.

c   *Note added at bottom of fol. 108ᵛ:* Puluis *[MS* Poluis*]* buffonum ist daz kupfer daz vom hamer felt, so mans schmihet *[?].*

PLATES

All the folios from 3r–108v of Clm 849 that contain magic diagrams or characters are reproduced.

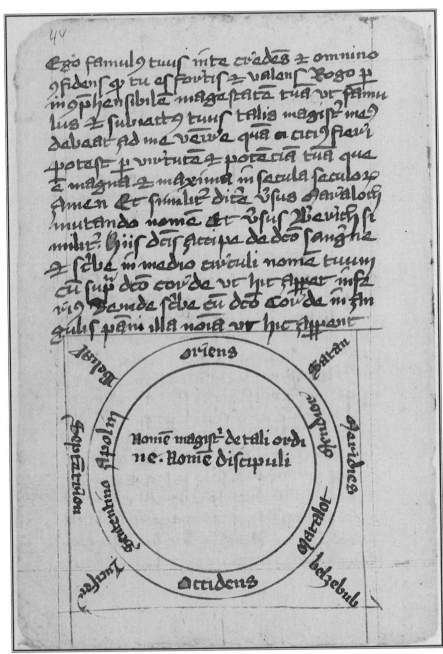

Fol. 4v, no. 1: Single band inscribed within a square; names of eight spirits inscribed in and around the band; cardinal directions marked; *Nomen magistri, de tali ordine* and *Nomen discipuli* marked in the centre.

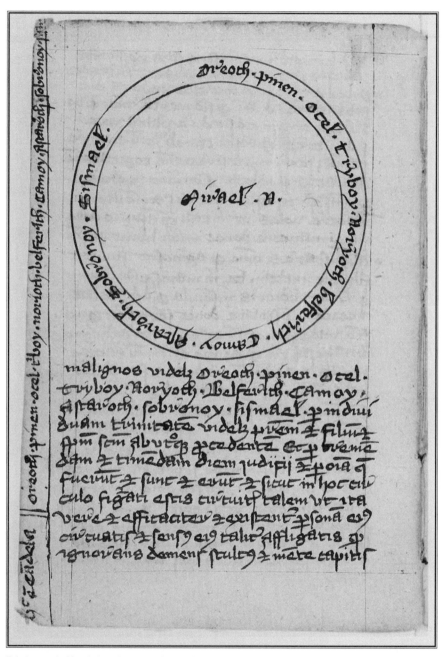

Fol. 6v, no. 2: Simple band; names of Mirael and victim in centre, names of ten demons in band.

Fol. 10r, no. 3: Simple band with names of eleven demons; position of the master marked in centre.

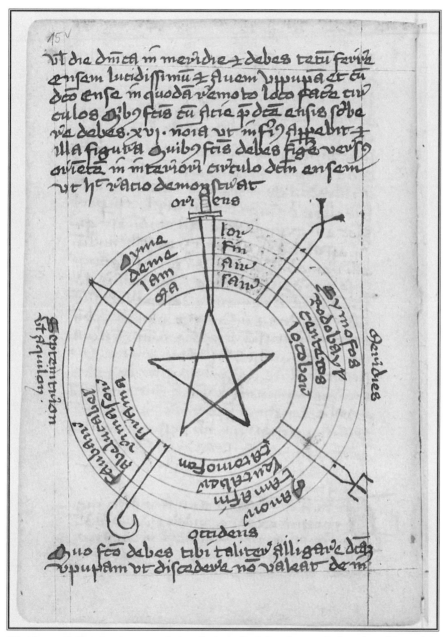

Fol. 15v, no. 6: Four bands; pentangle inscribed; cardinal directions marked; names of four spirits written in each band; position of sword marked to east; four other objects placed across the bands toward other directions.

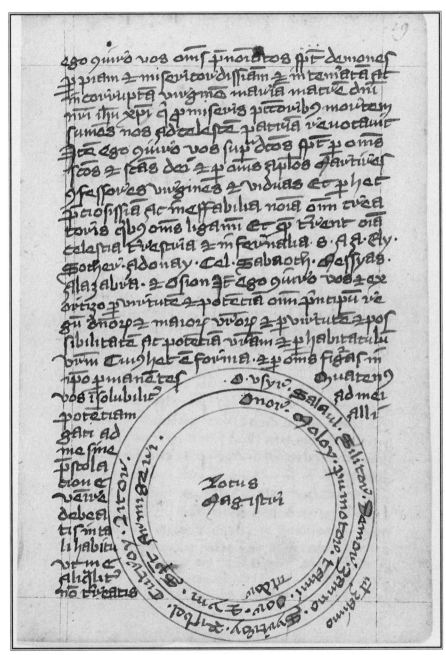

Fol. 19r, no. 7: Double band; names of nine spirits in outer band, six more ('arms-bearing spirits') in inner band, position of master marked in centre.

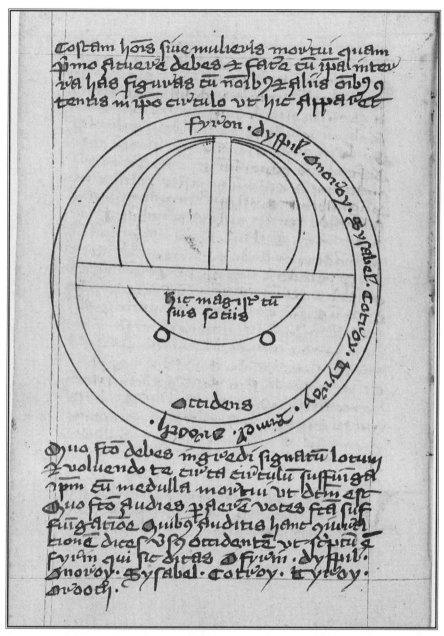

Fol. 21v, no. 8: Band with names of eight spirits, horizontal band across centre, vertical band across upper semicircle, all surmounted by crescent with two small circles, place of master and companions marked at bottom of crescent, east marked toward bottom.

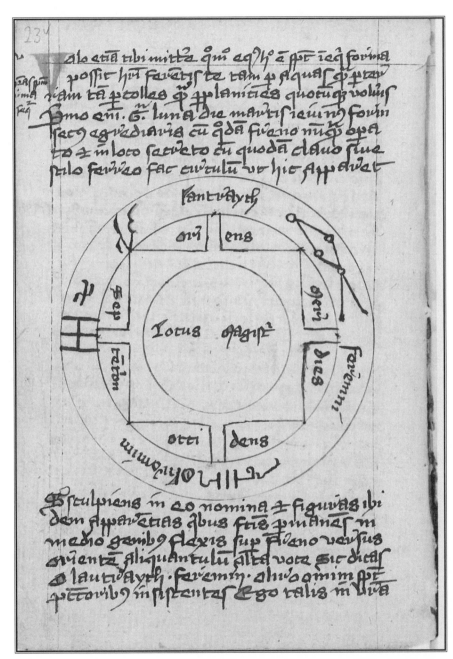

Fol. 23v, no. 9: Band containing three names, three characters, and crosses; square inscribed within circle, and arms protruding from the square, with cardinal directions; position of the master marked in centre.

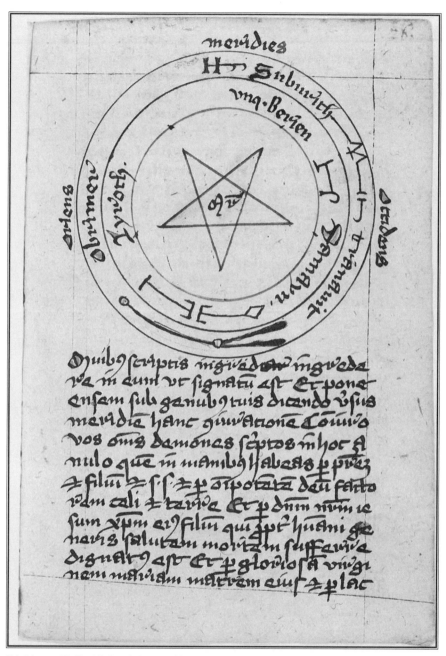

Fol. 26r, no. 10: Double band, drawn with sword; character and three names in each band; pentangle inscribed; cardinal directions indicated on sides; position of the master marked in centre.

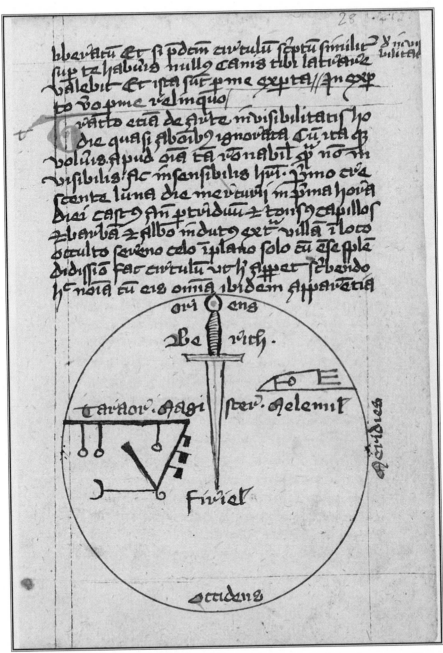

Fol. 28r, no. 11: Plain circle, with place of master and name Firiel marked near centre, name Taraor and elaborate character to left, name Melemil and further character to upper right.

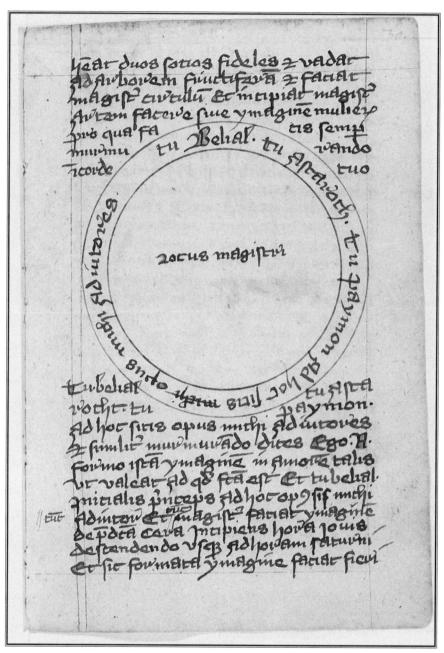

Fol. 30r, no. 12: Single band with invocation of Belial and two other spirits, and position of the master marked in centre.

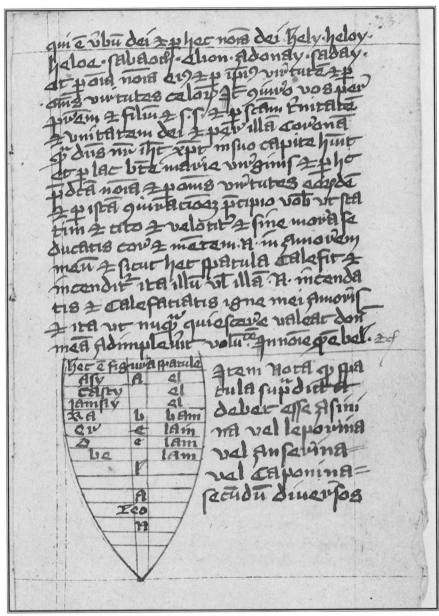

Fol. 33r, no. 13: Shield divided into sixteen horizontal bands, with one vertical band down the centre; names Asyel, Castyel, Lamsiyel, Rabam, Erlain, Olam and Belam in horizontal bands, each straddling the vertical band; A, B, E, L, A and N in the vertical band; *Leo* written across the intersection of the vertical band and the twelfth horizontal band.

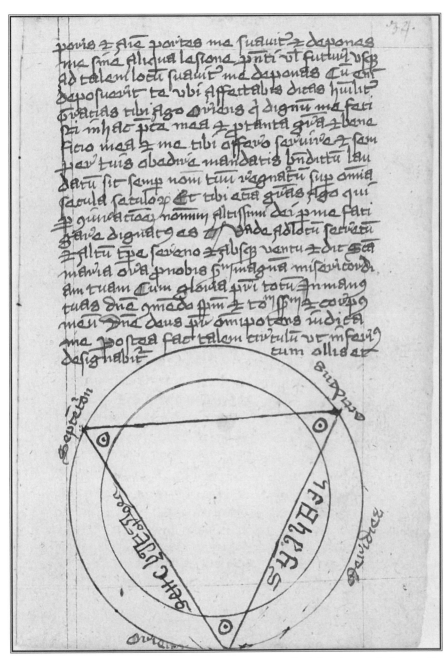

Fol. 34r, no. 15: Band, with triangle inscribed in outer circle, cardinal directions marked on outside, occult characters on two sides of triangle, positions of jars marked in angles.

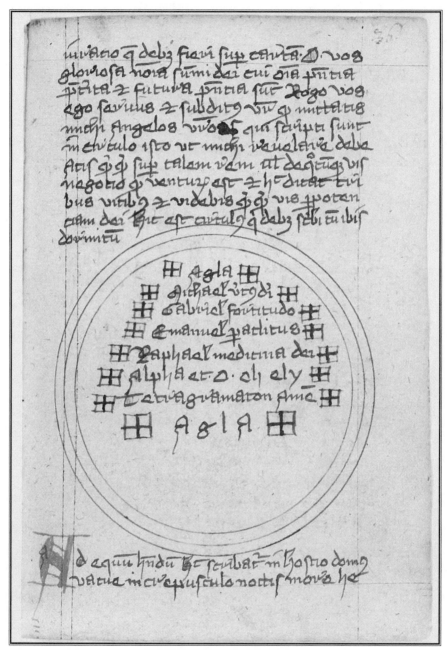

Fol. 36r, no. 16: Double band, with eight lines of text inscribed; cross inside square at either end of each line of text.

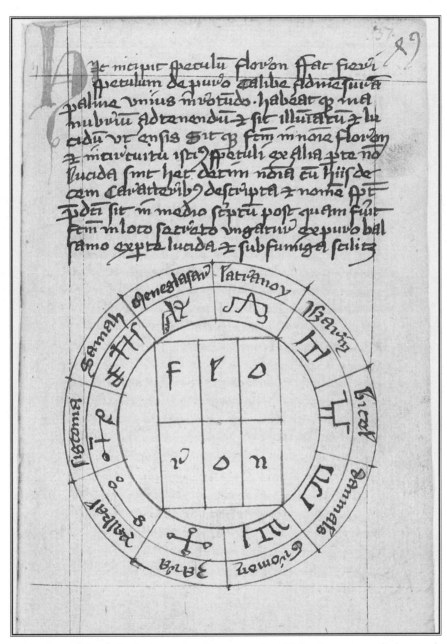

Fol. 37r, no. 18: Double band with ten segments; name of a spirit in outer part; occult character in inner part of each segment; inscribed and segmented vertical rectangle containing the letters F-L-O-R-O-N in segments.

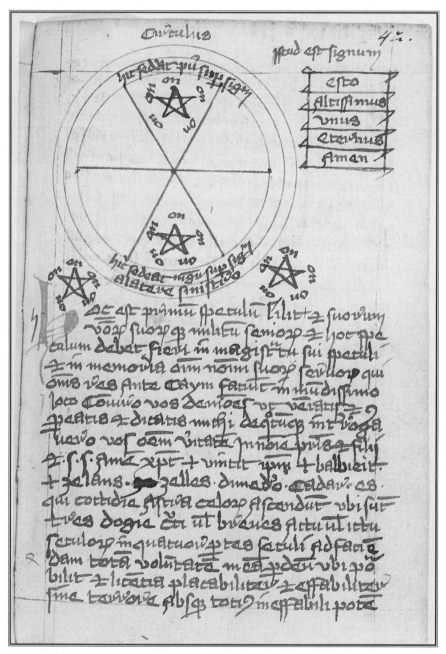

Fol. 42r, no. 22: Double band; interior divided into six wedges; pentangles (inscribed with *on*); positions of master and boy marked; lined column (with inscription) to right.

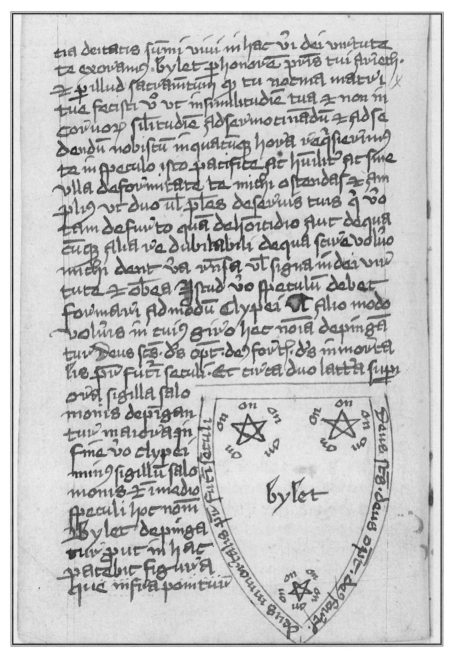

Fol. 42v, no. 23: Shield; inscription addressed to God; pentangles (*sigilla Salomonis*, inscribed with *on*);
name Lylet inscribed near centre.

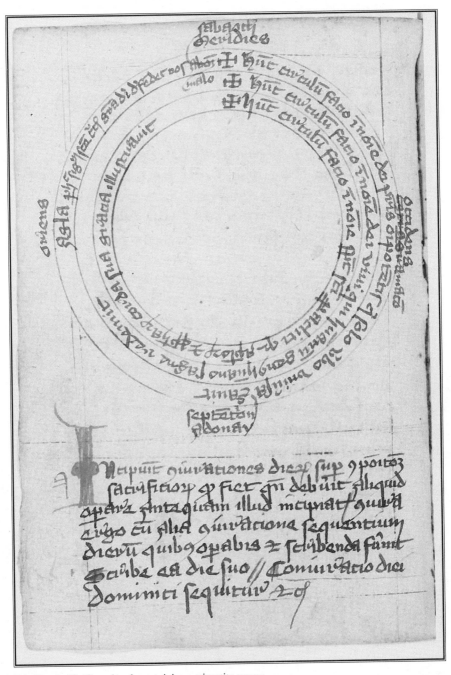

Fol. 68v, no. 36: Three bands containing a tripartite prayer.

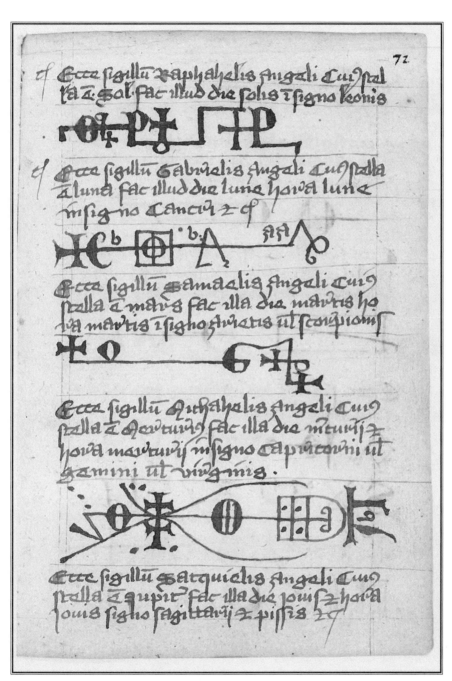

Fol. 72r, no. 37b: Seals for angels.

Fol. 72v, nos 37b–37c: Seals for angels, seals for planets and days of the week.

Fol. 73r, no. 37c: Seals for planets and days of the week.

Fol. 73v, no. 37c: Seals for planets and days of the week.

Fol. 74r, no. 37c: Seals for planets and days of the week.

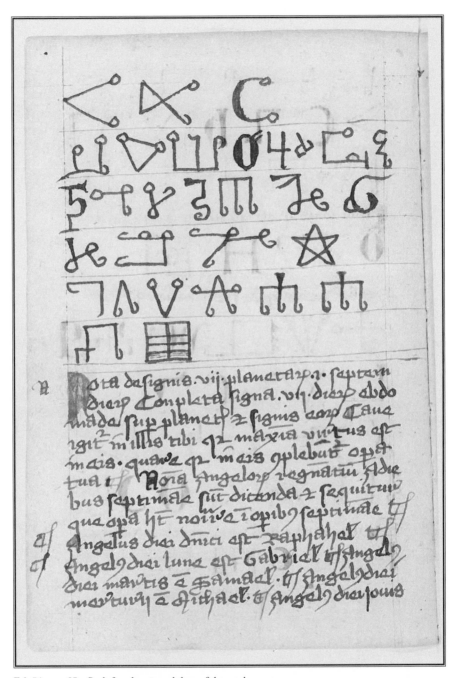

Fol. 74v, no. 37c: Seals for planets and days of the week.

Fol. 95v, no. 37r: Seal of Solomon (three characters).

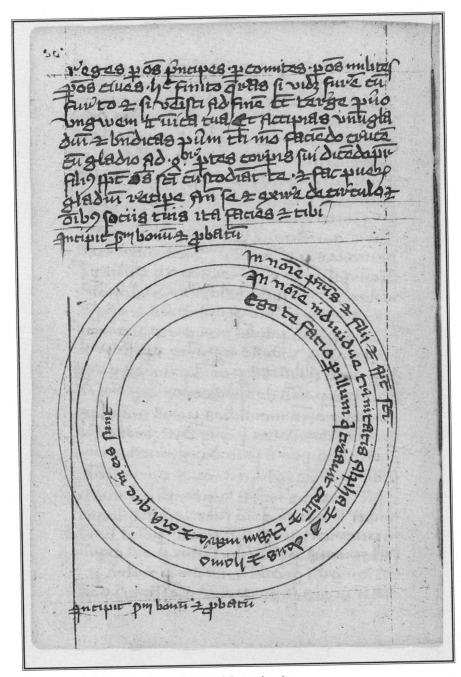

Fol. 99v, no. 39 (first circle): Three bands containing a tripartite prayer.

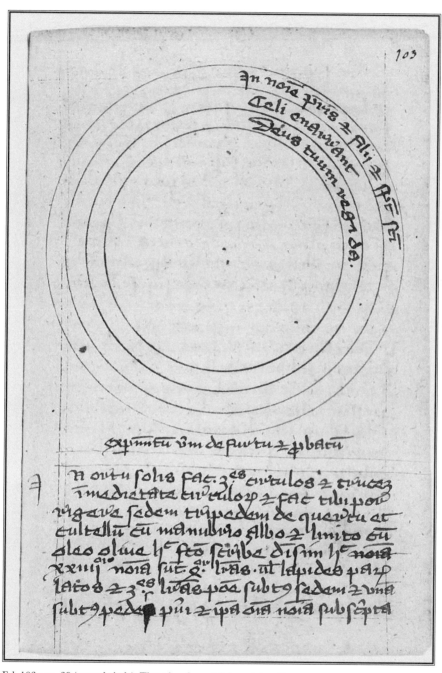

Fol. 103r, no. 39 (second circle): Three bands containing a tripartite prayer.

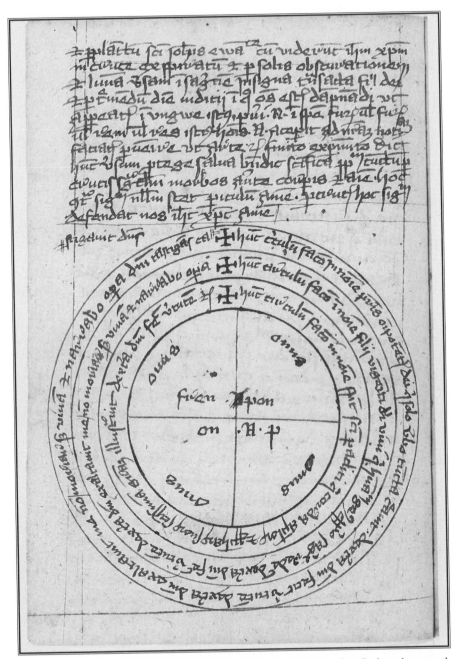

Fol. 105v, no. 40: Three concentric bands; centre of innermost divided into inscribed quadrants; each circle dedicated to member of Trinity.

Fol. 108r, no. 45: Complex character.

SELECTIVE BIBLIOGRAPHY

This list includes only the titles directly relevant to the present work and those cited repeatedly in the notes.

Bacon, Roger. *De Nigromancia*, ed. and trans. Michael-Albion Macdonald (Gillette, NJ: Heptangle, 1988)

Betz, Hans Dieter, ed. *The Greek Magical Papyri in Translation, including the Demotic Spells*, 1 (Chicago: University of Chicago Press, 1986)

Braekman, W. 'Magische experimenten en toverpraktijken uit een middelnederlands handschrift', *Verslagen en mededelingen van de Koninklijke Vlaamse Academie voor Taal en Letterkunde*, 1966, pp. 53–118; also published separately (Ghent: Seminarie voor Volkskunde, 1966)

Burnett, Charles. *Magic and Divination in the Middle Ages: Texts and Techniques in the Islamic and Christian Worlds* (Aldershot: Variorum, 1966)

Butler, E.M. *Ritual Magic* (Cambridge: Cambridge University Press, 1949)

Carey, Hilary M. *Courting Disaster: Astrology at the English Court and University in the Later Middle Ages* (New York: St Martin's Press, 1992)

Cohn, Norman. *Europe's Inner Demons: An Enquiry inspired by the Great Witch-Hunt* (London: Chatto, 1975)

Davidson, Gustav. *A Dictionary of Angels, including the Fallen Angels* (New York: Free Press, 1967)

Driscoll, Daniel, trans. *The Sworn Book of Honorius* [sic] *the Magician* (Berkeley Heights, NJ: Heptangle, 1983)

Duffy, Eamon. *The Stripping of the Altars: Traditional Religion in England, c. 1400–c. 1580* (New Haven: Yale University Press, 1992)

Eubel, Conrad. 'Vom Zaubereiunwesen anfangs des 14. Jahrhunderts (mit urkundlichen Beilagen)', *Historisches Jahrbuch der Görres-Gesellschaft*, 18 (1897), 609–31

Fürbeth, Frank. *Johannes Hartlieb: Untersuchungen zu Leben und Werk* (Tübingen: Niemeyer, 1992), 109–27

Gerson, Jean. *Œuvres complètes*, ed. Palemon Glorieux (Paris: Desclée, 1961–73)

Ginzburg, Carlo. *Ecstasies: Deciphering the Witches' Sabbath*, trans. Raymond Rosenthal (New York: Pantheon, 1991)

Greenfield, Richard P.H. *Traditions of Belief in Late Byzantine Demonology* (Amsterdam: Hakkert, 1988)

Hansen, Joseph. ed. *Quellen und Untersuchungen zur Geschichte des Hexenwahns und der Hexenverfolgung im Mittelalter* (Bonn: Georgi, 1901; repr. Hildesheim: Olms, 1963)

—— *Zauberwahn, Inquisition und Hexenprozeß im Mittelalter, und die Entstehung der großen Hexenverfolgung* (Munich: Oldenbourg, 1900; repr. Aalen: Scientia, 1964)

Hartlieb, Johann. *Das Buch aller verbotenen Künste, des Aberglaubens und der Zauberei*, ed. and trans. Falk Eisermann and Eckhard Graf (Ahlerstedt: Param, 1989)

Harvey, Margaret. 'Papal witchcraft: the charges against Benedict XIII', in Derek Baker, ed., *Sanctity and Secularity: The Church and the World* (Studies in Church History, 10) (Oxford: Blackwell, 1973), 109–16

Hyatte, Reginald, intro. and trans. *Laughter for the Devil: The Trials of Gilles de Rais, Companion-in-Arms of Joan of Arc (1440)* (Rutherford, NJ: Fairleigh Dickinson University Press; London: Associated University Presses, 1984)

James, M.R. 'Twelve medieval ghost stories', *English Historical Review*, 37 (1922), 413–22

Kieckhefer, Richard. 'Erotic magic in medieval Europe', in Joyce Salisbury, ed., *Sex in the Middle Ages: A Book of Essays* (New York: Garland, 1991), 30–55

Kieckhefer, Richard. *European Witch Trials: Their Foundations in Popular and Learned Culture, 1300–1500* (London: Routledge, 1976)

Kieckhefer, Richard. 'The holy and the unholy: sainthood, witchcraft and magic in late medieval Europe', *Journal of Medieval and Renaissance Studies*, 24 (1994), 355–85; and in Scott L. Waugh and Peter D. Diehl, eds., *Christendom and its Discontents: Exclusion, Persecution and Rebellion, 1000–1500* (Cambridge: Cambridge University Press, 1996), 310–37

Kieckhefer, Richard. *Magic in the Middle Ages* (Cambridge: Cambridge University Press, 1989; New York: Cambridge University Press, 1990)

Kieckhefer, Richard. 'Magie et sorcellerie en Europe au Moyen Âge', in Robert Muchembled, ed., *Magie et sorcellerie en Europe du Moyen Âge à nos jours* (Paris: Colin, 1994), 17–44

Kieckhefer, Richard. 'La negromanzia nell'ambito clericale nel tardo Medioevo', in Agostino Paravicini Bagliani and André Vauchez, eds., *Poteri carismatici e informali: chiesa e società medioevali* (Palermo: Sellerio, 1992), 210–23

Kieckhefer, Richard. 'The specific rationality of medieval magic', *American Historical Review*, 99 (1994), 813–36

Kittredge, George Lyman. *Witchcraft in Old and New England* (Cambridge, MA: Harvard University Press, 1929; repr. New York: Russell & Russell, 1956)

[Kramer, Heinrich, and (as ascribed) Jakob Sprenger], *The Malleus maleficarum*, trans. Montague Summers (London: Pushkin, 1928)

Peters, Edward. *The Magician, the Witch, and the Law* (Philadelphia: University of Pennsylvania Press, 1978)

Picatrix: The Latin Version of the Ghāyat Al-Hakīm, ed. David Pingree (London: Warburg Institute, 1986)

Robbins, Rossell Hope. *The Encyclopedia of Witchcraft and Demonology* (New York, 1959)

Scheible, Johann, ed. 'Semiphoras und Schemhamphoras Salomonis Regis', *Das Kloster*, 3 (1846), 289–330

Thorndike, Lynn. *The History of Magic and Experimental Science* (New York: Macmillan and Columbia University Press, 1923–58)

— 'Imagination and magic: force of imagination on the human body and of magic on the human mind', in *Mélanges Eugène Tisserant*, 7 (Vatican City: Biblioteca Vaticana, 1964), 353–8

— *Michael Scot* (London: Nelson, 1965)

INDEX